Introduction

This book is about the great and the good – and a few of the not so good: people from ancient times to the present day, and from all over the world, who have made their mark on history.

Who to put in and who to leave out

If you and a friend made separate lists of the 10 most famous people who have ever lived, you would probably find that you only agreed on two or three names. Imagine the difficulty if your list were to include 1000 people!

We assembled a team of nearly 50 consultants, all of them experts in areas as diverse as popular music and ancient history, and asked for their informed opinions on who should be included. We also consulted Oxford University Press offices around the world so that we could draw on their expertise to give the book an international perspective.

A particular challenge we faced was to compare the achievements of people doing different things or living at different times. For example, is the former US president *Ronald Reagan* more famous – or more important – than the athlete *Carl Lewis*? And does the fact that *Carl Lewis* could run the 100 metres faster than *Jesse Owens* make him a 'better' athlete – even though *Owens* was the winner of four gold medals at the Berlin Olympics of 1936?

There are no right or wrong answers to such questions, and that is why you will find a wide variety of people from all periods of history within these pages. Politicians, writers, and scientists sit side by side with the stars of sport and film. Because the list is limited to 1000 entries, there are bound to be well-known men and women who do not appear; at the same time, there are plenty of people you may not have heard of. But that's part of the fun: on the same page you can learn all about *Picasso* and then find out about *Phidippides*, the man who ran the first marathon.

A–Z Section

The 1000 entries are arranged alphabetically for easy reference. Each one starts with a short headpiece giving, at a glance, the person's name, a brief description of why they are famous, and their birth and (where appropriate) death dates. The abbreviation c. (short for *circa*, a Latin word meaning 'about') before a date means that it is only approximate. The main article then tells you more about the person's life: their inspirations, their achievements, their failures, or their evil deeds.

The entries are lavishly illustrated with nearly 500 carefully selected pictures. These show not only what some of these famous people looked like but also some of their inventions, their paintings, their designs, and so on. Twenty maps showing former empires and famous journeys have been specially created.

At the end of many of the articles you will find a 'see also' panel listing one or more names. This guides you to other people in the book who are linked in some way to the entry you are reading.

Special Reference Section

After the main section of 1000 entries you will find the Thematic and Chronological Directories. The first of these directories lists the people in the book by their area of achievement, thus grouping together the artists, the musicians, the scientists, and so on; the second lists them by their date of birth, starting with those born over 3000 years ago. These directories may be useful for project work and offer an alternative way of getting information from the book.

Fascinating stories and fantastic achievements – turn the pages and discover some of the people who have *really* made the world go round!

Peter **Abelard**

French philosopher and scholar
Born *1079* ***Died*** *1142 aged 63*

Born near Nantes, Peter Abelard's father wanted him to follow a military career but he chose to study instead. He taught theology (the study of religion) and founded a school which eventually became the University of Paris. In 1113 he tutored Heloise, the young niece of a church official. They fell in love, had a child, and married. Her uncle was outraged and had Abelard castrated. Abelard then became a monk and Heloise went into a nunnery. But they continued to write to each other, and these love letters have survived to tell their tragic story.

As a monk, and later a hermit, Abelard taught that people should defend the ideas of Christianity through logical thinking. He also wrote a book on ethics (the study of morals) and his autobiography, *The Story of My Misfortunes.* He was one of the leading philosophers, logicians, and theologians of medieval times. ◆

Abraham

Hebrew ancestor of both Jews and Muslims
Lived during the 20th century BC

According to the book of Genesis in the Bible, Abraham lived in the city of Ur in Mesopotamia (now mainly in Iraq). When he was about 75, God told him that he must leave his country and travel to Canaan, the promised land.

Abraham settled there, married, and had a son, Isaac. When Isaac had grown into a boy, God told Abraham to sacrifice him by placing him on an altar and killing him. Abraham and Isaac went into the mountains but before Isaac could be sacrificed, God told Abraham to stop. Abraham had proved that he would obey God and was even prepared to give him his own son. God blessed Abraham and his family and said that Isaac's children would be the founders of a great nation.

Abraham is important to Jews because he followed one God and because God led him to the promised land of Canaan or Israel, which the Jews have seen as their homeland ever since. He is important to Muslims because he was obedient to God. (According to Muslim tradition, Ishmael, the ancestor of the Arab peoples, was the son he nearly sacrificed.) And Abraham is important to Christians because he trusted in God's promises. ◆

Abu Bakr

First caliph of Islam
Born c.*573* ***Died*** *634 aged about 61*

In the year 610 near the Arabian town of Mecca, Muhammad began to receive messages from God. He soon began to preach the new religion of Islam, which means 'submitting to God'. Abu Bakr was one of the rich merchants who lived in the town of Mecca and was one of the first to believe in the new prophet. He became a close companion of Muhammad, who married Abu Bakr's daughter, Aisha. When the merchants of Mecca forced Muhammad to flee because they were worried that people would no longer come to Mecca to worship the pagan idols there, Abu Bakr went with him to Medina and became his chief adviser. When Muhammad died in 632, Abu Bakr was accepted as the 'successor of the Prophet of God', or Caliph of Islam. Abu Bakr extended the influence and rule of Islam by bringing the rest of Arabia under his

▼ *The tragic lovers were finally united in 1164 when Heloise died and was buried beside Abelard in Brittany.*

The

Oxford
Children's Book of
FAMOUS
PEOPLE

The Oxford Children's Book of FAMOUS PEOPLE

OXFORD
UNIVERSITY PRESS

Great Clarendon Street, Oxford OX2 6DP

Oxford University Press is a department of the University of Oxford.
It furthers the University's objective of excellence in research, scholarship,
and education by publishing worldwide in

Oxford New York

Auckland Bangkok Buenos Aires Cape Town Chennai
Dar es Salaam Delhi Hong Kong Istanbul Karachi Kolkata
Kuala Lumpur Madrid Melbourne Mexico City Mumbai Nairobi
São Paulo Shanghai Taipei Tokyo Toronto

Oxford is a registered trade mark of Oxford University Press
in the UK and in certain other countries

First published in 1994
First published in paperback 1996
Second edition 1999
Third edition 2002
Updated reprint 2006

British Library Cataloguing in Publication Data available

ISBN 0-19-910977-X

5 7 9 10 8 6 4

Printed in Italy by G. Canale & C. S.p.A

Consultants and Authors

Peter Aykroyd
Chris Baldick
George Bethell
Ephraim Borowski
Frederick Brogger
Malcolm Bull
Ian Chilvers
Mike Corbishley
Tony Drake
Canon John Fenton
Don Fowler
Gerald Haigh
Andrew Hawkey
Patrick Hickman-Robertson
Michael Hurd
Allan Jones

Paul Lewis
Bryan Loughrey
Howard Loxton
Deborah Manley
Peter Matthews
Colin McEvedy
Richard Milbank
Kenneth Morgan
Peggy Morgan
Daryl Moulton
Douglas Newton
Paul Noble
David Parkinson

R. B. Peberdy
Stephen Pople
Theo Rowland-Entwistle
Archie Roy
Steve Skidmore
Jennifer Speake
Louise Spilsbury
Richard Spilsbury
Richard Tames
Peter Teed
Nicholas Tucker
Trevor Williams
Elizabeth Williamson
Gillian Wolfe
Robert Youngson

control. He also began the Islamic conquests of Syria and Persia (modern Iran). ◆

see also
Ali   Muhammad

Chinua **Achebe**

Nigerian novelist
Born 1930

Born in eastern Nigeria, Chinua Achebe worked in broadcasting and the civil service before becoming a novelist. In his first and most famous novel, *Things Fall Apart* (1958), he describes the breakdown of African tribal life after the arrival of the British colonizers during the last century. In his memorable description of a traditional family, Achebe shows an understanding of the way the different cultures and rituals of Africa so often puzzle outsiders. Another novel, *A Man of the People* (1966), describes a dishonest African politician who wants to make as much money as he can while he has the chance. It is a funny-sad story, pointing out how difficult it can be for a country unused to political power to run itself properly during the first years of independence. Achebe has since written several children's books and has greatly helped younger African writers in their efforts to get their books published. ◆

John **Adams**

President of the United States of America from 1797 to 1801
Born 1735   Died 1826 aged 90

John Adams, the son of a farmer from Massachusetts, trained to be a lawyer at Harvard University.

He became a strong supporter of American independence from Britain and wrote articles for the Boston newspapers arguing for American rights against what many considered to be unfair British colonial laws.

▲ *John Adams lived longer than any other president of America; he died a few months short of his 91st birthday. He died on the same day as Thomas Jefferson, the man who succeeded him as president.*

He was elected to the House of Representatives (America's law-making body) and earned himself a reputation for being outspoken, blunt, and decisive. He helped to write, and signed, the historic Declaration of Independence document of 1776 which renounced connections with Britain. Three years later he went to France to negotiate the treaties that ended the American Revolution (War of Independence). This was the revolt against British rule that resulted in the establishment of the United States of America.

Adams was the first American ambassador to Britain. Then, from 1789 to 1797, he acted as America's first vice-president, before becoming its second president in

1797. Before he died, he saw his son, John Quincy Adams, become America's sixth president. ◆

see also
Jefferson   Washington

Aesop

Greek storyteller
Lived during the 6th century BC

Although Aesop is world-famous for his animal fables, we cannot be certain whether he actually wrote them or even if he was a real person! Tradition has it that Aesop was born in Thrace in Greece in the 6th century BC. He is said to have lived as a slave on the Greek island of Samos and on his release travelled extensively before being murdered at Delphi.

His fables, in which animals behave like humans, always end with a moral. Some of his moral catch-phrases, such as 'look before you leap', are still used today. His stories are short and entertaining and have been popular through the ages. Perhaps the most famous is *The Hare and The Tortoise*. ◆

▼ *An illustration from a 1912 edition of Aesop's The Hare and the Tortoise.*

Akbar

Emperor of the Mughal empire in northern India
Born *1542*   **Died** *1605 aged 63*

Akbar ruled the Mughal empire in India at the same time as Elizabeth I was queen of England. By the end of his reign, his lands covered an area as big as Europe, and he was more powerful than any European monarch.

Akbar was only 14 when he became emperor, and had to fight hard to build up his power. Sometimes he was ruthless. When he destroyed a rebel fort at Chitor, he built his enemies' heads into the walls of a tower. But Akbar preferred peace, and won most of his lands through treaties and marriages. The Mughal emperors were Muslims but the majority of Akbar's subjects were Hindus. To show that he respected their beliefs, he married a Hindu princess. He was much more tolerant about religion than European rulers living at the same time who forced their subjects to follow particular beliefs.

Akbar loved hunting with cheetahs, riding fierce camels and war elephants, and playing polo. He enjoyed painting, and also made tapestries and carpets. He had splendid palaces with beautiful gardens and he built the magnificent city of Fatehpur Sikri near Agra. It is still there today, almost unchanged, to remind us of Akbar's India. ◆

▼ *This map shows the extent of Akbar's Mughal empire in northern India.*

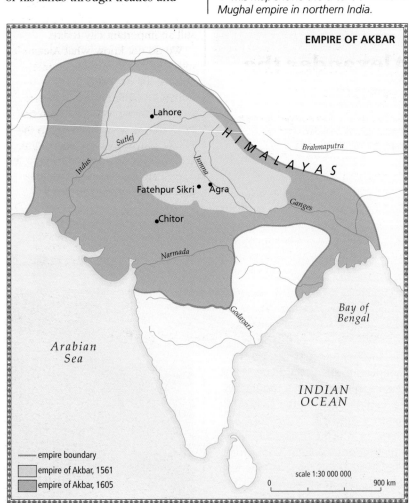

EMPIRE OF AKBAR

Lahore

Sutlej
Indus
HIMALAYAS
Brahmaputra
Jumna
Fatehpur Sikri • Agra
Ganges
• Chitor
Narmada
Godavari
Bay of Bengal
Arabian Sea
INDIAN OCEAN

—— empire boundary
☐ empire of Akbar, 1561
☐ empire of Akbar, 1605

scale 1:30 000 000
0   900 km

Alaric

Leader of the Visigoths
Born *370*   **Died** *410 aged 40*

In the late 4th century, the western part of the Roman empire came under attack from various peoples, including the Visigoths. They swept down, in huge numbers, from western Russia across the River Danube into Roman territory.

In 394 Alaric, the Visigoth leader, fought for the Roman emperor Theodosius. But in the following year he led an uprising against the Romans. Still seeking new lands for his people, Alaric led his forces into Italy in 401 and besieged Rome, the capital of the western empire, from 408–410. In 410 he broke into the city and captured it. Although he was briefly in control of Rome, Alaric still could not negotiate for lands for his people. He marched south to invade southern Italy but died while waiting to invade the island of Sicily. ◆

Alcock and Brown

English pilot and navigator who made the first non-stop flight across the Atlantic Ocean
John Alcock
Born *1892*   **Died** *1919 aged 27*
Arthur Brown
Born *1886*   **Died** *1948 aged 62*

John Alcock was a motor mechanic but his interest switched from cars to aircraft. He learned to fly and became a flying instructor. In World War I he was awarded for his bravery as a pilot. After the war, Vickers Aircraft recruited him as a test pilot: they wanted someone to make an attempt to fly an aircraft across the Atlantic Ocean.

▲ *John Alcock and Arthur Brown sitting inside what is probably a Vickers Vimy, the aircraft in which they made their record-breaking flight.*

At 4.13 pm on 14 June 1919, Alcock took off from St Johns, Newfoundland in a specially adapted Vickers Vimy bomber with Arthur Brown as his navigator. They landed the next day in a bog in County Galway, Ireland. The flight lasted 16 hours 12 minutes and covered 3025 km at an average speed of 190 kmph. Alcock and Brown shared a £10,000 prize and both received knighthoods. Alcock died in a plane crash shortly afterwards but Brown, who was also a pilot, eventually became a manager in the Vickers Company. ◆

👁 **see also**
Lindbergh

Louisa May **Alcott**

American author
Born 1832   Died 1888 aged 55

Louisa May Alcott had a strict and frugal upbringing in Philadelphia. However, in spite of this, she was a strong young girl. She was quite hard on herself and listed her faults as 'idleness, impatience, selfishness, independence, activity, wilfulness, vanity, pride, and the love of cats'.

When she grew up she tried to earn money to support herself by writing romantic thrillers for magazines. Then, at 35, she wrote *Little Women*. This classic novel was about family life during the American Civil War and was an idealized version of her own difficult childhood with the heroine, Jo, modelled on herself.

The book was a huge success. The popularity of *Little Women*, and of the follow-up volumes which Alcott wrote, at last freed her family from money worries. But her health had been damaged when she spent a brief spell as a nurse during the Civil War, and this, together with long-established habits of hard work and self-denial and her shyness with strangers, made it difficult for her to enjoy her fame. ◆

Alexander the Great

Ancient Greek king and general who conquered the Persian empire
Born 356 BC   Died 323 BC aged 32

Alexander became King Alexander III of Macedonia (northern Greece) at the age of 20. He devoted his reign to making Macedonia more important and to conquering the huge Persian empire to the east. He achieved this in a few years in a succession of brilliant battles and sieges. He reached India, and sent an expedition by sea from the mouth of the Indus to Babylon. He would have gone further, but his army refused. He wanted both Greeks and Persians to be rulers so he appointed Persians as well as Macedonians to high positions. He angered his army by adopting customs from the Persians, some of which involved honouring him as if he were a god.

Alexander had a famous horse called Bucephalus which his father had given him when he was a boy. When the horse died Alexander built a city and named it after him. He also built many new cities called Alexandria and settled soldiers and other Greeks in them. The most famous is the one in Egypt which is still an important city today.

We do not know what Alexander intended to do with his empire, because he died of a fever in Babylon before he had a chance to organize it properly. When he died no one was able to keep the newly won empire together. After years of war among his generals it was split up into several smaller kingdoms, including Babylonia, Egypt, and Macedonia itself. ◆

▼ *This 2nd–1st century BC Roman mosaic shows Alexander the Great riding into battle against the Persian ruler Darius III.*

Alexander, Earl of Tunis

British general
Born *1891* **Died** *1969 aged 78*

Harold Alexander was born into an aristocratic family. He originally wanted to be an artist but decided to make a career in the army and served as an officer in World War I. After the war he served in eastern Europe, Turkey, and India and showed a great talent for languages, learning to speak German, Russian, and Urdu. In 1937 he became the youngest major-general in the British army.

He distinguished himself in World War II, organizing the Allied retreats from France in 1940 and from Burma in 1942 (where he was nearly captured by the Japanese). He became General Eisenhower's deputy from 1943 and led the conquest of North Africa and the invasion of Italy. After the war he received many honours and served as a Governor-General of Canada and Minister of Defence. ◆

👁 **see also**
Eisenhower

Alfred

English King of Wessex from 871 to 899
Born *849* **Died** *899 aged 50*

Among the early kings of England, Alfred is the most famous. He lived at a time when Britain was made up of many separate kingdoms. His kingdom of Wessex extended from present-day Devon to Hampshire. Like his brothers, Alfred was brought up to hunt and fight, but he was also interested in studying.

Danish invaders, who already occupied other parts of England,

▲ *The man shown holding two sceptres on this 9th-century ornament is believed to be Alfred, King of Wessex.*

tried many times to take Wessex. Alfred led battles against them and even tried to pay them off. With a new army he finally beat them back and established a proper 'English' kingdom in southern England.

Alfred, who became known as 'Alfred the Great', was as famous for his peacetime work as his wartime exploits. He founded the first English navy and a number of new towns called burhs. He issued a new code of laws and encouraged the country's religious life by re-founding monasteries that had been destroyed. He also encouraged the use of the Anglo-Saxon language, and during his reign the Anglo-Saxon Chronicles were begun. ◆

Ali

Arab ruler; the fourth Caliph of Islam from 656 to 661
Born *c.600* **Died** *661 aged about 61*

Ali Ibn Abi Talib was the cousin of the prophet of Islam, Muhammad. Ali became a Muslim as a boy and married Muhammad's daughter Fatima. Pious, wise, and brave, in 656 Ali was chosen as the fourth Caliph – the leader of the Muslims and ruler of the expanding Arab empire. Al-Najaf, near Kufa in Iraq, became his capital and a great centre of learning.

A revolt against Ali's rule was led by Muawiyah, the governor of Syria and a member of the powerful Umayyad family. In 661 Ali was assassinated and his power was passed to the Umayyads, who ruled from Damascus. A group of Muslims, known as the 'Shiat Ali' (party of Ali), refused to accept Umayyad rule as they thought only descendants of Ali should be Caliphs. They became known in Muslim history as Shiites. ◆

👁 **see also**
Muhammad

Muhammad Ali

American world champion boxer
Born *1942*

After winning the amateur 'Golden Gloves' championship in 1959 and 1960, Cassius Clay from Louisville, Kentucky, became Olympic light heavyweight champion in 1960. He immediately became a professional and within four years was champion of the world.

Clay converted to the Islamic faith and changed his name to Muhammad Ali. Because of his beliefs, he refused to be called up into the American army to fight in

▲ *Muhammad Ali won a total of 56 boxing contests; 37 of these ended in knock-outs.*

the Vietnam War. His world title was taken away from him and he was banned from boxing from 1967 to 1970. He returned to the ring in the 1970s and, although he lost his title twice, he won in 1974 and 1978, thus becoming the first heavyweight boxer to win the world championship three times. ◆

👁 **see also**
Louis, Joe

André-Marie Ampère

French physicist
Born *1775*   **Died** *1836 aged 61*

As a child André-Marie Ampère was gifted at mathematics; he even taught himself Latin in order to read old books on the subject. His scientific interests were wide, but his greatest discoveries were in electricity.

In 1820 the Danish physicist Hans Christian Oersted discovered that an electric current in a wire would deflect (move) a nearby compass needle. Ampère worked out a mathematical law connecting the size of an electric current with the strength of the magnetic field it produced. This is now called Ampère's law. It is one of the most important laws in electromagnetism. Using it, Ampère was able to make instruments for measuring currents and voltages.

The unit of electric current, the ampere (sometimes shortened to 'amp') is named after him. ◆

👁 **see also**
Oersted

Roald **Amundsen**

Norwegian explorer and the first man to reach the South Pole
Born *1872*   **Died** *1928 aged 55*

Roald Amundsen began a career studying medicine, but gave it up to go to sea. Soon he became excited by the idea of polar exploration. He set out on his first expedition in 1903 aboard a small vessel with a crew of six. It took just over three years for Amundsen to become the first person to sail north from the Atlantic to the Pacific through the Arctic Ocean, north of Canada.

Amundsen decided to try to reach the North Pole next, but on hearing that an American, Robert Peary, had already done this, he sailed for Antarctica instead. It was to be a race between Amundsen and a British expedition led by Robert Falcon Scott, which had set out earlier. Amundsen and four companions, using sledges hauled by teams of dogs, reached the South Pole on 14 December 1911, almost a month before Scott's party. It was another first for Amundsen.

One of Amundsen's later adventures was in 1926 when he circled the North Pole twice in an airship. In 1928 Amundsen went to search for a friend who was missing on another airship flight over the North Pole. Amundsen set out to search for him, but his own plane was never seen again. ◆

👁 **see also**
Peary   Scott

▼ *Roald Amundsen pictured during an expedition to the North Pole in 1925.*

▲ *An illustration from Hans Christian Andersen's tale* The Emperor's New Clothes *in which a pompous ruler is taught a lesson by a clever tailor.*

Hans Christian **Andersen**

Danish children's story writer
***Born** 1805   **Died** 1875 aged 70*

H ans Christian Andersen was the only son of a poor shoemaker and of a mother who could hardly read. When he was 14 he walked all the way from his home in Odense to Copenhagen to try his luck in the big city. At the age of 17 he was put in a school with 12-year-olds. Because of this, and because he was so tall and clumsy, he was often mocked and bullied. Later in his life, when he began to write children's stories, he used this experience in the famous tale of *The Ugly Duckling*. He wrote his stories in simple language, just as he would have told them to a child. Even though such stories as *Thumbelina* and *The Little Mermaid* brought him fame throughout the world, Andersen remained a shy and lonely man. ◆

Elizabeth Garrett **Anderson**

Britain's first woman doctor
***Born** 1836   **Died** 1917 aged 81*

A t a time when all girls were expected to stay at home to be wives and mothers, the headmistress of Elizabeth Garrett Anderson's school encouraged her to seek a career.

When she was 22, Anderson decided that she wanted to be a doctor. (At this time, only men were allowed to be doctors.) She first trained as a nurse in London. Then, with the help of her professors, she studied in her spare time and was allowed to work as the first woman medical practitioner at the age of 29. But she was still not a fully-qualified doctor.

Anderson opened the St Mary's Dispensary for poor women and children, but she was still refused permission to study and become a doctor solely because she was a woman. So she went to Paris, studied there and passed her examinations, all in French and with six distinctions, and thus finally became a qualified doctor.

Elizabeth Garrett Anderson fought for the rights of women, especially women wanting to be doctors. Women in England were eventually accepted as medical students after the government passed the Medical Act of 1876. ◆

Saint **Andrew**

One of Christ's apostles and the patron saint of Scotland
Lived during the 1st century

A ndrew was a fisherman who lived in Capernaum. He was a disciple of John the Baptist and then became an apostle of Jesus. Jesus had told both Andrew and his brother, Simon Peter (who later became Saint Peter), that they would be 'fishers of men', so Andrew went out into the world preaching the Gospel. The people of Patras in Greece claimed that he was crucified there.

A later legend said that in the 4th century, a native of Patras had a dream in which an angel told him to take some of Andrew's bones to a land in the north-west. He obeyed, and travelled until he reached Scotland. The angel then told him to stop in Fife, where he built a church to hold the bones. The church was later called St Andrews. It became a centre for converting the Scottish people to Christianity. For this reason, Andrew was chosen to be the patron saint of Scotland. (He is also the patron saint of Greece and Russia.) His feast day is held on 30 November. ◆

see also

Jesus   John the Baptist   St Peter

Maya **Angelou**

American writer and performer
Born 1928

Marguerite Annie Johnson was born in St Louis, Missouri. She suffered a traumatic childhood and did not speak for several years. After moving to California, she gave birth to a son when she was only 16.

Before becoming a writer, Angelou was a performer and singer. In the 1940s she toured Europe and Africa in the opera *Porgy and Bess* before returning to America to work as a nightclub singer.

Angelou tells the story of her early life in *I Know Why the Caged Bird Sings* (1970), the first part of her much acclaimed three-part autobiography. Her other writing includes plays, poetry, songs, articles, and fiction.

Angelou is now professor of American Studies at Wake Forest University in North Carolina. ◆

◀ *Many of Maya Angelou's autobiographical works tell of her struggles growing up as a black woman in the American South. In another book, All God's Children Need Traveling Shoes (1986), she recounts her return to the West African country of Ghana in search of her family's past.*

Susan Brownell **Anthony**

American defender of women's rights
Born 1820   Died 1906 aged 86

Susan Brownell Anthony came from a well-to-do Quaker family in Massachusetts who brought all their children up to be independent and to stand up for themselves.

Anthony was a clever child, and could read and write by the age of three. For most of her adult life she used her abilities in a battle for votes and rights for women and for black people.

She showed great courage in the face of hostile opponents and newspapers which printed dreadful stories about her. She was a single-minded, energetic woman, who some said was not easy to know or to like! She had the satisfaction of seeing equal voting rights for women introduced into four states of America in her lifetime. ◆

Mark **Antony**

Roman politician and soldier
Born 83 BC   Died 30 BC aged 53

Although we know him as Mark Antony, his proper Roman name was Marcus Antonius. Like other young men from distinguished families in Rome, Mark Antony held several posts in the army and served under the general Julius Caesar. After Caesar had been murdered, Antony delivered a speech to the people of Rome at the funeral, stirring them up against the murderers. He was well placed to succeed him but hostility rose between him and Octavius, Caesar's adopted son and heir (and who later became Emperor Augustus). They ruled

▲ *A marble sculpture of Mark Antony, made during his lifetime.*

together with Lepidus for a while before splitting up the Roman Empire, with Antony taking the eastern area.

At first he co-operated with Octavius and married his sister, Octavia. However, he soon came under the influence of the queen of Egypt, Cleopatra. Although Cleopatra was very powerful she cost him a lot of support in Rome. He eventually left Octavia to marry Cleopatra and broke with Octavius, deciding to establish his power independently in the East. In 34 BC he declared Caesarion (Cleopatra's son allegedly by Caesar) as Caesar's heir instead of Octavius and divided the eastern empire among his family. War with the rest of the Roman Empire followed. The turning point of the war was when Antony's troops were defeated by Octavius's at the great naval battle of Actium in 31 BC. Antony and Cleopatra retreated to Egypt, pursued by Octavius. Realizing that all was lost, Antony committed suicide, shortly followed by Cleopatra. ◆

see also

Augustus   Caesar   Cleopatra

▲ St Thomas Aquinas depicted in a 16th-century stained glass window in Florence, Italy.

Saint Thomas Aquinas

Italian religious teacher and philosopher
Born *c.1225*   **Died** *1274 aged about 49*

Thomas Aquinas was the seventh son of the Italian Count of Aquino. His brothers were army officers but Aquinas persuaded his mother to let him join the Dominican order of preaching friars. He studied in Paris where he formed a school at which he taught until the pope called him back to teach in Italy.

The most famous of Aquinas's many writings are the *Summa Philosophica* and the *Summa Theologiae*. These are accounts of the Christian faith treated both philosophically, with reasoned argument, and theologically, as unquestioning belief in God.

Aquinas was declared a saint in 1323. His teaching is today accepted as standard by the Roman Catholic Church. ◆

Yasser **Arafat**

Palestinian leader
Born *1929*

Yasser Arafat has devoted his life to the struggle to create a homeland for the Palestinians who fled abroad when Israel fought for its independence from Britain in 1948. Arafat, the son of an Arab

▼ Yasser Arafat, leader of the Palestine Liberation Organization, seeks a Palestinian homeland free from Israeli rule.

merchant, was born in Jerusalem (which was then part of Palestine). In the 1950s he joined various guerrilla groups, including 'Fatah' (Victory) which organized raids against Israel. In 1969 he became leader of the Palestine Liberation Organization (PLO) which was recognized by Arab nations as the representative of all Palestinians.

After many years of attack and counter-attack, Arafat and the PLO reached an historic agreement with Israel in September 1993 in which the first steps were made towards a lasting settlement between both sides. ◆

Archimedes

Ancient Greek mathematician and engineer
Born *c.287 BC*
Died *212 BC aged about 75*

Archimedes was born in the town of Syracuse in Sicily, at that time ruled by the Greeks. He was the son of an astronomer and spent his life studying geometry and using his ideas to develop new types of machines. One of the most famous is the Archimedean screw for pumping out water.

There are lots of stories about Archimedes and even if some of them are not completely true they still give us an idea of what this great man may have been like.

One famous story tells of how Archimedes tried to work out whether the king of Syracuse's crown was made of pure gold or not. Archimedes could not solve the problem until one day, in his bath, he realized that the water level rose higher the more of his body he immersed. He leapt out of the bath and ran naked through the streets shouting 'Eureka!' which means 'I've got it!' The experiment was done with the crown. He noted how high the water level rose when he put it in a bath. Next he took a piece of pure gold weighing the same as the crown and immersed it in the water. Did the water level rise to the same height? No, so the crown could not have been made of pure gold! ◆

Aristophanes

Ancient Greek writer of comedies
Born *c.450 BC*
Died *c.385 BC aged about 65*

Aristophanes wrote such funny comedies that they are still frequently revived today. The most famous of these are *Frogs*, making fun of the celebrated Greek dramatist Euripides; *Clouds*, which mocked the famous Greek philosopher Socrates; and *Lysistrata*. This last comedy attacks the idea that war is a glorious activity. It tells the story of some women who, fed up with being left behind on their own, tell their soldier-husbands they will have nothing more to do with them until they have stopped fighting. The wives win, and peace comes at last. It was typical of Aristophanes that he should attack a subject such as war that many others of his time took very seriously. ◆

👁 **see also**
Socrates

Aristotle

Ancient Greek philosopher, teacher, and writer
Born *384 BC*   **Died** *322 BC aged 62*

At the age of 17 Aristotle joined Plato's Academy in Athens where he studied science and philosophy for 20 years. Shortly after Plato's death, Aristotle left the Academy and went to live on the Greek island of Lesbos, where he

continued to study. In 343 BC he was appointed tutor to the young Alexander the Great. When Alexander succeeded to the throne, Aristotle returned to Athens and set up his own school, the Lyceum. He directed the Lyceum for 12 years, devoting himself to a wide range of teaching, writing, and research. His output was enormous and included collections of historical information as well as scientific and philosophical works.

In the Middle Ages Aristotle's work was rediscovered by Arab scholars (including Averroës) and translated into Latin. He was regarded as the supreme authority in science and philosophy and his ideas remained a key part of university education in Europe from the 13th to the 17th centuries. ◆

👁 **see also**
Alexander the Great
Averroës   Plato

Richard Arkwright

English inventor of textile manufacturing machines
Born *1732*   **Died** *1792 aged 59*

Richard Arkwright was the youngest of 13 children. He had no schooling and did not learn to read and write until he was middle-aged. At the age of ten he was sent to work in a barber's shop. While working there he discovered a method for dyeing hair that

did not fade, and he became a rich and successful barber and wigmaker.

However, Arkwright's real claim to fame is his invention of the 'spinning frame', a machine for spinning cotton. He made it with the help of a skilled watchmaker, John Kay. Arkwright went on to invent and improve other machines used in textile manufacture. Many workers found their jobs were taken over by the new machines. They became very angry and tried to destroy the machines and even threatened Arkwright. But he was a determined man and his factories helped his home county of Lancashire become the centre of the world's cotton industry. ◆

▶ *Arkwright's spinning frame (1769) was driven by a water wheel.*

▲ *Louis Armstrong*

Louis **Armstrong**

*American jazz trumpeter, entertainer,
and singer*
Born *1901*   **Died** *1971 aged 70*

L ouis Armstrong had a poor but
happy childhood, even though
his parents were separated.
However, one day a silly prank
(firing a pistol in the street) ended
up with him being taken from his
family to live in a children's home.
It was there that he had his first
music lessons and learned to play
the cornet.

He left the home as a teenager
and gradually started to earn a
living as a musician. In the 1920s,
he formed various small groups of
his own, such as 'The Louis
Armstrong Hot Five', and made

some recordings that became
famous among jazz fans worldwide.

In 1936 Armstrong appeared in
his first film, *Pennies from Heaven*.
From then on he gradually became
a popular entertainer, famous for
his cheerful, gravelly singing voice.
His biggest popular song hits were
'Hello Dolly', recorded in 1964, and
'What a Wonderful World', recorded
in 1968. ◆

Neil **Armstrong**

*American astronaut; the first person to
set foot on the Moon*
Born *1930*

A s a young man, Neil Armstrong
was always interested in
flying. He earned his pilot's licence
at the age of 16, even before he had
learnt to drive a car. The following
year he became a naval air cadet,
and went on to fly in the Korean
War.

In the 1950s Armstrong became
a test pilot for NASA (National
Aeronautics and Space
Administration) before joining the
US space programme in 1962. In
1969 he joined astronauts Aldrin
and Collins on the *Apollo 11*
mission, and on 20 July he became
the first person to walk on the
Moon. As he stepped off the lunar

landing module, he said, 'That's one
small step for man, one giant leap
for mankind.' ◆

King **Arthur**

Legendary hero
Lived during the 6th century

T here are lots of tales about
Arthur, in many different
languages. The first written tales
date from around 800, although
Celtic people in Britain probably
told stories about him before then.
So who exactly was he? The simple
answer is – we don't know. There
was definitely no British king called
Arthur. But there might have been a
chieftain of that name who could
have led an army against Anglo-
Saxon invaders or against fellow
Britons in a civil war. Some
historians say his headquarters were
in the West Country. Others believe
that his base was in northern
England, or even Scotland.

The Arthur of legend was a
perfect Christian king who ruled
Britain and conquered most of
western Europe. He held court at
Camelot with his queen, Guinevere.
His 12 most trusted warriors were
called the Knights of the Round

▼ *A tapestry showing the quest for the
Holy Grail.*

Table. In many stories, these knights search for the Holy Grail, the cup which, according to Christian legend, was used by Jesus at the Last Supper. ◆

Aryabhata

Indian scientist
Born 476   Died c.550 aged about 74

Aryabhata was a pioneering mathematician and astronomer. At the age of 23, he summed up his knowledge in a poem of 121 verses, known as the 'Aryabhatiya'. It was written in Sanskrit, the ancient Indian language of learning. The poem explains how to work out many mathematical problems, including how to find the area of a triangle or a circle and the volume of a sphere or a pyramid. It also describes how to chart the paths of the Sun and the Moon, and predict their eclipses and explain why these eclipses happen. He was also able to calculate the length of the calendar year with great accuracy, and suggested that the Earth was a sphere, spinning on its own axis and revolving round the Sun. In India, scholars were still studying his works a thousand years after his death. In Europe, it took them the same length of time to discover for themselves his theory about the Earth's motion round the Sun. ◆

Asoka

Emperor of India from c.272 BC to 232 BC
Lived during the 3rd century BC

Asoka was the grandson of Chandragupta Maurya, the founder of the Maurya empire in ancient India. Asoka extended his empire to cover what is now Afghanistan, Pakistan, and most of India.

After coming to the throne Asoka waged many wars to extend his empire. However, he was deeply moved to see the suffering of wounded soldiers during one of his campaigns, and he was then converted to Buddhism. He declared that he would fight no more wars, and devoted the rest of his life to the spreading of Buddhism in India and abroad.

He governed according to the Buddhist principles of toleration and humanitarianism and believed in concern for human life and abstaining from harming animals. Asoka spread the teachings of Buddha throughout his empire by erecting pillars of stone with the main teachings of the Buddhist religion inscribed on them, and by sending missionaries to neighbouring countries. ◆

👁 **see also**

Chandragupta Maurya

Fred **Astaire**

American film actor and dancer
Born 1899   Died 1987 aged 88

Fred Austerlitz had a successful stage career dancing with his sister Adele from the age of seven. When Adele gave this up to get married, Fred looked for work in films. By 1933 he had changed his name to Fred Astaire and teamed up with Virginia ('Ginger') Rogers in *Flying Down to Rio*, the first of nine films they made together. Through films such as *Top Hat* (1935) and *Swing Time* (1936) they became cinema's most famous dancing couple.

Ginger Rogers also had a separate career as an actress in comedy films, winning an Oscar for *Kitty Foyle* in 1940. Astaire retired for a time in 1946, but returned to star in *Easter Parade* (1948) with Judy Garland. ◆

▶ *Fred Astaire and Ginger Rogers in Swing Time (1936).*

▲ *Atahualpa agreed to be baptised to avoid being burned to death. This is why he is holding a cross at his execution.*

Atahualpa

Last ruler of the South American empire of the Incas
Born c.1502   **Died** 1533 aged about 31

Atahualpa and his brother Huascar were the sons and heirs of the great Inca emperor Huayna-Capac. After the emperor's death in 1525, civil war broke out with the two brothers on opposite sides. Huascar was captured and killed, and Atahualpa became emperor, the supreme Inca, based in modern Peru.

As emperor, he was thought to be a god descended from the Sun. People approached him with great respect. He used only the richest of objects, which were kept for him alone. He had complete power over his people, but he was expected to be fair and generous and to follow the ancient traditions of the Incas.

Atahualpa was captured by a small Spanish army in 1532. Even in captivity he continued to rule his people with strength and authority. But despite paying a ransom of gold and silver, he was executed the next year and the Spanish, led by Pizarro, conquered the Inca people. ◆

👁 **see also**
Pizarro

Kemal **Atatürk**

President of the new Republic of Turkey from 1923 to 1938
Born 1881   **Died** 1938 aged 57

Mustafa Kemal was born in Thessalonika, now part of Greece. At military college in Istanbul, then capital of the Ottoman empire, he was so good at mathematics that he was given the name Kemal which is Arabic for 'perfection'.

▶ *Kemal Atatürk shown dressed in Turkish national costume.*

As an officer, he fought in World War I when the Ottoman empire joined the German side. In 1918, Kemal joined other Turkish politicians in calling for Turkey to become an independent nation free of foreign control.

With his military skill, the Turks defeated the Greeks when Greece and Turkey went to war in 1921. Shortly after that, the Ottoman sultans were deposed and in 1923 a Turkish National Assembly was elected with Kemal as president of the new republic.

As president he ruled as a virtual dictator. His main policy was the modernization of Turkey. In 1934, he introduced the idea of surnames and took the surname Atatürk ('father of Turks'). ◆

Attila

Leader of the Huns against the Roman empire
Born 406   **Died** 453 aged 46

Attila was born into the tribe of the Huns, a race of warring nomads who had moved from the Asian steppes right up to the borders of the Roman empire in the West.

When he became king of the Huns in 434, he united his scattered people in a campaign against the Roman empire. For the next 20 years the Huns under Attila conquered and plundered almost the whole of Europe. Attila's greatest desire was to destroy Rome, and the pope was forced to pay him huge sums of money to save the city.

While his followers lived in luxury, Atilla ate only meat out of a wooden bowl. He was a short man, with deep-set eyes and a gaze which was hard and arrogant.

Although far from handsome, he was married many times; some say he had 300 wives.

When Attila died, the Huns cut their cheeks so that they could mourn their leader with tears of blood. ◆

Clement **Attlee**

Prime Minister of Britain from 1945 to 1951
Born 1883   Died 1967 aged 84

Clement Attlee was born into a middle-class family in London. In 1906 he qualified as a barrister, and then worked as a college tutor. When he taught at the London School of Economics, he lived amongst poor people in the East End and was disturbed to see the problems they faced.

This led to him joining and, in 1935, becoming leader of the Labour Party. When he replaced Churchill as prime minister in 1945 with an outstanding election victory, his government immediately began to carry out major changes in Britain. It increased state benefits and pensions and, in 1948, created the National Health Service. The railways and the coal, gas, and electricity industries were nationalized (taken over by the state). Attlee's government also granted independence to Britain's Asian colonies: India, Pakistan, Burma (Myanmar), and Ceylon (Sri Lanka). ◆

W. H. **Auden**

British poet
Born 1907   Died 1973 aged 66

Wystan Hugh Auden's life falls into two almost equal parts, divided by the year 1939 in which he emigrated to America. As a young man in England, Auden was angered by the society around him. The rise of Hitler's Nazi Party in Germany made him strongly anti-fascist. The books of poetry such as *Look Stranger!* (1936) that he published in the 1930s established him as leader among the young left-wing English poets. With his friend Christopher Isherwood, he wrote the verse plays *The Ascent of F6* (1936) and *On the Frontier* (1938).

In 1939 Auden went with Isherwood to America and later took American citizenship. Much of his later poetry was complex and intellectually demanding, reflecting his conversion to Christianity. He returned briefly to England from 1956 to 1961 as professor of poetry at Oxford University. ◆

Saint **Augustine of Canterbury**

Sent by Pope Gregory to convert the English to Christianity
Date of birth unknown
Died 604 or 605 age unknown

Augustine was the prior (deputy head) of St Andrew's monastery in Rome when Pope Gregory I sent him and 40 of his monks to convert the people in Britain to Christianity. There had been Christians in Britain while it was a Roman province, and there were some Christian communities worshipping in western Britain when Augustine arrived in 597. He landed in Kent and the king of Kent, Ethelbert, was persuaded by his wife to allow Augustine's mission to begin.

On Christmas Day 597 Augustine converted 10,000 people. The main place for worship was the capital of Kent, Canterbury. Augustine was made Archbishop of Canterbury and Primate (chief bishop) of Britain by Pope Gregory in 601. He founded the first monastery in Britain in Canterbury. ◆

▶ *This 13th-century chair in Canterbury Cathedral is named after Saint Augustine. It is the seat in which every archbishop is enthroned.*

Saint Augustine
of Hippo

Important early Christian writer
***Born** 354 **Died** 430 aged 75*

Augustine grew up in a small town in North Africa, which was then part of the Roman empire. At the age of 16 he went to study law at Carthage University. By the time he was 22 he had a mistress and a son, but was able to support himself by teaching. Six years later he moved to Milan in Italy, where he taught the art of speech-making.

His beloved mother had been a Christian, but over the years Augustine felt he had grown away from God. Then suddenly one day, when he was looking again at an inspiring passage in the Bible, he decided to give up his career, leave his partner and son, and devote the rest of his life to God. His *Confessions* tells the story of his childhood, youth, and conversion.

When he wrote the *Confessions*, Augustine had just become Bishop of Hippo, a city near his home town in Africa where he remained until his death. He continued to write and in his most important work, *The City of God*, he urged Christians not to trust in Rome or in anything that it stood for, but to think of themselves instead as belonging to God's city in heaven. ◆

Emperor Augustus

First Roman emperor
***Born** 63 BC **Died** AD 14 aged 76*

Augustus started life as Gaius Octavius. His mother was the niece of Julius Caesar and, after his father died when Octavius was only four, Caesar adopted him and made him his heir.

When Caesar was killed, Octavius joined forces with Marcus Antonius (Mark Antony) against the murderers. Octavius ruled for a while with Mark Antony and

▼ *This map shows the full extent of the Roman empire under the rule of Augustus.*

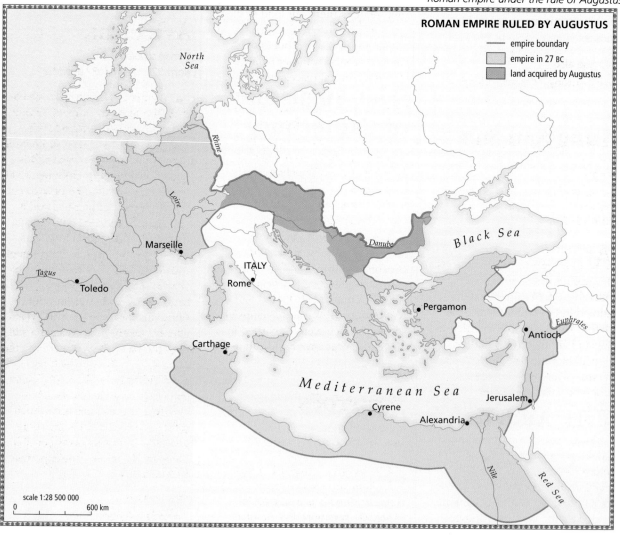

ROMAN EMPIRE RULED BY AUGUSTUS

— empire boundary
empire in 27 BC
land acquired by Augustus

North Sea

Rhine

Loire

Marseille

Tagus

Toledo

ITALY

Rome

Carthage

Danube

Black Sea

Pergamon

Euphrates

Antioch

Mediterranean Sea

Cyrene

Alexandria

Jerusalem

Nile

Red Sea

scale 1:28 500 000
0   600 km

Lepidus but before long civil war broke out in the Roman empire. Octavius defeated Antony (together with Cleopatra) and, in 29 BC, Octavius declared peace throughout the Roman world. He was now the most powerful man in Rome and took the name Augustus (meaning 'a person to be respected'). He established a new system of government: that of rule by one man, the emperor.

During his long reign he brought peace and enlarged the Roman empire. He also transformed the city of Rome. One writer said that Augustus 'could boast that he inherited it brick and left it marble'. On the deaths of his two grandsons he adopted Tiberius (his wife's son by a previous marriage) as his heir. ◆

👁 **see also**

Mark Antony   Caesar   Cleopatra

Aung San Suu Kyi

Campaigner for human rights in Burma (Myanmar)
Born 1945

Aung San Suu Kyi is the daughter of Aung San. He led Burma's struggle for independence, but was killed by a political rival. She studied in Burma and India, then at Oxford University. She married in England and had two children.

In 1988 Aung San Suu Kyi visited Burma. While she was there, a group of military leaders took power. She was appalled by their brutal rule, and helped form the National League for Democracy (NDL), who campaigned for a return to democracy. The NDL won elections held in 1990, but the government ignored the result and placed Aung San Suu Kyi under

house arrest until 1995. In 1991 she was awarded the Nobel Peace Prize for her 'non-violent struggle for democracy and human rights'. ◆

Jane **Austen**

English novelist
Born 1775   Died 1817 aged 41

Jane Austen was the seventh child of a country clergyman. Her father and mother always encouraged their children's imaginative play, converting the rectory barn into a little theatre for plays put on by the family during summer holidays. By the age of 12 Austen was writing her own stories and reading them out loud to the rest of the household.

She never married but instead moved around with her family, living in several places, including Bath, the setting for many episodes in her books. The family moved to Winchester in May 1817 seeking medical attention for her ill-health but Austen died two months later. She is buried in Winchester Cathedral.

Her books are famous for their witty insight into human failings and for their humour. The best-known novels are *Sense and Sensibility* (1811), *Pride and Prejudice* (1813), *Mansfield Park* (1814), *Emma* (1816), and *Northanger Abbey* and *Persuasion*, both of which were published in 1818, the year after her death. ◆

Averroës

Arab scholar
Born 1126   Died 1198 aged 72

The Arabian scholar Ibn Rushd was known as Averroës among learned Christians in the Middle Ages. He was born in Cordoba,

Spain and had such success as a doctor and a judge that he was appointed physician and adviser to the caliph (ruler) himself. However, Averroës is best known for his writings about the ideas of the Greek philosopher Aristotle. Averroës' thoughts about Aristotle were translated into Latin and it is through these translations that Christian scholars came to know about Aristotle. Averroës believed that faith and reason were separate ways of arriving at the truth, although this belief was not accepted by other Muslims. ◆

👁 **see also**

Aristotle

Avicenna

Persian scholar
Born 979   Died 1037 aged 58

Avicenna is the name by which Ibn Sina was known among learned Christians in the Middle Ages. He was born near Bukhara in Persia (now modern Iran) and is said to have written more than 200 books on a wide range of subjects. His philosophical works owed a great deal to the ideas of Aristotle and to some of Plato's followers. His greatest work was a huge book called the *Canon of Medicine* which was used as a basic medical textbook by both Muslims and Christians for more than 500 years after his death. In it, Avicenna still used the basic ideas about how the human body works which had been put forward more than 1000 years earlier by Aristotle and Galen. However, he also included much more accurate information about anatomy as well as many sensible ideas based on his own experience as a doctor. ◆

👁 **see also**

Aristotle   Galen   Plato

Charles **Babbage**

English mathematician
Born *1792*   **Died** *1871 aged 78*

Charles Babbage studied mathematics at Cambridge University. During his time there he calculated a correct table of logarithms which meant mathematical calculations could be done very accurately. However, most of his life was filled with his determination to build his own calculating machine.

He persuaded the British Government to invest £17,000 in the project (a very large sum of money in those days). He even invested £6000 of his own money. However, the project was never completed, mainly because the sort of machine that could be built at that time was too clumsy to do the work Babbage wanted it to do. Nevertheless, Babbage is often regarded as the 'grandfather of the modern computer' because of his original ideas. ◆

👁 **see also**

Pascal

J. S. **Bach**

German composer
Born *1685*   **Died** *1750 aged 65*

Johann Sebastian Bach was taught music by his father and then by his elder brother. Nobody seemed to teach him how to compose: he mainly taught himself by copying out the music of the composers he most admired. When he was 17 he took up his first important post as church organist in Arnstadt. He then worked as a court musician, first for the Duke of Weimar and then for Prince Leopold of Cöthen. His last and most important post was as organist and choirmaster of St Thomas's Church, Leipzig.

When working as a court musician, Bach wrote mainly chamber and orchestral works, including the six Brandenburg Concertos. When working for the church, he wrote organ music, cantatas, and great choral works, such as the *St Matthew Passion*.

Although he was very famous in his day (particularly as an organist), Bach's music was soon forgotten after his death. It was not until the 19th century that people began to realize how great it was.

He married twice and had 20 children. Two of them, Carl Philipp Emanuel (1714–1788) and Johann Christian (1735–1782), became, for a time, even more well known than their famous father. ◆

Francis **Bacon**

English politician and writer
Born *1561*   **Died** *1626 aged 65*

▲ *Although he was not a scientist himself, Bacon was central to the development of scientific methods and ideas.*

Francis Bacon was often ill as a child and spent a great deal of his time studying. He went to Cambridge University at the age of 12 and, after training to become a lawyer, spent most of his life working for the government.

Bacon is most famous for the 58 essays he wrote and published (1597–1625). People still enjoy reading what he had to say about human beings, their beliefs, and the world in which they live.

Bacon was knighted in 1603 and two years later published the *Advancement of Learning*, which gave his opinions on education at that time. In this and other books, he urged people to collect and classify facts about the world. He tried also to work out a method of using the facts collected to develop new scientific knowledge. In 1618 he became Lord Chancellor of England. ◆

Robert **Baden-Powell**

English founder of the worldwide Scouting movement
Born *1857*   **Died** *1941 aged 83*

Robert Baden-Powell was one of ten children. When he was 19 he joined the British army and was sent to southern Africa during the Boer War. One of his jobs there was to train some black African soldiers to scout out enemy country. He taught his scouts to notice details in the countryside, organizing them into small groups so that they could act more quickly.

When he returned to Britain he was surprised to learn that his *Aids to Scouting*, which he had written for his soldiers, was being taught in schools. He rewrote it as a book for boys and in 1908 founded the Boy

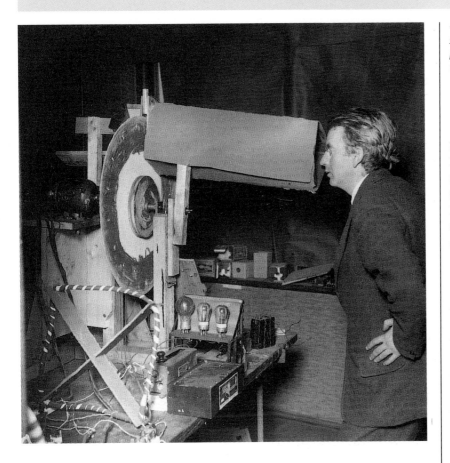

◀ Baird looking at a picture on the screen of his first television set. The picture is being 'drawn' by spots of light from holes in the rotating disc.

Scout Movement. His sister, Agnes, helped found the Girl Guide Movement in 1910, and later his wife, Olave, became World Chief Guide. ◆

▶ Baden-Powell seen wearing his soldier's uniform.

John Logie **Baird**

Scottish inventor of the first television
***Born** 1888   **Died** 1946 aged 57*

John Logie Baird's first jobs as an engineer were so miserable that when he was 26 he decided to become an inventor instead. His early ideas flopped and by the time he was 35 he was penniless. But in 1923 he started work on a machine that could transmit pictures, as well as sound, by radio. Soon he was able to send crude images by wireless transmitter to a receiver a few feet away.

Then, in January 1926, he gave the first public demonstration of television at the Royal Institution in London.

In 1929 the BBC made the first television

broadcast, using Baird's equipment. Baird was also responsible for the first sight and sound broadcast and the first outside broadcast (the Derby in 1931). A rival television system, which made use of cathode-ray tubes, took over from Baird's in 1933 and is still in use today. ◆

Vasco Núñez de **Balboa**

Spanish adventurer
***Born** c.1475   **Died** 1519 aged about 44*

Vasco Núñez de Balboa was a member of a noble Spanish family. In 1501 he sailed across the Atlantic Ocean to make his fortune. After settling briefly on the island of Hispaniola (Haiti), he stowed away aboard a ship that was carrying an expedition to found a new settlement on the coast of Central America.

He proved to be a born leader. Within a year he had made the little settlement a success, and the king of Spain made him its Governor.

Balboa was told by locals that there was another ocean nearby, and great wealth for the taking. He decided he would find this other ocean. With a small party of Spaniards and several hundred American Indians, he hacked his way through the jungle until from a hilltop he could see the Pacific Ocean. He rushed down the hill into the water, crying out that the sea belonged to the king of Spain. He was rewarded with the title of Governor of the South Seas. ◆

Honoré de **Balzac**

French novelist
Born 1799 *Died 1850 aged 51*

Honoré de Balzac was an extremely hard-working novelist, sometimes working 16 hours at a stretch. His vast collection of novels deals with every aspect of French society, from private life in the town or country to stories with a political or military

◀ *The sculptor Rodin was commissioned to make this statue of Balzac in 1897.*

setting. Taken together, this long series of novels became known as *La Comédie Humaine* (The Human Comedy). But Balzac was not really a comic writer; instead, he described a whole society as he saw it, with characters from one novel reappearing in another. The total impression is of a world so real it is hard to remember it all came from one man's imagination. Balzac's extraordinary powers of observation and understanding make his characters as believable as the settings in which they appear, which he always describes very vividly. ◆

Joseph **Banks**

English explorer and botanist
Born 1744 *Died 1820 aged 77*

Joseph Banks, the son of a wealthy doctor, became interested in botany at school. After inheriting his father's fortune, he was able to explore the world looking for new plants and animals. His first expedition, in 1766, was to Labrador and Newfoundland.

In 1768 Banks set sail with Captain Cook on the *Endeavour* bound for Tahiti and the South Seas. During the three-year voyage, Banks took part in the first exploration of Australia. The beautiful Australian plants *Banksia* are named after him.

In 1788 he became President of the Royal Society, the most important British scientific society. He was a friend of King George III, and advised him on the enlargement of the gardens at Kew and on his merino sheep, which were later so important in Australia. He was a friendly and hospitable person, and his natural history

▲ *A portrait of the botanist Joseph Banks from 1773.*

collections and library were always available for other scientists to use. ◆

👁 **see also**

Cook

Banting and Best

Canadian pioneers of the use of insulin
Frederick Banting
Born 1891 *Died 1941 aged 49*
Charles Best
Born 1899 *Died 1978 aged 79*

Frederick Banting graduated from the University of Toronto, Canada, and then served in World War I. He was awarded the Military Cross for his bravery.

After the war, whilst working as a doctor, he became interested in the disease diabetes. He managed to persuade Professor John MacLeod at Toronto to let him investigate the causes of this serious disease. Banting did not have much experience of research and so MacLeod appointed a young student, Charles Best, to help him.

Banting and Best carried out a

series of experiments on dogs. This proved that the hormone insulin, produced in the pancreas, can be used to treat diabetes. In 1922 a 14-year-old boy became the first person to be successfully treated using insulin.

Banting and MacLeod were awarded the Nobel Prize for Medicine in 1923. Banting was furious that Best had been left out and so generously shared his prize money with him. ◆

John **Bardeen**

American physicist
Born 1908   Died 1991 aged 83

Amplifiers, which make electrical signals stronger, and electronic switches were once big, expensive to operate, and broke easily. John Bardeen (with scientists William Shockley and Walter Brattain) made something better: the transistor.

Bardeen was born in Madison, Wisconsin, in America. He worked with Shockley and Brattain doing experiments on how electricity passed through materials called semiconductors. Just before Christmas 1947, one of the scientists spoke into a microphone and the world's first semiconductor transistor amplified the electrical signal to make the words sound louder. For this work, the team won the highest prize in science, the Nobel Prize, in 1956. The development of the transistor has made it possible to have such things as pocket calculators, digital watches, and portable computers.

Bardeen went on to study how some materials resist the flow of electricity whereas others, called superconductors, do not. By explaining how they worked, he won a share in a second Nobel Prize in 1972. ◆

Christiaan **Barnard**

South African surgeon who pioneered heart transplants
Born 1922   Died 2001 aged 78

Christiaan Neethling Barnard graduated from the University of Cape Town in South Africa in 1946. He went on to become resident surgeon at the Groote Schuur Hospital and then took a scholarship to the University of Minnesota in America from 1956 to 1958. While there he learnt a lot about heart surgery. He returned to Groote Schuur to concentrate on open-heart surgery, and designed an artificial heart-valve for use in operations. He began doing experimental heart transplants on dogs. When he felt he was ready, he and his colleagues at Groote Schuur performed the world's first transplant on a human patient, Louis Washkansky. They gave him the heart of someone who had died in a car accident. Unfortunately, complications set in and the patient died 18 days later. However, Barnard's work proved that, given the right conditions, heart transplant operations could work. ◆

Thomas **Barnardo**

British founder of Dr Barnardo's children's homes
Born 1845   Died 1905 aged 60

Thomas Barnardo was a small, sickly child with poor eyesight, but he was always clever and high-spirited.

At 21 he moved to London to study medicine, but he abandoned his studies to preach and teach among the poor families of the East End. Appalled by the plight of the homeless children he saw in that area, Barnardo began to raise money to provide homes for them.

Barnardo had lots of energy, remarkable powers of organization, and a flair for fund-raising. In his lifetime nearly 60,000 needy and handicapped children were sheltered and schooled in Dr Barnardo's Homes. He believed that no child should be denied help. His influence led to the state taking greater responsibility for protecting children against neglect and abuse. ◆

▼ *Children and carers in one of the first homes set up by Thomas Barnardo.*

J. M. **Barrie**

Scottish author and playwright
Born *1860*   **Died** *1937 aged 77*

James Matthew Barrie was born to a fairly poor household, the son of a handloom weaver. When he was six years old, his mother became seriously ill. While she lay in bed Barrie spent many hours with her, reading books or listening to her stories. It was then that he decided to become a writer.

He went to university, and then settled in London. His first novels were about life in his home town of Kirriemuir, which he called 'Thrums'. Then he began writing plays, and these brought him wealth and fame.

His most famous play, *Peter Pan*, was first performed in 1904, and with its mixture of fairies and pirates, it was an immediate success. Although *Peter Pan* is still popular, many of his other plays and books are too sentimental for modern taste and are now neglected. ◆

Béla **Bartók**

Hungarian composer and pianist
Born *1881*   **Died** *1945 aged 64*

Béla Bartók was only five when his mother began to teach him the piano. After graduating from Budapest's Academy of Music, he

◀ *One of Béla Bartók's critics once said that listening to his music was worse than going to the dentist. Today he is considered one of the greatest 20th-century composers.*

became well-known as a concert pianist, often performing his own works. Bartók loved Hungary, and when he discovered its folk music he began to collect and study it intensively. This gradually changed the nature of his own music and helped to give it a particular style. Many people, however, found his music aggressive and difficult to listen to.

In 1940 he emigrated to America because the political situation in Hungary had become intolerable to him. Although he was unhappy in America, he wrote two of his most colourful and popular works there: the Concerto for Orchestra, and the Third Piano Concerto. Bartók's music includes many folk-song arrangements and piano pieces, and six splendid string quartets. His body was reburied in Budapest after the fall of Communism. ◆

▶ *A theatre poster to advertise Barrie's play* Peter Pan. *This play grew from stories Barrie had made up for the five sons of some friends (to whom he gave a home when their parents died).*

Matsuo **Basho**

Japanese poet
Born 1644   *Died* 1694 aged 50

Matsuo Basho was born near Kyoto, Japan, the fourth of seven children of a poor samurai (warrior). At the age of nine he became a companion to the eldest son of his warrior lord, and together they studied literature, especially poetry. In 1672 Basho moved to the capital city of Edo (now Tokyo), where he became well-known as a poet. In the last ten years of his life he went on several long journeys on foot around Japan. This was an unusual thing to do since the roads were very bad and bandits were very common, making travel very dangerous. Basho's accounts of his journeys include many of his best and most famous poems. He is regarded as the greatest master ever of the haiku, the 17 syllable poem. In 1694 Basho started off on another journey, but fell ill and died at the city of Osaka in October. ◆

> On this Spring morning
> The moon shines pale through
>   the mist;
> It's a flower's face.
>   BASHO
> An example of his haiku poetry

Jean **Batten**

New Zealand solo aviator
Born 1909   *Died* 1982 aged 73

Born in Rotorua, New Zealand, Jean Batten had an early ambition to fly and came to Britain for training. By 1932 she was a skilful and daring pilot.

She obtained sponsors and soon made pioneering flights. In 1934 she set a record time for women flying solo from Britain to Australia.

◄ *Jean Batten and her plane,* Percival Gull.

Within the year, Batten became the first solo woman to make the return trip.

In 1935 Batten was the first woman to fly solo from Britain to Brazil, setting a speed record for both men and women pilots. In the next two years, she achieved two more absolute records – flying to New Zealand from Britain, and from Australia back to Britain.

Aviation historians rank Jean Batten as one of the top women solo pilots of the 1930s. She gave up flying when World War II began in 1939. ◆

👁 **see also**
Earhart   Johnson

Charles **Baudelaire**

French poet
Born 1821   *Died* 1867 aged 46

Charles Baudelaire first showed his rebellious side by misbehaving at his senior school in Paris. Deciding to become a writer, he lived in the Latin Quarter of Paris along with other struggling writers and artists, and became addicted to the drug opium. In 1841 his family sent him to India in an attempt to give him a fresh start. But he soon returned to his former life and quickly ran up huge debts. Turning to poetry, Baudelaire wrote about the pleasures and miseries of the

life he was leading, but his 1857 collection of poems, *Flowers of Evil*, proved to be very controversial. However, the way Baudelaire expressed the longing for something good to live for, gave these poems enormous power. Modern poets still regard Baudelaire as the first 19th-century poet to explore the inner secrets of the soul with the same sort of openness we expect today. ◆

Franz **Beckenbauer**

German footballer and manager
Born 1945

Footballer Franz Beckenbauer played his first game for Bayern Munich at the age of 18, and after just 25 games he was picked for West Germany. In 1966 he was in the team that lost the World Cup Final to England. Beckenbauer gained his revenge by scoring one of the goals that knocked England out of the 1970 World Cup, and then went on to captain West Germany to World Cup victory in 1974. As captain of Bayern Munich, he lifted the European Cup three times (1974–1976) and earned the name 'Kaiser' (Emperor) because he was such a good leader on and off the field. After retiring as a player, he went on to further success as coach and manager of the German national team. ◆

Saint Thomas **Becket**

Archbishop of Canterbury from 1162 to 1170
Born *1118*   **Died** *1170 aged 52*

After training as a lawyer, a priest, and a knight, Thomas Becket entered the household of the Archbishop of Canterbury, where he soon attracted the attention of the new king, Henry II. At the age of 36, Becket became the king's chancellor, and in 1162 was made Archbishop of Canterbury.

To everyone's surprise, Becket resigned as chancellor and began to live like a holy man. Saying that his duty to God as archbishop now came before his duty to the king, Becket angered Henry by challenging his claims to power over the Church.

Six years of quarrelling followed and Becket excommunicated (cut off from membership of the Church) any bishops whom he felt did not support him. The king flew into a rage, saying 'Will no man rid me of this turbulent priest?' Four of his

▼ *Thomas Becket and Henry II depicted in a stained-glass window at Canterbury Cathedral.*

knights took him at his word, went to Canterbury and slaughtered the archbishop at his cathedral altar. This sensational event shocked the whole Christian world. People saw Becket as a martyr and even compared his death with Christ's crucifixion. In 1172 the pope declared Becket to be a saint. ◆

Henri **Becquerel**

French physicist who discovered radioactivity
Born *1852*   **Died** *1908 aged 55*

Henri Becquerel followed in the footsteps of his father and his grandfather who had both been well-known physicists. He was interested in crystals which glow (fluoresce) after absorbing sunlight. When Röntgen discovered X-rays in 1895, Becquerel was fascinated: he wanted to find out whether fluorescent minerals emit X-rays. He put some crystals of a uranium compound on top of a photographic plate wrapped in paper and then left them in sunlight for several hours. When he developed the plate he found, as expected, the outline of the crystals.

Becquerel left some of the crystals and a photographic plate in a drawer. When he developed the plate he was surprised to see an image of the crystals. He had accidentally found that the effect was not due to sunlight but that something was coming from the crystals themselves. In fact it was radiation coming from the uranium.

His enthusiasm influenced Pierre and Marie Curie and in 1903 the three friends were awarded the Nobel Prize for Physics for their research into radioactivity. ◆

👁 **see also**
Curie   Röntgen   Rutherford

Ludwig van **Beethoven**

German composer
Born *1770*   **Died** *1827 aged 56*

Ludwig van Beethoven's father and grandfather were both professional musicians, so it was quite natural for him to follow in their footsteps. It was not long before, as a young man, he decided to leave Germany and seek his fortune in Vienna, Austria.

He made influential friends and was soon in demand as a fashionable pianist and teacher. However, from about 1796 he began to go deaf and by the end of 1802 his deafness was serious. At first he was in despair, but he pulled himself together and began to concentrate more fiercely than ever on composition.

The music he now wrote, including the Third and Fifth Symphonies, was more powerful and dramatic than anything anyone had ever written before. It seemed to tell of a life and death struggle between tremendous forces, ending always in triumph. For example, the

▲ *Despite his own misery, partly caused by his deafness (his ear-trumpet is shown above), Beethoven wrote inspiring music.*

heroine of his opera *Fidelio* defends her husband against an evil tyrant; and the *Missa Solemnis* (Solemn Mass) includes a prayer for deliverance from the horrors of war.

Some of Beethoven's music was considered to be unplayable at the time, but it was later realized that they were masterpieces.

His influence on later composers was enormous – Brahms, Mendelssohn, and Wagner all greatly admired him. ◆

Menachem **Begin**

Polish-born prime minister of Israel from 1977 to 1983
Born 1913   Died 1992 aged 79

Menachem Begin was a freedom-fighter who became a peace-maker. He studied law and became active in the Zionist movement to found a Jewish state in Palestine. He escaped the Nazi invasion of Poland and enlisted in the Polish Army. He went with it to Palestine and became a commander of a guerilla group which fought against the British army then occupying the country. A brilliant speaker, he became leader of the Herut (Freedom) party in 1948 and in 1970 became co-leader of the Likud (Unity) coalition. After 30 years in opposition he finally became prime minister in 1977.

Begin and the Egyptian president, Anwar Sadat, shared the Nobel Peace Prize in 1978 for their work in trying to bring peace to the troubled Middle East. ◆

see also
Sadat

Alexander Graham **Bell**

Scottish-born American inventor of the telephone
Born 1847   Died 1922 aged 75

Like other members of his family, Alexander Graham Bell trained to teach people to speak clearly. He went to America to continue this work and became convinced that he could teach totally deaf people to speak, even though they were unable to hear the sounds they were trying to imitate. He was also interested in other kinds of science, and was offered financial help towards his experiments from the parents of two deaf students whom he had taught to speak. One of his experiments led to his invention of the telephone, and he set up a company to develop and make telephones for sale.

In 1898 Bell became president of the National Geographic Society, and was so convinced that one of the best ways of teaching was through pictures that he started the *National Geographic* magazine, now world-famous for its superb colour pictures. ◆

▼ *This Bell telephone and terminal date from 1878. The Bell Telephone Company was the largest telephone company in the world for many years.*

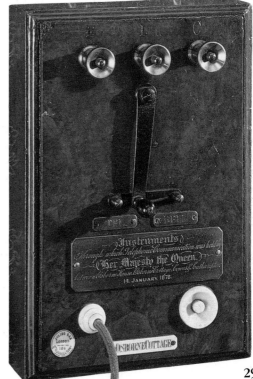

Jocelyn **Bell**

Bristish astronomer
Born 1943

Jocelyn Bell studied at the universities of Glasgow and Cambridge. In 1967, while working in Cambridge with a group of fellow radio astronomers, she noticed a highly unusual radio signal. It consisted of very rapid, regular pulses. Her observation led the team of scientists to make the important discovery of pulsars.

Pulsars are incredibly dense, rapidly rotating remnants of stars that have previously exploded as supernovae. These stars emit a beam of radiation which can be received on Earth each time the star rotates. This can be as often as once every 0.03 seconds. The leaders of the research team, Antony Hewish and Martin Ryle, went on to win the Nobel Prize for Physics in 1974, although Bell is regarded as the discoverer of pulsars. In her subsequent scientific career Professor Bell has been awarded many prizes for her work. ◆

Giovanni **Bellini**

Italian artist
Born 1430   Died 1516 aged 86

Giovanni Bellini was born in Venice, Italy, into an artistic family. His father, Jacapo, was a painter and he established a family workshop. His brother, Gentile, became a painter of considerable importance and his brother-in-law, Mantegna, also became a very famous painter.

Giovanni was at first much influenced by his father's ideas and sketches (his father's two sketch-books still survive) but later Mantegna was to become his strongest influence.

▲ *Giovanni Bellini's* Madonna and Child with St Paul and St George.

Bellini developed a large workshop where many apprentices and assistants helped him carry out the numerous requests for religious paintings and portraits. As a teacher he influenced many who later became great artists themselves. He eventually became chief painter to the state and is considered to be the most important and inventive of the Venetian 'Madonna' artists. ◆

David **Ben-Gurion**

Israel's first prime minister
Born 1886   Died 1973 aged 87

David Ben-Gurion has been called 'the George Washington of Israel', because like Washington he fought for his country's independence and led it in its early years. His original name was Gruen, but he changed it to Ben-Gurion, 'son of a lion-cub', after he emigrated from Poland to Palestine in 1906.

Palestine was then part of the Turkish Ottoman empire, and Ben-Gurion was expelled as a trouble-maker by the Turks. He went to America and joined the Jewish Legion, which fought in the British army in Palestine in World War I.

After the war Palestine came under British rule. Ben-Gurion became general secretary of the Histadrut (the Confederation of Palestine Jewish Workers), and organized the defence of the Jewish settlers against hostile Arabs.

When European Jews wanted to enter Palestine and were not allowed to do so, Ben-Gurion began campaigning for an independent Jewish state. In 1947 the United Nations decided that Palestine should be divided between Jews and Arabs, and in 1948 Ben-Gurion proudly read out the proclamation which declared Israel independent and he became prime minister. He retired in 1953, but was recalled in 1955 to serve again as prime minister until 1963. ◆

👁 **see also**

Begin   Weizmann

Karl **Benz**

German builder of the first practical motor car
Born 1844   *Died* 1929 aged 85

K arl Benz was determined that he would produce the first road vehicle to use the internal combustion engine. In the 1880s the internal combustion engine existed, and even though several engineers had tried fitting one on to a horse carriage, they had not been very successful in producing a practical motor car.

Benz, however, realized that the engine and the carriage had to be designed together. He went on to build a three-wheeled car which was patented in 1886. It was the first really successful automobile. He kept on improving his designs and by 1893 he was making four-wheeled cars that many people wanted to buy.

He teamed up with Gottlieb Daimler, his former rival, to start the great Daimler-Benz company. Benz's name still lives on in the Mercedes-Benz cars and lorries that are made today. ◆

👁 **see also**
Daimler

Vitus **Bering**

Danish explorer
Born 1681   *Died* 1741 aged 60

V itus Bering joined the Russian navy in 1703. He was a skilled navigator and in 1728 Tsar Peter the Great appointed him to lead an expedition to find out whether Asia and North America were connected by land. Bering sailed northwards along the coast of Asia and, when the coast turned westwards, he concluded that the two continents were separated by sea. In fact the distance between them, now known as the Bering Strait, is only about 80 kilometres. Five years later he headed the 600-man Great Northern Expedition along the Siberian coast. In 1741 he sailed west towards America and became the first European to sight Alaska, when he saw an Alaskan volcano. Foul weather and sickness forced him back. He was shipwrecked on a deserted island and died of scurvy with 19 of his crew. The survivors buried him on the island, which was later named Bering Island after him. ◆

▼ *Bering Island, Bering Sea, and the Bering Strait are all named after the Danish explorer Vitus Bering.*

Irving **Berlin**

Russian-born American songwriter
Born 1888   *Died* 1989 aged 101

I rving Berlin was born Israel Baline in Russia. When he was five his family left to go to New York. His father died when he was young and so, after only two years at school, he had to go to work. He worked as a newsboy, street singer, and singing waiter. Writing song lyrics got him a job with a music publisher and a printer's error gave him the idea for his professional name.

▲ *The 1948 film* Easter Parade, *starring two of Hollywood's greatest musical talents, Fred Astaire and Judy Garland, included many great Irving Berlin songs.*

Soon he started to write tunes too, although at the time he could not read music. In 1911 he hit the jackpot with 'Alexander's Ragtime Band', which sold 2 million copies by 1915. He wrote music and over 800 songs for shows and movies including *Top Hat* (1935), *Easter Parade* (1948), *White Christmas* (1954), and *There's No Business Like Show Business* (1954) which features stars such as Fred Astaire and Ginger Rogers, Judy Garland, Bing Crosby, Ethel Merman, and Marilyn Monroe. ◆

👁 **see also**
Gershwin   Porter

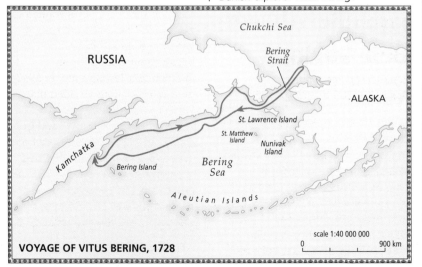

Chukchi Sea

RUSSIA

Bering Strait

ALASKA

St. Lawrence Island

St. Matthew Island

Nunivak Island

Kamchatka

Bering Island

Bering Sea

Aleutian Islands

scale 1:40 000 000
0   900 km

VOYAGE OF VITUS BERING, 1728

Hector **Berlioz**

French composer
Born *1803* **Died** *1869 aged 65*

Hector Berlioz first trained to be a doctor like his father, but his love of music proved too strong and from 1826 he studied music at the Paris Conservatoire. In the following year he fell passionately in love with an Irish actress, Harriet Smithson. She rejected him and he recorded his feelings about her in the extraordinary *Symphonie fantastique*. This seems to have made her change her mind because they married in 1833, although they parted eight years later.

Berlioz made his living as a music critic and conductor while he wrote a series of remarkable works, such as the *Roméo et Juliette* symphony. However, he never quite recovered from the failure of his operatic masterpiece, *Les Troyens*, and died a disappointed man. ◆

St Bernadette

French girl who saw a vision of the Virgin Mary at Lourdes
Born *1844* **Died** *1879 aged 35*

Marie-Bernarde Soubirous came from Lourdes, a French town close to the Spanish border. When she was 14 years old she announced that she had seen the Virgin Mary and that she had spoken to her. Neither her parents nor church officials believed her but she never changed her story.

Her claims aroused a great deal of public interest, so to avoid the publicity she was sent to a boarding-school. When she finally left school she went to live as a nun with the Sisters of Charity at Nevers. Here she was constantly plagued by sickness and suffered from asthma. Even when she was dying she

▲ *A souvenir postcard from Lourdes (1867) showing a vision of the Virgin Mary.*

showed considerable courage and good humour and won the admiration of her friends.

In 1933 Pope Pius XI canonized her as Saint Bernadette. Lourdes is now visited by thousands of pilgrims every year, particularly the sick. Many of them who are dipped in the water of a spring there claim to have been cured. ◆

Sarah **Bernhardt**

French actress
Born *1844* **Died** *1923 aged 78*

When she was young, Sarah Bernhardt enrolled in acting school and got a place in the French national theatre company. She was sacked for slapping a senior actress and it was some years before she became a leading actress famed for her musical 'silvery' voice. She was worshipped by her fans as 'The Divine Sarah' and travelled the world with her own company. Her most famous roles included the title role in Racine's play *Phèdre*, and Marguerite Gautier in *The Lady of the Camellias*. She also played male roles including the lead in *Hamlet*.

She was the first great actress to appear in movies. During the making of the film *Tosca* she injured her knee while jumping from some battlements. In 1915, after years of pain, her leg had to be amputated – but she went on acting in parts that she could play mainly sitting down. ◆

👁 **see also**

Irving

▼ *This theatre poster advertises Sarah Bernhardt's role in* The Lady of the Camellias.

◀ *This statue, The Ecstasy of St Theresa, is one of Gianlorenzo Bernini's most famous. The facial expressions of his subjects and the way their costumes are draped suggest drama and movement. Bernini was also a skilled architect and a painter.*

Gianlorenzo
Bernini

Italian sculptor
Born 1598   Died 1680 aged 82

Gianlorenzo Bernini grew up in a sculpting family. He was influenced by classical Greek and Roman sculpture, by Michelangelo, and by painters of his time. He founded the 'Baroque' style of sculpture: straightforward natural subjects which have balance and harmony and therefore directly appeal to the viewer. His sculptures are meant to be seen from a front view rather than from all around. Bernini attempted to show the real spirit of the person he was sculpting through their facial expression. His technique was to make small terracotta clay models first and then, with the help of many assistants, to make the large pieces. He liked to use coloured marbles or bronze to add a painterly effect to his sculptures. ◆

Bernoulli family

Swiss family of mathematicians
Jakob Bernoulli
Born 1654   Died 1705 aged 50
Johann Bernoulli
Born 1667   Died 1748 aged 80
Daniel Bernoulli
Born 1700   Died 1782 aged 82

Jakob Bernoulli's father wanted him to be a clergyman but he followed his passion for mathematics instead. As a young man he travelled to meet other mathematicians, and at 33 he was made professor of mathematics at Basel University, Switzerland. His special interests were curves, infinite series, and calculus. One curve, the logarithmic spiral, so fascinated him that he had it carved on his gravestone.

Johann Bernoulli became a mathematician against his father's wishes, just as his older brother Jakob had done. The two brothers had similar mathematical interests and became rivals. Sometimes one would claim the other's discoveries as his own. While visiting France, Johann met the Marquis Guillaume de l'Hospial and agreed to supply him with his mathematical discoveries in return for a salary. The Marquis then passed the discoveries off as his own.

Daniel Bernoulli was Johann's son. Johann taught him mathematics, but was not happy when Daniel became very successful. Daniel also studied philosophy and medicine, and for a while taught anatomy and botany at Basel. He made important discoveries in calculus, probability, and vibrations, but is most famous for his work on the pressure of flowing liquids. ◆

Leonard
Bernstein

American composer and conductor
Born 1918   Died 1990 aged 72

When Leonard Bernstein was ten, his family acquired a piano. Bernstein liked it and began lessons, soon making quick progress. He went on to study music at Harvard University and at the Curtis Institute of Music, Philadelphia. When he was in his mid-twenties he became assistant conductor of a great symphony orchestra, the New York Philharmonic.

From the 1940s Bernstein became known as a composer of musical shows. The most famous and successful of these was *West Side Story*, which opened on Broadway, New York, in 1957 and was later made into a film. He wrote many kinds of orchestral and choral music as well as music for the stage, and was a highly respected conductor and pianist. ◆

Chuck **Berry**

American rock and roll singer
Born 1926

In the 1950s Charles 'Chuck' Berry invented the ringing guitar sound which inspired many 1960s pop groups, especially the Beatles and the Rolling Stones. Born in San Jose, California, Berry did a number of jobs while he tried to become a full-time musician. Once he got a recording contract, he had a string of hits with witty story-lines. These songs mixed country music with rhythm 'n' blues and an irresistible dance beat.

His songs, including 'Rock'n'Roll Music' (1957) and 'Sweet Little Sixteen' (1958), are world-famous and have been performed by hundreds of other musicians. John Lennon of the Beatles once said of him, 'If you tried to give rock'n'roll another name, you might call it Chuck Berry.' ◆

👁 **see also**
Lennon and McCartney

Annie **Besant**

English campaigner for birth control, socialism, and the rights of women
Born 1847   Died 1933 aged 85

Annie Besant left her unhappy marriage when she was 26 and began working as a journalist. She cared deeply about poverty-stricken women who had to look after large families, and she began campaigning for birth control. When she published a book about it she was arrested and put on trial. Although she was released, her daughter was taken away from her.

The tragedy of losing her daughter pushed Besant into fighting for more reforms, especially for the London 'match girls'. These women worked long hours in unhealthy conditions making matches for four shillings (20 pence) a week. In 1888 they went on strike for better pay. Besant wrote about them in the newspapers and led a procession of match girls to the House of Commons. As a result, their strike was successful.

Besant then moved to India where she helped start the Central Hindu College at Varanasi (Benares). She believed strongly that India should be an independent country, free of British rule, and she started a newspaper to support this idea. She died before this dream became a reality. ◆

Henry **Bessemer**

English pioneer of steel manufacture
Born 1813   Died 1898 aged 85

Henry Bessemer's father was an engineer who fled from France during the Revolution. He established an engineering works in England and it was there that Henry Bessemer, after only a basic education, himself became an ingenious and skilled engineer. At 17 he founded a small business of his own in London, making a variety of products ranging from graphite for pencils to printing machinery. He flourished but his great success, in the 1850s, was a process for converting iron to steel by blowing air through it while molten. Steel was then scarce and expensive. By 1898, when Bessemer died, more than a million tonnes per year was being made in Britain alone by his process and it was also widely used abroad. Its only rival was the Siemens open-hearth process. Much of the steel produced by Bessemer's methods went into rails for the rapidly expanding railway system. ◆

👁 **see also**
Krupp   Siemens

◀ *One of Chuck Berry's songs was chosen as a sample of Earth music to go on board the Voyager space probe.*

◀ Benazir Bhutto was inspired to go into politics by her father's death.

Benazir **Bhutto**

Prime minister of Pakistan from 1988 to 1990 and from 1993 to 1996
Born 1953

After studying in Pakistan, Benazir Bhutto completed her education in America and England. She returned to Pakistan but after her father, prime minister Zulfikar Ali Bhutto, was executed, she spent a total of six years either in prison or under house arrest.

In 1986 she launched a campaign for open elections in Pakistan. The death of the president, General Zia-ul-Haq, in an air crash in 1988 did in fact lead to democratic elections. Benazir Bhutto's party won and she became prime minister at the age of 35. She was the first female leader of a Muslim state. In 1990, the opposition forced her out of office and charged her with corruption. She denied all charges and then campaigned to be re-elected as prime minister. She won the vote in 1993 with a small majority. Her coalition government lasted until 1996. ◆

👁 **see also**
Bhutto, Zulfikar

Zulfikar Ali **Bhutto**

President and then prime minister of Pakistan from 1971 to 1977
Born 1928   Died 1979 aged 51

The Bhutto family have been important in the politics of India and Pakistan for many years. Zulfikar Ali Bhutto was educated at the universities of California and Oxford before becoming a lawyer. At the age of 30 he joined Ayub Khan's cabinet and within five years had become Foreign Minister of Pakistan. In 1967, he started his own party, the Pakistan People's Party, which came to power in 1971. Bhutto was first president and later prime minister.

After the 1977 elections there were riots because some people thought Bhutto had rigged the vote. General Zia-ul-Haq staged a coup and overthrew Bhutto's government. Bhutto himself was arrested and charged with the murder of a political opponent. In spite of protests from around the world, he was hanged in April 1979. ◆

👁 **see also**
Bhutto, Benazir

Steve **Biko**

South African civil rights leader
Born 1946   Died 1977 aged 30

Stephen Biko went to the University of Natal in 1966 to study medicine. He soon became involved in student politics and in 1968 helped to found the South African Students' Organization. His main concern was for his own black people who suffered oppression under the apartheid system which deprived them of their basic rights. In 1972 Biko gave up his medical studies to help form the Black People's Convention, which worked to raise black people's awareness of oppression and to give them a sense of pride and hope for the future. His activities brought him into conflict with the government and he was often arrested and prevented from speaking in public. Then in 1977, after being arrested once again, he was so badly beaten in the police cells that he died before he could be brought to trial. Since his death he has become a symbol of the anti-apartheid movement. ◆

👁 **see also**
Mandela

35

Billy the Kid

American outlaw in the Wild West
Born 1859   Died 1881 aged 21

By the age of 12, William Bonney was already a gambler and card player, and had knifed a man for insulting his mother. In 1877, after more murderous exploits, he became involved in a war between two cattle-ranching families. As the leader of one of the gangs he was involved in one gun battle after another. He finally returned to cattle thieving and murdering when the war was over.

A sheriff called Pat Garrett was determined to catch Bonney, who was now known as Billy the Kid. He was captured in 1881 and sentenced to hang, but he managed to escape. Two months later, Garrett managed to corner him and shot him dead.

Billy the Kid murdered at least 21 people, but films have been made which show him as a popular hero. In reality, Bonney was a vicious murderer and a thief. ◆

Isabella Bird

British traveller and writer
Born 1832   Died 1904 aged 72

When she was 23 Isabella Bird visited Canada and America and carefully recorded much that she saw. Later she travelled to Australia, Japan, India, Tibet, Iran, Korea, and China and wrote successful books about her adventures. She married her family doctor and ceased her travels until his death five years later.

Isabella Bird often felt ill and depressed in England, but once abroad she rode great distances and lived under very hard conditions. She had 'the appetite of a tiger and the digestion of an ostrich'. At the age of 70, in pain from an injured spine, she rode a thousand miles through the Atlas Mountains in North Africa on a horse she mounted by stepladder. It was to be her last journey. ◆

Clarence Birdseye

American inventor and businessman
Born 1886   Died 1956 aged 70

Clarence Birdseye lived and died in New York but the idea for his most famous invention came to him when he was buying and selling furs in icy Labrador, Canada. During the severe winter, fresh food was hard to come by so the locals ate food that they had previously frozen. This fascinated Birdseye. When he returned home he began experimenting. He found that if he froze fish or vegetables very quickly between two metal plates, the flavour could be preserved.

In 1929 he became the first person to sell quick-frozen food in small packages. His idea was very successful and his food company grew and grew. Eventually he sold the company for a huge amount of money. Although he went on to invent many other things, he is best remembered for the packets of frozen food which still bear his famous name. ◆

Laszlo Biro

Hungarian-born inventor of the ball-point pen
Born 1900   Died 1985 aged 85

Laszlo Biro was born in Hungary, where he spent his early life as a journalist. With his brother Georg he worked on the idea of a pen with a tiny rolling ball at the tip instead of a pointed nib. This ball would allow a smooth flow of ink, although the problem was to get the ink right – not too runny, not too thick, and quick to dry.

In 1938 the brothers went to Argentina, away from the spreading Nazi influence in Europe. There they perfected and patented their ball-point pen – which has since become known simply as a biro.

At first biros were fashionable and expensive, but as time went by they became much cheaper. They were the most convenient everyday writing implements until the felt-tip pen was invented in the 1960s. ◆

▶ *Isabella Bird lived in this tent while travelling with a nomadic tribe in Persia (Iran).*

Georges **Bizet**

French composer
Born 1838   Died 1875 aged 36

Georges Bizet's parents were both musical and gave him his first lessons. He began to study at the Paris Conservatoire when he was only nine, and made a deep impression both as a pianist and composer. In 1857 he won the Prix de Rome, which enabled him to study in Italy for three years. On returning to Paris he had a hard struggle to make a living. Although he wrote music of all kinds, including a delightful Symphony in C, which was not performed until long after his death, opera was his first love. Some of his operas, such as *The Pearl Fishers* (1863) and *The Fair Maiden of Perth* (1867), were reasonably successful, but others failed. Even his masterpiece, *Carmen* (1875), shocked people by its realism and was coolly received at first. It is now one of the most popular of all French operas. Like all of Bizet's music, it is lively, colourful, and full of the most glorious melody. ◆

Otto von **Bismarck**

Prussian leader who helped create a united Germany
Born 1815   Died 1898 aged 83

Otto von Bismarck came from a noble family in Prussia, which was then only one amongst many German-speaking states. After serving in the army, he was elected to the Prussian parliament and in 1851 represented Prussia in the German Federal Diet, a parliament of all German states. He dreamed of uniting Germany under Prussian leadership.

In 1862 King Wilhelm of Prussia made Bismarck prime minister. Bismarck then started to pursue an aggressive policy against neighbouring countries. After capturing Danish territory with Austrian help, Prussian armies fought and defeated Austria in the Seven Weeks War of 1866. More success came in 1871 when Prussia defeated France and expanded Prussian borders.

These victories persuaded other German states to join a German

▲ *Bismarck's Prussian army bombards Strasbourg during the Franco-Prussian War, 1870–1871.*

Reich (empire) with King Wilhelm as Kaiser (emperor) and Bismarck as chancellor. The Reich gained colonies abroad and built up a fleet to compete with the British Royal Navy. In 1879 Bismarck made an alliance with the Austro-Hungarian empire. However, his career ended after Wilhelm died. His successor, Wilhelm II, was jealous of Bismarck's power and dismissed him in 1890. ◆

▼ *Maria Ewing plays the lead in the English Royal Opera's production of Bizet's Carmen.*

Tony **Blair**

Prime minister of the UK from 1997
Born *1953*

Tony Blair was educated at private schools in Durham and Edinburgh, then studied law at Oxford. He moved to London in 1976 to become a lawyer. He came from quite a rich family, but he wanted everyone to have a fair chance. So he went into politics as a member of the Labour Party and was elected to Parliament in 1983.

For the next 14 years Britain was governed by the Conservative Party. During that time, Blair played a large part in making the Labour Party more up-to-date, so that more people would vote for it.

In 1994 Blair became Labour Party leader. Then in 1997 a Labour government was voted into power, and Blair became prime minister. The following year he signed a peace settlement in Northern Ireland, after nearly 30 years of violence in the province. ◆

▼ *This is a page from William Blake's* Songs of Innocence and Experience.

William **Blake**

English poet, engraver, and artist
Born *1757*   **Died** *1827 aged 69*

As a boy, William Blake loved poetry and art. When he was 10, he went to a drawing school, and at 14 he was apprenticed to an engraver, learning how to prepare illustrations for books. He was for a time a student at the Royal Academy in London, but he later returned to engraving.

As a young man, Blake began to write poetry and illustrate it with pictures of biblical visions he had experienced. He etched his poems on copper plates and coloured the printed pages. Much of his poetry is happy and full of tenderness. His later poems, though, show more anger and sadness.

In his lifetime, few people valued Blake's poetry, and a lot of it was thrown away. But he produced so much that today we still have a large quantity of his poetry to enjoy. ◆

Louis **Blériot**

French airman
Born *1872*   **Died** *1936 aged 64*

Born in Cambrai, France, Louis Blériot first made a fortune making car headlamps. Then, when he was 30 he turned to aircraft design. In 1908 he created an aircraft control system not unlike that in use today – using elevators on the tail and later ailerons on the wings.

The first crossing of the English Channel by an aircraft was made by Blériot on 25 July 1909. He flew from Calais to Dover – a distance of some 34 kilometres. The flight took 37 minutes and won him a prize offered by the London paper, the *Daily Mail*. Blériot had designed this aircraft, his eleventh.

▲ *This illustration of Louis Blériot from the cover of a French magazine shows him flying over the cliffs at Dover after crossing the English Channel in his monoplane.*

It was a lightweight monoplane with a wooden frame and a fabric fuselage. ◆

Charles **Blondin**

French tightrope walker
Born *1824*   **Died** *1897 aged 72*

Born into a circus family, Charles Blondin was an 'aerobat' at five years of age. He did various tricks, but the tightrope, or high wire, became his speciality.

In 1859 he achieved the feat for which he will always be known. He rigged a high wire above Niagara Falls and walked across, the first person ever to do so. Having made it look easy, he repeated the walk many times, and then devised various ways of adding to it. His most fearsome trick was to call for volunteers to be carried across either piggyback or in a wheelbarrow. ◆

Enid **Blyton**

English author of children's books
Born 1897   Died 1968 aged 71

Enid Blyton began her career as a teacher, but soon switched to journalism, and often wrote about education. She then began to write children's books.

Her first book was a collection of poems for children. In the late 1930s, just before World War II, she started publishing the *Noddy* stories, for very small children, and adventure stories such as the *Famous Five* and the *Secret Seven*, for older children.

It was not long before she was writing her school story series, like *Malory Towers* and *The Naughtiest Girl*.

Enid Blyton wanted to educate her readers, and to give them a clear idea of right and wrong behaviour. Her stories have been enjoyed by a great many children, although teachers and librarians have often said that the plots are too simple and the style of writing is flat and uninteresting. ◆

Humphrey **Bogart**

American film actor
Born 1899   Died 1957 aged 58

'Bogey' was the son of a New York surgeon. He suffered a lip wound in the US Navy during World War I which gave him

▶ American actor Humphrey Bogart in the 1951 film Sirocco.

a distinctive appearance and voice when he later became an actor. His first film appearances in the 1930s were usually in gangster movies, but he became famous as the detective Sam Spade in *The Maltese Falcon* (1941). Then came the romantic drama *Casablanca* (1942), with Ingrid Bergman, before he teamed up with his wife Lauren Bacall in films such as *To Have and Have Not* (1944) and *The Big Sleep* (1946). He won an Oscar for his role in *The African Queen* in 1951. ◆

Niels **Bohr**

Danish physicist who helped discover the structure of atoms
Born 1885   Died 1962 aged 77

Niels Bohr studied physics at Copenhagen University, before becoming a professor there.

He moved to England in 1912 and worked with the great physicist Ernest Rutherford, trying to discover what atoms really looked like. Bohr's work showed that atoms have a nucleus at the centre and that electrons are arranged in orbits a fixed distance away from the nucleus. In 1922 Bohr received the Nobel Prize for Physics for his work on atoms.

During World War II Bohr worked hard to help Jewish scientists find new jobs, away from the tortures that they faced under Hitler. He himself made a dramatic escape from Denmark and fled to America. In 1943 he worked on the atom bomb project. However, he was so horrified by the potential effects of such a bomb that he spent the rest of his life working on peaceful ways of using atomic energy. ◆

◉ **see also**
Rutherford

39

Simón **Bolívar**

Venezuelan general
Born 1783   Died 1830 aged 47

As a young man Simón Bolívar travelled twice to Europe. There he was inspired by new ideas which claimed that all people should be free and equal. Eager to free his own country, Venezuela, from Spanish rule, he joined a group of rebels there. In 1810 they captured Caracas, the capital city, but the Spaniards fought back. Bolívar became a military leader in 1811, recaptured Caracas in 1813 and was given the title 'Liberator'.

A year later, Bolívar was forced to flee South America. But by 1817 he had returned to fight again. In 1819 his forces defeated the Spaniards in Colombia. That same year he founded Gran Colombia (a group of South American states), and became president.

In 1822, Bolívar met José de San Martín, who freed Argentina and Chile from Spanish rule. Bolívar later helped defeat Spanish armies still in Ecuador, Venezuela and Peru, bringing Spanish power in South America to an end.

In upper Peru, the people decided to form a separate republic, called Bolivia, in honour of Bolívar.

▼ *In 1821 Bolívar's army liberated Venezuela.*

Although Bolívar was respected, few agreed with his idea of uniting the whole of South America. When he died in 1830, Bolívar was hated by many for his dictatorial ways, but is also admired as South America's greatest liberator. ◆

👁 **see also**
San Martin

George **Boole**

English mathematician
Born 1815   Died 1864 aged 49

George Boole's father worked as a cobbler but was interested in mathematics and making optical instruments. He passed these interests on to his son who, by the time he was 15, was well-grounded in mathematics and had taught himself Latin, Greek, French, and German. In 1849, although he had no university degree, he was appointed professor of mathematics in Queen's College, Cork, and in 1857 was elected Fellow of the prestigious Royal Society. At Cork he wrote 50 mathematical papers and four books and developed what is still known as Boolean algebra. In this, logical statements are represented by algebraic equations, and the numbers 0 and 1 are used to represent 'false' and 'true'. Boolean algebra is fundamental to the operation of today's modern computers. ◆

Daniel **Boone**

Hero of the American Frontier
Born 1734   Died 1820 aged 85

Daniel Boone never went to school. Instead he hunted with the Native Americans who visited his father's farm. He grew up almost as skilled as they were in tracking animals.

On his first attempt to lead settlers to the West, Boone's 16-year-old son was captured and tortured to death by Native Americans. Two years later he completed the journey and founded Fort Boonesborough in Kentucky. For 20 years he led the defence of this settlement against attack.

Perhaps because of his childhood experience, Boone seemed reasonably at ease among the Native Americans. He once said 'I wouldn't give a hoot in Hell for a man who isn't sometimes afraid.' From Kentucky he took his family further west to Missouri. He died there in his sleep. ◆

Catherine and William **Booth**

English founders of the Salvation Army
William Booth
Born 1829   Died 1912 aged 83
Catherine Booth
Born 1829   Died 1890 aged 61

As a young man William Booth knew poverty, because his father went bankrupt and died early. He joined the Methodist Church, but left because he wanted to preach his own ideas. In 1855

▲ *While many of William Booth's peers went abroad to do missionary work, he stayed at home to help deprived people in Britain's city slums.*

he married Catherine Mumford, a social worker. Together they started the Salvation Army, a Christian organization to fight sin and poverty. William became the Salvation Army's first General.

Catherine Booth believed that women had as much right to preach as men. She made sure that the Salvation Army gave equal rights to all its members. She died in 1890, but William Booth continued their work. His book, *In Darkest England*, gave many ideas on how to help people suffering from poverty, homelessness, and alcoholism. With the help of their son, Bramwell, and daughter, Evangeline, the Salvation Army grew worldwide, and today it is still active in helping poor and homeless people everywhere. ◆

Jorge Luis **Borges**

Argentinian writer
Born *1899* **Died** *1986 aged 87*

Jorge Luis Borges experienced a wide variety of cultures in his youth. He was born in Buenos Aires, Argentina, and educated in Geneva, Switzerland. One of his grandmothers was English and from

an early age he read English literature. He also lived and wrote for a time in Spain. His great intellectual appetite was also fed by a wide reading of philosophy and theology from other cultures and ages.

He published many volumes of poetry, but he is most famous for his short stories; *Labyrinths* (1962) is an anthology of some of his best-known works. He used his great pool of knowledge to create unusual stories, some of which are often dream-like, cleverly blurring the boundaries between reality and fiction. ◆

Borgia family

Important Italian family in the late 15th and early 16th century
Alfonso Borgia
Born *1378*   **Died** *1458 aged 80*
Rodrigo Borgia
Born *1431*   **Died** *1503 aged 72*
Cesare Borgia
Born *1475*   **Died** *1507 aged 32*
Lucrezia Borgia
Born *1480*   **Died** *1519 aged 39*

The Borgias were an Italian family. The first Borgia to become famous was Alfonso. In 1455 he was elected Pope Calixtus III. He lived a simple life, but made his young nephew Rodrigo a cardinal and gave him great wealth.

Rodrigo Borgia worked in Rome for his uncle and for subsequent popes. Churchmen were forbidden to marry and have children. Rodrigo, however, had seven illegitimate children.

▶ *Rodrigo Borgia used corrupt means, blackmail, and bribery to be made Pope Alexander VI. He executed any who dared oppose his new position.*

In spite of this behaviour, he was elected as Pope Alexander VI in 1492. He then tried to make his children important and rich, especially his son, Cesare, and his daughter, Lucrezia.

Cesare wanted to conquer land in central Italy and make himself a prince. From 1499, with Pope Alexander's support, he attacked one city after another. But in 1503 Pope Alexander died. The new pope and his successor hated the Borgias. Cesare was arrested, and later taken to Spain and imprisoned. In 1506 he escaped, but died in 1507.

Lucrezia Borgia married three times, each time to a supporter of her father and brother. Her third husband was the duke of Ferrara. In Ferrara she encouraged leading painters and writers of the day. ◆

▲ *This is the centre panel of Hieronymus Bosch's triptych (painting on three panels) The Garden of Earthly Delights, his best-known work.*

Hieronymus **Bosch**

Flemish painter
Born *c.1450* ***Died*** *1516 aged about 65*

B osch's real name was Jerome van Aken; 'Hieronymus' is simply the Latin form of Jerome, and 'Bosch' is a shortened version of the name of the town where he lived – Hertongenbosch. This was a prosperous place (in what is now the southern part of the Netherlands) and Bosch was the town's leading artist. We know little about his life, for few records have survived. However, his paintings clearly show that he had one of the most vivid imaginations in the history of art, for there has been nothing else quite like them before or since. He often painted weird demons and monstrous creatures – sometimes half-human and half-animal – to show the follies and sins of mankind. His pictures are not only bizarre and sometimes baffling, but also very beautiful, for he had a wonderful sense of colour. ◆

Sandro **Botticelli**

Italian painter
Born *c.1445* ***Died*** *1510 aged about 65*

S andro Botticelli's real name was Alessandro Filipepi. 'Botticelli', meaning 'little barrel', was originally a nickname given to his chubby elder brother, but it stuck as a family name.

Botticelli lived almost all his life in Florence, which in the 15th century was a flourishing centre of art. The city was rich and proud, and Botticelli was one of its busiest artists, working for churches and noble families (who tried to outdo each other in splendour) as well as the civic authorities. At this time, most pictures were of religious subjects, but Botticelli's two most famous works are mythological scenes – *Primavera* (meaning 'Spring') and *The Birth of Venus*, both now in the Uffizi Gallery in Florence. They were painted for a member of the Medici family, who dominated political life in the city, and they were the first mythological paintings to be done on a large scale (each one is about three metres wide). They show the amazing gracefulness for which Botticelli is famous. In addition to painting, Botticelli was also commissioned to illustrate Dante's *Divine Comedy*. By the end of his career, however, his work had gone out of fashion. He was a sad and neglected figure when he died and his paintings did not become popular again until the 19th century. ◆

👁 **see also**
Dante   Medici family

Boudica

Queen of the Iceni tribe
Date of birth unknown
Died AD *61 age unknown*

T he Iceni tribe was one of the few tribes in Roman Britain that were allowed to govern themselves. However, when the king of the Iceni died in AD 59, the Romans decided to bring the area under full Roman rule. The Roman historian Tacitus wrote that the

▲ *This statue shows Boudica riding into battle. We do not know for certain if her chariot really did have sword blades attached to the axles. This could have been a myth spread among her terrified Roman victims, 70,000 of whom were said to have died during her rebellion.*

Romans plundered the kingdom, Boudica (the king's widow) was flogged, and her daughters were raped.

Tacitus described Boudica, whose name in her Celtic language meant 'Victory', as 'a very big woman, terrifying to look at, with a fierce look on her face'. She had a 'great mass of hair the colour of a lion's mane'. She gathered an army around her to fight the Romans. At first the rebellion went well as Boudica's army destroyed the towns of Colchester, Verulamium (now St Albans), and London. But then the Roman governor of Britain brought a great force from North Wales and destroyed the rebel army. Boudica poisoned herself to avoid capture by the Romans. ◆

David **Bowie**

English singer and songwriter
Born *1947*

David Robert Jones was born in Brixton, London. As David Bowie he became a songwriter and performer who remained a star by changing his looks and musical style to keep up with the times.

He was in many groups during the 1960s, but his first big hit was 'Space Oddity' in 1969. That led to a string of more than 40 hit records, including 'Let's Dance' (1983) which was No. 1 in both Britain and America at the same time.

When performing live, Bowie always liked to create a whole new personality for himself on stage, as he did in 1972 as 'Ziggy Stardust'. He also appeared in films and plays, but always returned to music. In 1983 he was paid 10.5 million US dollars for a concert in California, the highest sum ever paid to a rock star for a single show. ◆

Robert **Boyle**

Irish scientist
Born *1627*   **Died** *1691 aged 64*

Robert Boyle was a very clever boy and could speak Latin and Greek at the age of eight. In his twenties he took part in scientific experiments and discussions with a group who went on to found the Royal Society, a very prestigious association to this day.

Boyle did much to establish the method and ideas of modern chemistry. He wrote a famous book called the *Sceptical Chymist*. In this and other books he helped to explain ideas about atoms and elements. He insisted on the importance of doing experiments to test whether scientific ideas were really true. Boyle is best remembered for a law of physics: Boyle's law tells us mathematically how the volume of a gas will alter when the pressure is changed. ◆

Donald **Bradman**

Australian cricketer
Born *1908*   **Died** *2001 aged 92*

As a child, Donald Bradman practised cricket on his own by bouncing a golf ball against a wall and hitting it with a cricket stump. This practice paid off because he grew up to be the greatest run-scoring batsman of all time.

In his career he scored 28,067 runs at an average of 95 runs per innings. His highest-ever score was 452 not out, for New South Wales against Queensland, when he was 21. In his last Test innings as captain of Australia, he was bowled out for 0. Had it not been for that, he would have retired in 1948 with a Test average of over 100 runs per innings. ◆

William and Lawrence **Bragg**

English physicists
William Henry Bragg
Born 1862   Died 1942 aged 79
William Lawrence Bragg
Born 1890   Died 1971 aged 81

William and Lawrence Bragg shared the Nobel Prize for Physics in 1915 and were perhaps the most successful father and son team in the history of science.

In 1912 the German physicist Max von Laue showed that X-rays were waves and that they could be reflected from the layers of atoms inside crystals. William Bragg saw the importance of this and built the first spectrometer to measure the wavelengths of X-rays.

William and his son then worked together on the scattering of X-rays from different crystals. Lawrence worked out the formula that connects the wavelength of the X-rays to the spacing of atoms in the crystal structure. Scientists call this the Bragg law. ◆

see also
Becquerel   Röntgen

Tycho **Brahe**

Danish astronomer
Born 1546   Died 1601 aged 54

At university Tycho Brahe studied philosophy and other subjects. But on 21 August 1560 something happened which changed his life. It was predicted that on that day a small eclipse of the Sun would be seen in Copenhagen. Brahe was thrilled when the eclipse took place at the predicted time. He immediately turned his attention to astronomy and mathematics.

Brahe used various astronomical instruments for measuring the positions of stars and planets, but could only observe with the naked eye because Galileo's telescope was not yet invented. Before he died Brahe passed on his astronomical measurements to his assistant Johann Kepler, who later used them to produce the first accurate description of the movement of planets in our Solar System.

Brahe was a colourful figure who often courted trouble with other people. At the age of 19, during a midnight duel, his nose was cut off. From then on he had to wear a false metal nose. ◆

see also
Galileo   Kepler

▲ *Tycho Brahe pictured in the observatory he set up in Denmark.*

Johannes **Brahms**

German composer
Born 1833   Died 1897 aged 63

Johannes Brahms had his first music lessons from his father, who was a double-bass player. He began to study the piano when he was seven, and by the age of ten was performing in public concerts.

Although he was a fine pianist, Brahms really wanted to be a composer. His chance came when he met the composer Robert Schumann and his pianist wife, Clara. They treated him like a brother and did everything they could to encourage him. In 1863 he went to live in Vienna and his composing career really took off.

Brahms never married, though for a long time he was in love with Clara Schumann. What mattered to him most, however, was his music. He produced four great symphonies, chamber and piano music, songs, choral works such as the *German Requiem*, and also several fine concertos. ◆

see also
Beethoven   Schumann

Louis **Braille**

French inventor of a reading system for blind people
Born 1809   Died 1852 aged 43

Braille is a system of raised dots on paper that can be read by touch. It was invented by Louis Braille when he was only 15.

Born near Paris, Braille was blinded by an infection after an accident when he was three. He went to a special school where he excelled in music, becoming an organist and cellist. He decided to stay on at the school and became a teacher there.

Louis Braille spent most of his life improving and refining his reading system. It uses six dots in 63 combinations to provide letters, punctuation marks, numbers, and musical notation. Blind people can 'read' the dots by running their fingers lightly across the page. ◆

▲ *Constantin Brancusi's bronze sculpture* Mlle Pogany *(1913).*

Constantin **Brancusi**

Romanian sculptor
Born 1876   Died 1957 aged 81

Constantin Brancusi left home at the age of 11. He had no schooling until he attended art school in Bucharest. Later, when he was in Paris, he was fascinated by the work of the great sculptor Rodin, but refused to work with him because 'Nothing grows in the shade of big trees'.

Brancusi needed freedom to develop his ideas of completely streamlined shapes uncluttered by any fussy details. He was influenced by African art, Romanian folk art, and the exciting modern art of his time. His sculptures in polished metal, stone, and wood have grace, symmetry, and sleek lines.

Brancusi's masterpiece is a group of war memorial monuments including the 27-m high *Endless Column*. ◆

👁 **see also**

Rodin

Marlon **Brando**

American film actor
Born 1924   Died 2004 aged 80

When Marlon Brando studied acting in New York, he learned how to identify completely with the character he was playing. He also developed a realistic style of speaking which was well-suited to the types of young people he was portraying. His early films often showed him as a rebel, as in *A Streetcar Named Desire* (1951) and *The Wild One* (1953). He won an Oscar for *On the Waterfront* (1954).

Later he played powerful, older men such as the Mafia leader Don Corleone in *The Godfather* (1972), which won him another Oscar. In

▼ *Marlon Brando as a member of a motorbike gang in* The Wild One *(1953).*

Superman (1978) he was on screen as Superman's father for just nine minutes and was paid over 18 million US dollars. ◆

Willy **Brandt**

German chancellor and statesman
Born 1913   Died 1992 aged 78

Herbert Ernst Karl Frahm was a young man when the Nazis came to power in Germany. He opposed their policies and had to flee to Norway to escape the Gestapo. He changed his name to Willy Brandt and worked as a journalist in Norway and Sweden until Hitler and the Nazis were finally defeated in 1945.

Brandt returned to Germany and was elected to the Bundestag (parliament) in 1949 before becoming mayor of West Berlin in 1957. He led the city through the crisis of 1961 when the Berlin Wall was built by the Communists in the east of the city. This experience made him determined to improve relations with the Communist east. His chance came when he was elected chancellor of West Germany in 1969. He created policies of *Ostpolitik*, designed to reduce tension between east and west. For this he was awarded the Nobel Peace Prize in 1971. Just three years later Brandt was forced to resign when one of his assistants was found to be a spy. ◆

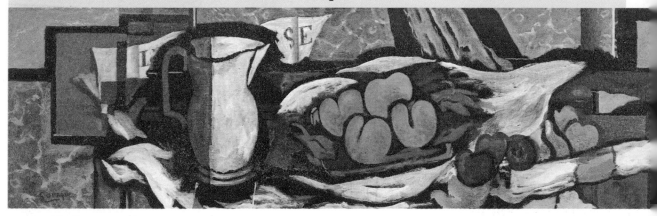

▲ *A still life of a bottle, some fruit, and a napkin by Georges Braque. It is an example of the Cubist style he and Pablo Picasso developed.*

Richard **Branson**

Chairman of the Virgin Group
Born 1950

Richard Branson is one of the UK's most successful businessmen. He says that he was successful by accident, going into businesses such as air travel because he was not happy with the existing service, rather than to make a fortune.

Branson left school early. He edited *Student* magazine, then set up the Student Advisory Centre (now called Help). In 1969 he started up Virgin, a successful record mail-order company. Soon afterwards he founded Virgin Records. The company expanded into publishing, recording, and selling other products, and changed its name to the Virgin Group.

Branson has continued to extend the Virgin brand into new areas, most notably Virgin Airways, Virgin Railways, Virgin Radio and Virgin Cola. In 1986 his boat won the coveted Blue Riband for the fastest crossing of the Atlantic by a boat. He was the first person to cross the Atlantic in a hot-air balloon in 1987, and has made several attempts to fly a balloon around the world. ◆

Georges **Braque**

French painter
Born 1882   Died 1963 aged 81

Georges Braque's father and grandfather were skilled painter-decorators. He was trained in this profession himself, but he took up art seriously when he was in his early 20s. At first he painted colourful landscapes, but in 1907 he met Pablo Picasso and this dramatically changed his outlook. Together, he and Picasso created the style known as Cubism, which was one of the great turning points in modern art. They specialized in still life pictures and painted objects as if we were seeing them from several angles at once. Their partnership come to an end during World War I. Braque was severely wounded during the war, but he recovered and later had a long and distinguished career as one of France's greatest painters. ◆

> *Art is meant to disturb, science reassures.*
>
> GEORGES BRAQUE

👁 **see also**
Picasso

Wernher von **Braun**

German rocket engineer
Born 1912   Died 1977 aged 65

Wernher von Braun was the son of a German baron. He became interested in rockets as a teenager after reading science fiction books.

It was during World War II that the real importance of rockets was recognized: unmanned rockets could carry bombs to enemy targets. Von Braun, a member of the German Nazi Party, headed a team that developed the first true missile. It was called the V-2 ('V' stood for *Vergeltung* which means 'vengeance'). This rocket was fuelled with alcohol and liquid oxygen and had an explosive warhead. It could travel a distance of about 300 km. Over a thousand V-2 rockets hit London during the war.

In 1945, when the war was over, von Braun surrendered to the Americans. They took him to America where he ran a rocket-building programme. This led to the building of the Saturn 5 rocket, used to launch America's manned missions to the Moon. ◆

Bertolt **Brecht**

German playwright and poet
Born 1898   Died 1956 aged 58

Bertolt Brecht was a major influence on 20th century drama. He explored a new style of drama, using unusual staging and different styles of acting in order to achieve his aim of making audiences think about the moral and political implications of his plays.

Brecht was born in Augsburg, Germany, and studied medicine and philosophy at the universities of Munich and Berlin. After serving in World War I he achieved success with his play *Drums in the Night* (1924). Throughout the 1920s and early 1930s he wrote many more plays. In 1933 Brecht and his wife were forced to flee from Germany after Hitler came to power. Brecht eventually reached America where he was investigated for having Communist beliefs. He left America and returned to East Berlin in 1947 where he founded The Berliner Ensemble, a theatre company that became world famous.

Among Brecht's plays that have become classics are *Mother Courage and her Children*, *The Caucasian Chalk Circle*, and *The Resistable Rise of Arturo Ui*. ◆

Benjamin **Britten**

English composer
Born 1913   Died 1976 aged 63

Benjamin Britten began writing music when he was only five. His Simple Symphony is made up of tunes he wrote as a child.

After studying at the Royal College of Music in London, Britten earned his living by writing music for documentary films and for concerts. He went to live in America at the beginning of World War II, but could not forget England. When he returned, it was to write the work that made him world-famous: the opera *Peter Grimes* (1945).

Many of Britten's operas were written for the world's great opera houses. Others, such as *The Turn of the Screw* (1954) (a chilling ghost story), were designed for the festival he started in Aldeburgh, the Suffolk town he made his home.

But it was not just opera that made his name. Britten wrote splendid orchestral music, songs, and choral works, none more fine, perhaps, than his great *War Requiem* of 1962. ◆

Brontë sisters

English novel-writing sisters
Charlotte Brontë
Born 1816   Died 1855 aged 38
Emily Brontë
Born 1818
Died 1848
aged 30
Anne Brontë
Born 1820
Died 1849
aged 29

Charlotte, Emily, and Anne were the daughters of a poor Irish clergyman. They lived in Haworth, a small town on the edge of the Yorkshire moors. Their mother died when Charlotte, the oldest child, was only five. After that, the sisters and their brother Branwell led their own lives mostly apart from their lonely father.

Later on, the sisters went to boarding school, and then became governesses. However, they hated being apart from each other, and eventually they all returned home where they started to write. In 1847 Charlotte wrote her masterpiece, *Jane Eyre*. This tells the story of a girl called Jane, who goes to a harsh school, and later becomes a governess. Jane falls in love with her employer, Mr Rochester. They are just about to marry when she discovers he has a wife already, a woman who is mad and locked up in a secret room in the same house.

Emily also wrote her only novel, *Wuthering Heights*, in the same year. Set in the bleak moors she knew so well, it tells the story of two very different boys, Edgar and Heathcliff, who both fall in love with the same girl, Catherine.

Anne had her novel *Agnes Grey* published in 1847. The sisters all wrote under pretend names, or 'pseudonyms'. Charlotte was 'Currer Bell', Emily was 'Ellis Bell', and Anne was 'Acton Bell': in those days it was easier to get published if you were a man!

Sadly, all three sisters died young. No other family of novelists has ever achieved so much as the shy and unworldly Brontës, whose books are still read very widely today. ◆

◀ *Laurence Olivier and Merle Oberon in the 1939 film adaptation of Emily Brontë's novel,* Wuthering Heights.

James **Brown**

American soul singer
Born 1928

James Brown had a hard childhood. When he was only 16 he was jailed for armed robbery. Turning to music kept him out of trouble, and in 1958 he had his first million-selling record, 'Try Me', a song in the gospel and rhythm 'n' blues styles. He gradually added hard, rhythmic guitars and frantic, punchy horns, creating a style which became known as funk.

His exciting live shows earned him the title Godfather of Soul. Hits like 'Papa's Got a Brand New Bag' (1965) and 'Living in America' (1986) confirmed his star status over a period of 20 years. ◆

John **Brown**

American anti-slavery campaigner
Born 1800   Died 1859 aged 59

'John Brown's body lies a-mouldering in the grave but his soul keeps marching on' goes a famous song. It celebrates the man who became a hero to Americans who were opposed to slavery.

John Brown was a white man with a large family. Seeking work, he settled down in a black township. He was angered by the way that the black slaves were treated. With five of his sons, he started illegally importing guns in to Kansas to help slaves fight for their freedom. One of their attacks on some slavery supporters ended in bloodshed. The attack, known as the 'Pottawatomie massacre', made him famous and much feared.

In 1859 he and 18 armed men captured a government armoury at Harpers Ferry in West Virginia, taking 60 hostages. They intended to arm the slaves and start a revolt. However, after two days marines stormed the armoury to free the hostages and capture Brown. He was tried and hanged shortly afterwards. ◆

👁 **see also**

Stowe   Tubman

◀ *A painting entitled* The Last Moments of John Brown.

▲ *The Pied Piper of Hamelin charms a group of rats.*

Robert **Browning**

English poet
Born 1812   Died 1889 aged 77

Robert Browning was the son of a bank clerk. Rather than go to school he stayed at home reading books from his father's large collection. He started writing poems from an early age and had his first published when he was only 21. He wrote his best-known poem, *The Pied Piper of Hamelin,* in 1842. It was based on an old German legend about a piper who charmed the rats out of the city with his music.

In 1846 Robert married Elizabeth Barrett, also a poet. Her father did not approve, so the couple had to run away to Italy to be together. They lived there happily, although sometimes Browning missed home.

After they had been married for

15 years, Elizabeth died. Very saddened, Browning returned to England. There, he wrote what many people consider to be his masterpiece, *The Ring and the Book* (1869), based on an Italian murder story. ◆

Anton **Bruckner**

Austrian composer and organist
Born *1824*   **Died** *1896, aged 72*

Anton Bruckner was the son of a poor village schoolmaster who was also the local church organist. Bruckner soon learned everything his father could teach him, and in 1837 was accepted as a chorister at the great Augustinian monastery of St Florian. He was a very modest man and went on studying long after he had made a name for himself as a composer and virtuoso. From 1868 he worked in Vienna as a professor at the prestigious Conservatoire.

Bruckner was greatly admired for his improvisations and undertook important concert tours to Paris and London. He wrote 11 symphonies, but discarded the first two and left the finale of his last symphony (known as No. 9) unfinished. Fortunately it could be completed from his detailed sketches, and so joined the others as some of the most important symphonic works of the late 19th century. ◆

Pieter **Bruegel** (the Elder)

Flemish painter
Born *c.1525*   **Died** *1569 aged about 44*

Pieter Bruegel was probably born in the village of Bruegel, near Breda in The Netherlands. There

is very little information about Bruegel's early life, but we do know that when he was in his twenties he travelled to Italy to see the great works of art there.

Although Bruegel was known for painting religious themes, he also painted people involved in ordinary village life. Some of his best-known paintings of such country folk are *Peasant Wedding* and *Peasant Dance*. Bruegel painted people honestly, with all their human failings, including drunkenness and greed. Some of his pictures carried strong messages about the good and bad, foolish and sensible things in life. His paintings are truly fascinating and need careful looking into to see all of the details.

His two sons, Pieter Bruegel the Younger and Jan Bruegel, are also well-known artists. ◆

Isambard Kingdom **Brunel**

British engineer
Born *1806*   **Died** *1859 aged 53*

As a boy, Brunel showed great skill at drawing and geometry. He trained with a maker of scientific

instruments in France before returning to England to work.

In 1830 he entered a competition to design a bridge to span the Avon gorge in Bristol. He won, but his design for the Clifton Suspension Bridge was not actually completed until 1864, after his death.

The turning point of Brunel's career came in 1833 when he was made chief engineer of the Great Western Railway Company. His main task was to build a railway between London and Bristol. It was one of the finest engineering achievements of its day.

While working on the Great Western Railway, Brunel became interested in steamships. His plan was that passengers from London to Bristol would be able to travel on to New York. Brunel built the first steamship to cross the Atlantic, the *Great Western*, which was launched in 1838. It had paddle wheels and was built of wood. His second ship, the *Great Britain*, was a revolution in design. Launched in 1843, it had a screw-propeller and was built of iron. It was the largest ship of its time and the forerunner of modern ocean-going vessels. ◆

▼ *Brunel's steamship* Great Eastern *was used to lay the first transatlantic telegraph cable.*

Filippo **Brunelleschi**

Italian goldsmith and architect
Born *1377* **Died** *1446 aged 69*

Filippo Brunelleschi grew up in Florence during the Renaissance – a time when scholars and artists were beginning to study the art and architecture of Ancient Rome and to encourage their use again. Brunelleschi, who trained as a goldsmith and did not turn to architecture until he was middle-aged, was the first architect to design buildings in this new spirit.

Brunelleschi took his ideas from the Florentine buildings he believed had been built by the Romans, but which had in fact been built hundreds of years after Roman times. His own buildings (churches, chapels, and a home for abandoned babies) have pleasing proportions which were quite new in Italian architecture. He also worked out the system for drawing in perspective that is still used today.

Brunelleschi was equally skilled as an engineer. He was given the job of providing Florence Cathedral with the largest dome to be built since Ancient Roman times and he invented a brilliant system for its construction. ◆

Sergey **Bubka**

Ukrainian record-breaking pole-vaulter
Born *1963*

Sergey Bubka took up pole-vaulting at the age of 12 and showed exceptional speed and strength. When he was 19 he became world champion at the 1983 Helsinki championships.

Bubka could not attend the 1984 Los Angeles Olympic Games because of the Soviet Union's boycott. But he seized gold at the Seoul Olympics in 1988 with a vault of 5.90 metres. His fans expected him to defend his title easily at the 1992 Barcelona Games, but he failed to qualify for the final. Yet that same year he vaulted 6.13 metres, another world best.

Sergey Bubka set the world record for the pole-vault over 30 times. ◆

▲ *From 1984 the pole-vaulter Sergey Bubka broke the world record on 35 occasions.*

Buddha (Siddhartha Gautama)

Indian religious teacher and founder of Buddhism
Born *c.563 BC*
Died *c.483 BC aged about 80*

Gautama was born at Lumbini (in modern Nepal). There is a story which says that a wise man predicted that Gautama would either be a great world ruler or a great religious teacher. His father, Suddhodhana, tried to turn his mind away from the religious life by keeping him within the gardens surrounding their home. Gautama married and he and his wife, Yasodhara, had a son called Rahula.

When Gautama was about 29 years old, he saw four signs, known to Buddhists as the 'heavenly messengers'. These changed his life.

▼ *A golden Buddha from the Wat Po temple in Bangkok, Thailand.*

They were an old man, a sick man, a corpse, and a wandering holy man who was seeking the truth. Their message of change, suffering, death, and the possibility of understanding the meaning of life led Gautama to leave his wife and child in the care of his family and go into the forest.

For six years he learnt from various religious teachers about meditation and strict disciplines of fasting and spiritual practice. At the end of that time he decided that depriving himself of sleep and extreme fasting weakened his body too much for deep reflection, so he broke his fast.

Gautama meditated for a whole night under a sacred tree, later called the Bodhi (enlightenment) tree. He made the breakthrough to understanding truth, which he called the Dharma. He discovered the causes of suffering, the nature of impermanence, and the need to purify the heart. His awakening to the truth is known as the Enlightenment.

After this, he was known as the Buddha (the Enlightened One) and spent the rest of his life teaching others the way to spiritual understanding. His first sermon at Sarnath near Varanasi (Benares) outlined the Four Noble Truths and the Noble Eightfold Path which form the core of his teaching. For the next 45 years he travelled widely in northern India and taught many people. He ordained both monks and nuns, and instructed them to continue to teach others. ◆

Buffalo Bill

Scout for the US Cavalry, actor, and Wild West showman
Born *1846*   **Died** *1917 aged 70*

Like many other people in the 'Wild West', William Cody (Buffalo Bill's real name) had little schooling and could just about write his name. At the age of 11 he was working to support his family. Later he fought in the American Civil War. After that he made his living supplying buffalo (bison) meat to railway workers. Cody's skill in shooting buffalo gave him his nickname.

▼ *A poster from 1899 advertising one of Buffalo Bill's popular Wild West shows.*

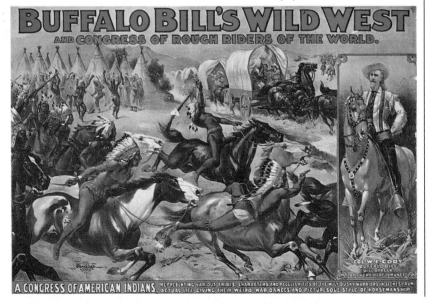

During the 1870s, Cody was a scout with the cavalry who were fighting the Indians. His hair-raising adventures made him famous, and he appeared on the stage in plays about himself. Cody became best known for his Wild West Show, an exhibition of horsemanship and mock battles which toured all over the world. ◆

👁 **see also**
Oakley

John **Bunyan**

English Puritan preacher and writer
Born *1628*   **Died** *1688 aged 59*

John Bunyan's family had very little money but he managed to learn to read and write, which was fairly unusual for someone so poor.

Bunyan got married in 1649. His wife had two religious books which had a great influence on her husband. He became a strict Puritan, gave up having a good time, and devoted his life to preaching.

Soon after Charles II became king of Britain in 1660, strict laws were passed against Puritan preachers, and Bunyan went to prison several times. In Bedford town jail he began to write his most important book, *The Pilgrim's Progress*, which was published in 1678. This is the story of the journey through life of a man called Christian. It is an allegory, which means that the events in the story have a deeper, religious meaning. Christian faces many dangers and temptations, meets lots of people, and sees many different places before finally reaching God's Heavenly City. The story shows how Christian learns to choose between right and wrong, and gets nearer and nearer to God. ◆

Robert **Burns**

Scottish poet
Born 1759 Died 1796 aged 37

Robert Burns was one of seven children of a struggling farmer in Ayrshire, Scotland. Burns began writing poetry at school, and decided to make full use of the words, rhythms, and sounds of his own Scottish dialect.

Burns worked as a farmer but had little success, and he caused so much trouble through his many love affairs that he came close to leaving Scotland. But when some of his poems were published in 1786, he was recognized as a poet of genius, and he decided to remain in Scotland. In addition to his poetry, Burns wrote or adapted traditional Scottish songs, including 'Auld Lang Syne', 'A Red Red Rose', and 'Ye Banks and Braes o' Bonnie Doon'.

For most of his life Burns had to worry about money, especially after

▼ *Some of Burn's possessions and commemorative art works.*

marrying in 1788 and starting a family. At first he returned to farming. Then in 1791 he took a full-time job as an excise-man (tax collector) in Dumfries. His last major poem, 'Tam o' Shanter', was published that same year.

Burns has been translated into more languages than any British poet apart from Shakespeare, and his birthday on 25 January is celebrated annually by Scots all around the world. ◆

George Walker **Bush**

President of the USA from 2001
Born 1946

George Bush was born in Midland, Texas in 1946. His father, George Herbert Bush, was in the oil business, and later became a politician. After university George joined the Texas Air Guard, flying fighter planes.

In the early 1970s he had several jobs, then in 1976 went into the oil business like his father. He married his wife Laura in 1977.

In 1988 George's father, George senior, became President of the USA. George junior helped his father in his election campaign.

In 1994 George junior decided to go into politics himself. He ran for the post of Governor of Texas, and won, even though most people thought that he had no chance. George was a very popular governor, and was elected for a second term in 1998.

In 1999, George decided to run for President in the 2000 elections. The election was very close-run, but George won, and in January 2001 became the 43rd President of the USA. ◆

▲ *Gatsha Buthelezi in traditional Zulu costume. He is the great-grandson of Cetshwayo, the former Zulu king.*

Gatsha **Buthelezi**

South African minister of home affairs
Born 1928

Gatsha Mangosotho Buthelezi is leader of the Inkatha Freedom Party (IFP). Its supporters are mostly Zulu-speakers from the province of KwaZulu-Natal.

In the 1960s Buthelezi opposed white domination and apartheid. He was against the establishment of separate 'homelands' for blacks from different ethnic groups. But in 1972 he became chief minister of

KwaZulu, a 'Zulu' homeland. In 1975 he re-established Inkatha (first formed in the 1920s) as an organization to unite Zulus and restore the rights of the king.

In the 1980s members of the African National Congress (ANC) criticized Buthelezi for opposing its call for sanctions against apartheid and for collaborating with the ruling National Party (NP). Many young, urban Zulu-speakers sided with the ANC, but most older, rural-dwellers backed Inkatha. Many thousands from both sides have died in fighting between the two organizations.

In South Africa's first democratic elections, held in April 1994, Inkatha came third behind the ANC and the NP. Inkatha won the election in KwaZulu and Buthelezi became a minister in the national government. ◆

👁 **see also**
Cetshwayo   de Klerk   Mandela

Josephine **Butler**

English campaigner for the rights of women
Born *1828*   **Died** *1906 aged 78*

Josephine Butler was a beautiful and educated woman. When she was quite young she saw that women were not allowed by law to be equal with men. She was happily married, but when her young daughter died, Butler decided to spend the rest of her life helping other women.

She began her work in Liverpool with prostitutes. At that time it was believed that prostitutes carried disease. Any woman suspected of being a prostitute could be arrested, examined by force, and imprisoned. Butler attacked this law and started what she called a 'Great Crusade' against it. Many people thought it was wrong to defend prostitutes, and she was attacked several times. However, Butler knew that most women became prostitutes because they were poor. As a brave woman and a great speaker, she won the support of thousands of people and the laws were eventually changed. ◆

Richard **Byrd**

American polar explorer
Born *1888*   **Died** *1957 aged 68*

Richard Byrd started exploring when he was in command of American naval aircraft assisting an expedition to Greenland. Unlike many other polar explorers, Byrd believed in using aircraft and modern navigational aids rather than only dogs and sledges. In 1926 he made the first flight over the North Pole. (After Byrd's death, an old friend claimed that this was a hoax.)

Byrd mostly explored the Antarctic. He named a range of mountains 'Rockefeller' after the millionaire John D. Rockefeller who had financed one of his expeditions. On one occasion, whilst mapping the Antarctic, Byrd was trapped alone in a hut for five months and had to be rescued. ◆

👁 **see also**
Rockefeller

Lord **Byron**

English poet
Born *1788*   **Died** *1824 aged 36*

George Gordon Byron was lame from birth, and rode on horseback whenever he could. When he was ten years old he inherited his great-uncle's estate, and became Lord Byron. As soon as

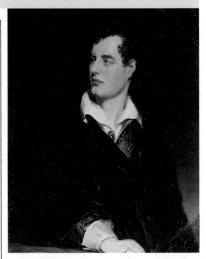

▲ *Byron's poems, although condemned on moral grounds, exerted a great influence on poetry, music, the novel, opera, and painting in Britain and Europe. He was regarded by many as a hero figure.*

he was old enough, he travelled through Europe on horseback. On his return to London he published a poem, *Childe Harold's Pilgrimage*, describing some of the wild landscapes he had seen. The poem was an immediate success.

Byron was a mixture of good and bad. He was described as 'mad, bad, and dangerous to know'. Many people were shocked by his numerous love affairs and he left England in bitterness. For a time he lived in Venice, where he wrote the long poem, *Don Juan*, which describes amazing adventures in extraordinary parts of the world.

In 1823 he went to Greece to help in the Greek struggle for independence from the Ottoman Turkish empire. However, before his soldiers could attack the Turkish fortifications, he caught a fever and died. ◆

> *'Tis strange – but true; for truth is always strange;*
> *Stranger than fiction.*
>
> LORD BYRON
> *Don Juan*

53

▲ *John Cabot departs from Bristol in 1497 in search of unknown lands.*

John **Cabot**

Italian discoverer of North America
Born c.1450
Died c.1498 aged about 48

John Cabot had an adventurous early life, during which he learned navigation. He settled in London in 1484. In 1496 King Henry VII of England heard of the expedition of Christopher Columbus to the West Indies and realized he was missing out on a chance of wealth and new colonies. So he instructed Cabot and his three sons Lewis, Sebastian, and Santius to sail in search of 'all heathen islands or countries hitherto unknown to Christians'.

The Cabots set off in 1497 in a tiny ship, the *Matthew*, with a crew of just 18 men. They reached the American coast after a voyage of 53 days, thus becoming the first Europeans to reach the North American mainland. However, Cabot thought that he was in north-east Asia!

On their return Cabot's report was so encouraging that the king sent him off on another expedition with a fleet of five ships. But Cabot found none of the gold or spices he was hoping for. ◆

👁 **see also**
Columbus

Gaius Julius **Caesar**

Roman general and dictator
Born c.100 BC
Died 44 BC aged about 57

Julius Caesar was born into an important Roman family and rose rapidly in his chosen career as a politician. He served his time in the army and then held various public offices. In 60 BC he was elected to the highest position in Rome, a consul. He was now in charge of the state's

▶ *A bust of Julius Caesar, the most famous of all Roman generals.*

administration and the armed forces, although he held power jointly with another consul. After his year of office he took on the governorship of provinces in northern Italy and Gaul (part of modern France). From here he conquered a vast new area in Gaul and Germany and invaded Britain twice, in 55 and 54 BC.

Caesar was now a very powerful leader with a huge army. He decided not to disband his troops, as he should have done by law, and marched into Italy in 49 BC. He crossed the River Rubicon which formed the boundary of Italy. From here there was no turning back. He had declared war on the Roman state. This meant civil war, and Pompey the Great fought against Caesar. The war lasted until 45 BC, and the next year Caesar declared himself 'dictator for life' – he was now the sole ruler. However, not everyone wanted to be ruled by one man, and on 15 March in 44 BC Caesar was stabbed to death.

We know a great deal about Caesar and his times because people who were there wrote about him and also because he wrote his own accounts of his adventures and battles. From his writing we can see what an intelligent and powerful man he was. At one time in his career he was the lover of Queen Cleopatra of Egypt, although he was married to Calpurnia. Cleopatra bore him a son called Caesarion who was executed by the Emperor Augustus. ◆

see also

Mark Antony   Augustus   Cleopatra
Pompey

Calamity Jane

American heroine of the Wild West
Born *about 1852*   **Died** *1903 aged 51*

Calamity Jane was born Martha Jane Burke in northern Missouri, America, but she grew up in western mining camps. She was a good horseback rider and an excellent shot with a rifle. In the rough life of the West she felt more comfortable dressed as a man.

She became attached to the 7th US Cavalry and some say she served as a scout to Colonel (later General) Custer. How she got her nickname is not clear. One story tells that she warned men that to offend her was to seek calamity.

By 1875 she was living in the gold-rush town of Deadwood in South Dakota. There she heroically helped the victims of a smallpox epidemic. She later married and moved to Texas, but returned to Deadwood and is buried there near the grave of Wild Bill Hickock. ◆

see also

Custer

▲ *Maria Callas pictured on the cover of a German magazine in 1959. She had the face and gift for dramatic expression and delighted audiences in such operas as* Madame Butterfly, Aïda, *and* Medea.

Maria **Callas**

American-born Greek soprano
Born *1923*   **Died** *1977 aged 53*

Maria Callas was born in New York. Her parents were Greek and her real name was Maria Kalogeropoulos. She trained in Athens and made her début there in 1941, but her international career began in 1947 when she sang Ponchielli's *La Gioconda* in Verona, Italy. Thereafter she appeared in all the major opera-houses, specializing in 19th-century Italian opera.

However, her stormy and self-critical temperament, and recurring vocal troubles, cast a shadow over her career. She was also the lover of the Greek shipping millionaire Aristotle Onassis, and for many years they made headline news. At her best, though, Callas was without equal as a dramatic soprano and spell-binding actress. She retired from the stage in 1965, but continued to make records. ◆

John **Calvin**

French-born Swiss Protestant Church reformer
Born *1509*   **Died** *1564 aged 54*

John Calvin was born and grew up in France and nearly became a priest in the Catholic Church. He studied law as well as religion. He was impressed by Martin Luther's teachings, and soon began to criticize the wealth and power of the pope and the Catholic Church.

It became too dangerous for him to stay in Catholic France, and he fled to the Protestant city of Basel in Switzerland. In 1536 he wrote a best-selling book, *The Institutes of the Christian Religion*. Calvin said Christians must use the Bible as their guide, not the pope or the Catholic Church. He taught that people could never be good enough to deserve to go to heaven, but God chose some people specially to be His 'elect'. He said that Christians might have a kind of vision which told them they were one of God's elect, but they should in any case live good and simple lives according to the teachings of Jesus.

In 1541 Calvin was asked to go to Geneva to lead the Protestants. There he organized schools and a university. There were all kinds of strict rules for everyday life; dancing, theatre-going, and card-playing were forbidden. Shopkeepers were punished if they charged too much. Unfaithful husbands and wives were executed, and a boy was beheaded for striking his parents. People had to wear plain clothes and avoid bright colours and women had to cover their hair. Calvin became the effective ruler of Geneva. By the time he died, his religious ideas were spreading across Europe. ◆

see also

Luther

Luis vaz de **Camoens**

Portuguese poet
Born *1524*   **Died** *1580 aged 56*

Luis vaz de Camoens' great poem, *The Lusiads*, is Portugal's national epic – in much the same way as Chaucer's *Canterbury Tales* is England's. It is the story of the spread of the Portuguese people around the world, and particularly of Vasco da Gama's voyage to the East.

Camoens studied for a life in the Church but did not become a priest. Instead he led a wayward and adventurous life. He was forbidden to marry the girl he loved and for whom he wrote his passionate poem, *Rimas*. He was banished for a time to Ceuta in North Africa, and there lost an eye. Back in Lisbon, his unruly behaviour got him banished again, this time to Goa in India rather than to jail.

In 1558 he was shipwrecked and lost almost everything except the manuscript of *The Lusiads*. Three years later it was published. The poem was a great success, but Camoens did not benefit much and died alone, in poverty. ◆

👁 **see also**

Gama

Albert **Camus**

French novelist
Born *1913*   **Died** *1960 aged 47*

Albert Camus was born in Algeria, of French and Spanish parentage. He grew up in North Africa where he had various jobs – he even played in goal for the Algiers football team!

When he moved to France he took up journalism and politics and fought heroically against the German occupation during World War II. After the war he decided to concentrate on writing. His most famous novels, *The Outsider* (1942) and *The Plague* (1947), express his idea of the 'absurd', the view that human life is meaningless and that happiness is only possible if we accept that life has no meaning other than what we give it.

Camus was awarded the Nobel Prize for Literature in 1957. He was killed tragically in a road accident only three years later. ◆

Giovanni **Canaletto**

Italian painter
Born *1697*   **Died** *1768 aged 70*

In the 18th century Venice was a great tourist attraction, just as it

▼ *One of Giovanni Canaletto's celebrated views of the Grand Canal in Venice.*

is today. However, 200 years ago the visitors were not people on package holidays, but aristocratic young gentlemen. They went to Italy to round off their cultural education, for no other country boasted such a wealth of art. Many of these young men took paintings and statues back to their own countries, and Giovanni Canaletto was the most famous of the artists who catered for this high-class 'tourist trade'. His views of Venice, packed with vivid detail, were like extremely large, very expensive postcards. Anyone who could afford one had a magnificent status-symbol souvenir. In the 1740s, war on the Continent made travel to Italy difficult and Giovanni Canaletto's business dried up. Most of his clients were British, so in 1746 he moved to England. He repeated his success there, staying for almost ten years painting views of London and of aristocrats' country houses. ◆

◀ *This silver penny bears the head of King Canute.*

Canute

King of England, Denmark, and Norway in the early 11th century
Born *c.994*   **Died** *1035 aged about 41*

Canute was the son of Swein I, King of Denmark. He came with his father on his invasion of England in 1013. Swein's Danish army had conquered the whole of England by the time he died, and Canute was declared king in February 1014. His reign in England nearly came to an end quickly, as the English king Ethelred (who had fled to Normandy when Swein invaded) returned. Canute went back to Denmark, but returned with an invasion force in 1015. By the end of the next year he really was the king of all England. He became king of Denmark in 1018 and king of Norway in 1030. ◆

Al **Capone**

Italian-born American gangster
Born *c.1899*   **Died** *1947 aged about 48*

Al Capone claimed that he was born in New York but it is more likely that he was born in Italy and emigrated with his family to America. Capone turned to crime very early, and was involved in New York street gangs when he was a teenager.

In 1920 the sale of alcoholic drinks was banned in America. This ban (called Prohibition) lasted for 13 years and many criminals, including Capone, made fortunes selling alcoholic drinks illegally. Capone operated in Chicago, becoming rich and influential through crime. He was very brutal, and was involved in the murder of seven members of a rival gang in the St Valentine's Day massacre. He was not arrested because he bribed many policemen and other officials.

Eventually, in 1932, Capone went to prison for not paying taxes. After only a few years he came out a sick man and died while still in his forties. ◆

▶ *This is a police mug shot of Al Capone taken in 1929. Capone was the crime king of Chicago during America's Prohibition years.*

Michelangelo Merisi da **Caravaggio**

Italian painter
Born *1571*   **Died** *1610 aged 38*

In Michelangelo Merisi da Caravaggio's day, all ambitious young painters wanted to make their reputations in Rome – the 'artistic capital' of Europe. He arrived there when he was about 20 and for several years struggled to earn a living. However, his reputation grew and he started to win important commissions from the Church. His paintings were bold and exciting. The people in them looked real and solid because he used real Roman people as models for his saints and madonnas, a practice which caused great controversy. He had a highly original way of using light and shade, so that the most important parts of the picture stood out dramatically from the background. At the age of 35 he was famous all over Europe, and half the painters in Rome were trying to imitate him. His success story was ended by his violent temper. In 1606 he killed a man over a petty argument and fled Rome. For the rest of his short life he was a wanderer, constantly worried that the law would catch up with him. He died of malaria. ◆

57

Chester **Carlson**

American inventor of modern photocopying machines
Born *1906*   **Died** *1968 aged 62*

Photocopying machines are now so commonplace that it is difficult to realize that they have only been generally available for about 30 years. At the touch of a button photocopiers can produce single or multiple copies of printed pages, enlarged or reduced if required, and some can reproduce in colour.

The person responsible for this revolution was a physicist called Chester Carlson. As a young man he worked with a firm in New York who required many copies of important documents. In 1938 Carlson produced his prototype photocopier based on electrostatic attraction of a black powder to paper. He called this process xerography (from the Greek word for dry writing). His method was not altogether successful and needed adapting. It was not until 1959 that the first commercial machine was put on the market, by the now giant Rank Xerox Corporation. Thanks to his skills, ingenuity, and perseverence, Carlson became a multi-millionaire. ◆

Andrew **Carnegie**

Scottish-born American businessman and benefactor
Born *1835*   **Died** *1919 aged 83*

When he was 12, Andrew Carnegie left Scotland for America with his parents and younger brother. They were very poor, so instead of going to school Carnegie went to work in a cotton factory. Later, whatever job Carnegie did, he tried to learn more about it. He worked very long hours, but read as much as he could in his spare time. Soon he was offered better jobs and he saved his money carefully.

During the American Civil War, railways were very important for moving troops and ammunition. Carnegie started a company in 1863 to make iron railway bridges instead of wooden ones. Ten years later his company began to produce steel too. This made Carnegie very rich. He was very generous with his money: before he died, he had paid for 2811 free public libraries around the world. He also established pension funds and gave financial help to universities in Scotland and in America. ◆

Lewis **Carroll**

English writer
Born *1832*   **Died** *1898 aged 65*

Lewis Carroll was the name used by Charles Dodgson, a mathematics teacher at Oxford University, when he was writing children's books and poems. Charles Dodgson was the third child in a family of 11, and he and his brothers and sisters spent ages playing literary games and drawing.

When he became a teacher at Oxford, Carroll used to take the daughters of his friend, Dean Liddell, for boat-rides on the river. On one of these river-trips he told the story of *Alice in Wonderland* to the young Alice Liddell. Later he wrote the story down, and it was published in 1865.

As well as *Alice in Wonderland* and *Alice Through the Looking Glass* (1872), he wrote poems and another children's book, *Sylvie and Bruno*. He was also a great letter writer and he invented games and puzzles. As an Oxford don, he also published mathematical works.

Carroll's story books are sort of

▲ *Two of Lewis Carroll's most famous creations, Alice and the Cheshire Cat.*

adventure stories, but they do not unfold like ordinary stories. Sometimes one thing will turn into another, as if in a dream, while at other times the people in the book seem to be moving about in a game, the rules of which are never quite clear. ◆

Jacques **Cartier**

French navigator and explorer who claimed Canada for France
Born *1491*   **Died** *1557 aged 66*

Jacques Cartier, an experienced navigator, was 43 when he set out with two ships and 61 men on his first voyage to North America. King Francis I of France had sent him on the expedition to search for gold. He first explored the coast of Newfoundland, then sailed up the Gulf of St Lawrence to the Gaspé Peninsula, where he set up a cross and claimed the land for France.

The next year, 1535, Cartier was sent on a second expedition. On 10 August, the feast day of St Lawrence, he arrived at a river which he named after the saint. He sailed upstream as far as the place where Quebec now stands. The smallest of his ships sailed on as far as a village called Hochelaga, at the foot of a mountain which he named Mont Réal. The city of Montréal now stands there. A third voyage in 1541 in search of precious stones failed, and Cartier retired to France, honoured as a great explorer. ◆

👁 **see also**

Champlain

▼ *In Jacques Cartier's first voyage to Canada he met a group of Iroquois Indians. Their chief let two of his sons sail back to France; they returned with Cartier on his second voyage.*

Henri **Cartier-Bresson**

French photographer
Born 1908

Henri Cartier-Bresson is celebrated for capturing significant moments of events on film. He became interested in photography after training as a painter. Since 1933, when he held his first photographic exhibition, he has covered the world's great events for the media, and has published many books of camera studies. As a young man he worked with the great French film director Jean Renoir.

Cartier-Bresson uses mainly black and white film and a hand-held camera. He rarely resorts to the complex photographic equipment favoured by other photographers. He records 'the decisive moment' (also the title of one of his books), relying on his own skill and experience. ◆

▲ *Henri Cartier-Bresson's style made an art form of news photography.*

Pablo **Casals**

Spanish (Catalan) cellist and conductor
Born 1876   Died 1973 aged 96

Pablo Casals was already a capable pianist, organist, and violinist before he took up the cello at the age of 11. He studied in Barcelona, Madrid, and Brussels. His solo career began in 1898, and he was soon regarded as the world's greatest cellist. He was also famous as a chamber musician, teacher, and composer of instrumental and choral works. In 1936 he went into voluntary exile in Prades, in the French Pyrenees, in protest against General Franco's Fascist regime in Spain, and from 1946 to 1950 even refused to play in public. In 1950 he founded the Prades annual musical festival, and in 1956 he went to live in Puerto Rico where he also founded another important festival, the Casals Festival. ◆

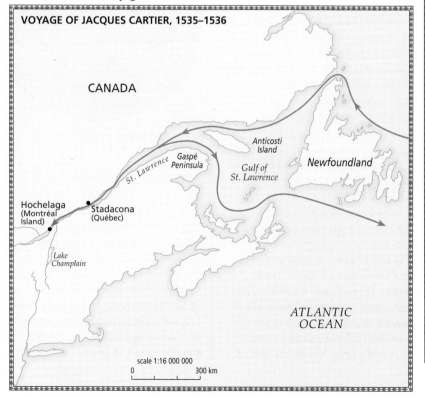

VOYAGE OF JACQUES CARTIER, 1535–1536

CANADA

Anticosti Island

Gaspé Peninsula

St. Lawrence

Gulf of St. Lawrence

Newfoundland

Hochelaga (Montréal Island)

Stadacona (Québec)

Lake Champlain

ATLANTIC OCEAN

scale 1:16 000 000
0   300 km

Giovanni **Casanova**

Italian adventurer
Born *1725*   **Died** *1798 aged 73*

G iovanni Casanova was a clever boy, and at first he studied to be a priest. However, he could not settle down to anything for very long, and he gambled, cheated, and lied his way through most of his life. He did not always keep out of trouble and he was in prison from 1755 to 1756, until he escaped and went to France. In his later years he settled down to be a librarian to the Count of Waldstein, in Bohemia.

What we know of Casanova comes from his very entertaining *Memoirs*. They are very boastful, especially about all his women friends, and it is not easy to know the truth. Even now, a man who boasts of many women friends may be called a 'Casanova'. ◆

Fidel **Castro**

Leader of the Communist revolution in Cuba
Born *1927*

U nder the harsh rule of General Batista, many poor Cubans lived in terrible conditions. Fidel Castro was amongst a group of people who decided to overthrow the government and for several years Castro led raids against government forces. He gathered more and more support until finally, in 1959, Batista fled the country.

Castro immediately began to change the Cuban way of life. He took over foreign-owned companies, but because many of these companies were American, the United States stopped all trade with Cuba. Castro then turned to Communist countries, such as the

▲ *A young Fidel Castro waves to his supporters.*

Soviet Union and China, for help.

In 1962, the Soviet Union tried to build nuclear missile bases in Cuba, with Castro's consent. The missiles were removed after the United States had blockaded Cuba and put pressure on the Russians.

Although Castro greatly improved conditions for the poor, many other Cubans wanted more freedom, and fled to America. ◆

Catherine the Great

Ruler of Russia from 1762 to 1796
Born *1729*   **Died** *1796 aged 67*

B orn Princess Sophia Augusta, she came to Russia from Stettin, Prussia (now in Poland) at the age of 14 and was given the name Catherine when she was received into the Russian Orthodox Church. At 15 she married Peter the

Great's grandson, Peter III. After 17 years of marriage, Peter became tsar in 1762. Almost immediately he was replaced by Catherine and put to death by his guards.

Catherine at once set about reforming Russia and turning it into a strong power. She took a great interest in education, particularly for girls, and also did a lot to improve the care of the sick.

During her rule Russia expanded eastwards towards the Pacific Ocean, westwards to take over much of Poland, and southwards to the coast of the Crimea and the Black Sea. Her own skilful diplomacy made sure that these gains became permanent.

▲ *An enamel and copper portrait of Catherine the Great.*

While the landowning nobles lived well, most Russian people were serfs, little better than slaves, and badly treated. Catherine, who needed the support of the nobles, gave them even more powers over their serfs. This led to a serfs' revolt in 1773–1775 which was brutally put down. Later the French Revolution of 1789 increased Catherine's fear of revolt, and in her later years she ruled with a rod of iron. ◆

Edith **Cavell**

British nurse executed during World War I

Born *1865*   **Died** *1915 aged 49*

Edith Cavell was the daughter of a clergyman. When she was 25 she went to Belgium as a governess, and later trained as a nurse. In 1907 she became matron of Belgium's first training college for nurses.

In 1914 German troops marched into Brussels. Edith Cavell joined a group of people who helped British and French soldiers, trapped behind German lines, to escape to The Netherlands. During the next year hundreds of soldiers passed through the cellars of her clinic. Then, on 5 August 1915, Edith Cavell was arrested. She was condemned to death by a German military court and was shot on 12 October. She met her death calmly and bravely. ◆

▶ *Nurse Edith Cavell with a small boy outside Shoreditch Infirmary, England, where she was working in 1903.*

Patriotism is not enough. I must have no hatred or bitterness towards anyone.

EDITH CAVELL
on the eve of her execution

Henry **Cavendish**

English scientist

Born *1731*   **Died** *1810 aged 78*

Henry Cavendish's family had aristocratic connections, and he was well-educated. Nevertheless he lived very modestly, even after he inherited a fortune at 40.

His mother died when he was two years old and for 50 years he lived with his father, who was a scientist. Cavendish's first scientific work was helping with his father's experiments. Soon he was making discoveries of his own, particularly in chemistry and electricity.

Cavendish found that hydrogen (which he called 'inflammable air') was a component of water, and investigated many of the properties of hydrogen gas. He also calculated the mass and density of the Earth.

Many of his discoveries remained unknown in his lifetime because he seldom spoke to anyone. Even his servants hardly ever heard him speak; he would write notes for them instead. He allowed other scientists to use his large library – provided he didn't have to meet them or talk to them. ◆

Camillo **Cavour**

Italian politician

Born *1810*   **Died** *1861 aged 51*

When Camillo Cavour was born, the French ruled Italy. After the defeat of the French emperor, Napoleon, Italy was divided between Austria (in the north), the Pope, and smaller kingdoms and areas ruled by dukes in the south.

Cavour, who came from a noble family in Turin, became an officer in the army. In 1847 he entered politics and in the following year sat in the parliament in the Piedmont kingdom. Cavour wanted to see all of Italy united and freed from foreign rule. He became prime minister of Piedmont in 1852. By the time of his death in 1861 Italy was free of foreign rule and united under one king, Victor Emmanuel II. ◆

👁 **see also**

Garibaldi   Victor Emmanuel II

William **Caxton**

English printer who set up the first printing press in England
Born c.1422   **Died** 1491 aged about 69

William Caxton liked to spend time writing, and in 1469 he started to translate into English a popular French romance called *The History of Troy*. Many people in England wanted a copy of this rather large book. Copies of books were once handwritten and so took a long time to complete. However, by this time books could be produced by the printing process introduced by Gutenberg in Germany some years earlier. Caxton learned how to do this, then set up his own press in Bruges, Belgium. Here he printed his English edition of *The History of Troy*, completing it by the end of 1473. In 1476, Caxton set up the first printing press in England, at Westminster in London.

During his lifetime, Caxton printed about 110 books. He also published Chaucer's *Canterbury Tales*, making this work available to many new readers. Before Caxton's printed editions, people spelt the same words in different ways. In his printing Caxton introduced a fixed spelling for words, a very important development in the standardization of English. ◆

👁 **see also**
Gutenberg

Benvenuto **Cellini**

Italian goldsmith, sculptor, and writer
Born 1500   **Died** 1571 aged 70

Benvenuto Cellini grew up in Florence in Italy and became the apprentice of a goldsmith. He was an excellent artist, but also a wild character. In 1516 he became involved in a fight and the city authorities sent him away. Throughout his life he was in trouble, and had to move from one city to another. But his work was so good that rich people were always asking him to make jewellery, medals, and sculptures.

In 1540 King Francis I invited Cellini to work for him at his court in France. He stayed for five years. During this time he made his famous gold salt-cellar for the king, topped with nude reclining figures. In 1545 he returned to Florence where he made the famous statue of Perseus and Medusa. When he was 58 Cellini began to write his *Autobiography*, in which he presented a lively picture of his life. ◆

Miguel **Cervantes**

Spanish writer
Born 1547   **Died** 1616 aged 68

The life of Miguel Cervantes reads like a tale of adventure. He spent his childhood travelling around Spain with his father, who supplied medicines for the poor. At the age of 21 he went to Italy and studied the work of the great Italian poets before enlisting as a soldier. He fought the Turks in the great sea battle of Lepanto in 1571 and was wounded three times. Later he was captured by pirates, and imprisoned for five years. He tried to escape, but had to be ransomed in the end.

Back in Spain his luck changed

▼ *Cellini's gold salt-cellar on which there are sea-horses, fishes, and animals, representing the union of Earth and sea.*

▲ *This illustration shows Cervantes' hero, Don Quixote, galloping to attack windmills which he has mistaken for giants waving their arms.*

when, in 1605, he published *Don Quixote*. It is a long book which is both funny and sad. It tells the tale of a poor hero who has many adventures, all caused by his own mistakes. The book was such a success that Cervantes could afford to spend the rest of his life writing. ◆

Cetshwayo

Last great Zulu king
Born c.1826   Died 1884 aged about 58

Cetshwayo was the nephew of Shaka the Zulu king. He fought as a warrior against white settlers at the age of 12, and in 1873 became king himself after the death of his father, Mpande. However, he could not claim his throne until six of his half-brothers had been killed and two more had fled. At first the British in South Africa supported Cetshwayo, but in 1878 they invaded Zululand. The Zulus won an early victory, wiping out a British regiment, but they were themselves defeated in 1879. Cetshwayo was captured and Zululand was divided

amongst 13 chiefs. Cetshwayo visited London to plead his case and the British restored him as ruler of central Zululand in 1883. However, he was soon expelled by his subjects and was forced to flee the country. ◆

👁 **see also**
Shaka

Paul **Cézanne**

French painter
Born 1839   Died 1906 aged 67

Paul Cézanne was born into an educated and wealthy family. He started studying law, but soon gave up in order to paint. His early pictures were not popular: people said they were hopelessly unskilled.

After studying art for a while in Paris, he settled in Pontoise, just north of Paris. After his father died, he returned to live in his birthplace, Aix-en-Provence, in southern France. As he had a lot of money he did not need to rely on selling his pictures to live. This gave him unusual freedom to develop his skills. He painted landscapes, still lifes, flowers, and portraits. By careful mixtures of colour and tone, he made his brush-strokes 'model' a hill or a figure without using an outline. His style of painting greatly influenced other artists. ◆

Marc **Chagall**

Russian painter
Born 1887   Died 1985 aged 97

Marc Chagall was brought up in the Jewish district of the small Russian town of Vitebsk. The people who surrounded him as a child, the stories they told, and the lively music they played, crop up again and again in his paintings.

As a young man he went to Paris at a time when there were a lot of changes going on in painting, writing, and music. Excited and influenced by these changes, Chagall went back to Russia, but his painting was not popular with the authorities, and he finally returned to Paris and settled there in 1923.

His work is highly imaginative, and blends reality with fantasy. Sometimes the figures in his paintings seem to be floating across the picture. He loved using clear, bright colours which shimmer on the canvas and glow in the stained-glass windows and tapestries which he designed in later life. ◆

▶ *Chagall's* Ecuyere aux colombes *(Circus rider and doves).*

Samuel de **Champlain**

French explorer and founder of Québec
Born 1567   Died 1635 aged 68

The first European settlers in Canada were the French. Because Samuel de Champlain was a fine navigator he was selected to go on an expedition to explore Canada's St Lawrence river. This was his first journey of exploration although he returned to North America many times.

In 1608 Champlain and 32 men founded the colony of Québec. Life was tough and death was commonplace on these expeditions. Only Champlain and eight others survived the first winter there. Champlain won the respect of the local American Indians by fighting in their wars, and he also traded with them for furs.

When the English attacked Québec in 1628, Champlain was in command of the colony. He was captured and sent to England. When England returned Canada to France in 1633, Champlain went back to Québec and died there. ◆

see also

Cartier

Chandragupta Maurya

Creator of the first empire in India
Lived during the 4th century BC

Chandragupta Maurya grew up in India over 2300 years ago. At that time there were many kingdoms in India. The most powerful was Magadha, in the north-east. Around 320 BC Chandragupta overthrew the king of Magadha and made himself king.

Chandragupta faced a crisis about 15 years later. The king of western Asia, Seleucus Nicator, and his army invaded north-west India. This threatened Chandragupta's lands. The armies of Seleucus and Chandragupta fought each other. Chandragupta's army won. In 303 BC the two kings made a treaty. It stated that Chandragupta would rule the Indus Valley (modern Pakistan) and adjoining lands. He thereby became the ruler of all of north India.

In 297 BC Chandragupta abdicated. The next two kings were his son Bindusara and his grandson Asoka. They extended the empire into central and south India. ◆

see also

Asoka

▶ *In his time, Chandragupta Maurya ruled three-quarters of the Indian sub-continent. His empire lasted for another 100 years after his death.*

Charlie **Chaplin**

British-born film actor and director
Born 1889   Died 1977 aged 88

Charlie Chaplin's mother was a music-hall entertainer in London and from the age of five Chaplin took part in her act. When she became ill, the young Chaplin was sent to an orphanage. In 1910 he moved to America and four years later he began to appear in films. He became the best-loved comedian of the silent cinema, famous for his moustache, bowler hat, baggy trousers, and cane. Soon he was writing and directing his own films, and in 1919 he joined other stars and directors in founding their own United Artists film company.

In his most famous films, such as *The Kid* (1920) and *The Gold Rush* (1925), Chaplin played a sad little tramp who was bullied and confused by powerful people. Usually, though, he bounced back and was always on the side of

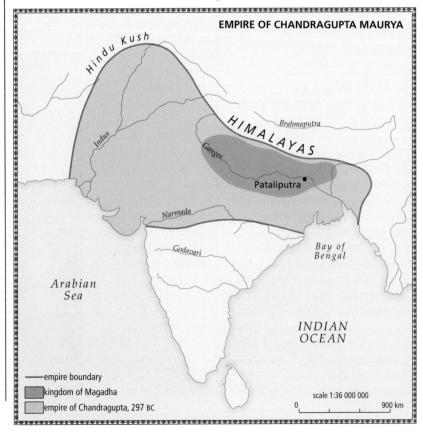

EMPIRE OF CHANDRAGUPTA MAURYA

Hindu Kush

Indus

HIMALAYAS

Brahmaputra

Ganges

Pataliputra

Narmada

Godavari

Arabian Sea

Bay of Bengal

INDIAN OCEAN

empire boundary
kingdom of Magadha
empire of Chandragupta, 297 BC

scale 1:36 000 000
0   900 km

weaker or poorer people. He also made successful talking pictures such as *The Great Dictator* (1940), a fierce but amusing attack on Adolf Hitler and his Nazi followers.

Later Chaplin was excluded from America because he was suspected of supporting Communism. However, in 1972 he returned in triumph to be awarded a special Oscar 'for the incalculable effect he has had in making motion pictures the art form of this century'. ◆

Charlemagne

Holy Roman Emperor from 800 to 814
Born 742   **Died** 814 aged 72

As the eldest son of Pepin, king of the Franks, Charlemagne was born into a very powerful family. The Franks were barbarians who invaded part of the Roman empire and settled in what is now France and Germany during the 5th century. When King Pepin died in 768, he divided his kingdom between his two sons, Charles and Carloman. Three years later Carloman died, and Charles became the sole ruler.

In 771 Charles's aim as king was to enlarge the kingdom that he had inherited, but at the same time to spread Christianity among the people whom he had conquered. During his long reign of over 40 years he organized military campaigns, and extended the kingdom of the Franks into an empire which stretched across what is now northern Germany, and parts of Poland, the Czech and Slovak Republics, Hungary, Italy, Spain, and former Yugoslavia. His conquests earned him the name of 'Charlemagne' (Charles the Great).

Pope Leo III asked Charlemagne to take over territory in Italy, and crowned him Emperor of the Holy

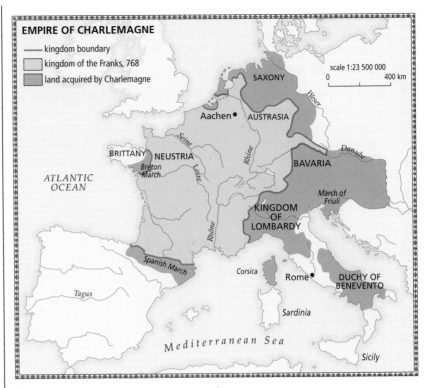

EMPIRE OF CHARLEMAGNE
— kingdom boundary
kingdom of the Franks, 768
land acquired by Charlemagne
scale 1:23 500 000
0   400 km

SAXONY
Aachen ● AUSTRASIA
Weser
BRITTANY   NEUSTRIA
Breton March
Seine
Loire
Rhine
Danube
BAVARIA
ATLANTIC OCEAN
March of Friuli
KINGDOM OF LOMBARDY
Rhône
Spanish March
Corsica   Rome ●
DUCHY OF BENEVENTO
Tagus
Sardinia
Mediterranean Sea
Sicily

▲ *After Charlemagne's death, the great empire he had created fell apart.*

Roman Empire in Rome on Christmas Day in 800. Charlemagne wanted to show that the new emperor in the West could recreate some of the splendour and learning of the old Roman empire. He built some magnificent palaces, particularly at his capital city, Aachen, which became centres of learning and art, and famous musicians and scholars were invited to spend time at them. ◆

Charles Edward Stuart

Last serious Stuart contender for the British throne
Born 1720   **Died** 1788 aged 67

Charles Edward Stuart is usually known as Bonnie Prince Charlie. His grandfather was King James II, who was expelled when the English people favoured the Protestant King William of Orange and his wife Queen Mary. But, like his grandfather, Charles was a Roman Catholic, and dreamed of going to Britain one day to claim the crown for himself.

Having lived in exile in Italy, Charles landed on the west coast of Scotland in 1745, in the reign of George II, with only 12 men. The Scottish Highlanders quickly rose to support the handsome prince, and four days later, with over 2000 supporters, Charles soundly beat an English army at Prestonpans, near Edinburgh. Charles and his army marched into England as far as Derby, but many of the Highlanders deserted on the march south so Charles retreated again to Scotland.

In 1746 his tattered army was beaten at Culloden Moor. For five months Charles was on the run, eventually escaping to France before finally settling in Italy. He turned to drink and did not do much with the rest of his life. ◆

Charles I

King of England and Scotland from 1625 to 1649
Born 1600   Died 1649 aged 48

Charles I was not born to be a king. He was backward and shy, and his brilliant elder brother, Henry, overshadowed him. But Henry died suddenly in 1612 and Charles became heir to the throne.

Charles was artistic, and his court was civilized and elegant. He was also very religious and wanted to make Church of England services more dignified and beautiful. However, Puritans and other critical people were afraid his strong-minded Catholic wife, Henrietta Maria, had too much influence and England would become Catholic again.

As king he ruled without parliament from 1629 until 1640, and tried to force his Scottish subjects to accept English church services. When this led to a war he could not afford, he promised to share some of his power with parliament. But many people in parliament did not trust him and England slid into civil war.

Although he was defeated, Charles did not believe he should give up his power, and he broke promises to his enemies. He tried to start another war in alliance with the Scots, which eventually led to his trial and execution – the only English king to be publicly beheaded. ◆

Charles II

King of England, Scotland, and Ireland from 1660 to 1685
Born 1630   Died 1685 aged 54

Charles II was 18 and in exile when his father Charles I was executed. In 1651 he returned to England, and spent six weeks on the run after Cromwell defeated his attempt to win back his crown. He disguised himself as a servant, and finally escaped to face nine more years of poverty and insecurity in France and The Netherlands.

When Charles II regained his crown in 1660 after the collapse of Cromwell's regime, he knew that he must rule with parliament and support the Church of England. So, although he was probably a Catholic, he kept quiet about it, and went along with parliament's laws which punished people for not attending Church of England services.

Charles's court was frivolous and worldly. He was easily bored by affairs of state and enjoyed the theatre, horse-racing, and gambling instead. He had many mistresses, including the actress Nell Gwynn. However, he was also a well-known patron of the arts and sciences, founding the Royal Society to encourage scientific research. ◆

👁 **see also**
Cromwell

Charles V

Habsburg emperor who ruled over vast territories
Born 1500   Died 1558 aged 58

Charles V, a devout Catholic, ruled over the largest

▼ *A painting depicting the execution of Charles I (seen top left).*

▲ *After retiring, Charles V spent much of his time worshipping God, listening to music, and dismantling and assembling mechanical clocks.*

collection of European lands since the time of Charlemagne. He inherited the throne of Spain through his mother in 1516, and three years later became ruler of Austria and The Netherlands and was elected Holy Roman Emperor. His Spanish subjects also conquered a vast new empire for him in Central and South America. His motto was *Plus ultra* (always further). His advisers wanted him to be 'God's standard-bearer', uniting all the Christian nations under his rule, waging war on the Muslim Ottoman Turks, and finally becoming 'Ruler of the World'.

Although Charles worked hard, he was not an inspiring leader of men; he always seemed to need more time, or money, to deal with the problems in his many scattered territories. By 1555 his long wars with France had led to no definite result, and he had failed to stop the Protestant ideas of Martin Luther from spreading in Germany, although he did manage to blunt the continued Ottoman attack on Christian Europe.

He retired in 1556, giving up the Empire to his brother and all his other lands to his son Philip. ◆

Ray **Charles**

American singer and musician
Born 1930   Died 2004 aged 73

Ray Charles Robinson had a tragic childhood: born in poverty, he lost his sight through illness at the age of seven, and both his parents had died by the time he was 15. He attended a Florida school for blind children where he learned to write musical arrangements in Braille. He became an accomplished pianist, and in time, one of the most inspirational musicians of the 20th century.

Recordings such as 'I Got A Woman' (1954) and 'What'd I Say' (1959) infuriated some churchgoers because they were basically rhythm 'n' blues songs with gospel-style vocals, although they were later recognized as being early examples of 'soul' music.

Other hits like 'Georgia On My Mind' (1960) and 'Crying Time' (1966) demonstrated his ability to play anything from jazz to country music, and earned Charles the widely-accepted nickname of 'The Genius'. ◆

Geoffrey **Chaucer**

English poet and writer
Born c.1340   Died 1400 aged about 60

When Geoffrey Chaucer was a small child, he was a page in the household of the Countess of Ulster, who was the wife of King Edward III's son, Lionel. When he was older, Chaucer became one of the king's 'squires', making beds and serving at the royal table.

In the war between England and France (1337–1453) Chaucer was taken prisoner, but in 1360 the king paid a ransom for his release. Later he became a diplomat, travelling to France and Italy on missions for the king. While in Italy he read books by the Italian writers Boccaccio, Petrarch, and Dante, and later used some of their stories in his own writing.

By 1374 he was made Controller of Customs in the Port of London, but left in 1386, and began writing his best-known work, *The Canterbury Tales*. This is a cycle of linked tales told by a group of pilgrims who meet in London before going on a pilgrimage to Canterbury. By that time he had already written many other long poems, including *Troilus and Criseyde* (1385), a very sad love story.

Chaucer was one of the most learned men of his age. He died in 1400 and is buried in Poet's Corner in Westminster Abbey. ◆

👁 **see also**

Dante   Petrarch

▼ *An illustration from an early edition of Chaucer's* Canterbury Tales.

Anton **Chekhov**

Russian dramatist
Born 1860   Died 1904 aged 44

Although he was born into a poor family, Anton Chekhov became an eminent doctor, at one time working with prisoners in a remote settlement near Siberia. He soon began writing, starting with short stories which combined humour with a deep understanding of the sometimes comic, sometimes tragic way in which others live their lives. When he was 29 he wrote the first of many plays, where once again he mixed seriousness with the lightest of touches. On stage, his characters talk about their fantasies and failures with honesty and regret. Although they can usually see where they have gone wrong, they generally remain unable to do anything about their mistakes. These plays made Chekhov famous, but at the height of his powers he was struck down with tuberculosis.

▲ *Anton Chekhov (left) with another of Russia's most famous writers, Leo Tolstoy.*

His last play, *The Cherry Orchard*, is one of the greatest dramas ever written. ◆

👁 **see also**

Tolstoy

Chiang **Kai-shek**

Ruler of China from 1928 to 1949
Born 1887   Died 1975 aged 87

Chiang Kai-shek trained as an army officer. In 1911 he helped in a rebellion to overthrow the dishonest rulers of the Chinese empire. China became a republic but was soon divided among warlords who kept power with their private armies.

Chiang Kai-shek joined the Nationalist Party, which believed in improving life for the peasants and poor workers. He became commander of the Nationalist armies after the death of Sun Yat-sen, who had been one of the original organizers of the Nationalist Party. Chiang Kai-shek used the armies to put down the warlords, and became ruler of China in 1928. He used his armies to try to crush the trade unionists and Communists but was not successful. Mao Zedong became leader of the remaining Communists.

When Japan invaded China in 1937, both Nationalists and Communists fought the Japanese occupiers. In 1945, when the Japanese had surrendered, the Communists started a civil war against the Nationalists. In 1949 Chiang Kai-shek had to flee to the island of Taiwan, which became known as the Republic of China (or Nationalist China). Chiang Kai-shek was its president until he died. ◆

👁 **see also**

Mao Zedong

Sun Yat-sen

Zhou Enlai

▶ *Chiang Kai-shek in 1930.*

▲ *A Chippendale mahogany bookcase.*

Thomas **Chippendale**

English 18th-century furniture maker
Born c.1718   **Died** 1779 aged about 61

Thomas Chippendale was born in Otley, Yorkshire, to a family of woodcarvers and cabinet-makers. We know nothing of his early life – even his date of birth is an estimate.

In 1727 the family moved to London, where there were many rich customers, and in 1749 Chippendale set up his own workshop to make furniture. At that time, wealthy people were looking for beautiful and fashionable things for their fine houses and they liked Chippendale's furniture very much.

Chippendale was especially good at making chairs, using his favourite dark mahogany wood. Many still exist today. They are beautifully designed and proportioned and although they look light and elegant, they are very strong and practical. He also made many dressers and chests of drawers, each one intricately decorated.

Thomas Chippendale had 11 children, and the family business carried on after his death. ◆

Chiyonofuji

Japanese sumo wrestler
Born 1955

Chiyonofuji (the professional name of Mitsugu Akimoto) is probably the most successful ever sumo wrestler. He made his début in 1970 at the age of 15. Because he was very light, he was at a physical disadvantage when faced by much heavier wrestlers. So, he decided to embark on a rigorous weight-training programme and increased his muscle-size and weight.

He became a *yokozuna* in 1981, which is the highest sumo rank, and he is the only wrestler to achieve 1000 career wins. He retired in 1991. ◆

▲ *Sumo wrestler Chiyonofuji is famous for his speed and power.*

Frederick **Chopin**

Polish pianist and composer
Born 1810   **Died** 1849 aged 39

It was always clear that Chopin would become a great pianist and composer of piano music. One of his compositions was published when he was seven, and he gave his first public concert a week before his eighth birthday.

Chopin loved Poland, but he realized that he would have to travel if his career was to prosper. Eventually he settled in Paris, but he never forgot his native land. The music he wrote – the brilliant polonaises and mazurkas, the powerful ballades – was Polish through and through. It was an inspiration to the Polish people in their struggle for independence from domination by Russia, Prussia, and Austria. Equally inspiring were his sparkling waltzes and romantic nocturnes. Chopin could make the piano talk. He could make it sing. ◆

Agatha **Christie**

English author of detective stories
Born 1890   **Died** 1976 aged 85

As a child, Agatha Christie did not go to school at all. During World War I she worked in a hospital dispensary, where she learned some of the details of chemicals and poisons which proved so useful to her in her later career of detective-story writer.

She was married twice, once to Colonel Archibald Christie, from whom she was divorced in 1928, and then to the archaeologist Max Mallowan. His care with fragments of evidence and her detective skills combined well together when she helped him in his excavation of sites in Syria and Iraq.

Agatha Christie wrote several plays and over 70 detective novels. Her books are excellent stories which make the reader desperate to know what will happen next. Since her death, several of her books have been successfully turned into films and television series. Her two most famous detectives are Miss Marple and Hercule Poirot. ◆

▲ An engraving of Queen Christina.

Queen **Christina of Sweden**

Queen of Sweden from 1632 to 1654
***Born** 1626 **Died** 1689 aged 62*

Christina was five when her father died. He was Gustavus Adolphus, King of Sweden. Christina immediately became Queen-elect, but did not rule until she was 18, in 1644. By then, the people of Sweden were tired of fighting wars. For 14 years Swedish soldiers had been fighting in Germany, in the 'Thirty Years' War'. In 1648 Christina helped to bring the war to an end.

Six years later, Christina suddenly gave up her throne and left Sweden. Everyone was shocked. She claimed that she was tired. In fact, she had secretly become a Roman Catholic. Sweden was a Protestant country and it was against the law of the country to become a Catholic. So, when Christina wanted to join the Roman Catholic Church, she had to go abroad.

Christina settled in Rome, where she became a friend of leading Catholic churchmen. She also supported musicians, writers, and painters, and made a large collection of paintings, medals, books, and manuscripts. ◆

👁 **see also**

Gustavus Adolphus

Winston **Churchill**

British statesman who led Britain during World War II
***Born** 1874 **Died** 1965 aged 90*

Winston Leonard Spencer Churchill was the grandson of the seventh Duke of Marlborough. He did not do well at school, but joined the army and had many adventures in Cuba, India, and the Sudan. In 1899 Churchill left the army and went to South Africa as a newspaper reporter during the Boer War, where he was captured by the Boers but managed to escape.

In 1900 he was elected to parliament as a Conservative, but in 1904 fell out with his party and joined the Liberals. He held several government posts, including President of the Board of Trade (1908–1910), when he introduced labour exchanges (which were later called Job Centres), and Home Secretary (1910–1911). Before and during World War I he served as head of the Admiralty, and then resigned from government to command troops in France for a time. After serving again as a Liberal minister after the war he returned to the Conservative Party, and was Chancellor of the Exchequer from 1924 to 1929.

During the 1930s Churchill was not a government minister. He warned that there was a danger of another world war, but many people ignored him. However, when World War II came the prime minister, Neville Chamberlain, put Churchill in charge of the Admiralty again. When German armies were overrunning Europe in May 1940, King George VI asked him to be prime minister and

◀ *Churchill poses for the camera after becoming prime minister. As well as being a politician, he was also a writer. He was awarded the Nobel Prize for Literature in 1953 for such books as* The Second World War.

lead a coalition government of all parties. His courage and his speeches inspired the people to withstand air raids and military defeats, and carry on to victory. His speeches were a triumph over difficulties, for in his early years Churchill had a stutter, and he had to fight hard to cure it.

Churchill remained prime minister until the general election of 1945 brought Labour to power, just before the war ended. He became prime minister again from 1951 to 1955, and finally gave up politics in 1964. ◆

> *Never in the field of human conflict was so much owed by so many to so few.*
>
> WINSTON CHURCHILL, 1940
> (on the skill and courage of British airmen)

Marcus **Cicero**

Roman politician, writer, and philosopher
Born *106 BC*   **Died** *43 BC aged 63*

Marcus Cicero lived during the last decades of the Roman Republic. He was born at Arpinum, about 100 kilometres from Rome. His father sent him to study in Rome and Athens. Cicero then became a lawyer in Rome; he was a powerful speaker and quickly became a top barrister. Then he went into politics. In 63 BC he served as consul; that is, he was one of the two rulers of the Republic, who held office for one year. During the year another Roman, Catiline, and his followers plotted to overthrow the government. Their plans were discovered and Cicero had the leaders killed.

Cicero's later life was difficult. From 49 to 45 BC there was civil war between Julius Caesar and Pompey. Cicero supported Pompey, but Caesar won. This put Cicero in danger, but Caesar died in 44 BC. Caesar was succeeded by Octavius (later called Augustus). In 43 BC Cicero criticized Octavius and as a result, Cicero was murdered. ◆

🔵 **see also**

Augustus   Caesar   Pompey

Eric **Clapton**

English guitarist and singer
Born *1945*

Eric Patrick Clapton first became interested in American blues music as a teenager attending Kingston Art College. His understanding of this music style

▼ *Fellow musicians regard Clapton as one of the finest of all rock guitarists.*

was so in advance of his contemporaries that by the mid-1960s he was the most famous blues virtuoso in the country.

His early recordings with The Yardbirds, John Mayall, and the 'supergroup' Cream helped define the role of the 'guitar hero', and have inspired musicians ever since. In 1970 his band Derek and the Dominos recorded the song 'Layla', one of the greatest of all rock singles, and possibly Clapton's most inspired performance.

His award-winning CD *Unplugged* (1992) introduced a whole new generation of listeners to the blues. ◆

Georges **Clemenceau**

French premier during World War I
Born *1841*   **Died** *1929 aged 88*

As a young man Georges Clemenceau was a journalist, but his republican ideas were not welcome in the France ruled by Emperor Napoleon III. He went to live in America from 1865 to 1869, where he taught French and horse riding. On his return to France in 1870 Clemenceau helped create the new French Republic and worked for many years as a journalist and politician. He was a Deputy in the French parliament from 1876 to 1893 and again from 1902 until 1920.

After serving as premier from 1906 to 1909, he returned to lead his country in 1917. So strong was his leadership during World War I he earned the names 'the Tiger of France' and 'Father of Victory'. After the war he helped to draw up the Treaty of Versailles with other Allied leaders. He stood for election as president in 1920, but he lost and retired from active politics. ◆

◀ *This is believed to be a model of Cleopatra's head.*

Cleopatra

Queen of Egypt
Born c.69 BC
Died 30 BC aged about 39

Cleopatra was the daughter of Ptolemy XII. It was the custom for brother and sister to marry and rule jointly. On her father's death, Cleopatra ruled Egypt with her younger brother Ptolemy XIII. However, Cleopatra's father had appointed Rome to be the guardians of his children. Egypt was no longer independent of the Roman empire.

Cleopatra was forced out of Egypt, but was restored to power by Julius Caesar, who allowed her to rule with another of her brothers. She lived with Caesar in Rome and bore him a son whom she called Caesarion. Caesar was assassinated in 44 BC, so Cleopatra then returned to Egypt and ruled jointly with her son.

A civil war soon followed in the Roman world, and Cleopatra became an ally and then mistress of Mark Antony. Antony permitted Cleopatra and Caesarion to be proclaimed joint rulers of Egypt and Cyprus. Cleopatra had three children by Antony, each of whom was proclaimed ruler of a part of the Roman empire.

In the civil war Antony and Cleopatra were defeated at the battle of Actium by Octavius (later the Emperor Augustus). They both committed suicide rather than be taken prisoner. Antony stabbed himself and Cleopatra let herself be bitten by a poisonous snake. ◆

👁 **see also**

Mark Antony   Augustus   Caesar

Bill **Clinton**

President of the United States of America from 1993
Born 1946

William J. Clinton grew up in Hot Springs, Arkansas, where he was inspired by his hero President Kennedy. From his early teens he too wanted to become a politician. After attending university at Washington, Oxford, and Yale, he became a professor of law. He married a lawyer, Hillary, in 1975 and began his political career as attorney general of Arkansas in 1976. Two years later he became the youngest U.S. Governor for 40 years. When he was defeated in 1980, it seemed that his political career was over. However, Clinton came back not only as Governor of Arkansas but also as the Democratic presidential candidate. He was elected president in 1992, and remained president until 2000. ◆

Robert **Clive**

English founder of British rule in India
Born 1725   **Died** 1774 aged 49

Robert Clive was sent to India as a clerk in the East India Company but he hated his work and lost no time in joining the East India Company's army.

Clive distinguished himself in the fighting against the French and their

▼ *Robert Clive meeting with the nawab (ruler) of Bengal.*

Indian allies in south India. In 1756, he commanded the Company's army which defeated the Indian ruler of Bengal. Bengal was still a province of the Mughal empire and was one of India's richest areas. After this victory, the Mughal emperor granted the Company the right to collect the revenues of Bengal. In effect, the Company became the masters of Bengal and Clive had laid the foundations for British rule in India.

In later years, as the first governor of Bengal, Clive did much to cut out corruption and provide firm government, although he did accept large gifts himself. He was bitterly attacked for this when he came back to England and, although cleared by parliament, he became very depressed and finally killed himself. ◆

Christopher **Cockerell**

English engineer and inventor of the hovercraft
Born *1910* **Died** *1999 aged 88*

Christopher Cockerell trained as an engineer and in electronics. He was fascinated by the idea of a hovercraft, a machine travelling on a cushion of air. Other scientists had already shown that a machine like an upside-down tea tray would float on a cushion of air pumped down from above, but the air quickly escaped around the edges. Cockerell showed that a 'wall' of air was much better at trapping the air cushion. In his first experiments he fitted a cat food tin inside a coffee tin and blew air from a vacuum cleaner down between them.

His first hovercraft tests in 1959 created a great sensation. His experimental hovercraft travelled along England's south coast at

30 knots (55 km/h), and then climbed onto the beach.

Cockerell's invention is of greatest use in countries with poor road and rail systems because it can travel up rivers and across deserts. ◆

Jean **Cocteau**

French poet, dramatist, artist, and film-maker
Born *1889* **Died** *1963 aged 74*

From boyhood, multi-talented Jean Cocteau was attracted to every kind of theatre from circus to classical drama. Friends organized a performance of his poems when he was only 16 and his first book of poems was published at 19. When he told the Russian impresario (showman), Diaghilev, that he wanted to create a ballet he was challenged 'Etonne-moi!' (Surprise me!). In collaboration with Picasso and composer Erik Satie he came

▼ *One of Cocteau's many talents was as an artist. He illustrated this poster for one of Diaghilev's Ballet Russe productions in Paris.*

up with the ballet *Parade* to music that incorporated typewriters and other unusual sounds. Novels, plays, movies, and distinctive drawings followed. Films such as *Beauty and the Beast* and *Orpheus* show his poetic use of cinematic effects. ◆

👁 **see also**
Diaghilev Picasso

Samuel **Coleridge**

English poet
Born *1772* **Died** *1834 aged 62*

As a young man Samuel Coleridge enlisted in the army. He was not suited for this life and was bought out by his brothers. He then moved to America, where he planned to set up a community which could live and educate its children on better principles than the rest of society. The plan failed and Coleridge moved back to Cambridge, where he had been a student.

He met the poet Wordsworth and moved to the Lake District to be near him. Coleridge had suffered from rheumatism all his life and the climate of the Lake District did not help. To relieve the pain he began taking the opium-based drug laudanum and he soon became addicted to opium itself.

Coleridge was one of the most important of the English poets. Together with Wordsworth he began what came to be known as the 'Romantic' movement in poetry. His most famous poems are *The Rime of the Ancient Mariner* and *Kubla Khan*. ◆

👁 **see also**
Wordsworth

Michael **Collins**

Irish statesman who helped to win independence for his country
Born 1890   Died 1922 aged 31

Michael Collins worked in an accountant's office in London from 1906 before returning to Dublin to take part in the Easter Rising of 1916. This was an armed rebellion to force Britain to grant Ireland independence, but it failed and Collins was captured. After he was released he became a Sinn Fein MP, although Sinn Fein did not join other British MPs in London. He helped to free the republican leader, Eámon De Valera, from Lincoln Jail and led the Irish Republican Army so successfully that the British government put a price of £10,000 on his head. When a truce was declared in 1921, Collins was one of the main Irish negotiators. The treaty he signed, which made most of Ireland independent but which left Northern Ireland under British rule, was not accepted by all republicans. In the civil war that followed Collins led the Irish government and its army, but was ambushed and killed by his opponents in West Cork. ◆

👁 **see also**
De Valera

Samuel **Colt**

American gun maker
Born 1814   Died 1862 aged 47

Samuel Colt was the inventor of a handgun that could fire one shot after another. The cylinder containing the bullets moved round as the gun was cocked for firing. Colt's 'revolvers' and rifles did not sell well at first and the company manufacturing them had to close down. But the US army liked them and when the government ordered 1000 pistols for the Mexican War, Colt was back in business. In 1855 he built the largest private armoury in the world, based at Hartford in Connecticut.

Colt's most famous gun was a

◀ *A Colt revolver, model 1873, known as the 'Peacemaker'.*

six-shooter called the Peacemaker. First sold in 1873, it became the gun of the cowboy and of the Wild West. ◆

Christopher **Columbus**

Italian explorer who travelled to the Americas
Born 1451   Died 1506 aged 54

Christopher Columbus, a skilled sailor, was a man with a dream. He knew that the Earth was round, and thought the easiest way to reach Japan was to sail west

▼ *On sailing west across the Atlantic Ocean, Columbus came upon America, a land which was unknown to Europeans at that time.*

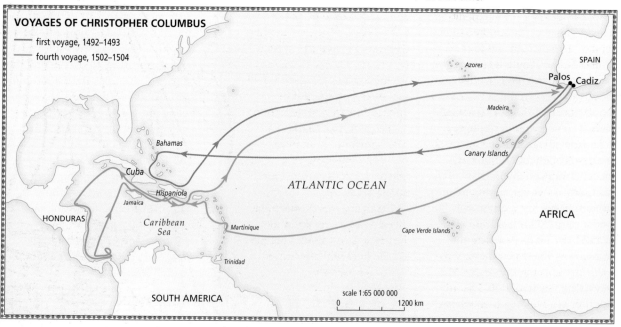

VOYAGES OF CHRISTOPHER COLUMBUS
— first voyage, 1492–1493
— fourth voyage, 1502–1504

SPAIN
Azores
Palos Cadiz
Madeira
Bahamas
Canary Islands
Cuba
Hispaniola
Jamaica
HONDURAS
Caribbean Sea
Martinique
Cape Verde Islands
AFRICA
ATLANTIC OCEAN
Trinidad
SOUTH AMERICA

scale 1:65 000 000
0   1200 km

around the globe. He looked for many years for a patron to finance such a voyage, and after many delays, he was eventually funded by Queen Isabella of Spain.

Columbus sailed with three small ships, *Santa Maria*, *Niña*, and *Pinta*, and about 90 men. After leaving the Canaries they sailed west until the morning of 12 October 1492 when a look-out sighted land. In fact it was one of the Bahama islands. Columbus was convinced it was the Indies and that he was very near Japan.

The *Santa Maria* was wrecked off the island Columbus named Hispaniola, so he decided to leave 40 men there to form a colony, and returned to Spain with the other two ships. He was hailed as a hero and was given the titles of Admiral of the Ocean Sea and Viceroy of the Indies. He set off again in 1493 with a fleet of 17 ships and 1200 men.

On his second arrival at Hispaniola Columbus found that all 40 of the men had been murdered. He founded another colony, and also visited Jamaica. Complaints were made about his harsh rule as viceroy, but in spite of this he was allowed to go on a third expedition in 1498. This time he reached the island of Trinidad and set foot on the mainland of South America.

However, Columbus was not a good governor and many more complaints about his rule reached Spain. A new governor, Francisco de Bobadilla, was sent to take over. He arrested Columbus and sent him back to Spain in chains.

Columbus was pardoned and in 1502 was allowed to make one more voyage. While exploring the coastline of Central America, he became convinced he was near the mouth of the Ganges in India. He returned to Spain and died shortly after, still believing he had reached the Orient. ◆

Nadia **Comaneci**

Romanian champion gymnast
Born 1961

Nadia Comaneci burst onto the gymnastics scene at the European championships of 1975 when, at the age of 13, she won four of the five gold medals. The following year she made Olympic history when she became the first gymnast ever to be awarded the perfect score (10·0) for her performance on the asymmetric bars. By the end of the competition, she had won gold medals for the asymmetric bars and the balance beam and was the overall Olympic champion, all at the age of 14. In 1989 she left Romania and settled in America. ◆

Confucius

Ancient Chinese teacher and writer
Born c.551 BC
Died 479 BC aged about 70

Confucius was the son of a poor nobleman. At the age of 15 he began work as an official in charge of public grain stores. When his mother died he followed the custom of returning home to mourn for three years. He gave up all pleasures and studied the ancient history and literature of the people of China. Afterwards he spent most of his life travelling as a teacher of young noblemen and officials.

Confucius's teachings were about what made an orderly society with contented people. He showed why the ancient books stressed the importance of polite behaviour and ceremonies. He said that noblemen and court officials should not plot to gain more power, but study music, poetry, and the history of their ancestors. Ceremonies should be a way of showing respect to ancestors, just as people should bow to their living rulers or to older people as a sign of obedience. Many of Confucius's sayings were written down in a collection called the *Analects*. The best known is 'Do not do to others what you would not have them do to you.' ◆

▼ *Confucius was a philosopher, rather than a religious leader. His teachings have become a widely held set of beliefs called Confucianism.*

Joseph **Conrad**

Polish-born English novelist
Born *1857*   **Died** *1924 aged 66*

Joseph Conrad, the adopted name of Jozef Korzeniowski, was born in what was then Russian Poland. He arrived in England aged 20, and worked as a merchant seaman for the next 16 years. Learning English during this time, he used his sea-faring experience to write some of his best novels, including *Lord Jim* (1900) and *The Shadow Line* (1917). However, Conrad was never interested in adventure for its own sake. In all his stories, individuals also battle against their own weaknesses as well as against natural dangers like storms, injury, or fire at sea. Conrad also had a fascination with human evil and despair, summed up unforgettably in his short novel, *Heart of Darkness* (1902). ◆

John **Constable**

English landscape painter
Born *1776*   **Died** *1837 aged 60*

John Constable's father was a corn merchant who owned Flatford Mill in East Anglia. He expected his son to continue the successful family business, but John did not seem happy. So his father allowed him to train as an artist and at the age of 23 John began at the Royal Academy School in London.

Constable devoted himself almost entirely to landscape painting. Unlike a lot of earlier landscape artists, who painted pleasant but imaginary scenes, Constable chose

▶ *John Constable's painting of Flatford Mill, Suffolk. Constable is particularly admired for the way he created a sense of time of day with his atmospheric lighting effects.*

to show real places under differing conditions of light and weather. He caught the scudding movement of clouds, and the drama of storms, painting with vigorous strokes of the brush. Most of all he enjoyed painting the places he knew and loved best, particularly the Suffolk countryside. ◆

Constantine I ('the Great')

Roman emperor from 306 to 337
Born *c.274*   **Died** *337 aged about 63*

By the time Flavius Valerius Constantinus, or Constantine, came to power in 306, the vast Roman Empire had been split into two parts: an eastern empire and a western empire.

Constantine, who was already a distinguished soldier, was with his father Constantius Chlorus, the emperor of the western empire, when he died in York in 306. The troops proclaimed the young Constantine as the new emperor of the west. For the next few years he fought many battles to defeat the emperor of the east and to win control over the whole empire and by 324 he had succeeded. He was then known throughout the huge empire as Constantine the Great.

He then set about building a new capital at Byzantium on the entrance to the Black Sea. He completed the task in 330 and called the city Constantinopolis, 'City of Constantine'.

Although he was not brought up as a Christian, he did not persecute Christians as earlier emperors had done. In 313 he issued an edict (order) allowing Christianity to be a recognized religion in the empire for the first time. He was baptized a Christian on his deathbed. ◆

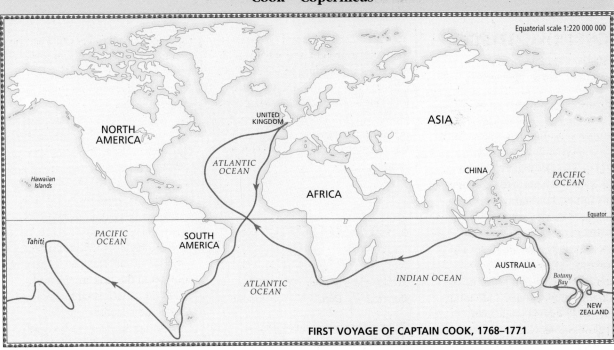

Equatorial scale 1:220 000 000

NORTH AMERICA

Hawaiian Islands

UNITED KINGDOM

ATLANTIC OCEAN

ASIA

CHINA

PACIFIC OCEAN

AFRICA

Equator

Tahiti

PACIFIC OCEAN

SOUTH AMERICA

ATLANTIC OCEAN

INDIAN OCEAN

AUSTRALIA

Botany Bay

NEW ZEALAND

FIRST VOYAGE OF CAPTAIN COOK, 1768–1771

James **Cook**

English navigator and explorer
Born 1728   *Died* 1779 aged 50

James Cook went to sea when he was 18 as a ship's boy on a coal ship. In 1755 Cook volunteered for the Royal Navy as a seaman. He soon proved himself to be an outstanding navigator and was quickly promoted.

In 1768 the Royal Society organized a scientific voyage to Tahiti. Cook was given command of the ship *Endeavour*, taking on board some famous scientists. The voyage lasted three years. On the journey, Cook insisted that the sailors ate plenty of fresh fruit, and so became the first captain to save his crew from scurvy, a terrible disease caused by lack of vitamin C.

Cook became the first European to chart the coast of New Zealand, and the first to discover the eastern coast of Australia. He claimed these lands for the British Empire. He named one bay 'Botany Bay' because of its many fabulous plants. It later became a dreaded prison colony for British convicts.

▲ *James Cook circumnavigated the world on his first voyage.*

On his second voyage (1772–1775), Cook sailed south to Antarctica and then charted the Pacific and its many islands.

On his third voyage (1776–1779), the Admiralty ordered him to explore a possible sea route around North America from the Pacific. He discovered the Sandwich Islands (Hawaii), explored the Alaskan coast, then passed through the Bering Strait, before returning to Hawaii where he was killed by islanders in a scuffle on shore. ◆

👁 **see also**

Tasman

Nicolaus **Copernicus**

Polish astronomer
Born 1473   *Died* 1543 aged 70

Nicolaus Copernicus was very well educated and studied mathematics, law, and medicine, before becoming an astronomer.

At that time everyone believed that the Earth was at the centre of the universe. But Copernicus realized that this picture did not agree with his observations. He worked out that the Sun was at the centre, with all the planets moving round it. He also said that our Earth takes a year to travel round the Sun, and revolves on its own axis once every 24 hours.

Copernicus wrote his theory in a famous book, *De Revolutionibus* (1543), which was published just before he died. His ideas were considered very controversial. They challenged the views about the Solar System held since the time of the Ancient Greeks. They also challenged the Church's belief that God created the Earth at the centre of the universe.

In 1616 Copernicus's book was regarded as a source of evil ideas and put on the *Index*, a list of books that Roman Catholics were forbidden to read. It was not until 1835 that Copernicus's book was removed from the *Index*. ◆

Aaron **Copland**

American composer
Born 1900   Died 1990 aged 90

Although he was born in Brooklyn, Aaron Copland's parents were Russian emigrants whose surname was originally Kaplan. His sister gave him his first piano lessons, but he soon outstripped her and went on to advanced studies. In 1920 he felt that he needed the stimulus of the European musical scene. He therefore decided to go to Paris to experience all the latest developments in music. On returning to America in 1924 he supported himself by teaching and playing the piano. Gradually he became known as a composer – especially after 1938 when he produced three highly successful ballets on American subjects that made use of folk-songs and jazz rhythms: *Billy the Kid* (1938), *Rodeo* (1942), and *Appalachian Spring* (1944). He wrote music of all kinds but it was through his use of folk-songs and jazz that he became the first serious composer to develop a recognizably 'American' style. ◆

Hernán **Cortés**

Spanish conqueror of the Aztecs
Born 1485   Died 1547 aged 62

Hernán Cortés studied law in Spain, but decided to try to make his fortune in the West Indies. In 1511 he became a soldier and joined an expedition to Cuba. In 1519 Cortés's fleet of 11 ships sailed to Yucatán, on the Mexican coast, to explore the country.

Cortés then marched inland to Tenochtitlán (now Mexico City), the capital of the Aztec rulers of Mexico. He had about 600

▲ *Hernán Cortés*

Spaniards with him, and several thousand Native Americans who were enemies of the Aztecs. The Aztec ruler, Montezuma, at first gave the Spaniards a friendly welcome. But Montezuma was killed by his own people in a riot, and Cortés and his men had to escape.

The Spaniards returned and besieged the city, bringing with them guns, steel armour and weapons, and horses – all new to the Aztecs. Unknown to both sides, the Spaniards also had a powerful but invisible weapon: smallpox. This disease, along with the war, killed thousands of Aztecs. By 1521 Cortés had conquered the whole country, and the great Aztec civilization collapsed. For nine years he ruled Mexico as governor, before returning home to Spain. ◆

👁 **see also**

Montezuma

Margaret **Court**

Australian tennis champion
Born 1942

Margaret Court (born Margaret Smith) won 64 Grand Slam tennis titles between 1960 and 1973, more than any other woman. The Grand Slam tournaments are Wimbledon and the French, Australian, and US championships.

Court was the first Australian woman to win Wimbledon (1963), and the second to take all four Grand Slam championships (1970). She captured the Australian title a record 11 times and has won a record 13 titles at the French championships. She was also three-times winner of the Italian, German, and South African championships.

She was also an outstanding all-rounder. For example, she won five doubles and eight mixed doubles titles at the US championships as well as five singles titles. She played with great power and stamina, yet sometimes lost because of nerves. ◆

Jacques Cousteau

French underwater explorer
Born 1910   Died 1997 aged 87

As a French naval officer, Jacques Cousteau was always keenly interested in exploring the oceans. In 1943 he helped invent the scuba or aqualung, a breathing device which allows divers to spend long periods under water. ('Scuba' stands for 'self-contained underwater breathing apparatus'.) He also developed the first underwater diving station and an observation vessel known as the diving saucer. Using his observation vessel and his scuba equipment, Cousteau made many amazing films and TV programmes about life in the world's oceans.

In 1960 Cousteau led a campaign to stop the planned dumping of

▼ *Jacques Cousteau is as famous for his environmental campaign work as for his films about ocean life.*

nuclear waste in the Mediterranean Sea. His fame helped swing public opinion behind him, and the plans were dropped. Since then he has continued to campaign for the conservation of the seabed, writing books and making more fascinating films about what goes on in the depths of the ocean. ◆

Thomas Cranmer

Henry VIII's Archbishop of Canterbury
Born 1489   Died 1556 aged 66

Thomas Cranmer was a quiet Protestant scholar who kept his beliefs to himself. He was the only one of Henry VIII's close advisers who avoided the king's wrath. Henry was particularly pleased when Cranmer arranged his divorce from Catherine of Aragon. Cranmer served the young Edward VI loyally, and compiled the Book of Common Prayer. This was used in churches in Edward's reign, and is still sometimes used today.

Cranmer's Protestant faith strengthened as time went on. However, when Catholic Mary became queen, she put him in prison for heresy (not accepting Catholic teaching). Because he was lonely and old, he signed a statement giving up his beliefs. However, when he heard that he was going to be burnt at the stake anyway, he realized he was wrong to have made such a decision. As the fire was lit around him, he put the hand which had signed the statement into the flames first, saying 'This is the hand that wrote it, therefore it shall suffer first punishment'. ◆

👁 **see also**

Henry VIII   Mary I

Crazy Horse

Native American leader
Born c.1849   Died 1877 aged about 28

It is said that Tashunca-uitco was given the name of 'Crazy Horse' because a wild horse galloped through his parents' village at the moment of his birth.

He grew up to be a fighting leader. He and his followers fought against the American government's policy of making Native Americans stay in areas called 'reservations'. However, the US Army eventually proved to be too powerful for him, and he had to surrender at Camp Robinson in 1877. When Crazy Horse realized he was going to be locked up, he tried to fight his way out but was killed in the attempt. ◆

▶ *The Sioux Indian chief, Crazy Horse.*

Crick and Watson

British and American discoverers of the structure of DNA
Francis Crick **Born** *1916*
James Watson **Born** *1928*

During World War II, Crick was a physicist working on the development of radar. After the war his interest turned to a new science called molecular biology. Physicists and chemists were working together to try to unlock the secrets of chemicals found in the body. There was special interest in the chemicals we inherit from our parents that make us look like them. This information is contained in tiny structures called chromosomes which are found in all the cells of the body. These chromosomes are made of a complicated chemical called DNA.

You cannot see the detailed structure of DNA under a microscope. Several scientists including Maurice Wilkins and Rosalind Franklin in London investigated DNA by firing X-rays at it. The X-rays produced patterns as they passed through the DNA, but they were difficult to understand.

A young American man called James Watson came to Cambridge and joined Crick in the difficult task of sorting out what those X-ray patterns meant. With a sudden flash of inspiration, Watson realized that a so-called double helix (a spiral within a spiral) could describe the structure of DNA. This led to an understanding of how DNA can make copies of itself. It was the key to all kinds of research on what animals and plants inherit from their parents, and in 1962 Crick, Watson, and Wilkins shared a Nobel prize. ◆

Davy Crockett

North American folk hero
Born *1786*   **Died** *1836 aged 49*

Davy Crockett was the son of poor settlers, who lived in Greene County, Tennessee. Many tales are told of his adventures as a bear hunter. He was also famous for braving the unknown forests further

◄ *Crick and Watson with a model of the double helix structure of DNA.*

▲ *An illustration of the last stand at the Alamo, 6 March 1836, a battle in which Davy Crockett lost his life.*

west in what is now the United States of America. He married and settled in Tennessee, and became an army colonel and a lawman.

In 1827 he was elected to the Congress of the United States, where he defended the land rights of poor farmers in western Tennessee. When he was not re-elected in 1835, he set out for Texas, which was fighting for independence from Mexico. He died in the battle of the Alamo against the Mexicans. ◆

Samuel Crompton

British inventor of the spinning mule
Born *1753*   **Died** *1827 aged 73*

Samuel Crompton learned to spin cotton on a spinning jenny. This was a machine for spinning raw cotton into thread, invented by James Hargreaves. But the spinning jenny annoyed Crompton because the thread kept breaking and so he set out to design a better machine.

To pay for it, he played his home-made violin in local theatres.

The 'spinning mule', as his machine was called, was very successful. The thread was fine and very even. People wanted to know Crompton's secret, and he even thought of destroying the machine to stop them finding out. Instead, he showed some manufacturers how it worked, thinking that his invention would make him rich. However, once they knew the secret, they became more successful than Crompton, and paid him very little. He remained bitter, and poor, for the rest of his life. ◆

see also

Arkwright   Hargreaves

Oliver **Cromwell**

Lord Protector of Britain from 1653 to 1658
Born 1599   Died 1658 aged 59

Oliver Cromwell was a boisterous schoolboy, but his stern schoolmaster had a great influence on him. Like many Puritans, he was brought up to believe that God had specially chosen him to do His will.

Cromwell's chance came when he was 41. He sat in the Long parliament of 1640, and was a strong supporter of parliament's powers. When civil war began, he trained his own cavalry. They joined parliament's victorious 'New Model Army', which Cromwell later commanded. He and his men never lost a battle.

After the war, Cromwell and other army leaders tried to make a deal with Charles I. But the king broke his promises.

Cromwell was clear about what to do, though many others were terrified. He put Charles on trial for bringing war to his people, and had him beheaded in 1649. After the collapse of parliamentary government, Cromwell declared that Britain was to be a republic ('the Commonwealth').

Cromwell fought several battles, crushing Irish resistance, and defeating the Scots in 1650 and 1651. His military victories made him the most powerful man in England. He was given the title Lord Protector (king in all but name) in 1653. He allowed more religious freedom than usual (except in Catholic Ireland), and gained a high reputation abroad as well. He tried to rule with parliament, though he also used his army to enforce what he thought was right.

▶ *An unfinished miniature of Oliver Cromwell.*

Parliament offered Cromwell the crown in the end but he refused it. He probably did not want to be 'King Oliver' anyway, but his old soldiers felt betrayed because he had even considered it. ◆

see also

Charles I   Charles II

Thomas **Cromwell**

Lord Great Chamberlain to Henry VIII
Born c.1485   Died 1540 aged about 55

Thomas Cromwell, the son of a blacksmith and innkeeper, rose to become one of the most powerful men in England. By 1513 he was making his living in England as a money lender and lawyer. Soon Cardinal Wolsey employed him as his legal and financial adviser. In 1523 Cromwell entered parliament and supported Wolsey's interests there.

When Wolsey died in 1530, Cromwell entered Henry VIII's service. He helped the king become Supreme Head of the Church of England and to divorce Catherine of Aragon. Cromwell promised to make Henry the richest king in England, and did so by organizing the closure of monasteries so that their wealth passed to the Crown.

Cromwell was a loyal servant of the king, and Henry showered him with honours. However, others hated him because of his ruthless use of power and he finally fell from favour. He was accused of treason and was beheaded. ◆

see also

Henry VIII   More   Wolsey

Tom **Cruise**

American film actor
Born 1962

Tom Cruise had to work part-time in his high-school years to help support his divorced mother and three sisters. He began his acting career in a school production of the musical *Guys and Dolls*. As a teenager he acted in adverts and on TV. His first Hollywood film was *Endless Love* (1981).

Top Gun (1985) established Cruise as a major movie star. He continued to be a huge box-office attraction, with films like *Rain Man* (1988), in which he starred alongside his boyhood hero Dustin Hoffman, *A Few Good Men* (1993), *Mission Impossible* (1995), and *Jerry MacGuire* (1996). For the film *Interview With The Vampire* (1994) he was paid over $20 million, making him one of Hollywood's highest-earning stars. ◆

Marie **Curie**

French physicist and chemist
Born 1867   Died 1934 aged 66

Marie Curie was born Marya Sklodowska in Poland's capital, Warsaw. Women were not allowed to go to university in Poland at this time, so Marya worked hard as a governess and saved some money so that she could go to study at the Sorbonne University in Paris. When living in France, she changed her name to the French 'Marie'.

In 1894 Marie met a successful chemist called Pierre Curie, and in a year they were married. Working with her new husband, Marie Curie spent her whole life studying radioactive substances. She invented an instrument to measure radioactivity, and found that a

▲ *Marie Curie at work in her laboratory.*

substance called pitchblende (the ore from which uranium is extracted) was a thousand times more radioactive than uranium itself.

After several years' work, Marie and Pierre managed to separate out the material that made pitchblende so radioactive. They called it radium and received a Nobel prize for their work. After her husband's death in a road accident, Marie carried on with her work and received a second Nobel prize in 1911.

The dangers of radioactivity were not properly understood at that time, and Marie Curie suffered throughout her life from radiation burns on her skin. She eventually died from a form of blood cancer called leukaemia. ◆

👁 **see also**
Becquerel Röntgen Rutherford

General George A. **Custer**

American Civil War general
Born 1839
Died 1876 aged 36

George Armstrong Custer wanted to be an army officer, but was almost expelled

for misbehaviour from the US Military Academy at West Point. After his training, Custer fought in the American Civil War from 1861 to 1865. His commanding officer called him 'gallant' but 'reckless'. The newspapers called him the 'Boy General' because he was only 23 when he was promoted. His long, golden hair streaming, he raced his cavalry to victory after victory and became a legendary hero for his courage.

After the Civil War, Custer was sent to fight the Native Americans who still roamed the Great Plains. He often fought rashly and did not treat his men well, but the newspapers still praised him.

Then in 1876, Custer and all 266 of his troops were killed at Little Bighorn, South Dakota, by a larger force of over 3000 Sioux Indians led by Chief Sitting Bull. ◆

👁 **see also**
Sitting Bull

▼ *Custer's defeat at Little Bighorn became known as 'Custer's Last Stand'.*

Cyrus the Great

Founder of the Persian empire
Date of birth unknown
Died *529 BC age unknown*

In about 550 BC Cyrus overthrew the King of the Medes and took possession of his capital. Within two years he had conquered the empire of Lydia, and taken the title of King of Persia. Then he added Babylonia, Syria, and Palestine to his empire and became master of all Asia from the Mediterranean to India. Soon he extended his rule from the Arabian desert to the Black Sea, the Caucasus, and the Caspian Sea.

Cyrus was a remarkable soldier who never executed or made slaves of the people he captured. Instead, he respected their religions and customs. He even allowed the Jews who were caught in Babylon to return to Jerusalem. ◆

see also
Darius

Louis Daguerre

French inventor of the first practical camera
Born *1789*   **Died** *1851 aged 61*

As a young man, Louis Daguerre worked as a tax collector and then became an artist. But what he really wanted to do was to produce an exact copy on paper of the world around him.

Daguerre was familiar with the camera obscura, where sunlight entered a dark box through a pinhole and produced on a screen an image, or picture, of what was outside the box.

In the 1830s Daguerre designed a box in which the image fell on a flat metal plate; the plate was coated with a chemical called silver iodide, which turned black in sunlight. The bright part of the picture became dark and the darker parts of the picture were left lighter. Although it took a long time to produce a rather fuzzy picture, this was how the very first photographs were taken. ◆

see also
Fox Talbot   Niepce

Roald Dahl

British author
Born *1916*   **Died** *1990 aged 74*

Roald Dahl's early life was almost as adventurous as any of his novels. As a young businessman working for Shell Oil, he was sent to work in Africa. After some extraordinary adventures, some involving wild animals, Dahl volunteered for the Royal Air Force when Britain declared war on Germany in 1939. After flying in East Africa, he crashed his plane in flames in the middle of the Western Desert. Despite dreadful injuries Dahl was soon flying again in Greece and Syria, before transferring to the USA in 1943.

After World War II he started writing stories, at first for adults and later for children. His most popular children's books include *Charlie and the Chocolate Factory, The BFG, Revolting Rhymes,* and *The Witches.* During the 1980s he was the most popular children's author in the world. ◆

Gottlieb Daimler

German pioneer of the internal combustion engine
Born *1834*   **Died** *1900 aged 66*

Gottlieb Daimler started his career as an apprentice gunsmith. Later, he studied engineering and became interested in the internal combustion engine. He wanted to improve on the gas-driven internal combustion engines of the time.

Daimler studied the work of other engineers, and in 1883 he built an engine that ran on petrol. It was much more powerful than any other internal combustion engine of the time. In 1885 he used one to make what was probably the world's first motor bike. He went on to build cars that used his engines.

Daimler did not invent the petrol engine or the motor car. But, because he made better engines, he has an important place in the history of the motor car. ◆

▼ *A 1903 Daimler car.*

Dalai Lama

Spiritual and political leader of the Tibetan people
Born 1935

Tenzin Gyatso was born in a cow shed to a poor farming family who lived in north-east Tibet. When he was only two-and-a-half years old, a group of Buddhist leaders declared him to be the reincarnation of the previous Dalai Lama who had died in 1933. They installed him as their new leader, whom they believed was the Buddha of Compassion come down to Earth.

When he was four years old he went to a palace called Potala in Lhasa, the capital of Tibet. Thousands of people greeted him and wept with joy that their Dalai Lama had been found. Although he was so young, he seemed to know exactly what to do during the long ceremony of enthronement and spontaneously blessed many of his people. Life in the Potala was quite strict and lonely for the Dalai Lama. He had to study extremely hard and take many exams in Buddhist philosophy, which he passed with flying colours.

When he was 16 the Dalai Lama faced his greatest crisis. The Chinese invaded Tibet, killing many people and destroying the great Buddhist monasteries. For nine years he tried to coexist peacefully with the Chinese, but in 1959, when his life was threatened, he made a daring escape over the Himalayan mountain passes to India. The Dalai Lama now lives in a small Himalayan hamlet in India from where he takes care of the 120,000 Tibetan refugees who had followed him into exile, and tries to get the world to help his people in Tibet. He has become respected worldwide for his message of universal peace, and was awarded the Nobel Peace Prize in 1989. ◆

▶ *One of Dali's quirky creations: the Lobster telephone.*

Salvador **Dali**

Spanish painter
Born 1904   Died 1989 aged 85

Dali was a brilliant, very talented, and ambitious young man. He believed that his name, Salvador, meaning Saviour, meant that he was expected to save the true art of painting which he defined as 'an instant colour photograph that you can hold in your hand, of superfine images'.

Dali's paintings are very realistic; that is, objects look as real as he could make them. Yet what he painted, his subject matter, is bizarre. His interest in Freudian psychology led him to create extraordinary paintings which extend the boundaries of the imagination. For example, some of his paintings show strange and eerie dream worlds (sometimes nightmare worlds) inhabited by burning giraffes, tiny people, huge insects, and monstrous figures. People react very differently to his paintings: some people are horrified by what they see, while others are amused.

Dali is one of the most famous artists of the 20th century. He has influenced the film world, fashion, and particularly the world of advertising. ◆

John **Dalton**

English chemist and physicist
Born 1766   Died 1844 aged 77

When John Dalton was only ten he went to work for a man called Elihu who was very interested in science. Elihu realized that Dalton was very bright and started to teach him mathematics. Dalton did so well that when he was only 12 he became the head of a small country school, teaching children of all ages. He later became a lecturer at New College in Manchester and then went to London to lecture at the famous Royal Institution.

In his early twenties he began to keep a diary, which was mainly notes and theories about the weather. When he died there were 200,000 entries. He suggested, correctly, that auroras, of which there was a specially brilliant display in 1787, were electrical in origin. However, his most important work was the development of his atomic theory. The Greeks of the ancient world had some ideas about atoms but John Dalton was the first modern scientist to suggest that atoms of different elements had different weights. ◆

Dante Alighieri

Italian poet and writer
Born 1265 **Died** 1321 aged 56

Dante Alighieri grew up in Florence, Italy. When he was nine years old, he met a girl who was younger than himself, and she changed his life for ever. When he was older he wrote a lot of beautiful poetry about her. Dante called her Beatrice. We know very little about her except that she married another man and died quite young. Dante saw her occasionally when he was a young man, but only among groups of friends.

▼ *An illustration of part of Dante's* The Divine Comedy. *The poem is often seen as a metaphor for Dante's own spiritual development.*

In 1302 Dante quarrelled with the supporters of the Pope in Florence and spent the rest of his life in exile in other cities of northern Italy. His great poem, *The Divine Comedy*, describes his journey through Hell, Purgatory, and Paradise. Throughout, he feels that the love of Beatrice directs him, and at the end she herself guides him among the blessed souls in Paradise.

Dante was one of the first great poets to write in the ordinary language of the people, rather than in Latin. He used his local dialect to create one of the most beautiful poems that the world has ever known. ◆

Georges **Danton**

French revolutionary leader
Born 1759 **Died** 1794 aged 34

Georges Danton was a huge man, with striking features and a very powerful voice. Originally from a farming family, he trained to be a lawyer and worked in Paris. There he became much

▲ *Danton's powerful words and manner attracted thousands of people to his cause.*

admired by the working-class population for his rousing speeches against the king, Louis XVI, and the aristocracy. He helped to organize the uprising on 10 August 1792 that led to the overthrow of the monarchy, and then in 1793 voted for the king's execution. A few months later he became a member of the dictatorial Committee for Public Safety, which was set up to run France, and for three months he virtually led the country.

The Reign of Terror began during this period, during which at least 12,000 political prisoners, priests, and aristocrats were executed. Danton, however, disapproved of the Terror, and his growing moderation brought him into conflict with his enemies, including Robespierre, the merciless revolutionary leader. This conflict eventually led to Danton's arrest, trial, and execution by guillotine. ◆

◉ **see also**

Robespierre

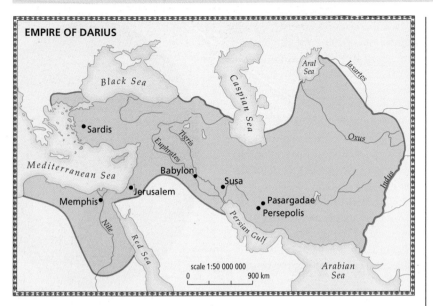

EMPIRE OF DARIUS

▲ The extent of the Persian empire in about 500 BC when it was ruled over by Darius I.

Darius I

Ruler of the ancient kingdom of Persia
Born c.558 BC
Died 486 BC aged about 72

Darius I took the throne of Persia in 521 BC. Persia was then a very large empire which controlled the countries along the eastern edge of the Mediterranean (now Turkey, Syria, Lebanon, Israel, Egypt, and Libya) and beyond to the east (now Iraq, Iran, Afghanistan, and Pakistan). As soon as Darius became king, he had to deal with revolts against him from all over the empire. He established peace by military force and then divided his empire into 20 provinces.

Darius went to war against Greece because they had helped Greek cities in Asia Minor (now Turkey) in their revolt against the Persians. The first fleet sent by Darius was destroyed in 492 BC off the north coast of Greece. In 490 BC Darius sent an army of perhaps 25,000 soldiers across to Greece. This ended in a disastrous defeat for the Persians. About 6400

Persian soldiers died compared to only 192 Greeks. Darius died a few years later and was succeeded by his son Xerxes. ◆

👁 **see also**

Xerxes

Charles **Darwin**

English scientist, best known for his theory of evolution
Born 1809   **Died** 1882 aged 73

Charles Darwin's father was a doctor and he decided that Charles should also study medicine. But Charles found that he could not stand the sight of blood, and, after two years, he went to Cambridge University to study classics instead. However, he soon found that he was more interested in geology and botany.

He became the friend of the professor of botany, who suggested that Darwin would be a suitable person to go as the naturalist and companion to the captain of a naval survey ship, HMS *Beagle*. Darwin set sail on 27 December 1831 for what was to be a five-year journey.

The most important part of the

voyage for Darwin turned out to be the few weeks spent in the Galapagos Islands, which lie on the Equator, about 1000 km from the coast of South America. These islands have plants and animals that are found nowhere else. Darwin was surprised to discover that each island had its own particular sort of tortoise. Why, wondered Darwin, should this be?

When he got home, Darwin realized that some of the birds from the Galapagos Islands were also closely related to each other but different in the shapes of their beaks. Yet the birds from any one island were similar. They were all rather like some small birds that live on the South American mainland, and Darwin decided that some of these must have reached the Galapagos Islands accidentally, perhaps by being blown off course during a storm, and had evolved (changed) in their new home.

After investigating all the animals he could, Darwin developed his theory of natural selection. This theory proposed that although most young animals die, the ones that

▼ Darwin was the target of many humorously critical attacks, including this comment on 'Darwinism' from the English magazine Punch in 1881.

PUNCH'S ALMANACK FOR 1882.

MAN·IS·BVT·A·WORM.

survive are those best suited to their way of life. If, every now and again, an animal is born which has some feature that gives it an advantage, it will survive, and so will its offspring that are like it. In this way a process of natural selection enables a particular population to evolve.

Darwin hesitated to publish his ideas, possibly because he knew they would upset many people. But in 1859 his book called *The Origin of Species* came out. It caused an uproar, as it contradicted the ideas found in the Bible. But few people nowadays doubt the basic truth of Darwin's arguments. ◆

David

Second king of Israel
Lived during the 10th century BC

According to the story in the Bible, as a boy David watched over his father's sheep and killed the Philistine giant, Goliath, with a stone from his sling. He was invited to the court of King Saul of Judah to play his harp. Jonathan, the king's son, became his friend, and Saul's daughter Michal was his first wife.

After Saul and Jonathan were killed in a battle against the Philistines, David became king of Judah. In seven years of warfare he defeated the Philistines and other enemies, captured Jerusalem, and took the Ark of the Lord containing the Ten Commandments to the city. David became king over all the tribes of Israel as well as of Judah. He ruled for over 30 years, and was succeeded by his son Solomon. The Jews regarded David as the ideal king and hoped there would one day be another king, descended from him, called the Messiah. ◆

👁 **see also**

Solomon

Jacques-Louis David

French painter
Born *1748* **Died** *1825 aged 77*

Jacques-Louis David began to study art at the age of 17 and at 26 he won a coveted prize (the Prix de Rome) which launched him on a highly successful career.

He became the most influential figure in the French art world. His early paintings were concerned with attention to detail, classic ideals, and 'republican' (i.e. anti-monarchy) ideas. During the French Revolution he voted for the execution of King Louis XVI and his portraits celebrated those who had died in the Revolution. His revolutionary activity led to a spell in prison.

Later, he passionately committed his painting to the cause of the Emperor Napoleon, but after Napoleon's defeat at Waterloo, David was forced to live abroad until he died. ◆

👁 **see also**

Louis XVI Napoleon I

▲ *A detail from* The Blessing of Josephine, *one of the works Jacques-Louis David completed while employed as court painter to Napoleon I.*

Saint David

Christian monk and bishop
Lived during the 6th century

We know almost nothing about the life of this saint. His monastery was at 'Menevia', which is now called St Davids, in Dyfed, south-west Wales. Later writers nicknamed him 'the Waterdrinker' because he led a very simple life and refused to drink wine or beer. It is said that he founded ten monasteries, including the one at Glastonbury in England. The monks in these monastaries led lives of great hardship.

Since the 12th century St David has been the patron saint of Wales. His feast day is 1 March, when the Welsh wear leeks or daffodils in his honour. No one knows for sure how this ancient tradition started. ◆

▲ *Bette Davis in a still from the film*
Jezebel (1938). A formidable actress, she
continued to make films until two years
before her death.

Bette **Davis**

American film actress
Born *1908*   **Died** *1989 aged 81*

Ruth Elizabeth Davis came from Lowell, Massachusetts, and studied acting in New York. Film directors did not think she was beautiful enough for romantic roles, but in the 1930s she established herself as a powerful actress playing forceful women. She won Oscars for her roles in *Dangerous* (1935) and *Jezebel* (1938).

In films such as *The Little Foxes* (1941) and *All About Eve* (1950) she played cruel and selfish characters. In others, like *Now, Voyager* (1942), she played more likeable women, but her strong personality always shone through. In later life she scared audiences of *Whatever Happened to Baby Jane?* (1962) when she terrorized her crippled sister, played by Joan Crawford. ◆

Jefferson **Davis**

American statesman
Born *1808*   **Died** *1889 aged 81*

Jefferson Davis was a soldier and cotton farmer in the southern US state of Mississippi. At that time all the work on the cotton plantations was done by black slaves. Davis treated his own slaves very well, and he did not consider that the whole system of slavery was a terrible evil.

In 1847 Davis became a national hero when he led Mississippian soldiers in a decisive stand against the Mexicans at Buena Vista. He then held important posts in the US government for some years. However, the rift between the northern states, which opposed slavery, and the southern states, which supported it, eventually led to him giving his complete support to the south.

During the Civil War that followed, Davis became president of the Confederate States of the south (1861–1865). He masterminded the Confederates' war effort against the much stronger northern states for four years until he was captured and imprisoned for treason. Although he was held in prison for two years, his case never came to court and he was released. ◆

Humphry **Davy**

English chemist, inventor of the miner's safety lamp
Born *1778*   **Died** *1829 aged 51*

As a boy Humphry Davy had an extremely good memory and was quite a showman. He used to stand on a cart in the market place and tell Cornish folk-stories to crowds of children. He was later apprenticed to a surgeon, and while he worked making up medicines and pills he became interested in chemistry. When he was 21 he began to study a gas called nitrous oxide, which is sometimes called laughing gas. It was later used to put people to sleep while they had their teeth pulled out.

Scientists today remember Davy because he discovered so many new chemical elements. However, he is generally remembered for his invention of the miner's safety lamp. In 1813 a dreadful gas explosion occurred in a mine and more than 90 miners were killed. Davy was asked to help prevent such accidents in the future. The safety lamp he invented, which had a flame enclosed in glass so that it could not ignite undetected gases, must have saved thousands of lives. He made many scientific discoveries, but he always said that his greatest discovery was a young man who came to work for him: his name was Michael Faraday. ◆

👁 **see also**
Faraday

James **Dean**

American film actor
Born *1931*   **Died** *1955 aged 24*

At school James Dean loved acting, and he went on to perform on stage and television before becoming a star at the age of 24 in *East of Eden* (1955). Within a few months he made two more films, *Rebel Without a Cause* (1955) and *Giant* (1956), but before they appeared in cinemas he crashed his sports car and died. Dean rapidly became a cult hero for teenagers who were angry at the way adults misunderstood them, just like the character he played in his second film, *Rebel Without a Cause.* ◆

Claude **Debussy**

French composer
Born 1862   *Died* 1918 aged 55

Claude Achille-Debussy began studying music at the Paris Conservatoire when he was ten. At first he hoped to become a great pianist, but he found that he was not quite good enough so he turned to composing instead.

As a composer he soon proved that he had genius. Such works as the *Prélude à l'après-midi d'un faune* (1892–1894) startled everyone. Instead of treating harmony according to the old rules, he used it freely, choosing chords for the sake of their effect, just as a painter chooses his colours.

Debussy's ideas set music free and opened up all sorts of possibilities for other composers to follow. He is therefore one of the most important composers of his day. Among his other works are the opera *Pelléas et Mélisande* (1892) and two important books of piano *Préludes* (1909–1910, 1911–1913). ◆

▲ *This illustration from Daniel Defoe's* Robinson Crusoe *(1719) shows the hero finding a footprint in the sand, proving that the island was inhabited.*

◀ *After the sudden and tragic end to his short film career, James Dean became a cult hero for young Americans in the 1950s.*

Daniel **Defoe**

English novelist
Born 1660   *Died* 1731 aged 71

Daniel Defoe, the son of a butcher, led an exciting and adventurous life. In 1685 he took part in the rebellion against King James II and was lucky to avoid execution. He was later put in prison for publishing opinions against the government, and even spent time as a secret agent.

Defoe is best known as the writer of *Robinson Crusoe*, which he published in 1719. Many people think of this as the first successful English novel. It tells how the hero survives after being shipwrecked on an island. Defoe also published his own newspaper, and wrote hundreds of pamphlets and articles on everything from politics to pirates. All his writing is vivid and realistic, like that of a good journalist. *A Journal of the Plague Year*, for example, tells exactly what it was like in London during the great plague of 1666. ◆

◄ *Degas' Danseuses au Repos (Dancers at Rest). In his paintings of ballet-dancers, Degas wanted to show the realities of the young dancers' hard work and exhaustion, not just the magic of the theatre as the curtain rises.*

Edgar **Degas**

French painter
Born *1834*   **Died** *1917 aged 83*

Edgar Degas was born into a wealthy Paris banking family. He wanted to be an artist from a young age, and his family had no objection to such an insecure life.

Degas was able to spend his time painting without worrying about money because his rich family supported him until he was well-known and established. Degas exhibited with the Impressionists, such as Monet and Renoir, but he was always an individualist rather than a member of a group. He realized that picture designs could break all the usual rules and that the artist need not place the main subject in the middle of the picture or show it complete. A picture showing just parts of people could look just as lifelike. He loved to paint scenes from unexpected angles, particularly ballet-dancers, because their bodies made exciting and unusual shapes. He was also a fine sculptor, making figures in wax which were then cast in bronze. His sculptures portrayed moving figures, mainly ballet-dancers. ◆

👁 **see also**
Monet   Renoir

Charles **de Gaulle**

President of France from 1958 to 1969
Born *1890*   **Died** *1970 aged 80*

As a child, Charles de Gaulle enjoyed playing war games. Later he went to St Cyr Military Academy. When he left in 1912 his reports said that he was 'average in everything except height'.

He was wounded and captured during World War I, and remained a soldier after the war. At the start of World War II he commanded a tank division. When France was invaded by the Germans in 1940, he escaped to England. From there he became the leader of all the French troops who had also escaped from occupied France. The Free French forces, with de Gaulle at their head, returned victorious to Paris in 1944 alongside the British and American troops.

De Gaulle was elected president of France in 1945, but resigned after only ten weeks. It was not until 1958 that he returned to power, when France was going through a political crisis. He survived a number of assassination attempts to become one of the most powerful presidents in French history. He insisted that France should be able to defend itself with its own nuclear weapons, and often argued with other leaders in Europe and the West. When he was defeated in a referendum (national vote) in 1969, he retired to his home village, where he died the following year. ◆

> *How can you govern a country which has 246 varieties of cheese?*
>
> Charles de Gaulle

F. W. **de Klerk**

President of South Africa from 1989 to 1994; deputy president from 1994
Born *1936*

Frederick Willem de Klerk became a lawyer after graduating from university. In 1972 he was elected to parliament for the National Party (NP). After 1978 de Klerk held a number of ministerial posts, including Internal Affairs and National Education. In 1989 he became president of South Africa.

Reacting to internal and international pressure, de Klerk surprised the world in 1990 by releasing political prisoners, including Nelson Mandela. De Klerk also legalized outlawed political parties such as Mandela's African National Congress (ANC). Negotiations between the ANC, NP, and other smaller parties led to the ending of apartheid. De Klerk and Mandela were awarded the Nobel Peace Prize in 1993 for their part in this achievement.

In 1994 the first election was held in which all adult South Africans could vote. It was won easily by the ANC. De Klerk became one of Mandela's two deputy presidents, but retired from active politics in 1997. ◆

👁 see also
Mandela

Eugène Delacroix

French painter
Born *1798* **Died** *1863 aged 65*

Eugène Delacroix was born into an important French family, but as an artist he had to struggle for recognition. His new style of painting shocked those who felt that his work was not in the great tradition of French classical painting. To us, looking at his work from a 20th-century viewpoint, it does not seem at all outrageous. At the time, however, his use of bright colours and free handling of paint shocked the art world. His subject matter ranged from lively animal studies to scenes from African, Arab, and Jewish cultures, and to portraits and exciting stories from literary subjects. ◆

Cecil B. **De Mille**

American film director and producer
Born *1881* **Died** *1959 aged 78*

Cecil B. De Mille started his career as an actor, but he soon became a director instead, and founded a film company which later formed part of Paramount Pictures. As a director he started making silent comedies, but he became more famous for *The Ten Commandments*, which he made twice, first as a silent film in 1923 and then again with sound and colour in 1956. This and his other 'epic' films based on stories from the Bible and from history were famous for their huge crowd scenes and their spectacular special effects, like the parting of the Red Sea in *The Ten Commandments*. ◆

▼ *Cecil B. De Mille (right) photographed during the filming of his 1956 film,* The Ten Commandments.

Deng Xiaoping

Chinese political leader
Born *1904* **Died** *1997 aged 92*

Deng Xiaoping came from a rich family, but in 1920 he became a Communist and helped to bring about the revolution in China in 1949. By 1956 he was one of the leading people in the Communist government, but the next 20 years were difficult as he did not support Mao Zedong's extreme ideas. When Mao turned against those who disagreed with him, Deng lost all his power.

Mao died in 1976, and two years later Deng was the most powerful leader in China. He used his power to improve the standard of living. More food was grown, and factories began to produce goods such as clothing, sewing machines, bicycles, and television sets. Deng allowed small private businesses to develop, and ended the most severe government censorship of television and newspapers.

However, many people began to protest about the lack of democracy in China. Deng's Communist government felt threatened. In 1989 troops were ordered to put down a massive protest in Beijing and hundreds of demonstrators were killed. ◆

👁 see also
Mao Zedong

Robert **De Niro**

American film actor
Born *1943*

Robert De Niro lived as a child in a part of New York called Little Italy. After training as an actor, De Niro had his first major part in the film *Mean Streets* (1973) directed by Martin Scorsese. Scorsese had lived in the same part of New York as De Niro and this film was set in the streets they had both known.

De Niro is well-known for becoming totally involved in the characters he plays. For the 1979 film *Raging Bull*, he put on over 30 kg to play the part of a boxer. He even took part in three proper boxing contests. This dedication brought him an Oscar for Best Actor. He also won the award for Best Supporting Actor for his role in the 1974 film *The Godfather*. ◆

▼ *In* The Deer Hunter *(1978) we see De Niro at work (as a steelworker), at play (deer-hunting), and as a volunteer in the Vietnam War.*

René **Descartes**

French philosopher and mathematician
Born *1596*   **Died** *1650 aged 54*

When René Descartes was 25, after studying, travelling, and serving in the army, he decided to devote his life to the study of philosophy and science. He settled in Holland, where he spent most of the rest of his life. He never married, although he had a daughter whose death at the age of five was said to be his greatest sorrow. He died of pneumonia in Stockholm, where he had gone to teach philosophy to Queen Christina of Sweden.

Descartes made a number of advances in mathematics, including the use of Cartesian coordinates in geometry. In philosophy he explored the certainty of knowledge. In his most famous philosophical book, *Discourse on Method* (1637), he argued that everything should at first be doubted because we can only be convinced of the truth after satisfying our doubts. This proved to him that he at least existed, because if he did not exist he could not think, much less doubt. And so he coined his most famous phrase: 'I think, therefore I am'. ◆

Eamon **De Valera**

Irish statesman
Born *1882*   **Died** *1975 aged 92*

The son of an Irish mother and a Spanish father, Eamon De Valera was born in America, but at the age of three he went to live in Ireland. When De Valera was older, he joined the Volunteers who rebelled in 1916 against British rule. The rebels had to surrender to the British, who shot most of their leaders.

De Valera was reprieved and later became leader of Sinn Féin (Ourselves Alone), which fought a guerrilla war against British rule from 1919 to 1921. Sinn Féin and the British then signed a treaty to set up an Irish Free State, but De Valera would not agree to it because Ireland was to be partitioned.

In 1926 he started a new party, Fianna Fáil (Warriors of Ireland). It won the 1932 general election, and Eamon De Valera was prime minister until 1948. He broke nearly all of Ireland's links with Britain, and in 1949 Ireland became a fully independent republic. For five years between 1951 and 1959 he was Taoiseach (prime minister) of the Republic, and between 1959 and 1973 he was president. ◆

Ninette **de Valois**

Irish-born ballet-dancer and founder of The Royal Ballet
Born *1898*   **Died** *2001 aged 102*

Ninette de Valois grew up in Ireland as Edris Stannus, but became famous as Ninette de Valois, dancing as a principal ballerina in England and Europe. By 1926 she was running her own ballet school, and in 1931 she formed the Vic-Wells Ballet. She was a brilliant organizer and teacher, and helped shape the careers of dancers such as Margot Fonteyn. Under her direction, the Vic-Wells Ballet became the Sadlers Wells Ballet, moved to Covent Garden, and was recognized in 1956 as The Royal Ballet.

Ninette de Valois created many famous ballets for her company. She worked hard so that Britain would have a great national ballet company and her achievement was recognized when she was made a Dame of the British Empire in 1951. ◆

👁 **see also**

Fonteyn

▶ *De Valois as a young dancer. She retired as director of The Royal Ballet in 1961.*

▲ *Princess Diana was able to talk easily and naturally with all kinds of people, especially small children.*

Diana, Princess of Wales

Born 1961   Died 1997 aged 36

Diana Spencer became Lady Diana in 1975, when her father became the eighth Earl Spencer. She did not do particularly well at school; she then moved to London to work in a nursery school.

In 1981 Diana married Charles, Prince of Wales, the Queen's eldest son and the heir to the British throne. They had two sons, William and Harry, born in 1982 and 1984.

Diana's beauty, elegance and kindness won her many fans, and she became a great supporter of charities and good causes. Sadly, Diana and Charles separated in 1992 and later divorced. Diana withdrew from public life for a while, but later took up her charity work once more, notably for the Red Cross campaign to ban landmines in war zones.

On 31 August 1997 Diana was tragically killed in a car crash in Paris, France, at the age of only 36.

There was a tremendous outburst of grief among the people of Britain and throughout the world. ◆

Bartolomeu Dias

Portuguese navigator and explorer
Born c.1450   Died 1500 aged about 50

Nothing is known of the early life of Bartolomeu Dias except that he was an experienced sea captain, and a knight at the court of the Portuguese king, João II. In 1487 João sent him on an expedition to sail south along the west coast of Africa, looking for a sea route to India.

A storm blew Dias and the three little ships under his command out to sea, until his crews feared they would fall off the edge of the Earth. When the storm subsided Dias turned east, then north, and reached the African coast at Mossel Bay. After sailing as far as the Great Fish River on the south-east African coast, his men then insisted on going home. But Dias had seen that the coast of Africa turned northwards leaving the passage to India clear. Dias named the south-western point of Africa the 'Cape of Storms', but King João changed the name to 'Cape of Good Hope'. ◆

◀ *This plate is illustrated with a scene from Dickens' Pickwick Papers.*

Mr Pickwick addresses the Club.

Charles **Dickens**

English novelist
Born 1812   Died 1870 aged 58

Charles Dickens was born in Portsmouth. His father was a naval clerk who frequently got into debt. When this led to his imprisonment, the young Charles, then aged 12, was taken out of school and put to work in a factory pasting labels onto bottles of shoe polish.

Later, he went to school again, and left at 15 to become a reporter covering debates in the House of Commons. His genius for describing comical characters and his anger about social injustice were soon noticed. In 1836 he began *The Pickwick Papers*. The book was so popular that by the age of 24 Charles was famous in both Britain and America.

Dickens went on to write such powerful stories that Parliament sometimes passed laws to stop the various scandals he described so vividly. For example, after publishing his book *Nicholas Nickleby*, some of the cruel boarding-schools he described were forced to close down following such bad publicity.

Dickens also had a wonderful gift for creating larger-than-life characters in his novels: the villainous Fagin in *Oliver Twist*, the bitter Miss Havisham in *Great Expectations*, the drunken nurse Mrs Gamp in *Martin Chuzzlewit*, and the optimistic, unreliable Mr Micawber in *David Copperfield*, a character based on his own father. When Dickens died of a stroke, he was mourned all over the world, and his books have remained popular ever since. ◆

👁 **see also**

Thackeray

Emily **Dickinson**

American poet
Born 1830   Died 1886 aged 55

Emily Dickinson was born at Amherst, Massachusetts, and lived almost all her life there. After a visit to Washington and Philadelphia in her early twenties she lived in seclusion at the family home at Amherst. For the last 25 years of her life she scarcely ever left her own room, except at dusk when she would creep out into the garden if no one else was around.

Emily had a few close friends with whom she exchanged long letters. She may even have fallen in love with one of the men she wrote to, but she was so secretive that no one knows for certain who this man was. From the 1850s she channelled all her energy into her poetry, which she wrote down in beautiful little handmade books. Very few of her 1700 poems were published in her lifetime, so it was only after her death that she was fully recognized as a gifted poet. ◆

Denis **Diderot**

French philosopher and writer
Born 1713   Died 1784 aged 70

As a young man, Denis Diderot chose to study law. Soon his wide interests in mathematics, philosophy, and literature led him to become a teacher and translator.

In 1745 Diderot was put in charge of producing a French encyclopedia. Gathering a brilliant team of scholars around him, Diderot used this opportunity to support the use of reason rather than religion as the best way of understanding and improving society. In 1750 he was briefly sent to prison for these attacks upon religious beliefs.

The first volume of his encyclopedia appeared in 1751, and the last came out in 1772. The ideas developed within it did much to prepare its readers for the massive reaction against old ideas and practices that developed during the French Revolution, five years after his death. ◆

▶ *Marlene Dietrich in a Hollywood publicity shot.*

Joe **DiMaggio**

American baseball star
Born 1914   *Died* 1999 aged 84

Joe DiMaggio, also known as 'Joltin' Joe' and 'the Yankee Clipper', played baseball for the New York Yankees from 1936 to 1951. He was a superb batter and was twice the top scorer for his team. In 1941, he set a new baseball record by making successful hits at least once in each of 56 consecutive games. He was also an excellent outfielder.

Even after he retired he remained in the public eye by marrying film star Marilyn Monroe in 1954. The marriage lasted only nine months. ◆

👁 **see also**

Monroe

▶ *Baseball star Joe DiMaggio in 1951.*

Rudolf **Diesel**

German inventor of the diesel engine
Born 1858   *Died* 1913 aged 55

Rudolf Diesel trained as an engineer in Munich, Germany. In the 1890s he began experiments on the internal combustion engine used to power cars. By 1897 he had perfected a simpler type of engine that did not need spark plugs and used a cheaper form of petrol, now called diesel. Diesel engines are widely used in lorries and are increasingly fitted into family cars. They are very economical to run, because they travel further per litre of fuel than ordinary cars with internal combustion engines.

Rudolf Diesel was not easy to work with and was often depressed. He died when he fell overboard crossing the English Channel. Some people think it may have been suicide. ◆

Marlene **Dietrich**

German-born American actress and singer
Born 1904   *Died* 1992 aged 88

Maria Magdalene Dietrich was born in Berlin, Germany. She first attracted attention for her appearances in the German and American versions of the film *The Blue Angel* (1930). She decided to stay in Hollywood, becoming a US citizen in 1937, and starred in such films as *Blonde Venus* (1932), *Destry Rides Again* (1937), and *Judgement at Nuremberg* (1961).

Not only was she an actress but she was also a singer, famous for her husky voice. She performed in cabarets for many years. She would often appear in trouser-suits, which was considered quite daring at the time. ◆

Diogenes

Ancient Greek philosopher
Born *c.400 BC*
Died *c.325 BC aged about 75*

D iogenes came to Athens with his father as an exile from his native city in the Black Sea region. Once in Athens, Diogenes studied philosophy. He developed his own ideas about how life should be conducted. He believed that people could become happy if they were content just to satisfy their own basic needs. He lived in extreme poverty himself. He taught that people should aim to become self-sufficient and train their bodies to need as little as possible and to have no shame. Diogenes was criticized by many people because of these views.

Diogenes and his followers were given the name 'Cynics', probably from the Greek word for dog, because dogs act without shame in public. ('The dog' was actually Diogenes' nickname.) ◆

Walt **Disney**

American cartoon film-maker
Born *1901*   **Died** *1966 aged 65*

W alter Disney grew up on a farm, and enjoyed sketching the animals. He established his own film company in Hollywood in 1923, creating Mickey Mouse in 1928 and Donald Duck in 1934. These quickly became the world's favourite cartoon characters. Then he made full-length animated films, including *Snow White and the Seven Dwarfs* (1937), *Pinocchio* (1940), and *Bambi* (1942). Sometimes he was criticized for changing famous stories to suit his cartoons.

His film company was the biggest producer of cartoons, but it also made children's films with real

© Disney

▲ *Some familiar characters from Walt Disney's cartoon adventure* Jungle Book, *made in 1967.*

actors, such as *Twenty Thousand Leagues under the Sea* (1954), and films like *Mary Poppins* (1964) which combined cartoon characters and real actors. In 1954 he opened Disneyland, the huge amusement park in California. He planned the even bigger Disneyworld in Florida, but this did not open until five years after his death. ◆

Benjamin **Disraeli**

Prime minister of Great Britain in 1868, and again from 1874 to 1880
Born *1804*   **Died** *1881 aged 76*

B enjamin Disraeli was Jewish by birth, and did not go to a well-known school. It was difficult for someone with his background to get to the top in Victorian Britain.

As a young man, he dressed in flashy clothes, and wore his black hair in long ringlets. He wrote some successful novels like *Coningsby* (1844) and *Sybil* (1846). However, although he became a Member of Parliament in 1837 and was chancellor of the exchequer several times, he did not have a long spell as prime minister until he was nearly 70!

He believed that the Conservative Party should improve the lives of ordinary people, especially when so many had the vote. In 1867, when he was chancellor of the exchequer, he introduced an important Reform Act which gave the vote to working men living in towns and cities. Between 1874 to 1880, when he was prime minister, he encouraged better housing for working people, and cleaner conditions in towns.

Disraeli wanted to see the British empire grow stronger than ever. He was supported in this by Queen Victoria, whom he charmed and flattered. In 1875 Britain took control of the newly-built Suez Canal. This canal formed the shortest route to India – an important part of the British Empire. ◆

👁 **see also**

Gladstone   Victoria

Donato **Donatello**

Italian sculptor
Born *1386*   **Died** *1466 aged 71*

Donato Donatello trained as an apprentice in the workshop of Ghiberti, a goldsmith, painter, and sculptor. Donatello then worked for 30 years at the Cathedral in Florence where he developed his individual style. He was much influenced by, and extremely knowledgeable about the classical sculpture of ancient Greece and Rome. Nevertheless he was the first sculptor to explore the new ideas about perspective, a sort of mathematical system to show distance and to create the feel of three dimensions.

He sculpted, carved, and decorated in marble, bronze, and wood. Later on he learnt to deliberately distort figures to make their impact more powerful. For example, in his carved and painted figure of the aged *Mary Magdalene* he chose to make her very ugly in order to emphasize the dramatic appeal of his subject.

Until the time of Michelangelo, Donatello was the greatest and the most influential sculptor in Florence. ◆

👁 **see also**

Michelangelo

▶ *Donato Donatello's sculpture,* Annunciation.

John **Donne**

English poet
Born *1572*   **Died** *1631 aged 59*

John Donne's first job was as an assistant to a senior government official. However, in 1601 his secret marriage to his employer's niece led to his dismissal. Already well-known as the author of some of the most passionate love poems ever written in Britain, he and his family led an uncertain existence until Donne decided to become a priest in 1615. His fame as a preacher grew quickly, and in 1621 he became dean of St Paul's Cathedral, a post he kept until his death. His poetry changed from its early interest in human emotion to the treatment of more religious themes. But even in this later work, Donne continued to write with immense feeling, in poems that were both complex and also very direct in their use of language. 'Death be not Proud' is the best-known of his Holy Sonnets. His sermons were also famous and attracted large congregations, and many are still in print today. ◆

> *Death be not proud, though some have called thee Mighty and dreadful, for thou are not so.*
>
> JOHN DONNE
> Holy Sonnets no. 6, 1609

Fyodor **Dostoevsky**

Russian novelist
Born *1821*   **Died** *1881 aged 59*

Fyodor Dostoevsky first trained as a military engineer before becoming a writer. His early stories described the dreadful poverty then existing in Russia, and in 1849 he was arrested as a suspected political agitator. Condemned to death, he was pardoned while actually facing a firing squad. He then spent four years as a convict in Siberia. Returning to St Petersburg, Dostoevsky lived in poverty. In 1866 he wrote *Crime and Punishment*, one of the world's greatest novels. It describes a poor student who murders a mean old lady for her money. The student believes that he is justified in doing this because of what he sees as his superiority over his victim. But his conscience finally forces him to confess his crime. Further novels, such as *The Brothers Karamozov* (1880), concentrated on the human struggle to live a spiritual life faced by personality weaknesses and the general despair caused by the corruption in Russia in the 19th century. ◆

Frederick **Douglass**

American anti-slavery campaigner
Born 1817   *Died* 1895 aged 78

Frederick Augustus Washington Bailey was born as a slave and was separated from his mother as an infant. After one attempt in 1833, he finally managed to escape from slavery in 1838. He ended up in Massachusetts, where he used the name Douglass to avoid recapture. In 1841 he began to speak against slavery for the Anti-Slavery Society, telling people his own life story. He later wrote this down as *The Life and Times of Frederick Douglass*. From 1847 to 1860 he edited his own newspaper, *The North Star*, and during the Civil War he was a consultant to President Lincoln. He believed that ex-slaves should be armed, and enlisted his own sons in the Union army. After the war he became the first black man to hold high office in the American government when he became the American ambassador to Haiti. ◆

👁 **see also**

Stowe   Truth
Tubman

Arthur Conan **Doyle**

Scottish writer
Born 1859   *Died* 1930 aged 71

Arthur Conan Doyle trained as a doctor, but he was never very successful in this profession. Soon he found that he could earn more money by writing, so when he was 32 he gave up medicine and took up writing full time.

Doyle wrote all sorts of books, from historical romances to adventure stories. But it was his detective stories, with the brilliant Sherlock Holmes as their hero, which brought him money and fame. *A Study in Scarlet* (1887) was the first book which introduced the character of Sherlock Holmes. Doyle also wrote some very successful short stories in *The Adventures of Sherlock Holmes* (1891–1893).

Later, Doyle became tired of writing about Sherlock Holmes. He tried to kill him off in a deadly struggle with the arch-villain, Moriarty. However, Doyle's readers complained so much that he had to write another story, in which Holmes reappears and tells of his amazing escape. ◆

Francis **Drake**

English sea captain, and the first English person to sail round the world
Born c.1540   *Died* 1596 aged about 56

At the time of Queen Elizabeth I, England and Spain were enemies (though they were not actually at war until the end of her reign). Elizabeth I allowed Francis Drake, an experienced sea captain, to plunder and steal from Spain's colonies, as long as he did it 'unofficially'. Drake went on several successful voyages, seizing treasure from Spanish colonies in South America and the West Indies. Drake was behaving little better than a pirate, but he was popular in England for his daring deeds.

Drake set out again in 1577 in his ship the *Pelican*, which was later renamed the *Golden Hind*. He plundered many South American settlements before sailing up the Californian coast. From there he crossed the Pacific Ocean, and returned home around the tip of Africa. For this remarkable

◀ *Anti-slavery campaigner Frederick Douglass.*

▲ *The English navy battles with the Spanish Armada in 1588.*

expedition, Elizabeth I honoured Drake by making him a knight.

In 1588 Spain planned to invade England with a great fleet of ships (or armada). When the Spanish Armada finally sailed towards England, Drake helped to defeat the fleet in the English Channel. ◆

👁 see also

Elizabeth I

Alfred **Dreyfus**

French army officer, unjustly accused of spying for Germany
Born *about 1859*   **Died** *1935 aged 76*

Alfred Dreyfus, a Jewish French army officer, was arrested in 1894 and accused of spying for Germany. He was found guilty and sentenced to life imprisonment on Devil's Island, the French penal colony in South America.

His family and friends, including the novelist Emile Zola, challenged the sentence, but the authorities refused a new trial until 1899. Anti-Jewish feeling was so strong in the French army that his second trial was a mockery. It was known that he was innocent but the military establishment tried to conceal it. Dreyfus was sentenced to ten years imprisonment, but within days was pardoned by the French president.

In 1906 his case was reviewed and, at last, Dreyfus was declared innocent, and returned to the army. In World War I he commanded one of the forts defending Paris. ◆

👁 see also

Zola

Alexandre **Dumas**

French writer
Born *1802*   **Died** *1870 aged 68*

Although Alexandre Dumas wrote many historical plays and stories, he is famous for creating the characters of d'Artagnan, Athos, Aramis, and Porthos in *The Three Musketeers* (1844–1845). Further adventures of the musketeers followed in *Twenty Years After* and *The Vicomte de Bragelone*. His other famous creation was *The Count of Monte Cristo* (1844–1845).

His successful writing career began in 1829 with the play, *Henri III*. Dozens of works followed this as Dumas kept up a hectic pace of writing and travelling. However, he almost never wrote a complete novel himself. He provided the plot and characters and often some of the important passages, and then left the main writing to a changing group of literary assistants. In this way he managed to produce many novels and stories. ◆

John **Dunlop**

Scottish inventor of the pneumatic tyre
Born *1840*   **Died** *1921 aged 81*

John Dunlop went to college to study to become a veterinary surgeon. He moved to Belfast, Ireland, when he was 27, and ran a successful vet's practice.

During the 1880s, bicycles were becoming very fashionable. They usually had solid rubber tyres, but Dunlop had the idea of a hollow tyre with air pressure inside it.

He patented his 'pneumatic' tyre in 1888. He never made a fortune out of it, though, for two reasons. One was that someone else, William Thompson, had patented an exactly similar idea in 1845, although it had not been made then because bicycles were much rarer. Another problem was that his pneumatic tyres were stuck to their wheels with glue, making it very difficult to mend punctures. It was not until other inventors came up with other methods of keeping pneumatic tyres fixed to wheels that they became really popular. ◆

▼ *A 1935 advert for the Dunlop Company, named after the inventor of the pneumatic tyre.*

Albrecht **Dürer**

German Renaissance artist
Born 1471   Died 1528 aged 56

Albrecht Dürer was one of 18 children; only three survived to adulthood. His artistic talent developed early. At the age of 13 he made a brilliant self-portrait, and at 15 he was apprenticed to a painter and book illustrator in Nürnberg, Germany. Four years later, when he had completed his apprenticeship, he went travelling to find out what other European artists were doing.

Although he produced many paintings, including water-colour landscapes, portraits, and studies of nature, his main achievement is in the difficult technique of print-making. He is one of the greatest-ever masters of engraving and making woodblock prints. The skill and beauty of his prints made him famous, and his work was often copied. He was a thoughtful, religious, and learned man, knowledgeable in many subjects. ◆

▼ *Dürer's woodblock print*
The Rhinoceros.

Antonín **Dvořák**

Czechoslovakian composer
Born 1841   Died 1904 aged 62

The Czechs are a very musical nation: therefore, it was quite natural for the young Antonín Dvořák to play the violin and join in the village music-making. When he was 12 he began to learn how to be a butcher, like his father and grandfather. However, he could not forget music, and eventually an uncle agreed to pay for him to have proper lessons.

When his studies were complete, Dvořák earned his living by playing the violin. He also wrote music, but it was not until he was nearly 40 that people began to recognize his importance as a composer.

Dvořák wrote many colourful operas, concertos, chamber music pieces, and nine symphonies, the ninth of which ('From the New World') was composed when he went to teach in America. His music is full of splendid, dance-like tunes that seem to have sprung out of the Czechoslovakian countryside. Dvořák made Czech music famous. ◆

Bob **Dylan**

American singer and songwriter
Born 1941

Robert Zimmerman was a wild and reckless teenager who ran off to travel across America. He took the name Dylan from Welsh poet Dylan Thomas, and performed as a singer in New York's Greenwich Village coffee bars during the early 1960s. Two of his own songs, 'Blowin' in the Wind' (1962) and 'The Times they are a-Changin'' (1963), became anthems for the Civil Rights movement in the USA. This started a new style, 'protest music', with songs about war, religion, politics, and racism.

Dylan's change from acoustic to electric instruments in the mid-1960s inspired a folk-rock craze, and he was called 'a spokesman for his generation'. His new writing technique, rich in strange images, bizarre characters, and hidden meanings, influenced many songwriters, including Lennon and McCartney of the Beatles.

For a time in the 1970s Dylan's music lost power, but in 1975 he recorded some of his best songs for *Blood on the Tracks*. He received a 'Grammy' award (similar to a film Oscar) in 1991 for lifetime achievement. ◆

👁 **see also**

Lennon and McCartney

Amelia **Earhart**

American pilot
Born 1898   Died 1937 aged 40

Amelia Earhart was always keen on aeroplanes, and as a young woman she took various odd jobs to pay for flying lessons. She was first noticed by the public when she flew across the Atlantic in

▲ *In 1932 Amelia Earhart became the first woman to fly across the Atlantic alone, completing the journey in 15 hours and 18 minutes.*

1928, even though she had really only been a passenger. However, she soon went on to make long-distance flights on her own and in 1932 she flew solo across the Atlantic. She became known as the 'Winged Legend'.

In 1937 she embarked on a trip around the world, with Fred Noonan as navigator. All the stops on the route were carefully planned, but one of them was at a small island in the Pacific Ocean. Her friends and advisers were worried about whether she and Noonan would be able to find it, even though they would be in radio contact. Their fears were justified. Although Earhart could be heard on the radio, she failed to find the island and the plane disappeared into the sea. ◆

👁 **see also**

Batten   Johnson

George **Eastman**

American founder of the Kodak photographic company
Born 1854   Died 1932 aged 77

As a young man, George Eastman was a keen amateur photographer, but he felt photography was too complicated. Photographers had to put chemicals onto a photographic plate and load it into the camera before taking a picture. So in 1888, he developed and mass-produced a small, cheap box camera that was easy to use. He called it a Kodak camera, and inside was a roll of film long enough for 100 pictures. When the film was used up, the camera was returned to the Kodak factory. Kodak developed the pictures, and returned them with the camera loaded with a new roll of film.

You press the button, we do the rest.

QUOTE FROM A
KODAK ADVERTISEMENT

Photography quickly caught on; Eastman made a lot of money and became known for his many generous charitable donations. ◆

👁 **see also**

Daguerre Fox Talbot Niepce

Clint **Eastwood**

American film actor and director
Born 1930

Clinton Eastwood worked as a swimming instructor and lifeguard while taking occasional small parts in films, before he found a regular part in the TV series *Rawhide* from 1959. His first big film success was in *A Fistful of Dollars* (1964). It was called a 'spaghetti' western because it was filmed outside America by the Italian director Sergio Leone. This was followed by several more western films.

In the 1970s Eastwood began directing his own films, and also appeared as the detective Harry Callaghan in *Dirty Harry* and other violent films. His directing career developed in the 1980s and he was highly praised for his film *Bird* (1988) about the life of jazz saxophonist Charlie Parker. He won an Oscar for Best Director for his 1992 western, *Unforgiven*, in which he also starred. ◆

▶ *Clint Eastwood in a familiar western role.*

Arthur Stanley **Eddington**

English astronomer
Born 1882   Died 1944 aged 61

Arthur Eddington won a scholarship at 16 to Owens College, Manchester. After graduating in physics in 1902 he went to Cambridge University, where his distinguished career led to his appointment as chief assistant at the Royal Greenwich Observatory. From then on his life was devoted to astronomy. Appointed director of the Cambridge Observatory in 1914 and a Fellow of the Royal Society, he specialized in finding out how stars move and what they are made of, and in studying Einstein's general theory of relativity. He made important contributions to all three subjects. His famous book, *Fundamental Theory*, published after his death, was the result of 16 years of study. A quiet man, Eddington had the rare ability to write and lecture so clearly that even very difficult ideas could be understood by ordinary people. ◆

Mary Baker **Eddy**

American founder of the Christian Science Church
Born 1821   Died 1910 aged 89

A sickly child and a widow at 22, Mary Baker gave up her only son when he was six and became a semi-invalid. Her second marriage brought little comfort but in 1862 her life was transformed by healer-hypnotist Phineas Parkhurst Quimby, who believed that illness was an illusion with purely mental causes. (At first Mary lectured

◀ *This picture of Edison is taken from the cover of a book called* World's Inventors. *It shows Edison with three of his inventions: the electric lamp; the phonograph; and a microphone to go inside a telephone receiver.*

enthusiastically about Quimby but later denied his influence.) Although she was temporarily paralysed by a bad fall in 1866, she claimed to have cured herself with the inspiration of the Bible, thus founding 'Christian Science'. Her ideas were set out in her book, *Science and Health* (1875), through a newspaper, the *Christian Science Monitor*, and with the skilful help of her third husband, salesman Asa Eddy. Despite quarrels, lawsuits, and scandals her following grew and she died immensely rich. ◆

Thomas **Edison**

American inventor of the phonograph and the electric lamp
Born 1847   Died 1931 aged 84

Thomas Edison's mother taught him at home and encouraged his interest in science. By the time he was ten he had made his own laboratory.

Edison set up his own company, which he called his 'invention factory'. One of his most important inventions was the world's first machine for recording sounds, the phonograph. The whole of our modern recording industry developed from this.

Edison also invented the electric lamp. It consisted of a wire inside a glass bulb from which all the air

had been taken out to create a vacuum. When an electric current was passed through the wire, called a filament, it glowed white-hot and gave out light. While experimenting, Edison found that a current could also flow across the vacuum to a plate inside the bulb. He did not understand why, but we know today it is due to electrons escaping from the filament: it is known as the Edison effect. This discovery led to the invention of electronic valves and was the beginning of our modern electronics industry. ◆

Edward the Confessor

King of England from 1042 to 1066
Born c.1003   Died 1066 aged about 63

Edward grew up as a prince in exile in Normandy while Danish kings ruled England. When the last Danish king died, a powerful English lord, Earl Godwin, arranged for Edward to return and become king.

Edward married Edith, Earl Godwin's daughter. At first Edward tried to balance the influence of Earl Godwin by bringing friends of his own from Normandy, but gradually he left most of the running of the country to Godwin and the other English earls. Edward preferred to concentrate on religious and charitable works, such as building the first great church of Westminster Abbey in London. Edward and Edith had no children; this caused a dispute about who should be king of England after him and led to the Norman invasion and conquest of 1066.

Edward is called 'the Confessor' because his whole life bore witness to ('confessed') his Christian faith. In 1161 he was made a saint. ◆

Edward I

King of England from 1272 to 1307
Born 1239   Died 1307 aged 68

Edward was only 12 when he started to help his father, Henry III, rule the kingdom, and he was married by the time he was 16. He first showed his strength in battle by defeating a group of barons who were rebelling against his father, and then proved himself a courageous knight on crusade to the Holy Land.

After Edward became king in 1272, he was faced with rebellion by a powerful Welsh prince, Llywelyn. Edward invaded Wales and within five years Llywelyn was dead, and all Wales was under his control. Edward built a string of fortresses in Wales to demonstrate

▲ *Part of a French manuscript showing a scene from the battle of Crécy, 1346, won by Edward III's army.*

English strength. However, when he tried to conquer Scotland he was not so successful. ◆

👁 **see also**

Llywelyn

Edward III

King of England from 1327 to 1377
Born 1312   Died 1377 aged 64

Edward's parents, Queen Isabella and Edward II, quarrelled bitterly and his mother took him to

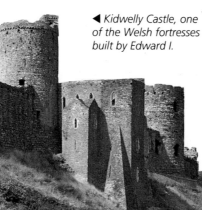

◀ *Kidwelly Castle, one of the Welsh fortresses built by Edward I.*

France. When Edward was 14, his mother and her lover, Roger Mortimer, murdered his father and crowned Edward king. Three years later, Edward had Mortimer killed.

Edward wanted to be a knight, fighting for fame and glory. In 1339 he invaded France, starting a war that was to continue for 100 years. Under Edward and his son, nicknamed the 'Black Prince', the English won many battles. The greatest was at Crécy in 1346. The English were so successful that Edward controlled almost as much territory in France as Henry II had done a century before.

By 1370, most of the fighting companions of Edward's youth were dead, as was his wife. And in France, a strong king was taking back the lands that Edward and his son had won. Edward lost his reputation as a true knight, and died a broken man. ◆

Gustave **Eiffel**

French engineer
Born 1832   Died 1923 aged 91

Gustave Eiffel was born in Dijon, France. He was interested in building with iron girders and he designed several large bridges and structures, including the framework for the Statue of Liberty, which stands in New York Harbor.

In 1889, there was a competition to design a monument for the anniversary of the French Revolution. Eiffel's winning design was an iron tower measuring over 300 m (984 ft) high. Although it was tall, it took only two years to build (1887–1889) and earned Eiffel the nickname 'magician of iron'. It was meant to last for 20 years but is still there today.

Eiffel also designed lock gates for the Panama Canal (1896). There was a scandal over the money for building it and Eiffel was one of those imprisoned. ◆

👁 **see also**

Lesseps

Albert **Einstein**

German-born physicist
Born 1879   Died 1955 aged 76

As a boy in Germany, Albert Einstein was very unhappy at school. His schoolmasters treated him badly because they thought he was not very clever. But, when he

▼ *The Eiffel Tower was built using 15,000 iron sections. Tourists can visit each of the four levels.*

▲ *Einstein and his wife Elsa visiting America in 1930.*

was 26, after moving to Zurich in Switzerland, he published several scientific papers that completely changed the way scientists think.

In 1914 he moved back to Berlin with his family. In 1921 he was awarded the top award in science, the Nobel prize, and modestly travelled third class to Stockholm to receive it.

It was not long before the Nazis started to gain military power in Germany. Although he was world-famous, Einstein suffered a lot of abuse because he was Jewish. Eventually he had had enough, and in 1933 he went to America where he lived for the rest of his life. He spent much of his time trying to persuade world leaders to abandon nuclear weapons.

Einstein's ideas in science were so new and strange that for many years ordinary people used to say that no one else could possibly understand them. But now his theories about time and space (relativity), about how very tiny particles like electrons and protons behave (quantum theory), and many others, are important parts of the courses that all physics students learn at university.

Not many people really deserve the title 'genius' but Einstein must be one of them. Nearly all branches of physics were changed by his theories, and without them lasers, television, computers, space travel, and many other things that are familiar today would never have been developed. ◆

Dwight **Eisenhower**

American president from 1953 to 1961
Born 1890   Died 1969 aged 78

From his childhood everybody called Dwight Eisenhower 'Ike', and his cheerful grin made him friends everywhere. He became a soldier during World War I and by World War II, although he had never been in action, he had risen to the rank of brigadier-general. His organizing skills led to his promotion to command American

▲ *A still from Eisenstein's film* Ivan the Terrible *(1944).*

forces in Europe in 1942.

Eisenhower held two more important army posts; he was chief of staff of the US Army, and in 1951 he was invited to be supreme commander of the NATO forces in Europe. In 1952 the Republican Party persuaded him to be its presidential candidate. He left the army, and his supporters swept him to power in the election with the slogan 'I like Ike'.

He served for two terms, winning a second election in 1956. During his presidency he brought the Korean War to an end and began the US space programme. ◆

Sergei **Eisenstein**

Russian film director
Born 1898   Died 1948 aged 50

Sergei Eisenstein's father wanted him to be an architect, but his real love was for the theatre. Surprisingly, his chance came when he had to leave his engineering training to serve in the army in the Russian Civil War of 1918. There were theatre groups in the army, and Eisenstein was able to join in as a helper and director.

After the Civil War, and until his death, he was more interested in directing films. Eisenstein showed his genius for putting together scenes in an interesting and exciting way. He believed that a film director should create something more than just a series of pictures. He called this the art of 'montage', and directors ever since have been influenced by what he did. ◆

El Cid

Spanish soldier and national hero
Born c.1043   Died 1099 aged about 56

When El Cid (whose real name was Rodrigo Díaz de Vivar) lived, Spain was divided into many small kingdoms. Most of these were ruled by Muslim invaders from North Africa; a few were governed by Christian Spanish kings.

Rodrigo collected an army of brave and loyal men around him.

Sometimes they fought for a Christian lord, sometimes for a Muslim king. Although Rodrigo was bloodthirsty, he was such a successful leader that the Muslims nicknamed him El Cid (the lord).

Fifty years after his death, one of the greatest poems of Spain, the *Cantar de mío Cid*, was written. In the poem El Cid is described as the perfect knight, the bravest soldier, and (because he fought the Muslim invaders) the best of Christians. ◆

Eleanor of Aquitaine

Queen of France from 1137 to 1152 and of England from 1154 to 1189
Born c.1122   Died 1204 aged about 82

High-spirited and beautiful, Eleanor was heiress to the duchy of Aquitaine in south-west France. She married King Louis VII of France in 1137 but the marriage was not very happy and they divorced in 1152.

Eleanor then married Henry of Anjou, who shortly afterwards became King Henry II of England. This meant that Aquitaine passed into English control, which caused prolonged conflict between France and England.

Although they had eight children, Eleanor and Henry did not get on, and she lived mainly in Aquitaine. In 1173 Henry's sons rebelled against him, assisted by Eleanor. After that Henry kept Eleanor in prison, but when he died she gave a lot of support to her sons, first Richard (the Lionheart) and then John, when they each became king of England. ◆

👁 **see also**

Richard I   John, King of England

Edward **Elgar**

English composer
Born *1857* **Died** *1934 aged 76*

Edward Elgar's father ran a music shop in Worcester, so although Edward could never afford to study at a college, he was surrounded by music. He played the violin in local orchestras and was happy to write music for anyone who asked him.

He was a sensitive man and was easily discouraged. It was only when he married, in 1889, that he found someone who really believed in him. After this, his music blossomed, and in 1899 the *Enigma Variations* for orchestra proved that he was a musical genius. Oratorios, two great symphonies, concertos for violin and cello, and a symphonic poem, *Falstaff*, were further proof.

In 1920 his wife died. Elgar was broken-hearted, and for the rest of his life wrote almost nothing. ◆

El Greco

Spanish painter
Born *1541* **Died** *1614 aged 73*

Even though Domenikos Theotcopulous was born on Crete, a Greek island, he lived in Toledo, Spain, from 1577 until he died. He became known by his nickname *El Greco*, which is Spanish for The Greek.

Little is known of his youth. He studied in Venice, under Titian, and in Rome, but it was in Toledo that he developed his own distinctive style. He mainly painted religious scenes, using distorted figures, which looked longer or shorter than in real life, and great contrasts of colour and light to express the great emotions of the spiritual events he portrayed. The strangeness of his art inspired theories that he was mad, but his paintings do express the intense religious feeling of his adopted country, Spain. ◆

▲ *El Greco's paintings, like* The Adoration of the Shepherds *(above), seem more like 'modern' art than those of other artists of his time. His work greatly influenced later artists.*

George **Eliot**

English Victorian novelist
Born *1819* **Died** *1880 aged 61*

George Eliot was the name adopted by Mary Ann Evans, the daughter of a Warwickshire estate manager. As an editor and journalist she worked with some of the most brilliant minds of the time. She finally started writing her own books under the name 'George Eliot' because she believed that male novelists were likely to be treated more seriously by critics.

Her first novel, *Adam Bede*, was set in the countryside she remembered so well. It is rich both in detail and in her understanding of country people. She then wrote *The Mill on the Floss*, drawing on her own childhood for its descriptions of the growing tension between the heroine and her family. But her masterpiece, *Middlemarch*, was still to come. Written in 1871, it describes a small town society, from rich landowners and clergymen to shopkeepers and labourers. To read it is to feel part of a community that has long since disappeared. ◆

T. S. **Eliot**

American poet
Born *1888* **Died** *1965 aged 76*

Although Thomas Stearns Eliot was born in the USA, he spent most of his life in England, first at Oxford University, then in London, where he worked as a bank clerk and as a publisher. His first important poem was *The Love Song of J. Alfred Prufrock*. Using language that is an intriguing mixture of the ordinary and the poetic, it describes the thoughts and feelings of a middle-aged man. In 1922 Eliot published an even more extraordinary poem, *The Waste Land*. This again combined everyday speech with highly unusual images in its description of what the poet saw as the worthless aspects of life in his own century. Traditional critics hated his modern approach, but younger ones saw it as an important breakthrough.

Later, Eliot became more religious and less daring. He turned to writing plays, including *Murder in the Cathedral* (about the death of Thomas Becket). In 1939 he wrote the jolly *Old Possum's Book of*

▲ *A newspaper caricature of T. S. Eliot.*

Practical Cats, which was the basis for the popular musical *Cats*, first performed in 1981. ◆

*Macavity, Macavity, there's no
    one like Macavity
There never was a Cat of such
    deceitfulness and suavity
He always has an alibi, and
    one or two to spare
At whatever time the deed took
    place – MACAVITY WASN'T
    THERE!*

T. S. ELIOT
Macavity: the Mystery Cat

Elizabeth I

Queen of England from 1558 to 1603
Born *1533* **Died** *1603 aged 69*

There was not much rejoicing when Elizabeth was born. Her father, Henry VIII, had wanted a son. When she was two, her mother, Anne Boleyn, was executed and Elizabeth then had four different stepmothers. Later, she was in great danger during her Catholic sister Mary's reign because she was a Protestant. The 25-year-old woman who became queen in 1558 was cautious, clever, quick-witted, and, unlike most girls of her time, very well educated.

Elizabeth could be very stubborn. She refused to change the Church of England set up in 1559, though at first neither Catholics nor Protestants were really satisfied. She would also often put off difficult decisions. Although Mary Queen of Scots was a great danger to her, Elizabeth took 17 years to agree to her execution. Even then Elizabeth tried to pretend she had allowed it by mistake.

Elizabeth did not like spending money either. She avoided an expensive war with Philip II of Spain for as long as possible, though she encouraged sailors like Drake to attack Spanish treasure ships, taking some of the treasure they captured. However, when the Spanish Armada set out to invade England, she became an inspiring war leader.

Queen Elizabeth I was a woman in a world of men. She cleverly controlled her powerful courtiers by being charming, witty, or angry. Everyone expected her to marry, and she promised parliament she would marry as soon as it was convenient – but it never seemed to be convenient. ◆

👁 **see also**
Drake   Henry VIII
Mary, Queen of Scots   Raleigh

▼ *Elizabeth I, 'Good Queen Bess', was a popular queen. During her reign England became powerful and prosperous, and arts and literature flourished.*

Elizabeth II

Queen of the United Kingdom and Northern Ireland and Head of the Commonwealth from 1952
Born 1926

Queen Elizabeth II is the 42nd ruler of England since William the Conqueror. Until she was ten years old she did not expect to be queen. It was only when her uncle, King Edward VIII, abdicated in 1936 that her father became King George VI and Elizabeth became heir to the throne. As a child she called herself 'Lilibet', a name that her family still use today. Her full names are Elizabeth Alexandra Mary.

Just before the outbreak of war in 1939, Elizabeth met a young sailor at a Royal Naval College. He was Prince Philip of Greece and was a distant relation. They married in Westminster Abbey when she was 21 and now have four children: Prince Charles, Princess Anne, Prince Andrew, and Prince Edward.

When her father King George VI died suddenly in 1952, Elizabeth was well-equipped to become queen. She had been taught much about the history of the United Kingdom and Commonwealth and had travelled all over Britain attending official duties. As queen, she undertakes more than 400 public engagements a year and has visited nearly every Commonwealth country at least once. In 1967 she introduced the 'walkabout' so that she could meet and talk with more of the general public. ◆

'Duke' Ellington

American jazz band leader, pianist, and composer
Born 1899   Died 1974 aged 75

Edward Kennedy Ellington's stylish clothes as a teenager

▶ *When Duke Ellington wrote music for his jazz orchestra he took into account the particular skills of his players. His music differed from other jazz routines because it was completely composed, not improvised.*

gained him the nickname Duke. He won a scholarship to art college, but was too busy learning jazz piano to attend.

In New York in 1927 he formed a ten-piece band, grandly calling it an orchestra, and became famous playing in Harlem's Cotton Club. Unlike most jazz musicians, he also wrote fully orchestrated works. Many hit records, including 'Don't Get Around Much Anymore' and 'It Don't Mean a Thing', spread his fame worldwide. Even the modern composer Igor Stravinsky counted Ellington as an influence.

He was the first black composer commissioned to write major film soundtracks and TV show themes. After 1965 he played many religious concerts in cathedrals, and continued working until his death. ◆

👁 **see also**
Stravinsky

Ralph Waldo Emerson

American philosopher and poet
Born 1803   Died 1882 aged 79

Ralph Waldo Emerson was born in Boston, one of five sons of a church minister. His father died when he was eight, leaving his mother and aunt to look after the brothers on a meagre income. He studied theology at Harvard University and became a clergyman at 26. However, he resigned only three years later, shortly after the death of his first wife, because of his unorthodox religious views.

He travelled to Europe and in England made friends with several writers, including Thomas Carlyle with whom he corresponded for 38 years. On his return to America he settled in Concord, Massachusetts, and devoted his life to lecturing all over the country and to writing philosophical essays and poems. His belief that people should rely on their own powers of intuition and his great respect for nature were hugely influential in America. ◆

Empedocles

Ancient Greek philosopher
Born c.494 BC
Died c.434 BC aged about 60

Empedocles came from an aristocratic Sicilian family but spent much of his life in exile. Like other great scholars of his time he was knowledgeable in many subjects and tried to explain all the changes that take place in the world around us. He believed that the world consists of four elements – earth, air, fire, and water. This view persisted until the 17th century. He thought of the universe as two hemispheres, one bright (day) and one dark (night), revolving around the Earth. In human anatomy he believed the blood ebbed and flowed like the tides, a view which was accepted until 1628 when William Harvey showed that blood circulates continuously. He also believed that the world had once been populated by creatures now extinct because they could not survive, thus to some extent anticipating Charles Darwin's theory of evolution. ◆

👁 **see also**
Darwin   Harvey

Jacob **Epstein**

American-born English sculptor
Born 1880   **Died** 1959 aged 78

Jacob Epstein was born in New York, but he came to Europe as a young man and lived in England for most of his life, becoming a

▲ The Rock Drill, *one of Epstein's most individual and impressive pieces of work, was sculpted in bronze in 1913. This mechanical monster hints at the influence primitive art had on his early sculpture.*

British citizen in 1911. He was the most controversial sculptor of his time and his statues were often savagely attacked by journalists and critics. Some of them thought that Epstein's nude figures were obscene, and others thought that his work was clumsy and ugly. It was certainly unconventional, for he was more concerned with creating figures that were bold and full of life than with making them look detailed and realistic. However, he was much praised for his portrait busts (some of the most famous men and women of the 20th century were portrayed by him), and by the end of his career he was regarded by many as the 'Grand Old Man' of British sculpture. ◆

Desiderius **Erasmus**

Dutch scholar
Born c.1466   **Died** 1536 aged about 70

Desiderius Erasmus was an orphan, and grew up in a monastery which he loathed. He

was allowed to leave, and spent the rest of his life in the universities of Paris, Oxford, Cambridge, and Basel. He taught and studied, and wrote many books, including a collection of proverbs called *Adages* (1500).

Erasmus thought the wealthy Catholic Church of his day had forgotten the teachings of Jesus. He made a new, accurate Latin translation of the New Testament (1516). He also wrote a best-selling book poking fun at worldly, lazy monks, *The Praise of Folly* (1511). However, he never wanted to leave the Church, and disagreed strongly with the Protestant ideas of Martin Luther. ◆

> *In the country of the blind the one-eyed is king.*
>
> DESIDERIUS ERASMUS

👁 **see also**
Luther

▼ *Erasmus was one of the key figures in the Renaissance – a 'rebirth' of the arts which involved a return to classical principles.*

Eric the Red

Viking leader and explorer
Lived during the 10th century

The Vikings, skilled sailors and fierce fighters, travelled from Scandinavia to invade and settle in many European countries. It is from the *Sagas* – poetic stories of Viking heroes and adventures – that we know of one of the most famous of them, Eric the Red.

Eric came from a Viking settlement in Iceland. In the year 984 he led an expedition which discovered Greenland; he returned the following year to start a settlement there which survived until about 1400. The achievements of Eric and his followers are difficult to imagine. They sailed the coldest and roughest seas in the world in small wooden ships. They then

▼ *Vikings used longships like the one below for coastal raids. But for ocean voyages and cargo carrying, they used broader, sturdier boats called* knarrs.

settled down to scratch a living from the meagre soil of Greenland, far from home and surrounded by an unknown and hostile land.

Eric the Red is remembered as perhaps the first of the long line of European explorers (including his son Leif Ericsson) who set out to find and colonize new lands across the sea. ◆

👁 **see also**
Ericsson

Leif **Ericsson**

Viking explorer
Lived during the 11th century

The son of Eric the Red, Leif Ericsson lived in the Viking colony of Greenland. In about the year 1000, Ericsson bought a ship and set off westwards towards land which others had seen but had not yet visited – North America.

Ericsson named three parts of North America – Helluland, Markland, and Vinland (these were probably Baffin Island, Labrador, and Newfoundland or New England). He and his crew stayed for the winter in Vinland ('Wine-land') which had a mild climate, and he returned with samples of the timber which grew there.

Ericsson never returned to Vinland, but others did, and for a time there was a Viking colony there. Archaeologists and historians have searched for many years for the remains of this colony, but no definite sign of it has ever been found, and no one is quite sure of Vinland's exact position.

A splendid statue of Leif Ericsson, in the city of Reykjavik in Iceland, is a reminder that he discovered the North American continent 500 years before Columbus. ◆

👁 **see also**
Eric the Red

M. C. **Escher**

Dutch graphic artist
***Born** 1898   **Died** 1972 aged 73*

Maurits Corneille Escher was one of the most brilliant engravers of the 20th century. He mastered several techniques of printmaking, especially woodcut and lithography. In woodcut the design is cut into a block of wood with metal tools, and in lithography it is drawn onto a specially prepared smooth stone. Escher was amazingly skilful at creating bewildering patterns and optical illusions. The most famous of his prints are the ones that represent 'impossible' buildings; they feature such visual tricks as staircases that seem to lead both up and down in the same direction, depending on

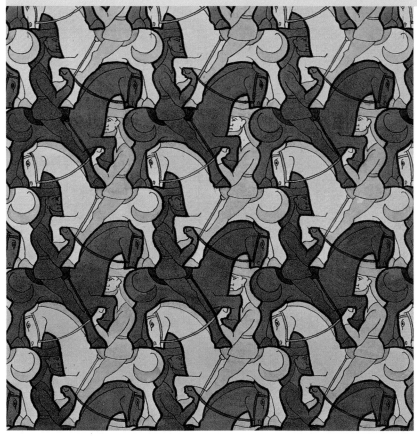

▲ Escher's *Symmetry Drawing E67*.

which way you look at them. Escher's prints are intriguing, and they have become very popular as posters. However, they have also provided serious food for thought for mathematicians and for psychologists interested in studying how the brain interprets what the eye sees. ◆

Euclid

Ancient Greek mathematician
Born c.330 BC
Died c.260 BC aged about 70

When Alexander the Great captured Egypt he set up a new city called Alexandria with a wonderful library and a university. It became the most important place in the world for people to go and study. Clever mathematicians such as Euclid moved from Greece to Alexandria to work.

Euclid was especially interested in geometry and wrote a textbook called *Elements of Geometry*. It has been described as 'the most studied book apart from the Bible'. For over 2000 years Euclid's textbook was the book all schoolchildren used as an introduction to geometry. Even the books used today are based on the way Euclid taught geometry. ◆

Leonhard **Euler**

Swiss mathematician
Born 1707   **Died** 1783 aged 76

In 1727 Leonhard Euler moved from his home in Switzerland to St Petersburg, Russia. There he published books on all aspects of mathematics including new theories on trigonometry and logarithms. He was a pioneer of pure mathematics and made major contributions to the fields of geometry, calculus, the theory of numbers, and to the practical application of mathematics. Perhaps as a result of his hard work he lost the sight in one eye.

In 1741 Frederick the Great invited Euler to join the Berlin Academy; he stayed there for 25 years. Frederick mockingly called him a 'mathematical cyclops' and Euler became increasingly unhappy. He returned to Russia, at the invitation of Catherine the Great, but soon after his arrival he lost the sight in his other eye. Blindness did not stop him, however, and he continued to apply his skills to the fields of mechanics, optics, acoustics, and astronomy. ◆

Fa Hsien

Chinese traveller and priest
Lived during the 5th century

Fa Hsien ('Splendour of Religious Law') was born in Shanxi province in China. He was a Buddhist priest who travelled from China to India so that he could visit the places where Buddha had lived and collect writings about the Buddha's teachings. He travelled to India in 402 and went on to Sri Lanka before returning home by sea. These long journeys involved crossing terrible deserts and freezing mountain passes, as well as being shipwrecked. He was still alive in 414 but other details of his life are uncertain. He wrote an account of his travels (*Record of Buddhist Kingdoms*) and also translated Buddhist teachings from Sanskrit into Chinese. ◆

 see also

Buddha

111

Peter **Fabergé**

Russian jewellery maker and designer
Born 1846   Died 1920 aged 74

Peter Fabergé inherited the family jewellery business in 1870. He soon became famous for making the kind of jewellery that the wealthy aristocracy of Europe liked – wonderful designs using gold, silver, jade, emeralds, and diamonds. His genius was such that these objects never looked vulgar. They were always beautiful and full of imaginative ideas.

He is particularly remembered for the jewelled Easter eggs which he made each year for the tsar of Russia to give to the tsarina.

▼ *The pictures at the top of this 1898 Fabergé egg are of Tsar Nicholas II and two of his daughters.*

In 1917 there was a revolution in Russia. The tsar was deposed and the new government of the people had no time for luxuries. Fabergé left Russia and lived out his remaining few years in Switzerland. ◆

Juan **Fangio**

Argentinian world champion motor racing driver
Born 1911   Died 1995 aged 81

Juan Fangio has been called the greatest racing driver of all time. He has won a record-breaking five world championships.

Born at Balcarce near Buenos Aires, Argentina, he became a travelling mechanic in 1928. He took up driving five years later and came to Europe in 1948 to try his luck. Before Fangio retired in 1958, he had won 24 Grand Prix races for manufacturers such as Mercedes-Benz and Ferrari.

Fangio's greatest race was the 1957 German Grand Prix, which he won after a pit stop had left him 48.5 seconds behind. He broke the lap record several times to catch and overtake his main rivals. ◆

Michael **Faraday**

English scientist
Born 1791   Died 1867 aged 75

As a young man Michael Faraday attended one of Sir Humphry Davy's lectures. He made careful lecture notes, bound them, and sent them to Davy, who was so impressed that he offered him a job. So, aged 22, Faraday became an assistant in the laboratories of the Royal Institution in London. In 1825 he succeeded Davy as director of the laboratory.

Faraday's most important work was to do with electricity and magnetism. Winding a coil of wire onto a piece of iron, he showed that when electricity was passed through the coil, the iron became a magnet. Then he wound another, separate coil onto the same piece of iron. When he switched on the current in the first coil he found that a current flowed in the second. He had, in fact, discovered the transformer. He then found that if he took a hollow coil and moved a magnet in and out, a current flowed in the coil. He had invented the dynamo. These were two very important discoveries which have helped shape the modern world.

Faraday also had the knack of explaining what he was doing in a simple way, so that ordinary people could understand. He started the famous Royal Institution Christmas Lectures in 1826. These science lectures for the general public have been held every year since, except for three years during World War I. ◆

👁 **see also**

Davy

Guy **Fawkes**

English conspirator who planned to blow up the Houses of Parliament in the Gunpowder Plot (1605)
Born 1570   Died 1606 aged 35

Guy Fawkes was brought up as a Protestant, but later became a Catholic. When James I became king in 1603, Guy Fawkes and other Catholics hoped for better treatment than they had received during Elizabeth I's reign. But James I allowed the persecution of Catholics to continue. In 1604, a small group of Catholics, led by Robert Catesby, plotted to kill the king. They invited Guy Fawkes to join them because of his ability to deal with explosives.

Concilivm Septem Nobilivm Angiorvm Conivrantivm in Necem Jacobi I.
Magnæ Britanniæ Regis, Totivsq Anglici Convocati Parliementi.

1.Bates - 2.Robert Winter - 3.Christopher Wright - 4.John Wright 5.Thomas Percy - 6.Guido Fawkes 7.Robert Catesby - 8. Thomas Winter

▲ *This print shows the conspirators in the Gunpowder Plot. Guy (Guido) Fawkes is third from the right.*

The plan was to blow up the House of Lords when the king came to open Parliament on 5 November 1605. They hired a cellar and filled it with gunpowder. Guy Fawkes agreed to light the fuse. But the plot was discovered, and on 4 November Guy Fawkes was arrested. Although he was tortured, at first he bravely refused to name the other conspirators. Eventually he signed a confession, and was tried and executed.◆

👁 **see also**
James I

Federico **Fellini**

Italian film director
Born 1920   Died 1993 aged 73

Federico Fellini grew up in Rimini, Italy, but at 18 he left for Florence and Rome. He worked as a cartoonist and journalist and scripted a radio serial before friendship with director Roberto Rossellini got him into movies as a writer and then director. The Oscar-winning *La Strada* (The Road)

(1954), made him internationally known. *La Dolce Vita* (The Sweet Life) (1960), a rather humorous look at fashionable society in Rome, was probably his greatest international success. However, it was less typical of his work than his films which mixed dream and reality, exploring personal memories and problems, such as *8½*, about a film director stuck in the middle of making a film and unsure how to go on. ◆

Ferdinand and **Isabella**

Rulers of Castile and Aragon in Spain
Ferdinand
Born *1452*
Died *1516   aged 63*

Isabella
Born *1451*
Died *1504*
aged 53

▶ *This 1496 dish bears the arms of Ferdinand and Isabella.*

When Ferdinand and Isabella were born, the Spanish peninsula contained five kingdoms. Three were small kingdoms: Portugal; Navarre (in the northeast); and Granada (in the south), which was inhabited by Muslims. The other two were Castile and Aragon. Isabella was the daughter of the king of Castile; Ferdinand was a son of the king of Aragon. In 1469 they married. As a result, they later became the joint rulers of the two kingdoms.

Ferdinand and Isabella acquired new income by several means, for example by forcing nobles to return land that had once belonged to previous rulers. They also demolished the castles of any nobles who opposed their rule. In 1492 they conquered Granada and expelled the Muslims. In 1503 they conquered the Kingdom of Naples in Italy, and in 1512 Ferdinand conquered Navarre.

Ferdinand and Isabella made Spain an important part of Europe. They supported Christopher Columbus, who discovered America for Spain. However, their reign also marked the start of the Spanish Inquisition, directed by Tomas da Torquemada. ◆

👁 **see also**
Columbus
Torquemada

Enrico **Fermi**

Italian-born American nuclear physicist
Born *1901*   **Died** *1954 aged 53*

Enrico Fermi was a physics professor at the University of Rome. In 1932 he heard about James Chadwick's discovery of the neutron, a particle in the centre of atoms. Fermi decided to do some experiments with neutrons himself. He set up a target made of uranium and bombarded it with neutrons, hoping to make a new substance. Although at the time he did not realize it, he had in fact discovered nuclear fission, the basis of nuclear power and atom bombs. For this work he was awarded the Nobel Prize for Physics in 1938. Later, Otto Hahn explained what was happening during nuclear fission.

During World War II, Fermi worked in America developing the first nuclear reactor. It was built in a squash court at the University of Chicago. This work led directly to the making of the atom bombs that were dropped on Hiroshima and Nagasaki in Japan in 1945 towards the end of World War II. ◆

👁 **see also**

Hahn

Ella **Fitzgerald**

American jazz singer
Born *1918*   **Died** *1996 aged 79*

Ella Fitzgerald was brought up in a New York orphanage. She became a singer because of a teenage dare. At 16 she was dared to sing in an amateur contest in Harlem, and won $25. Then, invited to sing with Chick Webb's band, she found success with hits like 'A-Tisket A-Tasket' (1938).

Fitzgerald brought jazz to new audiences as a star singer in the

▲ *Ella Fitzgerald is one of the most influential of popular jazz singers and her style is still much-copied even today.*

1950s. Her crystal-clear tones and perfect diction were unrivalled for singing popular songs. Indeed, Fitzgerald's finest achievement is her series of 'songbook' albums recorded in the late 1950s. Each contains the work of one popular writer, such as Cole Porter or George Gershwin. The albums are widely regarded as the best possible versions of the songs they contain, which include 'Manhattan' and 'Ev'ry Time We Say Goodbye'. ◆

👁 **see also**

Gershwin   Porter

F. Scott **Fitzgerald**

American novelist and short story writer
Born *1896*   **Died** *1940 aged 44*

Francis Scott Key Fitzgerald lived the same sort of life that he described in his novels, one of glamour, fame, and success. Born in Minnesota, he was educated at Princeton University and even as a youth he was determined to succeed in social, athletic, and literary fields.

He achieved instant fame with his first novel, *This Side of Paradise* (1920), and shortly after married the glamorous Zelda Sayre. Their pleasure-seeking lifestyle of party-going and big spending made them symbols of the high-living young generation of the 'Roaring Twenties'. Among Fitzgerald's most famous novels are *The Great Gatsby* (1925) and *Tender is the Night* (1934), which portray and analyse the mood of the times in which he lived.

Scott Fitzgerald died suddenly in Hollywood of a heart attack hastened by chronic alcoholism, leaving his final novel, *The Last Tycoon*, unfinished. ◆

Gustave **Flaubert**

French writer
Born *1821*   **Died** *1880 aged 58*

The son of a wealthy doctor, Gustave Flaubert first trained in law before withdrawing due to illness and turning to literature. His first published novel, *Madame Bovary* (1857), was also his greatest. Written over a period of five years, it describes the sad life of a romantic young village girl married to a dull, unsuccessful husband. In search of something better she has two love affairs, both of which end unhappily. She finally poisons herself, leaving her unsuspecting husband heart-broken. Flaubert records this whole story in great detail, as if it were something that had happened in real life. This made *Madame Bovary* the most realistic novel of its time, setting a pattern for future novelists all over the world. ◆

▲ *This stained glass window in St James's Church, London, depicts Alexander Fleming at work in his laboratory.*

Alexander **Fleming**

English discoverer of penicillin
Born *1881*   **Died** *1955 aged 73*

Alexander Fleming trained as a doctor at St Mary's Medical School, London, and then spent his entire working life there. He became interested in the infections caused by bacteria that resulted in so much disease. He joined researchers looking for vaccines that would kill such bacteria.

One day in 1928 when Fleming was working in his laboratory, he noticed that a mould had formed on one of his experimental dishes containing live bacteria. The bacteria next to the mould were dying. Fleming realized that the mould was producing a substance which killed the bacteria. The mould was called *Penicillium notatum*.

Fleming showed that penicillin could kill many dangerous bacteria, but he was slow to see that it could be used as a medical treatment and,

in any case, he found it very hard to produce, except in very small quantities. So there was little interest in penicillin until 1941, when Howard Florey, an Australian pathologist, Ernst Chain, a German-born biochemist, and other scientists at Oxford University found a way of making enough penicillin to begin treating patients with serious infections. The results were spectacularly successful. In 1945 Fleming, Florey, and Chain shared a Nobel prize for their work. ◆

Margot **Fonteyn**

English classical ballet dancer
Born *1919*   **Died** *1991 aged 72*

Margot Fonteyn, the adopted name of Peggy Hookham, grew up in Hong Kong where she studied dance. When she came back to England she quickly became very successful, dancing from 1934 onwards with Sadler's

Wells Ballet, later to become the Royal Ballet. While still in her teens, she took on some of the great classic roles, including Odette-Odile in *Swan Lake*. For nearly 30 years, Fonteyn was the company's leading ballerina. Her remarkable technique and warm personality made her very popular.

Fonteyn had two great partnerships. One was with the choreographer Frederick Ashton, who created many outstanding roles for her. The second, from 1962, was with the brilliant Russian dancer Rudolf Nureyev.

Fonteyn continued to dance, create new roles, and teach until she was well into her fifties. ◆

👁 **see also**

Nureyev

▼ *Margot Fonteyn was one of the world's greatest classical ballerinas. In 1979 she gave new insights into the world of dance by writing and presenting a television series.*

▼ In this picture Henry Ford is seen standing next to the ten-millionth Model T, produced in June 1924, and the very first Model T, built in 1908.

Henry **Ford**

American manufacturer of early cars
Born *1863*   **Died** *1947 aged 83*

Henry Ford was born on his family's farm in Michigan, America, but he did not like farming. At 15 he became an apprentice in a machine shop, and in 1893 he built his first car. He drove it for about 1500 kilometres, then sold it and built two bigger cars. Then, in 1903, he started the Ford Motor Company.

Using light, strong steel, he built cheap cars for everyone to buy. In 1908, he built the first Ford 'Model T', the 'Tin Lizzie', which sold for $825. He was soon selling a hundred cars a day. By 1927, 15 million Model Ts had been made, and the Ford Motor Company was worth 700 million dollars.

The cars were made on an assembly line: as they slowly moved the 300 metres through the factory, workers completed simple single tasks on them. It was boring work, but Ford paid the highest wages in the industry.

Early Fords were simple, cheap, and reliable: 'Anyone can drive a Ford' was one slogan. But keeping things simple sometimes meant less choice. 'You can have any colour you like,' said Henry Ford of his Tin Lizzie, 'so long as it's black'. ◆

John **Ford**

American film director
Born *1895*   **Died** *1973 aged 82*

John Ford, the adopted name of Sean O'Feeney, got his first job in movies as a props man before beginning to direct films. He developed his skills on dozens of short films and westerns, with a lot of emphasis on action. *The Iron Horse* (1924), a big-scale silent movie set around the building of the Union-Pacific intercontinental railway, was his first huge success. Human dramas such as *The Grapes of Wrath* (1940), *How Green Was My Valley* (1941), and *The Quiet Man* (1952) also gained acclaim (and Academy Awards). Ford is best remembered, though, for directing classic westerns such as *Stagecoach* (1939). ◆

👁 **see also**
Griffith   Wayne

Jean **Foucault**

French scientist
Born *1819*   **Died** *1868 aged 49*

The son of a poor bookseller, Jean Foucault's original ambition was to become a reporter for a newspaper, recounting the latest scientific news. He acquired a reputation for the clarity of his writing and in 1855 was appointed physicist at the Paris Observatory. This gave him the opportunity to try out some ideas and he is famous for two important experiments. First, in

▼ Foucault demonstrates his pendulum at the Panthéon in Paris.

1850, he demonstrated the rotation of the Earth by using a very long pendulum. This was set swinging along a line marked on the floor but as the Earth slowly turned, the direction of the swing of the pendulum deviated more and more from the line. His second great experiment was to measure the speed of light over a distance of 20 metres, by means of apparatus involving rotating mirrors. Previously, the speed of light could be deduced only from astronomical observations. Foucault's value was 298,000 kilometres per second: the precise value is 299,792 kilometres per second, so Foucault's rather basic experiment in fact produced a very accurate result. ◆

see also

Galileo   Huygens

George **Fox**

English founder of the Society of Friends (the Quakers)
Born 1624   Died 1691 aged 66

George Fox grew up as a strong Christian. However, he became confused about the best way to worship God, believing that there was an 'inner light' in everyone which helped them to understand Christ's teachings. He thought that people should meet together to worship God quietly as equal friends, without priests and ceremonies. He began to win followers, who became the 'Society of Friends'.

Fox travelled around preaching. He ignored the manners of the time, speaking as an equal to upper-class people, and never taking his hat off to show respect. This soon got him into trouble. Once,

◀ *George Fox, seen here in a painting from 1654, believed in looking for the good in everyone.*

when on trial, Fox told the magistrate that he should quake before the Lord: in response the magistrate called him and his followers 'Quakers'.

He was imprisoned eight times, but he kept the Friends together in spite of persecution. His teachings have lived on in the Quaker movement today. ◆

William **Fox Talbot**

English scientist remembered for his work on photography
Born 1800   Died 1877 aged 77

William Fox Talbot was a bright boy, who was especially interested in science. While he was at school he caused so many explosions with chemicals that his housemaster forbade him to do further experiments. Instead, Fox Talbot found a friendly blacksmith who, in the housemaster's words, 'lets him explode as much as he pleases!'.

When Fox Talbot was 33 and on holiday in Italy, he was looking at a camera obscura (rather like a pin-hole camera) and thought how wonderful it would be if the pictures could be recorded on paper. Six years later he had invented the photographic process in which a negative is made first and then a print is made from the negative. We still use the same idea today.

In 1851 Fox Talbot had the idea of breaking up a picture into tiny dots so that photographs could be produced on a printing machine. If you look through a magnifying glass at any of the photographs in this book you will see they are made up of tiny dots. ◆

see also

Daguerre   Niepce

▲ *This painting by Giotto is entitled St Francis Preaching to the Birds.*

Saint **Francis of Assisi**

Italian founder of the Franciscan order of friars
Born 1182   Died 1226 aged about 44

Francis had all the makings of a successful man of the world. Then, when he was 22, he suffered a serious illness and began to feel that helping the poor was more important than making money. The new Francis worked for no money, let robbers beat him up, and kissed lepers. He was still searching for a pattern to follow in his life. He found it in the instructions given by Christ to his disciples: 'Go to the lost sheep… Heal the sick… Cleanse lepers… Provide no gold, silver or copper to fill your purse, no pack for the road, no second coat, no shoes, no stick: the worker earns his keep.'

Francis became a travelling preacher, owning nothing but his coat and living on the food that people gave him. Francis inspired others to live like him, and in 1210, with the permission of the Pope, he set up a new order of 'friars' (brothers), called the Franciscans. At this point there were just 12 of them. Within nine years there were Franciscans all over Europe, but Francis himself was not interested in running such a large organization and refused to be their leader. He travelled to Egypt in 1219 to preach to the Muslims and made other missionary journeys. But for most of his life he stayed near his home town of Assisi with a small group of followers, praying and preaching until his death in 1226. ◆

Francisco **Franco**

Spanish dictator from 1939 to 1975
Born 1892   Died 1975 aged 82

Francisco Franco was born into a navy family, but he decided to be a soldier. He became an officer at 18 and was gradually promoted until he was one of Spain's top generals. Then, in 1931, King Alfonso XIII left the country and Spain became a republic. Franco often criticized this republican government for the disorder in Spain.

In 1936 there was a military uprising against the republican government. Franco joined the rebels and soon became their leader. Civil war began between the two sides, and Franco was given military aid by Mussolini and Hitler. One million people died before Franco won the war in 1939.

Franco then became *caudillo* (dictator) and ruled Spain, without allowing any opposition or criticism, for 36 years. Before he died, he named Juan Carlos, grandson of Alfonso XIII, to be king after his death. ◆

Anne **Frank**

Jewish girl who wrote a diary when in hiding during World War II
Born 1929   Died 1945 aged 15

After the rise of Hitler and the Nazis in Germany, Anne Frank's father, Otto, moved his family to Amsterdam in The

▼ *Since Anne Frank's diary was first published in 1947 it has been translated into over 30 languages.*

Netherlands. When the Germans invaded and the family heard of the plans to put all Jews into concentration camps, they went into hiding. They concealed themselves in a hidden room in Otto Frank's former warehouse with four other Jews. Dutch friends smuggled them tiny rations of food.

Anne kept a lively diary, noting down daily events in these cramped quarters. She always seemed to remain cheerful. In spite of everything, she wrote 'I still believe that people are really good at heart.'

Two years later, on 4 August 1944, the secret room was broken into and the families sent to concentration camps. Anne, her mother, and her sister all died. Otto survived and published Anne's diary in 1947. The Franks' hiding place in Amsterdam has been converted into a museum. ◆

Aretha **Franklin**

American singer
Born 1942

Aretha Louise Franklin was the daughter of a baptist minister. She began her career in his Detroit church, and was a gospel-singing prodigy at the age of 12.

Columbia Records made her sing jazz when they signed her in 1960, but she eventually found her feet at Atlantic Records seven years later when she was restyled as 'The Queen of Soul'. A string of hits such as 'Respect', 'Chain of Fools' (both 1967), and 'Think' (1968), established her as possibly the finest female vocalist of her generation.

In recent years she has enjoyed chart success singing duets with famous admirers such as George Michael, Whitney Houston and Lauryn Hill. ◆

▼ *Models used in Benjamin Franklin's lightning rod experiments.*

Benjamin **Franklin**

American statesman and scientist
Born 1706   Died 1790 aged 84

As a young man Benjamin Franklin tried a number of jobs in America and in England. In America he set up his own publishing business, and by the age of 23 was printing all the money for Pennsylvania. In 1753 he became the postmaster for that colony.

He was always interested in science, and proved that lightning was just a giant electrical spark. He took the risk of flying a kite up into a thundercloud and showed that an electrical spark would jump from a key tied to the wet string. This famous experiment resulted in the development of the lightning conductor or rod.

In 1757 he was appointed to be the representative of Pennsylvania in London. He spoke in Parliament against the British government's tax policies towards the American colonies. Then, after helping Thomas Jefferson write the Declaration of Independence in 1776, he served in Paris. Here he managed to persuade France to support the American colonists in their fight for independence against the British during the American Revolution (War of Independence). ◆

👁 **see also**
Jefferson

John **Franklin**

English arctic explorer
Born 1786   Died 1847 aged 61

In the early 19th century, it was thought that a way could be found to the Pacific round the north of Canada – the so-called 'North-west Passage'.

In 1845 the experienced explorer Sir John Franklin sailed for the Northwest Passage with two ships, *Erebus* and *Terror*. They were never seen again.

Many search parties looked for Franklin. In 1857, after official efforts stopped, Lady Franklin paid for a further search. This party found the remains of some of the expedition on King William Island. A note explained that Franklin had died in 1847.

The exact cause of the deaths of the Franklin party is a mystery. A modern theory says that they were poisoned by the lead in the food cans they took with them, but nobody is really sure. ◆

Dawn **Fraser**

Australian Olympic swimming champion
Born 1937

Dawn Fraser is the only swimmer to win the same event, the 100 metres freestyle, at three successive Olympic Games – Melbourne (1956), Rome (1960), and Tokyo (1964).

The youngest of a Sydney family of eight children, Fraser began competitive swimming when she was aged 11. She trained hard and estimates she swam 10,000 kilometres in ten years. She was the first woman to swim 100 metres in under one minute. She also broke the 100 metres world record nine times.

Fraser was a very popular figure but her high spirits annoyed Australian swimming officials. In 1965 she was suspended from competition for three years over a prank carried out at the Tokyo Olympic Games. She never swam as well again. ◆

Frederick **I**
('Barbarossa')

Holy Roman Emperor from 1155 to 1190
Born c. 1123
Died 1190 aged about 67

In the Middle Ages Germany and northern Italy formed an empire – the Holy Roman Empire. In Germany the princes were very important because they elected the king of Germany and the king was then crowned emperor by the pope. Frederick was the son of the Duke of Swabia in south-west Germany, and nephew of Emperor Conrad III. When Conrad died in 1152, the German princes elected Frederick to be king. He was crowned emperor in Rome by Pope

Adrian IV. The Italians called him 'Barbarossa' meaning 'red beard'.

Frederick made many attempts to increase his power in Italy but he was eventually forced to give in to Pope Alexander III, who did not approve of him, in 1177 after a long, humiliating struggle. However, Frederick still managed to assert his power in Germany. Once this was assured he left the empire in the hands of his son and went to fight in the Crusades in the Holy Land. He won two victories against the Muslims but was later drowned while crossing a river. ◆

▼ *This bronze and gold head of Frederick I dates from 1160.*

Frederick **II**
('the Great')

King of Prussia from 1740 to 1786
Born 1712   Died 1786 aged 74

Born in Berlin, Frederick II was son and heir to Frederick William I, the king of Prussia. Prussia's lands were in various places. They included territories around Berlin and further to the east. Frederick was an unhappy child. His father spent much of his time with the army. Frederick, however, hated army life; he preferred books and music.

When Frederick became king he conquered Silesia, a rich territory, south-east of Berlin, which was ruled by Austria. Austria twice tried to take it back, but failed. In 1772 Prussia joined Russia and Austria in seizing parts of Poland. Frederick thereby obtained the land between the two main parts of Prussia, which was now much larger and richer: Frederick had made it a leading power in Europe. ◆

> *My people and I have come to an agreement which satisfies us both. They are to say what they please, and I am to do what I please.*   FREDERICK II

Sigmund **Freud**

Austrian psychologist
Born 1856   Died 1939 aged 83

As a doctor Sigmund Freud worked with patients who were very depressed or who often had strange ways of behaving that made other people think them extremely odd. The usual sort of treatment for mental illness at that time was lots of rest in the hope that things would gradually get better on their own. Freud decided instead to talk to such people at great length. He believed strange behaviour was often linked to past worries, worries which often reappeared in dreams and nightmares.

Although patients could not at first remember what it was that had once made them so unhappy, Freud found that, given time, troubled memories often came back. After talking to Freud openly about such things, many patients felt much better, at last able to shed problems that had been poisoning their lives without their knowing it.

By the time of Freud's death many other doctors were treating patients in similar ways, listening carefully to all they had to say and so helping them to get better. ◆

👁 **see also**

Jung

Robert **Frost**

American poet
Born 1874   Died 1963 aged 88

R obert Frost was 11 when his father died and his family moved across America from San Francisco to New England. The people and landscapes of New England were to provide an inspiration for Frost's rhythmical, rural verse that made him one of America's most popular poets.

The turning point in Frost's career came in 1912 when he sold his farm and moved to England in order to concentrate on his writing. He met up with several poets and in 1913 published his first volume of poetry, *A Boy's Will*. This was followed a year later by *North of Boston*. He returned to America to great public acclaim and became a professor at Amherst College, Massachusetts. He

published several more volumes of poetry and won many literary prizes, including the Pulitzer Prize four times. He became professor of poetry at Harvard between 1939 and 1943 before returning to Amherst where he remained until his death in 1963.◆

Elizabeth **Fry**

English prison reformer
Born 1780   Died 1845 aged 65

E lizabeth Gurney was the daughter of a wealthy Quaker banker. In 1800 she married Joseph Fry, a London merchant. Although she had a large family, she still found time to work amongst the poor. She became particularly concerned about prison conditions, believing firmly that prisoners should always be helped to become better citizens.

At that time prisons were often very violent places and full of disease, but Fry insisted on visiting some of the worst in Britain and Europe. She was responsible for ensuring that women prisoners were always looked after by women staff. She also managed to get prisons to start educating or training some of their prisoners, so that it was sometimes possible for them to get jobs when they were released. Near her own home, Fry opened a free school and began the first proper training course for nurses. When she died she was mourned by thousands. ◆

▼ *Prison reformer Elizabeth Fry visiting women inmates at Newgate prison.*

Athol **Fugard**

South African playwright
Born 1932

Athol Fugard studied at Cape Town University. It was while he was in Cape Town that he first became involved in the theatre and acting world. In 1958 he moved to Johannesburg with his wife who was herself an actress.

Fugard's many plays explore the former South African policy of racial discrimination known as apartheid. They include *The Blood Knot* (1961) about the troubled relationship between two black brothers, *Boesman and Lena* (1968) about the lives of a homeless black couple, and *Master Harold and the Boys* (1982) which portrays the relationship between a white teenager and two of his family's black servants. ◆

Yukichi **Fukuzawa**

Japanese writer who introduced Western ideas to 19th-century Japan
Born 1835   Died 1901 aged 66

Fukuzawa came from a poor samurai (warrior) family. He was one of the first Japanese to visit America and Europe, and in 1866 published the first volume of his best-selling book, *Conditions in the West,* in which he described everyday life in Western countries.

In 1868 a new government came to power, keen to learn more about the West and spread new ideas. For the rest of the 19th century Fukuzawa was the most influential commentator on Western ideas. His school, which he founded in 1868 (and which later became a famous university), trained many of Japan's leaders, and his books and other writings were read by thousands of Japanese. He is known as one of the founders of modern Japan. ◆

Robert **Fulton**

American steamboat pioneer
Born 1765   Died 1815 aged 49

When he was 17, Robert Fulton left his home town to go to Philadelphia. A few years later he set sail for England where he became involved in designing and building machinery, locks, and aqueducts for the rapidly expanding canal system.

In 1797 he went to France and spent several years there. He experimented with a steamboat on the Seine and designed a submarine, *Nautilus,* a periscope, and torpedoes which would have been used against British ships. He then returned to America and in 1806 designed the *Clermont,* a steam-powered boat, 40 metres long, propelled by 4.5-metre wide paddle wheels. It sailed 240 kilometres up the Hudson river from New York to Albany and back in less than three days. This proved that steam propulsion could be used commercially, and before long Fulton had built many steamboats. This new development marked the beginning of the end of the era of sailing ships. ◆

👁 **see also**

Brunel

▶ *In this self-portrait, Fulton is seen demonstrating his submarine periscope.*

▲ *Clark Gable in his famous role as Rhett Butler in* Gone with the Wind *(1939).*

Clark **Gable**

American film actor
Born 1901   Died 1960 aged 59

Clark Gable was a factory worker and oil-driller before he started acting. At first he appeared in films as a villain, but in 1934 he found success with the romantic comedy *It Happened One Night*, for which he won an Oscar. During the 1930s he was the most popular 'leading man' in Hollywood films, famous for his muscular good looks.

His greatest role was as the handsome Rhett Butler in the American Civil War drama *Gone*

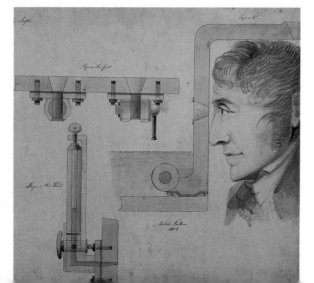

with the Wind (1939). He was still acting in films at the time of his death. His last film, *The Misfits*, with Marilyn Monroe, came out the year after he died. ◆

Yuri **Gagarin**

Soviet cosmonaut; the first man in space
Born *1934*   **Died** *1968 aged 34*

Yuri Gagarin was born into a poor farmer's family in a village, now renamed Gagarin, near Smolensk in Russia. While at college, he joined an air club near Moscow and learned to fly. Soon after college he joined the air force and began to fly fighter planes.

Because Gagarin was daring and skilled, he was singled out for space training. Being small also helped, as the first spacecraft did not have enough room inside for tall people.

His spaceship, *Vostok*, was launched from the Baykonur site in the Kazakh desert on 12 April 1961. Although his flight around the Earth took only 1 hour 48 minutes, it was the first human journey into space.

Only seven years later Gagarin was killed while testing a new plane. He was buried with honours alongside the Kremlin wall in Moscow's Red Square. ◆

Thomas **Gainsborough**

English painter
Born *1727*   **Died** *1788 aged 61*

Thomas Gainsborough was born in Sudbury, Suffolk, and he loved the local East Anglian countryside. Landscape painting was his greatest joy, but he could make more money by painting portraits, so he reluctantly

> *Painting and punctuality mix like oil and vinegar.*
> THOMAS GAINSBOROUGH, 1772

devoted most of his time to that. He worked in Ipswich and Bath, and in London where he settled in 1774. His only real rival as the leading British portrait painter of his time was Sir Joshua Reynolds. They were completely different in temperament (Gainsborough was easygoing and often unpunctual in his work; Reynolds was sober-minded and the complete professional), but they had great mutual respect. Gainsborough painted some of the most graceful and dignified portraits (particularly of beautiful women) in the history

▼ *A typical portrait by Thomas Gainsborough, entitled* Giovanna Baccelli.

of art, and although landscape remained a 'sideline' for him, he was an inspiration to his great East Anglian successor, John Constable. ◆

👁 **see also**
Constable

Galen

Greek medical doctor
Born *c.130*   **Died** *c.200 aged about 70*

Claudius Galenus (Galen) was a famous doctor of the Ancient World. He was born in the Greek town of Pergamum, where he studied to be a doctor and tended the wounds of a troop of gladiators. This taught him a lot about the human body and how to try to heal it. He noticed that when nerves are cut, muscles may not work. He also found that arteries carried blood, not air as many people believed. However, he was not always right. For instance, he believed that our bodies have four liquids: phlegm, black bile, yellow bile, and blood and that when we have the right balance between them we are healthy.

Galen became doctor to the Roman emperors and was very famous. However, he was quarrelsome and was not always very popular. ◆

👁 **see also**
Hippocrates

123

Galileo **Galilei**

Italian astronomer; the first person to use a telescope to look at the Sun, Moon, and planets
Born *1564*   **Died** *1642 aged 77*

Galileo Galilei is nearly always referred to just by his first name. He was the eldest of seven children, whose father was a musician and scholar from one of the noble families of Florence. Galileo himself became a good organist and enjoyed playing the lute, but it was his contributions to science that made him famous. His father sent him to the University of Pisa to study medicine, but he was much more interested in mathematics and physics. In 1589 he became a professor of mathematics.

In 1609 Galileo made a small telescope, having heard about this new invention in The Netherlands.

▼ *Galileo's sketches of the phases of the Moon. He saw that instead of having a smooth surface it was covered in craters and mountains.*

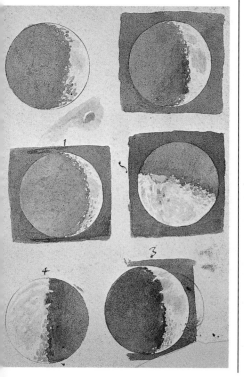

Through his observations of the planets, he discovered four moons circling the planet Jupiter, craters on the Moon, spots on the Sun, and rings around Saturn. He also observed that the planet Venus has phases like the Moon's. This could only mean that Venus travelled around the Sun. Galileo became convinced that the Earth and all the other planets orbit the Sun.

At that time the Christian Church thought any idea that the Earth was not the centre of the Universe went against the Scriptures. The book published by the astronomer Copernicus in 1543, setting out such a theory, had been officially banned by the Church.

Galileo's views on the subject and the books he wrote were to get him into serious trouble with the Church. As the Church was very powerful in those days Galileo was forced to say publicly that he did not agree with Copernicus in order to avoid torture or even execution. Although he made this declaration, he never changed his real belief. ◆

👁 **see also**
Copernicus

Luigi **Galvani**

Italian doctor and physicist
Born *1737*   **Died** *1798 aged 61*

Luigi Galvani was born in Bologna, Italy, where he trained to be a doctor. He began to do experiments to test what electricity would do to muscles. In those days there were no batteries like the ones we have today. Instead, Galvani used a machine to generate electricity. He sent electricity through frogs' legs and noticed that the legs jumped. He then discovered he could do the same thing without the electrical

machine. He touched the legs with a copper hook hanging from an iron rail and the legs twitched. He thought he had discovered 'animal electricity' but really he had found the starting point for making a simple battery. However, he was right to say that our muscles work using electricity. ◆

👁 **see also**
Volta

Vasco da **Gama**

Portuguese explorer, the first European to complete the sea route to India
Born *c.1469*   **Died** *1524 aged about 55*

Vasco da Gama had already distinguished himself as a brave soldier in the service of the King of Portugal when he was chosen to lead a voyage to India around the Cape of Good Hope in southern Africa. Since Christopher Columbus had failed to find a westward sea route to India, the Portuguese were determined to find the eastward route.

Da Gama sailed in 1497 with four small ships and 170 men. Unlike earlier navigators he did not hug the African coast, but sailed boldly into the Atlantic before turning east to round the Cape. The little fleet ran into a storm, and many men mutinied, but da Gama had the ringleaders arrested.

The fleet reached the coast north of the Cape of Good Hope after three months without seeing land. They cruised along the coast, stopping at various places. To their astonishment, they found flourishing Arab towns with stone houses on the coast of what is now Mozambique. Da Gama found a friend in the Sultan of Malindi, who supplied two Arab pilots to guide him to India.

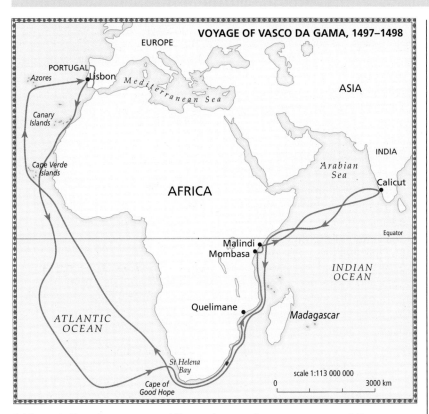

VOYAGE OF VASCO DA GAMA, 1497–1498

EUROPE

PORTUGAL
Azores
Lisbon
Mediterranean Sea

ASIA

Canary Islands

Cape Verde Islands

AFRICA

INDIA

Arabian Sea

Calicut

Equator

Malindi
Mombasa

INDIAN OCEAN

ATLANTIC OCEAN

Quelimane

Madagascar

St Helena Bay

scale 1:113 000 000

0   3000 km

Cape of Good Hope

▲ Vasco da Gama's voyage round the coast of Africa to India (1497–1498) opened up an important new trade route by sea between Europe and Asia.

With their aid he made a peaceful voyage across the Indian Ocean to south-west India. Da Gama set up a trade agreement with the local people and returned to Portugal with a rich cargo of spices, two years after he set out. He had lost two-thirds of his men and half his ships, but he had done what he set out to do.

Da Gama made two more voyages to India. In 1502 he took 19 ships to help the Portuguese settlers in Goa. Then in 1524, after 20 years in retirement, he went as viceroy (local ruler) to Goa, where the Portuguese colonial government was having difficulties. However, he died of fever only two months after he arrived. ◆

👁 **see also**
Columbus   Dias

Indira **Gandhi**

Prime minister of India from 1966 to 1977 and from 1980 to 1984
Born 1917   Died 1984 aged 66

Indira Priyadarshani was the only child of Jawaharlal Nehru, India's first prime minister. After her mother died she became a close companion to her father. She married a journalist, Feroze Gandhi, with whom she had two sons: Rajiv and Sanjay. Sanjay died in a plane crash when he was only 33.

Indira Gandhi followed her father's interest in politics and was elected president of the Indian National Congress, the country's main political party, in 1959. During these early political years, she worked as her father's aide while he was prime minister. She became Minister for Information and Broadcasting in 1964 and two years later she became prime minister.

For several years she was quite successful and popular. However opponents in the Congress party thought she had too much power. In 1975, faced with the growing opposition threat, she declared a state of emergency. Opponents of her policies were even sent to prison. This made her very unpopular and she lost the general election of 1977.

She came back to power with a large majority in 1980. Soon after this she was faced with unrest in the Punjab where some Sikhs were demanding their own state. A group of armed Sikhs occupied the Golden Temple, the holiest Sikh shrine, in Amritsar. In June 1984 Mrs Gandhi ordered her troops to storm the Golden Temple and a large number of people were killed. A few months later, Mrs Gandhi was shot dead by one of her Sikh bodyguards in revenge for the attack in Amritsar. She was succeeded by her son Rajiv ◆

👁 **see also**
Nehru

▼ Prime minister Indira Gandhi during one of the happier moments of her two often troubled periods of rule.

Mahatma **Gandhi**

Indian leader in the struggle for independence from British rule
Born *1869*   **Died** *1948 aged 78*

Mohandas Karamchand Gandhi was a shy, nervous boy, but when he was 18 he travelled alone to study in London. He returned to India in 1890 and struggled to make a living as a lawyer.

In 1893 Gandhi accepted an offer to represent a firm of Indian merchants in a court case in South Africa. Soon after his arrival, he realized how many problems blacks, Asians, and other non-whites faced, and he decided to stay on to help his fellow countrymen. Gandhi represented them in court and became quite wealthy. But he soon rejected his wealth and lived more simply.

During this time, Gandhi developed his strategy of non-violence. The idea was to oppose unjust laws by non-violent protest. He was sent to prison three times, but by imposing hardship upon himself and also showing no sign of anger or hatred, Gandhi believed that he could persuade his opponents that his cause was just.

When he first returned to India in 1915, Gandhi was not opposed to British rule. But after a massacre in 1919, when soldiers opened fire on a crowd of unarmed Indians, killing nearly 400 people and wounding over 1000, Gandhi changed his mind. Over the next 20 years, Gandhi led the Indian National Congress party in three major campaigns against British rule, but on each occasion he was arrested and sent to prison.

During these years Gandhi campaigned to improve the status of the untouchables, the lowest group in the Hindu social order. He also believed that people and nations should be self-sufficient. He set an example by devoting part of each day to spinning home-made cloth. In his eyes, industrialization, as in Europe and North America, usually led to exploitation, greed, and squalor.

Gandhi struggled in vain to overcome the growing gap between the Hindu and Muslim populations, which led in 1947 to the creation of the separate Muslim state of Pakistan. When India and Pakistan became independent from Britain in 1947, there was an explosion of violence between the different communities. Gandhi appealed for peace. He was assassinated by a Hindu extremist in January 1948.

Although his real name was Mohandas Gandhi, he was known by millions of people as Mahatma, meaning Great Soul. ◆

👁 **see also**
Jinnah   Nehru

◀ Gandhi pictured on the step of 10 Downing Street, London in 1931 before meeting Prime Minister Ramsay MacDonald.

Greta **Garbo**

Swedish-born American film actress
Born *1905*   **Died** *1990 aged 85*

Greta Gustafsson grew up in Stockholm, Sweden, and worked as a model before she started acting in films. She travelled to Hollywood and became a star in romantic silent films such as *The Torrent* (1926). When talking pictures came in, her Swedish accent meant that she was given roles as distinguished European ladies, such as the great Swedish queen in *Queen Christina* (1933) and the tragic heroine of *Anna Karenina* (1935). She was famous for her beauty and for her serious expression, but she was also very private and disliked publicity. She made her last film in 1941. ◆

▼ Famed for her serious expression, it was headline news when Garbo smiled for the first time on screen (in Ninotchka, 1939).

Gabriel **Garcia Marquez**

Latin-American writer
Born 1928

Born in a poor town in Colombia, Garcia Marquez still managed to study law and journalism at university. He soon began writing short stories which mixed close attention to detail with dream-like descriptions of magical events. His most famous novel is *One Hundred Years of Solitude* (1967). This describes the adventures of a family settled in a new town in the middle of a South American jungle. Myth and legend combine with ordinary human affairs in an unforgettable way. This magical-realism style has since encouraged many other novelists to experiment with fantasy in their own books. Garcia Marquez is not always popular with his government for criticizing the huge gaps between rich and poor in South America. He was awarded the Nobel Prize for Literature in 1982. ◆

Giuseppe **Garibaldi**

Italian guerrilla fighter who helped to unite Italy
Born 1807   Died 1882 aged 74

As a young man, Garibaldi worked as a sailor, becoming a sea captain in 1832. After taking part in an unsuccessful mutiny in 1834, he escaped to France and then to South America. There he led an adventurous life, driving cattle and fighting in rebel armies.

Well known now as a brave but sometimes reckless fighter, Garibaldi led a group of Italians back to northern Italy in 1848, to

▲ *A wall-painting showing Garibaldi and Victor Emmanuel II meeting in 1860.*

help in the war against Austria. The next year he helped to defend Rome against the French, before being forced into exile in 1849. He returned to Italy in 1854, and retired to the island of Caprera.

> *I can offer you neither honours nor wages; I offer you hunger, thirst, forced marches, battles, and death. Anyone who loves his country, follow me.*
>
> GIUSEPPE GARIBALDI

He came out of retirement to fight for Victor Emmanuel II, the King of Piedmont. In 1860 he led 'the Thousand' (*i Mille*) guerrilla volunteers in red shirts in a successful revolt in Sicily, and then defeated the army of the King of Naples. Southern Italy became united under Victor Emmanuel. Garibaldi's name is still famous in Italy. Almost every town has a square or street named after him. ◆

◉ **see also**
Cavour   Victor Emmanuel II

Marcus **Garvey**

Jamaican campaigner for the rights of black people
Born 1887   Died 1940 aged 52

As a young man, Marcus Garvey worked as a printer, but no one would employ him after he had led a strike. He then took jobs in Central America and was shocked to see the discrimination against West Indians.

In 1914 Garvey started the Universal Negro Improvement Association (UNIA) in Jamaica. He said the black peoples' struggle for fair treatment was like the African countries' fight against European rule. In 1917 he started branches of the UNIA in America. It printed newspapers, ran a shipping line, and opened community centres called Liberty Halls.

Garvey's movement soon had branches all over the world. Then the UNIA was banned in African countries and Garvey was accused of fraud and deported from America to Jamaica. He died in poverty in London. However, his ideas inspired many others to work to win equality for black people. ◆

Bill **Gates**

*American founder of Microsoft and
major figure in the computer world*
Born 1955

Bill Gates began writing
computer programs at 13.
He went to Harvard University, and
while he was there he developed
BASIC, a simple and easy-to-use
computer programming language.
He believed that personal
computers (PCs) would eventually
spread to every home and office. So
in 1975 Gates and his school friend
Paul Allen founded the company
Microsoft to develop software
(computer programs) for PCs.
Microsoft expanded, and in 1981
produced MS-DOS, the operating
system used on most PCs. 1983 saw
the creation of Windows, a program
in which the user points at icons
(small pictures) with a hand-held
pointer (a mouse) and clicks on
them to open files and programs.

By 1993 Microsoft had become
the world's largest computer-
industry company, and Gates was
massively rich: by mid-1997 his
personal fortune was estimated at
$42 billion, making him the richest
person in the world. In recent years,
Microsoft has been accused of
trying to monopolise the industry,
particularly access to the Internet. ◆

Antoni **Gaudí**

Spanish architect and designer
Born 1852   Died 1926 aged 74

Antoni Gaudí was proud of his
family of coppersmiths. From
them he learned to appreciate
craftsmanship and to use it in all
his buildings. He also passionately
loved his native country (the part
of Spain called Catalonia) and was
inspired by its Gothic and Arab-
influenced architecture.

◀ *A Gaudí mosaic 'dragon'
in a Barcelona park.*

Gaudí's church of the Holy
Family (the Sagrada Familia) in
Barcelona is one of the most
extraordinary buildings in Europe.
Gaudí worked on it for 43 years –
over half his lifetime – but the huge
church is still unfinished. A forest of
tall openwork towers soars above
walls encrusted with plants and
animals (mostly carved by Gaudí
himself) and with colourful pottery
mosaics – a Gaudí trademark. ◆

Paul **Gauguin**

French artist
Born 1848   Died 1903 aged 54

Although he was born in Paris,
Paul Gauguin's mother
was Peruvian and he spent his
childhood in Lima. Later he joined
the merchant navy and eventually
settled in France where he became
a successful businessman. However,
when he was 35 years old, he
decided to give up his job and
devote all of his time to his hobby:
painting.

Gauguin became convinced that
European artists had forgotten how
to express true feelings in simple,
direct ways. At first he studied
peasant art in Brittany, but finally
he left Europe altogether to find
his own way of painting.

He went to Tahiti, an island in
the South Pacific Ocean. There he
painted the local people going
about their daily tasks and he
developed a strong personal style
of his own. When his paintings
were shown in Paris, he was proud
that many people were shocked by
what they saw.

At the age of 54 Gauguin died
in the Marquesas Islands in the
Pacific, after years of ill health,
disappointment, and poverty. ◆

▼ *A typical painting by Paul Gauguin. He
usually painted the Tahitians and their
island in these bright, strong colours.*

Karl **Gauss**

German mathematician, astronomer, and physicist
Born *1777*   **Died** *1855 aged 77*

Karl Gauss's father was a poor labourer who could not afford to pay for his son to go to school. Fortunately for Gauss, his great mathematical talent was noticed and the Duke of Brunswick offered to pay for his education.

When he was only 30, Gauss was appointed director of the observatory at Göttingen in west Germany, and he remained there for the next 47 years. His breadth of interest was enormous, embracing arithmetic, algebra, and geometry; probability and statistics; astronomy and physics; mechanics and optics; surveying and telegraphy. His scientific results were recorded in several hundred publications. Through these, and by correspondence and personal contact, Gauss influenced scientific and mathematical thought throughout Europe. He also profoundly influenced later generations and Einstein could scarcely have formulated his theory of gravity without knowledge of Gauss's work. ◆

see also

Boole   Einstein   Euler   Pascal

Joseph **Gay-Lussac**

French physicist and chemist
Born *1778*   **Died** *1850 aged 71*

After studying in Paris, Joseph Gay-Lussac joined a team of young scientists and started to investigate gases, with the help and guidance of an older scientist. After various experiments, Gay-Lussac found that equal volumes of gas expand by equal amounts when their temperatures are raised – unlike solids and liquids. Later he discovered that gases combine in simple volume ratios. For example, two volumes of hydrogen combine with one volume of oxygen to form water. This is now called Gay-Lussac's law.

Ever curious, Gay-Lussac wanted to know whether the Earth's magnetic field altered at high altitudes. In 1804 he tried to find out by going up in a hydrogen balloon. Even at a height of 7 km he discovered that the magnetic field was the same as at ground level. No one had ever been so high in a balloon before. ◆

Genghis Khan

Mongol emperor
Born *1162*   **Died** *1227 aged 65*

Genghis Khan was first called Temujin. He was married when he was nine, as was the custom in his tribe. But in the same year his father was poisoned by his Tartar enemies. Temujin was not old enough to lead his father's men, and they deserted him.

As soon as he could, Temujin begged 20,000 soldiers from a friendly chief and set about making himself leader of all the Mongol tribes. His methods were brutally efficient: to make sure there was no rebellion from defeated tribes, he killed everyone taller than a cart axle – all the adult warriors – while everyone shorter had to swear loyalty to him.

By 1206 Temujin was recognized as lord of all the Mongols, having united eastern and western Mongolia. He took the title 'Genghis Khan', which means 'Ruler of All'. Now he led his armies against the Chinese empire.

By the time of his death his empire extended from the shores of the Pacific to the northern shores of the Black Sea. This empire had been won through brilliant leadership, iron discipline, and unimaginable cruelty, particularly against conquered peoples. His grandson, Kublai Khan, carried on his empire and finally completed the conquest of China. ◆

see also

Kublai Khan

▼ *Before his death, Genghis Khan and his followers created the Mongol empire, the largest empire in history.*

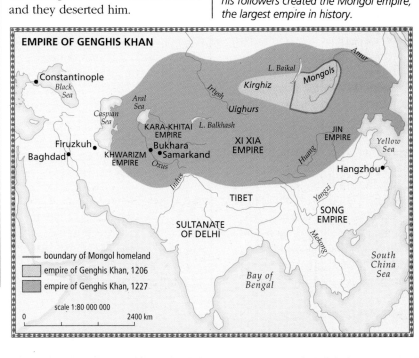

EMPIRE OF GENGHIS KHAN

Constantinople
Black Sea
Caspian Sea
Aral Sea
L. Baikal
Kirghiz
Mongols
Irtysh
Uighurs
Amur
L. Balkhash
KARA-KHITAI EMPIRE
Firuzkuh
Baghdad
KHWARIZM EMPIRE
Bukhara
Samarkand
Oxus
Indus
XI XIA EMPIRE
Huang
JIN EMPIRE
Yellow Sea
Hangzhou
TIBET
Yangzi
SONG EMPIRE
SULTANATE OF DELHI
Mekong
Bay of Bengal
South China Sea

— boundary of Mongol homeland
empire of Genghis Khan, 1206
empire of Genghis Khan, 1227

scale 1:80 000 000
0   2400 km

▲ *A 15th-century carving showing St George and the dragon.*

Saint **George**

Christian martyr who became the patron saint of several countries
Lived during the 3rd century

We know very little for sure about this saint and martyr. George was probably a soldier, who was killed in Palestine for his Christian faith by the Romans. However, centuries later, a famous story grew up about him.

It told of a dragon which was terrorizing a whole country. The dragon demanded first sheep and then a human being to keep it satisfied. The first victim was to be the king's own daughter, but George attacked the dragon, and led it away. Then he told the people that if they became Christians, he would rid them of the monster. Fifteen thousand men agreed to be baptized, and George killed the dragon.

Venice, Genoa, Portugal, and Catalonia, as well as England, took George as their patron saint. His feast day is on 23 April. ◆

George I

King of Great Britain from 1714 to 1727
Born 1660   Died 1727 aged 67

When Queen Anne died in 1714 she had no children, so the crown was passed to the German George of Hanover. He was the great-grandson of James I of England, and as a German prince had fought with the British against the French. Once in Britain George became rather shy and lazy. He had never learned to speak English, and so was forced to talk to his ministers in French. Although he was disliked, his reign provided stability in Britain. He was happy to leave all important decisions to Parliament and his ministers, especially Robert Walpole. He missed Germany, however, and on one of his visits to Hanover he died there of a stroke. ◆

👁 **see also**

James I   Walpole

George III

King of Great Britain from 1760 to 1820
Born 1738   Died 1820 aged 81

George was known as one of the most expert botanists in Europe. Unfortunately, when he succeeded his grandfather George II, he was not such a success as king. This was partly because he interfered rather awkwardly in the country's politics and lost many friends.

When the American colonies objected to the taxes the British made them pay, George was firmly against giving in to them. This led to the American Revolution in 1775, and George became even more unpopular when the British were driven out of America in 1781 after a long and bitter conflict.

In his own family George was a loving but very jealous father. When his sons broke away from him he was so upset he suffered periods of mental illness. Doctors now suspect he was really suffering from porphyria, a disease which produces some of the symptoms of madness. From 1811 until his death, his son ruled as Prince Regent in his place. ◆

Geronimo

Apache Indian chief
Born 1829   Died 1909 aged 80

Geronimo's name comes from the Spanish for Jerome; his Apache name, Goyaale, means 'the clever one'.

Geronimo grew up in Mexico. In about 1877 the American government, wanting land for settlers, moved the Apaches onto a reservation in Arizona. Geronimo escaped and fought against the troops. He was returned to the reservation, but fled to Mexico with a band of men. From concealed mountain camps they made raids on both sides of the border. Soon he was recaptured, but he fled again briefly in 1885, before finally surrendering. He ended his days in Oklahoma, where he became a farmer and dictated his life story. ◆

George Gershwin

American composer
Born 1898   Died 1937 aged 38

George Gershwin was the son of Jewish parents who had emigrated from Russia to New York. He did badly at school, and showed no interest in music until one day when he was ten he heard another schoolboy playing the violin. He started having piano lessons and made very quick progress.

As a young man he started writing songs for shows. During the 1920s and 1930s he turned out a stream of music, much of which is still sung and played: songs such as 'Somebody Loves Me', 'Fascinating Rhythm', and 'A Foggy Day'. Many of the words of his songs were written by his elder brother Ira.

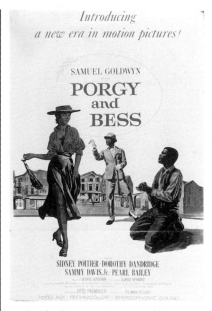

▲ *Gershwin's opera* Porgy and Bess *shows the influence black American jazz and blues music had on his own compositions.*

Gershwin always wanted to be a more serious composer, and he wrote orchestral and piano music, and an opera, *Porgy and Bess* (1934–1935). Sadly, he died of a brain tumour when he was only 38. ◆

👁 **see also**
Porter   Rodgers

J. Paul Getty

American multi-millionaire oilman
Born 1892   Died 1976 aged 83

Jean Paul Getty went to university in southern California and in Oxford before joining his father's oil company. By the age of 24 he was a millionaire, and in 1930, when his father died, he took over the company. Before long he had taken over other companies to form a business empire of more than 100 companies, headed by his own Getty Oil Company.

Outside of business his main interest was in art, and he used his considerable fortune to buy many paintings and sculptures. In 1953 he founded the J. Paul Getty Museum, in Malibu, California, to house his art collection. ◆

Alberto Giacometti

Swiss sculptor
Born 1901   Died 1966 aged 64

Alberto Giocometti was the son of a painter, so art was in his blood. For most of his life he lived and worked in Paris, the centre of the art world at the time. However, it was an exhibition of his work in New York in 1948 that made him internationally famous. At this exhibition he showed sculpture in a new style he had created. His figures were tall and extremely thin, with a gaunt, wasted look. World War II had only recently ended and many people thought that Giacometti's strange, tragic figures captured the spirit of the time in a moving way. This sudden success did not go to Giacometti's head, because he lived only for his art and did not care about fame or riches. ◆

◀ *Giacometti's* Trois Hommes Qui Marchent (Three Men Walking) *(1948) is typical of his post-World War II sculpture.*

André **Gide**

French novelist
Born 1869   Died 1951 aged 82

André Paul Guillaume Gide was born in Paris in 1869. His father, who died when he was only 11, was professor of law at the Sorbonne, the University of Paris. Gide was an only child and had a lonely youth. He was educated at home and then in a Protestant secondary school.

Gide loved all kinds of literature and wrote poetry, biography, fiction, drama, travel journals, and literary criticism. He rejected his strict Protestant upbringing in his life and work, and for young French people in the years after the end of World War I, he symbolized their rebellion against conventional attitudes.

His work is almost entirely autobiographical and includes *The Immoralist* (1902), *Strait is the Gate* (1909), *The Counterfeiters* (1926), and an almost lifelong *Journal* published in four volumes (1947–1951). He was awarded the Nobel Prize for Literature in 1947. ◆

Gilbert and **Sullivan**

English playwright and composer who wrote operettas together

William Gilbert
Born 1836   Died 1911 aged 74

Arthur Sullivan
Born 1842   Died 1900 aged 58

Before William Gilbert and Arthur Sullivan worked closely together writing their 14 operettas, they had independent careers. Gilbert trained as a barrister, but soon became known for his plays and comic verse, such as the *Bab Ballads*. Sullivan published his first

▲ *A scene from Gilbert and Sullivan's operetta* HMS Pinafore.

anthem in 1855 when he was still a chorister of the Chapel Royal. He then studied in London and Leipzig, and made his name with some music written for a performance of Shakespeare's *The Tempest* in 1862.

Gilbert and Sullivan's operettas, which include *HMS Pinafore* (1878), *The Pirates of Penzance* (1879), and *The Mikado* (1885), were so successful that the theatre manager and producer Richard D'Oyly Carte built the Savoy Theatre especially for their works. But things did not always run smoothly: Gilbert had a quick temper, and Sullivan suffered greatly from ill health. Their partnership ended in 1896. ◆

Giotto di Bondone

Italian painter
Born c.1267   Died 1337 aged about 70

Giotto di Bondone lived in Florence with his wife and their eight children, and painted frescos (wall paintings on plaster) of religious subjects. Perhaps the most splendid are those in the Arena Chapel in Padua which tell stories from the lives of Jesus Christ and the Virgin Mary. There is a famous series of frescos in Assisi which

show scenes from the life of St Francis, but it is not certain whether Giotto actually painted these.

Giotto developed a style that was unique at that time. He used paint to give the impression that people are solid objects, and not merely flat shapes. For the first time, figures looked like real people, showing human emotions.

Because of his fame and success, Giotto was given the job of designing a bell-tower for Florence Cathedral, but the building was not completed until after his death. ◆

William **Gladstone**

English prime minister four times between 1868 and 1894
Born 1809   Died 1898 aged 88

William Ewart Gladstone's father was a rich Scottish businessman who educated his son at Eton and Christ Church, Oxford. Gladstone was clever and deeply religious. He was also very energetic, working a 16-hour day even when he was an old man.

Gladstone was 23 when he first became a Member of Parliament, and was prime minister for the last time aged 84. He began as a Conservative but later created the

▲ *A cartoon caricature of William Gladstone from 1869.*

Liberal Party. He believed that people should have the chance to help themselves. In 1870, when he was prime minister, school education was provided for every child under ten. In 1884 ordinary men – but not women – in the countryside got the vote.

Unlike his great rival Benjamin Disraeli, Gladstone did not have an easy relationship with Queen Victoria. She was never comfortable in his presence and disapproved of his policies, which she considered to be revolutionary.

Gladstone wanted above all to bring peace to Ireland. He fought hard to give Home Rule (the right to run their own home affairs) to the Irish. Many people in the British Parliament and in Ulster bitterly opposed him. In 1894 poor health forced him to resign as prime minister, and he died four years later. ♦

👁 **see also**

Disraeli   Victoria

John **Glenn**

American astronaut who was the first American in space

Born 1921

John Glenn was working as an American air force pilot, and had more than 2000 hours of flight time, when he was picked for the NASA astronaut training programme along with six other former pilots. The programme to put a man into space was accelerated after the Russian cosmonaut Yuri Gagarin made a successful flight in 1961. John Glenn was chosen to be the first American to be launched into space. His flight was postponed ten times because of bad weather and computer failures, but eventually he took off on 20 February 1962 for a flight that took him three times round the Earth.

After retiring from NASA, Glenn entered politics as a senator. Then in 1998, at the age of 77, he became the oldest ever astronaut when he flew on a 9-day mission in the Space Shuttle *Discovery*. ♦

Owain **Glyndwr**

Leader of the last Welsh revolt against English rule

Born c.1354
Died c.1416 aged about 62

Owain Glyndwr was a northern Welsh landowner who was angered by the way his countrymen were being crippled by English taxes. In 1400 a local quarrel between Glyndwr and an English lord flared up into a national uprising. Glyndwr proclaimed himself Prince of Wales and summoned his first independent Welsh parliament at Machynlleth in 1404.

Henry IV, the king of England, could do little to stop the revolt. Worse still, Glyndwr was a natural ally for English lords plotting against the king, and in 1403 Glyndwr lent his support to the rebellion led by the Percy family in the north of England.

In 1405 the tide turned against Glyndwr, especially after Prince Henry, later to become Henry V, took over the English campaign. Within three years Glyndwr had lost his main strongholds. But even when his supporters abandoned him, he still fought on as an outlaw. Centuries after his death, he remained an inspiring legend for many Welsh people. ♦

👁 **see also**

Henry V   Llywelyn the Great

◄ *John Glenn was the first American to orbit the Earth. He did so in the spacecraft* Friendship 7, *in a flight lasting five hours.*

Gobind Singh

Tenth and last Sikh Guru
Born *1666*   **Died** *1708 aged 41*

Gobind Singh was born in Bihar, India, the son of the ninth Guru, whose name was Tegh Bahadur. Guru Gobind Singh was very well educated, a good horseman, and trained to fight in self-defence. He also had a very generous and kind nature and Sikhs consider him an ideal human being.

In 1699 when the Sikhs came together for the festival of Baisakhi at Anandpur, Guru Gobind Singh asked for five Sikhs who were prepared to give their lives for their faith. These five went through a new form of initiation into the order of the Khalsa (the order of Sikhs dedicated to following the Guru in all respects). Many more followed them. All the men added Singh (lion) to their names and the women added Kaur (princess), to show their equality and unity, like brothers and sisters.

Guru Gobind Singh was killed by a mystery assassin. As he lay dying, he said that the Sikh holy book was to succeed him in guiding the community rather than another human being. The book became known as the *Guru Granth Sahib*. ◆

👁 **see also**

Nanak

Joseph Goebbels

German Nazi leader
Born *1897*   **Died** *1945 aged 47*

Paul Joseph Goebbels, the son of a factory foreman, attended eight universities and became a doctor of philosophy at Heidelberg

▶ *Joseph Goebbels*

University in 1921. Rejected by the army because of a club foot, he joined the newly formed Nazi party in 1924. At first he edited the party newspaper and later was put in charge of Nazi propaganda. He organized party rallies and demonstrations and when Hitler came to power in 1933 Goebbels became minister of propaganda. This meant that he was in control of the press, broadcasting, education, and culture throughout Germany. This enabled him to spread hatred against Jews and any other people who did not fit the Nazi idea of a perfect German. He remained at the centre of the Nazi government throughout World War II. When the Nazis finally faced defeat, Goebbels committed suicide in Berlin with Hitler, first killing his wife and six children. ◆

👁 **see also**

Hitler

Hermann Goering

German Nazi leader
Born *1893*   **Died** *1946 aged 53*

Hermann Wilhelm Goering flew in World War I with the

famous Richthofen squadron. Later he went to university but gave up his studies to join the Nazi movement in 1922, and became one of Adolf Hitler's close advisers. In 1928 he was elected to the German Reichstag (parliament) and became its president in 1932. He was made commander of the German air force in 1934 after Hitler had come to power, and began secretly to build up the Luftwaffe (air force). He later helped form the Gestapo (secret police) and Germany's first concentration camps.

At the start of World War II Hitler made him a Reichsmarshal, but Goering fell out of favour when the Luftwaffe lost the Battle of Britain in 1940. He was dismissed from the Nazi Party in 1945 after his unauthorized attempts to make peace with the Allies. He was sentenced to death for war crimes at the Nuremberg trials, but swallowed poison to avoid execution. ◆

👁 **see also**

Hitler

Johann von Goethe

German poet
Born *1749*   **Died** *1832 aged 82*

Johann Wolfgang von Goethe is considered the founder of modern German literature and in his old age people would make pilgrimages to his Weimar home to visit him. His writings show that he was influenced by many people, such as great philosophers, Shakespeare, Byron, folk singers, and, not least, by the many women he fell in love with.

Goethe was amazingly versatile: he made important discoveries in

▲ *This illustration shows and scene from Goethe's drama Faust. Faust is guided by the devil who takes the form of Mephistopheles (seen right).*

science; he was a good actor, and also a theatre director. But he is best remembered for his great plays, his novel *The Sorrows of Werther* (1774), his many songs, and above all the poetic drama *Faust* (1808) in which the hero sells his soul to the devil in exchange for enjoying all that the world can offer him. ◆

William **Golding**

English novelist
Born 1911   Died 1993 aged 82

Born in Cornwall, William Golding studied at Oxford University before becoming a schoolteacher. After many initial rejections from publishers, his first novel, *Lord of the Flies* (1954), quickly became a classic. In it Golding describes a group of junior schoolboys stranded alone on an island. Although they manage to agree among themselves over some matters, quarrels between them soon lead to disaster. Other novels by Golding also explore the best and worst in human nature, including *The Inheritors* (1955) and *Pincher Martin* (1956). In 1983 he was awarded the Nobel Prize for Literature and he was knighted five years later. ◆

Samuel **Goldwyn**

American pioneer film producer
Born 1882   Died 1974 aged 81

Samuel Goldfish was a Polish orphan who emigrated first to London, then America. He worked in a glove factory and as a salesman before he and his brother-in-law set up as film-makers. Taking the name Goldwyn, he became a top producer and an influential star-maker. When his own company became part of M.G.M. (Metro-Goldwyn-Mayer) in 1924 he left to become an independent producer. Films such as *Wuthering Heights* (1939), which made Laurence Olivier a star, and *The Little Foxes* (1941) were typical of his use of famous writers and adaptations of their work. He insisted on only making films suitable for the whole family to see. Some of his amusingly illogical remarks, such as 'Include me out' (known as 'goldwynisms'), have become as famous as his pictures. ◆

> *A verbal contract isn't worth the paper it is written on.*
> SAMUEL GOLDWYN

▼ *A camera man and a sound man attempting to film a lion (who is supposed to be roaring!) to make the logo that appears before all M.G.M. movies.*

▲ *Mikhail Gorbachev with the American president Ronald Reagan at the Geneva Summit in 1985. Their interpreters can be seen behind them.*

Mikhail
Gorbachev

Leader of the USSR from 1985 to 1991
Born 1931

Mikhail Gorbachev was born on a farm in the Stavropol region of Russia. He studied hard at school and gained a place at Moscow University to study law. A bright and popular student, he joined the Communist Party in his second year. At the early age of 39 he became Party leader of the Stavropol region. In 1985, at the age of 54, he became General Secretary of the Communist Party and in doing so took over the leadership of the whole of the USSR.

For the first time in 60 years, the USSR had a relatively young and reforming leader. He launched three new policies: *perestroika*, meaning 'restructuring', to make the economy more efficient; *glasnost*, to make the country more open and honest; and *demokratizatsiya*, to give people initiative. His policies were popular abroad: he withdrew Soviet troops from Afghanistan so ending a long war there, and he signed an agreement with America to reduce the number of short-range nuclear missiles.

But problems grew at home. The economy was in trouble. The nationalities (Latvians, Ukrainians, Moldavians, and others) began to demand more independence. His reforms displeased the Party's conservatives and they tried to overthrow him in 1991. Even though he survived that coup, his power was much weakened. When Russia and the other states of the union formed a new Commonwealth of Independent States, Gorbachev resigned. He had introduced sweeping reforms but could not hold the Soviet Union together. ◆

👁 **see also**

Yeltsin

Nadine
Gordimer

South African writer
Born 1923

The prize-winning writer Nadine Gordimer was born in Springs, Natal and educated at a convent school and at the University of Witersrand, Johannesburg. Her first book was *Face to Face*, a collection of short stories published in 1949. This was followed by another collection, *The Soft Voice of the Serpent*, in 1952.

She is renowned for her many novels set in South Africa. As an opponent of apartheid (the former policy of racial segregation), she explores the life of the white middle classes and how political racism and bigotry affect them. Her novels include *The Lying Days* (1953), *A Guest of Honour* (1970), the Booker Prize winning *The Conservationist* (1974), and *My Son's Story* (1990). She was awarded the Nobel Prize for Literature in 1991. ◆

Francisco de
Goya

Spanish painter
Born 1746 Died 1828 aged 82

Francisco de Goya spent most of his career in the Spanish capital, Madrid. There he worked mainly for the court, and in 1799 he was appointed King Charles IV's principal painter. He painted many portraits of the royal family and courtiers, designed tapestries for the royal palaces, and also produced religious pictures for churches.

His most original works, however, are of a much more unusual kind. When he was 46 he suffered a mysterious illness that temporarily paralysed him and left him stone-deaf for the rest of his life. This traumatic experience made him think deeply about human suffering and inspired him to paint imaginative scenes, often involving terror or the supernatural.

After Spain was invaded by the French armies of Napoleon in 1808, Goya also produced a number of anti-war paintings and prints. ◆

▲ Although he is perhaps best-remembered for the horrific images he painted, Goya was also a great portrait painter, as this study shows.

W. G. **Grace**

English cricket hero
Born 1848   Died 1915 aged 67

William Gilbert Grace was born near Bristol, and was taught to play cricket, along with his two brothers, by his mother. Mrs Grace must have been a very good coach, because all three Grace brothers

▲ This illustration of cricketer W. G. Grace, England's best all-rounder in his day, is from an 1896 calendar.

ended up playing first-class cricket for Gloucestershire.

'W. G.', as he was known, made his début at the age of 16. Although he later qualified as a doctor, he carried on playing cricket until the age of 60. He completely changed the way cricket was played and was so popular with spectators that notices were sometimes displayed outside grounds, saying: 'Admission sixpence; if Dr Grace plays, one shilling.' During his career, which lasted nearly 45 years, Grace scored 54,896 runs (including 126 centuries), took 2876 wickets, and held 877 catches. ◆

Steffi **Graf**

German tennis player
Born 1969

Steffi Graf became a professional tennis player at 13, and within three years had become one of the top 10 tennis players in the world. From August 1987 to March 1991

she reigned as the world's top female player, winning a record number of international tennis tournaments.

In 1988 Graf completed an unequalled 'Golden Grand Slam', winning the four most important individual tournaments (the US Open, the French Open, Wimbledon, and the Australian Open), plus the Olympic gold medal. Graf retired from professional tennis in 1999, and married tennis star Andre Agassi in 2001. She has earned her place in history as one of the world's greatest sportswomen. ◆

Martha **Graham**

American modern dancer and choreographer
Born 1894   Died 1991 aged 97

Even as a very small child Martha Graham loved dancing, and as soon as she had completed her formal schooling she devoted her life to dance. She studied dance in Los Angeles and when she was 25 she became a professional dancer. At first she toured America with a dance company, but eventually appeared in New York dancing on her own.

Graham developed her own style of ballet, dancing to classical and modern music. She also made up her own very unusual, imaginative dances. When she was 35 she formed her own dance company, employing modern artists and composers to design colourful sets, costumes, and music for her ballets. Her dances were based on many unusual themes, including ancient Greek legends and the lives of Native American Indians. She stopped performing when she was 75, but continued to teach and to make up ballets. ◆

Kenneth **Grahame**

Scottish writer
Born 1859   *Died* 1932 aged 73

Kenneth Grahame's mother died when he was five and he and his brothers and sisters went to live with his grandmother. Grahame did well at school but instead of going to university he got a job with the Bank of England. He eventually rose to be its Secretary – the person whose signature you see on currency notes.

When he was in his twenties he began to write essays in his spare time. Later came stories about a family of orphans, collected in *The Golden Age* (1895) and *Dream Days* (1898). However, he is best known for *The Wind in the Willows* (1908). Its hero, Toad, and his riverside friends, Ratty, Mole, and Badger, first appeared in bedtime stories and letters to Grahame's son, Alastair. ◆

▼ *A scene from* Toad of Toad Hall, *a popular play based on Grahame's* Wind in the Willows.

Cary **Grant**

British-born American film actor
Born 1904   *Died* 1986 aged 82

Archibald Leach (Cary Grant's real name) was born in Bristol, England. He always wanted to be an entertainer and in 1920 he went to America to try his luck. At first he worked as a singer and an actor in stage musicals before becoming famous as an actor in Hollywood films. A lot of his success was due to his good looks and his witty and charming personality. He rose to fame alongside Marlene Dietrich in *Blonde Venus* (1932). His best-remembered films include comedies such as *Bringing up Baby* (1938) and *Father Goose* (1964), and suspense dramas such as *To Catch a Thief* (1955) and *North by Northwest* (1959), in which he was directed by Alfred Hitchcock. He received an Academy Award ('Oscar') in 1970 for his contribution to the film world. ◆

👁 **see also**

Dietrich

Ulysses S. **Grant**

Commander of the Union armies in the American Civil War; American president from 1869 to 1877
Born 1822   *Died* 1885 aged 63

After 11 years in the army Ulysses Simpson Grant resigned and tried farming. He failed, and so took a job in his father's leather goods business. When the American Civil War broke out in 1861 he volunteered for the Union Army of the northern states. Within four months his expertise and skill as a commander had earned him promotion to brigadier-general. A series of victories, including Vicksburg and Gettysburg in 1863, led President Abraham Lincoln to appoint Grant commander-in-chief of all the Union armies. Grant's drive and ruthlessness forced the Confederates of the southern states to surrender in April 1865.

Three years later, in 1868, Grant won the American presidential election for the Republicans with the slogan 'Let us have peace'. Even though scandals and bribes rocked

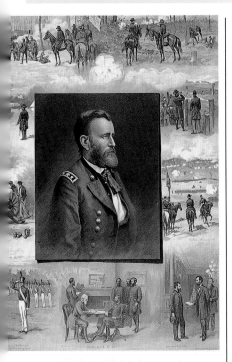

▲ *Published in 1885, this series of pictures traces Ulysses S. Grant's military career.*

his government, he managed to win re-election in 1872.

Grant refused to run for a third term, and retired in 1877. He invested his considerable savings in a firm which went bankrupt in 1884, leaving him with heavy debts. To make money he wrote his memoirs. It was a race against time, for he knew he was dying of cancer. Almost as soon as he finished the work he died, but the book earned his family $450,000. ◆

👁 **see also**

Lee   Lincoln

Graham **Greene**

English writer
Born 1904   Died 1991 aged 87

Graham Greene was the son of a headmaster and he attended his father's school as a pupil. From early on he was very aware of the difficult position this put him in; he owed loyalty both to his fellow pupils and also to his father. This may be why in novels like *Our Man in Havana* (1958) or *The Honorary Consul* (1973) Greene often describes characters who are also split between conflicting duties.

Finally he ran away from school, later becoming a journalist, then an author and playwright. Some of his novels can be read like detective stories. Others, like *Brighton Rock* (1938) or *The Power and the Glory* (1940), take on important issues like belief in God or how far the poor and oppressed should rebel against their own, often corrupt, political leaders. ◆

Gregory I

Italian religious leader, and the first monk to become pope
Born c.540   Died 604 aged about 64

Gregory came from a rich and noble Christian family. His great-great-grandfather had been pope, three of his aunts lived as nuns, and his father was an official in the government in Rome. Gregory himself was made chief magistrate of Rome. However, in 574 he gave up everything in order to become a monk. He lived in the family house, which he turned into a monastery.

This peaceful life was frequently interrupted by official duties for the pope. Then, in 590, Gregory himself was chosen by the people of Rome to become pope. Although he was sad to leave the quiet of his monastery, he was very active in his papal duties. He sent his monks out to preach all over Italy and also to Britain. He reformed the way in which the Church carried out its business and how its services were presented and sung. Through his writings and by the way he lived his own life, he changed the way Church leaders behaved. Gregory showed how it was possible to combine a monk's existence of reading and prayer with a pope's life of action and power. ◆

Wayne **Gretzky**

Canadian ice-hockey star
Born 1961

Wayne Gretzky was born in Brantford, Ontario. He began skating before he was three and was playing organized ice hockey by eight. In 1979, when he was 18, he joined the Edmonton Oilers and became the youngest player to score 50 goals and more than 100 points in a season.

In the 1981–1982 season Gretzky scored a record 92 goals. In 1985–1986 he achieved another record by scoring 215 points. He became the National Hockey League's most valuable player of the season for a record ninth time in 1989. He has also broken the NHL's all-time scoring record of 1850 points. ◆

▼ *Wayne Gretzky in action for the Los Angeles Kings in 1993.*

Edvard **Grieg**

Norwegian composer and pianist
Born *1843* **Died** *1907 aged 64*

Edvard Grieg's family originally came from Scotland. His mother taught him to play the piano when he was six years old. When he was 15 the great Norwegian violinist Ole Bull advised him to study at the famous Leipzig Conservatoire, for in those days German music and German methods dominated the whole of Europe. After an unhappy time in Leipzig, Grieg lived for a while in Copenhagen, supporting himself by giving piano recitals and gradually adding to his own compositions. In 1867 he married his cousin, Nina Hagerup, who had a fine soprano voice. He wrote many songs for her, and together they toured Europe giving recitals. Grieg loved Norwegian folk music, and his own compositions soon took on a distinctive Norwegian flavour themselves. His many songs and piano works brought him fame and popularity, in particular his Piano Concerto in A minor and the incidental music he wrote for Henrik Ibsen's play *Peer Gynt*. ◆

👁 **see also**
Ibsen

Walter Burley **Griffin**

American architect and city planner
Born *1876* **Died** *1937 aged 61*

Walter Burley Griffin, one of Australia's best-known architects, was really an American. He was born in Chicago, and was working there in 1912 for Frank Lloyd Wright when he won the competition for planning a new capital city for Australia – Canberra.

The Australians did not really want a new capital city and they certainly did not like the idea of an American designing it. Despite this, Griffin managed to lay out most of the roads of the new city before he gave up and moved to Sydney. Canberra today has the shape that Griffin intended, thanks to his persistence. Griffin made the most of the mountainous countryside of New South Wales and created a magnificent chain of lakes which runs right through the city centre. The centre is very grand, with broad, straight avenues focused on the headquarters of the Australian government – the Capitol. ◆

👁 **see also**
Wright, Frank Lloyd

D. W. **Griffith**

American film pioneer and director
Born *1875* **Died** *1948 aged 73*

David Wark Griffith left school early to work as a lift-boy to help support his family before becoming a touring actor. He tried

▼ *D. W. Griffith (in the white hat) directs a close-up shot on one of his early film sets.*

to write plays and in 1908 he sold some story ideas to early film-makers and this brought him the chance to direct a movie. He made over 400 silent films (usually lasting only 12 minutes) in which he and cameraman 'Billy' Blitzer developed the use of many basic cinema techniques: close-ups, long-shots, fades, and cutting between shots. Then came two great epics of the silent cinema: the hugely profitable three-hour *The Birth of a Nation* (1915) and the even more ambitious but financially unsuccessful *Intolerance* (1916). Griffith made more movies, some with sound, but in the 1930s he found it impossible to raise backing for the kind of films he wanted to make. ◆

Grimm brothers

German brothers who recorded and published fairy tales
Jakob Grimm
Born *1785* **Died** *1863 aged 78*
Wilhelm Grimm
Born *1786* **Died** *1859 aged 73*

Sons of a German lawyer, Jakob and Wilhelm Grimm both went to university with the intention of

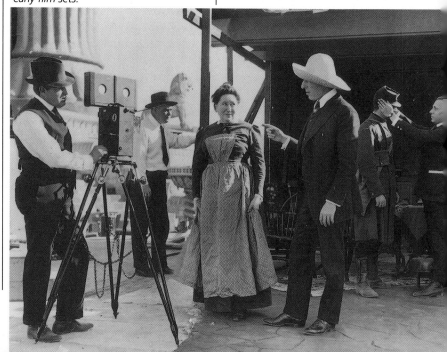

▲ *An illustration from* Sleeping Beauty, *one of the fairy tales the Grimm brothers recorded.*

becoming civil servants. But once there they became more interested in folk tales, spending their time listening to and studying the stories, songs, and poems that people had told and sung long before the invention of printing. Between 1812 and 1815 they published around 200 of the best stories; these included *Snow White, Sleeping Beauty, Hansel and Gretel, Cinderella,* and *Little Red Riding-hood.*

At the time the brothers said that they wrote down the tales exactly as they heard them. But in reality it is believed that they rewrote most of the stories in order to make them longer and more satisfying to readers. Even so, the Grimm brothers were very important in the effort to keep fairy tales alive, so that people can still read them today long after the older, spoken versions have been forgotten.

Together they also compiled a huge German dictionary. They saw the study of language and the collecting of fairy tales as equally important tasks in their quest to hold on to the heritage of the German language. ◆

Walter **Gropius**

German architect
***Born** 1883 **Died** 1969 aged 86*

Walter Gropius was the son of an architect. From early on he designed buildings that used only modern materials. In 1914 he built some factories constructed purely from glass and steel. He also borrowed ideas from modern art, sometimes making his buildings look like abstract paintings. In 1919 he founded the 'Bauhaus' in Germany, a school of design that used the most outstanding artists, sculptors, and architects of the day. Students there were taught how to use smooth surfaces, bright colours, and three-dimensional design in their buildings.

In 1933 the Bauhaus was closed down by the Nazis. Gropius, who had left the Bauhaus five years before that, moved to England in 1934 because of the growing power of the Nazi government. After designing more striking modern buildings in Britain he finally settled in America. There he worked closely with other designers in his search for truly modern architecture fitting for life in the 20th century. ◆

Che **Guevara**

Latin American revolutionary
***Born** 1928 **Died** 1967 aged 39*

Ernesto Guevara de la Serna was born in Rosario, Argentina. He led a comfortable early life, and trained to be a doctor. However, after going on a long journey through Latin America, the poverty he saw convinced him that there had to be a revolution to improve life for the poor. So in 1956 he joined Fidel Castro's campaign to overthrow the Cuban dictator Batista. Guevara fought as a guerrilla leader and then, when Castro won, he became a diplomat and a minister in the Cuban government.

But Guevara was not happy doing routine work; he wanted to spread the revolution to other poor countries. He travelled secretly in Africa and South America before he surfaced in Bolivia where he was captured and executed by the army. After his death Che Guevara became a romantic symbol of revolution and his face appeared on millions of posters throughout the world. ◆

👁 **see also**
Castro

▼ *A poster of Che Guevara, hero of revolutionaries all over the world.*

▲ *King Gustavus Adolphus, who strived to make Sweden the most important power in northern Europe.*

Gustavus Adolphus

King of Sweden from 1611 to 1632
Born *1594*   **Died** *1632 aged 37*

Gustavus Adolphus was only 16 when he succeeded his father as king of Sweden. At that time Sweden was in danger: it was fighting with Denmark, Poland, and Russia. To save his kingdom, Gustavus II made a treaty with Denmark (1613) and stopped fighting Poland. But he continued the war against Russia, to stop Russia from taking Sweden's land to the east of the Baltic Sea. Russia finally made peace in 1617.

During the rest of his reign, Gustavus strived to make Sweden even more powerful. He founded schools and encouraged industry, especially mining. He improved the army and equipped it with the latest weapons.

In 1618 war began in Germany between Protestant rulers in the north and Catholic rulers in the south. During the 1620s the Catholics conquered northern lands and reached the Baltic Sea, which meant that they could stop Sweden's trade with Germany. Gustavus, who was a Protestant, resolved to fight back. Between 1630 and 1632 Swedish forces fought their way to south Germany, but, during the ensuing Battle of Lützen, Gustavus was killed. ◆

👁 **see also**
Christina

Johann Gutenberg

German inventor of printing in Europe
Born *c.1400*
Died *c.1468 aged about 68*

Before Johann Gutenberg's invention, most books were handwritten, with a few produced using carved wooden blocks. Both methods were slow, so few books were available and these were very expensive. Only monasteries, universities, and the very wealthy could afford them.

Gutenberg was skilled at working with metals, and invented a mould with which he was able to cast a lot of identical copies of each letter of the alphabet on metal stamps. The stamps could be put together to form words, and arranged to make whole pages. After ink had been applied to the metal stamps, any number of copies could be made on paper, using a specially constructed press.

Gutenberg's best-known work is called the *42-line Bible* or *Gutenberg Bible*. He began to print pages of this Bible in 1452 and it took him until 1456 to finish the whole work and print only 300 copies. He gave up printing altogether in 1460. He had made little money out of it, and died a poor man. ◆

Fritz Haber

German chemist
Born *1868*   **Died** *1934 aged 65*

At the end of the 19th century many people felt that the world faced starvation if new forms of nitrogenous fertilizers were not found to increase food production. Ten years later Fritz Haber devised a process for 'fixing' the abundant

▼ *The chemist Fritz Haber was also the inventor of the gas mask, worn here by German anti-aircraft crew in World War I.*

nitrogen in the air by combining it with hydrogen derived from water. Haber's method is still one of the most important of all industrial chemical processes. In 1918 this was recognized by the award of the Nobel Prize for Chemistry.

After Germany's defeat in World War I Haber tried to restore his country's fortunes by using his chemical expertise in other ways. However, his brilliant career came to a sudden end in 1933 when the Nazis forced him to leave the country because he was Jewish. He died soon afterwards having settled in Switzerland. ◆

Hadrian

Emperor of Rome from AD *117 to* AD *138*
Born C. AD *76*   **Died** AD *138*
aged about 62

Hadrian's full name was Publius Aelius Hadrianus and he was born in Spain, then part of the Roman empire. He held important posts in the Roman government and was adopted by Emperor Trajan as his son and heir after his own parents died. Hadrian worked hard for his adopted father, serving both in the army and as governor of several provinces before becoming emperor on Trajan's death.

Hadrian travelled throughout his lands, more than any other Roman emperor (he visited Britain in AD 121). He made many improvements to the armies and governments of the Roman colonies he visited. He loved culture and was particularly fond of Athens where he paid for many new buildings. He also built a splendid country house for himself on the outskirts of Rome at a place now called Tivoli.

He was also responsible for one of the most impressive monuments to survive from the Roman world – the great stone wall known as

▲ *Hadrian's Wall ran 117 km from the mouth of the River Tyne in Northumberland to the Solway Firth. It formed a strong defensive barrier between what was then Britain and Caledonia.*

Hadrian's Wall. It was built to protect the northern boundary of the Roman province of Britain from attacks by the Scots. ◆

👁 **see also**
Trajan

Otto **Hahn**

German chemist
Born *1879*   **Died** *1968 aged 89*

Otto Hahn's parents wanted him to be an architect, but he was drawn instead to chemistry. During the 1930s he began to investigate uranium. This has the heaviest atoms of any natural element. He discovered that bombarding uranium atoms with neutrons (extremely small particles) breaks the atoms into smaller, lighter ones. This process is called nuclear fission. As the atoms break up, they release enormous amounts of energy. This meant that nuclear fission could be used as a new power source, or as a new type of weapon. During World War II, many scientists worked on atomic weapons, but Hahn worked on other projects. After the war he became an opponent of further research on atomic weapons.

He received the Nobel Prize for Chemistry in 1944 and the Enrico Fermi Award in 1966. ◆

👁 **see also**
Fermi   Oppenheimer   Rutherford

Haile Selassie

Emperor of Ethiopia
Born *1892*   **Died** *1975 aged 83*

Haile Selassie became king of Ethiopia in 1928 and emperor in 1930. Before that he was known as Prince Ras Tafari.

In 1935 Italy invaded Ethiopia. Haile Selassie asked the League of Nations for its help but none was given. He was forced to seek exile in Britain, where he remained until the British helped him drive the Italians out in 1941. Once he was restored to the throne, he initiated a slow programme of economic and social reforms in an effort to modernize Ethiopia. However, he seemed to lose touch with the problems of the country and his extravagent lifestyle made him unpopular. In 1974 he was overthrown by an army revolt and died – possibly murdered – the next year. Nonetheless, he is revered by followers of the Rastafarian religion in the Caribbean who regard him as a messenger of God. ◆

Edmond **Halley**

English astronomer remembered for his work on Halley's comet
Born 1656   Died 1742 aged 85

While studying at Oxford University Edmond Halley became a good astronomer and mathematician. He was so keen on astronomy that he left Oxford before getting his degree to spend two years on the island of St Helena in the South Atlantic, making charts of the southern sky.

Halley also made studies of the Earth's magnetism, tides, and weather. From 1696 to 1698 he was deputy controller of the mint (where coins are made) at Chester, and after that he commanded a Royal Navy ship for two years. In 1703 he became a professor at Oxford, and in 1720 was made Astronomer Royal.

Halley worked out that a bright comet seen in 1682 was the same one that had appeared in 1531 and 1607. He correctly predicted that it would be seen again in 1758, although he did not live to see it. It is now called Halley's Comet. ◆

Frans **Hals**

Dutch portrait painter
Born c.1581   Died 1666 aged about 85

In the 16th century Holland was ruled by Spain, but after a long struggle it won independence in 1609. The Dutch developed a great feeling of national pride, and Frans Hals was the artist who best represented his countrymen's new optimism and self-confidence. His most famous works were group pictures of civic guards – volunteer part-time soldiers who were ready to defend their country against any further threat from Spain.

Hals had a great gift for depicting

▲ *Frans Hals's picture of* The Laughing Cavalier *(1624) shows his remarkable ability to capture a sense of fleeting movement and expression.*

lively expressions and a sense of movement, and he made most earlier group portraits look like stiffly-posed school photographs. In spite of his popularity, Hals was constantly in trouble because he lacked money (he was twice married and had ten children to support) and he died in poverty. ◆

Hammurabi

King of Babylon from 1792 BC to 1750 BC and creator of the first Babylonian empire
Lived during the 18th century BC

Hammurabi lived almost 4000 years ago in Mesopotamia. Mesopotamia was an area in the Middle East between the rivers Tigris and Euphrates. (Most of Mesopotamia is now in modern Iraq.) In 1792 BC Hammurabi became King of Babylon, which was one of about 30 cities in southern Mesopotamia. Each city was independent and ruled by its own king.

Hammurabi was a cunning man. One by one, he attacked and conquered other cities in southern Mesopotamia, until he had brought them all within an empire ruled from Babylon. The empire – known as the Babylonian empire – was almost 800 kilometres long and

▼ *Through carefully planned attacks, Hammurabi extended the lands he inherited until he ruled over the Babylonian empire.*

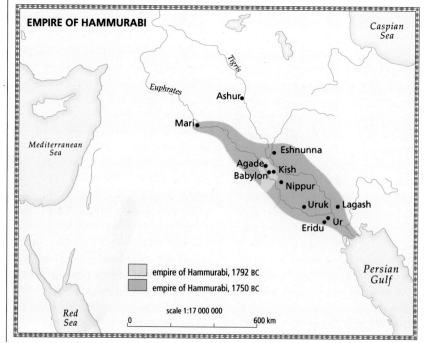

EMPIRE OF HAMMURABI

Caspian Sea

Tigris

Euphrates

Ashur

Mari

Mediterranean Sea

Eshnunna

Agade
Babylon • Kish
• Nippur

Uruk • Lagash
Ur
Eridu

Persian Gulf

Red Sea

☐ empire of Hammurabi, 1792 BC
▨ empire of Hammurabi, 1750 BC

scale 1:17 000 000
0   600 km

about 250 kilometres wide. It stretched from Mari, north-west of Babylon, down to the Persian Gulf to the south-east. Hammurabi issued laws and governed the empire through officers to whom he sent orders. He was regarded as a careful planner and an efficient ruler. He was also much more than a warrior; he encouraged agriculture, literature, and intellectual pursuits and his reign become known as 'the golden age of Babylon'. ◆

George Frideric Handel

German composer
Born *1685*   **Died** *1759 aged 74*

George Handel's father wanted him to become a lawyer and he was very unhappy when the boy insisted on studying music instead. When he was 18 Handel went to Hamburg to work as an orchestral player and learn all he could about opera. He wrote two operas. One of

▼ *A portrait of Handel from the house where he was born in Halle.*

them, *Almira*, was a great success and he was invited to Italy, the home of opera in the 18th century.

He stayed in Italy for nearly three years and wrote many successful works. However, he was still restless. In 1710 he visited London and was so happy there that he decided to make it his home, even though he had already accepted an appointment in Hanover. Fortunately, the Elector of Hanover became King George I of England in 1714 and he forgave the composer, so Handel was able to continue working in England.

Handel wrote orchestral works, such as the *Music for the Royal Fireworks* and the *Water Music* suite, and many fine concertos. However, he is probably best known for his oratorios (a kind of opera without scenery or costumes), including the famous *Messiah* (1742). ◆

Tom Hanks

American film actor
Born *1956*

Tom Hanks spent much of his childhood on the move, because his father was a travelling cook. While at school in Oakland, California, he took up acting, and he continued to act throughout school and college.

After college Hanks went first to New York, then to Los Angeles looking for work. He acted in his first film in 1979, but it was his role in *Splash* (1984) that brought him to international attention. He had mixed success for the next few years, but *Big* (1988) and *Sleepless in Seattle* (1993) were huge box-office successes. In 1995 Hanks became only the second person ever to win the Oscar for Best Actor two years running. He won it in 1994 for his role as a person with

Aids in *Philadelphia*, then in 1995 for his role as the slow-witted hero of *Forrest Gump*. He was the voice of Woody in *Toy Story* and *Toy Story 2*. ◆

Hannibal

Carthaginian general
Born *247* BC   **Died** *183* BC *aged 64*

Carthage, a colony founded by the Phoenicians in North Africa, became a powerful and wealthy trading nation. In 264 BC it clashed with the other great power at the time, Rome. Hannibal's father, Hamilcar, was the general in charge of Carthaginian forces in this first war. The Romans defeated Carthage and made it pay huge fines.

At the age of nine, Hannibal was taken to Spain by his father on a campaign. His father made him swear to be a lifelong enemy of Rome and the Roman empire.

In 221 BC, at the age of 25, Hannibal took over the command of the Carthaginian forces in Spain. He attacked the town of Saguntum in northern Spain, and war broke out again. Although the Romans sent an army against him, Hannibal outwitted them by marching right across the Alps into Italy. He started with about 40,000 soldiers and 37 elephants (mainly to frighten the Roman troops) but, after the crossing, only 26,000 men and 12 elephants were left.

Hannibal raised a new army and defeated the Romans in several major battles. The Romans were in despair of ever defeating Hannibal, until they appointed a new general, Cornelius Scipio. He finally defeated Hannibal's army at Zama in North Africa in 202 BC. Hannibal returned to Carthage, but eventually committed suicide to avoid being captured by the Romans. ◆

James Keir
Hardie

Scottish politician and first leader of the modern British Labour Party
Born *1856*   **Died** *1915 aged 59*

James Keir Hardie was born in a one-roomed house, and by the age of ten he was working in a coal mine. Here he saw miners risking appalling injuries and even death in return for very low wages. Hardie thought trades unions could improve conditions for working people, and by 1886 he was a full-time union organizer in Ayrshire. Later he realized a new political party was needed to speak up for working people in Parliament. In 1892 he stood for Parliament in West Ham, Essex, and became the first independent Labour Member of Parliament. He wore a soft tweed cap, which angered the other, smartly dressed MPs, but 'the man in the cloth cap' became a working-class hero.

Hardie spoke out in Parliament against unemployment and poverty, and demanded votes for women. At first his was a lone voice, but by 1906 the number of Labour MPs had grown to 29, and Hardie became the new party's first leader. Hardie was a pacifist, and when World War I broke out in 1914 he hoped that an international strike would stop it. He was bitterly disillusioned when most of his Labour and socialist colleagues supported the war, and died a disappointed man. ◆

Thomas **Hardy**

English novelist and poet
Born *1840*   **Died** *1928 aged 87*

The son of a stonemason, Thomas Hardy was born – and spent much of his life – in Dorset. He even set many of his novels there and in the surrounding counties (calling the area 'Wessex').

Hardy first worked as an architect and church-restorer in London, but he also began writing novels and poetry. After the success of his fourth novel, *Far From the Madding Crowd* (1874), he returned to his beloved Dorset.

▲ *A drawing of Thomas Hardy from an 1892 edition of the magazine* Vanity Fair. *At that time he was a very popular and successful novelist.*

This novel was one of many describing the ups and downs of country life in the West Country. However, the good humour running through his early work began to disappear in favour of a sadder approach to life. He increasingly saw his characters as victims of a cruel and uncaring world. For example, in *Tess of the D'Urbervilles* (1891), he describes an innocent girl destroyed by a villainous lover and a series of unlucky mishaps.

In 1874 Hardy married, but the relationship was never easy. He described the type of difficulties he and his wife had in his novel *Jude the Obscure* (1895). However, readers were not ready for this sort of honesty about marriage, and the outcry against him caused Hardy to abandon novels and concentrate on poetry. Hardy experimented with different rhymes and verse forms; his *Collected Poems*, published two years after his death, contains over 900 poems.

The death of his wife in 1912 led to some beautiful poems in which Hardy expresses his regrets about their past unhappiness together. In 1914 he married again and lived quietly until his death. ◆

James
Hargreaves

English inventor of the spinning 'jenny'
Born *c.1720*   **Died** *1778 aged about 58*

Spinning wheels have been used for thousands of years to twist the wool fibres from sheep into the long threads or 'yarns' used for weaving. In about 1764 an uneducated weaver from Lancashire called James Hargreaves invented a machine which one person could use to spin several threads at the same time. He called this machine a 'jenny' after his young daughter.

Other spinners thought that Hargreaves' machine would put them out of work because it was so much faster than the old methods. They broke into his house and destroyed his jennies and his weaving loom. This scared him and so he moved his family to Nottingham. He and a partner set up a small mill to spin yarn and he worked there for the rest of his life.

In 1770 Hargreaves received a patent for his invention but he never became rich even though there were thousands of jennies in use by the time he died. ◆

👁 **see also**
Arkwright   Crompton   Jacquard

Harun al-Rashid

Arabian ruler from 786 to 809
Born c.764   Died 809 aged about 45

Harun al-Rashid was brought up in the Islamic religion. He fought against the Christians in Constantinople and earned the title 'al-Rashid' (the one following the right path). After being governor of Tunisia, Egypt, Syria, Armenia, and Azerbaijan he became Caliph (ruler) of the entire Arab empire in 786. The empire stretched from the Mediterranean Sea to India.

Harun al-Rashid's palace in

▼ *Though believed to be a cruel and extravagent ruler, Harun al-Rashid is the hero in many of the stories in* The Arabian Nights.

Baghdad became famous for its riches and jewels, and its food, wine, women, poetry, and song. The empire was also rich and produced textiles, metal goods, and paper (at this time paper was unheard of in Europe). Harun al-Rashid's fabulous wealth and his many wives passed into legend in the stories of *The Arabian Nights*. ◆

William **Harvey**

English physician who discovered how blood travels round the body
Born 1578   Died 1657 aged 79

William Harvey was the eldest of seven sons of a wealthy farming family. His brothers all did well as merchants in London, but he went off to study medicine. He was a very successful doctor, and became court physician to King James I and then to King Charles I.

▲ *William Harvey (right) demonstrates his theory of the circulation of the blood to King Charles I, who employed Harvey as his doctor.*

Harvey made a careful study of the heart and blood vessels (veins and arteries) in the dozens of different animals which he cut up. For more than 1500 years doctors had followed the writings of the ancient Greek physician Galen, who taught that blood moves backwards and forwards in the vessels that carry it. But Harvey found that valves in the blood vessels allow the blood to move in only one direction.

Harvey showed that blood is pumped from the heart all the way round the body and back to the heart, where it begins its journey again. He was the first person to describe the circulation of the blood accurately. ◆

👁 **see also**
Galen

Vaclav **Havel**

President of Czechoslovakia from 1989 and then president of the new Czech Republic from 1992 to 2003
***Born** 1936*

Vaclav Havel's family was anti-Communist, even though they lived in Communist Czechoslovakia. Havel worked in a theatre as a stage-hand and later became a playwright. His plays became very popular but when the Russians invaded Czechoslovakia in 1968, Havel, who was known for his views on human rights, found that his plays were banned. He managed, however, to continue to write and to publish abroad.

From 1979 to 1983 he was imprisoned for helping to create Charter 77, a declaration for human rights, and in 1989 he was jailed again for inciting a rebellion against the government. After his release he helped form Civic Forum, an organization which led mass protests to demand freedom and democracy. After a general strike was threatened, the Communist

▼ *Vaclav Havel, the most famous campaigner for democracy in former Czechoslovakia.*

government resigned. Havel was elected president by a landslide victory. He tried to preserve a united Czechoslovakia, but the federation broke up in 1992 and was split into Slovakia and the Czech Republic. Havel became president of the Czech Republic. ◆

👁 **see also**
Masaryk

Robert **Hawke**

Prime minister of Australia from 1983 to 1991
***Born** 1929*

Robert (Bob) Hawke was born in South Australia. After graduating from the University of West Australia he went to England to study at Oxford University. On his return to Australia he worked as a lawyer for the Australian Council of Trade Unions. Later he became its president and from 1970 until 1980 he was a skilful negotiator on behalf of trade unionists. In 1980 he was elected to parliament and three years later became leader of the Labour Party. Within a month he was prime minister as the Labour Party swept to victory in the election. In all he won four general elections between 1983 and 1990 before being replaced as leader of the party and as prime minister by Paul Keating. He retired from politics in 1992. ◆

Stephen **Hawking**

English physicist
***Born** 1942*

Stephen Hawking, one of the most brilliant thinkers of modern times, has been Lucasian Professor of Mathematics at

▲ *In his* A Brief History of Time, *Hawking argues that our universe and an infinite number of universes like it, are all part of one great 'super-universe'.*

Cambridge University since 1979, the same position Isaac Newton once occupied. He is a worthy successor to that great scientist because his research into the nature of black holes, relativity, gravitation, and cosmology has been outstandingly important, influencing in a profound way the work of many other scientists.

Hawking has travelled and lectured widely. Apart from his technical papers and books, he has also written highly successful publications for the general reader: his *A Brief History of Time* (1988) was a huge best-seller. His lengthy list of fellowships, prizes, medals, and honorary degrees awarded by the most prestigious institutions in the world is an acknowledgement of his intellectual service to humankind. To achieve all this he has triumphed over a crippling neurological handicap which has confined him to a wheelchair for much of his career. ◆

Nathaniel **Hawthorne**

American writer
Born *1804* **Died** *1864 aged 59*

Nathaniel Hawthorne was born in Massachusetts. His father was a sea captain who died when his son was four. After living a sheltered life with his mother, Hawthorne decided to become a writer. One of his ancestors had been a judge in 1692 when some innocent people were executed in Salem for the supposed crime of witchcraft. Troubled by this cruel story, Hawthorne wrote about the harsh attitudes of the early American settlers in *Twice-told Tales* (1837). His most famous novel, *The Scarlet Letter* (1850), tells the story of one of the early settlers in America named Hester Prynne, condemned to wear a large scarlet 'A' for life because she had once committed adultery. She eventually finds happiness, helping others in distress and so setting an example to those who once condemned her.

Hawthorne later became the American consul in Liverpool, England, from where he visited Italy, the inspiration for his last completed novel, *The Marble Faun*, published in 1860. ◆

Franz Joseph **Haydn**

Austrian composer
Born *1732* **Died** *1809 aged 77*

Franz Joseph Haydn's father was poor and could do little to help a son who wanted to become a musician. Fortunately a relative agreed to pay for Haydn's education, and in 1740 the organist of Vienna's great cathedral, St Stephen's, took him into the choir, where he remained until he was 17.

Although he did not receive any formal lessons, he learned all he could, and taught himself to compose by studying the music he most admired. In 1759 he obtained his first official appointment, as musician to Count Morzin, and in 1761 he went to work for Prince Esterházy, at the prince's splendid palace at Eisenstadt. Haydn served the Esterházy family for 30 years. He wrote operas for their private opera-house, and church music for their private chapel. He also wrote symphonies and quartets, concertos, songs, and piano music for their day-to-day entertainment.

His fame spread far beyond the walls of the Eisenstadt palace. When the time came for him to retire, his music was known and loved throughout Europe. Haydn's music is ingenious and inventive. Without him, the symphony, of which he wrote 104, and the string quartet might never have become such important musical forms. ◆

▼ *The luxurious Neptune pool in the grounds of newspaper tycoon William Hearst's grand Californian castle.*

William Randolph **Hearst**

American newspaper tycoon
Born *1863* **Died** *1951 aged 88*

William Randolph Hearst left university early to take control of the *Examiner* newspaper in San Francisco, which was owned by his father. After making it very successful, Hearst then bought the *New York World* newspaper. He increased its circulation by printing sensational and often exaggerated stories that people liked to read. Using the money he made, he bought other papers and by 1927 he owned a total of 25 newspapers and magazines.

Hearst became very rich and powerful. He built a huge and extravagant castle for himself at San Simeon in California and invited lots of Hollywood stars to stay there. In 1941 the film-maker Orson Welles made and starred in *Citizen Kane*, a film about a newspaper tycoon which many people believe is really about Hearst. ◆

◉ **see also**
Welles

Georg **Hegel**

German philosopher
Born *1770* **Died** *1831 aged 61*

Georg Hegel was born in Stuttgart and spent much of his life teaching in various German colleges. At first he studied theology (religion), although even at that time he was writing and editing pieces on philosophy. He also worked as a newspaper editor and was even a headmaster of a school for a while. Then, in 1818, he became professor of philosophy at Berlin University. He remained there until he died during a cholera epidemic in 1831.

Hegel's philosophy, found in such works as *The Phenomenology of Mind* (1807) and the later *Encyclopedia of the Philosophical Sciences* (1817), is notoriously difficult. This is partly because he tried to bring all knowledge and systems of thought into just one all-embracing reality through his idea of the 'dialectic'. In his dialectic, Hegel stated that the truth to any given question could only be found by combining the two opposite answers to that question. This, and his ideas on society, religion, history, and art influenced many later thinkers. ◆

Henry **Heinz**

American businessman
Born *1844* **Died** *1919 aged 73*

Even when he was a child, Henry Heinz was interested in selling food. By his 16th birthday he already had employees working for him, growing food for the market in the city of Pittsburgh.

Heinz's first company was set up to sell horseradish. In 1876 he reorganized it and began building it into a major national company.

▲ *An early poster advertising Heinz spaghetti. Henry Heinz kept an eye on every stage of the production of his foods, from the farming to the advertising.*

By 1905 it was the largest producer of pickles, vinegar, and ketchup in America and Heinz had acquired the nickname 'Pickle King'. He especially enjoyed being involved in the marketing of his products and the '57 varieties' slogan was chosen in 1896 because he liked the sound of it. He was a thoughtful man who cared about the welfare of his staff, and supported 'Pure Food' laws at a time when most of his competitors opposed them.

The Heinz family controlled the company until 1969 and they are still the largest shareholders. ◆

Werner Karl **Heisenberg**

German physicist
Born *1901* **Died** *1976 aged 74*

Werner Karl Heisenberg studied at the German universities of Munich and Göttingen. Then, from 1924 to 1926, he went to work in Denmark with Neils Bohr. At that time the world's physicists were struggling with the problem of wave-particle duality – the fact that the electron sometimes behaves like a particle and sometimes like a wave. Heisenberg said that it was wrong to think of the electron in this way and suggested that we can only know about it by observing the light that it emits. Using this idea he put together a mathematical method of predicting the behaviour of atomic particles. He was awarded the 1932 Nobel Prize for Physics for this work.

Heisenberg went on to show that we cannot measure an atomic particle's speed and position at the same instant. Each can be measured separately, but measuring one of them alters the other – so we cannot know both exactly. This is known as Heisenberg's Uncertainty Principle. During World War II Heisenberg was made director of Hitler's atomic bomb programme, but Germany was defeated before the work could be completed. ◆

👁 **see also**

Bohr

Ernest **Hemingway**

American writer
Born 1899   *Died* 1961 aged 62

Much of Ernest Hemingway's writing is based on his own adventurous life. He drove an ambulance in World War I and was a war correspondent in World War II and the Spanish Civil War. He was a big-game hunter, a deep-sea fisherman, and loved bullfighting. He was considered a hard drinker, a fighter, and was married four times.

His books reflect his life and interests. His first major success, *A Farewell to Arms* (1929), dealt with his experiences in Italy in World War I; *Death in the Afternoon* (1932) was a study of bullfighting; *For Whom the Bell Tolls* (1940) was set in the Spanish Civil War; and *The Old Man and the Sea* is about an aged fisherman trying to catch a huge marlin. His writing skills were rewarded with the Pulitzer Prize in 1953 and the Nobel Prize for Literature in 1954.

Despite his success, Hemingway became depressed by his failing health and shot himself in 1961. ◆

Jimi **Hendrix**

American rock singer and musician
Born 1942   *Died* 1970 aged 27

James Marshall Hendrix was one of the most exciting, unusual, and imaginative rock guitarists ever. He began his career in his Seattle home by imitating records of blues guitarists. He then played the guitar with many top soul groups. He started his own band in New York, but moved to London in 1966 to form the trio The Jimi Hendrix Experience. He immediately found success with 'Hey Joe' (1967) and, despite the strangeness of his sound, followed it with five more hit singles and three albums before his death in 1970. Many later guitarists have imitated Hendrix, but none have managed to play quite like him. ◆

▼ *Jimi Hendrix's group, The Jimi Hendrix Experience, disbanded in 1969, but he continued to record and perform until his death a year later.*

◀ *Sonja Henie brought artistic as well as athletic skills to the sport of ice-skating.*

Sonja **Henie**

Norwegian ice-skater and film actress
Born 1912   *Died* 1969 aged 57

When she was just 11 years old, and already a champion in her own country, Sonja Henie caused a sensation by performing in the 1924 Olympic Games. She went on to win gold medals in the Olympic Games of 1928, 1932, and 1936. She also won a record ten world titles and was European champion six times.

When Henie retired from competitive skating she started a new acting career. She starred in 11 popular Hollywood films, earning more money than any sportsperson had done before. She became an American citizen in 1941. ◆

151

▲ *This is a detail from the Monument to Discoveries in Lisbon, Portugal. Henry the Navigator is on the right.*

Henry the Navigator

Portuguese prince who organized and paid for Portuguese exploration in the 15th century
Born 1394   Died 1460 aged 66

Henry was the son of King John I of Portugal. After a time as governor of a town in Morocco, he became governor of the Algarve province in Portugal.

Although he did not go on any voyages, Henry devoted his life to exploration. He provided ships and finance for the Portuguese captains who were pushing further and further down the coast of Africa and into the Atlantic. As a result, Portugal become a powerful sea-trading nation, seeking new countries to trade with and new products to bring back to Europe.

By the time Henry died, Portuguese ships had explored the African coast as far as what is now Sierra Leone, and had sailed up the Gambia river. Contacts made with the African people eventually gave rise to the Portuguese slave trade. ◆

Henry IV

King of France from 1589 to 1610
Born 1553   Died 1610 aged 56

Henry was born into a French noble family in the mid-16th century. At this time the people of France were bitterly divided. In the Middle Ages all French people had been Catholic Christians. But from the 1530s many had become Protestant Christians, or 'Huguenots'. From the 1560s Catholics and Huguenots fought each other.

Henry was brought up as a Huguenot and later fought in wars against the Catholics, who were led by the King of France. In 1584, however, the king's brother died and Henry became heir to the throne. Then in 1589 the king died and Henry was crowned king. Catholics, however, would not accept this because Henry was a Huguenot. Another war broke out and Huguenots again fought Catholics, but could not defeat them.

Wanting peace for France, Henry became a Catholic in 1593 and the fighting finally stopped in 1598. At the same time Henry established political rights and some religious freedom for the Huguenots, and before too long France began to prosper again. Henry died in 1610 when a Catholic fanatic stabbed him to death. ◆

Henry V

King of England from 1413 to 1422
Born 1387   Died 1422 aged 35

Henry's father, Henry Bolingbroke, was at one time a trusted adviser to King Richard II. But when Richard banished Bolingbroke, the young Henry was left in the king's care. The next year (1399) Henry's father came back, seized the English throne from Richard, ruled as Henry IV, and declared young Henry to be heir to the kingdom of England.

Henry V became king on his father's death in 1413. King Charles VI of France did not take the new English king seriously, and Henry vowed to make him regret this. He

▼ *The battle of Agincourt, 1415, at which Henry V defeated the French army.*

152

made careful preparations for war and invaded France in 1415. Within two months Henry had destroyed the French army at Agincourt. Henry kept up the military pressure for the next five years, until the French king had to agree to let Henry marry his daughter, and so become heir to the French throne.

Henry was now the most powerful ruler in Europe, and he even started making plans to go on crusade to the Holy Land. But seven years of fighting had exhausted him. During another long French siege he caught fever and died, leaving a nine-month-old baby as his successor. ◆

Henry VIII

King of England and Wales from 1509 to 1547
Born 1491   Died 1547 aged 55

When Henry VIII came to the throne in 1509 he seemed to have everything. He was tall, handsome, and good at hunting and

jousting. He was religious, well educated, and musical. He was devoted to his new wife Catherine of Aragon, and he soon found an energetic and loyal minister in Thomas Wolsey, whom he made Lord Chancellor.

But Henry wanted a son to succeed him, and was prepared to stop at nothing to get his own way. He grew tired of Catherine, who had given him a daughter, Mary. He wanted to marry a woman of the court, Anne Boleyn. Wolsey failed to persuade the pope to give the king a divorce, and so he was dismissed from the post of minister.

Henry, with his new minister, Thomas Cromwell, and the Archbishop of Canterbury, Thomas Cranmer, found a more ruthless solution. Henry broke with the pope and the Catholic Church. He married Anne Boleyn (and divorced Catherine afterwards), became Supreme Head of the English Church, and destroyed the monasteries because he wanted their wealth. Henry dealt ruthlessly with those who opposed him. Few people close to him, especially his wives, escaped trouble.

The old Henry was a terrifying figure. He had a painful ulcer on his leg, and was so overweight that a machine had to haul him upstairs. But to many of his people he was a great king. When he died his councillors did not dare announce the news for three days.

Henry VIII married six times and his wives suffered various fates. They were: Catherine of Aragon (divorced), Anne Boleyn (beheaded), Jane Seymour (died), Anne of Cleves (divorced), Catherine Howard (beheaded), and Catherine Parr (survived). He had three children: Mary I (daughter of Catherine of Aragon), Elizabeth I (daughter of Anne Boleyn), and Edward VI (son of Jane Seymour). ◆

▲ *A famous portrait of Henry VIII by Hans Holbein.*

👁 **see also**
Cranmer   Elizabeth I   Mary I
More   Wolsey

Katharine Hepburn

American film actress
Born 1907   Died 2003 aged 96

Katharine Hepburn's first film, *Bill of Divorcement*, made her a star in 1932. She was then identified with witty comedies, such as *Bringing Up Baby* (1938) and a series of movies with Spencer Tracy (her partner in private life). She also triumphed in mature roles, in *The African Queen* (1951), *The Lion in Winter* (1968), and as the elderly mother in *On Golden Pond* (1981), for which she was awarded one of her four Academy Awards (Oscars). This was despite a trembling caused by Parkinson's disease and an eye ailment, the result of dunkings in a Venice canal for scenes in *Summer Madness* (1955). ◆

Barbara Hepworth

English abstract sculptor
Born 1903   Died 1975 aged 72

Like her friend, the sculptor Henry Moore, Barbara Hepworth went to Leeds School of Art and then to the Royal College of Art in London. A scholarship took her to Italy, where she learnt to carve marble. Her work progressed from basic carving of stone or wood to using bronze, sometimes curving metal into shapes joined by thin metal rods resembling strings of musical instruments. Much of her work is abstract, not intended to represent anything. It focuses on shape, texture, size, and surface. After World War II she gained an international reputation as one of the greatest modern sculptors, and carried out many commissions for public places. She died in a fire at her studio in St Ives, Cornwall. ◆

👁 **see also**

Moore

▼ *Barbara Hepworth's sculpture in wood entitled* Single Form.

Hereward the Wake

English Anglo-Saxon leader
Dates of birth and death unknown

Very little is known about Hereward the Wake's life. He was a tenant of the abbey of Peterborough in Lincolnshire. In 1070 a Norman abbot, Turold, got control of that abbey, and Hereward, with other Anglo-Saxon tenants and some Danish pirates, decided to rebel against him. They burnt and plundered the abbey, and made off with its treasure to the Isle of Ely, a marshy area that Hereward could easily defend.

Anglo-Saxons from other parts of the country, who were resisting the Normans, came to Ely to join Hereward. In 1071 King William I (William the Conqueror) decided to take action, and attacked the rebel stronghold. Hereward managed to escape but what happened to him then is not really known. Hereward has lived on in many people's imaginations as an outlaw hero who defied the power of the Normans. ◆

👁 **see also**

William I

Hero of Alexandria

Ancient Greek inventor
Lived during the 1st century AD

We know very little about Hero of Alexandria's life. However, we do know about his marvellous inventions because copies of the books he wrote have been passed down through the centuries. His books contain descriptions of mechanical toys and playthings he invented. The most famous was a small ball which whizzed round by the force of steam. This was the first use of a steam-engine, but it was to be another 1700 years before anyone thought of using steam to drive machines other than toys. He also produced several toys using water; they have been given such names as 'Hero's magic fountain' and 'Hero's magic jug'.

Apart from toys, Hero also invented useful devices, such as his 'dioptra'. This could measure the distance between far-off points and also their height. It was similar to the theodolite used by surveyors today, when examining land before plans can be made for building houses or roads. ◆

Herod

King of the Jews at the time when Jesus was born
Born c.74 BC   Died 4 BC aged about 69

Herod was appointed king of the Jews in 40 BC. Although he was given the province of Judaea (now modern Israel) by the Romans, he had to fight to make it his kingdom. This Herod (there were several) was called 'the Great' because of the forceful way he ruled. But the Jewish population would probably not have agreed with this title, since he ruthlessly put down rebellions.

Herod's first job was to besiege Jerusalem, and eventually he took control there. When he found out about the birth of Jesus, whom people were calling the future king of the Jews, he ordered all children under the age of two in Bethlehem to be put to death. Jesus and his family escaped to Egypt, and Herod died the same year.

Throughout his life Herod was a suspicious man, always thinking that there were plots against him.

▲ *This illustration depicts Herod's massacre of innocent children and Jesus' escape to Egypt.*

For this reason he executed his own son and those of his sister, Salome, and he also executed his wife, her mother, and the High Priest. ◆

Herodotus

Ancient Greek historian
Born *c.484* BC   **Died** *c.424* BC

Herodotus came from the Greek town of Halicarnassus (now on the coast of Turkey) but spent years travelling throughout Greece, Asia, and Africa. In 444 BC he sailed to southern Italy as one of the founders of a new Greek colony called Thurii. Once there Herodotus devoted his time to writing a nine-volume history of Greece. He particularly wanted to record the struggles between the Greeks and the Persians. Herodotus is thought to be an important historian today because he did not just accept what other writers had said before but collected evidence for himself. ◆

William and Caroline Herschel

German-born British astronomers
William Herschel
Born *1738*   **Died** *1822 aged 83*
Caroline Herschel
Born *1750*   **Died** *1848 aged 97*

William Herschel started his working life following in his father's footsteps as an oboist in a German military band. In 1757 he came to England and worked as a musician, eventually settling in Bath. His sister Caroline joined him there in 1772. Gradually his interest in astronomy grew and he started to build his own telescopes.

In 1781 he discovered the planet Uranus, the first planet to be found with the help of a telescope. This discovery changed his life. King George III supported Herschel financially so he could devote himself completely to astronomy.

Herschel directed his tremendous energy towards making many observations of a much higher quality than anyone had done before. He made catalogues of nebulas and double stars, and discovered moons around Uranus and Saturn.

Caroline Herschel soon became his devoted assistant and an expert herself. She went on to do research of her own, discovering new comets and nebulas. She was awarded the Gold Medal of the Royal Astronomical Society for making a huge catalogue of her brother's observations. ◆

▼ *This huge mirror telescope was built and used by William Herschel.*

155

Heinrich **Hertz**

German physicist
Born *1857*   **Died** *1894 aged 36*

Heinrich Hertz was born into a rich and well-educated family. He studied hard and in 1878 went to the University of Berlin.

Earlier, in 1865, the physicist James Clerk Maxwell had written down the laws of electromagnetism. These predicted the existence of electromagnetic waves which could travel through a vacuum. Hertz was encouraged to try to find them.

In 1888 he set up his most famous experiment. He used an electrical circuit to make sparks jump across a gap between two metal rods. He noticed that this caused pulses of electricity in a similar circuit some distance away. He had become the first person to broadcast and receive radio waves.

Unfortunately Hertz was not a very healthy man. He died at the age of 36 just before Marconi demonstrated that radio waves could be used to send messages over long distances.

The unit of frequency is called the *hertz* in his honour. ◆

👁 **see also**

Marconi   Maxwell

Thor **Heyerdahl**

Norwegian explorer
Born *1914*   **Died** *2002 aged 87*

Thor Heyerdahl always had his own definite ideas about how human civilization might have spread during the world's early history. He was convinced that early progress was spread by those from advanced communities travelling to other parts of the world.

To prove that this might have been so, he and five companions

▶ *In their papyrus reed craft* Ra, *Thor Heyerdahl and a crew of six set off from the port of Safi in Morocco in 1969 to cross the Atlantic.*

built a simple balsa-wood raft called the *Kon-Tiki*. In 1947 they sailed it from Peru to Eastern Polynesia to prove that Indians from South America could once have made this journey. Their journey involved great danger but to everyone's delight the *Kon-Tiki* expedition landed safely.

Heyerdahl's next project was to cross the Atlantic from Morocco to the Caribbean, this time in *Ra*, a reproduction of an ancient Egyptian boat made of papyrus. His idea was to suggest that South America could once have been influenced by ideas from Egyptian civilization. Heyerdahl wrote popular books about both of these expeditions.

While many scholars were not convinced by his theories, they all admired Heyerdahl's bravery and skill. ◆

Rowland **Hill**

English reformer of the postal system
Born *1795*   **Died** *1879 aged 83*

When he was 12, Rowland Hill began to teach mathematics at his father's school. Their school became famous because the pupils made their own rules and enforced them without corporal punishment.

Hill was very interested in the

▼ *The Penny Black and the Two Pence Blue, two of the first adhesive stamps, are now valuable collectors' items.*

postal system in England at the time. In 1837 he published a pamphlet suggesting that instead of making very expensive charges, all letters weighing up to half an ounce (14 grams) should be delivered anywhere in the country for one penny. He also recommended the use of 'a bit of paper just large enough to bear the stamp and covered at the back with a glutinous wash' – in other words, an adhesive postage stamp.

Post Office officials opposed it, but most people thought it was an excellent idea, and the 'Penny Post' came into use in 1840. Later Hill was knighted by Queen Victoria for giving Britain the world's first proper postal service. ◆

Edmund **Hillary**

New Zealand mountaineer who was one of the first men to climb Everest
Born *1919*

Edmund Hillary worked as a bee-keeper before taking up mountain-climbing. After climbing in the New Zealand Alps and the Himalayas, he became a member of the British Everest expedition in 1953. When almost at the summit, it was left to Hillary and Tenzing Norgay, a Sherpa tribesman from Nepal, to make the final climb. This they did on 29 May. News of their success reached Britain on the day of Queen Elizabeth's coronation. Hillary was knighted by the new queen in July 1953.

Since then he has made other trips to Everest, becoming a good friend to the local Sherpa people. With them he has worked on schemes for building new schools and hospitals. ◆

👁 **see also**
Tenzing Norgay

Hipparchus

Greek astronomer and mathematician
Lived during the 2nd century BC

Although his dates of birth and death are unknown, and few of his writings survive, Hipparchus was probably the greatest astronomer of ancient times.

He carried out much of his work on the Greek island of Rhodes, for many years carefully observing the Sun, Moon, planets, and stars, using astronomical instruments of his own invention. Lenses had not been invented yet, so he made all his observations with the naked eye. He was the first person to make a scientific link between the movement of the Sun, stars, and planets and the Earth's seasons. His calculations were amazingly accurate. He compiled the earliest-known star catalogue of the 'positions' of 850 stars, and measured their brightness on a scale of 'magnitudes' where the brightest stars are of first magnitude, the faintest being of sixth magnitude. This method is still the basis of modern astronomical brightness scales. He was also the inventor of trigonometry, in which the angles of triangles and the lengths of their sides can be calculated. ◆

Hippocrates of Cos

Greek physician, sometimes called the 'father of medicine'
Born *c.460 BC*
Died *c.370 BC aged about 90*

Unfortunately we do not know much about Hippocrates, but the little we do know shows him to have been a kind and sensible doctor. He was born and worked

▲ *Two sides of a coin minted in Hippocrates' honour in 50 BC.*

on the Greek island of Cos where there was a medical school. In his time most people believed that illnesses were caused by evil spirits or bad magic, but Hippocrates taught that disease was often caused by not eating good food or by living in a dirty place. He is reported to have written 70 books about medical treatment. Apart from Galen, no other doctor had more influence on Western medicine than Hippocrates.

Hippocrates kept careful records of people's illnesses and how they responded to treatment. He was a good surgeon and could set broken bones straight. He taught his methods to other doctors, including his own two sons.◆

👁 **see also**
Galen

Emperor **Hirohito**

Emperor of Japan from 1926 to 1989
Born 1901   Died 1989 aged 87

Hirohito was the eldest son of Crown Prince Yoshihito of Japan. Hirohito visited Europe in 1921, the first crown prince of Japan to travel abroad. When he returned, his father retired because of mental illness and Hirohito became prince regent, ruling in his place.

He became emperor in 1926 and although his reign was foreseen as being one of *Showa* ('bright peace'), Japan soon became involved in war. First Japan invaded China and then joined World War II on the side of Germany and Italy.

Hirohito did not want war against America, but he could not stop his military leaders from attacking Pearl Harbor, an American naval base in Hawaii. Only at the end of the war did Hirohito overrule his generals. Speaking on the radio for the first time, he announced Japan's surrender in 1945.

After the war he stayed on as emperor, but real power was given to the people and their elected politicians. Japan became friendly with its old enemies in the West, but even after his death many could not forgive Hirohito for the things his armies had done during World War II. ◆

Alfred **Hitchcock**

English film director
Born 1899   Died 1980 aged 81

Alfred Hitchcock was the son of a London poultry dealer. He was good at drawing and got a job writing and designing captions for silent films. He soon worked his way up to become a film director.

▲ *In Alfred Hitchcock's thriller* The Man Who Knew Too Much *(1956), James Stewart and Doris Day play a couple whose son is kidnapped by spies.*

In 1926 *The Lodger* began his long series of suspense thrillers, in which he makes a very brief appearance each time. His film *Blackmail* (1928) was the first British talking picture. He directed *The Thirty-Nine Steps* (1935) and several other films in England, but then moved to Hollywood and became even more famous as a director of frightening thrillers such as *Rebecca* (1940), *Psycho* (1960), and *The Birds* (1963). ◆

Adolf **Hitler**

Austrian-born dictator of Nazi Germany
Born 1889   Died 1945 aged 56

Adolf Hitler's father died when his son was 14. As a young man Hitler frittered away his inheritance so he then had to earn his own living. He painted postcards and advertisements in Vienna, Austria, until World War I when he fought in the German army and was awarded the Iron Cross for bravery.

When Germany lost the war, Hitler was so angry about the terms of the peace treaty that he turned to politics. He joined the National Socialist (Nazi) Party and soon became its leader. Many joined the

▼ *Adolf Hitler pictured at a rally in 1934, the year in which he succeeded Hindenburg as head of state.*

Nazi Party, and in 1923 they tried to seize power in Munich. This attempt failed and Hitler went to prison.

> *The broad mass of a nation . . . will more easily fall victim to a big lie than to a small one.*
>
> ADOLF HITLER
> *Mein Kampf,* 1923

There he wrote *Mein Kampf* (My Struggle) (1923) which set out his ideas: he believed Germany's problems were caused by Jews and Communists and that Germany needed a strong Führer (leader) to be great again. Times were hard and his ideas caught on. Although he got only 37 per cent of the votes in the presidential election, Hitler was invited by President Hindenburg to become chancellor (chief minister) in 1933.

When Hindenburg died in 1934, Hitler became president, chancellor, and supreme commander of the armed forces. All opposition to his rule was crushed. Millions of people were sent to concentration camps, and Jews gradually lost all their rights. Hitler became an ally of Fascist Italy and began to push Germany's boundaries outwards. In 1938 he invaded Austria and in 1939 occupied Czechoslovakia and finally attacked Poland too.

This started World War II. Hitler took personal command of Germany's war plans, including a disastrous invasion of the USSR. However, after almost six years, and having ordered the deaths of millions of Jews and others in extermination camps, he was defeated by the Allied powers. He shot himself in his underground shelter in Berlin. ◆

👁 **see also**

Goebbels   Goering
Mussolini   Rommel

Thomas **Hobbes**

English philosopher
Born *1588*   **Died** *1679 aged 91*

Thomas Hobbes's early life was mainly spent as tutor to the Duke of Devonshire's family. When the English Civil War broke out, Hobbes fled to France for 11 years, believing that his theories about the state put him in danger. These theories, set out in his treatise *Leviathan* (1651), say that all power comes from the people; they hand it over to a monarch, who protects them in return for their absolute obedience.

Hobbes's opinion that religion too should be subject to the state led to accusations of atheism. However, he was protected by King Charles II, so he was able to continue defending his controversial views on almost everything right up until his death. ◆

Ho Chi Minh

Founder of the Vietnamese Communist Party and president of North Vietnam
Born *1890*   **Died** *1969 aged 79*

Ho Chi Minh (meaning 'He who shines') was born Nguyen Tat Thanh in Vietnam when it was part of Indo-China, a colony ruled by France. While working in London and Paris he met French Communists who believed it was wrong for France to rule over colonies. They helped him travel to the Soviet Union, where he trained as a Communist organizer. He went to live just outside Vietnam so he could organize a Communist Party inside Indo-China without being arrested, founding the Indo-China Communist Party in 1930.

In 1941, during World War II, Japan entered Indo-China and Ho set up an underground movement,

▲ *When the city of Saigon was captured by the North Vietnamese in 1975, it was renamed Ho Chi Minh City in Ho's honour.*

the Vietminh (supported and funded by the Allies), to fight them. He hoped to take over when the Japanese left in 1945, but the French returned. In 1946 Ho declared war on the French: his forces finally won in 1954.

Vietnam was then divided at the Geneva Conference and Ho became President of North Vietnam. Non-Communist South Vietnam was supported by America, but Ho was determined to reunite the two. He backed the South Vietnam Communists, called the Vietcong, who were fighting their government and the Americans.

In 1965 the United States began to bomb North Vietnam. Its people spent much of their lives in shelters, but the bombing made them even more loyal to Ho. Six years after his death, the two Vietnams were united under the rule of the Communist Party. ◆

Dorothy **Hodgkin**

English chemist
Born 1910   *Died* 1994 aged 84

Dorothy Hodgkin was born in Cairo but most of her life has been spent in her chemistry laboratory in Oxford.

If a chemist wants to make a new drug or copy a chemical that occurs naturally, it is necessary to know what sort of atoms it contains and how they fit together. In other words a plan or design is needed, just as you would need one to build a house. Professor Hodgkin is the world's leading expert in solving this kind of problem.

In 1964 she became only the third woman ever to be awarded the Nobel Prize for Chemistry (the other two were Marie Curie and Irène Joliot-Curie). She received it for finding out how the atoms are arranged in penicillin and vitamin B12. The following year she became only the second woman to be awarded the very special Order of Merit (Florence Nightingale was the other). ◆

William **Hogarth**

English painter and engraver
Born 1697   *Died* 1764 aged 66

William Hogarth was the most important British artist of his period. For generations, foreign artists (such as Van Dyck) had dominated British painting, but Hogarth showed that he could be just as good and just as original as the competition from across the Channel. He was a superb portrait painter, but because he refused to flatter the people he portrayed, he was not able to earn his living this way. Instead he invented a new type of picture – or rather series of pictures. In a series of six or eight scenes he represented successive incidents from a story that illustrated the reward of goodness and the punishment of wickedness. He not only attacked cruelty and injustice, but also poked fun at pompous people, and his pictures had tremendous impact. Engravings of them sold in large numbers and pirate publishers made their own

copies. Hogarth was a strong character and he successfully campaigned to have a Copyright Act passed by Parliament to prevent people cashing in on his work. ◆

Katsushika **Hokusai**

Japanese painter and printmaker
Born 1760   *Died* 1849 aged 89

Katsushika Hokusai is the most famous Japanese artist and one of the greatest of any country or time. Completely dedicated to his art and a master of every subject he chose to depict, he produced a huge number of paintings, prints, and drawings – about 30,000 works in all. Like most Japanese artists of his time, he made his living mainly through coloured prints made from engraved woodblocks; his most famous work is the set of prints *Thirty-six Views of Mount Fuji* (1826–1833), showing Japan's

▼ *The artist William Hogarth specialized in scenes from London life, such as this one,* The Election – Canvassing for Votes.

▲ *Katsushika Hokusai was an expert at creating scenes with just a few simple lines in his woodblock prints. In the Well of the Great Wave of Kanagawa (above) is one of the most famous of his prints.*

sacred mountain in a marvellous variety of views and weather conditions. In the 1850s his prints became well-known in Europe; they influenced the Impressionist artists with their freshness, vigour, and love of life. ◆

Hans **Holbein** the Younger

German painter
Born 1497   Died 1543 aged 46

Hans Holbein was born in Augsburg in the south of Germany, where his father and uncle were painters. Holbein decided to become a painter as well. He worked with his father and then travelled around Germany to learn from other painters. He

eventually settled in Basel (in modern Switzerland), where he became a friend of the churchman and scholar Erasmus. In Basel he produced portraits and prints, including three portraits of Erasmus, and he illustrated a Bible.

In 1526 Holbein went to England, where he met friends of Erasmus and painted their portraits too. One of the people he met, and later painted, was the politician and author Thomas More. Holbein's paintings were so lifelike and colourful that they attracted the interest of Henry VIII. Holbein was appointed court painter. He painted over 100 pictures of Henry, his family, and English nobles. ◆

👁 **see also**

Erasmus   Henry VIII

Billie **Holiday**

American jazz singer
Born 1915   Died 1959 aged 44

Billie Holiday's father played banjo and guitar in a jazz band, and at 15 she was in New York singing in jazz clubs. Her distinctive voice and emotional appeal brought her rapid success. All through the 1940s and 1950s she toured and recorded, making two trips to Europe, in 1954 and 1958. Her best-known records are probably 'Strange Fruit', 'Fine and Mellow', 'Lover Man', and 'Violets for my Furs'.

At the time when Holiday was touring, there was still a great deal of prejudice against blacks in the American South, and as a black singer, Holiday came across a lot of racism.

Her personal life was also filled with problems, particularly her addiction to drugs. This eventually brought about her tragic early

death, at a time when she should have been reaching the peak of her artistic abilities. ◆

Buddy **Holly**

American singer and songwriter
Born 1936   Died 1959 aged 22

Like many early rock'n'roll musicians, Texas-born Charles Hardin Holley began by playing country music but, as leader of Buddy Holly and the Crickets, he went on to become one of rock'n'roll's greatest songwriters. He was also, in 1956, the first musician to use two guitars, bass, and drums, which became the standard line-up for pop groups in the 1960s. His hits, including 'That'll be the Day' (1957), 'Rave On' (1958), and 'It Doesn't Matter Any More' (1959), have been recorded by many artists and still sound fresh today.

Tragically, Holly died in a plane crash at the peak of his success, when he was only 22. ◆

▼ *Buddy Holly had an instantly recognizable 'hiccuping' singing style. The music he wrote influenced many later pop musicians.*

Gustav **Holst**

English composer
Born *1874*   **Died** *1934 aged 59*

Gustav Holst's family originally came from Sweden. His parents were both pianists and wanted him to be a concert pianist but a crippled arm made this impossible. However, from the age of 18 Holst made his living through music as a choir director, a trombonist in a dance band and an orchestra, and finally as director of music at St Paul's Girls' School and at Morley College in London.

The inspiration for Holst's composition came from several varied sources – English folk music, Hindu scriptures, and from the poems of John Keats, Walt Whitman, and Thomas Hardy. His most famous work is *The Planets* orchestral suite, composed between 1914 and 1916.

He lectured at the Royal College of Music in London, where he had been a student, and at universities in Britain and America, and he has had a long-lasting influence on musical education in schools. His experience as a teacher developed his interest in works for small choirs and orchestras, such as his *St Paul's Suite* (1913) which was written for amateur string-players. ◆

Homer

Greek poet
Lived during the 8th century BC

Homer is believed to be the author of two very long poems about the gods and heroes of ancient Greece. These are the *Iliad*, about the capture of the city of Troy (Ilium), and the *Odyssey*, an account of the adventures of the hero Odysseus during his long journey home to Greece from Troy.

We know almost nothing about Homer. Later Greek and Roman writers thought that he was a blind, wandering poet. It is also thought that he came from one of the cities in Asia Minor (now Turkey). Some people think he may not have existed at all, and his poems were just collections of verses which were recited in royal courts by travelling storytellers. However, most experts of this early Greek period and its literature now believe that there was a man called Homer who composed these long, epic poems. They think that Homer did not write the poems down but took famous stories and put them all together, before reciting them from memory. His poems were probably not actually written down for another 100 years. ◆

▼ *In Homer's* Odyssey, *the hero Odysseus survives many trials such as storms, fierce monsters, and strange temptations such as the 'Sirens' depicted on this vase from c.480* BC.

Soichiro **Honda**

Japanese car and motor cycle manufacturer
Born *1906*   **Died** *1991 aged 85*

Soichiro Honda was always interested in cars and machinery. In 1948 he started a business making motor cycles using ex-army tools and parts. At that time, machinery and vehicles were scarce in Japan because many resources had been used up in World War II. However, Honda still managed to build up what became the largest motor cycle firm in the world. In the 1960s Honda started making cars as well, and these were just as successful.

Honda was always more interested in making things than in having business meetings, and it was his instinct for knowing what motor cyclists and motorists wanted that made him successful. He was one of a group of business leaders who made Japan into a leading industrial nation. ◆

Robert **Hooke**

English physicist, chemist, and inventor of the compound microscope
Born *1635*   **Died** *1703 aged 67*

As a child, Robert Hooke was very bright, and was said to have mastered a geometry course and learned to play the organ in one week. Unfortunately he grew up to be very bad-tempered and was always having rows with other scientists. He was so worried these scientists might steal his discoveries that he sometimes left proof of his experiments in code. The result of his secrecy and grumpiness was that he did not get the credit for all his discoveries.

Hooke studied the way metals behave when they are stretched and described it in a way that we still call 'Hooke's Law'. He also developed a new version of the microscope. A Dutch scientist called Leeuwenhoek had shown how useful microscopes could be in many branches of science, but he only had a microscope with one lens. Hooke invented a much more powerful one with several lenses, called the compound microscope. He described his invention and many other pieces of apparatus in his book *Micrographia*. ◆

👁 **see also**

Leeuwenhoek

William **Hoover**

American businessman
Born *1849*   **Died** *1932 aged 83*

People often talk of 'hoovering' the carpet when they mean cleaning it with a vacuum cleaner. William Hoover never liked his name to be used in this way. He may have been embarrassed because he knew that it was

An early advertisement for the 'Hoover', now a household name.

actually J. Murray Spangler who invented the first upright household vacuum cleaner. (Perhaps we should talk of 'spanglering' our carpets!) Spangler was caretaker at a department store in Ohio when Hoover met him. Spangler's original invention looked very similar to some of today's 'Hoovers', with its dust-bag on the outside of the upright handle. Hoover talked Spangler into selling him the rights to his invention and then set up the Hoover Suction Sweeper Company to manufacture it. In 1908 the company produced its first cleaner which proved to be a great success. ◆

Harry **Houdini**

Hungarian-born American magician and entertainer
Born *1874*   **Died** *1926 aged 52*

Harry Houdini was the stage name of Erich Weiss. His family had emigrated to America from Hungary when he was a child. He began his career as a trapeze artist, but it was as a magician who could perform amazing escapes that he became famous.

Houdini taught himself how to escape from all kinds of chains and bindings. He toured America and Europe, attracting publicity for his show by performing stunts, such as escaping from a strait-jacket or prison cell. He even escaped from an airtight tank full of water, but his most famous trick was the 'Chinese torture cell' into which he was locked, hanging upside down, with his ankles held by stocks.

All Houdini's acts were tricks which depended on his physical strength, skill, and fitness. He was annoyed whenever it was suggested that he had special powers, and he would expose others who claimed that they had supernatural powers, such as fraudulent mind-readers, by performing their tricks himself. ◆

▼ *During his career, Houdini invented many new acts, including making an elephant disappear and walking through a brick wall.*

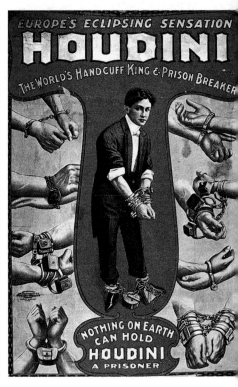

Edwin **Hubble**

American astronomer
Born *1889* **Died** *1953 aged 63*

Edwin Hubble trained as a lawyer but in 1913 began astronomical research at Yerkes Observatory, Wisconsin. This was to be the beginning of a distinguished career during which his observations and brilliant deductions showed that many so-called nebulae (gas and dust clouds) were in fact galaxies far outside our own Milky Way galaxy. By ingenious methods Hubble managed to measure their distances and speeds. Many of Hubble's pioneering discoveries were made in California with the Mount Wilson Observatory's 2.5 m wide telescope which came into operation about the time (1919) Hubble joined its staff. He discovered that the universe is expanding and that the speeds at which galaxies are moving away from us are proportional to their distances from us. Known as Hubble's Law, this theory is the basis for modern cosmology's concept of the Big Bang, the explosion that began our universe. Hubble also introduced a useful classification of types of galaxies according to shape, which is still in use today.

Older astronomers who worked at Mount Wilson many years ago still remember Hubble, pipe in mouth, standing in the cold, darkened dome of the observatory, guiding the enormous telescope with which he mapped the universe. ◆

Henry **Hudson**

English explorer and navigator
Born *c.1565* **Died** *1611 aged about 46*

The first part of Henry Hudson's life is a mystery. The earliest report of him is that on 1 May 1607 he sailed from London as captain of

▲ *English explorer Henry Hudson and his crew coming ashore and meeting Native American Indians in 1610.*

the tiny ship, *Hopewell*. He was looking for a sea route to China to the north of Europe and Asia. This and a second voyage proved to be unsuccessful.

Hudson then took a job with the Dutch East India Company, and in a slightly larger ship, the *Half Moon*, he explored the east coast of North America, and in particular the Hudson River, which was later named after him.

In 1610 Hudson set sail on board the ship *Discoverie*, with a small crew and a boy, his own son John. He was hoping to reach China by way of the North Pole. He discovered what became known as Hudson Bay, where he had to spend the winter. Next summer the crew mutinied and set Hudson, his son, and some of the others adrift in a small boat. They were never seen again. ◆

Howard **Hughes**

American businessman and film producer
Born *1905* **Died** *1976 aged 70*

Howard Hughes took over the successful Hughes Tool Company, which made and sold oil-drilling equipment, when his father died in 1924. He used some of his inherited wealth to produce Hollywood films, the most famous of which include *Hell's Angels* (1930), *Scarface* (1932), and *The Outlaw* (1944). He was also interested in flying and set up the Hughes Aircraft Corporation. In 1935 he set a new record speed of 563 km per hour in a plane he designed himself. All in all, he broke the world speed record three times. Less successful was his design for a giant flying boat to carry 750 passengers; the *Spruce Goose*, built in 1947, flew just 1.5 km. For the last 25 years of his life Hughes was a recluse, living a secret life out of public view. He died while being flown to Houston for medical treatment. ◆

Langston **Hughes**

American writer
Born *1902* **Died** *1967 aged 65*

James Mercer Langston Hughes was born in Joplin, Missouri and educated at Lincoln University. He rose to prominence in the 1920s as part of the Harlem Renaissance, an influential black American literary movement.

Hughes's first major poem, 'The Negro Speaks of Rivers', was published in 1921. This was followed by the experimental and influential volumes of poetry, *The Weary Blues* (1926) and *The Dream Keeper and Other Poems* (1932). In these collections Hughes showed his knowledge of folk culture through his use of lyrical verse, jazz, and blues.

Hughes continued to express the life of black Americans in his writing which included his two-volume autobiography, *The Big Sea* (1940) and *I Wonder as I Wander* (1956), and the *Simple* stories ◆

Victor **Hugo**

French poet, novelist, and dramatist
Born *1802*   **Died** *1885 aged 83*

Victor-Marie Hugo was the son of an officer in Napoleon's army and he spent a lot of his boyhood travelling around Europe. By the time he was in his early teens he was writing poetry and plays. When he was just 17 he was

▼ *A poster for the richly entertaining 1939 film version of Victor Hugo's* The Hunchback of Notre Dame.

already busy founding a literary magazine and had won three prizes for his poetry. He was also involved in politics and in the 1840s his anti-monarchy opinions led to him being banished from France by the emperor, Napoleon III. He lived in exile from 1851 until 1870, mainly in the Channel Islands.

Hugo produced a great number of novels, poems, and plays but is perhaps best known for the novels *The Hunchback of Notre Dame* (1831), about a deformed bell-ringer and the beautiful woman he falls in love with, and *Les Misérables* (1862), about an innocent man condemned to life imprisonment. ◆

Baron von **Humboldt**

German scientist and explorer
Born *1769*   **Died** *1859 aged 89*

Friedrich Heinrich Alexander von Humboldt was a member of a noble German family, and a man of many talents. He studied biology, geology, metallurgy, mining, and politics at university. From 1799 to 1804 he and a companion explored the rainforests surrounding the Amazon and Orinoco rivers in

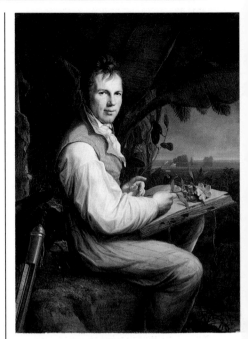

▲ *Baron von Humboldt spent over 20 years writing up an account of his travels in South America.*

South America, travelling nearly 10,000 km. He studied the Peru Current, sometimes called the Humboldt Current, a flow of cool water along the coast of Peru, and reported that guano (the excrement of sea birds) would make good fertilizer. He also identified the cause of mountain sickness and gathered over 60,000 plant specimens.

For over 20 years Humboldt lived in Paris, working on scientific experiments and writing up the results of his explorations, before returning to his birthplace, Berlin. In 1829 he spent six months in Siberia, investigating the geography of that region and studying its weather and geology. He then organized the setting up of a chain of weather stations around the world. For a time he was sent on diplomatic missions by the government of Prussia. Humboldt spent the rest of his long life writing a five-volume book about the universe, entitled *Cosmos*. ◆

Charles **LAUGHTON** in "The **HUNCHBACK** of **NOTRE DAME**" with **MAUREEN O'HARA · THOMAS MITCHELL · EDMOND O'BRIEN** *DIRECTED by* **WILLIAM DIETERLE**

▲ *A wall painting in a town in Iraq portraying Saddam Hussein as a mighty military leader.*

David **Hume**

Scottish philosopher and historian
Born 1711   Died 1776 aged 65

Although he was born and died in Edinburgh, David Hume spent several years in France, where he wrote his major philosophical work, the *Treatise of Human Nature* (1739–1740). Doubting the existence of God, Hume directed his investigations towards providing natural and, if possible, scientific explanations for the way in which human beings think and experience the world. In particular, he was interested in cause and effect: we can see that something may follow after something else, but how can we be really certain that it is caused by it?

A leader in Scottish intellectual life, Hume extended his reputation beyond philosophy with his best-selling historical works, *Political Discourses* (1751) and *History of England* (1754–1762). ◆

Saddam **Hussein**

President of Iraq from 1979 to 2003
Born 1937

Saddam Hussein came from a poor peasant family. When he was 22 he took part in a plot to kill the prime minister of Iraq. Saddam was shot but escaped, cutting the bullet out of his leg with his penknife. After living in exile in Egypt and being imprisoned, he helped overthrow the government of Iraq in 1968. Although he had never been in the army, he appointed himself general and became president in 1979, giving top jobs to his relatives and friends.

In 1980 Saddam launched an eight-year war against Iran that cost hundreds of thousands of lives, and in 1990 he invaded the oil-rich state of Kuwait. A powerful army from many countries, backed by the United Nations, expelled Iraq after six months, but Saddam himself remained in power. In 2003 the USA and UK, claiming Saddam illegally held weapons of mass destruction, went to war against Iraq and forced him into hiding. ◆

Christiaan **Huygens**

Dutch mathematician who developed the pendulum clock
Born 1629   Died 1695 aged 66

Christiaan Huygens's parents realized he was a brilliant mathematician when he was very young. His father was an official in the Dutch government and Huygens had a good education.

▼ *Christiaan Huygens built the first pendulum clock, thereby heralding the beginning of truly accurate time measurement.*

Huygens was not only a great mathematician but he was also good at making things. He made a lot of improvements to the telescope (invented by Galileo in 1609), which made it possible to observe the rings around Saturn for the first time. Huygens also built the first pendulum clock, which was more accurate than other clocks at that time.

He also studied light, and concluded that it moves in waves that spread out, just as the ripples on a pond travel outwards when a stone is dropped into the water. But many scientists preferred Newton's idea that light is a stream of tiny particles. Huygens's 'wave theory' was ignored for 150 years until Thomas Young was able to prove that light really does behave like a wave. ◆

👁 **see also**
Galileo   Newton   Young

Ibn Batuta

Moroccan traveller and writer
Born *1304*   **Died** *1368 aged 64*

When he was a boy, Ibn Batuta studied the Koran very thoroughly. By the age of 21 he was an expert in Muslim theology and law, and he set out on a pilgrimage to Mecca. At first he was homesick, but he was to go on to travel more than 120,000 kilometres over the next 28 years.

Ibn Batuta journeyed to Damascus and joined a pilgrimage there. At Mecca he joined other pilgrims returning to Persia (now Iran). He continued to travel in Asia Minor (now Turkey), observing and keeping records, relating tales and

▼ *Ibn Batuta was one of the greatest Muslim travellers. This map shows some of his journeys around India between 1332 and 1344. He recorded his travels around the world in his book* Rihla (Journey), *which is valued by historians because of the information it gives about the time in which he lived.*

wonders. He then travelled north to Kazan on the River Volga, and on to Constantinople.

Ibn Batuta crossed the Hindu Kush mountains and remained in the service of the Sultan of northern India for eight years. He was sent to accompany a returning Chinese embassy, but a storm destroyed the fleet of junks before they could leave. He was left with only his prayer mat and ten pieces of gold. He eventually reached China in 1344, before finally returning home. Later he travelled throughout Spain and crossed the Sahara to Timbuktu before dictating a fascinating account of his travels. ◆

Ibn Khaldun

Arab historian
Born *1332*   **Died** *1406 aged 74*

Ibn Khaldun was the first person to try to write about why events happened in history and not just to record what happened. He was born in Tunis, North Africa and lived at a time of many changes, when wars, plagues, famines, and trade could make some kingdoms suddenly poor and others suddenly rich. He travelled widely throughout the Arab world, serving as a high official, a general, a professor, and a judge. He was also robbed, imprisoned, and shipwrecked. When the world-conqueror Tamerlane conquered the city of Damascus and took captives, he was so interested to meet Ibn Khaldun that he set him free afterwards. These adventures gave Ibn Khaldun plenty of knowledge of life in different countries and helped him write a great history of the world as he knew it. ◆

👁 **see also**
Tamerlane

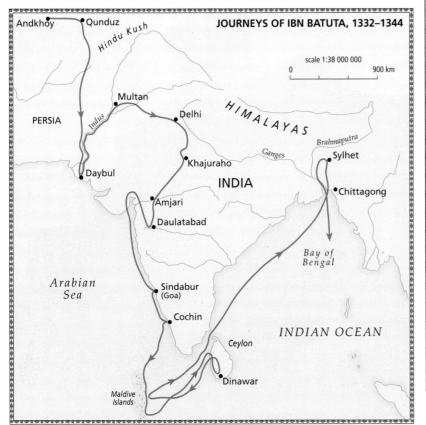

JOURNEYS OF IBN BATUTA, 1332–1344

Andkhoy   Qunduz   Hindu Kush

scale 1:38 000 000
0   900 km

Multan
PERSIA   Indus   Delhi
HIMALAYAS
Daybul   Khajuraho   Ganges   Brahmaputra   Sylhet
INDIA
Amjari   Chittagong
Daulatabad

Arabian Sea
Sindabur (Goa)
Bay of Bengal
Cochin
INDIAN OCEAN
Ceylon
Dinawar
Maldive Islands

Henrik **Ibsen**

Norwegian playwright
Born *1828*   **Died** *1906 aged 78*

Henrik Ibsen became a chemist's assistant when he was 15. He planned to go to university but failed the entrance exam. He turned to journalism instead and also began writing poetry and plays. Then, in 1851, he was given a job as stage director and resident playwright at the Norwegian Theatre. Here he began to formulate his ideas about drama and the psychological development of characters.

He married in 1858 and in 1864 moved to Italy and then to Germany. During the next few years, Ibsen wrote several plays which established him as the founder of modern drama and one of the world's greatest playwrights. These include: *A Doll's House* (1879), *Ghosts* (1881), and *Hedda Gabler* (1890). He returned to Norway in 1891 but was forced to abandon writing after suffering a stroke in 1900. ◆

Muhammad **Iqbal**

Indian poet and political leader
Born *1877*   **Died** *1938 aged 61*

Muhammad Iqbal studied in Lahore, Cambridge, London, and Munich. He earned his living as a university teacher and a lawyer but his fame came through his poetry. He wrote about the past glory of Islam and the need for Muslims to revive it.

In his role as a political leader, Iqbal at first supported the struggle to free India from British rule. However, later he became convinced that Indian Muslims needed a separate country of their own. In 1930 he spoke to the annual meeting of the Muslim League at Allahabad and called upon his fellow Muslims to set up such a state. The League finally decided to do this in 1940, two years after his death. The new country – Pakistan – came into being in 1947.

Iqbal had written his poetry in Persian and in Urdu, and Urdu became the national language of Pakistan. Pakistanis regard Muhammad Iqbal as the father of their country and Iqbal Day is celebrated in his honour every year. ◆

👁 **see also**
Jinnah

Henry **Irving**

English actor-manager
Born *1838*   **Died** *1905 aged 67*

John Henry Brodribb worked as a merchant's clerk but was fascinated by the theatre. An inheritance provided him with enough money for the costumes, swords, and wigs he needed to equip himself as an actor. He also bought his way into the lead role in an amateur production of Shakespeare's *Romeo and Juliet* at a London theatre. Success as Romeo encouraged him to turn professional under the stage name Henry Irving. He spent many years working in touring companies before gaining his place as a leading actor, playing a conscience-stricken murderer in the melodrama *The Bells* in 1871. From 1878 he took over the management of the Lyceum Theatre in London. Here, for over 20 years, he presented plays by Shakespeare and romantic dramas. In 1895 he became the first actor to be knighted, bringing a new respectability to the acting profession. ◆

👁 **see also**
Garrick   Kean

◀ *Henry Irving dressed for playing the role of Cardinal Wolsey. His successful managerial partnership of the Lyceum Theatre with the actress Ellen Terry lasted 24 years.*

Isaiah

Hebrew prophet
Lived during the 8th century BC

Isaiah was an important Hebrew teacher whose writings are found in the section of the Bible known as the Prophets. In the Bible, a prophet is someone who speaks for God rather than foretells future events. There are 15 such men in the Prophets, and Isaiah, Jeremiah, and Ezekiel are renowned as the major ones. Many of Isaiah's teachings appear in the book of the Bible which has been given his name. His name actually means 'salvation of God'. He looked forward to the time when the God of Israel would appear on Earth to be worshipped by everyone. He thus urged his people 'Prepare ye the way of the Lord', warning that the unfaithful could be punished. Many Christians believe that Isaiah was probably referring to the coming of Jesus Christ. ◆

Ito Hirobumi

Japanese statesman who served four times as prime minister
Born 1841   Died 1909 aged 68

Ito Hirobumi was the son of a peasant. He became an attendant in a samurai (warrior) family and at the age of 14 was adopted by the family. In 1862, together with four other young samurai, he secretly boarded a British cargo ship, and went to London. When he returned he took part in the revolution which overthrew the rule of the Tokugawa shogun (warlord) in favour of the emperor. He spent the rest of his life working for the newly formed government, which wanted to reform the country and take on some western ideas. Ito helped to organize a new tax system and

▲ *Ito Hirobumi was an influential figure in the modernization of Japan.*

travelled abroad again in order to study European constitutional models before writing the Japanese constitution which set up a Diet (parliament). He served four times as prime minister, the first time in 1885 and the last in 1900.

In 1904–1905 Japan defeated Russia in a war over which country should control Korea. Ito was sent to govern Korea for the Japanese. He wanted to work with the Koreans rather than ruling by force but he was assassinated by a Korean nationalist. ◆

👁 **see also**
Tokugawa Ieyasu

Ivan the Terrible

Tsar of Russia from 1547 to 1584
Born 1530   Died 1584 aged 53

Ivan became Grand Prince of Moscow when he was only three years old. At 16 he had himself crowned 'tsar and grand prince of all Russia'. (Tsar is Russian for 'Caesar', meaning emperor.) His rule marked a turning point for Russia in foreign affairs. In 1552 he defeated the Mongol-Tartars at Kazan, so ending their 300 years of domination. The eastern road across Siberia to the Pacific was now open. Russia also tried to expand its borders westwards towards the Baltic Sea, but, even after 20 years of war, Ivan failed to keep the land he had gained.

Ivan lived up to his name 'the Terrible': in an orgy of terror in 1581 he killed not only his enemies but also his friends, and even his own son. After his son's death he became quite insane and his mad howls could be heard ringing through the Kremlin. He died in a sudden fit in 1584. ◆

▼ *By the age of 16 Ivan the Terrible was ruler of Russia.*

Andrew **Jackson**

President of the United States of America from 1829 to 1837
Born 1767   Died 1845 aged 78

Andrew Jackson was born two months after his father died. A slave on his uncle's plantation remembered him as 'the most mischievous of youngsters thereabouts'. Jackson avoided school and loved fighting and racing horses. As a 14-year-old soldier in the American Revolution (War of Independence), he was captured by the British. In prison he caught smallpox, and while he was ill his mother died. Jackson survived, and gambled away the money he had been left by his father. Later he apprenticed himself to a lawyer, but his wild ways won him few clients. He moved west, and caused a scandal by marrying his landlady's daughter before her divorce was final. Even so, his new family helped him to become a politician, a judge, and a major-general.

In 1812 America declared war on Britain because Britain was opposed to the westward expansion of the United States and was also trying to limit American trade with Europe. Jackson also fought against the Creek Indians, who had joined the British, and was nicknamed 'Old Hickory' because of his toughness. In 1815 he slaughtered British troops who were attacking New Orleans, an act that made him a hero to the American people.

Jackson was elected as the seventh president of America in 1828, and again in 1832. He was the first president to represent the pioneers of the West. These people wanted to farm the hunting grounds of the Native American Indians. President Jackson tried to move all Native, American Indians to the west of the Mississippi River, a policy that caused great suffering to them. ◆

Michael **Jackson**

American singer and songwriter
Born 1958

Michael Jackson was hailed as a singing and dancing genius from the age of six. He began his show-business career in 1970 when he and his brothers formed a group called The Jackson Five. In 1971 he began his solo career.

While filming *The Wiz*, a 1978 remake of *The Wizard of Oz*, Jackson met producer Quincy Jones and began to work with him. They produced three best-selling albums: *Off the Wall* (1979), *Thriller* (1982) and *Dangerous* (1987). During the 1990s Jackson had a short, troubled marriage to Lisa-Marie Presley, and lost his sponsors Coca-Cola. However, his 2001 album *Invincible* topped the charts. ◆

◀ *Michael Jackson is famous for his amazing dance routines as well as his singing.*

Joseph-Marie **Jacquard**

French inventor of the automatic loom
Born 1752   Died 1834 aged 82

Weaving plain cloth on a loom is easy because the cross-thread (weft) passes over one long thread (warp) then under the next, then over the next, and so on. Making patterned cloth is complicated because the weft passes under a different set of threads each time it crosses the loom. If the operator makes a mistake then the pattern is ruined.

In 1805 Joseph-Marie Jacquard invented an automatic loom. This used a chain of cards punched with holes to control needles and hooks attached to the warp threads. Where a card had a hole the needle went through and the hook was lifted up. This lifted the correct set of warp threads. By using a different set of cards a different pattern could be woven.

Local weavers thought that Jacquard's loom would put them out of work. They burnt his machines and tried to drown him in the river Rhône. He survived and the French government paid him for his invention. Jacquard's design was so successful that it quickly spread throughout the world and is still used today. ◆

● **see also**
Arkwright   Compton
Hargreaves

▲ *Mick Jagger is renowned for his famous pout and energetic live performances.*

Mick **Jagger**

English singer and songwriter
Born 1943

Michael Philip Jagger's father was a P.E. instructor who stressed the importance of physical fitness. Jagger heeded his father's advice and became one of the most athletic of all musical performers, the unforgettable frontman of the rock group the Rolling Stones.

The group emerged from London's thriving rhythm and blues scene in the early 1960s, and at first they were content to copy the blues songs which had inspired them. By 1963, however, Jagger was writing songs with guitarist Keith Richards, and together they produced such rock classics as 'Satisfaction' (1965), 'Jumpin' Jack Flash' (1968), and 'Brown Sugar' (1971).

Jagger has also occasionally acted, and made solo records, and in 1985 he duetted with David Bowie on a chart-topping single, 'Dancing in the Street', which raised a lot of money for famine relief in Africa. ◆

👁 **see also**
Bowie

James I

James VI of Scotland from 1567 to 1625;
James I of England from 1603 to 1625
Born *1566*   **Died** *1625 aged 58*

James did not have a very happy childhood. His father, Lord Darnley, was murdered, and his mother, Mary, Queen of Scots, was executed. James became king of Scotland when he was only a baby, and was brought up strictly by Scottish nobles.

James was a highly intelligent man. He loved peace, and, unlike many others, did not want to persecute people for their religion. But he was lazy, extravagant, and rather undignified. He was criticized for having favourites and for giving them too much power.

When James became the first Stuart King of England he hoped for an easier life. But in 1605 a group of Catholics nearly blew him and his Parliament up in the Gunpowder Plot. The Puritans were also dissatisfied, as he did not change the Church of England as they demanded. However, in his reign a fine new English translation of the Bible was made, now called the 'King James Bible', or the 'Authorized Version'. ◆

👁 **see also**
Fawkes   Mary, Queen of Scots

▼ *Like many kings at that time, James I believed his power came from God.*

Henry **James**

American writer
Born *1843*   **Died** *1916 aged 72*

Henry James was born into a wealthy New York family. Determined to be a writer, he believed that Europe would provide him with more ideas for his books. In 1876 he went to Britain, and he stayed there for the rest of his life.

Altogether he wrote 20 novels and over 100 short stories. In his writing he aimed to create characters so lifelike that readers would eventually feel that they knew them as people. Such very detailed descriptions take time, and James's novels are often very long. In his shorter stories he sometimes described supernatural events, most famously in *The Turn of the Screw* (1898).

James's fiction had a large influence upon future writers who also tried to achieve the same degree of characterization and realism in their novels. ◆

Jesse **James**

American outlaw
Born 1847 Died 1882 aged 34

At the age of 15, Jesse James joined a group of southern guerrillas and fought against the Unionists in the American Civil War.

When the war ended in 1865, Jesse and his brother Frank formed a gang of outlaws. During the next ten years they carried out many daring robberies and hold-ups. Then, in 1876, one bank robbery went wrong. Most of the gang were killed or captured, but Jesse and Frank escaped and formed a new gang. There was now a price on their heads, and in 1882 a gang member shot Jesse and claimed the reward.

Legend has turned Jesse James into a hero, but he was really the leader of a ruthless gang who murdered at least ten people. ◆

▶ A wanted man: Jesse James.

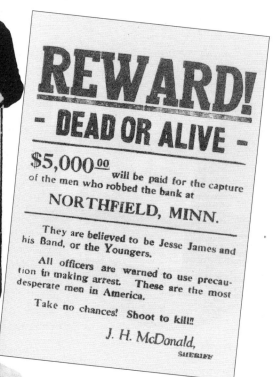

Thomas **Jefferson**

President of the United States of America from 1801 to 1809; author of the American Declaration of Independence
Born 1743 Died 1826 aged 83

Thomas Jefferson was born in Virginia, a colony still ruled by Britain. He later inherited a large plantation there, worked by slaves. He became a successful lawyer before going in to politics and being elected to the local government. He joined in many debates on the Colonies' independence from Britain and he was so respected that he virtually wrote the Declaration of Independence himself. (It later became the basis for the American Constitution.) This declaration resulted in the American War of Independence (1776–1783).

Jefferson was elected governor of Virginia (1779–1781), and then rose up the political ladder, eventually becoming the third president of America in 1801. Perhaps his greatest achievement then was the purchase from Napoleon of the territory of Louisiana, which was soon explored by Merriweather Lewis and William Clark. However, Jefferson was probably most proud of his last great achievement, the foundation of the University of Virginia in 1819. ◆

👁 **see also**
Lewis and Clark
Washington

Edward **Jenner**

English discoverer of the smallpox vaccination
Born 1749 Died 1823 aged 73

In Edward Jenner's time there were regular outbreaks of a deadly disease called smallpox and it claimed tens of thousands of lives in England alone. Jenner heard stories of milkmaids claiming that they could get protection from smallpox if they caught cowpox, a mild disease which affected cows, and he decided to investigate.

In 1796 Jenner took the contents of a blistering pimple from the arm of a milkmaid suffering from cowpox and injected it into an eight-year-old boy. The boy became ill with cowpox but soon recovered from this mild infection. Jenner then injected him with smallpox. The boy did not become ill; the cowpox had made him immune to smallpox.

In 1798 Jenner published the results of his work, and within three years people as far away as America and India were receiving the new protection from smallpox. Jenner's discovery made him rich; he was rewarded by parliament with sums totalling £30,000, an enormous amount of money in those days. ◆

👁 **see also**
Pasteur

REWARD!
- DEAD OR ALIVE -

$5,000.00 will be paid for the capture of the men who robbed the bank at
NORTHFIELD, MINN.

They are believed to be Jesse James and his Band, or the Youngers.

All officers are warned to use precaution in making arrest. These are the most desperate men in America.

Take no chances! Shoot to kill!!

J. H. McDonald,
SHERIFF

Jesus

Jewish prophet and teacher who became the founder of Christianity

Born C.4 BC*
Crucified C.AD 28 or 29 aged about 32 or 33

There are four written accounts of the life of Jesus, called the gospels of Matthew, Mark, Luke, and John. They are found in the New Testament section of the Bible. The gospels gather together many stories about Jesus. According to these stories, Jesus' mother was Mary but his father was God, instead of Mary's husband, Joseph. Apart from the story of his birth in a stable in Bethlehem, not much is known about Jesus' childhood.

At about the age of 30, Jesus was baptized by his cousin, John the Baptist. After this, Jesus began to preach and large crowds gathered to listen to him. Jesus taught them to love God and their neighbours, particularly those in need. He explained that God cares more about what goes on in our hearts than about just keeping rules. He called people to be sorry for their sins, in preparation for the 'kingdom' of God. He told them that God is a father who looks after us and forgives us, and he taught them the Lord's Prayer.

Jesus' followers came to believe that he was the Messiah or Christ (a king whom the Jewish people were waiting for, to come and save them). Jesus chose 12 men from among his followers to help preach his message of love, humility, and trust in God. They were called Apostles, 'those who are sent out'.

Jesus was very popular and the Jewish religious leaders felt that he was a threat to them. Realizing that his life might be in danger, Jesus made a special occasion of his last meal with his apostles (known as the Last Supper). He took bread and gave it to them to eat, saying 'This is my body', and gave them wine to drink, saying 'This is my blood'.

Later that night, Jesus was arrested, after Judas, one of the Apostles, had shown the Jewish religious authorities where to find him. He was put on trial before the Roman governor, Pontius Pilate, and sentenced to death by crucifixion (being nailed to a wooden cross). This day is now marked as Good Friday.

On the third day after Jesus' death, news spread that he had risen from the dead. Easter Sunday is the day when Jesus' resurrection from the dead is celebrated. Jesus' followers became known as Christians. Soon there were many non-Jewish as well as Jewish Christians, thanks to early preachers like Paul, who travelled widely through the Roman empire.

▲ *Part of a stained glass window showing Jesus blessing little children.*

Muslims also think Jesus was a prophet, but they do not believe, as Christians do, that he was God himself, who had become a human being to save the world from sin and death. ◆

*At the time when Jesus was born, the Romans dated years from the legendary foundation of Rome. About 500 years after the lifetime of Jesus, Christian scholars worked out a new system, counting from what they thought was the year of his birth. Historians now know that he was born a few years earlier than this, in about 4 BC.
BC stands for Before Christ.
AD stands for Anno Domini, 'in the year of our Lord'.

👁 **see also**

John the Baptist   Mary
St Paul   St Peter

▶ Jinnah's portrait on a banknote from Pakistan. He is shown wearing Western clothing which was quite unusual for a Muslim leader at that time.

Mohammed Ali Jinnah

Founding father of the state of Pakistan
Born 1876   Died 1948 aged 71

While he was working as a lawyer in India, Mohammed Ali Jinnah became involved in politics. He joined the Indian National Congress, an organization which wanted India to become an independent country, free from British rule. Jinnah believed that unity between Hindus and Muslims was the best way to make this happen. However, he became concerned that the Congress was interested only in the Hindu population of India. He left and joined the Muslim League, which represented Muslim interests.

Under his leadership, the Muslim League grew in importance. During the independence negotiations with the British, Jinnah and the Muslim League fought hard for a new separate state for Muslims. Despite bitter fighting between Hindus and Muslims, this new state – Pakistan – was formed in 1947. Jinnah became governor-general of Pakistan, but he only lived for another 13 months.

In Pakistan, he is known as Qaid-i-Azam, 'the great leader'. ◆

👁 **see also**

Gandhi, Mahatma   Iqbal

Joan of Arc

French peasant girl who led the French against the English
Born 1412   Died 1431 aged 18

Joan, the daughter of a peasant, grew up in north-east France. She was a devout and intelligent child and, unlike many children then, she could also read and write.

As Joan later remembered: 'I was in my thirteenth year when God sent voices to guide me. At first I was very frightened.' The voices kept returning and she stopped being afraid. She recognized them as St Michael, St Catherine, and St Margaret, the patron saints of France. They spoke about the sufferings of France since the English had invaded, under Henry V. The true heir to the French throne, Charles the Dauphin, had not yet been crowned king. The saints told Joan to put on men's clothes to lead the fight against the English.

Joan managed to persuade Charles of her mission. He sent her with troops to Orléans, the last city in northern France still resisting the English. Within a week of her arrival in May 1429, the siege of Orléans ended. Two months later, the English had been defeated and Charles was crowned king of France in Reims Cathedral.

Known as 'the maid of Orléans', Joan carried on the fight. However, after a year she was captured by the duke of Burgundy, an ally of the

▼ A portrait of Joan of Arc from 1420.

English. King Charles of France made no attempt to rescue her.

The English put Joan on trial as a witch and a heretic (a person who disagrees with the Church's teaching). They insisted that the Devil inspired her to wear men's clothes and to claim such power. Joan was found guilty and was burnt at the stake in Rouen in May 1431. Twenty-five years later, the French king proclaimed her innocent, and nearly 500 years after her death the pope declared her a saint. ◆

👁 **see also**

Henry V

Sir Elton **John**

English singer and songwriter
Born 1947

Reginald Dwight went to Pinner Grammar School, then to the Royal Academy of Music in London. After college he played piano in a hotel, then later joined a local group. In 1967 he changed his name to Elton John. He went to America to appear in a concert in 1970, and became an 'overnight success'. His first international hit was 'Your Song' (1971), followed by a string of hit records and sell-out concerts. His involvement with good causes brought him into close contact with Diana, Princess of Wales, and at her funeral in Westminster Abbey he sang a specially written version of his song 'Candle in the Wind' in tribute to her. ◆

👁 **see also**

Diana, Princess of Wales

▶ *The head of a statue of King John in Worcester Cathedral.*

King **John**

King of England from 1199 to 1216
Born 1167   Died 1216 aged 48

John was the youngest son of Henry II and Eleanor of Aquitaine. From an early age he was nicknamed 'Lackland' because, while his older brothers were all given some of Henry's lands to look after, he had nothing.

When he was king, John went too far in attacking his enemies, and he did not respect his friends enough. His supporters began to lose trust in him, and let the French king invade Normandy. In the fight to win the land back, John used every means he could to raise money in England. Finally his subjects refused to pay any more because the king was acting illegally. In 1215 they made a great list of their rights called Magna Carta (the Great Charter), and John had to agree to respect it. He died the next year, a humiliated king. ◆

👁 **see also**

Eleanor of Aquitaine   Richard I

Pope **John XXIII**

Italian Pope from 1958 to 1963
Born 1881   Died 1963 aged 81

Angelo Roncalli came from a large farming family. They were so poor he sometimes had to carry his shoes to school to save the leather. At the age of 12 he went to the seminary (school for priests) in Bergamo and from there to Rome. In World War I he was a hospital chaplain. After the war the pope sent him to various European countries as his ambassador, and then in 1953 he became bishop of Venice.

He was unexpectedly elected pope in 1958, at the age of 76. He visited children in hospital and prisoners in jail, and was especially concerned with helping the poor and with movements for international peace. He was on good terms with the Protestant and Orthodox churches and with Jews, and this helped to change the image of the pope. He also asked the Catholic bishops from across the world to help him solve the problems of the Roman Catholic Church. More than 2000 bishops met in Rome between 1962 and 1965 at the Second Vatican Council. Unfortunately, 'good Pope John' died before the council ended. ◆

John the Baptist

Jewish prophet who lived at the same time as Jesus
Born *c.4 BC*
Died *c.AD 28 aged about 32*

According to the Bible, John was the son of a priest, Zacharias, and his wife Elizabeth, who was the cousin of Mary, the mother of Jesus. In about AD 27 John began preaching on the banks of the River Jordan. He asked people to be sorry for the wrong they had done and to lead a new life. To show that they had repented and that their sins were washed away, John immersed them in the River Jordan. This sign of cleansing is called baptism and gives John his title. Jesus himself was baptized by John.

John criticized the Jewish ruler, Herod Antipas, for marrying his brother's wife, Herodias. So Herodias had John arrested and put in prison. At a banquet, Herodias persuaded her daughter Salome to dance for the king and his guests and to ask for the head of John the Baptist as her reward. Herod did not want John killed, but he had promised Salome that she could have whatever she wished, so John was beheaded. The severed head was carried in on a dish and presented to Salome, who gave it to her mother. ◆

👁 **see also**
Jesus   Mary

Pope **John Paul II**

Polish-born Pope from 1978
Born *1920*

Before becoming pope, John Paul II was called Karol Wojtyla (pronounced Voy-ti-wa).

▲ *John Paul II has travelled more widely and been seen by more people than any other pope in history.*

His father was a soldier and his mother, who died when he was nine, was a teacher. 'Lolek' (as he was known) was good at studies and sports, especially football and skiing.

By the time his father died in 1941, Poland had been occupied by Nazi Germany and the Soviet Union. During World War II, Karol was forced to work in a stone quarry. His first ambition was to be an actor, and six of his plays were later published. But he thought the Polish people needed priests more urgently, so in 1946 he became a priest and went to study in Rome. In 1964 he was made Archbishop of Kraków and three years later he became a cardinal.

His election as pope in 1978 was a complete surprise. The pope before him, John Paul I, had died after only 33 days in office. Wojtyla was chosen because he was only 58, which was young by papal standards. As pope he is very strict on sexual morality, wants priests to stay out of politics, and is opposed to women priests. ◆

Amy **Johnson**

English pilot
Born *1903*   **Died** *1941 aged 37*

As a young woman, Amy Johnson became interested in flying and joined the London Aeroplane

▼ *Amy Johnson photographed in 1930 standing by her aeroplane Jason I, a De Havilland Gipsy Moth. This was the plane in which she made her record flight to Australia.*

Club.

In 1930 she became the first woman to fly to Australia, unfortunately just failing to beat the existing record for the journey, made by another pilot, Jim Mollison. Shortly afterwards they were married.

In the early 1930s she made a number of long-distance flights; some with Jim Mollison, and some alone. In 1941 her aircraft plunged into the sea and was lost in mysterious circumstances. ◆

Lyndon B. Johnson

President of the United States of America from 1963 to 1969
Born *1908*   **Died** *1973 aged 64*

Lyndon Baines Johnson was born in Texas, where he later worked as a teacher. He entered politics in 1931 as a Democrat and was elected to the House of Representatives in 1937 and to the Senate in 1949. He became vice-president when J. F. Kennedy was elected president in 1960. This meant that when Kennedy was assassinated in Dallas three years later, Johnson automatically became president himself.

America was badly shaken by the assassination and Johnson helped to restore calm by acting firmly and with dignity. This earned him a great deal of public respect. When presidential elections were held the following year, he won by a massive majority of 15 million votes.

During his time as president, Johnson improved health care for the elderly and civil rights for black Americans. However, he lost a lot of popular support when he increased American involvement in the Vietnam War, and he refused to stand for re-election. ◆

Michael Johnson

American sprinter, the greatest ever at 200 and 400 metres
Born *1967*

Michael Johnson was born in Dallas, Texas. Having concentrated on running at college, when he left in 1990, he was ranked the world number 1 at both 200 and 400 metres.

In 1991 Michael won his first world championship (at 200 metres). But at the 1992 Olympics he had a stomach bug, and did not win an individual medal. Then at the 1996 Olympics he won both the 200 and 400 metre races, shattering the world record at 200 metres. No-one had ever won both events before.

In 1999 Michael at last broke the 400 metres world record. The following year he won Olympic gold at 400 metres for a second time: the only athlete ever to do this. ◆

Samuel Johnson

English poet, critic, and lexicographer
Born *1709*   **Died** *1784 aged 75*

Samuel Johnson was born in Staffordshire, where he later opened a private school with his wife. When this proved to be unsuccessful he went to London and began a career as a writer. Although he did not make much of a living at first, he soon became well-known in the book trade.

He was then asked to write a dictionary. This took nearly eight years to complete. The dictionary was published in 1755 and made him very famous. It remained in use for over a century.

Johnson was also renowned for his conversation and wit as well as being regarded as the leading critic and literary scholar of his day. ◆

Michael Jordan

American basketball player
Born *1963*

Born in Brooklyn, Michael Jordan was a leading college basketball player at the University of North Carolina. He then began an outstanding career with the Chicago Bulls, becoming the National Basketball Association's most valuable player in 1988.

Jordan is renowned in professional American basketball for his high scoring. By 1992 he had achieved a record average of 32.3 points in 589 games for the Bulls. He is known as 'Air' Jordan because of the height he can leap.

He competed in the Barcelona Olympics in 1992 with the 'Dream Team'. This US team consisted of top professional players instead of the usual college amateurs. Not surprisingly, the team easily won the Olympic gold medal. ◆

▼ *Michael Jordan retired from basketball in 1998, but came back and joined the Washington Wizards for 2002 and 2003.*

177

Joseph

Hebrew adviser to the Pharaoh of Egypt
Lived during the 18th century BC

According to a story in the Bible, Joseph was the son of Jacob and Rachel. Jacob gave Joseph a coat of many colours and Joseph dreamed that he would be a great man. His jealous half-brothers sold him to merchants travelling to Egypt and told their father that his favourite son was dead.

Joseph was sold as a slave in Egypt and was sent to prison for offending his master's wife. In prison he told people the meaning of their dreams. When Pharaoh, the ruler of Egypt, had some strange dreams, Joseph was sent for. He said that the dreams foretold a famine. Pharaoh ordered Joseph to oversee the building of granaries to store corn before the famine came.

When Joseph's brothers travelled to Egypt to buy corn, they did not recognize him. But he knew who they were. His younger brother and father joined him to live in Egypt.

The stories of Joseph are found in the Book of Genesis in the Bible. There is a chapter named after him in the Muslim scriptures, the Koran, too. ◆

▲ *Joule used this electromagnet in some of his experiments.*

James **Joule**

English scientist who experimented with heat
Born *1818*   **Died** *1889 aged 70*

James Joule's father was a wealthy brewer. In his twenties, Joule helped run the brewery, but he always managed to find time for doing experiments. He had no proper education, but taught himself whatever he needed to know.

Joule was fascinated by heat: he measured the amount of heat produced by all kinds of processes. He noticed that doing work always produces heat. The 'work' could be as different as boring a hole in a piece of metal with a drill, or pushing a wheel round with water. He found that a certain amount of work always produced a certain amount of heat.

Joule wrote about something we call 'energy', and explained that energy is never destroyed; it is just changed into different forms. When you jump up and down you use lots of energy; when you stop jumping where has the energy gone? The ground you were jumping on will have got hot, and so will you. Your jumping energy has become heat energy. This is a very important rule in science and became known as the 'law of the conservation of energy'. ◆

▼ *An illustration from the story of Joseph.*

James **Joyce**

Irish novelist
Born *1882*   **Died** *1941 aged 58*

The eldest of ten children from a poverty-stricken family, James Joyce still managed to go to university. Deciding early on to become an author, he then moved to Paris, surviving by writing and teaching. His popular book *Dubliners* (1914) contains some of the best short stories ever written. Two years later he wrote an autobiographical novel, *A Portrait of the Artist as a Young Man*. This also proved popular, although it seemed shocking to some people. But this public unease was nothing compared with the scandal following Joyce's masterpiece *Ulysses* (1922). This extraordinary novel deals with one day in the life of an unsuccessful Irish businessman. It deals equally with all sides of life and also constantly experiments with different uses of language. With its publication, Joyce became one of the most famous 20th-century novelists. ◆

> '*All moanday, tearsday, wailsday, thumpsday, frightday, shatterday.*'
>
> JAMES JOYCE
> Ulysses

Carl **Jung**

Swiss psychologist
Born 1875   Died 1961 aged 85

Carl Jung believed, as Sigmund Freud did, that people with mental troubles could be helped by talking about them with a doctor. But unlike Freud, Jung believed that we are all born with certain problems which have to do with what sort of people we are.

Some people, for example, will always feel better in company; Jung called these 'extroverts'. Others are happier on their own; in Jung's terms, 'introverts'. Jung believed it was important for us to feel at home with both types of behaviour,

otherwise we can sometimes become rather unbalanced.

Jung discovered that his patients' dreams could sometimes give them a good idea about where they were going wrong in their lives. For example, if someone always dreamt about fierce, wild animals, Jung might suggest this was because they were refusing to face up to their own angry feelings. He would suggest that they try to turn all this energy into something creative like painting or writing.

This interest led Jung to study art and myths from all over the world. The strong similarities he found within them proved to him that all human beings are much the same at heart. ◆

👁 **see also**
Freud

Justinian

Emperor of the Byzantine Empire from 527 to 565
Born 483   Died 565 aged 82

Justinian was born in the countryside, about 180 kilometres north-west of Constantinople (modern Istanbul),

which was then the capital of the Roman Empire. In Constantinople Justinian had an uncle, who was made emperor in 518. The new emperor, however, lacked a son to succeed him, so he made Justinian his heir. In 523 Justinian married Theodora, a beautiful and strong-minded woman who had once been a child actress. She became very influential and played an important part in the government of the empire.

The empire had once included all the lands round the Mediterranean, but before Justinian's birth Germanic tribesmen had conquered western Europe and north-west Africa. When Justinian became emperor, in 527, he was determined to reconquer the lost lands. His armies won back north-west Africa, Italy, and south-east Spain.

Justinian also strengthened his government. His officers compiled three collections of laws, so that people could know which laws were in use. He also encouraged the Church. In Constantinople alone he paid for 30 new churches, including Hagia Sophia, one of the largest and most magnificent churches ever built. ◆

▼ *6th-century mosaics from Ravenna, Italy, showing Justinian and Theodora.*

Franz **Kafka**

Czechoslovakian writer
Born *1883* ***Died*** *1924 aged 40*

Franz Kafka was born in Prague and lived most of his life there, but he wrote in German, which was then Czechoslovakia's official language (it was still part of the Austrian empire). He lived quite an uneventful life, working for an insurance company until illness – tuberculosis – forced him to retire. In his lifetime he published only a few stories, and he left instructions for his unpublished works to be destroyed. However, the person in charge of his will, Max Brod, disregarded these instructions. Two of Kafka's novels, *The Trial* (1925) and *The Castle* (1926), published after his death, gained him a reputation as one of the most powerful and original writers of the 20th century. They are written in a beautifully clear style, but they portray a nightmarish world in which individuals are frightened and bewildered by sinister and oppressive forces of authority. ◆

Kalidasa

Indian writer
Lived during the 5th century

Kalidasa was probably the greatest Indian writer of all time. He wrote in Sanskrit, the Indian classical language of learning and religion, and is known to have been the author of at least three dramas and three long poems. He was a Hindu, possibly a Brahmin priest, and took his stories from Hindu mythology. His name means 'servant of Kali', Kali being the wife of the god Siva. Kalidasa was expert at describing the pains of love and the beauty of nature. His most famous play, *Sakuntala*, tells the story of King Dusyanta who falls in love with the beautiful forest nymph, Sakuntala. Their love is placed under a curse by the sage Durrasas, but they are eventually reunited. Their son, Bharata, became the legendary founder of India (which is officially called 'Bharat' in Hindi). ◆

▼ *An illustration from Kalidasa's* Sakuntala. *King Dusyanta and Sakuntala meet by a river bank in the forest.*

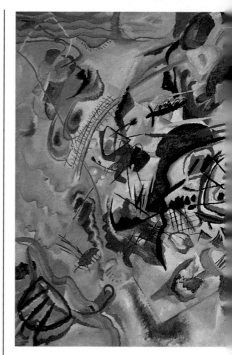

Wassily **Kandinsky**

Russian artist
Born *1866* ***Died*** *1944 aged 77*

At the age of 30 Wassily Kandinsky gave up a promising career teaching law and went to art school in Munich. Since childhood he had been fascinated by colour and later on by science and music. Once he became an experienced artist he began to make experimental pictures in which colour was all important.

Kandinsky is famous as the first artist to paint pictures that did not look like anything recognizable: he was the first 'abstract' artist. He decided that painting recognizable objects harmed his pictures. Instead he wanted to make his pictures seem somehow like music: they did not mean anything in particular but they had a deep effect on the viewer. Just as musical sounds affect people deeply, Kandinsky believed colours and forms could also express and inspire emotions. These

▲ *Before Kandinsky, no one had dreamt that a work of art might not easily be recognizable as something real. His pictures, such as this one,* Composition No.7 *(1919), are more to do with what goes on in the mind.*

'colour music' pictures astonished the world.

Although Kandinsky was always strongly influenced by his Russian background, he travelled widely around Europe, becoming first a German and later a French citizen. His thoughts, teachings, writings, and artwork caused an artistic revolution. ◆

Immanuel **Kant**

German philosopher
Born *1724* ***Died*** *1804 aged 79*

Immanuel Kant was born in the town of Königsberg (renamed Kaliningrad in 1945), then part of the German state of Prussia. He taught in its university for 42 years.

He is regarded by many as the greatest Western philosopher since Socrates. His *Critique of Pure Reason* (1781) looked at the basic philosophical question of how we know or experience something: is it because of the qualities of the object itself or because there are some ideas within ourselves that enable us to make sense of that object? Kant decided that, in addition to 'things in themselves', there exist inborn ideas, which he called 'categories'. Kant also wrote other works, including two other *Critiques* on what it means to act morally and on issues such as what we really mean when we say something is beautiful. ◆

Gary **Kasparov**

Soviet chess champion
Born 1963

Gary Kasparov was born Harry Weinstein in Azerbaijan. He was Soviet junior chess champion at 12, and an international Grand Master five years later. In 1981 he won the USSR national title,

▼ *Gary Kasparov was only 22 when he became world chess champion in 1985.*

replacing his fellow countryman Anatoly Karpov at the top of the world rankings. He challenged Karpov for the world title in 1985, and beat him to take the title. This made him the youngest-ever world champion.

Kasparov defended his world title several times against Karpov and other opponents. In 1996 he beat the IBM supercomputer 'Deep Blue' four games to two, but then lost a rematch to an improved 'Deeper Blue' in 1997. In 2000 Kasparov lost the Brain Games World Championship to Vladimir Kramnik. However, he is still considered the greatest chess player of all time. ◆

Kenneth **Kaunda**

President of Zambia from 1964 to 1991
Born 1924

Kenneth David Kaunda was born in Lubwe, Northern Rhodesia (now Zambia), the son of a teacher. He worked as a teacher and headmaster in Lubwe from 1943 to 1948. In 1950 he joined the African National Congress (ANC), which was seeking independence for Zambia (and other central African countries) from Britain. He worked for the ANC for many years, facing arrest and imprisonment for his activities. Then in 1958 he broke away from the ANC to form the Zambia African National Congress (ZANC). A year later Kaunda was arrested again. On his release he became president of the United National Independence Party (UNIP). In 1964 UNIP won the national elections and Kaunda became the first president of an independent and newly-named Zambia. He remained in power for 27 years until he was defeated in elections in 1991. ◆

Yasunari **Kawabata**

Japanese novelist
Born 1899   Died 1972 aged 72

Yasunari Kawabata became an orphan early on in his life and had a lonely childhood. After leaving Tokyo University he wrote *The Izu Dancer* (1924). This autobiographical novel contains a lot of powerful descriptions, as if Kawabata were determined to make his readers experience what he was writing about as vividly as possible.

Kawabata was very influenced by ancient Japanese poetry, and his most famous novel *Snow Country* (1956) has the atmosphere of a long poem, with one event running into another as if in a dream. In his work Kawabata often conveys an image of beauty but there is also a feeling of loneliness and a constant interest in death. He was awarded the Nobel Prize for Literature in 1968 but only four years later he committed suicide after the death of an old friend. ◆

Edmund **Kean**

English actor
Born 1789   Died 1833 aged 44

Edmund Kean was a child singer, dancer, and acrobat. However, he was not very happy at home and ran away to live with his uncle. At 15 he was working as an actor wandering from town to town looking for work, but it was ten years before he got his big chance – to act at the famous Drury Lane theatre in London.

With his flashing eyes and expressive style of acting, Kean soon became noted for playing wicked and villainous characters. He was considered one of the greatest tragic actors but was less successful in romantic roles. Scandals in his private life damaged his career and drink ruined his health. He collapsed while acting in Shakespeare's play *Othello* at the Covent Garden theatre in London, and died nine weeks later. ◆

Buster **Keaton**

American star of silent films
Born 1895   Died 1966 aged 70

Joseph Keaton's parents were comedians. They trained him when he was very young to perform in their stage act. He was given his name 'Buster' when he fell down the stairs and survived unhurt. When he was 21 he joined the comedian Roscoe 'Fatty' Arbuckle in making short films.

From 1919 he started making his own films, such as *Our Hospitality* (1923) and *The Navigator* (1924), in which he escaped from one disaster after another with hardly a single change of expression. He was nicknamed 'Great Stone Face' because of this. In his greatest film, *The General* (1927), he played an engine-driver caught up in the American Civil War. Sadly, his career ended with the arrival of the 'talkies' (talking pictures). ◆

👁 **see also**
Chaplin

John **Keats**

English poet
Born 1795   Died 1821 aged 25

John Keats's father died in a riding accident when John was only eight years old. Six years later his mother died of tuberculosis. When he was 16 he started to train as a doctor and later studied medicine at Guy's Hospital, London. But by this time he was determined to be a poet, and in 1817 he published his first book of poems.

While Keats never doubted his own talents, bad reviews meant that he could never earn enough money from writing alone. Even so, he went on to write some of the best-known poems in the English

▼ *Buster Keaton, seen here in a still from the 1925 film* Go West, *was one of the greatest comedians of the silent screen.*

language, including 'Ode to a Nightingale', 'The Eve of St Agnes', and the mysterious 'La Belle Dame Sans Merci'.

Keats became seriously ill after a walking tour in Scotland and later died in Rome of tuberculosis. ◆

Fast-fading violets covered up in leaves;
And mid-May's eldest child,
The coming musk-rose, full of dewy wine,
The murmurous haunt of flies on summer eves.

JOHN KEATS
'Ode to a Nightingale' (1820)

Helen **Keller**

American writer who achieved success despite being deaf and blind
Born 1880 Died 1968 aged 87

Helen Keller had a severe illness when she was a baby, which left her deaf and blind. As a result she could not make any recognizable sounds. Desperate to help her, Keller's parents employed 20-year-old Anne Sullivan, once blind herself, as her teacher. Patiently, Sullivan taught Keller the names of objects by pressing letters into her hand. She taught her to speak by letting her feel the vibrations in her own throat. Keller soon showed that she was an intelligent student. She learned to read and write fluently in Braille, and eventually studied for a university degree.

Keller tried to help as many people like herself as she could. Her own amazing success was a great inspiration, and she toured the world giving lectures. She wrote many books, including *The Story of My Life*, published in 1902. ◆

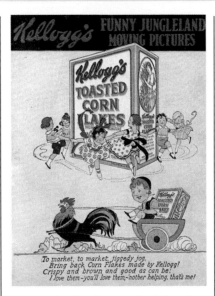

▲ *An early advertisement for Kellogg's cornflakes. Today Kellogg's is a thriving multi-million pound business.*

William **Kellogg**

American businessman and founder of the Kellogg Company
Born 1860 Died 1951 aged 91

William Kellogg worked with his brother John at a hospital in Battle Creek, Michigan. Because his brother was the director of the hospital, Will Kellogg was able to try out all sorts of cereal foods in an attempt to improve patients' diets. Toasted cornflakes proved to be so popular that Kellogg started to sell them to the general public, first of all by mail order. Although cornflakes were not entirely new, they had never before been sold as a breakfast food. The Kellogg Company was set up in 1906 to manufacture them and Kellogg advertised them energetically: they were a big success. Cornflakes dramatically changed American breakfast-eating habits and made Kellogg a fortune. In 1930 he started the W. K. Kellogg Foundation, a charity which gave large sums of money for social improvements. It particularly supported work to help children. ◆

Ned **Kelly**

Australian outlaw
Born 1855 Died 1880 aged 25

Ned Kelly's father was transported as a criminal from Ireland to Australia. From the age of 15 Kelly was also constantly in trouble. Between 1878 and 1880 he operated in the Kelly Gang with his brother and two others. They were famous for holding up and killing three policemen in 1878, and had a price of up to £2000 on each of their heads.

The police seemed powerless against them. Many were outraged by their crimes, but to others Ned Kelly became a hero. He claimed to be fighting for justice for the poor against the rich and powerful.

The final shoot-out with police came after an attempted train ambush. Kelly tried to escape in a suit of armour, but was shot in the legs. He was tried for murder and hanged in Melbourne jail. ◆

◄ *The home-made suit of armour worn by Ned Kelly.*

William **Kelvin**

British physicist
Born *1824* **Died** *1907 aged 83*

William Thomson Kelvin was born in Ireland but when he was six his family moved to Scotland. His father taught him and William proved to be a brilliant student. He went to Glasgow University at the age of ten and was writing important scientific papers when he was just 16. In 1892, after making many contributions to science and industry, he was made Baron Kelvin of Largs. (Largs is a Scottish town.)

Kelvin was a pioneer in the study of electromagnetism. He and Michael Faraday put forward the idea of an electromagnetic 'field'. Later James Clerk Maxwell used this suggestion in his famous theory on electromagnetism.

Kelvin was very practical and he invented several devices concerned with sending messages through wires. In 1866 Queen Victoria knighted him for designing a transatlantic telegraph cable.

Kelvin also did important work in the field of thermodynamics. Most importantly, he put forward the idea of absolute zero – the temperature at which all molecules and atoms stop moving. The scientific unit of temperature is named after him. ◆

see also

Faraday Joule Maxwell

John Fitzgerald **Kennedy**

President of the United States of America from 1961 to 1963
Born *1917* **Died** *1963 aged 46*

John Kennedy was one of nine children. His elder brother Joe

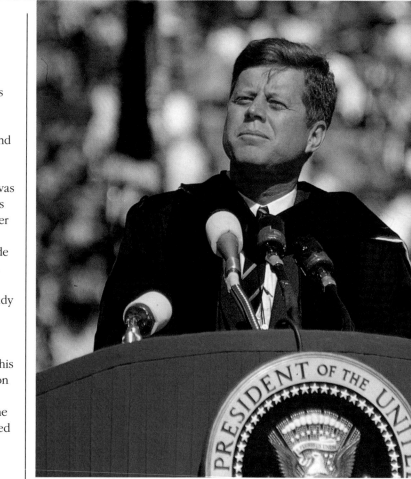

▲ *J. F. Kennedy was the youngest man to be elected as the president of America. He was also the youngest to die while in office.*

was killed in 1944. Kennedy's father had decided Joe would be president one day; John now took Joe's place.

The whole family helped Kennedy win his first election as a Democratic member of the House of Representatives in 1946. One opponent said, 'It's that family of his. They're all over the state.' He received the same support in 1952 when he became a senator from Massachusetts.

In 1960 he was elected president of America. Handsome and inspiring, in his first speech he said, 'My fellow Americans, ask not what your country can do for you, but what you can do for your country'.

Although he was energetic and intelligent, Kennedy soon faced problems. He gave American help to Cuban refugees trying to invade Communist Cuba. They failed, making America look foolish. Nevertheless, Kennedy did stop the USSR from building nuclear missile bases on Cuba in 1962. He also sent military advisers and troops to Vietnam, which led, after his death, to American involvement in the Vietnam War. At home, he proposed laws to give black Americans equal rights, but Congress did not pass these laws in his lifetime.

> *Mankind must put an end to war or war will put an end to mankind.*
>
> JOHN KENNEDY, 1961

In November 1963 Kennedy travelled to Dallas, Texas, to gather support in the American South. He was shot and killed by a sniper while travelling in an open car. The world mourned Kennedy not only for what he did, but for the good he could have done had he lived. ◆

see also
Khrushchev

Jomo **Kenyatta**

President of Kenya from 1964 to 1978
Born *c.1894*   **Died** *1978 aged about 84*

Kamau wa Ngengi was born into the Kikuyu tribe in Kenya. He was baptized Johnstone Kamau and educated by Scottish missionaries before getting a job in Nairobi. Jomo Kenyatta, as he became known, joined the Kikuyu Central Association and visited London on their behalf. He lived in Britain during the 1930s and studied anthropology.

Back in Kenya, Kenyatta became president of the Kenya African

▼ *Jomo Kenyatta, first president of the independent Republic of Kenya.*

Union in 1947. At this time many Kikuyu formed a secret group called 'Mau Mau' which used violence to drive white farmers from Kikuyu lands. Although he denied it, Kenyatta was suspected by the British rulers of Kenya of leading Mau Mau. In 1953 he was sentenced to seven years' hard labour. Although released from prison in 1959 he was kept under close watch until 1961. Then, when Kenya became independent of Britain in 1963, Kenyatta became the first prime minister. In the following year he was made the first president of the Republic of Kenya. His years in power brought some stability and prosperity to the country. ◆

Johannes **Kepler**

German astronomer
Born *1571*   **Died** *1630 aged 58*

Johannes Kepler was the son of a soldier. His early intention was to be a Lutheran Church minister and he studied theology at university. But it turned out that he had a flair for mathematics, and his interest in astronomy grew.

In 1594 he became a professor of mathematics at Graz, where he settled and married. Four years later the family was forced to flee because of religious persecution and he went to work for the Danish astronomer Tycho Brahe. When Brahe died in 1601, Kepler got his job. He also inherited a huge number of Brahe's astronomical observations.

Using Brahe's observations of Mars, Kepler proved that the planet's orbit around the Sun is an oval shape and not a circle. Later he worked out two more important laws about the orbits of the planets.

Kepler's whole life was afflicted by war, religious persecution, bad

▲ *Johannes Kepler discovered three important laws of planetary motion.*

luck, and ill health. Yet he is remembered as one of the greatest astronomers of his age. ◆

John Maynard **Keynes**

English economist
Born *1883*   **Died** *1946 aged 63*

John Maynard Keynes was a successful pupil at Eton school and at Cambridge University, where he went on to become a lecturer. During World Wars I and II (1914–1918 and 1939–1945) he was an adviser on economics to the government.

Economics is the science which studies trade, industry, employment, finance, and banking. Keynes believed in an economy planned by the government. He proposed that financial crises and unemployment could be prevented if the government intervened and took control of interest rates and public spending. Politicians and economists have argued about Keynesian economics ever since. Some say his ideas do not work; others say that they have never been properly tried. ◆

Imran **Khan**

Pakistani cricketer and politician
Born 1952

Imran Khan perfected his cricket at school in Lahore, Pakistan, and in Worcester, England, before going to Oxford University where he captained the cricket team in 1974. He then took up county cricket, playing for Worcestershire and for Sussex.

He made his test début for Pakistan in 1971 and became captain in 1982. He played for his country 88 times and is only the third player to score over 3000 test runs and take 300 test wickets.

After retiring from cricket in 1992, Imran Khan raised money to build a cancer hospital in Lahore, in memory of his mother, whom he saw slowly die of the disease. The hospital, which opened in 1994, was damaged by a bomb two years later, and since then Imran Kahn has been actively involved in his country's politics. ◆

▶ *Imran Khan captained Pakistan to victory in the World Cup in 1992.*

▲ *Ayatollah Khomeini (second from left) ruled Iran under strict and traditional Islamic religious principles.*

Jahangir **Khan**

Pakistani squash champion
Born 1963

The name 'Jahangir' means 'conqueror of the world', and that is exactly what Jahangir Khan became in the world of squash. He came from a family of squash players and at 15 won the World Amateur championship of 1979.

In 1981 he lost to the Australian Geoff Hunt in the final of the British Open championship. Astonishingly he did not lose another game until 1986, when he was beaten by Ross Norman of New Zealand in the world championship final. In the course of that remarkable run of victories, Khan become world squash champion five times in a row (1981–1985). He won the world championship again in 1988. ◆

Ayatollah Ruhollah **Khomeini**

Iranian religious leader
Born 1900   Died 1989 aged 89

Ayatollah Ruhollah Khomeini was born in Khomein, central Iran. He spent most of his life studying the Islamic faith and teaching at the holy city of Qum, where he was recognized as an 'Ayatollah' (guide sent from God). It was not until he was in his sixties that he became directly involved in the world of politics.

In the 1960s he spoke out against the shah (king) of Iran who was using Iran's oil-wealth to change the country's old way of life. Khomeini was against giving more freedom to women and taking land and education out of the hands of religious leaders. In 1964 he was forced to live abroad because of his opposition to the shah. However, the rapid changes in Iran made the shah so unpopular that in 1979 he fled abroad and Khomeini returned.

For the next ten years Khomeini was the most important person in Iran. He did not actually govern but little could be done without his approval. In the name of Islam, opponents of his rule were imprisoned, tortured, and executed.

> *Anybody wanting to banish theft from the world must cut off the thief's hands.*
>
> AYATOLLAH RUHOLLAH KHOMEINI

Iran was feared by neighbouring countries and the West as a supporter of terrorists. A war with Iraq was fought from 1980 to 1988 with great loss of life on both sides. When Khomeini died in 1989 there were scenes of wild grief in Iran. ◆

Nikita Khrushchev

Soviet leader who denounced Stalin
Born 1894   Died 1971 aged 77

Nikita Sergeyevich Khrushchev was a metal worker who joined the Communist Party in 1918. He became a party worker in Kiev and Moscow, where he became First Secretary in 1935. He became Secretary of the Ukraine region in 1938, but resigned during World War II to organize resistance in the Ukraine against German forces. When Stalin died in 1953 there was a power struggle amongst the Communist leaders. Khrushchev emerged as First Secretary of the Communist Party. In an historic speech at the Party Congress in 1956 he took the bold step of denouncing Stalin. People finally realized the bad things Stalin had done, and Khrushchev's power grew. In 1958 he became prime minister. Although he wanted peace with America he almost went to war with them over the Cuban missile crisis in 1962. Two years later he was replaced by Brezhnev and Kosygin who initially shared power. ◆

👁 **see also**
Kennedy Stalin

Khufu

Egyptian pharaoh; builder of the Great Pyramid
Lived during the 26th century BC

Khufu is best known as the builder of the Great Pyramid at Giza on the banks of the River Nile. The pyramid, together with others nearby, was one of the seven wonders of the ancient world.

The ancient Egyptians made elaborate preparations for the journey after death to the next world. The Great Pyramid was made mainly of locally quarried limestone. About 2,300,000 blocks weighing about two-and-a-half tons each were used to build the structure, which was originally 146 metres high. Building such a pyramid required great skill – the construction had to be carefully measured and the stones cut to fit accurately. Each of the pyramid's four sides was built at an angle of exactly 52 degrees. Today the Great Pyramid still dominates the skyline even though many of its outside blocks of stone have been rubbed away over time. ◆

▼ *The Great Pyramid, built on the order of the Egyptian king Khufu.*

Nicole Mary Kidman

Australian film star
Born 1967

As a teenager Nicole Kidman was tall and gawky. She thought that she was 'the ugliest person on Earth'. But she loved drama, and spent as much time as she could at the St Martin's Youth Theatre in Melbourne.

At 14, Nicole appeared in her first film, a TV movie called *Bush Christmas*. She made several more Australian films, and won praise or her role in the TV series *Vietnam*.

In 1989 Nicole was invited to play opposite Tom Cruise in the Hollywood movie *Days of Thunder*. During the filming Nicole and Tom fell in love, and they were married in 1990.

For the next few years Nicole was better known as 'Mrs Tom Cruise' than as a film actor. But in 1995 she had a great success with *Batman Forever* and as a ruthless killer in *To Die For*, and in 1996 with *Portrait of a Lady*. She was becoming a star in her own right.

In 1999 Nicole appeared on stage in London, in a play called *The Blue Room*. The play won a drama award, and moved to Broadway. In 2000 Nicole separated from her husband Tom Cruise. She also made the musical *Moulin Rouge*. The film came out in 2001, and was nominated for an Oscar. ◆

◀ B. B. King's albums include Blues is King (1967) and Lucille Talks Back (1975).

B. B. **King**

American blues guitarist and singer
Born 1925

Riley King was born to sing the blues: he grew up during the Great Depression, a poor black farm boy in the tough southern state of Mississippi. He was always musical, singing in church when he was four, and learning guitar as a teenager. He became known as 'Blues Boy', a nickname he later shortened to 'B. B.' King.

He started recording in 1949, and his distinctive guitar playing on such early classics as '3 O' Clock Blues', 'Please Love Me', and 'You Upset Me Baby' immediately revealed him to be a master musician. King has remained both popular and influential over the years, and together with his faithful guitar 'Lucille' he is one of the most familiar figures in blues music. ◆

Martin Luther **King** Jr

American civil rights leader
Born 1929   Died 1968 aged 39

At the age of 15 Martin Luther King Jr went to college on a special programme for gifted students. After gaining his degree in divinity in 1948, he trained to be a Baptist minister as his father and grandfather had been before him.

He became a pastor in Montgomery, Alabama, two years later, and joined the struggle for black people's rights straight away. He led a boycott of the buses in Montgomery because they had separate seats for blacks and whites. The blacks shared cars or walked until the bus company gave in and allowed all passengers to sit anywhere they chose.

This victory convinced King that the best way for black people to win their rights was to break laws in a non-violent way. In Atlanta and Birmingham, he led 'sit-ins' by blacks in 'whites only' eating places. In spite of being attacked, arrested, and imprisoned, King and his followers kept up their campaign. In August 1963, 200,000 people joined their march on Washington. At the end of this march, he gave his famous 'I have a dream' speech, which inspired millions of people throughout the world to campaign for civil rights. Here is an extract:

'I have a dream that one day this nation will rise up and live out the true meaning of its creed: "We hold these truths to be self-evident; that all men are created equal." I have a dream that one day on the red hills of Georgia the sons of former slaves and the sons of former slave-owners will be able to sit down together at the table of brotherhood. I have a dream that my four little children will one day live in a nation where they will not be judged by the colour of their skin but by the content of their character.'

▼ *Martin Luther King Jr waves to the crowd during the civil rights march in Washington in 1963.*

The next year the Civil Rights Bill was made law and King was given the Nobel Peace Prize. However, other black leaders opposed him because they believed that blacks should fight violence with violence.

In 1968 he was killed by a sniper in Memphis, Tennessee. Only the night before his death, King said: 'I may not get to the promised land with you, but I want you to know tonight that we as a people will.' ◆

see also
Malcolm X

William Lyon Mackenzie **King**

Prime minister of Canada from 1921 to 1930 and from 1935 to 1948
Born *1874* **Died** *1950 aged 75*

William Lyon Mackenzie King was named after his grandfather, William Lyon Mackenzie, who had been the first mayor of Toronto. He had led a rebellion in 1837 demanding a better deal for the hard-working pioneer farmers. King wanted to help ordinary people too.

He began his career in politics in 1900, and as minister of labour drafted a law to help people settle strikes. He became leader of the Liberal Party in 1919 and was elected prime minister in 1921. King's government introduced Canada's first old-age pension and developed a foreign policy independent of Great Britain.

The problems caused by the world economic crisis in 1929 led to King's government losing the 1930 election to the Conservatives. However, he returned to power in 1935 and led his nation through the war years 1939–1945. After the war his government provided free training for returning soldiers. It also introduced family allowances and unemployment insurance to protect people from hardship. ◆

Mary **Kingsley**

English explorer and traveller in Africa
Born *1862* **Died** *1900 aged 37*

Mary Kingsley's father was a doctor who spent most of his time travelling abroad. Her mother was constantly ill and Mary looked after her and her little brother. She was never given any schooling, but she learned to read and taught herself Latin, physics, chemistry, mathematics, and engineering from her father's library. From his letters and books she learned about warm countries beyond England with strange plants and animals.

Her parents died when she was 30 and she was left poor and alone. However, she was determined to visit the places she had read about.

During 1893 and 1894 she travelled in West Africa to collect specimens of fish for the Natural History Museum in London, and to gather information about African religions. She explored the forests north of the River Zaïre (Congo) on foot and by paddling in a dugout canoe. She became very interested in the lives of the African people.

She wrote two successful books and became a popular lecturer. In 1900 she went to South Africa to nurse the soldiers in the Boer War. She died there of fever. ◆

▶ Mary Kingsley was one of the most famous travellers in Africa during the 19th century. Through her journeys and her encounters with the local population, she challenged the accepted view of the 'primitive' native.

Rudyard **Kipling**

Indian-born English author
Born *1865*   **Died** *1936 aged 70*

When Rudyard Kipling was only six years old he was sent by his British parents from their home in India back to England. There he spent five miserable years staying with a foster-mother he hated. However, he became much happier when he went to boarding school, and was quickly noticed as a budding young writer.

At 16 he returned to India and began writing short stories and poems describing the lives of the British and Indian people. In 1894 he wrote *The Jungle Book*, which includes stories about an Indian child, Mowgli, brought up by a family of wolves.

Kipling next wrote the *Just So Stories*: a series of fables describing how the leopard got its spots, the camel its hump, and many others. His finest novel, *Kim*, about an orphan boy of the same name, appeared in 1901. Kipling was the first English writer to win the Nobel Prize for Literature (in 1907). ◆

▲ *An illustration by Kipling for one of his* Just So Stories, *'How the Elephant Got His Trunk'.*

Horatio **Kitchener**

British soldier
Born *1850*   **Died** *1916 aged 65*

Horatio Kitchener was born in south-west Ireland. He decided to become a soldier and joined the British army in 1871. Before long he was promoted to senior posts. From 1892 to 1899 he was commander-in-chief in Egypt, and defeated Sudanese Muslims at the famous battle of Omdurman (1898). From 1900 to 1902 he led the British army in the Boer War, and defeated the Afrikaner people of South Africa. He served in India as commander-in-chief (1902–1909) and in Egypt (1911–1914).

In 1914 war broke out in Europe. Germany and Austria-Hungary stood on one side; France, Russia, and Britain on the other. Britain's prime minister, Herbert Asquith, made Kitchener secretary of state for war. Kitchener feared that the war would be long and gruelling and Britain would need a bigger army. He modernized the British forces and soon recruited a million men. In summer 1916 he sailed for Russia, but his ship hit a mine and sank. Kitchener drowned. ◆

▲ *Kitchener calls for volunteers on a World War I army recruiting poster.*

Paul **Klee**

Swiss painter
Born *1879*   **Died** *1940 aged 60*

Paul Klee is one of the best-loved artists of the 20th century. He produced a huge amount of work (oils, water-colours, drawings, prints), but he had an astonishingly vivid imagination and never repeated himself. Some of his paintings are purely abstract, but most of them are based on the things that he saw around him. They are full of radiant colours and a joyous love of life.

Klee spent most of his career in Germany, where he was much admired as a teacher of art as well as for his work as a painter. When

Hitler came to power in 1933, however, he opposed all modern art and Klee was forced to give up his teaching post in Dusseldorf and return to Switzerland. In the last five years of his life he suffered from a painful illness and was depressed by political events as Europe headed for war. He continued to paint superb pictures, but in them a grim humour often replaced the playful wit of his earlier work. ◆

John **Knox**

Scottish religious reformer who set up the Protestant Church of Scotland
Born 1505   **Died** 1572 aged 67

John Knox was a devout Protestant as a young man when Scotland was still a Catholic country, ruled with French help. He went to England, and became a chaplain to Edward VI, but when Catholic Mary I came to the throne he and many other Protestants had to escape. He spent most of his exile in Geneva, Switzerland, where he was influenced by John Calvin.

In 1559 he returned to Scotland, determined to set up a Protestant Kirk (Church) like Calvin's at Geneva. His fiery preaching helped to begin a rebellion, which forced out the Catholics. He drew up the 'Scottish Confession', a statement of Protestant beliefs. No one was supposed to go to Catholic services, nor obey the pope.

Although the Catholic Mary Queen of Scots arrived in Scotland in 1561, the Protestant Kirk grew stronger. Knox made things very

The First Blast of the Trumpet Against the Monstrous Regiment of Women.
                        JOHN KNOX
Title of one of his pamphlets

difficult for Mary and she lost her throne in 1567, partly because of him. His preaching and writing played an important part in the formation of the Protestant Church in Scotland. Protestants there who followed him were afterwards called Presbyterians. ◆

see also
Calvin   Mary I   Mary, Queen of Scots

Robert **Koch**

German bacteriologist
Born 1843   **Died** 1910 aged 66

Robert Koch studied medicine at the University of Göttingen in Germany. His teacher there believed that diseases were caused by microscopic organisms. Koch spent his life identifying these organisms and applying his knowledge to the world's most deadly diseases. He and his assistants devised a method of growing bacteria outside the body so that the bacteria can then be studied.

Koch started work on the animal disease, anthrax. He studied the life cycle of the tiny bacteria that cause anthrax and also found the tiny spores which infect the land where animals graze.

Koch then studied tuberculosis (TB). Today TB can be prevented by inoculation but it used to be a deadly killer causing thousands of deaths each year. The bacteria responsible are extremely small but Koch used his superb practical skills to identify and grow them. This work enabled others to develop a vaccine against the disease.

Koch spent the rest of his life studying other diseases such as cholera, bubonic plague, and malaria. He was awarded the Nobel Prize for Medicine in 1905. ◆

see also
Jenner   Pasteur

▼ *Koch was also a teacher, and many of his students became great scientists.*

Helmut **Kohl**

German chancellor from 1982 to 1998
Born 1930

Helmut Kohl became an active member of the German Christian Democratic Union (CDU Party) in 1947, and in 1959 he was elected to the local parliament in West Germany. In 1973 he became the CDU Party's national chairman, and in 1982 chancellor (prime minister) of West Germany.

Kohl is a passionate believer in international co-operation. He made strong links with the USA, and strengthened the ties between West Germany and the rest of the European Community (now the European Union, or EU). After World War II Germany was split into two parts, and Berlin was divided by a huge wall. When the Berlin Wall fell in 1989, Kohl was instrumental in bringing East and West Germany together. When they merged in 1990 to become the Federal Republic of Germany, Kohl became chancellor. He was re-elected for the last time in 1994. ◆

Paul **Kruger**

President of the first South African Republic from 1883 to 1904
Born 1825   Died 1904 aged 78

Paul Kruger's parents were Boer farmers in southern Africa. The Boers were the descendants of Dutch settlers who did not like the power that the British had in southern Africa. In 1835 Kruger's family, along with many other Boers, travelled north to form their own independent country. They settled in territory they called the Transvaal.

In 1877 Britain decided that the Transvaal should also come under its rule. Kruger, by this time a respected politician, led the opposition to this and became a general in a rebel army against British troops. In 1883 the Transvaal regained its independence from Britain and Kruger was elected as its first president. He was re-elected three times.

However, more trouble was to come. When gold was first discovered, prospectors from all over the world rushed out to South Africa. The new settlers were not

▲ *A sketch of Paul Kruger from a 1900 edition of the magazine* Vanity Fair.

popular with the Boers, and Kruger did his best to exclude them from the Transvaal, banning them from full citizenship until they had been in the country for at least seven years. The British government objected to this, and the second Boer War followed. After the Boers were defeated, Kruger went to Europe and eventually died in Switzerland. ◆

Alfred **Krupp**

German industrialist
Born 1812   Died 1887 aged 75

As a young man Alfred Krupp inherited a share in a nearly bankrupt steel works in Essen from his father Friedrich. Gradually he restored the business, bought out his co-heirs, and founded one of the world's great industrial dynasties. His steel was in huge demand for railways, steamships, and later for armaments.

In 1862 he introduced the Bessemer steel-making process from Britain and secured control of German coal and Spanish iron-ore supplies. He was a stern employer but noted for his concern for his employees. He was succeeded by his son Friedrich (1854–1902) and later his daughter Bertha (1886–1957). In World Wars I and II the Krupp firm supplied vast quantities of arms to the German government. Krupp's grandson Alfred was imprisoned by the Allies for war crimes, but soon released: once again the House of Krupp flourished, but this time as a public corporation. ◆

👁 **see also**

Bessemer

Kublai Khan

Mongolian general and ruler
Born 1215   Died 1294 aged 79

Kublai Khan was a grandson of Genghis Khan, one of the most terrifying soldiers in history, who had begun life as an obscure chief of a wandering tribe and ended it as ruler of a huge empire in central Asia. When Kublai was ten years old, he fought on horseback in his grandfather's last campaign.

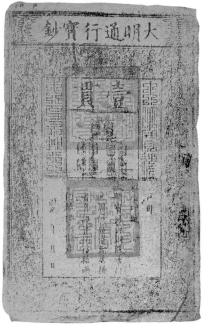

▲ *One of the first banknotes issued by the Mongolian ruler Kublai Khan.*

When Kublai grew up and became leader (Great Khan) of the Mongols he completed his grandfather's conquest of China and established his capital at Khanbalik (now Beijing). Kublai added Korea and Burma to his Yuan (Mongol) empire, which now stretched from the Black Sea to the China Sea. His rule was reported to be harsh and he enforced obedience. He appointed many foreigners, including the Venetian explorer Marco Polo, to work for him. It is through Polo's praise of the wonderful riches that he found in the East that the name of Kublai Khan became known in Europe. ◆

👁 **see also**

Genghis Khan   Marco Polo

▶ *A character from Kurosawa's 1954 western-style masterpiece,* Seven Samurai.

Akira **Kurosawa**

Japanese film director
Born 1910   Died 1998 aged 88

After the tragedy of the great Kanto earthquake of 1923, Japanese audiences were ready for light entertainment, and Akira Kurosawa remembered the imported films that he saw in the following year. They helped shape the style of his films when he became a director.

Sanshiro Sugata, his first film, was criticized by the army in 1943 for being too foreign. After the war, *They Who Tread on the Tiger's Tail* was banned by the American authorities because it was thought to be 'anti-democratic'. Many of his films tell dramatic stories from violent periods in Japanese history; some of them have been called 'eastern westerns'. Kurosawa was awarded a special Oscar in March 1990 for his unique contribution to cinema. ◆

Marquis de **Lafayette**

French soldier, revolutionary, and politician
Born 1757   Died 1834 aged 77

The Marquis de Lafayette was as famous in America as he was in his native France. He became a popular American hero when he joined the French, who were fighting alongside American colonists against the British in the American Revolution (War of Independence). He was at the battle of Brandywine and at the final conflict at Yorktown in 1781. Several American towns were even named after him, including ones in Louisiana, in Alabama, and in Indiana.

During the French Revolution, which began on 14 July 1789, the people formed a National Assembly to rule the country. Their slogan was 'liberty, equality, fraternity'. Lafayette became the vice-president of the National Assembly and introduced a declaration of citizens' rights similar to the American Declaration of Independence.

Hated by king and court, Lafayette was forced to flee his country in 1792. He returned later and played a leading part in the revolution of 1830. ◆

Lao Tzu

Chinese thinker
Lived during the
6th century BC

▲ *The Chinese philosopher Lao Tzu is commonly regarded as the founder of Taoism.*

Chinese scholars traditionally held Lao Tzu to be the author of *Tao Te Ching* (The Book of Changes), which sets out the basic ideas of the Taoist religion. However, it is now thought that *Tao Te Ching* dates from the 3rd century BC, while western scholars believe Lao Tzu may have lived in the 6th century BC and that the book was written by several authors. At least 350 other books have tried to explain its teachings.

Taoists believe that all things are connected and the aim of life is peace and harmony. Taoism tells people to trust their senses and instincts rather than reason and official laws as Confucius taught. Under the T'ang dynasty (618–907)

A journey of a thousand miles must begin with a single step.

LAO TZU

Lao Tzu was worshipped as an ancestor of the emperors. Even after Taoism lost official favour it remained popular with ordinary people and was a great influence on Chinese art. There are still 2000 Taoist temples in Taiwan. ◆

see also

Confucius

Pierre Laplace

French mathematician and astronomer
Born 1749
Died 1827 aged 77

Pierre Simon Laplace came from a poor farming family but showed such intelligence that neighbours paid for his school education. By the age of 18 he had been appointed professor of mathematics at the Paris Military School. His success led to him becoming a Count of the Napoleonic Empire and a Marquis.

His work as an astronomer is reckoned by scientists to be second only to Isaac Newton's. Laplace proved the stability of the Solar System (showing that no two planets could collide), studied the orbit of the Moon, and worked on the shape and rotation of Saturn's rings. He also introduced the nebular hypothesis of the origin of the Solar System: the theory that the Solar System originated from a cloud of gas. He wrote a

number of very important and influential books yet, at the end of his long life, he said 'What we know is minute; what we are ignorant of is vast'. ◆

see also

Newton

René **La Salle**

French explorer
Born 1643   Died 1687 aged 44

René La Salle was born into a wealthy family in Rouen, France. As a young man he went to 'New France' – the French colonies in Canada. There he began to explore, with a view to seeking new land for the French settlers.

His biggest achievement was to travel the length of the Ohio and Mississippi rivers to the Gulf of Mexico, claiming the lower valley of the Mississippi for France in 1682 and calling it 'Louisiana' after the French king, Louis XIV.

La Salle's last expedition was by sea, with a fleet of ships, to the Gulf of Mexico. He wanted to see if a colony could be set up at the mouth of the Mississippi. However, the fleet got lost, and after two years searching for the Mississippi delta, La Salle's men mutinied and killed him. ◆

Laurel and **Hardy**

English and American comic actors
Stanley Laurel
Born 1890   Died 1965 aged 75
Oliver Hardy
Born 1892   Died 1957 aged 65

Stanley Laurel, whose real name was Arthur Stanley Jefferson, was an English comedian who played in pantomimes before travelling to America. He started appearing in films there in 1917. Oliver Norvell Hardy came from Georgia, America, where he first appeared on stage at the age of eight. He started acting in films in

▼ *Laurel and Hardy, one of the most successful comedy partnerships.*

1914. Both appeared in dozens of silent films before they began their successful partnership in the 1927 silent comedy *Putting Pants on Philip*.

In the next 30 years they made over 100 silent and talking pictures, and achieved great success with films such as *Sons of the Desert* (1934), *Way Out West* (1937), and *Blockheads* (1938). Their humour came from the contrast between the small, thin, confused Laurel and the big, fat, irritable Hardy. ◆

Rod **Laver**

Australian tennis player
Born 1938

At 13, Rod Laver was selected for a tennis coaching course by a Brisbane newspaper. As a left-handed player, called 'the Rockhampton rocket' after his home town, he became good enough to win the Australian Amateur championship in 1960. Two years later he did the 'Grand Slam', winning the Australian, French, US, and Wimbledon championships in the same year.

He then turned professional, and was barred from these championships until they became 'open championships' (for both amateur and professional players) in the late 1960s. In 1969 Laver won the Grand Slam once again. ◆

Antoine **Lavoisier**

French chemist who became known as the 'father of modern chemistry'
Born 1743   Died 1794 aged 50

As a young man Antoine Lavoisier became interested in improving street lighting and studied how different fuels burnt in

▲ *This is the apparatus used by Lavoisier to investigate burning. The substances to be burned were placed in the furnace (left). The change in water level in the bell jar (right) showed how much air was used up during the burning.*

lamps. Burning became a subject that interested him and his careful experiments of burning substances in air, and those of the English chemist Joseph Priestley, made Lavoisier realize that air contains two gases; he called one 'oxygen' and the other 'azote', which we now know as nitrogen. He proved that when a substance is burnt it combines with oxygen in the air. This really moved chemistry into the modern age. Lavoisier went on to give chemicals many of the names we now use and arranged them into family groups.

Lavoisier came from a wealthy family and invested his money in a business called tax-farming. The tax-farmers were paid by the government to collect all the taxes. Their profits provided Lavoisier, and other investors, with a great deal of money. But many of the people were poor and hated tax-farmers. During the French Revolution they rebelled, and by 1794 France was ruled by people who hated the king, the aristocracy, and tax-farmers. Lavoisier was found guilty of being a tax-farmer and was executed by the guillotine. ◆

◉ **see also**
Priestley

D. H. **Lawrence**

English novelist
Born 1885 Died 1930 aged 44

David Herbert Lawrence was the son of a coal-miner and a schoolteacher. He went to Nottingham University and trained as a teacher. By this time he had started writing, and in 1913 produced his greatest novel, *Sons and Lovers*. This describes his childhood and the strong relationships he had both with his mother and with friends. In other novels, such as *The Rainbow* (1915), Lawrence describes his characters' most secret feelings.

Later on, Lawrence felt that British industrial society was too cut off from nature and genuine feelings. With his wife, Frieda, he travelled extensively in search of the ideal surroundings for his restless spirit. His poor health gradually got worse, and he finally died in France of tuberculosis. ◆

T. E. **Lawrence**

English hero who helped in the Arabs' struggle for independence; also known as Lawrence of Arabia
Born 1888 Died 1935 aged 46

As a young man, Thomas Edward Lawrence enjoyed exploring castles and following the routes of the crusaders in Palestine. He learnt Arabic and travelled around North Africa.

In 1914 Lawrence went to Cairo as a British intelligence officer to help Arab troops to free their country from Turkish rule. Lawrence led dashing camel-back raids to dynamite railway lines. The Turks offered a high price to anyone who could capture 'al-Urans, destroyer of engines'. In 1917 he was captured and tortured. After the Turks were defeated, Lawrence became a hero. But he refused all honours and retired to write *The Seven Pillars of Wisdom*, which describes his experiences in the Arabs' struggle. Lawrence was bitterly disappointed when Britain and France did not give the Arabs complete independence.

Lawrence died in 1935 when he swerved on his motorbike to avoid two boys on a country road. ◆

▼ *T. E. Lawrence photographed in the traditional Arab clothing that he often wore.*

Leakey family

British archaeologists who discovered fossil humans in East Africa
Louis Leakey **Born 1903**
Died 1972 aged 69
Mary Leakey **Born 1913**
Died 1996 aged 83
Richard Leakey **Born 1944**

Louis Leakey is best remembered for his archaeological work in East Africa, where he made his first discoveries between 1925 and 1936.

Louis and his wife Mary concentrated their explorations for fossils in the Olduvai Gorge in Tanzania. In 1959 Mary discovered a skull of a large 'southern ape', *Zinjanthropus* (later called *Australopithecus*) *boisei*, which dated back about 1.7 million years. The Leakeys also discovered the remains of *Homo habilis*, at that time the earliest human known, and *Homo erectus*, the maker of many beautiful implements found throughout Africa.

After Louis' death, Mary continued at Olduvai Gorge, uncovering living places and implements of East Africa's earliest inhabitants. Then, at Laetoli, in Tanzania, she discovered the footprints of our ape-like ancestors who lived more than 3.5 million years ago.

Their son Richard Leakey has made important discoveries of human fossils at many places in East Africa and Ethiopia. In 1984 he discovered an almost complete *Homo erectus* skeleton at Lake Turkana in Kenya. His first love, though, is wildlife, and he is now in charge of Kenya's game parks. ◆

Edward **Lear**

English poet who wrote limerick verse
Born *1812*   **Died** *1888 aged 75*

Edward Lear was the 20th child of a wealthy stockbroker and his wife. But when he was 13 his father lost all his money and went to prison, and the children had to find work.

At 19, Edward produced a book of drawings of the parrots at London Zoo, and the Earl of Derby invited him to his estate to draw his animals too. While he was there, Edward made up limericks and illustrated them for the earl's grandchildren. He published them in *A Book of Nonsense* in 1846, and they were an immediate success.

He spent most of his life travelling, painting, and writing 'nonsense' verse. In these verses nutcrackers, chairs, birds, and creatures like the Dong with the Luminous Nose, the Pobble, and the Jumblies were given human feelings and characters. Lear invented words such as the 'runcible' spoon and the 'scroobious' bird. ◆

Le Corbusier

European architect
Born *1887*   **Died** *1965 aged 77*

Le Corbusier – the name adopted by Charles-Edouard Jeanneret – was born in Switzerland. He became famous for his campaign to construct new types of buildings. He thought that houses should be on columns, to free the ground underneath, with flat roofs for terraces and gardens. In flats with limited space, Le Corbusier mixed large, open-plan, sometimes split-level rooms, with much smaller rooms for sleeping.

Le Corbusier believed that modern towns could offer decent living conditions to large populations. In 1925 he designed a workers' city of 40 houses in France. However, local people were suspicious of his designs, and he had more success planning individual houses. Then in 1947 he was given another opportunity and designed a large housing complex for 1800 people in Marseille. The plan for this *Unité d'Habitation* included a school, a hotel and, on the roof, a nursery, open-air theatre, and gymnasium.

Although he had many fresh modern ideas for housing, some people still preferred more traditional ideas – an argument that continues to this day. ◆

Robert E. **Lee**

Commander of the Confederate troops during the American Civil War
Born *1807*   **Died** *1870 aged 63*

Robert Edward Lee studied at the US Military Academy at West Point, before becoming an

▲ *This picture shows the Battle of Winchester (September 1864) during the American Civil War of 1861–1865. After winning several battles between 1862 and 1863, Lee's Confederate army of the South finally surrendered in 1865.*

army officer. In the war between America and Mexico (1846–1848), his bravery made him famous.

Many years later, when the Civil War broke out, Lee decided to return to Virginia where he was born. In April 1861 he resigned from the US army and trained the Confederate army of the South. They won several major victories but were poorly equipped; they did not have enough guns and had little food.

At the battle of Gettysburg in 1863 Lee's forces were outnumbered and defeated. For the next year and a half he was forced back on the defensive until his ragged and hungry army surrendered at Appomattox Courthouse in April 1865.

Lee spent the last five years of his life as president of Washington College in Virginia. ◆

 see also
Grant   Lincoln

Lee Kuan Yew

Prime minister of Singapore from 1959 to 1990
Born *1923*

After studying law at Cambridge University, England, Lee Kuan Yew founded the People's Action Party in Singapore in 1954. He became the first prime minister of independent Singapore in 1959 and helped to make the country one of the most prosperous in Asia, with excellent public housing, transport, health, and education services. He insisted on discipline and order, imposing strict laws against litter, long hair, and chewing-gum. Impatient of criticism, he was quite prepared to lock up awkward journalists, strikers, and political opponents and to ban satellite television because, unlike the local news media, he could not control it. Lee gave up office in 1990 but remained powerful behind the scenes. ◆

Anton van Leeuwenhoek

Dutch pioneer of the microscope
Born *1632*   **Died** *1723 aged 90*

Anton van Leeuwenhoek worked in a fabric shop in Amsterdam. When he was 22 he went home to Delft, opened his own shop, and stayed there for 70 years.

He was always interested in scientific things and made a simple microscope with just one lens. Until that time, people had treated the microscope more like a toy than a useful scientific instrument. Leeuwenhoek used his microscope to study the fibres of the fabrics he worked with and then began to look at leaves and flowers, and

▲ *A portrait of Anton van Leeuwenhoek from 1695.*

small creatures such as bees and lice. He also studied blood, skin, and hair. He was the first person to describe blood cells and to see that blood flowed in tiny veins known as capillaries. ◆

👁 **see also**
Hooke

Gottfried Leibniz

German philosopher, mathematician, and physicist
Born *1646*   **Died** *1716 aged 70*

Leibniz was one of the greatest thinkers of the 17th century. He tackled philosophical questions and was devoted to the cause of world peace. He was a scientist, too, and met Huygens and Boyle among others, and suggested new ideas about force, time, and energy.

> *Two things are identical if one can be substituted for the other without affecting the truth.*
> GOTTFRIED LEIBNIZ, 1704

His greatest achievement was the discovery of a new mathematical method called calculus. Scientists use this to deal with quantities that are constantly varying. Newton had developed a similar method for his work on gravity and so there was a bitter row about who had been first. Newton had started work on it in 1665 but Leibniz published his results in 1684, three years before Newton. In fact, they probably discovered the method simultaneously. ◆

👁 **see also**
Boyle   Huygens   Newton

George Lemaitre

Belgian astronomer
Born *1894*   **Died** *1966 aged 72*

George Lemaitre was born in Charleroi, Belgium and studied to be an engineer. After being a soldier in World War I his interest changed to science.

During the 1920s, astronomers noticed that the universe seemed to be spreading out in all directions and this puzzled them. Lemaitre suggested that everything in the universe was once squashed together like a snowball. This exploded, blowing everything apart, like bits flying away from a snowball when it hits a wall. Although this happened a long time ago, the parts of the universe – the galaxies and stars we see today – are still moving apart, long after the 'big bang'. Today, many astronomers agree with Lemaitre's 'big bang' theory of the universe. ◆

👁 **see also**
Hubble

198

Vladimir **Lenin**

*Communist ruler of the new USSR
from 1917 to 1924*
Born *1870*   **Died** *1924 aged 53*

When Lenin was 17, his elder brother was hanged for trying to kill the Russian tsar. This opened Lenin's eyes to the problems of his country: a weak tsar, a corrupt Church and nobility, and millions of poor and angry peasants and factory workers. Like many people, Lenin saw revolution and the Communist ideas of Karl Marx as the only solution.

Within a few months of going to university in 1887 to study law, he was expelled for taking part in a student protest meeting. After getting his degree in 1891, he continued his political activity, and was sent first to prison and then into exile in Siberia. While he was in Siberia he took the name 'Lenin', from the River Lena.

In 1898 the Russian Social-Democratic Workers' Party was formed. In an effort to gain power, Lenin helped to split the party in 1903, leading the Bolsheviks ('Majority') against the Mensheviks ('Minority'). The Bolsheviks later became known as the Russian Communist Party.

From 1905 until 1917, Lenin lived in exile. He returned to Russia when the tsar was overthrown and a new government began to rule. Lenin called for a revolution to put a Bolshevik government into power and this revolution led to him becoming the real ruler of Russia. In 1922 the old Russian empire was transformed into the Union of Soviet Socialist Republics (USSR). It lasted until 1991. Lenin's embalmed body is kept in a mausoleum in Red Square, Moscow. ◆

see also

Gorbachev Marx Stalin Yeltsin

Suzanne **Lenglen**

French champion lawn tennis player
Born *1899*   **Died** *1938 aged 39*

Suzanne Lenglen came from a poor family, but her parents backed her ambition to succeed as a tennis player. She won her first big championship aged 15 and her first Wimbledon title in 1919.

▲ *On the 100th anniversary of his birth, a third of the people of the world were living in countries run by Communist governments inspired by Lenin's first successful Communist revolution.*

After that, she lost only one match until 1926. In seven years, Lenglen captured six Wimbledon singles and doubles titles as well as the Olympic championship in 1921. She became a professional player in 1926, which meant she could no longer compete in amateur tennis tournaments such as Wimbledon and the Olympics.

Most all-time rankings of women tennis players place Suzanne Lenglen first. Her success made women's tennis a popular and important sport. ◆

◀ *Suzanne Lenglen in action during the 1922 Wimbledon championships.*

Lennon and McCartney

English songwriters and musicians
John Lennon
Born *1940*   **Died** *1980 aged 40*
Paul McCartney
Born *1942*

When they met in 1957, John Winston Lennon and James Paul McCartney were just two Liverpool teenagers with a passion for rock 'n' roll. Lennon was wild and rebellious while McCartney was more studious, but this unlikely partnership was to revolutionize popular music in the 1960s.

They were the principal songwriters in the Beatles, and the incredible success of their songs kept the group at the top of the charts for seven years. These songs ranged from catchy pop to psychedelic rock, and included such all-time favourites as 'She Loves You' (1963), 'Yesterday' (1965), 'Yellow Submarine' (1966), and the classic album *Sgt. Pepper's Lonely Hearts Club Band* (1967).

Lennon and McCartney started recording separately in 1970 when the Beatles split up. Neither was as consistent on his own, although McCartney in particular has enjoyed some enormous solo hits. Lennon's peace anthem 'Imagine' (1971) has become a much-loved classic and was widely played at the time of his murder in 1980. ◆

▼ *McCartney and Lennon singing together in the incredibly successful group, the Beatles.*

▲ *The mysterious half-smile of Leonardo da Vinci's* Mona Lisa *still fascinates visitors at the Louvre Museum, Paris.*

Leonardo da Vinci

Italian artist, scientist, and inventor
Born *1452*   **Died** *1519 aged 67*

The young Leonardo da Vinci was described as handsome, strong, and charming, a talented musician and an excellent conversationalist. At 15 he was apprenticed to a leading Italian artist who taught him painting, sculpture, metal casting, mosaics, jewellery, and costume design. At 20 he was a master painter but considered himself to be as much an engineer as an artist.

He began many grand paintings but actually finished very few. Although his artistic output was small he brilliantly solved the problem of how to make faces and people look three-dimensional on a flat surface by shading light into dark. His painting *Mona Lisa* is probably the most famous portrait in the world. Another of his great masterpieces is a wall painting of *The Last Supper*.

Leonardo wanted to understand and know about everything he saw. He was one of the first to dissect human bodies and understand how muscles and bones work, and how a baby grows in the womb.

He examined all of nature: how plants and trees grow, how rocks are formed, and what laws govern the wind and oceans. He even suggested that the Sun stood still, and did not move around the Earth as most people believed. He also planned buildings, and worked out how to divert a river and how to construct canals. He invented weapons and acted as military adviser to the Duke of Milan. His skills also included arranging festivals and grand theatricals and inventing amusing mechanical toys.

Although Leonardo was both greatly admired and highly respected he was not really understood. His scientific work was far ahead of that of his contemporaries, including a flying machine nearly 400 years before the first powered aircraft, and most of his ideas remained in his notebooks undeveloped. It is amazing that one man could have created so much. ◆

Ferdinand de **Lesseps**

French engineer and diplomat
Born 1805   Died 1894 aged 89

Between the ages of 21 and 44, Ferdinand de Lesseps worked as a diplomat in several countries. During his late twenties he worked in Egypt. While working there, he had the idea for the Suez Canal. It would connect the Mediterranean Sea to the Red Sea through Egypt. At that time, ships sailing between Europe and Asia had to pass round Africa – a very long route.

Work began in 1860, thanks to Lesseps's enthusiasm and planning (and despite British opposition at first). Progress was expensive and slow, but in 1869 the canal was opened. Lesseps became a national hero in France, and was honoured in Britain.

His next project was the Panama Canal, begun in 1881, linking the Pacific and Atlantic oceans. It was dogged by technical and financial problems, and in 1893 Lesseps was found guilty of bribery. By then, however, he was very ill, and he died shortly afterwards. ◆

👁 **see also**
Eiffel

Carl **Lewis**

American athlete
Born 1961

Carl Lewis comes from a sporting family. His father is a sports teacher, his mother and sister are international athletes, and his brother is a soccer player. Lewis's own career is one of the most successful ever in athletics history. Not only has he had the longest run of long jump victories ever, but he has also been the world's best sprinter.

In 1983 he had three wins at the Helsinki world championships. Then, at the 1984 Olympics, he equalled Jesse Owens's record of four gold medals, triumphing in the 100 m, 200 m, long jump, and 4 × 100 m relay. He retained his gold medals for 100 m and the long jump at the 1988 Seoul Olympics. ◆

C. S. **Lewis**

English author
Born 1898   Died 1963 aged 64

After a lonely childhood, partly spent playing imaginative games with his older brother, Clive Staples Lewis became an outstanding scholar who taught at both Oxford and Cambridge universities. He wrote academic books and science fiction for adults and then decided to write books and stories for children too.

The Lion, the Witch and the Wardrobe was the first of a series of seven stories which describe the activities of a family of children who stray into the fairyland world of Narnia. In each story they are faced by a choice between good and evil. The adventures are so exciting that many young readers miss the fact that Lewis is using the stories as an allegory to preach a Christian message. His great hero, Aslan the lion, is a symbol for Jesus Christ. ◆

◀ *Olympic gold-medal winner Carl Lewis.*

◀ *A painting of Lewis and Clark on the Columbia River during their expedition to the Louisiana Purchase territory (1804–1806).*

Lewis and Clark

Leaders of the first expedition to cross the American continent
Meriwether Lewis
Born *1774*   **Died** *1809 aged 35*
William Clark
Born *1770*   **Died** *1838 aged 68*

In 1803 the US government bought from France a large piece of land in North America called 'The Louisiana Purchase'. President Thomas Jefferson decided to send an expedition to explore it and to cross the Rockies to reach the Pacific Ocean.

Jefferson chose Meriwether Lewis to lead the expedition, and he then chose William Clark, an expert on Native American Indians, to go with him. With about 40 other men, mostly soldiers, they started out in 1804 from St Louis, in boats and canoes up the Missouri river.

Eventually, they left the river and climbed a pass through the Rocky Mountains. They had many adventures, including close encounters with grizzly bears, which no white man had seen in America before. In November 1805 they reached the Pacific Ocean. After the winter they returned by roughly the same route.

The explorers brought back a lot of information about the land, the Native American Indian population, and the plants and animals. The expedition's many journals and maps were studied for years afterwards. ◆

◉ **see also**
Jefferson

Abraham Lincoln

American president from 1861 to 1865
Born *1809*   **Died** *1865 aged 56*

As a child, Abraham Lincoln hardly ever went to school, but he loved reading. Books were scarce and expensive then; he read the Bible and *Aesop's Fables* over and over again.

Lincoln tried various jobs before becoming a lawyer, a politician, and eventually a candidate for the presidency of the United States. During his campaign to be elected president, one of his main concerns was the split between Americans who thought slavery was wrong, and those who thought it was right. In a speech in 1858, he said 'I believe this government cannot endure permanently half slave and half free.' Two years later he was elected president.

After the American Civil War began in 1861, Lincoln was criticized at first because the North did not win quickly. Then, on 1 January 1863, he introduced the Emancipation Proclamation, freeing all US slaves. (Southerners, of course, did not free their slaves until they had lost the war.)

In 1863, Lincoln made a speech after the terrible battle of Gettysburg, saying that the soldiers had died so 'that government of the

▼ *The statue of Abraham Lincoln at the Lincoln Memorial in Washington, DC. It stands 5.8 m tall.*

people, by the people, for the people, shall not perish from the earth'. Later, Americans realized that Lincoln had summed up the spirit of democracy.

Lincoln had plans for healing the wounds caused by the war, but was killed before he could carry them out. He was shot by a fanatical supporter of the southern states. ◆

👁 **see also**

Grant   Lee

Charles Lindbergh

American aviation pioneer
Born 1902   Died 1974 aged 72

Charles Lindbergh always had an ambition to fly aeroplanes. He went to college in 1920, but soon left so that he could learn to fly. After a time in the Army Air Service he had a regular job flying mail across America.

In 1926 a prize was put up for the first non-stop flight from New York to Paris. Several famous airmen decided to attempt this. Some were killed in the attempt. On 20 May 1927 Lindbergh took off in a specially built aeroplane called the *Spirit of St Louis*. He landed at Le Bourget Airport, Paris, 33½ hours later, having flown 5800 km.

Lindbergh became a hero on both sides of the Atlantic, and went on to be an important adviser during the growth of long-distance air travel. Towards the end of his life he became interested in conservation, and opposed the development of supersonic aeroplanes as he believed they would have a bad effect on the Earth's atmosphere. ◆

▶ *Lindbergh described his journey across the Atlantic in a book,* Spirit of St Louis, *which won him a Pulitzer Prize.*

Carolus **Linnaeus**

Swedish botanist
Born 1707   Died 1778 aged 70

Carolus Linnaeus was fascinated by plants from an early age and was lucky enough to live at a time when many new plants and animals were being discovered.

When he was older, Linnaeus worked out a method of giving two-part names to every different species. In this way each kind of plant and animal had a name which was not used for any other. It was said at the time that 'God created; Linnaeus set in order', for his system made it possible for each new discovery to be slotted into an arrangement of similar species.

Linnaeus was made professor of medicine and then of botany at Uppsala University, Sweden, where he had been a student. In 1753 he became a Knight of the Polar Star in recognition of his work, and later he was made a count.

Wherever he went he collected

plants and made notes on all that he saw. He published over 180 works, the most important of which is *Systema Naturae*, which is still used today by scientists who classify the living world.

Linnaeus was born Carl Linné but became known as Carolus Linnaeus as all his works were in Latin. ◆

Joseph **Lister**

British surgeon who introduced sterilization in operating theatres
Born 1827   Died 1912 aged 84

Joseph Lister trained to be a doctor and attended one of the first operations to be performed under anaesthetic. He was appalled at the huge number of people who died after surgery. Surgeons, working in their ordinary clothes, and with unwashed hands, boasted that they could cut off a leg in 25 seconds. Not surprisingly, many of the patients died.

Lister tried moving the patients' beds further apart to prevent infection, but things were no better. Then he read Louis Pasteur's findings about bacteria in the air, and began to look for something that would keep operating theatres perfectly clean.

Lister suggested that as carbolic acid was used to purify sewage, perhaps it would kill bacteria in surgery too. Carbolic acid was sprayed into the air during operations, and heat was used to kill bacteria on the knives and instruments that were used. At first no one believed Lister's success, but by 1879, most of the London hospitals were using his methods, and many patients lived who would have died without them. ◆

👁 **see also**

Pasteur

Franz **Liszt**

Hungarian composer and piano virtuoso
Born *1811*   **Died** *1886 aged 74*

Music came naturally to Franz Liszt. He began to play the piano when he was only five, and gave his first public concert when he was nine. A group of Hungarian noblemen were so impressed they gave him money to study in Vienna and Paris. By the time he was 12 he was being compared with the greatest adult pianists of the day.

◀ *Liszt was a handsome young man whose piano recitals made him as popular and wealthy in his own time as the pop stars of today.*

Liszt was more than just a great pianist: he was also a fine composer. His music was technically brilliant and very adventurous, and pointed the way to new musical developments. One of his inventions was the symphonic poem, an orchestral work that told a story in terms of music. *Les Préludes*, *Mazeppa*, and *Hamlet* are examples, but he also wrote vast quantities of music of all kinds. ◆

David **Livingstone**

Scottish missionary and explorer
Born *1813*   **Died** *1873 aged 60*

Although his family was poor, David Livingstone worked very hard and saved enough money to train as a doctor. In 1841 he sailed for southern Africa to join a Christian mission station in what is now Botswana.

In 1853 Livingstone began his first great expedition to search for new trade routes through Africa. He walked from the middle of Africa to the Atlantic coast, then headed east until he reached the Indian Ocean. He was the first European to see the Victoria Falls. When Livingstone returned to Britain in 1856 he was hailed as a hero because he was the first European to cross Africa from west to east.

Livingstone's second expedition, up the Zambezi River by steamboat, was a disastrous failure. His wife died of fever and many other lives were lost before the expedition collapsed in 1864.

Livingstone's third expedition, to find the source of the River Nile, began in 1866. He vanished and some people thought he had died. But in 1871 the American journalist Henry Morton Stanley found Livingstone on the shore of Lake Tanganyika. 'Dr Livingstone, I presume,' were Stanley's famous words when they met.

Livingstone died in 1873. His body was shipped to England and buried in Westminster Abbey. ◆

◀ *An elephant trumpets a greeting as Livingstone's boat, the Ma Roberts, passes by on a voyage along the Shire River in Malawi, Africa.*

David **Lloyd George**

British prime minister from 1916 to 1922
Born 1863   Died 1945 aged 82

As a young Liberal Member of Parliament, David Lloyd George began to fight for a better life for poorer people. By 1908 he was appointed Chancellor of the Exchequer, and in 1911 he introduced new legislation making richer people pay more in taxes to help the sick and unemployed.

When World War I broke out in 1914, Britain was poorly prepared and at first did not do very well. Two years later the prime minister, Asquith, was pushed out and Lloyd George took his place. He set about winning the war, and struggled to make people, especially the army generals, change their old-fashioned ways. In 1918 victory came, and Lloyd George easily won the general election that followed. He began the task of helping to rebuild Europe, and helped set up the League of Nations to keep the peace. In 1922 he was forced to resign by his opponents, but he remained an important figure in British politics until the 1940s. ◆

Llywelyn the Great

Medieval Welsh ruler
Born c.1172   Died 1240 aged about 67

Although he was heir to the kingdom of Gwynedd (Snowdonia) in north Wales, Llywelyn spent his childhood in exile. When he was older he fought back, and by 1194 he had deposed his uncle David. By 1200 he had become master of most of northern Wales. Five years later he married the illegitimate daughter of King John of England, and began to threaten English lands in the south. This was too much for King John, who invaded Wales in 1211.

Fortunately for Llywelyn, John's troubles in England meant that he had little time to deal with the Welsh. Seizing his chance, Llywelyn forced Welsh rulers to recognize his leadership. Two years after John's death, the English acknowledged that Llywelyn was ruler of most of Wales. Shortly before his death, he became a monk, after a lifetime spent encouraging the Welsh to think of themselves as a united people. ◆

👁 **see also**
King John

John **Locke**

English philosopher
Born 1632   Died 1704 aged 72

John Locke was one of the most learned men of his time, educated in the sciences, politics, religion, and philosophy. But he was a practical as well as an academic man. He would advise young people, whose company he greatly enjoyed, not to waste their free time on playing games, but to find pleasure in doing useful things like gardening or carpentry.

He published a number of books which have greatly influenced political and philosophical thought. His most famous, *Essay Concerning Human Understanding*, explores the idea that experience is the only source of knowledge. He was also a firm believer in the rights of the individual, and wrote that no one, whether priest or ruler, has the right to force another person to take on his/her beliefs. ◆

Henry Wadsworth **Longfellow**

American poet
Born 1807   Died 1882 aged 75

The son of a lawyer, Henry Wadsworth Longfellow was a university teacher before deciding to concentrate on writing. He soon became the most famous American poet of his time. His works include 'Paul Revere's Ride', 'The Wreck of the Hesperus', and 'Excelsior'. These have strong rhythms and tell their exciting

▲ *Hiawatha, the hero of Longfellow's epic poem, sails into the sunset in this 1910 edition of* The Song of Hiawatha.

stories in vivid language. Longfellow's most famous poem is the longer *The Song of Hiawatha*. This describes the life of Hiawatha, an Indian brave who was brought up by the daughter of the Moon. He becomes leader of his tribe before hard times lead to the death of his lovely wife, Minnehaha. Before his own death Hiawatha warns about the coming of the white man. The whole poem is told in a catchy, almost sing-song rhythm. ◆

Louis XIV

King of France from 1643 to 1715
Born *1638*   **Died** *1715 aged 76*

Louis XIV became King of France at the age of four on the death of his father. His mother, Anne of Austria, at first ruled for him, helped by her powerful chief adviser, Cardinal Mazarin.

After Mazarin died, Louis was determined to rule alone. As he said himself, 'L'état, c'est moi' ('I am the state'). He became known as the Sun King because he chose the Sun as his royal badge.

Although he brought some improvements to France, there were darker sides to his reign. He fought expensive and unsuccessful wars and at home he was cruel to the Huguenots (Protestants), telling them that they had to become Roman Catholics. Two hundred thousand of them refused and left the country.

Louis had a magnificent palace built in Versailles. However, the life of luxury that he and his court enjoyed angered those who were struggling to survive. After ruling for 72 years, he died a lonely figure, no longer respected by his people. ◆

Louis XVI

King of France from 1774 to 1792
Born *1754*   **Died** *1793 aged 38*

Louis XVI came to the throne at the age of 19. A weak man, he often relied on the advice of his strong-minded wife, the beautiful Marie Antoinette of Austria, even though she was unpopular because of her high spending. Eventually the French nobles began to oppose much that Louis tried to do.

In 1788 he summoned the estates-general (a sort of parliament) to

▲ *This plate commemorates the execution of King Louis XVI in 1793.*

help him get his way against these nobles. However, it only added to his troubles by demanding reforms on behalf of the people. When the French Revolution started in 1789, Louis and his family were taken away and kept under guard.

Instead of trying to come to an agreement with the new forces in France, Louis and his family fled from Paris in a horse and carriage in 1791, but he was recognized and brought back. In 1792 he was found guilty of treason for having dealings with enemies of the Revolution, and in 1793 he was beheaded by guillotine. Nine months later Marie Antoinette met a similar fate. ◆

👁 **see also**
Danton   Marie Antionette
Robespierre

Joe **Louis**

American world-champion boxer
Born *1914*   **Died** *1981 aged 67*

Joseph Louis Barrow was born in Lafayette, Alabama. He became a professional boxer in 1934 and world heavyweight champion in 1937 when he knocked out the reigning champion James Braddock. He was the first black man to be allowed to fight in the world championship for 22 years.

Nicknamed the 'Brown Bomber', Joe Louis successfully defended his title a record 25 times over a period of almost 12 years. Out of 66 professional fights, he won 63; 49 were by knockouts.

He retired in 1949, but made two unsuccessful comebacks. His last important fight was in 1951 when he lost to Rocky Marciano. ◆

Ignatius **Loyola**

Spanish founder of the Society of Jesus (also known as the Jesuits)
Born 1491   Died 1556 aged 65

B orn in Spain, Ignatius Loyola became a knight and fought in battles. In 1521, however, he was hit in the legs by a cannon-ball. He was badly wounded and underwent two operations. While recovering, he read books about Jesus and the saints which affected him deeply.

▲ *A portrait of Saint Ignatius Loyola by Rubens.*

After this spiritual transformation Loyola lived in a cave for a year, thinking and praying. After visiting Jerusalem in the Holy Land, he returned to Spain to study to be a priest. He also studied in Paris, where he met a group of like-minded companions.

When in Rome shortly afterwards, Loyola and his companions decided to create a new 'order' of religious men. Called the Society of Jesus, its members ('Jesuits') aimed to spread the ideas of Christianity. In 1540 Pope Paul III gave his approval for the Society. Loyola became leader, and wrote the Society's rules. He also completed his famous book of prayers, *The Spiritual Exercises*. By the time of Loyola's death there were over 1000 Jesuits, working in many countries. ◆

Lumière brothers

French inventors of the first films
Auguste Lumière
Born 1862   Died 1954 aged 91
Louis Lumière
Born 1864   Died 1948 aged 83

A uguste and Louis Lumière's father, Antoine, was an artist and photographer. The boys were extremely clever and when Louis was only 18 they started a factory for making photographic plates.

In 1894 Antoine visited Paris where he saw Thomas Edison's 'kinetoscope', a machine where you looked through a hole at a series of pictures inside a spinning drum. He was amazed by the appearance of movement this created. When he told his sons about it, they immediately set about solving the problem of projecting moving pictures on to a screen. Louis, inspired by watching the action of a sewing machine, designed a mechanism for holding each 'frame' in front of the light beam for a split second before moving the next one into position.

In 1895 the Lumière brothers demonstrated their *cinématographe* in Paris. Even though their first film only showed workers leaving the Lumière factory, the audience was wildly enthusiastic and the cinema industry was born. ◆

👁 **see also**

Edison

▼ *Auguste and Louis Lumière opened the world's first cinema in Paris to show their films.*

▲ *A page from Martin Luther's German translation of the Bible (c.1530).*

Martin **Luther**

German religious reformer
Born 1483   Died 1546 aged 62

As a young monk, Martin Luther was worried that the Catholic Church had become too wealthy and powerful and that many churchmen had forgotten the teachings of Jesus.

Luther became a priest in 1507 and a teacher of theology (religion) at the University of Wittenberg in Saxony. However, it was not long before an argument began between Luther and other churchmen. He said that people must study the Bible for themselves, and did not need to say a certain number of prayers, or go to special church services. This implied that priests, and the whole organization of the Catholic Church, were not really so important.

Soon Luther was in trouble. In 1520 he was expelled from the Catholic Church by the pope. In the following year, the Holy Roman Emperor, Charles V, ordered Luther to appear before a special meeting of all the princes in Germany. Luther still refused to give up his beliefs, even though the emperor condemned him, and he was in danger of being put to death.

Fortunately for Luther, the ruler of Saxony protected him and some other German princes supported him too. He was able to spend the rest of his life teaching and writing. He also got married and raised a large family.

By the time Luther died, his followers (called 'Lutherans') had formed a new Protestant Church which was quite separate from the Catholic Church. ◆

🕮 **see also**
Calvin

Albert **Luthuli**

Zulu leader who campaigned peacefully against apartheid
Born 1898   Died 1967 aged 69

Albert Luthuli was born into a Christian Zulu family in Southern Rhodesia (now Zimbabwe). His father was a Christian missionary. After teaching for 15 years Luthuli was elected tribal chief in his family home at Groutville, Natal.

After World War II he joined the African National Congress (ANC) which was working for black people to be given full political rights in South Africa. Luthuli did not believe in violence; instead he led campaigns of peaceful disobedience against the apartheid laws that kept people of different races apart.

When he was elected president of the ANC in 1952, the government responded by taking away his chieftainship. Later he was arrested, and in 1959 he was banned from leaving his home district for five years. The following year the ANC itself was banned. Despite the ban, Luthuli was allowed to go to Oslo in 1961 when the Swedish government awarded him the Nobel Peace Prize for all that he had done in opposing discrimination against black people in South Africa. ◆

🕮 **see also**
Buthelezi   Mandela

Douglas **MacArthur**

Commander of the United States army during World War II
Born 1880   Died 1964 aged 84

Following in his father's footsteps, Douglas MacArthur joined the US army. He was an outstanding soldier. In 1930 he was appointed

▼ *General Douglas MacArthur photographed in the Philippines in 1944.*

◀ A scene from a production of Shakespeare's Macbeth *in which Macbeth, holding the bloodied weapons he has used to kill Duncan, discusses the terrible deed with his wife.*

Chief of Staff, and from 1935 he organized American defences in the Philippines (a US territory).

In December 1941, more than two years after the beginning of World War II, Japanese armies landed in parts of south-east Asia, including the Philippines. MacArthur and his forces resisted the invasion at first but were eventually forced out. MacArthur was transferred to Australia and for two years commanded Allied attacks against the Japanese. Finally, in the spring of 1945, American troops recaptured the Philippines.

MacArthur, who was now the commander of all US army forces in the Pacific, received the Japanese surrender in September 1945. He was then placed in command of the Allied occupation of Japan and took an active role in many reforms.

Five years later, North Korea invaded South Korea. The United Nations agreed to support the South and MacArthur was ordered to oppose the invasion. His forces pushed the North Koreans back, but were forced to retreat from an invading Chinese army. He eventually repelled the Chinese but then had ideas about attacking China itself. President Truman would not agree to this plan and MacArthur was dismissed. ◆

Macbeth

King of Scotland from 1050 to 1057
Born *c.1005*
Died *c.1057 aged about 52*

M acbeth was a king of Scotland who became the subject of the play *Macbeth* written by William Shakespeare in 1606. Shakespeare based some of his play on facts he found in *Chronicles of England, Scotland, and Ireland* (1577) by Raphael Holinshed, the 16th-century historian. Macbeth was commander of the forces of Duncan I, king of Scotland. He seized the Scottish throne after he had defeated and killed Duncan in battle in 1040. In Shakespeare's play, Macbeth murders Duncan after a prophecy spoken by three witches, and with encouragement from his wife, Lady Macbeth.

Macbeth's reign was prosperous until he himself was defeated in 1054 by Malcolm III, son of Duncan, and Siward, Earl of Northumberland. However, Macbeth remained king until he was killed by Malcolm in 1057. Lulach, Macbeth's stepson, then reigned for a few months before Malcolm succeeded him. ◆

◉ **see also**

Shakespeare

John A. Macdonald

First prime minister of Canada, from 1867 to 1873 and from 1878 to 1891
Born *1815*   **Died** *1891 aged 76*

J ohn Alexander Macdonald emigrated with his family from Scotland to Kingston, Upper Canada (now Ontario) when he was five years old. When he was ten he was sent to a boarding school. At the age of 15 he began to work in a law office and before he turned 21 he opened his own office and became a successful lawyer. Macdonald's personal life was not always happy. His first son, John Alexander, died when just a baby. His first wife, Isabel, spent most of her life sick in bed. A daughter from his second marriage was an invalid.

Macdonald was first elected to government in 1844. In 1865 he and a former rival, George Brown, began persuading others to unite Britain's six North American colonies to form a single country – or 'confederation'. He chaired the London conference of 1866 to create the Dominion of Canada and he was chosen to be Canada's first prime minister the following year.

During his years as prime minister, Canada expanded territorially with the new provinces of Manitoba, British Columbia, and Prince Edward Island, and also experienced growth in its economy. Macdonald encouraged the building of a railway across the country and the development of industry. ◆

Ramsay **MacDonald**

Prime minister of Britain in 1924 and from 1929 to 1935
Born 1866   Died 1937 aged 71

Ramsay MacDonald, the son of a Scottish maid, became a Labour Member of Parliament in 1906. He became leader of the Labour Party in 1911, but resigned at the start of World War I because of his unpopular belief in negotiation, not war, with Germany. He was re-elected as party leader in 1922 and in 1924 became the first Labour prime minister, serving from January until November. He won a second term in 1929. However, unemployment was very high and in 1931 MacDonald recommended a cut in unemployment benefits to help solve the financial crisis. His cabinet rejected this idea but MacDonald was able to continue as leader by forming a national coalition government with the support of Conservatives and Liberals. The Labour Party called him a traitor and expelled him. Nevertheless he remained in office until failing health forced his resignation in 1935. ◆

Niccolò **Machiavelli**

Italian political writer
Born 1469   Died 1527 aged 58

Niccolò Machiavelli was born near Florence in Italy. Little is known about his life until 1498, when he was appointed to an important post in the government of Florence. For most of the 15th century, Florence had been dominated by the Medici family. However, in 1494 the Medicis had been driven out. Machiavelli worked for the new government. Between 1500 and 1508 he visited the courts of many foreign rulers, including that of Cesare Borgia, a ruthless prince in central Italy.

In 1512 the Medici family returned to Florence and expelled their enemies, including Machiavelli. He went home to the family farm, but he really wanted to return to work. He wrote several books about politics to try to please the Medici family. In 1520 they gave him a minor post, but in 1527 they were again driven out of Florence. Machiavelli also lost his job and died soon afterwards.

Machiavelli is famous for his writings, notably his book *The Prince* (1513). This book tells rulers how to increase their power, often through the cruel manipulation of other people. ◆

👁 **see also**

Borgia family   Medici family

Charles Rennie **Mackintosh**

Scottish architect, designer, and painter
Born 1868   Died 1928 aged 60

Charles Rennie Mackintosh was the son of a police superintendent. As a child in Glasgow he had only one aim – to be an architect. He studied in Glasgow where he became friendly with some painters and designers of stained glass, jewellery, furniture, and embroidery. They became known as the 'Glasgow Group' and Mackintosh became the group's leading light. He and his friends wanted to combine the best of Scottish art with the New Art (Art Nouveau) from Europe. In his most famous building, the Glasgow

▲ *The library of the Glasgow School of Art is typical of Mackintosh's clear, bold design style.*

School of Art, we can recognize the cragginess of Scottish castles combined with the flowing plant forms of Art Nouveau. Glaswegians flocked to the tearooms that Mackintosh designed for the city. Each one had different and unusual decoration and furniture. They have now mainly been destroyed.

Mackintosh did not find much success in his lifetime and he gave up architecture when he was only 41 to spend the rest of his life painting. However, he is now regarded by many as a pioneer of modern design. ◆

James **Madison**

President of the United States of America from 1809 to 1817
Born 1751   Died 1836 aged 85

James Madison was born in Port Conway in the state of Virginia. In 1776 Virginia and 12 other states broke away from British rule to form the United States. In 1787 Madison represented Virginia at a conference to plan the organization of the government of the new country. He favoured a strong central system with upper and lower houses of elected members, and helped to draft the American Constitution (the basic principles of government). Two years later, he was elected to the House of Representatives. There he planned the Bill of Rights, which made the Constitution fairer in operation.

Madison was secretary of state in Thomas Jefferson's government (1801–1809) before becoming president himself in 1809. As president he took the United States into the war of 1812 with Britain. This ended after three years with the signing of the Treaty of Ghent, which restored all territories conquered in the war to their original owners. ◆

👁 **see also**

Jefferson

Madonna

American singer
Born 1958

Madonna Louise Ciccone was born in Michigan, America. She was the most successful female singer of the 1980s. She studied dancing and then combined this with singing when she moved to New York.

Her hits include 'Into the Groove' (1985), 'Vogue' (1990) and Music (2001). She has achieved lasting success, reinventing her image several times.

Madonna has also acted in several films, including *Desperately Seeking Susan* (1985), *Dick Tracy* (1990), and *A League of Their Own* (1992).

She has been married twice, first to actor Sean Penn in 1985, and currently to film director Guy Ritchie. ◆

Ferdinand **Magellan**

Portuguese navigator and explorer
Born c.1480   Died 1521 aged about 41

Ferdinand Magellan was the son of a noble Portuguese family. He was a page at the Portuguese court before serving in the army, and then sailing with merchants to Indonesia.

Magellan thought there must be a way around the Americas to the East Indies. The king of Portugal rejected his plan for a voyage of discovery, so he offered his services to King Carlos of Spain.

Magellan set sail in 1519 with five small ships. When the fleet anchored for the winter in San Julián Bay, in Argentina, his Spanish captains mutinied. Magellan hanged one of the ringleaders.

When the fleet finally continued on its journey, one ship was wrecked in a storm, and another turned back to Spain. Magellan battled against the bad weather conditions through the straight between Tierra del Fuego and the mainland of South America. (The strait is now called the Magellan Strait after him.) He emerged into calm sea, which he named the Pacific (peaceful) Ocean.

The ships still sailed on and eventually reached the Philippines. Magellan had at last succeeded in reaching the East Indies by sailing westwards. However, before he could sail for home he was killed in a skirmish there. ◆

▼ *After Magellan's death, one of his ships, the Vittoria, carried on to Spain. It thus became the first vessel to circumnavigate the world.*

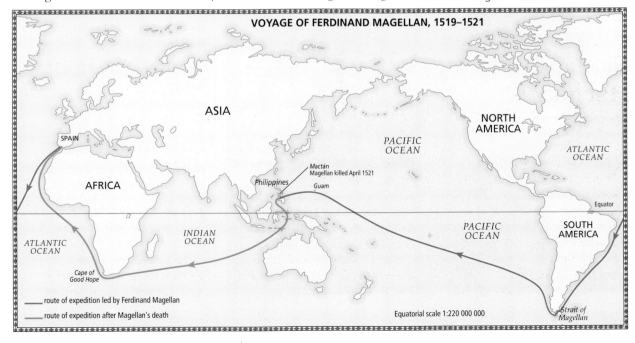

VOYAGE OF FERDINAND MAGELLAN, 1519–1521

ASIA

NORTH AMERICA

PACIFIC OCEAN

ATLANTIC OCEAN

SPAIN

AFRICA

Mactán
Magellan killed April 1521

Philippines

Guam

Equator

ATLANTIC OCEAN

INDIAN OCEAN

PACIFIC OCEAN

SOUTH AMERICA

Cape of Good Hope

___ route of expedition led by Ferdinand Magellan

___ route of expedition after Magellan's death

Equatorial scale 1:220 000 000

Strait of Magellan

René **Magritte**

Belgian painter
Born *1898*   **Died** *1967 aged 68*

René Magritte was one of the most famous of the Surrealist painters. The Surrealists were a group of artists and writers who wanted to explore the power of their subconscious minds; Surrealist paintings often look more like what we might see in dreams than representations of the real world. Once the novelty of this style had worn off, many such paintings looked repetitive and contrived. Magritte, however, seemed to have limitless imagination, and he kept freshness and wit in his work throughout his career. His paintings are full of bizarre images including enormous rocks that float in the air and fishes with human legs, all presented with a delightful kind of deadpan humour, but also a sense of mystery. ◆

▼ *Magritte delighted in placing everyday things in unfamiliar situations, as in Golconda (1953), where men wearing bowler hats fall like rain from the sky.*

Mahavira

Indian religious leader
Born *c.599 BC*
Died *c.527 BC aged about 72*

Mahavira ('Great Hero') is often called the founder of the religion known as Jainism but he probably only reformed a religion which already existed. He is said to have lived around the same time as Buddha. Both lived in the Ganges valley, left their families when they were 30, and lived lives of extreme poverty and deep thinking. When they felt sure that they understood the meaning of human life and how it should be lived, they spent the rest of their lives teaching their beliefs to others. Mahavira is said to have starved himself to death when he was 72: the highest goal for a Jain monk or nun is to die of starvation, although this does not happen very often.

Both Jains and Buddhists believe that all living things are reborn many times and that the true aim of life is to escape rebirth by living

▲ *An illustration from a 15th-century version of the Kalpasutra, the Jain Holy Scriptures.*

correctly. Both believe that this involves not harming any other living thing. Jains go even further than Buddhists in this respect. They are such strict vegetarians that they take great care not to hurt even the tiniest of insects. Jain nuns and monks even carry brooms to sweep all surfaces to avoid crushing insects accidentally.

Buddhism spread through much of Asia but Jainism, which now has about 3 million followers, is found mainly in India. ◆

👁 **see also**
Buddha

Gustav **Mahler**

Austrian composer and conductor
Born *1860*   **Died** *1911 aged 50*

Gustav Mahler was one of 12 children born to a poor inn-keeper and his wife. He is said to have begun composing at around the age of four and was sent to study music in the Czech capital,

Prague, when he was only ten. As a student at the Vienna Conservatory of Music, he had to give music lessons to support himself. Later he made his fortune as a brilliant conductor, working with great orchestras in Budapest, Hamburg, Vienna, and New York.

Mahler loved writing long, complicated works for large orchestras. These include nine completed symphonies. Some are unusual because they combine solo singers or choirs with the orchestra. This is also true of one of his most famous compositions, *Das Lied von der Erde* (Song of the Earth) (1909), where an alto, a tenor, and an orchestra perform songs based on ancient Chinese poems.

Mahler's music was mostly ignored for 50 years after his death but he is now praised as a pioneer of modern classical music and an important influence on composers such as Schoenberg, Shostakovich, and Britten. ◆

see also
Britten   Schoenberg   Shostakovich

Margaret **Mahy**
New Zealand children's writer
Born 1936

Margaret Mahy was a school librarian in Christchurch, New Zealand, when she began writing children's stories. The very first to be published, *A Lion in the Meadow* (1969), won a medal from the New Zealand Library Association. *The Haunting* (1982), a tale of a boy who is possessed by a ghost, won the Carnegie Medal, which is awarded in Britain to the outstanding children's writer of the year. Her lively and imaginative books have pictures by top illustrators such as Helen Oxenbury. They often play on the interaction

of fantasy and reality in stories such as *Mrs Discombobulous*, who gets sucked into her washing-machine and comes out into another world, and *The Dragon of an Ordinary Family*, about a pet dragon. ◆

see also
Blyton   Dahl

Malcolm X
American civil rights leader
Born 1925   Died 1965 aged 39

As a boy, Malcolm Little, son of a Baptist minister, saw his home burned down by the Ku Klux Klan (a group dedicated to terrorizing black people). He later moved to Boston where he was imprisoned for seven years for burglary. Here he became a follower of Elijah Muhammad, founder of the Black Muslims. Working for the Black Muslims, Malcolm toured and lectured, campaigning for black Americans to seek self-government, not equality with whites. He told them that they had to be prepared to use violence as a means of self-defence. It was during this time that

▼ *Malcolm X awaiting his turn to speak at a Black Muslim rally in Washington DC in 1961.*

he changed his name to Malcolm X.

After quarrelling with Muhammad, Malcolm X left the Black Muslims and gradually modified his views on separatism. In 1964 he formed the Organization of Afro-American Unity to promote links between black people in Africa and America. Hostility continued between his followers and the Black Muslims and he was shot and killed at a rally in New York City. *The Autobiography of Malcolm X* (1965) remains a best-seller and a film about his life was released in 1993. ◆

Thomas **Malory**
English writer
Lived during the 15th century

No one knows for sure who Thomas Malory was, but many believe him to have been a knight who was imprisoned in London for unknown crimes for 20 years. It was possibly during this time that Malory finished his great book about King Arthur's knights of the Round Table and their quest for the Holy Grail. Much of this work was translated from French sources, but Malory added his own touches while keeping the original French title, *Le Morte d'Arthur* (The Death of Arthur). In 1485 the whole work was published by William Caxton, the first British printer. The stories about King Arthur, his bride Guinevere, the magician Merlin, and the gallant Sir Lancelot, soon proved popular with readers. Malory's beautiful use of language also has a magic of its own. Many future writers went on to write their own versions of these stories, including the poet Alfred Tennyson in his *Idylls of the King*. ◆

see also
Arthur   Caxton   Tennyson

Thomas **Malthus**

English economist and philosopher
Born *1766*   **Died** *1834 aged 68*

Thomas Malthus was a clergyman who looked for the underlying causes of the misery of poor people in the England of his time. He believed that population growth was the problem, and that the production of food and other resources would not be enough to supply the expanding population. He felt that unless the birth-rate was controlled, starvation, war, and disease would prevent many people from advancing beyond the most basic standard of living.

When his short *Essay on Population*, setting out these views, was first published in 1798, it caused furious controversy. Malthus revised and enlarged the *Essay* in 1803, and his later views were rather more optimistic about the future of humankind. ◆

Nelson **Mandela**

President of South Africa from 1994
Born *1918*

Nelson Mandela is related to the Xhosa royal family, but spent much of his childhood herding cattle. After going to university, he qualified as a lawyer.

Mandela helped form the Youth League of the African National Congress (ANC) in 1943. The Youth League stressed the need for the ANC to identify with the hardships and struggles of ordinary black people against racial discrimination.

The ANC led peaceful mass protests against apartheid ('separate development'), the policy introduced by the National Party (NP) in 1948 to justify and strengthen white domination.

▲ *Nelson Mandela (left) and F. W. de Klerk were awarded the Nobel Peace Prize in 1993 for their efforts to end apartheid in South Africa.*

Many protesters were imprisoned or killed. In 1960 the ANC was outlawed. In reply, Mandela and others established 'Umkhonto we Sizwe' (Spear of the Nation), a guerrilla army, in 1961.

In 1964, after months in hiding, Mandela was arrested and imprisoned for life. Offered a conditional release by the government, he refused to compromise over the issue of apartheid. Eventually, as a result of internal and international pressure, Mandela was released in 1990 by President de Klerk. He led the ANC in negotiations, and these resulted in the first democratic elections to be held in South Africa. The ANC won easily, and in 1994 Mandela became president. He retired from office in 1999, and his deputy Thabo Mbeki became president. ◆

👁 **see also**
Buthelezi   de Klerk   Tutu

Benoit **Mandelbrot**

Polish-born American mathematician
Born *1924*

Benoit Mandelbrot was born in Warsaw, Poland, and moved to Paris with his family in 1936. There he met an uncle who was an important mathematician. His uncle advised him to avoid geometry, but Mandelbrot liked geometry best of all branches of mathematics and continued to study it.

After World War II Mandelbrot

▼ *A fractal image generated by a computer. The patterns of such fractal images repeat endlessly.*

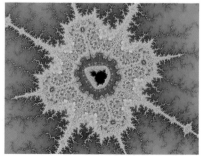

moved to America and worked on various projects. He soon became interested in what he called 'fractal geometry' – a term used to describe shapes that are repeated indefinitely, each time smaller. Fractals can be generated on a computer screen and often resemble natural shapes. Because of this similarity, fractals can be used to create models of natural changes, for example how a coastline may change through erosion, or how tree roots branch out. Fractals can also create amazing computer art. ◆

Edouard **Manet**

French painter
Born 1832   Died 1883 aged 51

Edouard Manet came from a wealthy family, and no one looked less like a 'bohemian' artistic rebel than he did. He was every inch a gentleman. However, he had unconventional ideas about art. Most painters of his time followed tradition, but Manet liked to look at

▼ *Manet's paintings were mainly of everyday life, such as this one of a couple at a Parisian café,* Chez le Père Lathuille's *(1879).*

everything freshly. He chose subjects from everyday life that no one had thought of painting before, and he painted with broad, sketchy brushstrokes, rather than with fine detail as was the current trend. Many art critics were outraged. However, a group of up-and-coming young artists – known as the Impressionists – loved his work and he became associated with them. By the end of his career the critics had come to appreciate the sparkling beauty of his paintings. Two years before his death Manet was made a member of France's Legion of Honour – a great distinction. ◆

👁 **see also**
Monet   Pissarro   Renoir

Mao Zedong

One of the founders of the People's Republic of China in 1949
Born 1893   Died 1976 aged 82

Mao Zedong was one of the first to join the new Chinese Communist Party in 1921. They worked alongside the Guomindang (Nationalist Party), led by Chiang Kai-shek, until 1927, when the Nationalists had many Communists

killed. Mao helped the remaining Communists to survive by setting up a 'soviet' (elected council). At first the Communists fought off the Nationalists, but in 1934 the attacks became too strong. Mao then led the Communists on the 'Long March', nearly 10,000 km over mountains and deserts to a new base. Thousands died on the way.

In 1937 the Japanese invaded China. Chiang Kai-shek retreated to the mountains, but Mao sent the 'people's liberation army' to help people in occupied villages. When the Japanese finally left, Mao received great support from the people in the civil war against Chiang Kai-shek.

By 1949 Mao's forces had captured Beijing and set up a People's Republic, making Mao leader of a quarter of the world's people. He encouraged peasants to overthrow their landlords and work together on collective farms.

In 1957 he ordered the peasants to join their collective farms into large 'communes'. Some peasants worked in 'brigades' on the fields, while others were told to open factories or furnaces to make iron. This was all part of Mao's plan for a 'great leap forward' in industry. However, many of the schemes did not succeed because not enough money was being spent on new technology or education.

In 1959 Mao retired from the post of chairman of the Republic but re-emerged in 1966 to start the 'Cultural Revolution'. This new movement was intended to keep Chinese Communism free from outside influence and to ensure that Mao and his ideas remained at the forefront of life in China. The Cultural Revolution finally ended when Mao died. ◆

👁 **see also**
Chiang Kai-shek   Deng Xiaoping

Diego **Maradona**

Argentinian footballer
Born 1960

Diego Maradona was born in Buenos Aires and quickly showed the skills that made him an Argentinian league footballer by the age of 15. He was voted South American Footballer of the Year in 1979 and 1980. After leading Argentina's youth team to World Cup success in 1979, he joined the full national squad in their unsuccessful attempt to keep the World Cup in 1982.

In 1986, as Argentina's captain, he lifted up the World Cup after brilliant performances throughout the tournament. He led Argentina once again in the 1990 World Cup final, although they were beaten 1–0 by West Germany. ◆

Guglielmo **Marconi**

Italian pioneer of radio
Born 1874   Died 1937 aged 63

Guglielmo Marconi began his experiments on sending radio signals in Italy before deciding to move to England.

He realized that if signals were to travel long distances he needed to have a very high aerial, so he began to use balloons and kites. In 1897 he sent a signal just over 14 km across the Bristol Channel. In 1899 he set up his apparatus in two American ships and was able to report on the America's Cup yacht race. This caused great excitement and Marconi became famous. But some scientists still did not believe that you could send signals very far. They thought the waves would go straight up and get lost in space.

In 1901 Marconi finally convinced everyone by sending a signal all the way from Cornwall to Newfoundland. It was later proved that the waves bounced back off special layers in the atmosphere, and that was how they were able to travel round the world. ◆

Maria Theresa

Empress of Austria-Hungary from 1740 to 1780
Born 1717   Died 1780 aged 63

Maria Theresa was the eldest daughter of Charles VI, who was the head of the Habsburg family and ruled Austria, Hungary, and other lands. Normally only a male could become ruler of the Habsburg lands, but Charles's only son died. Charles declared that Maria Theresa should inherit the family lands.

When Charles died in 1740, foreign rulers would not accept Maria Theresa as ruler, and tried to invade some of her territories. Frederick II of Prussia seized an area of her land called Silesia. Between 1757 and 1763 her forces fought the Prussians, but failed to recapture their land.

Maria Theresa was a well-loved ruler. She introduced many reforms to help the poorer people and built up agriculture and industry, so increasing the wealth of the empire. ◆

Marie Antoinette

French queen who was beheaded after the French Revolution
Born 1755   Died 1793 aged 37

Marie Antoinette was the 11th daughter of the Holy Roman Emperor Francis I of Austria and Maria Theresa. In 1770 she married Louis, who later became King Louis XVI of France. Marie Antoinette kept to her own small circle of friends, and her extravagance helped to create enormous debts for Louis. At the same time discontent in France led to the Revolution of 1789. Marie Antoinette tried to

▶ *A portrait of Empress Maria Theresa.*

persuade Louis to seek refuge with his army away from Paris, but he refused. Later they and their children were held prisoner in Paris, and in 1792 the palace was stormed and the monarchy was overthrown. Marie Antoinette was accused of betraying France to the Austrians and was guillotined in October 1793. ◆

👁 **see also**
Louis XVI   Maria Theresa

Duke of **Marlborough**

English general and statesman
Born 1650   *Died* 1722 aged 72

John Churchill, the first Duke of Marlborough, became powerful during the reign of James II. But he was an Anglican and disliked James's attempt to turn the country back to Catholicism. In 1688 Churchill deserted James for William of Orange (William III) and became a general in William's army, but he was not trusted and William dismissed him. However, at the end of his life, William saw that Marlborough was the man to lead the fight against Louis XIV's France and appointed him Commander-in-Chief of the English army.

In the early years of Queen Anne's reign, Marlborough was the most famous Englishman in Europe: he was the statesman who held together the Grand Alliance against Louis, and the general who led their armies to a string of dazzling victories. He lived until 1722, dying in Blenheim Palace, Oxfordshire. The palace was the grateful nation's gift for his victories although it was only partly completed before he died. ◆

👁 **see also**
Louis XIV   William III

Bob **Marley**

Jamaican reggae singer and songwriter
Born 1945   *Died* 1981 aged 36

Bob Marley was born to a black mother, and a white father who left home before Bob was born. He lived with his mother in Trenchtown, in Kingston, Jamaica, where living conditions were harsh. When he joined the group the 'Wailin' Wailers' he wrote many songs about life in Trenchtown.

By 1965 the Wailers' reggae music was attracting listeners far beyond Jamaica. A recording contract in the United Kingdom brought world fame in the 1970s. Unfortunately, in 1977 he contracted cancer in the foot. It spread throughout his body and he died just a few years later. ◆

Marx Brothers

American actors and entertainers
Groucho (Julius) Marx
Born 1890   *Died* 1977 aged 87
Chico (Leonard) Marx
Born 1891   *Died* 1961 aged 70
Harpo (Adolph, later Arthur) Marx
Born 1893   *Died* 1964 aged 71
Zeppo (Herbert) Marx
Born 1901   *Died* 1979 aged 78

The Marx brothers were trained by their mother to be a singing and dancing group. They later switched successfully to comedy. Each of them had a distinctive character. Zeppo played straight, romantic roles. Groucho, with his moustache, cigar, and funny walk, was always cracking jokes. Harpo, whose name came from his beautiful harp playing, never spoke. He communicated by strange noises, gestures, and funny faces. Chico spoke with an Italian accent and was often seen playing the piano. Most of their films concentrate on the three most famous and comical of the brothers: Chico, Harpo, and Groucho. ◆

I never forget a face, but in your case I'll be glad to make an exception.
GROUCHO MARX

◄ *Harpo, Chico, and Groucho Marx playing the fools for a Hollywood publicity photograph.*

◄ *Karl Marx in a poster from about 1920. In the years before he died, Marx suffered ill-health. Had it not been for the money that Engels gave him, he would not have been able to support his family or continue his work.*

Karl **Marx**

German philosopher
Born *1818*   **Died** *1883 aged 64*

Karl Marx studied at the University of Bonn and then moved to Berlin in 1836. Here Marx developed ideas that were to change his life.

In 1843 Marx, now a journalist, began a journey round Europe. He moved to Brussels where he met Friedrich Engels. Together they worked for the Communist League, and in 1848 wrote *The Communist Manifesto*, which ended with the words: 'The workers have nothing to lose but their chains. They have a world to win. Workers of all countries, unite!'

Ideas like these led to Marx being expelled from Brussels and then from France and Germany. In 1849 he fled with his family to London. There, with the help of Engels, he developed his Communist ideas.

Marx wrote that 'Communism (is) the positive abolition of private property'. Under Communism, people would own all things in common and share them fairly. Marx believed this would happen, but only if working people organized themselves. That is why he became one of the leaders of the International Working Men's

Association (the 'First International'). By 1869 it had 800,000 members and Marx had published Volume I of *Das Kapital* (Capital), the most important work of his life. After Marx's death, Engels published Volumes II and III. ◆

👁 **see also**

Lenin   Stalin   Trotsky

Mary

Mother of Jesus
Dates of birth and death unknown

The significant events in the life of Mary are recorded in the Gospels. According to Luke, Mary was visited by the angel Gabriel, who told her that she would give birth to Jesus. When she was pregnant Mary travelled to Bethlehem with her husband Joseph to take part in a population census. The familiar nativity stories are told by Matthew and Luke.

According to Matthew, Joseph and Mary fled to Egypt while Jesus was still young to escape Herod. They returned to Nazareth and Jesus was taken to the temple in Jerusalem as a boy. At His crucifixion, Jesus spoke to His mother from the Cross and entrusted her to His disciple John.

Over the centuries, different

Christians have held a variety of beliefs about the religious significance of Mary. She is regarded by many as the Mother of God who listens to prayers. She is also thought by many believers to be responsible for miracles of healing. She is respected by Muslims and is mentioned in the Koran. ◆

Mary I

Queen of England and Wales from 1553 to 1558
Born *1516*   **Died** *1558 aged 42*

Mary was the daughter of Henry VIII and the Catholic Catherine of Aragon. Soon after she became queen, on the death of her half-brother, Edward VI, she married Philip II of Spain. She hoped he would help her make England Catholic again, as she was determined to stamp out Protestant belief. During her short reign over 300 Protestants, including Archbishop Cranmer, were burnt at the stake because the queen considered them heretics (for not accepting Catholic teaching).

Mary was a sick woman, and she died after a reign of only five years. She was succeeded to the throne by Elizabeth I. ◆

👁 **see also**

Cranmer   Elizabeth I   Henry VIII
Philip II of Spain

Mary, Queen of Scots

Queen of Scotland from 1542 to 1567
Born *1542*   **Died** *1587 aged 44*

Mary was the daughter of King James V of Scotland. He died a week after her birth, so she became queen of Scotland when she

▲ *Mary's beauty, the drama of her life, and the bravery of her death have ensured a lasting fascination in her.*

Thomas **Masaryk**

Czechoslovak politician and philosopher
Born 1850   Died 1937 aged 87

Thomas Masaryk was born in Moravia (now Slovakia), which was then part of the Austro-Hungarian empire. The empire's inhabitants included Germans, Hungarians, Czechs, Slovaks, and other peoples. Masaryk became a philosopher, and in 1882 he was appointed a professor in the Czech University of Prague.

In Prague, Masaryk became interested in politics. When World War I broke out in 1914, he saw that the Austro-Hungarian empire would be defeated. Masaryk thought that the Czechs and Slovaks should have their own independent country, and he went to the enemy countries – Britain, Russia, and the USA – to win support for the idea. When the war ended in 1918, the victorious Allies created the independent country of Czechoslovakia. Its people elected Masaryk as their first president. ◆

👁 **see also**
Havel

Henri **Matisse**

French artist
Born 1869   Died 1954 aged 84

Henri Matisse began a career in law and took drawing classes only as a hobby. He proved to be exceptionally talented. He developed a colourful free style, often considered shocking. He made a famous portrait of his wife, nicknamed 'Green Stripe' because he boldly painted green shadows on her face!

The human figure dominated Matisse's drawings, prints, book illustrations, paintings, and sculpture. Later he used North African patterns and shapes in his pictures, and later still cut and pasted paper to create coloured pictures of simplified shapes.

Matisse said that for more than 50 years he had not stopped working for an instant. He even worked from his wheelchair in old age. ◆

▼ *A colourful Matisse cut-out picture entitled* The Sadness of the King.

was only a few days old. She was born at a time of conflict between Scotland and England, and was brought up in the French court for safety. In 1558 the English throne passed to Elizabeth I, a Protestant, but many Catholics viewed Elizabeth as illegitimate and thought Mary had a better claim to the throne. She returned to Scotland in 1561, but her ambitions lay in England.

At first Mary managed to remain a Catholic queen without offending the powerful Scottish Protestants. However, she was accused of being involved in several scandals, including a plot to murder her second husband, the Earl of Darnley, and in 1567 she was forced to abdicate (give up the throne). She sought safety in England, but Elizabeth feared her and kept her in captivity for 19 years. Eventually Mary was found guilty of involvement in a Catholic plot to kill Elizabeth, and she was beheaded in 1587. ◆

👁 **see also**
Elizabeth I

▲ *In 1956 Stanley Matthews became the first European Footballer of the Year.*

Stanley **Matthews**

English football player
Born *1915*   **Died** *2000 aged 85*

As a boy, Stanley Matthews kicked a small rubber ball around everywhere he went. Practising like this earned him the name 'the Wizard of the Dribble' because of his skilful ball control.

Matthews played his first football league match in 1931 and his first for England in 1934. He won an FA Cup winners' medal while playing for Blackpool Football Club in 1953. He helped to set up three goals in this amazing match after Blackpool were losing 3–1 to Bolton with only minutes to go. This extraordinary game is now known as the 'Matthews final'.

Matthews was still playing first division football when he retired at the age of 50. ◆

Guy de **Maupassant**

French writer
Born *1850*   **Died** *1893 aged 42*

Guy de Maupassant was the son of a Normandy aristocrat. He served in the army and worked as a government clerk before being encouraged to become a writer by the novelist Gustave Flaubert. Flaubert encouraged him to aim for the highest standards and never to be content until he had found exactly the right word.

Maupassant wrote six novels and about 300 short stories which were immensely popular in his lifetime and remain much admired today. These stories, considered by some critics to be the greatest of the short-story genre, are written in a direct and free-flowing style, realistically describing the details of the characters' lives. ◆

👁 **see also**

Flaubert

▼ *Guy de Maupassant endured mental illness for much of his adult life, and was insane when he died.*

James Clerk **Maxwell**

Scottish physicist
Born *1831*   **Died** *1879 aged 47*

At 14 James Clerk Maxwell was asked to speak to scientists of the Royal Society of Edinburgh about his work in geometry, and when he was only 24 he became professor at Aberdeen University. He retired ten years later to write about his theories on electricity and magnetism. Then, at the age of 40, he was invited to become the first professor of experimental physics at Cambridge and, while he was there, the famous Cavendish Laboratory was built.

Some years before, the scientist Michael Faraday had talked about magnets and electric currents having 'lines of force' and made pictures of them. Maxwell heard about this and developed a mathematical theory that explained it. He suggested that if the magnet moved back and forth it would make waves run along the lines of force Faraday had discussed.

Maxwell then made the amazing suggestion that light is in fact incredibly rapid waves on the lines of force. The waves are called 'electromagnetic waves'. He was able to prove that this is true. His mathematics also suggested that there ought to be other kinds of electromagnetic waves with shorter and longer wavelengths than light. Sadly he died before any of the others could be discovered, but we now know that radio, infra-red, ultraviolet rays, X-rays, and gamma rays all belong to Maxwell's electromagnetic wave family. ◆

👁 **see also**

Faraday

John **McAdam**

Scottish engineer
Born 1756   *Died* 1836 aged 80

John McAdam was nearly 60 when he took the job which was to make him famous. He had been a merchant for most of his life but when he was in his middle forties he became interested in roads. He spent years travelling thousands of miles at his own expense to study the appalling state of Britain's muddy roads.

In 1815 he was made General Surveyor of the Bristol roads. McAdam believed that most of the roads should be dug up and remade by laying 25 cm of small broken stones, each no bigger than 2.5 cm, on a flat well-drained bed. The wheels of the carriages using the road would then compact the stones until the surface was smooth, hard, and easy to maintain.

McAdam's system worked so well in Bristol that soon it was known all over the country, and a new word for it, 'macadamizing', had entered the language. Even today the word 'tar-macadam', or 'tarmac' for short, preserves his name. ◆

Joseph **McCarthy**

American politician who campaigned against suspected Communists
Born 1908   *Died* 1957 aged 48

Joseph McCarthy, a farmer's son from Wisconsin in the American mid-West, first studied to become a lawyer. Then, after World War II, he was elected a Republican senator. He found fame in 1950 by making a speech in which he said he knew the names of 205 Communists in the US State Department. Although he provided no proof he attracted a lot of support, and many people in public life were accused of 'un-American activities'. Many books and films were censored because they were suspected of encouraging revolts against the government. Then in 1954 McCarthy accused US army officers of being Communist sympathizers. The hearings were shown on television and McCarthy appeared to the American public as a bully and a liar. In December that year he was publicly criticized by the senate and the 'McCarthyism' era was effectively over. ◆

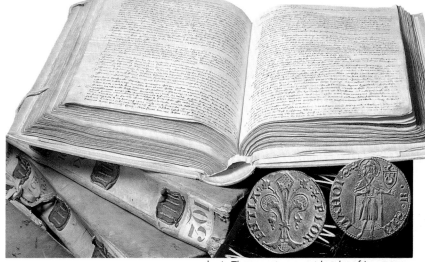

▲ *The secret account books of Lorenzo and Cosimo de Medici alongside two Italian gold florins, Europe's most stable currency at the time of the Medicis.*

Medici family

Italian aristocratic family who dominated the city of Florence from the 15th to the 18th century

In the Middle Ages Florence was a rich and important city. Among its leading families was the powerful Medici family, whose members were bankers and traders. In theory Florence was a republic, governed by leading inhabitants rather than a monarch or a nobleman. But during the 15th century, the supporters of the Medici family dominated the city government. The Medici decided on policies for the city in private, which their supporters then implemented. The first Medici to rule in this way was Cosimo the Elder (1389–1464, ruled from 1434), regarded as the model for Niccolò Machiavelli's book *The Prince*. He was followed by Piero the Gouty (1414–1469, ruled from 1464), and Lorenzo the Magnificent (1449–1492, ruled from 1469).

The Medici family always had enemies in Florence. At various times these enemies drove them out of the city, but they were always restored to power again eventually. Members of the Medici family – Piero di Lorenzo, Alexandro, Cosimo, and their descendants – ruled Florence on and off until the middle of the 18th century.

The Medici family wanted to make Florence the most beautiful city in the world. They are famous for their generous support of Florence's numerous artists and sculptors, including Brunelleschi, Botticelli, and Michelangelo. ◆

👁 **see also**
Borgia family   Brunelleschi
Botticelli   Machiavelli
Michelangelo

Mehemet Ali

Egyptian ruler
***Born** 1769   **Died** 1849 aged 80*

An Albanian by birth, Mehemet Ali entered the service of the sultan (king) of the Ottoman empire. In 1798 he was sent to Egypt to fight off French invaders, and in 1805 he used the strength of his troops to make himself 'Pasha' (ruler) of Egypt. With French help he set up a modern European-style army and navy and improved agriculture and education. Between 1820 and 1822 he conquered the Sudan and in 1823 founded Khartoum as its capital. Although his troops fought on the Ottoman side during the Greek War of Independence, this did not stop him trying to take Syria from the Ottomans in the 1830s. He was too ill to rule in person during the last two years of his life, but members of his family continued to rule Egypt until 1952. Mehemet Ali is regarded by many as the founder of modern Egypt. ◆

Golda **Meir**

Prime minister of Israel from 1969 to 1974
***Born** 1898   **Died** 1978 aged 80*

Golda Mabovitch was born in the Ukraine, the daughter of a carpenter. She was brought up in Milwaukee, America, and trained to become a schoolteacher. In 1917 she married, and emigrated to Palestine four years later.

She became an active member in the Zionist movement, which fought for a homeland for Jews in Palestine. On the eve of Israel's independence in 1948 she was sent to America to raise funds for defence, returning with $50 million.

She held various government posts before being appointed foreign minister in 1956 – a position she held for nine years. Now a widow, she changed her name to Meir, the Hebrew form of her married name, Myerson.

In 1969 the prime minister died suddenly, and Meir was asked to take over until elections. She was such a success that after the elections she was asked to carry on. She took a tough line with Israel's Arab enemies, while trying to reach a lasting peace. In 1973 the Yom Kippur War, the fourth conflict between Israel and the Arab

▼ *Golda Meir, prime minister of Israel from 1969 to 1974, was one of the world's first women prime ministers.*

countries, broke out. Although peace was soon negotiated, her government was severely criticized because of early defeats, and she resigned. ◆

👁 **see also**
Ben-Gurion   Weizmann

Lise **Meitner**

Austrian-born Swedish physicist
***Born** 1878   **Died** 1968 aged 89*

Lise Meitner was born in Austria and studied at Vienna University. Afterwards she moved to Berlin to study theoretical physics. Sexual prejudice at that time meant that she was not allowed to use the same laboratories as the men and so she had to work in an old carpentry shop. In spite of this, she and her colleague Otto Hahn did important work on radioactivity. In 1918 she and Hahn announced the discovery of a new radioactive element – protactinium.

After World War I Meitner returned to Berlin but when Hitler came to power she was forced to flee Germany because of her Jewish origins. She took refuge in Sweden where she eventually became a citizen. She continued working and in 1939 published a paper explaining how uranium nuclei could split after being bombarded with neutrons. For this explanation of nuclear fission she was awarded a share in the 1966 Enrico Fermi Prize for Atomic Physics. She was horrified when this discovery was used to make bombs and refused to work on the atom bomb. ◆

👁 **see also**
Fermi   Hahn

▲ *Australia's Nellie Melba was the leading singer of her generation.*

Nellie **Melba**

Australian soprano
Born *1861*   **Died** *1931 aged 69*

Nellie Melba derived her stage name from Melbourne, the city of her birth. Her real name was Helen Porter Mitchell. In October 1887 she made her operatic début, in Brussels, as Gilda in Verdi's *Rigoletto*. Triumphant appearances in London and Paris soon followed, and by 1892 the operatic world was at her feet. She even had two famous foods, Peach Melba and Melba toast, named in her honour!

London's Covent Garden Opera House remained especially dear to her, and she made her last appearance there, in her favourite role of Mimi in Puccini's *La Bohème*, on 8 June 1926. She made many recordings between 1904 and 1926 which preserved the quality and natural agility of her exceptional voice. Her singing partnership with the tenor Enrico Caruso was particularly memorable. ◆

◉ **see also**
Sutherland   Te Kanawa

Herman **Melville**

American writer
Born *1819*   **Died** *1891 aged 72*

Herman Melville had to leave his New York school early because his father became bankrupt, and then died, when Herman was only 12. In 1839 he took a job as cabin boy on a ship bound for England, and then worked on a whaling ship. Life at sea was hard and he escaped to a South Sea island. After a difficult and adventurous journey home to America, he published two novels based on his experiences, *Typee* (1846) and *Omoo* (1847).

Several more of Melville's books were also inspired by his own adventures at sea. The most famous is *Moby-Dick*. Published in 1851, it tells the story of Ahab, the captain of a whaling ship, and his obsession with the huge whale (Moby Dick) who had bitten off his leg in a previous encounter.

Melville also published several volumes of verse and completed another novel, *Billy Budd*, just before he died. ◆

▼ *A poster for the 1956 film version of Herman Melville's* Moby-Dick.

Mencius

Chinese philosopher
Born *c.371 BC*
Died *c.289 BC aged about 82*

Mencius was the most influential follower of the great Chinese thinker Confucius. He was born in Shantung, taught by the grandson of Confucius, and himself became a teacher. What he really wanted, however, was to be trusted adviser to a powerful and well-meaning king. He spent much of his life travelling from court to court looking for such a ruler but never found one. Instead he spread his ideas through his writings, which were studied in China over the following 2000 years. Mencius believed that people were naturally good – but that their goodness needed to be encouraged by a wise ruler. If the ruler was fair and kind, his subjects would want to obey him willingly, but if he was cruel or wicked Mencius declared that it would be right for them to rebel against him. ◆

◉ **see also**
Confucius

WARNER BROS. present
GREGORY PECK
in JOHN HUSTON'S "U"
"MOBY DICK"
Colour by TECHNICOLOR

Gregor **Mendel**

Austrian monk who developed the theory of genetic inheritance
Born *1822* **Died** *1884 aged 61*

As a young man Gregor Mendel joined a monastery and became a monk. The monastery supplied schools with teachers, and Mendel was sent to university to train as a science teacher. He spent his life teaching science in a local school and living a quiet religious life in the monastery.

Mendel had his own little garden in the monastery where he grew edible peas, and also sweet peas with pretty coloured flowers. He became interested in how the different characteristics, such as size and colour, were passed down from parent plants. He kept careful records of what all the parent plants looked like and what sort of young plants their seeds produced. He grew many generations of pea plants and finally worked out a set of rules to explain how the different characteristics were passed down (the subject we now call genetics).

He published his work in a local magazine for botanists, but at the time it went unrecognized. Then, 16 years after Mendel's death, the Dutch botanist Hugo de Vries discovered Mendel's paper, and Mendel's Laws of Heredity became the basis of all studies of heredity. ◆

Dimitri **Mendeléev**

Russian chemist who first arranged the 'periodic table' of chemical elements
Born *1834* **Died** *1907 aged 72*

Dimitri Mendeléev studied science in France and in Germany and then became a professor of chemistry in the Russian university of St Petersburg. He was interested in the atomic weights of different elements and made a list of all 63 of the chemical elements known at that time, putting them in order of increasing

▼ *Dimitri Mendeléev, the youngest of 15 children, had a troubled youth. His father was blind and his mother ran a factory to support a large family. Both his parents died before he was 20.*

atomic weight. He then rearranged the list into a continuous pattern of rows and columns and found that all the elements in the same column were similar to each other. This arrangement of chemical elements is called the 'periodic table'.

When Mendeléev worked out this table he found there were gaps, and he predicted that new elements would be discovered to fill these gaps. He looked at the sort of elements in the same column as the gap and was able to say what the new element would be like.

At first scientists were rather suspicious of Mendeléev's predictions, but within a few years some of these new elements were discovered and Mendeléev became a world-famous scientist. ◆

Felix **Mendelssohn**

German composer and conductor
Born *1809* **Died** *1847 aged 38*

Felix Mendelssohn was handsome, intelligent, highly educated, and born into a very wealthy family. He gave his first public concert when he was nine. By the time he was 16, and had completed his String Octet, it was clear to everyone that he was also a musical genius.

Good fortune followed him through the rest of his life. He became one of the most popular composers of the day in England as well as in Germany. His music, such as the 'Italian' Symphony, *The Hebrides* overture, the music for *A Midsummer Night's Dream*, the Violin Concerto, and the oratorio *Elijah*, pleased everyone. However, he took his duties seriously and worked so hard as a teacher and conductor that he undermined his

▲ *Felix Mendelssohn composed this music to accompany the words of a song written by Heinrich Heine.*

health. When his beloved sister, Fanny, died, Mendelssohn seemed to lose the will to live and died only a few months later. ◆

Yehudi **Menuhin**

American-born British violinist
Born 1916   Died 1999 aged 83

Yehudi Menuhin was the eldest of a family of remarkable musicians. He began violin lessons when he was four years old, and made his first public professional appearance (in San Francisco) in 1924. A sensational Paris début in February 1927, followed by an even greater success in New York in November, launched him on an international career. Concert tours followed throughout the world, and he began recording in 1927.

In 1959 Menuhin made his home in London (eventually taking British citizenship in 1985). He has directed important festivals and appeared frequently as a conductor. In 1963

he founded a specialist school for exceptionally talented young musicians. He was knighted in 1965 and made a Peer in 1993. ◆

Robert **Menzies**

Australian statesman and prime minister from 1939 to 1941 and 1949 to 1966
Born 1894   Died 1978 aged 83

Robert Gordon Menzies was born in Jeparit, Victoria, and studied at Melbourne University. After working as a lawyer he started a career in politics, first in Victoria and then with the United Australia Party. Within a few years he was a member of the Federal Government and in 1939 became prime minister of Australia. He was forced to resign two years later when colleagues were dissatisfied with his leadership of Australia's war effort during World War II but returned to the premiership in 1949. The United Australia Party had by now become the Liberal Party and Menzies remained its leader for 17 years. During his time in office Australia changed considerably. Its industry became more advanced, people moved to the country from all over Europe and Asia, and Menzies created closer ties with America.

Menzies was knighted for his services to Australia in 1963, three years before his retirement. ◆

Gerardus **Mercator**

German map-maker
Born 1512   Died 1594 aged 82

Born in Germany, Gerhard Kremer was later known by the Latin version of his name – Gerardus Mercator. He was a skilled engraver, instrument-maker, and surveyor, which were all excellent qualifications for a map-maker.

At that time, European explorers were setting off to distant and unknown places. Mercator was the best of the map-makers who were putting the explorations and discoveries on paper and trying to make a sensible map of the world. He produced a beautifully drawn world map in 1569 which today shows how much of the world had been discovered and how much was still unknown.

Mercator started work on a book of 100 maps; when he died his son completed it. It was the first map collection to be called an 'Atlas'. Mercator's name is now given to a 'projection' of the Earth's surface on a flat sheet of paper. Although this projection is commonly used, it does give a distorted idea of the true areas of some countries. ◆

▼ *This map of the world is from Gerardus Mercator's* Atlas. *It shows his method of portraying the roughly spherical Earth on a flat piece of paper.*

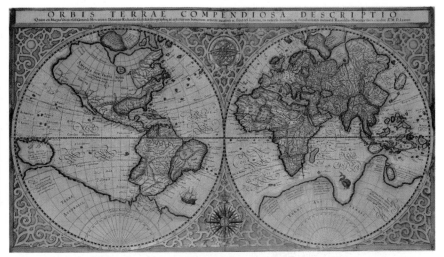

Eddy **Merckx**

Belgian champion cyclist
***Born** 1945*

Eddy Merckx was born just outside Brussels, the Belgian capital. He was a very good student at school and enjoyed playing soccer and basketball. Then, at the age of 14, he discovered cycling and made such rapid progress that he was world amateur champion when he was only 18.

The following year he became a professional, and an amazing run of success ensued. Between 1966 and 1978, when he retired, he triumphed five times in the Giro d'Italia (Tour of Italy) as well as winning the Tour de France five times. However, he was always the first to admit that he owed much of his success to the loyal team of riders who supported him. ◆

Klemens **Metternich**

Austrian chancellor and foreign minister
***Born** 1773   **Died** 1859 aged 86*

In the 19th century Europe was made up of a number of large empires (such as the Austrian Empire) or confederations of smaller states (such as the German Confederation).

Although Klemens Metternich was born in Germany, his father was an Austrian diplomat. Metternich studied at Strasbourg University and followed in his father's footsteps. In 1794 he was sent as a diplomat to England. Later he held various government posts and became Austria's foreign minister in 1809. The Austrian emperor made Metternich a prince in 1813. His skill in negotiating put Austria in a strong position after the defeat of the French emperor, Napoleon. Although Metternich continued to rise in the government of Austria (he was made chancellor in 1821), a revolution in 1848 forced him to resign. He lived in exile in England for many years but returned to Vienna in 1851, where he died eight years later. ◆

Michelangelo Buonarroti

Italian sculptor, painter, poet, and architect
***Born** 1475   **Died** 1564 aged 88*

At the age of 13, against his family's wishes, Michelangelo

▼ *This part of Michelangelo's Sistine Chapel fresco tells the story of Adam and Eve's expulsion from Paradise.*

became apprenticed to a painter, and a year later he went to study at a school for sculptors.

He longed to understand exactly how the human body worked. He dissected corpses at a hospital, and the things he learned from his dissections made him able to paint, draw, or sculpt figures with an accuracy that astounded everyone.

For all his gifts, Michelangelo was a difficult personality. He quarrelled easily and was often depressed, imagining enemies everywhere. He was furious when Pope Julius II asked him in 1508 to paint the ceiling of his chapel. He thought it was a plot by his enemies to keep him away from sculpting. But the painting which he did on the ceiling of the Sistine Chapel turned out to be one of the most astonishing creations in the history of art. It took four years to complete.

Michelangelo then worked for some years at the great church of St Peter in Rome and is mainly responsible for its magnificent dome. Later in his life his work changed in feeling, and his final painting in the Sistine Chapel, completed in 1541, is sombre and heavy. In his later sculpture his forms merge into each other and are very emotional compared to the serenity of his earlier work, such as the huge statue of David made between 1501 and 1504. ◆

Arthur **Miller**

American dramatist
Born 1915

Arthur Miller's father was a small New York manufacturer who lost his money in America's economic slump in the 1930s. After working in a warehouse, Miller saved up to go to university and he soon began writing plays. *Death of a Salesman* (1949) is considered to be his masterpiece. It describes a pleasant but weak hero who instead of facing reality lives a false life of public cheerfulness and optimism. When the gap between this fantasy life and his own failures becomes too great, he finally kills himself.

Miller's other great play, *The Crucible* (1962), describes the hysteria that accompanied witch-hunting in 17th-century America. Miller makes a direct contrast here between this fanatical behaviour and the persecution of American Communists in his own time.

In 1956 Miller married the actress Marilyn Monroe. They divorced in 1961, and his play *After the Fall* (1964) describes some of the difficulties of their relationship. ◆

👁 **see also**
Monroe, M

Glenn **Miller**

American bandleader and trombonist
Born 1904   Died 1944 aged 40

Glenn Miller went to university before becoming a professional trombonist. He was in demand as an instrumentalist but had less success at forming his own band until he started the Glenn Miller Orchestra in 1937. With his 'new sound', made by increasing the number of saxophones, this 'big band' soon became popular, with compositions such as 'Moonlight Serenade', 'Pennsylvania 65000', and 'Little Brown Jug'. The band even appeared in two Hollywood movies: *Sun Valley Serenade* (1941) and *Orchestra Wives* (1942).

Miller was given a commission in the US army during World War II and led the air force band playing in Europe. Returning to London from performances in Paris, his plane disappeared and no trace of it has ever been found. ◆

▲ *Glenn Miller's composition 'Moonlight Serenade' became famous as his band's signature tune.*

A. A. **Milne**

English writer
Born 1882   Died 1956 aged 74

Some writers are less famous than the characters they create. This is certainly true of Alexander Alan Milne, the creator of Winnie the Pooh and Christopher Robin. In real life, Christopher Robin was Milne's son (also called Christopher) and the stories that Milne wrote about Christopher's teddy bear (Pooh) and other toys have become classics.

Winnie the Pooh was published in 1926 and *The House at Pooh Corner* followed two years later. The books were illustrated by Ernest Shepherd.

Milne also wrote two books of verse for children: *When We Were Very Young* (1924) and *Now We Are Six* (1927).

Although Milne wrote magazine articles, essays, plays, and a detective novel, he will always be remembered for creating Pooh, Piglet, Eeyore, and the rest of the characters who lived in the Hundred Acre Wood. ◆

John **Milton**

English 17th century poet
Born *1608*   **Died** *1674 aged 65*

At Cambridge University John Milton first thought of becoming a clergyman, but decided instead to put his great gifts into poetry. One of his first major poems was *Lycidas*, written in memory of a friend who had drowned. Like other poets he was greatly influenced by Latin and Greek literature, but Milton also brought to this poem his own strongly Christian vision of life. He created a new form of poetry, one which was both passionate and scholarly at the same time.

When the English Civil War began in 1642, Milton sided with Parliament against King Charles I. He wrote many articles and pamphlets attacking the monarchy and defending people's freedom to choose their own leaders as well as to publish and read what they liked.

Milton's work led to serious eye-strain, and in 1652 he went blind. When Charles II was restored to the throne in 1660, Milton was arrested, but eventually pardoned. At about this time he wrote one of the greatest poems in existence, *Paradise Lost*. This is a very long poem re-telling the Bible story of how Satan tempted Adam and Eve into disobeying God. Composed entirely in Milton's head and dictated to members of his family, *Paradise Lost* uses poetic language to create an effect that is both magnificent and moving. ◆

Minamoto Yoritomo

Japanese shogun
Born *1147*   **Died** *1199 aged 52*

Minamoto Yoritomo was the first samurai (warrior) to rule Japan as 'shogun' (supreme commander) in the name of the emperor.

When he was a young man his family, the Minamoto, led a rebellion against the Taira family, who held almost all the power in government. In 1185 forces led by his half-brother Yoshitsune defeated the Taira on land and sea, and Yoritomo ensured every last one of the Taira was hunted down. Then he became jealous of Yoshitsune's success. Yoshitsune raised a revolt which failed, so he fled north, but was eventually killed. This left Yoritomo as master of the whole country. Rather than make himself emperor – which might have made him new enemies – he forced the child-emperor of the time to say he was ruling in his name. Yoritomo decided to make the eastern coastal city of Kamakura, near present-day Tokyo, his military headquarters, and this effectively became the central government of Japan. This shogunate was to last until 1333. ◆

👁 **see also**

Tokugawa

Joan **Miró**

Spanish painter
Born *1893*   **Died** *1983 aged 90*

Apart from Picasso, Joan Miró was the greatest Spanish

▼ Animal Composition *by Joan Miró. His style includes simple forms, bright colours, and a sense of fun.*

painter of the 20th century. His most famous pictures are dream-like fantasies featuring strange insect-like creatures with human expressions. They are colourful, bizarre, and amusing. Miró said they were inspired by hallucinations brought on by hunger when he was a poor young artist. He also worked with many other art forms including stained glass and pottery.

Miró was extremely versatile and hard-working. He was still learning new techniques when he was in his eighties and worked up to the day of his death. From 1919 to 1940 he lived mainly in Paris, and after that on the island of Majorca, but he always kept strong links with his birthplace, Barcelona. ◆

👁 **see also**
Picasso

Joni **Mitchell**
Canadian singer and songwriter
Born 1943

Roberta Joan Anderson displayed a talent for painting in high school, but she abandoned plans for a career in art when she learnt to play the guitar and became interested in folk music. Her skill as a songwriter was soon noticed, and her songs were sung by others before she recorded them herself under the name Joni Mitchell.

Her early albums *Clouds* (1969) and *Ladies of the Canyon* (1970) contained many of her best-loved songs: 'Both Sides Now', 'Chelsea Morning', 'Big Yellow Taxi', and 'Woodstock', which became one of the definitive statements about the 'hippie' generation. Her later jazz-influenced recordings have proved less commercial, but her reputation as one of pop's premier songwriters remains undiminished. ◆

▲ *Joni Mitchell abandoned her art studies and plans to become a commercial artist. Instead she became a successful singer and songwriter.*

François **Mitterand**
President of France from 1981 to 1995
Born 1916   *Died* 1996 aged 79

François Mitterand studied law and politics, and graduated from the University of Paris in 1938. A year later his country was at war with Germany and Mitterand joined the army. He was wounded and captured by the Germans. He managed to escape at his third attempt and joined the French resistance, fighting against the German occupation of France. After the war he entered politics and was elected to the National Assembly. During the 1950s he served as a government minister in a number of posts and then in 1971 became leader of the Socialist Party. He stood unsuccessfully for the post of President of France on two occasions before finally being elected in 1981. Although he encountered many problems during his first seven years of office, he was re-elected in 1988. ◆

Molière
French playwright and actor
Born 1622   *Died* 1673 aged 51

Molière was the son of a successful upholsterer. His real name was Jean-Baptiste Poquelin. He first studied law at university, then left home to become an actor, adopting the stage name Molière. He toured France with a group of friends and began to write plays for this new company.

In 1658, after about 12 years of touring, the group was given a permanent theatre in Paris by King Louis XIV. From that time on, Molière wrote many more delightful plays. Although most of these were comedies, they often had a serious side too, attacking human failings such as snobbishness, hypocrisy, and meanness. One of his funniest plays is called *Le Malade Imaginaire* (The Imaginary Invalid). It is about someone who always thinks he is more ill than he really is. Tragically, one night Molière, who was acting the main part, collapsed and then died only a few hours later. ◆

▼ *A 17th-century portrait of Molière, one of France's greatest playwrights.*

Piet **Mondrian**

Dutch painter
Born *1872*   **Died** *1944 aged 71*

Piet Mondrian was one of the most important painters in the creation of abstract art – art that does not represent anything, but exists purely for the sake of its shapes and colours. He was rather an odd character, and was obsessively tidy and self-disciplined.

Until he was about 50 he had little financial success, for his kind of painting was slow to win admirers. He used only right-angled shapes and the most basic colours – blue, red, and yellow, and black and white. Gradually, however, people realized that his pictures had a beauty and elegance of their own, and many other artists imitated him. He lived in Paris for most of his career, but left in 1938 because of fears about impending war; he spent two years in London, then settled in New York in 1940. ◆

▲ *Monet designed and planned every aspect of his garden at Giverney himself. His paintings of the garden became increasingly abstract towards the end of his life.*

Claude **Monet**

French painter
Born *1840*   **Died** *1926 aged 86*

As a child in Paris, Claude Monet hated school and spent his time making cartoon-style pictures of his teachers. He became so clever at it that at the age of 16 he was earning pocket money making quick portraits.

When he first became an artist, Monet struggled for many years in poverty while his art was ignored, laughed at, and considered the work of a lunatic. He insisted on working outdoors to make on-the-spot pictures, but because the weather continually changed he had to work quickly, energetically applying pure, bold colour straight onto the canvas. His colourful pictures did not attempt to copy a scene; they gave an impression of it (hence the term Impressionism), concentrating on the effects of light and atmosphere.

From his mid-fifties, Monet was regarded as the famous grand old man of Impressionism. His output of paintings was enormous. He particularly liked to paint the same subject many times in different weather conditions and seasons. He painted the Thames in London in different lights, and at home in his garden he made a series of wonderful pictures of water-lilies. In fact, his garden at Giverny, 65 km northwest of Paris, provided the greatest single inspiration for Monet's artistic work for over 40 years. ◆

👁 **see also**
Manet   Pissarro

Mongkut

King of Siam from 1851 to 1868
Born *1804*   **Died** *1868 aged 64*

As a young man Mongkut became a Buddhist monk and a learned scholar. Unusually for a member of the royal family he was able to travel freely around Siam (now called Thailand). Meetings with American and French missionaries made him intensely interested in western languages and science. After becoming king in 1851 (when he became known as Rama IV) he encouraged trade between Siam and western countries. Although he was unable to make many changes to Siam's traditional way of life, he ensured that his sons learned as much as possible about western culture so that they could begin to introduce great reforms. The life of the royal family's English governess, Anna Leonowens, was later made into a musical play, *The King and I.* ◆

James **Monroe**

*President of the United States of America
from 1817 to 1825*
Born 1758   Died 1831 aged 73

James Monroe was born in
Virginia, North America, when
Virginia was still a British colony. In
1775, while Monroe was at college,
the American Revolution (War of
Independence) broke out between
Britain and its American colonies.
The following year, Monroe joined
the American army. He fought in
several battles, in which he showed
great courage. In 1779, after three
years away, he returned to Virginia.
Two years later, the British forces
surrendered.

Having helped the 'United States'
to win independence, Monroe
entered politics. Between 1782 and
1816 he served in the Virginia
legislature and the national
Congress; was governor of Virginia;
was an American diplomat in
Europe; and was secretary of state.
In 1816, he was elected president.

At this time, much of Central and
South America consisted of Spanish
colonies. From 1818 onwards the
Spanish colonists overthrew their
foreign rulers and founded new
countries (such as Argentina and
Mexico). To help preserve the
independence of these countries,
Monroe declared in 1823 that
European countries should not
interfere in American countries. (In
return, the United States would not
interfere in Europe.) This policy was
followed for almost a century. It was
called 'The Monroe Doctrine'. ◆

Marilyn **Monroe**

American screen idol
Born 1926   Died 1962 aged 36

Marilyn Monroe was born
Norma Jean Mortenson. She
had a miserable childhood in Los

▲ *Marilyn Monroe in one of her classic
Hollywood publicity poses.*

Angeles foster homes because her
mother was mentally ill.

After working as a model and in
minor film roles, Monroe starred in
her first big role in *Niagara* in 1953.
Two of her best-known films,
Gentlemen Prefer Blondes (1953)
and *Some Like it Hot* (1959), show
she was a fine comic actress.
However, she also took serious,
dramatic roles in films like *The
Misfits* (1961), her last film.

She was married three times,
including to baseball star Joe
DiMaggio and playwright Arthur

Miller, who wrote *The Misfits* for
her. She died from a drug overdose
in 1962. Even now, many years after
her death, she is remembered as
one of the most beautiful stars of
cinema history. ◆

👁 **see also**
DiMaggio   Miller, Arthur

Joe **Montana**

American football quarterback
Born 1956

From the age of eight it was
obvious that Joe Montana had
great football ability. He played
brilliantly for Notre Dame, the
college renowned for football, and
was signed up by the San Francisco
49ers in 1979. He suffered a serious
back injury in 1986 which put his
future as a player in doubt but
amazingly he recovered.

His exploits with the 49ers have
made him possibly the best
attacking quarterback ever to play
American football. Despite many
injuries, he led his team to victory
in four Superbowl matches.

In 1992 he joined the Kansas City
Chiefs on a three year contract and
retired from NFL football in 1995. ◆

▼ *Joe Montana seen here playing for the
Kansas City Chiefs.*

▲ *Maria Montessori with children being taught by the methods she devised.*

Maria
Montessori

Italian developer of a new system of educating young children
***Born** 1870   **Died** 1952 aged 81*

Maria Montessori was the only child of a civil servant. In 1890 she became Italy's first woman medical student and graduated with distinction.

As a doctor Montessori publicized the plight of disturbed children who were kept in asylums meant for insane adults. In 1900 she became director of Rome's first special school for 'degenerates', as children with severe learning difficulties were then called. She taught these children by new methods, and they did as well in the state examinations as 'normal children'.

In 1906 she opened a school for three- to six-year-olds on a poor estate. She began to notice that the children's urge to master their surroundings was so strong that they could be left to organize their own learning when given the right equipment and materials. Visitors from abroad were astonished to find the children calm, tidy, courteous, and absorbed in what they were doing. They learned to read and write without difficulty.

From 1912 until her death she travelled and lectured on her methods and worked hard to keep up the standards of the many Montessori schools that opened all over the world. ◆

Claudio
Monteverdi

Italian composer
***Born** 1567   **Died** 1643 aged 76*

Claudio Monteverdi studied with the organist of Cremona Cathedral and made such good progress that he published a collection of short choral compositions when he was only 16. Several collections of madrigals (songs for voices, usually without instruments) soon followed. In 1592 he entered the service of the Duke of Mantua, whose court was one of the most musical in Italy. There he worked as a singer, instrumentalist, and composer. Apart from madrigals, which were often very colourful and dramatic, Monteverdi wrote operas. His *Orfeo* (1607) is regarded as the first great masterpiece of the operatic form that had only just been invented.

In 1612 he became Master of Music at St Mark's Cathedral, Venice. This gave him the chance to write magnificent music for the services, but when the first public opera-house was opened in Venice (1637) he turned again to opera. Like *Orfeo*, Monteverdi's last operas, *The Return of Ulysses* (1641), and *The Coronation of Poppea* (1642), are regarded as masterpieces. ◆

Montezuma II

Emperor of the Aztecs for 18 years
***Born** c.1480   **Died** 1520 aged about 40*

The Aztecs controlled most of Mexico and parts of Central America for over 100 years before they were conquered by the Spanish. Aztec emperors were elected by government, army, and religious leaders. They ruled with the help of a group of nobles to advise them. They had every

▼ *This mask represents one of the most important Aztec gods, Tezcatlipoca.*

possible luxury, but they and the people who served them were restricted by many rituals and customs. Emperors were remote, mysterious figures, rarely showing themselves to the common people.

Montezuma II became emperor in 1502. He was greatly feared. Unlike the previous emperor, he gave greater power to his own family and the nobility, and took it away from other people such as members of the merchant class. During his reign, his army conquered many cities, and he brought lands ruled by the Aztecs more firmly under his control.

Then, in 1519 the Spanish, led by Hernán Cortés, entered the Aztec capital of Tenochtitlán. Montezuma was killed during one of the battles. ◆

👁 **see also**

Cortés

▲ *A 19th-century plate commemorating the Montgolfier brothers' great ballooning achievements.*

Montgolfier brothers

French designers of the hot-air balloon
Joseph Montgolfier
Born *1740* **Died** *1810 aged 69*
Jacques Montgolfier
Born *1745* **Died** *1799 aged 54*

The Montgolfier brothers worked as paper-makers and they owned a factory at Annonay, near Lyon. At that time nobody believed that people would ever fly, but that did not stop the Montgolfiers experimenting. They discovered that a smoke-filled bag would rise above a fire made of straw and wool, and thought they had discovered a new gas, which they called 'electric smoke'. In fact this was only hot air, as they realized later.

On 5 June 1783 they flew a silk balloon, lined with paper, and filled with hot air from a burning brazier. It travelled over a kilometre in its ten-minute flight. The brothers were determined to make the first balloon to carry passengers.

On 15 October, François Pilâtre de Rozier went up in the brothers' tethered balloon. All was then ready for the first free-flight attempt to take place. The intrepid Pilâtre de Rozier, and his friend the Marquis d'Arlandes, took off in Paris in the Montgolfiers' balloon on 21 November 1783. They travelled 9 km in 25 minutes, until the brazier they carried burnt a hole in the balloon. ◆

Field Marshal Montgomery

English commander of Allied forces during World War II
Born *1887* **Died** *1976 aged 89*

Bernard Law Montgomery trained at the military academy at Sandhurst and fought in World War I. He stayed in the army after the war and by the time of the outbreak of war in Europe again in 1939, he commanded the 3rd Division of the British Army. He took part in the invasion force to France and its evacuation from Dunkirk. In 1942 he took command of the 8th Army and it was under his leadership that the British won one of the most important battles of the war in the Middle East, at El Alamein. Montgomery continued the offensive against the German army (led by Rommel) in North Africa. Then, in February 1943 Montgomery's forces came under the command of the American General, Dwight Eisenhower. They took part in the invasion of France in June 1944 and Montgomery received the German surrender at his headquarters on 3 May 1945. In the following year he was created Viscount Montgomery of Alamein, taking the title from his most famous victory. ◆

L. M. **Montgomery**

Canadian author of children's novels
Born *1874* **Died** *1942 aged 67*

Lucy Maud Montgomery was just two years old when her mother died and she was sent to live with her grandparents on Prince Edward Island. When she grew up she became a teacher, but she left this job to take care of her grandmother after her grandfather died.

She had kept a diary for many years, and eventually she began writing stories and poems, which were published in one of the local newspapers. Her first novel, *Anne of Green Gables*, was published in 1908. It was an instant best-seller. In the book, an elderly brother and sister ask for a boy from an orphanage to help on their farm. They are sent a girl, Anne, by mistake, and they come to love her very much. Montgomery continued to write a great deal and produced seven sequels to *Anne*, other novels for children and adults, an autobiography, and many poems and short stories. ◆

Henry **Moore**

English sculptor
Born *1898* **Died** *1986 aged 88*

By the time he was 11, Henry Moore had decided to become a sculptor. After fighting in World War I he returned to Yorkshire, where he had been born. He started teaching but disliked it so much that he enrolled at Leeds School of Art. After a scholarship to study at the Royal College of Art in London, he travelled to Italy in order to widen his understanding of sculpture.

Henry Moore's work was always based on nature: rock formations, stones and bones, landscape itself, and the human figure. He never tried to copy precisely the source of his ideas, but rather to suggest a likeness.

He was 50 before he was internationally recognized. He had exceptional energy, finally completing about 800 sculptures in wood, stone and bronze, 4000 drawings and 500 prints. ◆

👁 **see also**

Hepworth

◀ *Sculptures such as this* Family Group *(1948–1949) are among Henry Moore's most famous works. They simplify the human form using smooth, gently curving lines.*

Thomas **More**

English scholar executed by Henry VIII
Born *c.1477* **Died** *1535 aged about 58*

Thomas More was a devout Catholic, who, as a young man, nearly became a monk. Henry VIII enjoyed More's company, but More was not deceived by the king's favour. He once said, 'If my head could win him a castle in France, it would not fail to go.' More was also a successful lawyer and scholar, and wrote a popular book called *Utopia* about an imaginary perfect world.

▲ *Portrait of Thomas More from 1527.*

After Cardinal Wolsey had failed to grant Henry VIII his divorce from Catherine of Aragon, the king made Thomas More his chancellor. But More believed the king was wrong to divorce his wife, and to break with the Catholic Church to get his way. He refused to swear an oath accepting Henry's actions, even after being imprisoned in the Tower of London for 17 months. He was beheaded, saying on the scaffold: 'I die the king's good servant, but God's servant first.' ◆

👁 **see also**

Henry VIII   Wolsey

▲ *William Morris created many colourful designs like this for fabric and wallpapers.*

William **Morris**

English artist, poet, and socialist politician
Born 1834   Died 1896 aged 62

After getting a degree from Exeter College, Oxford, William Morris started work as an architect, but he soon gave up architecture to become a painter like his friends Edward Burne-Jones and Dante Gabriel Rossetti. Later he helped to set up his own firm of fine art craftworkers who designed furniture and wallpaper. He was also an accomplished poet, basing many of his poems and stories on ancient sagas of Icelandic origin.

In 1883 he joined a socialist political party, the Social Democratic Federation, and travelled the country to speak at meetings and lead marches. When he quarrelled with the leaders of the Social Democratic Federation, he helped to start another party, the Socialist League.

Five years before he died he began yet another venture, setting up the Kelmscott Press which published beautifully bound and illustrated books. ◆

👁 **see also**
Rossetti

Samuel **Morse**

American inventor of Morse code
Born 1791   Died 1872 aged 80

Samuel Morse studied painting in London and worked as a successful portrait painter in America for many years.

But Morse was also a scientist. On a return voyage to America, a fellow passenger demonstrated some electromagnetic devices. Morse realized he could adapt them to make an electric current put dots and dashes on paper, and he invented a dot-and-dash code for each letter of the alphabet. He used it to send coded messages along a wire to an electrical receiver, which printed the dots and dashes. It was the quickest way to communicate over long distances, and more successful than rival telegraph systems in Europe.

In 1843 Morse constructed a 65-kilometre telegraph between Baltimore and Washington for the American government. Soon other towns and cities were linked by Morse's telegraph system, and he became rich and famous. ◆

Moses

Leader and prophet of the Hebrews
Probably lived in the 13th century BC

According to the Bible, Moses was born while the Hebrews were slaves in Egypt. Pharaoh, the ruler of Egypt, had ordered that all Hebrew baby boys must be killed. So Moses' mother hid him in a basket in the bulrushes (reeds) on the banks of the River Nile. Pharaoh's daughter found him and he grew up in the palace.

Moses had to run away to Arabia after attacking an Egyptian who was ill-treating a Hebrew slave. In Arabia he felt the presence of God when he saw a burning bush, and he knew that he had to return to his people.

Back in Egypt he and his brother Aaron asked Pharaoh to release the Hebrew slaves. Pharaoh refused so God sent ten plagues to Egypt. Pharaoh agreed to let the people go and Moses led them in the 'Exodus' (departure) across the Red Sea.

They wandered in the wilderness for 40 years. During this time Moses received the Ten Commandments on two tablets of stone at Mount Sinai and bound the people to God in a covenant (agreement) that they would keep His laws. Moses died before the people reached the 'promised land' of Canaan. ◆

👁 **see also**
Joseph

▲ *To many musicians, Mozart is, quite simply, the greatest of all composers.*

Wolfgang Amadeus **Mozart**

Austrian composer
Born 1756   Died 1791 aged 35

When the Salzburg violinist Leopold Mozart realized that his children, Maria Anna and Wolfgang Amadeus, were exceptionally musical, he set about teaching them all he could. But even he must have been surprised when he discovered just how talented his son was. By the time Wolfgang was five he was able to compose quite good pieces of music, and as a performer of the harpsichord and violin he could outshine much older musicians.

In 1762 Leopold took his children on tour to Munich and then Vienna. In the following year they travelled around Germany, France, and England. In 1770 they toured Italy. Everywhere they went, young Mozart impressed all the leading musicians he met.

When eventually the touring had to stop, Mozart joined his father as one of the Archbishop of Salzburg's court musicians. However, he hated being treated like a servant. In 1781 he went to Vienna, determined to earn a living as best he could.

He taught and gave concerts. He composed music of all kinds and, for a while, was successful. However, things began to go wrong, and his last few years were spent in comparative poverty. He was given the cheapest of funerals and his grave was soon forgotten.

Mozart wrote 41 symphonies and 27 piano concertos, besides much chamber and solo piano music. The complete list of his works contains over 600 titles. Finest of all, perhaps, are his operas: *The Marriage of Figaro, Così fan tutte, Don Giovanni,* and *The Magic Flute.* ◆

Robert **Mugabe**

First prime minister of independent Zimbabwe
Born 1924

Robert Mugabe was born at a Catholic mission north of Salisbury, the capital of Southern Rhodesia (now Zimbabwe). His mother hoped he would become a priest, but he trained to be a teacher instead.

Rhodesia was then a colony ruled by Britain. Robert Mugabe travelled to other countries in Africa in the 1950s and saw people fighting for independence from British rule. With others, he founded the Zimbabwe African National Union (ZANU) to fight for majority rule by black people in his own country. ZANU was banned and Mugabe was sent to prison.

He then joined the ZANU guerrilla fighters who were attacking Rhodesian forces from Mozambique. A cease-fire was declared and free elections took place in 1980. He was elected president of Zimbabwe in 1987. Since the 1990s he has come under increasing criticism for his increasing use of violence to stay in power. ◆

Muhammad

Islamic prophet
Born c.570   Died 632 aged about 62

Muhammad's father, Abdullah, died before he was born, and his mother, Aminah, died when he was only six. Therefore, he was brought up under the protection of his grandfather, Abdul Muttalib, and his uncle, Abu Talib. They came from the powerful Quraish tribe who looked after the Kaaba, the central religious shrine in the city of Mecca in Arabia.

Muhammad became a shepherd. He was known as *al-amin*, the trustworthy one.

Muhammad used to pray alone in a cave on Mount Hira outside Mecca, and there he received his first revelations from God. Muhammad believed that he had to preach to the people of Mecca that there is only one God, Allah, and that they were wrong to worship idols (images). The people laughed at him. A few believed in his message and encouraged him to continue to preach.

In 619 Muhammad's wife and uncle died. With the loss of these two important supporters, some of the Meccans plotted to kill Muhammad. In 622 he emigrated

▼ *The Dome of the Rock mosque in Jerusalem, built 691–692, covers the sacred spot from which Muslims believe Muhammad ascended to Heaven.*

from Mecca to Medina with his followers. This move is called the *hijra* (migration) and marks the beginning of the Muslim calendar.

In Medina Muhammad taught people about religion and he organized armed resistance to anyone, including the Meccans, who was hostile to the new Muslim community. He led various campaigns and defeated the Meccans. In 630 Muhammad entered Mecca peacefully. The people there became Muslims and destroyed the idols. By the time of Muhammad's death most of the tribes in the Arabian peninsula had acknowledged his authority. He was buried in Medina.

For all Muslims, Muhammad is their model husband, parent, statesman, soldier, honest trader, and man of God. ◆

👁 **see also**

Ali

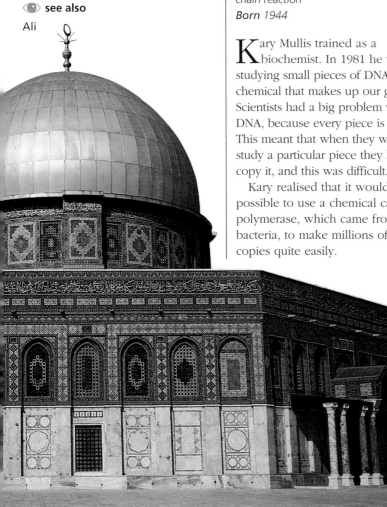

▲ The Dance of Life *by Munch.*

Kary Banks **Mullis**

American inventor of the polymerase chain reaction
Born 1944

Kary Mullis trained as a biochemist. In 1981 he was studying small pieces of DNA, the chemical that makes up our genes. Scientists had a big problem with DNA, because every piece is different. This meant that when they wanted to study a particular piece they had to copy it, and this was difficult.

Kary realised that it would be possible to use a chemical called a polymerase, which came from bacteria, to make millions of DNA copies quite easily.

His idea became the polymerase chain reaction, one of the most important tools in the study of genetics. In 1993 he received a Nobel Prize for his work. ◆

Edvard **Munch**

Norwegian painter
Born 1863   Died 1944 aged 80

Edvard Munch had a miserable childhood. His mother died when he was five, his sister died when he was 11, and his father became almost insane with grief. The one compensation was that Edvard was looked after by a kind aunt, who encouraged his gift for art.

All this suffering affected his paintings. He depicted people, showing their fears and anxieties, in a way that no other artist had done before. Gradually he was recognized as a genius. At the age of 44 he had a mental breakdown. When he recovered, he had a more cheerful outlook, and he painted new subjects such as landscapes. However, he never quite recaptured the magic of his early work. ◆

Rupert **Murdoch**
Australian media magnate
Born 1931

Keith Rupert Murdoch's father was an Australian newspaper publisher. After graduating from Oxford University, Murdoch worked on British newspapers until his father died in 1952. He then returned to Australia to run the family newspapers. Immediately he changed their style, introducing more gossip and sport, so that they sold more copies. His newspaper empire grew and in the 1970s and 1980s he bought control of British newspapers, including *The Sun* and *The Times*. Many workers lost their jobs when he introduced new print technology and there were angry scenes at his News International company. In 1985 he became an American citizen and bought the film company 20th Century Fox, and in 1989 he launched the satellite TV station which became BSkyB. ◆

Benito **Mussolini**
Dictator of Italy from 1926 to 1943
Born 1883   **Died** 1945 aged 61

Benito Mussolini was involved in politics from an early age and was often arrested for his activities. He began to believe that the only way to change society was through the use of violence.

After World War I, many people were scared that there would be a revolution in Italy, as there had been in the Soviet Union. In 1919 they gave Mussolini funds to set up the Fascist Party to oppose the Socialists and Communists. His Fascists attacked trade unionists, broke up strikes, and then 'marched' on Rome in 1922.

The king asked Mussolini to be prime minister and Mussolini gradually took more power for himself. By 1926, *il Duce* ('the Leader'), as he was now known, had become a dictator.

In 1935, to increase Italy's power and his own glory, Mussolini invaded and conquered Ethiopia. His great friend in Europe was Hitler. They formed an alliance, which took Italy into World War II on Germany's side in 1940. However, Mussolini's armies suffered many defeats. By 1943 Mussolini had been overthrown and placed under arrest. German paratroops rescued him and put him back in power in northern Italy. The end, though, was not far away. When Italy was finally defeated, Mussolini was shot by his Italian enemies and his body was hung upside-down in the Piazza Loreto in Milan. ◆

◉ **see also**
Hitler

◀ *Benito Mussolini in 1928.*

Modest **Mussorgsky**
Russian composer
Born 1839   **Died** 1881 aged 42

Although Modest Mussorgsky was taught the piano by his mother, and played a concerto when he was nine, music was not thought to be a proper career for the son of a wealthy landowner. He therefore entered the St Petersburg Cadet School and in due course took a commission in the army. However, he continued to play the piano and compose short pieces, and in 1858 he left the army in order to become a full-time composer.

Despite some success, life became a struggle and he began to drink heavily. The result was that he left many compositions unfinished, or in a very muddled state. His music, however, showed great power and originality, such as his historical operas *Boris Godunov* and *Khovanshchina*, the symphonic poem *St John's Night on the Bare Mountain*, and the piano suite *Pictures at an Exhibition*. After his death his works were 'polished', but not always improved, by such composers as Rimsky-Korsakov. ◆

◉ **see also**
Rimsky-Korsakov

Eadweard **Muybridge**
English photographer
Born 1830   **Died** 1904 aged 74

When Edward James Muybridge emigrated to America at the age of 22 he changed his name to Eadweard to sound more 'Anglo-Saxon'. He became a professional landscape photographer in

▲ *Eadweard Muybridge's famous photographs showing a horse running at full gallop.*

Guru **Nanak**

First leader of the Sikhs
Born 1469   Died 1539 aged 70

Nanak was born a Hindu, but when he grew up he worked for a Muslim and learned about the Muslim religion too. When he was older he became a religious teacher, preaching a new faith using ideas from both Hinduism and Islam. This new religion, called Sikhism, was based on one God and on the equality of all human beings.

Nanak believed that he had seen God and wrote about his experience in one of his early songs. This song can be found in the Sikh holy book, the Guru Granth Sahib. To reach unity with God he said people should meditate, pray, sing hymns, and follow the advice of a spiritual guide ('guru').

Nanak travelled a great deal to teach people about God's path. Eventually he settled in the village of Kartarpur and lived as the teacher of ordinary men and women. They listened to Nanak's teachings and followed his advice and example. Nanak became known as Guru Nanak. Before he died, Nanak appointed his most trusted follower, Lehna, as his successor. Lehna was given the name Guru Angad. ◆

▼ *Amritsar, a city in the Punjab region of India, is the holy city of Sikhism. The Golden Temple (below) is the holiest of all Sikh temples.*

California, but when asked to photograph a horse at full gallop he became fascinated with the idea of photographing movement. In 1877 and 1878 he succeeded, using 24 cameras and a system of trip wires stretched across a track. As a horse ran past, its hooves broke the wires and triggered the shutters. This was the first time anyone had shown that a galloping horse lifts all its feet off the ground at the same time. Muybridge went on to photograph many animals, publishing his famous book *Human and Animal Locomotion* in 1887. ◆

Vladimir **Nabokov**

Russian-born American writer
Born 1899   Died 1977 aged 78

Vladimir Nabokov was well educated and spoke Russian, English, and French at a very young age. As a teenager he published two volumes of poetry before his family was forced to flee Russia following the Communist Revolution of 1919.

Nabokov studied at Cambridge University before living in Berlin and Paris. During this time he wrote poems, short stories, and plays as well as nine novels including *Despair* and *Invitation to a Beheading*. These were published under the false name V. Sirin. In 1940, Nabokov and his family moved to America and he became an American citizen. He taught at Stanford, Wellesley, and Cornell universities while continuing to write. Known for his imaginative writing, Nabokov received public and financial success with his novel *Lolita* (1955). ◆

Fridtjof **Nansen**

Norwegian explorer and scientist
Born *1861*   **Died** *1930 aged 68*

Fridtjof Nansen began his varied career as a zoologist. On a whaling voyage he saw Greenland, and decided to lead an expedition to cross it. With five other men he made the first crossing of the island in 1888–1889.

Later Nansen led a more daring expedition. He left his specially designed ship, the *Fram*, drifting slowly across the frozen Arctic Ocean whilst he tried to reach the North Pole on foot. Eventually he had to turn back, but had got nearer to the Pole than anyone before him.

Nansen then worked as a scientist, becoming first a professor of zoology, and then a professor of oceanography, the study of oceans. In 1921 he was appointed League of Nations High Commissioner for refugees, and was awarded the Nobel Peace Prize in 1923 for his work in this field. ◆

Napoleon I

Emperor of France from 1804 to 1814 and again in 1815
Born *1769*   **Died** *1821 aged 51*

Napoleon Bonaparte was only ten when he entered military school. After graduating, he was rapidly promoted and soon commanded an entire army and conquered northern Italy for France. Next he invaded Egypt in 1798, but his fleet was defeated by Nelson at the battle of the Nile. By this time, the French Revolution had been going on for ten years. However, the Directory, who were in charge, were in a mess so Napoleon returned to Paris because he believed France needed firm government. In November 1799, after a coup d'état (overthrow of a government), he became the new leader of France. Over the next five years, Napoleon worked hard and made many changes to improve ordinary people's lives. At the same time, his armies were successful abroad. In 1804 he became emperor, and by 1807 his was the largest empire in Europe since the days of Rome.

But then things began to go wrong. The Spanish, with British help, drove the French out of Spain. Then, in 1812, Napoleon made his worst mistake by invading Russia. The Russians steadily retreated, drawing Napoleon's army deeper into Russia and further from its supplies. Napoleon reached Moscow, but still the Russians refused to make peace, and Napoleon realized that he had to retreat. His army was now caught by the bitter Russian winter, and his frozen, starving men died in their thousands.

By now many French people were disillusioned with Napoleon's rule. After his defeat at the battle of Leipzig and the invasion of France in 1814, Napoleon was banished to the Mediterranean island of Elba.

In 1815 he escaped and landed in France. The soldiers who were sent

▼ Napoleon Crossing the Alps *by Jacques Louis David.*

to stop him welcomed him as emperor instead and he returned to Paris. But after his defeat at the battle of Waterloo, Napoleon was again exiled, this time to the island of St Helena in the south Atlantic. He died six years later. ◆

see also

Napoleon III   Nelson   Wellington

Napoleon III

Emperor of France from 1852 to 1870
Born 1808   Died 1873 aged 64

After Napoleon Bonaparte was banished from France with the rest of his family, the French king, Louis Philippe, was put back on the throne. Louis Napoleon, Bonaparte's nephew, dreamed of returning to France as a great ruler himself. In 1836 and 1840, he tried to start rebellions in France against the king. Both these failed and he was first exiled to America, and then later spent six years in prison before escaping to England.

In 1848, Louis Philippe was expelled from France. Louis Napoleon returned, this time to be elected president, and then became Emperor Napoleon III in 1852. His style of rule was undemocratic but he brought industrial development to France. His foreign policy was less successful, because he was always interfering in other countries' affairs.

From 1856 he suffered ill health, and eventually allowed his ministers to assume more power. In 1870 France declared war on Prussia but was heavily defeated. Louis Napoleon was again thrown out of France, and died just three years later in England. ◆

see also

Napoleon I

Gamal Abdel Nasser

President of Egypt from 1956 to 1970
Born 1918   Died 1970 aged 52

As a boy Gamal Abdel Nasser joined demonstrations against the British, who ruled Egypt with the help of the Egyptian king. Then, when he was in the army, he joined a secret group who managed to overthrow King Farouk in 1952 and get rid of the remaining British troops. Two years later Nasser became prime minister and then, in 1956, president.

In that year Egypt was invaded by Britain, France, and Israel after Nasser took over the Suez Canal from its foreign owners. Their action was criticized by many nations and they soon withdrew, leaving Nasser with even more power in Egypt.

He tried to use this power to unite Arab countries, but their divisions proved too deep. In 1967 Egypt was defeated in the Six Day War by Israel. Nasser died of a heart attack three years later. ◆

▼ *Nasser addressing a huge crowd in Cairo in 1961. When he died in 1970, he was greatly mourned. He had helped to turn Egypt into a politically powerful country.*

◀ *Martina Navratilova*

Martina Navratilova

Czech-born American tennis champion
Born 1956

Martina Navratilova was born in Czechoslovakia, but moved to America in 1975 when she started to become a successful tennis player. In 1981 she became a US citizen and the following year was the first woman professional tennis player to earn more than one million dollars in a season.

Her favourite championship has always been Wimbledon, where she has won nine singles finals (1978–1979, 1982–1987, and 1990), beating the record set by fellow American, Helen Wills Moody. She was the most outstanding woman tennis player of the 1980s. ◆

Nebuchadnezzar

King of Babylon from 605 BC to 562 BC
Born *c.630 BC*
Died *c.562 BC aged about 68*

Nebuchadnezzar II was the last great ruler of the ancient city of Babylon, which stood by the river Euphrates in the territory of modern Iraq. Nebuchadnezzar extended Babylonian power over a huge area by successful military campaigns in Syria, Palestine, and Egypt. Two of his campaigns, in 597 and 587 BC, were against the city of Jerusalem. The Bible reports how he destroyed Jerusalem and took its inhabitants, including the young Jewish prophet Daniel, as captives to Babylon.

Nebuchadnezzar built massive defensive walls around Babylon and enlarged and adorned its temples and palaces. He also built the Hanging Gardens, an artificial hill with terraces and trees, for his wife, a foreign princess who was homesick for her own country. These hanging gardens were one of the seven wonders of the ancient world. ◆

▼ *Part of the Ishtar Gate, which was the main entrance to the city of Babylon.*

Pandit Jawaharlal Nehru

First prime minister of independent India, from 1947 to 1964
Born *1889*   **Died** *1964 aged 74*

At the age of 15, Pandit Nehru was sent away from home to study in England. He studied science at Cambridge University and later studied law in London. He returned to India in 1912 and joined his father's law practice.

Nehru supported Mahatma Gandhi and became one of the most prominent leaders of the Indian nationalist movement. In 1920 he started working for the Indian National Congress, an organization that led India's struggle to gain freedom from British rule. He served as its president in 1929 and again from 1936 to 1937. However, he was frequently sent to prison for his opposition to British rule.

In 1946 he was again elected president of the Indian National Congress. He led the team that negotiated with the British government the terms and timetable for India's independence. He became the first prime minister of independent India in 1947, and remained prime minister until he died 17 years later.

Nehru strongly believed in parliamentary democracy and brought rapid economic development to his country. His government concentrated on establishing large-scale industrial units and new hydroelectric projects to generate power to meet India's needs.

Nehru's reputation at home and abroad suffered a severe blow when China invaded India in 1962. Many Indians blamed Nehru and his policies for the unprepared state of the Indian army at the time of the invasion. He died two years later after a stroke. ◆

The light has gone out of our lives and there is darkness everywhere.

NEHRU, JANUARY 1948
Speech following
Gandhi's assassination.

◉ **see also**

Gandhi, Indira   Gandhi, Mahatma

Horatio **Nelson**

Britain's greatest admiral
Born *1758*   **Died** *1805 aged 47*

Although he was never a strong child, Horatio Nelson was always determined to go to sea. At the age of 12 he accompanied his sailor uncle to the Falkland Islands. At 15 Nelson joined the navy, and six years later was given command of his own ship.

Despite frequent illnesses, Nelson made a name for himself as a skilled and popular commander. His success began during Britain's war against the French in 1793. Despite being blinded in his right eye

▲ This illustration shows Nelson explaining the plan of attack to his officers prior to the battle of Trafalgar.

during a battle, Nelson was soon made an admiral. More injuries followed, including the loss of his right arm from below the elbow. But still he pursued the French, destroying their navy in 1798 at the battle of the Nile.

▼ The uniform Nelson was wearing when he was shot.

Nelson is most famous for the battle of Trafalgar in 1805. His 27 ships encountered 33 French and Spanish vessels. Nelson signalled to his fleet, 'England expects that every man will do his duty' and once again the French navy was beaten. However, during the fighting Nelson was shot by a French sniper and died on the deck of his ship, the *Victory*. ◆

👁 **see also**

Napoleon I

Nero

Emperor of Rome
Born AD 37   *Died* AD 68 aged 30

Nero was adopted by his mother's uncle, the Emperor Claudius, in AD 50. He married Claudius' daughter Octavia and so became part of the ruling household. Nero's mother Agrippina made sure that her son became emperor after Claudius by poisoning the true heir, Britannicus.

Nero was said to be a cruel man, even arranging for his own mother and

wife to be murdered. We do not know that he actually started the Great Fire of Rome in AD 64, as some historians suggest, but he used the opportunity to rebuild large parts of the city and to build an enormous palace for himself, called the Golden House. He blamed the Christians for the fire and used it as an excuse to persecute and massacre them.

In AD 68 there were uprisings against him starting in southern Gaul (now France). He committed suicide when he realized that everyone, including his own bodyguard, had deserted him. ◆

Thomas Newcomen

British inventor of an early steam-engine
Born 1663   *Died* 1729 aged 66

Thomas Newcomen was a blacksmith. In 1698 he used his skill in working with metal to build a steam-engine. Seven years earlier a military engineer called Thomas Savery had built the first steam-engine. It could be used to pump water out of a mine or well, but it was very dangerous to use because it required enormous steam pressure which could easily burst the pipes. Newcomen developed a much safer engine, but it was rather slow and could not do a lot of work. About 60 years later James Watt found a way of making Newcomen's engine work much better, and this new type of engine was used to drive machines in many different industries. The steam-engine was one of the important developments that led to the Industrial Revolution. ◆

see also

👁 Watt

◀ *Isaac Newton was knighted for his contributions to the world of science in 1702 and elected president of the Royal Society in 1703. This is his original manuscript for his book on the theory of light and colour.*

Nicholas II

Tsar of Russia from 1894 to 1917
Born *1868*   **Died** *1918 aged 50*

The tragedy of Russia's last tsar (emperor) was that he was a weak man who tried too hard to be a strong one. At first Nicholas II made all the big decisions about running the country himself, without a representative government. But this proved to be a disaster because he lived a completely different life from his people and was ignorant of the country's real problems.

Russia's disastrous defeat by Japan in 1904–1905 was one of the main causes of the revolution that took place in Russia in 1905. Nicholas was forced to allow a

Isaac **Newton**

English scientist
Born *1642*   **Died** *1727 aged 84*

Isaac Newton went to Cambridge University when he was 19, and was already doing important research in his second year. But then, because of the great plague, he had to go home to Lincolnshire for two years until the danger of catching the disease was past.

Many people have heard the story of Newton watching an apple fall from a tree. He was only 23 but was already thinking about the movement of the Earth, the Moon, and the planets. He realized that, just as the force of gravity pulled the apple to Earth, gravity keeps the Moon in its orbit. It is rather like a piece of string tied to a stone that you whirl around your head; if the string breaks, the stone is flung away. Without gravity the Moon would fly off into space.

Newton tried to make a telescope to study the stars, but found that if he used lenses the bright images had coloured edges. In trying to find out why this happened, he invented the mirror telescope. This does not give coloured edges, and many of our present-day telescopes are based on Newton's design. He was so persistent in asking

questions about the coloured edges that he was the first person to discover that white light is a mixture of all the different colours. Raindrops make a rainbow and a prism makes a spectrum by splitting up the white light. Before Newton, people thought that the raindrops or the prism added the colour.

Newton's greatest book, written in Latin and usually called *The Principia* (1686–1687), has had an enormous effect on the way scientists, and especially physicists, have thought ever since. ◆

👁 **see also**

Huygens   Leibniz   Young

◀ *This picture of Tsar Nicholas II and his family was taken not long before they were all murdered in 1918.*

Duma (parliament) to be elected. A period of relative prosperity followed and Nicholas won popular support for the war against Germany (1914). However, he then unwisely took personal command of the armies, leaving the government to the tsarina Alexandra and the priest Rasputin. (Rasputin was a rogue who seemed to have enormous influence over Alexandra after he had helped to treat the crown prince who suffered from a rare blood disease.) Mismanagement of Russia's part in World War I and government chaos resulted in Nicholas giving up the throne in February 1917. He was imprisoned with his family until they were murdered in July 1918 near Ekaterinburg by the Communist revolutionaries. ◆

👁 **see also**

Rasputin

Jack **Nicklaus**

American champion golfer
Born 1940

Jack Nicklaus started to play golf at the age of 10 and played a round of only 69 shots over a 6.49-km course when he was 13. While still at Ohio State University, he became US amateur champion. Then, when he turned professional in 1961, he began his run of tournament successes by winning the US Open championship in 1962.

Since then the 'Golden Bear', as he is known to his fans, has won more major tournaments than anyone else in golfing history, including four US Opens and five US Masters championships. He retired as a professional in 1990. ◆

👁 **see also**

Palmer

Joseph **Niepce**

French pioneer of photography
Born 1765   Died 1833 aged 68

Like his brother Claude, Joseph Niepce began life as an army officer but both retired around 1800 to live on the family country estate near Chalons-sur-Saône.

The two brothers were familiar with an early steamship – the *Pyroscaphe* – which had undergone trials on the Saône river. In 1807 they designed and patented a kind of internal combustion engine, the pyréolophore, which they hoped – vainly as it happened – might be used for ship propulsion. In 1816 Claude went to England to promote the pyréolophore and Joseph turned his hand to the reproduction of pictures by the then popular technique of lithography. This led him to study possible methods of making permanent photographs (he called them heliographs) on a pewter plate, and later on paper. In order to develop his invention Niepce went into partnership with another French photographic pioneer, Louis Daguerre, in 1826, but ultimately contributed little more. ◆

👁 **see also**

Daguerre   Eastman   Fox Talbot

Friedrich **Nietzsche**

German philosopher
Born 1844   Died 1900 aged 55

Born into a strict Protestant family in Saxony, Germany, Friedrich Nietzsche broke with Christianity in his twenties and devoted himself to classical literature and philosophy. The composer Richard Wagner

▲ *Nietzsche suffered from ill-health in his thirties and in 1889 had a permanent breakdown brought on by overwork and loneliness.*

influenced him greatly at first, but Nietzsche later rejected him and most German culture of the time.

In books such as *Thus Spoke Zarathustra* (1883–1892), Nietzsche challenged cultural values passed down through many centuries from classical, Jewish, and Christian traditions. He held that notions of 'the good', 'the true', and 'the beautiful' are illusions; what matters is 'the will to power' – man's quest for a higher form of existence. (Nietzsche discounted women except as mothers of future 'supermen'.) He was isolated from mainstream philosophy by his extreme views, and suffered ill-health for the last decade of his life.

His philosophy is notorious because the Nazis misused it as justification for their racist policies, even though his ideas and theirs were not really compatible. ◆

👁 **see also**

Wagner

▲ Florence Nightingale, the 'lady with the lamp', pictured doing her nightly rounds during the Crimean War.

Florence **Nightingale**

English founder of modern nursing
Born 1820   Died 1910 aged 90

Florence Nightingale decided she wanted to be a nurse, but this caused bitter arguments with her family, who thought that nursing was not a job for respectable women. It was not until 1851 that Nightingale got her own way and started work in a small London hospital. She was so successful that the Secretary of State for War asked her to go to the Crimean War to take charge of the nursing of wounded British soldiers.

She set sail in 1854 with 38 nurses. Within a month they had 1000 men to look after. Nightingale worked 20 hours a day to improve the nursing of ordinary soldiers. Every night she visited the wards, and the soldiers loved her as 'the lady with the lamp'. Her story was published in newspapers back home and she became a national heroine. The public donated

£45,000 for her to spend as she saw fit. In 1860 she spent it on the development of the Nightingale training school for nurses at St Thomas's Hospital, London.

In 1907 she became the first woman ever to be awarded the Order of Merit. ◆

👁 **see also**
Seacole

Vaslav **Nijinsky**

Russian ballet-dancer
Born 1890   Died 1950 aged 60

Vaslav Nijinsky's parents were dancers, and both he and his sister followed in their footsteps. When he was ten he was enrolled in the Imperial Ballet School in St Petersburg, Russia. By the time he was 20 he was touring the world. The great ballet producer,

◀ Nijinsky in a scene from the ballet Scheherazade.

Diaghilev, made him the star of many of his ballets. Nijinsky was always looking for new techniques and styles, and he often offended classical ballet fans. Much of what he did, though, was later recognized and used in modern ballet.

Nijinsky's later life was tragic. By the time he was in his 30s he was showing signs of mental illness. This became progressively worse and he spent much time in hospital. He died, after much sadness and suffering, in London in 1950. He was reburied in Paris in 1953. ◆

👁 **see also**
Diaghilev   Nureyev

Richard **Nixon**

President of the United States of America from 1969 to 1974
Born 1913   Died 1994 aged 81

Richard Nixon began his career as a lawyer, and served as an aviation ground officer in World War II. In 1946 he was elected to the House of Representatives, and after four years he became a senator. When Eisenhower became president in 1953, Nixon was his vice-president. Nixon himself failed to win the election for president in 1960, but won in 1968.

At the time US troops were involved in the Vietnam War. Nixon realized that the Communists could not be defeated, and so from 1971 he began to withdraw the soldiers. Afterwards he improved relations with Communist China and the Soviet Union.

Nixon was easily re-elected in 1972, but his second term of office was rocked by scandals. During the 1972 election campaign, some of Nixon's supporters burgled the Watergate Hotel, the headquarters

246

of the opposing Democratic Party. Nixon denied all knowledge of the break-in, but eventually he had to admit he had helped to cover up the facts. He resigned in 1974. ◆

Kwame **Nkrumah**

Leader of Ghana from 1957 to 1966
Born 1909   Died 1972 aged 62

Originally a teacher, Kwame Nkrumah later studied in America and in England. In both countries he met people who were working for the rights of black people and they inspired him. He decided to return to the Gold Coast to fight for his country's independence from Britain.

He founded the Convention People's Party in 1949 and called for 'positive action'. This led to his imprisonment in 1950. While in prison, he won an election so easily that not only was he released, he was also made 'Leader of Government Business'. In 1954 he became prime minister. The Gold Coast gained independence in 1957 and was renamed Ghana. Nkrumah became its president in 1960.

There followed many problems for Nkrumah's government and it became increasingly unpopular. While he was on a trip to China in 1966, he was deposed. He died in exile in Guinea in 1972. ◆

Alfred **Nobel**

Swedish inventor of dynamite who left a fund for the Nobel prizes
Born 1833   Died 1896 aged 63

Alfred Nobel's father invented a submarine mine, and went on to manufacture explosives.

Alfred became obsessed with what his father was doing. During his own experiments, Alfred's factory blew up, killing his brother. But he continued experimenting and invented a much safer explosive which he called 'dynamite'. This was used for blasting through rock. He also invented another explosive which was used for shooting bullets out of guns.

Nobel died a wealthy but sad man because people thought of him as someone who manufactured destruction. He had hoped that terrible weapons would prevent war because no one would dare use them. He was wrong. In his will he left a fund of over $9 million to give prizes (Nobel prizes) in five fields: literature, physics, chemistry, physiology and medicine, and peace. (In 1969 a sixth prize – for economics – was added.) They have become the highest award anyone can be given. ◆

Sidney **Nolan**

Australian painter
Born 1917   Died 1992 aged 75

Sidney Nolan was the most internationally famous of all Australian painters. He worked at various odd jobs before becoming a full-time artist when he was 21. He is best-known for his paintings of landscapes and scenes from Australian history. His most famous paintings are those representing Ned Kelly, the 19th-century outlaw who became an Australian folk-hero. Nolan painted in a highly original way, showing the dramatic mood of his subjects without treating them realistically. He travelled all over the world and found inspiration in the strange beauty of Antarctica and New Guinea as well as in his own country. ◆

▼ *Sidney Nolan's* Dog and Duck Hotel.

Michael **Nostradamus**

French physician and astrologer
Born 1503   Died 1566 aged 63

Was a man living in the 16th century able to predict the Great Fire of London of 1666, the French Revolution, World War II, the rise of both Napoleon and Adolf Hitler and that Man would walk on the moon? The answer is 'yes', only if we are to believe the claims of the supporters of the French astrologer, Nostradamus.

Michael Nostradamus (the Latinized form of his real name, Michel de Notredame) was a well-known doctor when he wrote a series of over 900 predictions about the future of the world in two books called *The Centuries* (1555–1558). The problem with these predictions is that they are very vague and could be made to mean almost anything. They are written in several languages, contain anagrams and riddles and are not placed in chronological order.

We should hope that Nostradamus was not always accurate in his predictions. He even claimed that the world will end in 1999:

Like the great king Angolmois
The year 1999, seventh month,
The great king of terror will
    descend from the sky,
At this time, Mars will reign for the
    good cause.

This verse supposedly predicts the end of the world, although some people claim that it predicts an invasion from outer space! ◆

Rudolf **Nureyev**

Russian ballet-dancer and choreographer
Born 1938   Died 1993 aged 55

When Rudolf Nureyev was a child he was a member of a children's dance group which travelled about performing traditional folk dances. Later he joined his local ballet company. In 1955 he went to the Kirov ballet school in Leningrad (now St Petersburg), one of the top ballet schools in Russia. From there he joined the Kirov Ballet and became a principal dancer.

In 1961 Nureyev went to Paris with the Kirov. While he was there he decided not to go back to the Soviet Union. He asked for 'political asylum' (protection and refuge from a country) and stayed on in the West. He became famous throughout the world, dancing all the great ballet roles. He was admired for his powerful personality as well as the strength which showed in his dancing. ◆

👁 **see also**

Fonteyn   Nijinsky

Julius **Nyerere**

President of Tanzania from 1964 to 1985
Born 1922   Died 1999 aged 77

Julius Nyerere was born the son of a chieftain at a village on Lake Victoria, Tanganyika (now Tanzania). After going to university and working as a teacher, he helped to form the Tanganyika African National Union (TANU), which did very well in Tanganyika's first elections of 1958. Tanganyika became independent in 1961 as a result of TANU's success. Nyerere was elected prime minister. He resigned after a short time, but became President of the Republic of Tanganyika in 1962.

◀ *This is the first official portrait of Julius Nyerere, made in 1963.*

In 1964 Tanganyika and Zanzibar decided to merge to form 'the United Republic of Tanzania. Nyerere became its first president. He was regularly re-elected at five-yearly intervals, and became one of the longest serving leaders in Africa until he retired in 1985. His views were respected throughout the world and Tanzania has remained one of the most politically stable countries in Africa. ◆

Annie **Oakley**

American star of Wild West shows
Born 1860   Died 1926 aged 66

Phoebe Anne Moses learned to shoot when she was very young. When she was a child she hunted game which she sold for money to pay off the mortgage on the family farm. She married a marksman whom she met in a shooting competition. They started their own trick-shooting act, and together they toured variety shows and circuses.

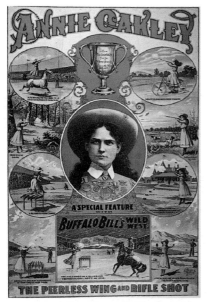

▲ *A 1901 poster for Buffalo Bill's Wild West Show featuring Annie Oakley.*

When Annie Oakley (her stage name) was 25 she and her husband joined the famous 'Buffalo Bill' Cody's Wild West Show. For 17 years, she amazed audiences with her rifle-shooting skills. She was such a good shot that she could split a playing card held edge-on from 30 paces away. She could also hit a coin thrown in the air, and even shoot cigarettes held in her husband's lips. ◆

👁 **see also**
Buffalo Bill

Daniel **O'Connell**

Irish political campaigner
Born 1775   Died 1847 aged 71

Daniel O'Connell was a lawyer who had a great gift for speaking in public. He was one of the main campaigners for rights which the Catholic Irish people had lost when their country was joined to Britain in 1801 and their parliament in Dublin was closed.

His first campaign was to change the law forbidding Catholics to hold positions of power. He set up a Catholic Association, which even the poorest peasants were invited to join. In 1828 he won an election even though it was illegal for him, as a Catholic, to be a candidate. The British parliament gave in and passed a law for Catholic freedom in 1829 and he became an MP.

In the 1840s O'Connell led his second campaign to undo the 1801 Union of Britain and Ireland. His work was only the start of a struggle which went on until 1921. He is remembered for his efforts to unite all classes of Irish people, and because he always stood for political campaigns, not violence, to win what he thought was right. ◆

Hans Christian **Oersted**

Danish physicist who discovered electromagnetism
Born 1777   Died 1851 aged 73

Hans Oersted was the son of a chemist and so started life surrounded by scientific apparatus. He studied at the university of Copenhagen and, to complete his education, travelled to meet Europe's leading scientists. He learnt a lot and in 1806 was given a job at his old university.

He also gave public lectures which became very popular. At one of these, in April 1820, Oersted tried an experiment he had never done before. He put a compass underneath a wire and then switched on an electric current: the magnetized compass needle moved!

Oersted realized the importance of what he had seen. Up to that time, scientists believed that electricity and magnetism were different forces. He had proved that they were connected.

Other scientists took up the study of this 'electromagnetism'. Their work produced new scientific theories and many important inventions such as the dynamo and the electric motor. ◆

👁 **see also**
Ampere   Faraday

▼ *The equipment used in Oersted's famous compass experiment.*

Georg **Ohm**

German physicist
Born *1787*   **Died** *1854 aged 67*

After leaving university, Georg Ohm held a series of teaching jobs. In 1817 he started teaching mathematics and physics at a Jesuit school in Cologne, Germany. Here he did some original research into electricity. In 1827 he published *The Galvanic Circuit Treated Mathematically*. This book contains an explanation of his famous law which shows that the current flowing in an electric circuit is proportional to the voltage (i.e. the current increases when the voltage increases). This became known as Ohm's law. Resistance to the current in an electrical circuit is measured in units called ohms.

Ohm's law makes the relationship between voltage and current very simple to understand but at first scientists in Germany did not take the idea seriously. Finally, in 1841, the Royal Society of London acknowledged the importance of Ohm's work by awarding him its prestigious Copley medal. His fame then spread in Germany where he was eventually made a professor of physics at Munich University. ◆

Georgia **O'Keeffe**

American painter
Born *1887*   **Died** *1986 aged 99*

Georgia O'Keeffe was born into a prosperous dairy-farming family in Wisconsin, America. She hated school and by the age of 12 decided that she would be an artist.

Much of her work was influenced by the landscapes of New Mexico and south-west America. She was considered very 'avant-garde' (innovative) because she adopted an abstract style for her subject

▲ *Georgia O'Keeffe's* Yellow Walnut Tree Leaves with Daisy *looks abstract because it shows such enlarged, though precise, details of the subject.*

matter, usually based on plant-life and landscapes. Her paintings are very expressive, and include huge flower paintings which seem to magnify the structure of petals and stamens, gently revealing the most intimate parts of the plant, thus making us look at something familiar in a new way. ◆

Laurence **Olivier**

English actor
Born *1907*   **Died** *1989 aged 82*

Even when he was still a child people noticed how good Laurence Olivier was at acting, so when he left school he went to study at the Central School of Speech and Drama in London.

The first 'hit' that he acted in was *Private Lives* by Noel Coward, but he became really well known in 1935 when he played Romeo in Shakespeare's play *Romeo and Juliet*. A year later he was the leading actor at the Old Vic, an important London theatre, and took several major parts in Shakespeare plays. He then became an international star when he appeared in films such as *Wuthering Heights* (1939) and *Henry V* (1944). He was knighted in 1947.

As well as being an actor, Olivier directed many plays and in 1962 he was made the first Artistic Director of the National Theatre company. He was made a life peer, becoming Lord Olivier, in 1970. ◆

Omar Khayyam

Persian poet and scientist
Born *1048*   **Died** *1123 aged 75*

Omar Khayyam was born in Nishapur, Persia (now Iran); his surname may mean that he was the son of a tent-maker. He proved to be a brilliant scholar, excelling in history, law, medicine, and, above all, astronomy and mathematics. He wrote a famous textbook on algebra which was known in Europe as well as in the East. He was put in charge of reforming the calendar to make it more accurate and also set up an observatory and school of astronomical research in Isfahan.

Omar Khayyam is also world-famous as a poet – thanks to an English poet, Edward Fitzgerald, who lived over 700 years after Omar's death. His four-line poems (rubaiyat) praise the pleasures of life but also show that he thought deeply about religion. At least 250 of them survive. Fitzgerald had the idea of putting them together and translating them as though they were one long poem. Since he published his version in 1859 – *The Rubaiyat of Omar Khayyam* – they have been translated into many other languages. ◆

▲ *An illustration from* The Rubaiyat of Omar Khayyam.

J. Robert Oppenheimer

American nuclear physicist
Born *1904*   **Died** *1967 aged 62*

Julius Robert Oppenheimer was a student at Harvard University before going to study in Europe, where he met the world's leading physicists. He then returned to America to conduct research into sub-atomic particles.

During World War II, Albert Einstein and others warned that if Nazi Germany developed a nuclear weapon then the rest of the world would be in great danger. In response the American government gathered together a group of scientists to build their own atomic bomb. Oppenheimer set up a laboratory at Los Alamos, New Mexico, and led the project. On 16 July 1945, Oppenheimer's team successfully tested the first atomic bomb. Three weeks later 'A-bombs' were used to destroy the Japanese cities of Hiroshima and Nagasaki, killing thousands of people.

In 1963 the American president, Lyndon Johnson, presented Oppenheimer with the Enrico Fermi Award for Atomic Physics. ◆

👁 **see also**
Einstein   Fermi

George **Orwell**

English novelist
Born *1903*   **Died** *1950 aged 46*

George Orwell, the pen-name of Eric Blair, was born in India and educated in England. He served for five years in the Burmese police force and also spent some time living as a tramp, earning a bit of money by washing dishes. These experiences were later used in some of his novels, as were memories of his time spent fighting for the Republicans in the Spanish Civil War.

Orwell was a great journalist, but he only became famous as a novelist in the last few years of his life. In 1945 he wrote *Animal Farm*, an allegory describing how some farm animals first get rid of their harsh master, Mr Jones, only to suffer even worse cruelties from their own ruthless pig-rulers. In fact, Orwell was really attacking the way that the Russian Revolution of 1917 was betrayed by the tyrant Stalin, who ended up behaving even more badly than the former tsar (emperor).

Four years later Orwell wrote *Nineteen Eighty-Four*, a novel set in what was then the future. It described a bleak world where workers must exercise every day in front of a 'tele-screen' which also spies on them. Anyone showing any signs of independence is caught and executed. It is a powerful novel describing the horrors of total dictatorship. ◆

▼ *George Orwell working as a radio jounalist in 1945. From 1947 he suffered from tuberculosis and he was in and out of hospital until his death in 1950.*

Nikolaus **Otto**

German inventor and industrialist,
Born *1832*   **Died** *1891 aged 59*

The son of a farmer, Nikolaus Otto left school at 16 to work for a local merchant. He soon left to seek his fortune in Cologne and there became interested in a new kind of engine which had been developed by a French engineer, Jean Lenoir. Like the steam-engine, it depended on a piston working in a cylinder but the power was provided by the explosion of a mixture of gas and air instead of by steam. This was the ancestor of the internal combustion engine which – using petrol or oil as a fuel – was destined to revolutionize transport on land, sea, and in the air.

▲ *Otto's four-stroke engine was a great success. It was reliable, efficient, and relatively quiet.*

Otto's engine used a four-stroke firing sequence, which was different from Lenoir's two-stroke version, and he was granted a patent in 1876. During the next ten years he sold 30,000 of his engines – the 'silent Otto' – but then his patent was declared invalid. Unknown to Otto the principle of his engine had already been patented, but not developed, in 1862 by another Frenchman, Alphonse Beau de Rochas. ◆

🕮 **see also**
Benz   Diesel

▲ *Jesse Owens winning one of four gold medals – for the 100 yards, 220 yards, 4 × 100 yards relay, and long jump – at the 1936 Olympic Games in Berlin.*

Wilfred **Owen**

English poet during World War I
Born *1893*   **Died** *1918 aged 25*

Wilfred Owen was already a poet when World War I began. After he enlisted in the army in 1915, the atmosphere in his poems soon changed from romance to bitter anger against the slaughter then going on in the trenches. As he puts it himself in his poem 'Anthem for Doomed Youth':

> What passing-bells for these
>   who die as cattle?
> Only the monstrous anger of
>   the guns.

In 1917 he returned to England with injuries, but went back to France the following year. He was shot dead one week before the end of the war. His poems, published after his death, did much to change the notion that war was still a brave and noble thing. Instead, he painted an unforgettable picture of the pointless waste, stupidity, and cruelty that had led to the deaths of so many young men on both sides in the trenches. ◆

Jesse **Owens**

American champion athlete
Born *1913*   **Died** *1980 aged 67*

James Cleveland (J. C., thus 'Jesse') Owens from Alabama was 22 when he took part in an athletics meeting in Michigan. Within 45 minutes he had equalled the world record for the 100 yards, and broken the records for the 220 yards, the 220 yards hurdles and the long jump. His long jump world record lasted for 25 years.

The next year, 1936, was Olympic year. Adolf Hitler, the leader of Nazi Germany, wanted the Berlin Games to show the world that what he called 'the Aryan race' of white Europeans was superior to any other. After Jesse Owens had demolished that myth by winning four gold medals, Hitler refused even to shake hands with the black American athlete. ◆

Niccolò **Paganini**

Italian violinist and composer
Born 1782   Died 1840 aged 57

Although he began, at the age of five, to learn to play the mandolin, Niccolò Paganini soon turned to the violin. Urged on by an ambitious father, he made such good progress that he performed in public when he was only 12. In the following year the great violinist Alessandro Rolla declared that Paganini had nothing left to learn, but recommended that he study composition with Ferdinand Paer.

In 1801 Paganini broke away from his tyrannical father and worked as an orchestral player until 1809. He then began the career of a virtuoso soloist, travelling all over Italy and mesmerizing his audiences with his fabulous technique and strong sense of showmanship. Having conquered Italy, he then proceeded to conquer the rest of Europe, amassing great wealth in the process. Such was his technical wizardry that many people believed the rumour that he had been taught by the devil himself. ◆

Thomas **Paine**

British political thinker
Born 1737   Died 1809 aged 72

Thomas Paine devoted his life to speaking out for freedom, which meant he was loved and admired by many people, but hated and feared by others. In 1774 he emigrated to America, where he wrote a pamphlet called *Common Sense* (1776), a rousing call for independence from Britain. He also wrote against slavery and in favour of women's rights. In 1787 he returned to England where he wrote *The Rights of Man* (1791– 1792), in which he supported the French Revolution and called for an end to illiteracy, poverty, unemployment, and war. Fearing arrest for treason, he fled to France in 1792 and was warmly welcomed. However, he was imprisoned when he opposed the execution of Louis XVI. He returned to America in 1802, but his last great book, *The Age of Reason* (1794–1795), had made him unpopular there; its plea for religious tolerance was considered anti-Christian. ◆

Palladio

Italian architect and writer
Born 1508   Died 1580 aged 72

Andrea di Pietro da Gondola, who became known as Palladio, was one of the greatest of all Italian architects. He began as a humble stone carver and at the age of thirteen was apprenticed to a carver in Padua. However, before long he ran away to Vicenza, a rich city near Venice. When he was 27 he was befriended by a group of gentlemen and scholars and, through them, began to learn about the architecture of Ancient Rome.

Palladio was particularly interested in the measurements and proportions that Ancient Roman architects had used and in the kinds of buildings they had designed. The houses (villas) that he designed in the countryside outside Venice are based on Roman country houses and farms. Like all his buildings, these houses had to be useful as well as beautiful.

Palladio wrote four books and illustrated them with examples of classical Roman architecture and his own buildings. These books have influenced architects ever since, particularly British architects of the eighteenth century who, following Palladio's example, invented a 'Palladian' style. ◆

▼ *Palladio used Ancient Roman principles of balance, proportion, and symmetry to design a range of fine buildings with elegant rooms, such as this one in the Villa Barbaro in Italy.*

Arnold **Palmer**

American champion golfer
Born 1929

Professional golf in America and Britain has achieved such wide popularity today thanks to the attacking style of Arnold Palmer in the 1950s and 1960s.

Pennsylvanian-born Palmer won the American amateur title in 1954. In his first major professional championship, the 1958 US Masters, he snatched a dramatic victory on the last two holes. Palmer went on to win all of the world major professional trophies except the US PGA championships, at a time when golf was becoming popular with television viewers. He was a strong and exciting player and attracted large crowds of fans wherever he competed.

After his best playing days were over, Palmer became a designer of golf courses around the world. ◆

👁 **see also**

Nicklaus

Emmeline and Christabel **Pankhurst**

Leaders of the suffragette campaign to win votes for women in Britain
Emmeline Pankhurst
Born 1858   Died 1928 aged 69
Christabel Pankhurst
Born 1880   Died 1958 aged 77

Emmeline Goulden married a lawyer, Richard Pankhurst, who believed that women should have the same rights as men. In 1903, after her husband had died, she and her forceful eldest daughter Christabel founded the Women's Social and Political Union, the 'suffragettes'. They and their supporters interrupted political meetings, smashed shop windows, and did all they could to win women the right to vote. When they were arrested they went on hunger strike. Christabel escaped to Paris in 1912 so that she was free to organize the campaign. They became quite ruthless, and even broke with Emmeline's younger daughter, Sylvia, because she worked independently from them with poor women in London's East End. When war came in 1914, Emmeline and Christabel urged women to work for their country.

Eventually, in 1918, women over the age of 30 in Britain were given the vote and in 1928, a month after Emmeline Pankhurst's death, all women in Britain were given the same voting rights as men. ◆

> *We are here to claim our rights as women, not only to be free, but to fight for freedom. That is our right as well as our duty.*
> Christabel Pankhurst, 1911

▼ *Emmeline and Christabel Pankhurst posing in prison uniform to rouse sympathy and admiration for the suffragette campaign.*

▶ *This Land League poster from 1881–1882 urged tenant farmers to refuse to pay rent while Charles Parnell and others were imprisoned for the cause. The campaign worked and they were released.*

Mungo **Park**

Scottish explorer who located the River Niger in West Africa
Born 1771   Died 1806 aged 34

Having first studied medicine, Mungo Park went to London where a group of gentlemen interested in African exploration chose him to search for the River Niger in West Africa.

In 1795 he set out on horseback from the mouth of the River Gambia. He travelled inland from one African kingdom to the next before being captured by Muslim nomads, who made him beg for his food and drink from a cattle trough. Park escaped and on 21 July 1796 had his first sight of the River Niger near Ségou. He followed it to Sansanding, where the onset of the rainy season forced him to return.

In England his book *Travels in the Interior Districts of Africa* was very successful, and in 1805 he was asked to lead a military expedition to follow the Niger to the sea. He set out with 42 British volunteers, but the rains came and many of the men died. At Sansanding he built a boat but by the time he launched it, only four men remained alive. Ill and in fear of the Muslim tribesmen, they travelled down river firing into the bush. They were attacked at Bussa and Park was last seen jumping overboard. ◆

▶ *Mungo Park led one of the first European expeditions to investigate the course of the River Niger. He played an important part in early European exploration of Africa.*

and believed that the Irish should have their own government instead of being ruled from London as part of the United Kingdom.

He became an MP in the British Parliament in 1875, and was soon noted for his long speeches. In 1880 he became leader of the Home Rule Party. He was also president of the Land League which backed farmers who refused to pay rents for the land. The government imprisoned Parnell for this, but with so much support in Ireland they had to release him and help farmers to pay their debts and buy their own land.

By 1885 the demand for Home Rule had become so popular in Ireland that Parnell's party had 86 MPs and the British prime minister, William Gladstone, needed his help to stay in power. Gladstone decided to give Home Rule to Ireland but it did not come for another 35 years, because some MPs voted against the Bill. Parnell led more campaigns for Home Rule up to 1890 but then became involved in a divorce case. The Home Rule Party voted against him as their leader; he died the following year. ◆

👁 **see also**
Gladstone

Charles **Parnell**

Irish political leader
Born 1846   **Died** 1891 aged 45

Charles Parnell was a Protestant landowner in Ireland. However, he sympathized with the poverty of Catholic farmers

Blaise **Pascal**

French mathematician
Born 1623   **Died** 1662 aged 39

Blaise Pascal was a mathematical genius. By the age of 12 he had worked out the first 32 theorems of the Ancient Greek mathematician Euclid. At 16 he published a geometry book about parts of cones called conic sections. The French philosopher and mathematician René Descartes hardly believed that a 16-year-old could produce such advanced mathematics.

By the time he was 19 Pascal had invented a calculating machine for adding and subtracting numbers. Unfortunately it was too expensive to make and was never used.

Pascal was also very interested in Evangilista Torricelli's work with barometers. Pascal proved that the atmosphere really does have weight by sending his brother-in-law up a mountain with a barometer. The level of mercury in the tube dropped the higher he went.

Ten years before his death Pascal became a devout Catholic, abandoned his scientific and mathematical work and instead devoted his time to writing about religion and philosophy. ◆

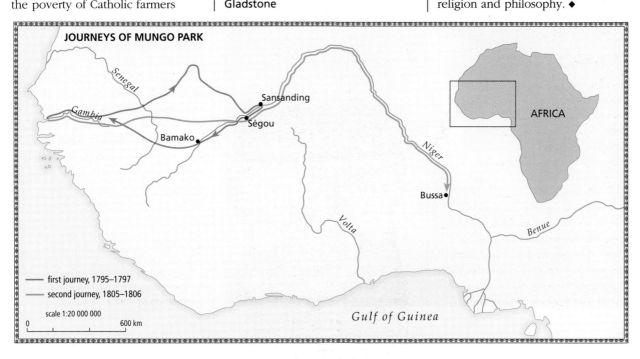

Louis **Pasteur**

French scientist who discovered that bacteria cause disease
Born *1822*   **Died** *1895 aged 72*

L ouis Pasteur was not a very clever boy at school and was mainly interested in painting. But his life changed when he began to study chemistry. He became fascinated by the subject, worked very hard, and in his twenties had already become famous for his experiments.

In 1856 Pasteur was asked to help the French wine industry because much of the wine was going sour. He showed that this was caused by a tiny living organism, a yeast, which could be killed by heat. This heating process was named 'pasteurization' and is used today to make milk safe to drink.

Pasteur's most important work, however, was his study of what causes disease. He showed that microscopic living organisms, 'germs' (bacteria), carried disease

▼ *Pasteur's scientific achievements included a life-saving vaccine against rabies.*

from one person to another. He made a special study of a disease called anthrax which kills cattle and sheep. He isolated the anthrax bacteria and prepared a weak form which he injected into sheep; this gave them immunity to the disease. A similar method had been used by Edward Jenner for preventing smallpox in people.

Louis Pasteur then made a life-saving vaccine for treating and preventing the deadly disease called rabies. He spent his whole life dedicated to his work, and died a respected and well-loved man. ◆

👁 **see also**
Jenner   Koch

Saint **Patrick**

The patron saint of Ireland
Born *c.390*   **Died** *c.460 aged about 70*

P atrick was born into a family of Christians in Roman Britain. At the age of 16 he was captured by Irish pirates. He spent the next six years as a slave in Ireland, where there was no practised religion,

before escaping back to Britain. According to his own later writings, he was now a much changed person. He trained to become a priest, and in about 435 he returned to Ireland. From then on he devoted his life to converting the Irish people to Christianity. He worked mainly in the north, where he had his own bishopric at Armagh.

He is still the most popular saint in Ireland, although no one is sure where he died and was buried. His feast day is 17 March, and in pictures he is often shown treading on snakes because, among many other legends, St Patrick is supposed to have driven all the snakes out of Ireland. ◆

Saint **Paul**

Christian saint and apostle
Born *c.3*   **Died** *c.65 aged about 62*

T his Christian saint was originally named Saul, after the first king of Israel. He was Jewish by birth and was also a Roman citizen. He was so gifted that he was sent to Jerusalem to train as a rabbi (a Jewish religious teacher). In the years after the crucifixion of Jesus he joined others in persecuting Jesus's followers.

The story of Saul's conversion to Christianity tells how he was travelling to Damascus one day when he saw a light and heard the voice of Jesus asking, 'Saul, Saul, why do you persecute me?'. Blinded for a while by the great light, he was led to Damascus and there he was baptized as a Christian.

He spent three years quietly praying and thinking, and then joined other Christians in Jerusalem. This was the beginning of a life of missionary journeys, teaching people about Jesus. Paul, as he was

▲ *This 15th-century fresco shows St Paul (right) visiting St Peter, another Christian saint, in jail.*

now called, taught and wrote letters to the Christian congregations to help them to understand their new religion and follow its teachings.

Paul's life was very difficult. He was shipwrecked, beaten for his beliefs, and often criticized by those who had been followers of Jesus right from the beginning. Roman soldiers arrested him in Jerusalem after a mob of people attacked him because they thought he had ignored Jewish laws. He used his right as a Roman citizen to 'appeal to Caesar', which meant going to Rome to be tried. In Rome he was imprisoned for two years. He was probably killed in the reign of the Emperor Nero. ◆

👁 **see also**

Jesus

Linus **Pauling**

American chemist
Born *1901*   **Died** *1994 aged 93*

L inus Pauling was awarded the 1954 Nobel Prize for Chemistry for his work on the structure of molecules. He used information from X-ray diffraction and other techniques to find the lengths of the bonds holding the atoms together and the angles between them. He then used quantum mechanics to explain how the bonds were formed. His ideas explained the shape of simple molecules and helped scientists to understand some very complicated molecules such as proteins.

Pauling was a pacifist and campaigned for many years against the testing of nuclear weapons. He published his views in a book called *No More War!* and also took a petition, signed by over 11,000 scientists, to the United Nations calling for a ban on weapons testing. He was awarded the 1962 Nobel Peace Prize for his efforts, thus making Pauling one of the few people to receive two different Nobel Prizes. ◆

Luciano **Pavarotti**

Italian tenor
Born *1935*

I n 1961, after a period of study, Luciano Pavarotti won an international singing competition and made his début as Rodolfo in Puccini's *La Bohème*. He was first heard outside Italy in 1963 when he went to Holland and London, and in the following year he toured Australia with Joan Sutherland. He made his American début in 1968, since which time he has appeared in all the world's great opera houses and is widely regarded as one of the greatest tenors of the day.

Pavarotti is a great favourite with the general public, partly because of his larger-than-life personality and remarkable physical appearance. He has been closely associated in friendly rivalry with the tenors Placido Domingo and José Carerras. ◆

👁 **see also**   **Sutherland**

▼ *Luciano Pavarotti singing in his usual flamboyant manner.*

257

Ivan **Pavlov**

Russian physiologist whose experiments led to the study of behaviour in animals
Born *1849*   **Died** *1936 aged 86*

Ivan Pavlov's father was a priest and Pavlov himself started to prepare for the priesthood. However, he soon became more interested in science and decided to study science and medicine at university.

He became intrigued by the way we digest food and did lots of experiments with dogs. He knew that when a hungry dog is shown food it will immediately start to dribble saliva. This is called a reflex action. Pavlov cut open the cheeks of his dogs to reveal their salivary glands, so that he could observe the dribbling more clearly. He then rang a bell every time food was brought to the hungry dogs. After a while, ringing the bell alone was enough to make the dogs dribble. The dogs had learnt to expect food when the bell rang. Dribbling had become a reflex response to the bell ringing as well as to food.

Pavlov's experiments made scientists think more about why animals behave the way they do and how they learn different types of behaviour. ◆

Anna **Pavlova**

Russian-born ballerina
Born *1881*   **Died** *1931 aged 49*

Anna Pavlova's unusual talent for dancing was spotted while she was still at school. She was enrolled at the St Petersburg Imperial Ballet School and in 1906 the Imperial Russian Ballet gave her the title of prima ballerina. A year later she danced *The Dying Swan*, a ballet specially created for her.

By 1913 Pavlova had decided to leave Russia to set up her own company. Her aim was to bring ballet not only to the great European and American cities, but to places such as India, Africa, and South America where it had hardly ever been seen.

Over a period of 20 years she covered thousands of miles and gave nearly 5000 performances, amazing audiences with her lightness and grace. From 1912 she was based in London, where she was an inspiration to many younger English dancers. ◆

👁 **see also**

Fonteyn

▼ *Anna Pavlova holding the final pose in a performance of* The Dying Swan, *her most famous role.*

Lester Bowles **Pearson**

Canadian politician who played an important role in international affairs
Born *1897*   **Died** *1972 aged 75*

As a young man, Lester Bowles Pearson worked as a stretcher-bearer in Greece with the Canadian army during World War I. He joined another regiment in 1917 and went to England. On his return home he completed a degree at the University of Toronto and tried careers in law, business, and teaching before he joined the Department of External Affairs.

Eventually he became a diplomat, working in London and also in Washington. He represented Canada when the United Nations was set up in 1945, and was president of the UN General Assembly in 1952. When there were problems between Israel and Egypt he suggested sending in a UN peacekeeping force. The idea worked well, and Pearson won the Nobel Peace Prize in 1957.

Pearson became leader of the Canadian Liberal Party in 1958. His party was in opposition at first, but in 1963 it won the election and Pearson became prime minister. Before he retired in 1968 his government had introduced welfare programmes, including a pension plan and a scheme to provide medical care for everyone. ◆

Robert **Peary**

American Arctic explorer
Born *1856*   **Died** *1920 aged 63*

On 6 April 1909, accompanied by four Inuits (Eskimos) and a black American friend, Matthew Henson, Robert Peary reached the North Pole after a long and very exhausting sledge journey. At least that is what everyone thought at the time. But during the 1980s, when Peary's record books were re-examined and his calculations checked, it seems that he got it wrong and probably missed the North Pole by about 80 kilometres. Nevertheless Peary can claim fame for the many journeys that he made across the Arctic ice-cap.

Robert Peary spent all of his working life in the United States navy and led many expeditions to little-known areas of the frozen north. Over a period of 20 years he studied Greenland and its isolated inhabitants. The native people befriended him and assisted him on his expeditions. Peary was the first person to prove beyond doubt that Greenland is an island. ◆

Robert **Peel**

British prime minister from 1834 to 1835 and from 1841 to 1846; he also founded the first police force
Born 1788   Died 1850 aged 62

Robert Peel was a tall, handsome man who became a brilliant scholar at Oxford University. Thanks to his father's money and influence, he became a Member of Parliament when he was only 21, supporting the Tory (Conservative) Party. He held a number of government posts in Britain and Ireland before becoming home secretary, where he was in charge of law and order. He started the London Metropolitan Police force, and policemen were called 'bobbies' and 'peelers' after him.

Peel became a baronet in 1830 when his father died, and was briefly prime minister from 1834 to 1835. Then, as leader of the Conservative Party, he became prime minister again in 1841, staying in power until 1846. To

▲ *Robert Peel is best remembered for starting the police force in London. The arrival of 'peelers' helped to stop a lot of petty crime, particularly amongst young boys.*

help poorer people he reduced the taxes on goods, especially food, and brought back income tax instead. His party split, though, when he repealed the Corn Laws (which had kept the price of bread high by putting taxes on imported grain), and he resigned as prime minister. He was afterwards thought of as the founder of modern conservatism. ◆

I. M. **Pei**

Chinese-born American architect
Born 1917

Ieoh Ming Pei was born in Canton in southern China. When he was 18 he went to America to study architecture and has worked there ever since. He became an American citizen in 1948 and is considered one of the country's most successful architects. Most of his buildings have bold and simple forms, like gigantic pieces of sculpture. Some of them (for instance, his extension to the National Gallery of Art in Washington D.C.) look from the outside like huge blocks of stone or concrete. Others (like the tall and slender John Hancock Tower in Boston) are made of steel and glass, which reflect the sky and the Sun. Pei is most famous in Europe for the pyramids of steel and glass in the courtyard of the Louvre in Paris. They look like sculpture, but they are there to let light into a great underground hall – Pei's new entrance to all the museums in the Louvre. ◆

▼ *Pei's elegant glass pyramids act as the roof for the Louvre's new subterranean service area and make it feel light and airy.*

▲ *Pelé, who wore the number 10 team shirt, is thought by many to be the greatest football player of all time.*

Pelé

Brazilian football player
Born *1940*

Edson Arantes do Nascimento was given the nickname 'Pelé' by the friends he played football with as a boy. He showed so much promise for his first club, Noroeste, that he was signed by the top club Santos and was picked to play for the national Brazilian team when he was only 16. A year later, in 1958, he scored two goals to help Brazil win the World Cup final.

In a career that lasted until 1977, Pelé showed that he was the complete footballer, combining speed and ball-control with fierce and accurate shooting. Before leaving Santos to play for the New York Cosmos in 1971, he had scored 1216 goals in 1254 games. He also played 110 games for Brazil, winning World Cup winners' medals in 1958 and 1970. ◆

William **Penn**

English Quaker who founded the colony of Pennsylvania
Born *1644*   **Died** *1718 aged 73*

William Penn was very religious from an early age and eventually converted to the Quaker faith. Quakers believe that each person must look for true religion in their own heart and in their own way. The Anglican Church (Church of England) at the time found this hard to accept, preferring instead that everyone should worship in the same style. Penn was expelled from Oxford University for refusing to go to compulsory Church of England services and was later imprisoned for preaching his own faith.

On his release Penn met other Quakers who were all looking for a place where they could follow their own beliefs in freedom. In 1680 Penn asked King Charles II for a gift of land in the Americas in return for a large debt the king owed Penn's father. The gift came, made up of land on the east coast between Maryland and New York. It was called Pennsylvania ('Penn's woods'). Penn sailed out there with other Quakers. Once established, he was so honest and just in his dealings with the local Native Americans that there was very little trouble between them and the Quakers, although he did have some difficulties with his own often unruly followers. ◆

🏈 **see also**

Fox

Samuel **Pepys**

English diarist
Born *1633*   **Died** *1703 aged 70*

On 1 January 1660, Samuel Pepys (pronounced 'peeps') started writing a diary. He wrote in code, probably because he did not want his wife to read it. His diary shows that although he was fond of her, he also enjoyed flirting and

▼ *The Fire of London in 1666 was recorded by Pepys in his diary.*

having affairs with other women.

Pepys had a good job organizing supplies for the navy. He travelled in the ship which brought Charles II back to England in 1660, and also attended his coronation. Pepys's boss was the king's brother, the Duke of York (later James II).

Pepys lived through the terrible plague of 1665, and the Fire of London the following year, and recorded these events in his diary. He kept his diary for nine years. When you read it, you can almost step straight back into the London of Charles II. ◆

see also

Charles II

Pericles

Ancient Greek statesman
Born *c.495 BC*
Died *c.429 BC aged about 66*

Pericles dominated the city of Athens' affairs from 461 BC. He helped to make Athens a great city

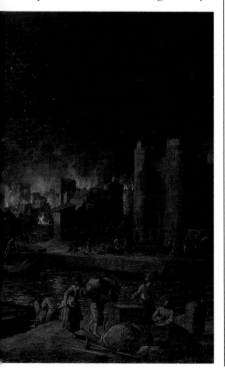

and developed the way it was organized, so that all the male adult citizens could meet in a large assembly and make decisions about peace and war and new laws. These decisions were inscribed on stone and publicly displayed. This was the first recorded democracy.

Pericles also made Athens strong by extending the city's walls and by making sure the navy was capable of controlling the seas around Greece. Athens was then able to build an empire from the cities and islands that looked to it for protection. Pericles also arranged for beautiful buildings to be built on the hill of the Acropolis. The most famous of these is the Parthenon, a large temple to the city's goddess Athene.

Pericles had enemies, and not everyone thought that democracy was the best way of running the city. Many of the comic plays written at the time made cruel fun of him. However, Pericles was such a good speaker in the assemblies that he remained in control for many years. He was elected 'general' (a political office as well as a military one) fifteen times.

Pericles wanted Athens to be at peace but he could not avoid a war with Sparta, a city in southern Greece. War broke out in 431 BC and Athens was eventually defeated. Pericles died in a great plague that hit Athens soon after the beginning of the war. ◆

Eva **Perón**

Argentinian political leader
Born *1919*   **Died** *1952 aged 33*

Maria Eva Duarte was born near Buenos Aires, Argentina. Her family was poor so she went to Buenos Aires at the age of 15 to become an actress. She met Juan

▲ *Eva Perón (Evita) became immensely popular with the Argentinian public because she devoted herself to helping the poor, and improving education and women's rights.*

Perón there in 1944 when she was a successful radio actress and married him the following year.

Juan Perón had held various government posts since 1943. When he became president of Argentina in 1946, Eva (or 'Evita' as she was known) virtually ran the ministeries of Labour and of Health. By 1947 she owned or controlled almost every radio station in Argentina, and had closed or banned over 100 newspapers and magazines.

She was a gifted speaker and campaigned hard for women's rights. However, her bid to become vice-president was blocked by military leaders who feared she might one day become president and be in charge of them. Her death from cancer shortly afterwards contributed to the decline of her husband's regime. ◆

Henri Philippe
Pétain

*French general and head of state from
1940 to 1944*
Born *1856*   **Died** *1951 aged 95*

Henri Philippe Omer Pétain was a soldier who became an instructor at army school, before being made a general in 1914. In World War I he became a national hero for organizing the halting of the German advance at Verdun in 1916, and in 1917 he was made French commander-in-chief.

He served in a number of posts before retiring from the army in 1931 to enter politics. As minister for war from 1934 he was responsible for preparations for World War II. In 1940 he became prime minister and signed a truce with Germany which surrendered three-fifths of France to German control. From 1940 to 1942 Pétain was head of a French government

▼ In this poster, Henri Pétain, the hero of World War I, tries to reassure the French people that, as prime minister, he will help them through the difficult times – namely World War II.

set up in the town of Vichy. This government had no real power, and had even less when German forces completed their occupation of France.

At the end of World War II Pétain was arrested by the Allies and tried for treason because he had worked closely with the Germans. He was sentenced to death but this was altered to life imprisonment. ◆

Peter the Great

Tsar of Russia from 1682 to 1725
Born *1672*   **Died** *1725 aged 52*

Peter came to the throne as joint tsar with his half-brother Ivan at the age of ten, but spent his childhood playing and being educated in the countryside outside Moscow. His stepsister, Sophia, ruled in his place until she tried to take power for herself. In 1689 Peter took charge and sent Sophia to a nunnery.

After Ivan's death in 1696, Peter became sole ruler. He spent two years in western Europe studying various industries, and brought back

▲ This painting portrays Peter the Great as a ship's carpenter. Carpentry was a hobby at which he became highly skilled.

to Russia teachers of all the arts and crafts which his country most needed. The reforms he introduced with the help of foreign statesmen and craftsmen turned Russia into a more modern country, with an army and navy, schools and universities, and its first public newspaper.

Peter was also a soldier tsar and spent much of his life at war. His greatest victory was against the Swedes at Poltava in 1709 during the 21-year 'Northern War'. His victories in this war enabled him to build a new capital city for Russia, St Petersburg, on the Baltic coast.

Peter had a son, Alexei, by his first wife Eudoxia, but Alexei plotted against Peter and was put to death in 1718. As he had no other heir, Peter's second wife, Catherine, became Catherine I, Empress of Russia, when he died in 1725. ◆

Saint Peter

Leader of the 12 apostles, the first followers of Jesus
Lived during the 1st century

Peter (originally called Simon) and his brother, Andrew, were

J'AI ÉTÉ
AVEC VOUS
DANS LES JOURS
GLORIEUX

JE RESTE
AVEC VOUS
DANS LES JOURS
SOMBRES...

SERVIR

1918   1940

fishermen who lived near the Sea of Galilee. One day when they were out fishing, Jesus called to them to follow him and become 'fishers of men'. From then on Peter and Andrew were especially close to Jesus until his death.

Jesus gave Simon the name Cephas, which means a stone. Peter comes from the Greek equivalent, *petra*. Peter seems to have been the first person to say that Jesus was the Messiah (the Jewish leader prophesied in the Old Testament of the Bible). In Matthew's gospel Jesus says that Peter and his faith are the rock on which the Church will be built.

There are many stories about Peter in the gospels. He seems to have been a person who made mistakes as well as showing great faith. When Jesus was arrested in Jerusalem and taken away to be tried, Peter, in a state of panic, denied three times that he knew him. Afterwards he wept bitterly at his betrayal.

After the crucifixion of Jesus, Peter preached that Jesus was alive. He was imprisoned twice, but escaped and travelled round the Mediterranean telling people about Jesus and his teaching.

There is a tradition that Peter spent the last years of his life, before being crucified for his beliefs, as the first bishop of Rome. ◆

◉ **see also**

Jesus

Francesco Petrarch

Italian poet and scholar
Born *1304*   **Died** *1374 aged 70*

Francesco Petrarch (Petrarca in Italian) was the son of an Italian exile. He spent his childhood

▲ *Riders prepare to form a procession on this frieze from the Parthenon which is now in the British Museum, London. Phidias directed all of the sculpture for the Parthenon.*

in Italy and France, before attending university in Bologna in 1320 to study the classics. He returned to Avignon, where he had spent some time as a child, on the death of his father in 1326. A year later he saw and fell in love with a woman whom he called Laura. Her true identity is still a mystery but she was the inspiration behind the love lyrics of Petrarch's *Canzoniere* (1342), a book of sonnets, songs, and madrigals.

Petrarch's association with the wealthy Colonnas and Visconti families allowed him to travel extensively in Europe and he became known for his genius and great learning. His writing includes the epic poem *Africa* (1338–1341), *The Life of Solitude* (1344), and several volumes of letters. ◆

Phidias

Ancient Greek sculptor
Born *c.490 BC*
Died *c.430 BC aged about 60*

Phidias was the most famous artist of ancient Greece. Sadly, all of his sculptures have long been

destroyed, so we have to rely mainly on the writings of ancient Greek and Roman authors to get an idea of his genius. He was renowned for the grandeur of his work and no one else portrayed so nobly the majesty of the gods and goddesses. His statue of Zeus, the king of the gods, in his huge temple at Olympia, was one of the seven wonders of the ancient world. It was made of gold and ivory, as was his statue of Athena in her temple – the Parthenon – at Athens.

Phidias was the director of all the decorative sculpture of the Parthenon, and fortunately much of it survives (most of it is in the British Museum). He probably did not carve any of it himself, but he must have approved it and it gives some idea of how beautiful his own work must have been. One other direct link with him survives; in the 1950s archaeologists excavated his workshop at Olympia and found a cup with the inscription 'I belong to Phidias' – the ancient equivalent of his tea-mug. ◆

Phidippides

*Greek soldier who ran the first
'marathon'*
Lived during the 5th century BC

In 490 BC Persian invaders landed on Greek shores at Marathon. Legend has it that Phidippides, one of the Greek soldiers, ran to seek help from the Spartans. To do this he covered a distance of about 240 km. Some say that he then ran back to take part in the battle. Eventually, the Greeks managed to beat off the Persian attack, losing only about 190 men while the Persians lost over 6000.

According to the legend, the Greek general, Miltiades, sent Phidippides to carry the news of the victory to Athens. He raced the 40 km to Athens, announced the victory, and dropped down dead.

The long-distance race which we call the marathon derives its name from Phidippides's run. The length of the race varied for a while but eventually settled at 26 miles (42 km – similar in length to Phidippides's legendary run). An extra 385 yards was added at the 1908 Olympics held in London so that the race could finish in front of the Royal Box; 26 miles and 385 yards (42.2 km) has remained the official length of the marathon ever since. ◆

Philip II of Spain

King of Spain from 1556 to 1598
Born *1527*   **Died** *1598 aged 71*

Philip II of Spain was the richest, mightiest ruler in Christian Europe. His empire included parts of Italy, the Netherlands, and vast stretches of South and Central America, as well as Spain and Portugal. From 1559 he never left these last two kingdoms. As his reign went on he spent more and more time in his monastery-cum-palace, the Escorial, several miles from Spain's capital, Madrid.

Philip was a very serious Roman Catholic, at a time when wars to do with religion were ravaging Europe. He involved his peoples in many of these wars, but he rarely let his religious aims get in the way of more worldly ones. For example, when he sent the Spanish Armada

▼ *A detail from a Dutch stained-glass window showing Philip II of Spain and his wife, Mary, Queen of England.*

to attack England in 1588, it was for military and not religious reasons. His reign was part of the so-called 'Golden Age' of Spain. However, Philip spent so much of Spain's wealth on his wars that the Spanish era of power and prosperity was almost over by the time he died.

Philip's second wife was Mary I of England. ◆

👁 **see also**

Mary I

Pablo **Picasso**

Spanish painter and sculptor
Born *1881*   **Died** *1973 aged 91*

Pablo Picasso showed a truly exceptional talent for art when very young. By the age of 11, he was writing and illustrating art magazines as a hobby. He hated school and never learned to write well. He loved painting and worked at nothing else.

He often helped his father, a painter, with his work. One evening his father left Picasso to finish a picture of pigeons. On his return, he saw an astonishingly lifelike painting. He gave his son his own palette and brushes and never painted again. Picasso was just 13.

Many people realized that Picasso was a genius, but he wanted to do things in his own way, even if he disappointed those who expected him to become a traditional painter. At first he suffered years of poverty, but he was both courageous and self-disciplined, with an enormous appetite for hard work.

As his extraordinary talents developed, he was constantly breaking the rules of artistic tradition; he shocked the public with his strange and powerful pictures. He intentionally avoided 'copying' real life in his paintings,

◄ *Many of Picasso's figure paintings shocked audiences with their distorted views of their subjects, like this one, Portrait of Dora Maar.*

I paint objects as I think them, not as I see them.
PABLO PICASSO, 1959

but designed new forms to give fresh ways of seeing things in the world around us.

Picasso made drawings, paintings, collages, prints, theatre sets, sculptures, pottery, and ceramics. His style changed many times, but he is probably best known for his 'Cubist' pictures, which used simple geometric shapes and only a few colours. His life's work entirely changed our ideas about art. ◆

👁 **see also**

Braque

Auguste **Piccard**

Swiss engineer and scientific explorer
Born *1884*   **Died** *1962 aged 78*

With his twin brother Jean, Auguste Piccard qualified as an engineer in Zurich. Together they developed a keen interest in ballooning – ultimately to investigate what happens high in the Earth's atmosphere – and in 1913 made a 16-hour ascent. During World War I they both joined the balloon section of the Swiss army. After the war, Jean emigrated to America to follow a university career, but Auguste continued his ballooning while professor of physics at Brussels University.

▼ *Auguste Piccard with a sketch of his 'mesoscaphe' – an under-sea 'helicopter'. This was a diving boat with a rotor propellor which would allow it to descend and ascend vertically to depths of 1800 m.*

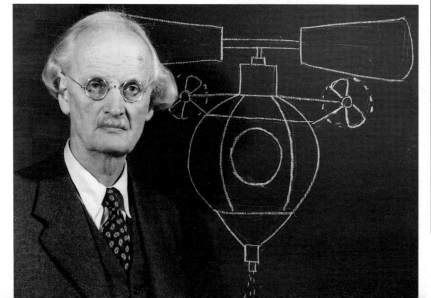

In 1931 he attracted worldwide publicity with an ascent of nearly 16,000 m, using the first balloon to be equipped with a pressurized gondola. Two years later he reached over 16,200 m. But his dream had always been 'to plunge into the sea deeper than any man before', to explore the ocean depths. This he achieved, with his son Jacques, in a self-propelled diving machine called a bathyscaphe. Together they descended to over 3000 m in 1953; Jacques – in a later vessel, the *Trieste* – went down to almost 11,000 m in 1960. ◆

👁 **see also**

Gay-Lussac   Montgolfier brothers

Mary **Pickford**

American film star
Born *1893*   **Died** *1979 aged 86*

Mary Pickford was the stage name of Canadian-born Gladys Smith. She was acting when she was only five years old and at 15 was already appearing on stage in New York, earning a living for her family.

She began working in movies as an extra for D. W. Griffith's Biograph Company and became the first star of the silent screen. From 1913, as Mary Pickford, a succession of sweet and innocent roles, such as *Rebecca of Sunnybrook Farm* (1917) and *Pollyanna* (1920), made her 'America's sweetheart' – and also one of America's richest women. In 1919 she formed United Artists with Charlie Chaplin, Douglas Fairbanks (her husband) and Griffith, to ensure film profits went to them rather than the studio bosses. ◆

👁 **see also**

Chaplin   Goldwyn

Piero della Francesca

Italian painter
Born c.1415   **Died** 1492 aged about 75

Piero della Francesca was one of the most important painters in one of the greatest periods of Italian art. He was a mathematician as well as an artist and his paintings have an almost geometric harmony.

They are mainly on religious subjects, although he also did a few portraits. Sometimes they can look a little stiff at first sight, but they have a solemn dignity and a subtle beauty of colouring which other painters could not match. Piero was born and died in the little town of Sansepolcro, about 40 miles from Florence, and most of his best paintings are in places that until recently were not much visited by travellers. Because of this, they were virtually ignored for four centuries after his death. It was not until the early 20th century that he was 'rediscovered' by art historians and took his deserved place among the great masters. ◆

▼ *One of Piero della Francesca's most famous paintings, entitled* The Baptism of Christ.

Lester **Piggott**

English champion jockey
Born 1935

Lester Piggott rode his first winner in 1948 at the age of 12, and soon established a winning habit as a flat-race jockey. He had his first Derby winner in 1954 and, by 1983, had ridden a record nine winners in that classic race.

Between 1964 and 1971 he was champion jockey each season. He retired from the saddle in 1985 to become a trainer, by which time he had ridden over 4000 winners. Because he did not pay as much income tax as he should have done, he was sent to prison for tax evasion in 1987. Piggott returned to racing in 1990 but retired finally in 1995. ◆

Camille **Pissarro**

French painter
Born 1830   **Died** 1903 aged 73

Camille Pissarro was one of the leading Impressionists – the artists who revolutionized painting with their bright colours and sketchy brushwork. He was the oldest of the group, and the others tended to regard him as a kindly father figure. Like the other Impressionists, he endured great poverty early in his career, and it was only in the last ten years of his life that he achieved any financial success. By this time his eyesight was failing and he had to give up painting landscapes out of doors: many of his late pictures were views of Paris that he painted while looking out of windows. Eventually he became completely blind. ◆

see also

Manet   Monet

William **Pitt** (the younger)

Prime minister of Britain from 1783 to 1801 and from 1804 to 1806
Born 1759   Died 1806 aged 46

William Pitt, the younger son of the Earl of Chatham, who was also named William Pitt, became a member of Parliament in 1781 at the age of 22. In 1783, at the age of 24, he became the youngest person to hold the office of prime minister.

For the next ten years his government worked hard to ensure Britain's economic recovery after the American War of Independence. During this time he raised taxes to pay off Britain's debts, and reduced widespread smuggling.

When France declared war on Britain in 1793 after the French Revolution; Pitt fought back hard, forming an alliance with Russia, Sweden, and Austria. He censored the newspapers and sometimes imprisoned without trial those who wanted a revolution in Britain too. Nearer to home, he secured the Union of Great Britain and Ireland in 1800 after the Irish uprising two years earlier. However, the strain of so many wars eventually seemed to be too much for him, and he died only two years into his second term as prime minister. ◆

Francisco **Pizarro**

Spanish conqueror of the Inca empire
Born c.1474   Died 1541 aged about 67

As a young man, Francisco Pizarro looked after a herd of pigs. He then decided to go to Hispaniola in the Caribbean to try his fortunes there and to take part in several exploring expeditions.

In 1522 he was scratching a living as a landowner in Panama when he heard rumours of the Inca empire in Peru and its fabulous wealth. Having made an expedition to check that it really existed, he returned to Spain in 1528 and asked permission from the king, Emperor Charles V, to conquer the land.

▲ *Once Francisco Pizarro had conquered the Inca empire, it was not long before the Spaniards had conquered the whole country of Peru.*

In 1532 Pizarro arrived in Peru to find the country split by civil war. He seized the emperor, Atahualpa, and demanded a huge ransom of gold and silver. After the money was paid, Pizarro had Atahualpa executed on the grounds that he was plotting against the Spaniards. Spain now ruled the Incas – Pizarro had conquered the Inca empire of several million people with an initial force of just 180 men. But he did not enjoy his victory for very long. In 1541 he was killed by rival Spaniards. ◆

see also

Atahualpa   Charles V   Cortés

Max **Planck**

German physicist
Born 1858   Died 1947 aged 89

Max Planck was appointed professor of physics at Kiel and then Berlin universities. He spent much of his early research on thermodynamics – the branch of physics that deals with the transformation of heat into other forms of energy. In 1900 he solved a problem that had troubled scientists for a long time: hot objects radiate heat energy but the energy stops suddenly instead of tapering away gradually as scientists expected. Planck explained this by saying that energy is always transferred in fixed amounts, rather like money. Just as in money there is a smallest-value coin, and a donation of money cannot be less than this, so energy has a smallest value. It is called a quantum of energy. Different currencies have different smallest coins. Similarly, different energy exchanges have different-sized quanta – though they are always extremely small. Planck's 'quantum theory' was developed further by other scientists, and was one of the most important discoveries of the 20th century. Planck was awarded the Nobel Prize for Physics in 1918. ◆

see also

Fermi   Heisenberg   Schrödinger

Sylvia **Plath**

American novelist and poet
Born *1932*   **Died** *1963 aged 30*

Since Sylvia Plath's death by suicide, she has been one of the most discussed women writers of the 20th century. She has become a feminist heroine, seen as both a rebel and a victim. In 1956 she married the English poet Ted Hughes, but they separated in 1962 and she lived alone in London.

Shortly before her death, her only novel, *The Bell Jar* (1963), was published; it tells of a woman student's emotional breakdown. Plath also published two volumes of poetry in her lifetime, but it was the collection published after her death, *Ariel* (1965), that made her reputation. Her best-known poems deal hauntingly with personal pain and tragedy, but she wrote tender and witty poems as well. ◆

Plato

Ancient Greek philosopher
Born *429 BC*   **Died** *347 BC aged 82*

Plato was born into an important Athenian family. He was well educated and at the age of 20 became a pupil of Socrates. The teachings of Socrates had an enormous influence on Plato's thinking and on what he wrote.

When Socrates was put to death in 399 BC, Plato went to live for a time in Megara, west of Athens. He also travelled for the next 12 years throughout Greece and to Egypt, Italy, and Sicily. In 387 BC he returned to Athens and started a school of philosophy. Most schools were held in the open air, in shady walks or under the colonnaded verandas of public buildings. His school was established in a park and gymnasium (sports ground)

about 2 km outside the city walls. This park was sacred to Academus, and so Plato's school became known as the Academy (a word still used for some types of school). The Academy of Plato lasted until 529.

Plato believed, like Socrates, that the right way to teach was to ask questions and then let the pupils discover the truth for themselves. A great deal of this teaching was published in his *Dialogues,* which were discussions between various people. Probably Plato's most famous work was *The Republic*, in which he discusses the ideal state or society. Plato describes the last hours and thoughts of Socrates in a book called *Phaedon.* ◆

👁 **see also**

Avicenna   Socrates

▼ *A detail of* Aristotle and Plato *(right) from* Raphael's painting School of Athens.

Plutarch

Ancient Greek historian
Born *C.AD 46*
Died *c.120 aged about 74*

The son of a philosopher, Plutarch studied philosophy himself in Athens and later lectured on this subject in Rome. In his travels through Egypt, Greece, and Italy, he set about collecting as much information as possible about the Greek and Roman heroes he later described in his greatest book, *Plutarch's Lives.* This was written in order to encourage respect between Greeks and Romans by describing the lives of the most noble citizens from both countries. Plutarch's short biographies did not stop simply at details of his subject's childhood, achievements, and death. He also added interesting stories about them, aiming to please as well as educate his readers. Translated

into English in 1579, *Plutarch's Lives* greatly influenced William Shakespeare. In plays like *Julius Caesar*, *Coriolanus*, and *Antony and Cleopatra*, Shakespeare often quotes whole passages taken from Plutarch with little alteration. Plutarch also wrote about philosophy and religion. ◆

👁 **see also**
Shakespeare

Pocahontas

Native American girl who befriended some English settlers in America
Born *1595* **Died** *1617 aged 22*

▲ *This portrait of Pocahontas, painted by an unknown artist in 1616, shows her dressed like an English lady.*

Pocahontas (her name means 'the little playful one') was the favourite daughter of Powhatan, chief of the area where the first English settlement was established at Jamestown, Virginia in 1607. She was about 12 when one of the settlers, Captain John Smith, was dragged before her father to be clubbed to death. Pocahontas pleaded successfully for his life to be spared.

Some years later, Pocahontas was taken hostage by the English in Jamestown who wanted her father to return his English prisoners. During her time in Jamestown she converted to Christianity and, to cement Anglo-Native American relations, she married a tobacco planter, John Rolfe. He took her and their baby son to London and they lived there for a year. However, she became homesick and decided to return home. She joined a ship that was sailing for Virginia, but died of smallpox before it had left England. ◆

Edgar Allan **Poe**

American poet and writer
Born *1809* **Died** *1849 aged 40*

Edgar Allan Poe's mother died when he was only three and he was adopted by a wealthy merchant who took him to England. After going to school in London, Poe returned to America to study at the University of Virginia. He then joined the army, but managed to get himself discharged for neglect of duty in 1831.

By this time, Poe had already published two volumes of poems and he decided to make his living by writing. He edited newspapers and magazines, and wrote stories, verse, and critical essays. Although he was admired as a poet – *The Raven and Other Poems* was

published in 1845 – he is most famous for his horror stories, such as *The Fall of the House of Usher* (1839), which tells the tale of a madman who buries his sister alive. Many of his stories have inspired horror movies.

Poe failed to earn much of a living by writing, and became an alcoholic. After his wife's death in 1847 he became more depressed and wrote less and less. ◆

Jackson **Pollock**

American painter
Born *1912* **Died** *1956 aged 44*

Jackson Pollock was the most famous representative of a style of painting known as Abstract Expressionism. In this, the artist virtually attacks the canvas with paint to express emotions directly and powerfully. Pollock also often laid his canvases on the floor and dripped paint on to them, a form which became known as 'Action Painting'.

Abstract Expressionism is now recognized as one of America's most original contributions to art, but Pollock endured poverty and mockery before he achieved success – one magazine article even dubbed him 'Jack the Dripper'. ◆

▼ *Jackson Pollock's* Mural *(1943) is typical of his work.*
University of Iowa Museum of Art, Oil on canvas. Gift of Peggy Guggenheim.

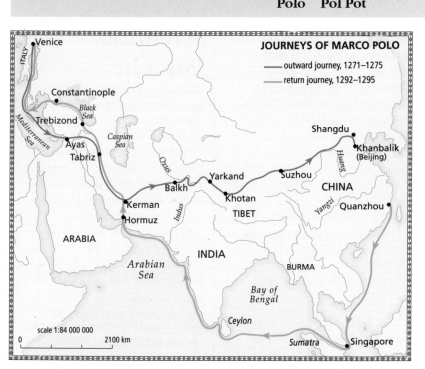

JOURNEYS OF MARCO POLO
— outward journey, 1271–1275
— return journey, 1292–1295

scale 1:84 000 000

0   2100 km

Marco **Polo**

Italian merchant and traveller
Born c.1254   *Died* 1324 aged about 70

In the 13th century, Cathay, as people then called China, was a romantic, unknown land to most Europeans. When Marco Polo was 18 he was invited by his father and uncle, Niccolò and Maffeo, to go with them to the court of the emperor Kublai Khan at Khanbalik (Beijing). Niccolò and Maffeo had already visited Kublai Khan, the first Europeans to do so.

The three merchants set out from their home in Venice in 1271. They went by ship to the Mediterranean coast of Turkey, and the rest of the way overland. They took the southern branch of the Silk Road, along which merchants from China regularly brought silk to Europe. The road runs north of the Himalayas, and across the Gobi Desert. The whole journey took nearly four years.

Kublai Khan received them warmly at court. Marco, who had a gift for languages, became a civil

▲ *The book Marco Polo wrote on his return from the Chinese empire contained descriptions of Kublai Khan's court and of the countries he visited.*

servant and travelling diplomat for Kublai. He was sent on many missions, visiting India, Myanmar (Burma), and Sri Lanka.

After 17 years the Polos decided it was time to return home. They went by sea, by way of Singapore, Sri Lanka, and the Persian Gulf. They arrived back in Venice in 1295 with a fortune in jewels, having been away 24 years.

Marco spent the last 30 years of his life as a Venetian merchant. At one time he was captured by the Genoese and became a prisoner of war in Genoa. While there he dictated the story of his travels. This is not a story of his personal adventures but a description of the almost unknown Mongol Empire. Many readers thought he was making things up, and Venetians called him *Il Milione*, meaning 'he of the million lies'. Later, though, people realized his account was mostly true. It influenced

Christopher Columbus's decision to look for a westward route to China and Japan. ◆

👁 **see also**
Columbus   Kublai Khan

Pol Pot

Prime minister of Cambodia from 1975 to 1979, and leader of the Khmer Rouge
Born 1928   *Died* 1998 aged 69

Pol Pot grew up in Cambodia, when Cambodia was part of Indo-China – a French territory. Having trained as a Buddhist monk and been educated at a French university, he joined the anti-French resistance under Ho Chi Minh. Cambodia achieved independence from France in 1953.

In 1960 Communists in Cambodia founded their own Communist Party, which was later called the Khmer Rouge. Pol Pot, who had risen to a high position within the Party, organized country people to

▼ *Visible evidence of the many people who died in Cambodia at the hands of Pol Pot's Khmer Rouge.*

fight the government. In 1975 they won control and Pol Pot became prime minister.

Between 1975 and 1979, his government forced the inhabitants of the capital city, Phnom Penh, to move into the countryside. He ordered that enemies of the Khmer Rouge should be killed; over 2 million people may have died. Something had to be done to stop the killing: in December 1979, the Vietnamese army invaded Cambodia and Pol Pot fled into Thailand. In his absence, he was sentenced to death for some of the worst crimes in history. ◆

see also

Ho Chi Minh

Pompey

Roman general and politician
Born *106 BC*   **Died** *48 BC aged 58*

In 510 BC the inhabitants of Rome drove out their king. Thereafter, they elected two consuls each year to rule the city for a year. The system worked well until the 1st century BC, when wars broke out between rivals for power. Between 88 and 81 BC there were wars between Sulla and Marius (who died in 86 BC), then between Sulla and Marius's followers.

Pompey raised an army to support Sulla, and thereby became one of Rome's most important politicians. Between 83 and 81 BC he destroyed Sulla's enemies, and then put down other revolts against the Roman government. Pompey's success gave him great prestige: he was elected consul in 80 BC, and for the next 20 years he held important government posts.

The other leading Roman at this time was Julius Caesar. Pompey and Caesar worked closely together at

first, but in 49 BC they quarrelled and began a civil war. Pompey and his supporters fled to Greece, where Caesar defeated them at Pharsalus (48 BC). Pompey fled to Egypt, but was murdered later the same year. ◆

see also

Caesar

Alexander **Pope**

English poet
Born *1688*   **Died** *1744 aged 56*

Alexander Pope educated himself at home with the help of his father. He was unable to go to school because of a crippling spinal disease and later was banned from studying at university because of his Roman Catholic background.

Pope started writing poetry when he was very young, soon showing mastery of the rhyming couplets which were so popular then. When only 23 he wrote *An Essay in Criticism,* a witty poem which includes the now famous line, 'To err is human, to forgive, divine'. Three years later he wrote his mock epic poem, *The Rape of the Lock.* He also translated Homer's *Odyssey* and *Iliad,* edited an edition of Shakespeare's works, and wrote many poems which were sharply critical of the writers and politicians of his time. His brilliant poetry gave much pleasure to others, except, of course, to those he was attacking. ◆

see also

Homer

Ferdinand Porsche

German car designer
Born *1875*   **Died** *1951 aged 76*

As a young man Ferdinand Porsche was an engineer with the Daimler-Benz company before becoming a designer for the Auto-Union racing team in 1930.

In 1934 he designed a revolutionary new type of car, to be produced cheaply, with the engine, unusually, at the rear. This idea was taken up enthusiastically by the Nazi government. In 1936 they promised to produce the Volkswagen (German for 'people's car') in large numbers for the civilian (non-military) market. This car became known as the Beetle, and proved to be immensely popular worldwide. By the late 1980s over 20 million had been sold.

Ferdinand Porsche also designed the Porsche sports car, first built in 1948. His son formed the Porsche Company in the same year. ◆

▼ *Two of Ferdinand Porsche's most famous car designs: a 1947 version of his VW Beetle (bottom), and a 1951 soft-top version of his up-market Porsche (top).*

Cole **Porter**

American songwriter
Born 1891   Died 1964 aged 73

Cole Porter started to play the violin when he was six and the piano when he was eight. He had even written an operetta and had a waltz published by the time he was eleven. The son of wealthy parents, he went to both Yale and Harvard universities, studying law and music. After World War I Porter took classes with composer Vincent d'Indy in Paris.

> *In olden days a glimpse of stocking*
> *Was looked on as something shocking*
> *Now, heaven knows,*
> *Anything goes.*
>
> COLE PORTER
> 'Anything Goes', 1934

See America First (1916) was his first musical on Broadway but his most successful shows were *Anything Goes* (1934), *Kiss Me Kate* (1948), *Can Can* (1953) and *Silk Stockings* (1955). A horse-riding accident in 1937 left him confined to a wheelchair and in great pain. However, this did not stop the flow of songs with their cleverly rhymed lyrics and sparkling tunes. ◆

👁 **see also**

Berlin Gershwin Rodgers

Beatrix **Potter**

English writer and illustrator of children's stories
Born 1866   Died 1943 aged 77

Beatrix Potter enjoyed sending letters to her friends' children; when she ran out of news, she filled the pages with her own pictures and a story about a rabbit

◀ *An illustration from Potter's* The Tale of Peter Rabbit.

called Peter. The children loved them so much that she sent *The Tale of Peter Rabbit* to six publishers, but none of them would publish it. Instead, she had the book printed with her own money, and gave copies of it to children. It became so popular that in 1902 a publisher named Frederick Warne agreed to reprint *Peter Rabbit* for her. Thousands of copies were sold.

With the royalties from *Peter Rabbit*, and other tales such as *Squirrel Nutkin* and *The Tailor of Gloucester*, Potter bought a small farm in the Lake District. During the next ten years she wrote *The Tale of Tom Kitten*, *The Tale of Jeremy Fisher*, and many more, using the landscape and the animals around her for inspiration. She stopped writing after her marriage in 1913. ◆

Nicolas **Poussin**

French painter
Born 1594   Died 1665 aged 71

Nicolas Poussin grew up in Normandy, northern France. When he was about 17, a painter came to the nearby town to paint pictures for the church. The painter aroused Poussin's interest in art and he made up his mind to become a painter. He went to Rouen and Paris to study.

In 1624 Poussin decided to go to Rome, which was then an important artistic centre. Many artists in Rome painted pictures that showed a lot of action and excitement. Poussin tried to paint in the same way but his paintings seemed dull. Instead he developed his own way of composing pictures, often showing small groups of people enjoying the countryside. Poussin's works attracted much interest and he soon became famous. In 1640 Poussin returned to Paris, becoming the court painter to King Louis XIII until 1643. He then went back to Rome.

The careful composition of his paintings, and their special atmosphere, influenced other painters and made Poussin one of France's foremost landscape painters in the 17th century. ◆

Elvis **Presley**

American rock and roll singer
Born 1935   Died 1977 aged 42

Elvis Presley was born into a poor family in Mississippi. As a teenager he spent much of his time with black musicians, learning a lot about blues and gospel music. In 1953 he paid to make a record for his mother's birthday at Sun Records in Memphis. The owner liked his unusual mixture of styles, and offered him professional recording work.

His first local hit was 'That's All Right' in 1954, and he created a sensation on television by swivelling his hips while singing. Adults were outraged, but teenagers loved it. By 1956 he was a national

▼ *For many years Elvis Presley was the most popular singer in the world.*

star, making huge hits like 'Hound Dog', 'Blue Suede Shoes', and 'Jailhouse Rock'. Known as the 'King of Rock 'n' Roll', Presley eventually recorded 94 gold singles and over 40 gold albums. He also starred in 27 films.

He continued touring and recording during the 1960s. During the 1970s he spent more and more time at Graceland, his huge house in Memphis. He died there of heart failure in 1977. Many thousands of his fans still visit Graceland every year. ◆

Joseph **Priestley**

English chemist who discovered oxygen
Born 1733   Died 1804 aged 70

Joseph Priestley was a minister in the Unitarian Church and also very interested in politics. Although he had no scientific education, he also became very keen on doing experiments.

Priestley's real claim to fame is his outstanding work studying gases, and particularly his identification of oxygen, which he called 'dephlogisticated air'. The importance of oxygen in burning was shown by the great French chemist Antoine Lavoisier.

Priestley's political opinions got him into a great deal of trouble. He fled to London with his family when a mob burned down his home because of his support for the ordinary French people during the French Revolution. Before long it was not safe for him to remain in England and he quickly left for the United States of America. He was warmly welcomed and spent the rest of his life working mainly for the Unitarian Church. ◆

👁 **see also**

Lavoisier

▲ *Sergei Prokofiev composed seven symphonies, including the popular First Symphony (1917).*

Sergei **Prokofiev**

Russian composer
Born 1891   Died 1953 aged 61

Sergei Prokofiev had his first music lessons from his mother, who was an excellent pianist. He began composing when he was five, could play Beethoven sonatas when he was nine, and by the age of 11 had written two operas. When he was 13 he went to study at the St Petersburg Conservatory of Music.

His first important compositions, two piano concertos, caused a great scandal. People thought them far too noisy. But later works, such as the popular First Symphony (the 'Classical'), helped them to change their minds. Other compositions by Prokofiev include operas, piano and violin concertos, and ballets such as *Romeo and Juliet* (1935).

After the 1917 Russian Revolution, and the founding of the USSR, Prokofiev spent many years in America and France. But he could not stay away and returned home in 1927 and again in 1934. One of the first pieces he wrote on his return was the delightful children's tale *Peter and the Wolf* (1936). ◆

▲ *Alain Prost driving for Ferrari in 1990.*

Alain **Prost**

French champion motor-racing driver
Born *1955*

Although Alain Prost was very talented at football, he chose to be a motor-racing driver instead. In 1980 he drove in his first Formula One Grand Prix for the McLaren team. He later drove for the Renault, Ferrari, and Williams teams.

By the end of his career Prost had won 51 races, more than any driver in history (a record broken since only by Michael Schumacher) and scored close to 800 points. He also won the world championship on four occasions, the last of them in 1993, the year he retired.

Prost was famous for the care with which he planned for each race. This is how he earned the nickname 'The Professor'. ◆

Marcel **Proust**

French author
Born *1871*   **Died** *1922 aged 51*

Marcel Proust suffered from asthma throughout his life, and his growing ill health led him gradually to withdraw from people into his own company. But by this time he had wide knowledge of the ways of rich French society, which he used in the writing of his seven-part novel *Remembrance of Things Past*.

Proust's work is not easy, and was originally refused by so many publishers he eventually had to pay for its publication himself. But over the years *Remembrance of Things Past* has come to be seen as one of the great classics of literature, full of revealing ideas about human thoughts, feelings, and relationships. ◆

Claudius **Ptolemy**

Egyptian astronomer and geographer
Lived during the 2nd century

Ptolemy lived and worked in Alexandria from 127 to 151. His great book *The Almagest* was published in about 140. It was an encyclopedia of all that was known in astronomy in Ptolemy's day and was accepted as the truth about the Solar System for about 15 centuries. It taught that the Earth was the centre of the universe with the Sun, Moon, planets, and stars all revolving about our planet. Ptolemy also published an important book on the principles of geography in which he dealt with the problems of constructing accurate maps using mathematics. The book contained a map of the known world.

Ptolemy's books were preserved and much later were translated and studied by Arabian astronomers who found that they had to modify his theories to fit their more accurate observations. Ultimately Ptolemy's Earth-centred theory of the universe was replaced by Copernicus's Sun-centred theory. ◆

👁 **see also**

Copernicus

Giacomo **Puccini**

Italian composer
Born *1858*   **Died** *1924 aged 65*

Giacomo Puccini was the last and greatest of a long line of composer-musicians who lived and worked in Lucca, Italy. At first it seemed that he would become a church organist like his father, but he was increasingly drawn to opera.

▲ *Puccini's opera* La Bohème *is famous for its dramatic effect and realism.*

After studying at the Milan Conservatory, Puccini entered a competition for a one-act opera. He failed to win a prize, but so impressed the great music publisher Giulio Ricordi that he was offered a contract to compose a full-length work. Although this first project was not successful, Ricordi still had faith in Puccini, and was rewarded by a series of wonderfully melodious and theatrically effective operas that are among the most popular ever written. The most famous are *Manon Lescaut* (1893), *La Bohème* (1896), *Tosca* (1900), *Madame Butterfly* (1904), and *Turandot* (produced posthumously in 1926). ◆

Henry **Purcell**

English composer and organist
Born 1659   Died 1695 aged 36

Henry Purcell became a chorister of the Chapel Royal – the musicians and clergy employed by the English monarch for religious services. In 1674 he was appointed tuner of the Westminster Abbey organ, and in 1677 succeeded Matthew Locke as 'composer to the King's violins'. Two years later he became organist of Westminster Abbey.

Purcell wrote many fine choral works for royal occasions, as well as anthems and chamber music. He also wrote incidental music for many plays, and a series of 'semi-operas' (plays with much music), such as *King Arthur* (1691) and *The Fairy Queen* (1692). His only real opera, *Dido and Aeneas* (1689), was very dramatic and emotional and is considered to be his masterpiece. Purcell is universally regarded as one of the greatest of all English composers. ◆

Alexander **Pushkin**

Russian poet, playwright, and novelist
Born 1799   Died 1837 aged 37

Alexander Pushkin was born into a wealthy family in Moscow and educated in St Petersburg, where his talent for poetry was noticed. After leaving school he worked for the government, but continued to write poetry. His political poems angered the government and he was banished to southern Russia. Here he started one of his greatest works, the novel *Eugene Onegin*, which portrayed current trends in Russian life.

The public read his poems eagerly and his fame grew. The tsar, recognizing his popularity, summoned him to Moscow and gave him a personal pardon. But his writing continued to be censored, and he was spied on. In 1836 he was wounded in a duel with a French baron who admired his wife and died two days later. ◆

▼ *The famous Russian writer Alexander Pushkin in a portrait from 1827.*

Pythagoras

Ancient Greek mathematician
Born c.582 BC
Died c.497 BC aged about 85

At the age of about 40 Pythagoras set up a strange religious community in southern Italy. It was called the Pythagorean Brotherhood and its members lived according to rules made by Pythagoras. The Pythagoreans lived a very strict, simple life and spent much of their time doing mathematics. Pythagoras believed that mathematics held the key to all the secrets of the universe, and he believed some numbers were magical.

He is best remembered for 'Pythagoras's theorem', a simple rule in geometry linking the lengths of the sides of right-angled triangles. But Pythagoras also did some of the very first scientific experiments by listening to the sounds of stretched strings of different lengths and working out the mathematics of octaves and harmony. Pythagoras's mathematical ideas became important to the philosopher Plato, and through him influenced other scientists such as Galileo, Kepler, and Newton. ◆

◉ **see also**

Galileo Kepler Newton Plato

Mu'ammar al-**Qaddafi**

Libyan leader from 1969
Born 1942

Mu'ammar al-Qaddafi's father was a Bedouin (nomadic Arab) farmer. Qaddafi was educated at the University of Libya and at the Military Academy. He came to power in Libya in 1969 as the leader of an army revolt which overthrew the country's king, Idris, and made himself president in 1977. He used Libya's oil-wealth to improve living conditions in his otherwise very poor country, and also to buy modern planes and weapons for the armed forces.

Qaddafi's government has been involved in a number of incidents with neighbouring countries, including Chad, Sudan, and Uganda. He has also been unpopular with some Western countries because of his support for terrorist and revolutionary groups. In 1986 the American president, Ronald Reagan, authorized the bombing of the Libyan capital, Tripoli, in retaliation for alleged acts of terrorism against American nationals. Some of Qaddafi's own children were killed and injured in the raid.

Qaddafi is a strict Muslim and in 1973 he outlawed alcohol and gambling in Libya. Many of his theories, based on the ideas of Mao Zedong, are kept in his *Green Book*. ◆

👁 **see also**
Mao Zedong   Reagan

François **Rabelais**

French writer
Born c.1494   Died 1553 aged about 59

The son of a rich landowner, François Rabelais became a Franciscan monk before qualifying as a doctor. However, he is more famous for his work as a writer. In 1532 he published his comic masterpiece *Pantagruel*, followed two years later by *Gargantua*. Both books describe the adventures of a giant father and son, both of whom have huge appetites. They are aided by a trouble-making monk called Frère Jean, whose behaviour is so un-Christian that both books were eventually banned by the Church authorities in Paris.

Although Rabelais constantly makes his readers laugh, his books also attack the worst political, educational, and religious abuses of his time. Although for some years his books could only be read outside France, he had a large

▼ *An illustration from François Rabelais' humorously critical novel about the giant Gargantua.*

influence on future French writers, as well as upon British authors such as Jonathan Swift. ◆

👁 **see also**
Swift

Yitzhak **Rabin**

Prime Minister of Israel from 1974 to 1977 and from 1992 to 1995
Born 1922   Died 1995 aged 73

After graduating from agricultural college, Yitzhak Rabin joined the Jewish Defence Force during World War II. He later played an important part in Israel's victory over the Arab troops in the Six-Day War (June 1967). In 1973 Rabin became a Labour member of parliament, and a few months later prime minister. From 1984 to 1986 he was defence minister in a coalition government, then became prime minister again in 1992.

Rabin believed that Israel should withdraw from the Arab territories it had occupied since the Six-Day War. He began negotiations with Yasser Arafat, head of the Palestine Liberation Organization. This outraged many Jewish people, and there were demonstrations and violent clashes between Jews and Palestinians. Tragically Rabin was assassinated in October 1995, by a Jew determined to end the peace process. ◆

Jean **Racine**

French playwright and poet
Born 1639   Died 1699 aged 59

Jean Baptiste Racine was brought up by his Catholic grandmother who sent him to a strict religious school. Later, however, he moved away from a possible career in the Church and left for Paris where he started to write poetry. He found favour at the court of King Louis XIV and began to write plays. His earliest were *The Thebiad* (1664) and *Alexander the Great* (1665). These were followed by many others, including his masterpiece, *Phèdre* (1677). The subjects for his plays often came from Greek mythology. The plots were simple, but his characters expressed a whole range of complex emotions.

In 1677 Racine retired from dramatic writing, married, and settled down in domestic happiness until his death in 1699. ◆

Sergey **Rakhmaninov**

Russian composer and pianist
Born *1873*   **Died** *1943 aged 69*

Sergey Rakhmaninov studied music first at the St Petersburg Conservatory and then (1888) at the Moscow Conservatory. His first opera, *Aleko* (1893), was a success, but his First Symphony failed completely. He became very depressed, and even lost faith in his ability to compose. Fortunately, he was helped to recover by a course of hypnosis.

The success of his second piano concerto (1901) finally restored his confidence. As a pianist he began touring in 1899, visiting America for the first time in 1909. He left Russia after the 1917 Revolution and settled in America, where he pursued the hectic career of a popular concert pianist. Although this greatly reduced the time he could devote to composition, he wrote many fine songs and piano pieces, as well as four piano concertos, *Rhapsody on a Theme of Paganini* for piano and orchestra, and three symphonies. ◆

▲ *This drawing of Sergey Rakhmaninov was made when he was 43. His dramatic and emotional style of music thrilled concert audiences.*

Walter **Raleigh**

English courtier and explorer
Born *c.1552*   **Died** *1618 aged about 66*

Walter Raleigh supposedly first pleased Elizabeth I when he laid his fine velvet cloak over a puddle so the queen's shoes would not get muddy. He was certainly a great favourite of her's after he came to court in 1581. However, he did not always please her, especially when he married Elizabeth Throgmorton, a lady-in-waiting. He was sent to the Tower of London, and then banished from court for a time.

Raleigh was an accomplished soldier who had fought in France and Ireland, and helped to prepare England's defences against the Spanish Armada. He was also fascinated by the riches of America. He never went there himself, but his expeditions probably brought potatoes to Britain for the first time, and whether he brought tobacco from America or not, Raleigh made pipe-smoking fashionable at court. In 1595 he went to South America and searched unsuccessfully for El Dorado, a mythical land said to be full of gold.

James I, who became king in 1603, distrusted Raleigh, and imprisoned him in the Tower of London for over 12 years. Raleigh wrote a *History of the World*, and did many scientific experiments while he was there.

In 1616 James allowed Raleigh to go back to South America to search for gold. However, his expedition found no gold and got into a fight with the Spanish instead. Raleigh returned home a sick man, and, in 1618, James finally ordered his execution. ◆

> *I have a long journey to take, and must bid the company farewell.*
>
> WALTER RALEIGH, 1618
> (his last words before being executed)

▼ *Although Queen Elizabeth I enjoyed Walter Raleigh's company, she did not think he was reliable, and never gave him any real power.*

Ramakrishna

Indian holy man and religious teacher
Born 1836   Died 1886 aged 50

Gadadhar Chatterji was the son of a poor family. His only language was Bengali; he spoke no English or Sanskrit. From a very early age his only real interest was his religious spiritual quest. His eldest brother, Ramkumar, offered to pay for his education, but he declined, saying he wanted no 'mere bread-winning education'. Instead he devoted himself to prayer. First he worshipped the Hindu goddess Kali. Then he became a sannyasin (monk) and took the name Ramakrishna. Later he learned about Islam and Christianity, and came to the conclusion that all religions were equal paths to the same goal.

Thousands came to listen to him speak and his followers began to collect his sayings so that they could be written down and published throughout the world. These followers kept his memory alive long after his death. His wife, Sarada-devi, whom he married when she was five, became a saint and was known as Divine Mother to Ramakrishna's disciples. ◆

Rameses II

King of Egypt from 1304 BC to 1237 BC
Lived during the 13th century BC

In ancient times, the kingdom of Egypt was one of the richest places in the world. Rameses became king (pharaoh) of Egypt in about 1304 BC. He wanted to increase Egypt's land and power. For 16 years he and his army fought against Egypt's main enemy, the Hittites, who ruled a powerful empire in an area which is now modern Turkey. Eventually the two

▲ *Rameses II was pharaoh for 66 years, probably the longest time an Egyptian king ever ruled.*

sides made peace and Rameses married a Hittite princess.

During Rameses' long reign, Egypt prospered and there was a substantial programme of building. He founded a new capital city in the flat delta of the Nile and called it 'Pi-Riamses', the 'Land of Rameses'. Throughout Egypt he built numerous temples. One of these, at Abu Simbel in south Egypt, is very famous because the front consists of four enormous statues of Rameses himself. ◆

Raphael

Italian painter
Born 1483   Died 1520 aged 37

Raffaello Sanzio (Raphael's real name) was apprenticed at the age of seven to his father, an artist. He began by learning to mix up colours for his father's pictures.

He was already a master painter by 17 and worked in Florence and then in Rome. He was employed by the pope to work on the Vatican and the Sistine Chapel, for which he designed tapestries.

His great interest was in painting the human figure, especially the Madonna and Child (Mary and Jesus). By showing tender glances and reaching-out gestures, he made them look loving, unlike the cool and formal pictures people were

▶ *One of the things people like about Raphael's paintings is the naturalness of his figures, like the rounded characters in this fresco,* Galatea (1513).

used to. He had amazing skill at taking ideas from others and, by varying and changing them, making something quite new of his own. His work shows exquisite beauty and harmony; he painted nothing ugly, horrible, or shocking.

He crammed an astonishing amount of artistic achievement into his short life, and received many honours for his wall paintings, portraits, huge figure compositions, engravings, and tapestry designs.

He died on his 37th birthday, and left behind an idea of 'perfection' in painting. For centuries he was regarded as the greatest painter of all time. ◆

> *Raffaello was quite right to be jealous of me, for all he knew of art he learned from me.*
>
> MICHELANGELO
> talking about Raphael

Rasputin

Favourite of the Russian royal family
Born *1871* **Died** *1916 aged around 45*

Rasputin was the son of Russian peasants. He presented himself as a holy man who could heal people. In 1905 in St Petersburg – the capital of Russia at the time – he met the Russian empress (tsarina), Alexandra, and the emperor (tsar), Nicholas II. Their son, Alexei, suffered from haemophilia. This meant that if he cut himself, the bleeding would not stop. Because Rasputin was able to make Alexei feel calm, he became popular with Alexandra.

In 1914 Russia went to war with Germany. The following year, the tsar left the court and took command of the Russian army. While he was away, Alexandra, under Rasputin's influence, dismissed government ministers, and replaced many of them with incompetent men. Rasputin and Alexandra were largely responsible for the tsar's failure to respond to the ever rising tide of discontent amongst the Russian people, which eventually led to the Russian Revolution (1917). A group of noblemen tried to kill Rasputin, to remove his evil influence. They

▲ *The famous Russian priest, Rasputin.*

poisoned him, shot him, and then threw him in the River Neva where he drowned. ◆

👁 **see also**

Nicholas II

Maurice **Ravel**

French composer
Born *1875* **Died** *1937 aged 62*

Joseph Maurice Ravel first became well-known as a pianist and a conductor and he made a number of concert tours. However, apart from these excursions, he led a quiet and retiring life devoted to composing music.

Ravel had studied music at the Paris Conservatoire, under the direction of the composer Gabriel Fauré among others. Ravel turned to many different composers for inspiration, but developed his own uniquely personal style. He often drew on unusual sources, such as fairy tales or magic, for his themes.

His main works are songs and piano pieces, but he also wrote orchestral pieces such as the famous *Boléro* (1928), two piano concertos, ballets, and two short operas. One of his most famous piano works, *Gaspard de la Nuit*, is one of the most difficult to play that has ever been written. ◆

Satyajit **Ray**

Indian film director
Born 1921   Died 1992 aged 71

With a musician mother, writer father, and writer and painter grandfathers, Satyajit Ray was brought up in artistic circles. He, however, originally planned a career in science but changed his plans while studying with the poet Rabindranath Tagore (a family friend) and became interested in book illustration instead.

Working on the story of Apu, a Brahmin boy growing up in poverty in a Bengal village, made Ray want to film this book. Helping French director Jean Renoir to film *The River* on location in India increased his interest in cinema.

▲ *Satyajit Ray (left) directing one of his films. He liked spontaneity and preferred to use the first filming of a scene rather than a retake.*

Over the next five years, using amateur actors and filming mainly at weekends, he made *Pather Panchali* (completed 1955). It won a major prize at the Cannes Film Festival and was followed by two other films continuing Apu's story called *Unvanquished* (1956) and *World of Apu* (1959). Among the best of his other films are *The Music Room* (1958) and *The Chess Players* (1977). ◆

👁 **see also**
Tagore

Ronald **Reagan**

President of the United States of America from 1981 to 1989
Born 1911   Died 2004 aged 93

Ronald Reagan came from a poor family in Illinois. After working his way through college, he became a radio sports announcer. He then got a Hollywood contract in 1937, and he made the first of 50 films.

For several years after the war he was president of the Screen Actors Guild. He was so good at making speeches that many people told him he should be a politician.

Reagan joined the Republican Party in 1962 and was elected governor of California in 1966. Having lost the Republican presidential nomination in 1968 and 1976, he won it in 1980 and became president. He was re-elected for another term in 1984. During his presidency, military expenditure increased while less money was spent on welfare benefits for the poor. In 1987 a treaty was signed with Mikhail Gorbachev of the Soviet Union to eliminate all ground-based, intermediate-range nuclear missiles. ◆

👁 **see also**
Gorbachev

Steve **Redgrave**

British rowing champion
Born 1962

Steve Redgrave was brought up in Marlowe, near Henley, UK. At school he was good at all kinds of sports, but in 1976 he began to concentrate on rowing.

By 1984 Steve was a world-class rower. In the Olympics that year he won his first rowing gold medal. In 1986 he teamed up with Andy Holmes and won the coxless pairs world championships. The pair then won Olympic gold in 1988. After Andy Holmes retired, Steve paired up with Matthew Pinsent. From 1993 to 1996 they were unbeaten, winning four world championships and two Olympic golds. In the 2000 Olympics Redgrave won a record fifth gold medal in the coxless fours. ◆

Rembrandt van Rijn

Dutch painter
Born 1606   Died 1669 aged 63

Rembrandt went to university when he was only 14. A year later he left to develop his artistic talent. He used his family as models, and mastered the skill of painting facial expressions. He particularly loved to paint portraits. Indeed he painted himself 60 times, from a young man to old age.

Rembrandt's sufferings began with the death of three of his children, then of his mother and of his wife, Saskia, leaving him with one son, Titus.

As he grew older, Rembrandt became extra-sensitive to the real person behind the face he was painting. He no longer bothered with people's clothes or with backgrounds, but concentrated on the true personality. ◆

Pierre Auguste **Renoir**

French painter
Born 1841   Died 1919 aged 78

Pierre Auguste Renoir was the son of a tailor, and grew up knowing that good craftsmanship was essential in the making of

▲ The Luncheon of the Boating Party *by the French artist Pierre Auguste Renoir shows his use of bright colours and interest in lively scenes.*

quality work. At the age of 13 he was apprenticed to a porcelain manufacturer to produce hand-painted designs. He later moved over to painting fans and then to decorating blinds.

However, Renoir became dissatisfied with this work, and began to study figure drawing and anatomy at evening classes. He worked in a famous studio where he met other young artists who were interested in capturing the dappled effects of light and shadow in their paintings. With them he founded the group of painters known as the Impressionists, who held their first exhibition in 1874. Renoir's early work suffered ridicule, but he soon became successful as a portrait painter. He also enjoyed painting busy scenes of ordinary people in bright colours, using bold brushstrokes without fussy detail. He continued to work up until his death and produced over 6000 paintings. ◆

👁 **see also**
Manet Monet Pissarro

Paul **Revere**

American patriot during the American Revolution
Born 1735   **Died** 1818 aged 83

At the age of 13 Paul Revere was apprenticed to his father, a Boston silversmith. Later he set up his own workshop and became an ardent patriot who wanted his country to be free of British rule. Along with others, and disguised in war-paint and feathers, he threw crates of tea into the sea at the so-called 'Boston Tea Party' to protest against British taxation.

On 16 April 1775 a single lantern in the North Church steeple in Boston signalled that the British troops were marching inland to capture a munitions store and two patriots, Hancock and Adams, who were hiding at Lexington. Paul Revere rode through the night to warn the country people and to urge them to resist. At Lexington the British soldiers were fired on by armed farmers, and they were made to retreat by a larger force. This was the beginning of the American Revolution (War of Independence). Revere took an active role and in 1776 was put in command of Castle William, defending Boston Harbour.

After the war Revere established the first copper-rolling mill in the United States. He eventually died a wealthy and successful merchant and manufacturer. ◆

▼ *A print showing the 'Boston Tea Party' protest against British taxation on 16 December 1773.*

▲ The giant statue of a sun god on the island of Rhodes, the Colossus of Rhodes, was one of the seven wonders of the ancient world. This cartoon, 'The Rhodes Colossus', from the British magazine Punch, gives an idea of how important Cecil Rhodes was in Africa by 1895.

Cecil **Rhodes**

British colonist in southern Africa
Born 1853   **Died** 1902 aged 48

As a boy Cecil Rhodes suffered from weak lungs, so he went to southern Africa where the climate would be better for him. He worked on a cotton farm but later moved to Kimberley to mine for diamonds.

Between 1873 and 1881, Rhodes spent time at Oxford University studying for a degree. During these years he decided that the British should extend their rule throughout Africa. He began to make the money to fulfil his dream in the mines at Kimberley. By 1891 his company, De Beers, owned 90 per cent of the world's diamond mines.

Rhodes had entered parliament in the Cape Colony in 1881, and he became prime minister in 1890. Against opposition from Paul Kruger and the Boers of the Transvaal, he pushed British rule northwards, creating a new colony which was called Rhodesia (now Zimbabwe) after him.

In 1895 Rhodes supported the 'Jameson raid', which attempted to overthrow Kruger's government in the Transvaal. It failed, and Rhodes had to resign as prime minister. When he died he left £3 million in his will to pay for overseas students to go to Oxford University. ◆

👁 **see also**

Kruger

Richard I

King of England from 1189 to 1199
Born 1157   **Died** 1199 aged 41

Richard was the third son of Henry II and Eleanor of Aquitaine. In 1173 his mother persuaded him to rebel, with two of his brothers, against Henry. The revolt failed, but 16 years later Richard forced his ageing father to

▲ Richard I, portrayed here at rest on his tomb, was known as Richard the Lionheart because of his bravery in battle.

make Richard heir to all his lands in England and France, leaving nothing for John, Richard's younger brother.

Once in power, Richard went on the Third Crusade to the Holy Land with the other kings and nobles of Europe. They failed to capture Jerusalem, but Richard defeated Saladin, the Muslim leader, at Arsuf. On the way back to England, Richard was taken prisoner by one of his enemies, the Duke of Austria. His government in England had to pay a huge ransom for his release.

Although he was king for ten years, Richard spent a total of only five months of his reign in England; the last five years of his reign were devoted to fighting the King of France. He died of blood poisoning, caused by an arrow in his shoulder, while besieging a town in the French kingdom of Aquitaine. ◆

👁 **see also**

Eleanor of Aquitaine   Saladin

Richard III

King of England from 1483 to 1485
Born 1452   **Died** 1485 aged 32

The son of the Duke of York, Richard lived in the shadow of his elder brother, who became King Edward IV in 1461, while Richard was created Duke of Gloucester. In the continuing feud for the English throne between the house of York and the house of Lancaster, Richard helped his brother defeat Lancastrian challenges. This struggle, which lasted for 30 years, became known as the War of the Roses because of the red rose badge worn by the Lancastrians and the white rose badge worn by the Yorkists.

When Edward died in 1483, Richard did away with the nobles

▲ Triple Portrait of the Head of Richelieu. *During the reign of King Louis XIII (1601–1643), Armand Jean Richelieu was the most powerful man in France.*

the French monarchy, given order and unity to the country, and won for France a leading position in European affairs. However, his excessive taxation, his refusal to operate any form of democratic government, and his crushing of the power of the French nobility meant that he created many enemies for himself, and there were several attacks on his life. ◆

Nikolay **Rimsky-Korsakov**

Russian composer and teacher
Born 1844   Died 1908 aged 64

Nikolay Rimsky-Korsakov's first ambition was to be a sailor, and in 1856 he became a naval cadet. However, he was also inspired by the new spirit in Russian music and at the age of 15 began to write a symphony. Apart from a few piano lessons, he was entirely self-taught and almost completely ignorant of musical theory. He made strenuous efforts to catch up on his musical knowledge and, though still a naval officer, eventually became a professor at the St Petersburg Music Conservatory in 1871. He proved to be a fine teacher (Stravinsky was one of his pupils). He was also a great admirer of Russian music and produced his own versions of Borodin's incomplete opera *Prince Igor*, and Mussorgsky's opera *Boris Godunov*. His own finest compositions are distinguished by their brilliant orchestration. They include such operas as *The Legend of Tsar Sultan* (1900) and *The Golden Cockerel* (1907), and the symphonic suite *Sheherazade* (1888). ◆

◉ **see also**

Stravinsky

who might become his enemies, imprisoned his brother's two sons (the rightful heirs to the throne) in the Tower of London, and had himself proclaimed king – all within three months. Until then he had been a popular and trusted man, but now he began to lose support. When England was invaded by Henry Tudor, a Lancastrian bethrothed to the Yorkist heiress, Elizabeth of York, Richard was deserted by many of his followers. He was killed on the battlefield at Bosworth and his crown was found on a thorn-bush. ◆

Armand Jean **Richelieu**

French cardinal and politician
Born 1585   Died 1642 aged 57

Armand Jean Richelieu became a bishop when he was only 22. He later came to the notice of Marie de Medici, then acting as regent for her son, Louis XIII. Through her influence Richelieu won a place at the French court and in 1622 was made a cardinal.

When he was 39 Richelieu became chief (prime) minister and together with Louis XIII, who was now king, he virtually ruled the country. One of his major aims was to restore the monarchy to its former absolute power. To do this he tried to curb the politically strong and ambitious nobles, who enjoyed virtual independence from royal authority. Richelieu's foreign policy was directed at restoring French influence and power in Europe, especially against Austria and Spain which were controlled by the Habsburg dynasty.

By the time of his death in 1642, Richelieu had restored the power of

Diego **Rivera**

Mexican painter
***Born** 1886   **Died** 1957 aged 70*

Diego Rivera studied art and politics in Europe from 1907 to 1921. At that time he was much influenced by Pablo Picasso, the famous Spanish master of modern art. But when Rivera went home to Mexico, he deliberately turned his back on fashionable European styles of painting. He said he was more interested in 'art for the people'. He revived older methods of painting such as fresco (using water-colours on wet plaster) and encaustic painting (using heat to fuse wax colours onto a surface).

Rivera loved to paint scenes from Mexican life and history, particularly the history of ordinary people. He also much admired the American Indians, and painted huge murals (paintings that decorate walls and ceilings) in vivid colours, showing how the Aztecs were destroyed by the Spaniards. His sympathy for Communism, though, sometimes got him into trouble. His huge mural for the American Rockefeller Center in New York was removed

▲ *Many of Diego Rivera's paintings, like this one,* The Market at Tenochtitlan, *portray the culture and history of Mexico.*

because it contained a picture of Lenin, the first leader of the Communist Soviet Union. ◆

👁 **see also**
Picasso

José **Rizal**

Filipino nationalist
***Born** 1861   **Died** 1896 aged 35*

José Rizal is known as the father of Filipino independence – though he himself had never really campaigned for it.

The son of a wealthy landowner, Rizal proved himself to be a brilliant medical student in Spain and Germany. While abroad he became leader of a group of students who wanted reforms in the Philippines, which were then a Spanish colony. Rizal wrote two novels which called for an end to the wealth and power of Spanish friars in his country. He also wanted equal rights for all Filipinos and Spaniards although

he did not call for complete independence from Spain. Returning home, he founded a school and hospital but was falsely accused of plotting revolution and was executed. This convinced Filipinos that Spanish rule must come to an end. ◆

Robert I

King of Scotland from 1306 to 1329
***Born** 1274   **Died** 1329 aged 54*

Robert 'the Bruce' came from an aristocratic Scottish family. He was very ambitious, and grew up wanting to become king of Scotland. To gain the Scottish throne, Bruce stabbed his main rival in a quarrel, and a month later he was crowned King Robert I.

At first things went badly for the new king. England was at war with Scotland, and wanted to have control over its neighbour. Many of

▼ *Robert I pictured with his second wife in 1306. As king of Scotland, he won independence for his country from England.*

Robert's family and supporters were captured and savagely treated by the English king, Edward I. Robert was forced to go into hiding and almost lost heart. There is a story that while he was sheltering in a cave, he saw a spider struggling again and again to climb up to her web and not giving up. The spider's example inspired him to keep on fighting against the English. Finally, in 1314, he overwhelmed Edward II's army in the fierce battle of Bannockburn.

King Robert's victory did not end the fighting with England, but at least Scotland was once again an independent kingdom. He died of leprosy in 1329, a great hero. ◆

👁 **see also**

Edward I

Julia Fiona **Roberts**

American film star
Born 1967

As a child Julia Roberts wanted to be a vet, but later she decided to study acting like her older brother and sister.

In 1990 Julia became a star almost overnight for her part in the romantic comedy *Pretty Woman*. Between 1993 and 1997 she made a range of different movies. Then in 1997 Julia returned to romantic comedy with *My Best Friend's Wedding*. In 1999 another romantic film, *Notting Hill*, was very popular.

Julia was now one of the top stars in Hollywood. She was paid $20 million – the most ever paid to a screen actress – to appear in the film *Erin Brockovich*. This dramatic film was a huge success, and won her an Oscar in 2001. ◆

Paul **Robeson**

American classical actor and singer
Born 1898 Died 1976 aged 77

Paul Robeson studied law at university, but in the 1920s, when he qualified, it was difficult for black people to get work as lawyers. So instead he became an actor and a singer. He played the title role in Shakespeare's *Othello* in London and New York. He also starred in films, including *Sanders of the River* (1935), and *Show Boat* (1936).

Robeson had a wonderful, natural bass voice which captured listeners' attention. The song 'Ol' Man River' from *Show Boat* is always associated with him, as are such songs as 'Water Boy' and 'Ma Curly Headed Babby'.

After visiting the Soviet Union in the 1930s, Robeson became interested in Communism. In 1950 the American government took away his passport because he would not deny being a Communist. This caused him great grief and bitterness and seriously affected his career. He eventually left America and stayed away until 1963, when he returned for health reasons. ◆

Maximilien **Robespierre**

Famous leader in the French Revolution
Born 1758 Died 1794 aged 36

After studying in Paris, Maximilien Robespierre returned to his home town, Arras, where he worked as a lawyer until he was 30. In 1789 he was elected as a deputy to represent his province in the Estates-General (parliament). Unlike many other deputies, Robespierre saw himself as representing the poor as well as the rich.

▲ *Robespierre is mostly remembered for the thousands of people he sent to the guillotine before he himself was executed, rather than for his ideas.*

The French Revolution started in 1789 and Robespierre made a name for himself through the power of his speeches. He pressed for the ideas of the Revolution – liberty for all, equality for all, and fraternity (brotherhood) of all.

By 1793 there was civil war in the west, an invasion in the north-east, and people were starving. Robespierre and his supporters, the Jacobins, decided that ruthless action was needed to feed the people, to raise a citizen army, and to get rid of the Revolution's enemies. He joined the Committee of Public Safety, which organized these activities.

This was the time of 'the Terror', when anyone might be accused of treason, quickly tried, and executed. Robespierre thought this was necessary, but as thousands were killed, many saw it as brutal tyranny. By the summer of 1794, people were sick of the Terror. Robespierre's revolutionary colleagues rose against him and he was sent to the guillotine. ◆

👁 **see also**

Danton

285

John D. **Rockefeller**

American industrialist and multimillionaire
***Born** 1839* ***Died** 1937 aged 97*

John Davison Rockefeller was a businessman when the first oil well was drilled in America in 1859. Four years later he started an oil refinery in Ohio. By 1870 his company, the Standard Oil Company, began to buy up many other oil companies.

By 1882 Standard Oil had 95 per cent of all the refining business in America. This monopoly made him into a multimillionaire. Once he had made his fortune Rockefeller began to look for good and useful ways to spend his money. In 1891 he paid for the University of Chicago to be established, and he later set up the Rockefeller Institute for Medical Research (which became Rockefeller University) in New York City. In 1913, after retiring from the oil business, he began the Rockefeller Foundation to finance charitable activities. ◆

Richard **Rodgers**

American composer of musicals
***Born** 1902* ***Died** 1979 aged 77*

As a schoolboy, Richard Rodgers wrote songs for amateur shows and was determined to become a composer. Then, when he was 16, he met 23-year-old lyric writer Lorenz Hart. 'Fly With Me' (1919), written for Columbia University amateurs, began a 25-year writing partnership. Their Broadway hits include 'On Your Toes' (1936) and 'Pal Joey' (1940). In 1943, the year Hart died, Rodgers found a new lyricist in Oscar Hammerstein II – a friend since

▲ *The screen version of Rodgers and Hammerstein's stage musical* South Pacific *was filmed in 1958.*

1914 with whom he had worked occasionally. Among the shows they wrote together are *Oklahoma!* (1943), *Carousel* (1945), *South Pacific* (1949), *The King and I* (1951), and *The Sound of Music* (1959), all filmed by Hollywood. Although Rodgers always composed to reflect the character and situation of the storylines, the result was a succession of hit songs. ◆

◉ **see also**

Gershwin Porter

Auguste **Rodin**

French sculptor
***Born** 1840* ***Died** 1917 aged 77*

Auguste Rodin was sent to boarding school for a short time to improve his poor studies, but his only interest was drawing. When he was older he began work as a stonemason, carrying out the designs of others for decorations on buildings. His techniques became highly skilled and he began to study

the works of famous sculptors in museums.

He was powerfully influenced by the statues of Michelangelo and visited Italy to see more of them. His own figures eventually became famous for their unusually life-like quality and sense of movement. They were so realistic that he was even accused of taking a cast from a live model.

Like other artists at the time, Rodin discovered that sculpture need not look entirely finished to be effective or powerful. However, his work caused endless quarrels amongst his critics. Many changes were usually requested before his figures could be placed in public places. One of his most famous, 'The Thinker', was attacked and damaged by a vandal. ◆

Erwin **Rommel**

German field commander in North Africa in World War II
***Born** 1891* ***Died** 1944 aged 52*

Erwin Rommel joined the German army in 1910 and won medals for gallantry in World War I. Remaining in the army after the war, he also wrote books about military tactics. At the start of World War II he was in charge of the guards at Hitler's headquarters, but in 1940 he moved to a Panzer tank division and headed the invasion of France in May. Then, when Italian forces collapsed in North Africa, Rommel was sent out as head of the Afrika Korps. He fought a successful campaign until he was defeated at El Alamein in October 1942. Rommel then served in France as Inspector of Coastal Defences.

He had become unhappy with Hitler's leadership and gave his support to a plot to assassinate the Nazi dictator. In July 1944 the plot

▲ *General Erwin Rommel leading German troops in North Africa in 1941.*

failed and Rommel's involvement was discovered. Already badly injured by an Allied air attack on his car, he took poison to save his family from trial and execution. ◆

👁 **see also**

Hitler

Wilhelm **Röntgen**

German scientist who discovered X-rays
Born 1845   **Died** 1923 aged 77

In 1895 Wilhelm Röntgen was doing experiments in which he applied a strong electric current to metal plates inside a glass tube from which most of the air had been removed. His tube was covered with black cardboard and the room was dark. To his amazement, he noticed that a chemical on the bench across the room was glowing. After many further experiments he decided that the tube was giving out rays that went through both the glass and the cardboard. He called these mysterious rays X-rays. (The letter X is often used to mean unknown.) Today, X-rays are commonly used in hospitals or at the dentist to see inside the human body. For his work on X-rays, Röntgen was awarded the Nobel Prize for Physics in 1901. ◆

▼ *This cartoon from 1900, five years after X-rays were discovered, imagines what a beach scene might look to their discoverer, the physicist Wilhelm Röntgen.*

Eleanor **Roosevelt**

American humanitarian and First Lady
Born 1884   **Died** 1962 aged 78

Eleanor Roosevelt was orphaned when she was ten and brought up by her strict grandmother. She was taught at home, until at 15 she went to school in England. When she was 17 her uncle, Theodore Roosevelt, became president of the United States of America.

Eleanor married a distant cousin, Franklin Delano Roosevelt, and supported him when he became a politician. Then he caught polio. To save his career, Eleanor became 'the legs and eyes of a crippled husband'. On his behalf, she visited mines, slums, hospitals – all places he could not go to himself.

Eleanor Roosevelt always spoke up for the poor, Black people, and women. Many thought she should keep quiet when her husband became president in 1932, but others admired her honesty.

After her husband's death in 1945, Eleanor Roosevelt continued to make speeches and write for newspapers. She was also a US delegate to the United Nations and in 1946 became the chairwoman of the United Nations Human Rights Commission. ◆

👁 **see also**

Roosevelt, Franklin D.
Roosevelt, Theodore

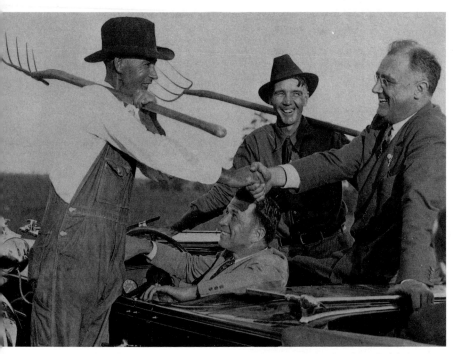

▲ *The 'New Deal' programme of social and economic reform launched by Franklin D. Roosevelt (seen here, right, in 1932) made him popular with working people.*

Franklin D. Roosevelt

President of the United States of America four times, from 1933 to 1945
Born 1882   Died 1945 aged 63

Franklin Delano Roosevelt, a cousin of the former American president, 'Teddy' Roosevelt, had to fight hard to overcome a physical handicap. He developed polio at the age of 40, and his legs were almost paralysed.

By this time however, Roosevelt, a Democrat, had already served in the New York State senate, and as Assistant Secretary for the Navy. Although he was badly crippled he soon returned to politics. In 1928 he was elected governor of New York State, and four years later became president of America.

At this time, America was in a terrible state. One worker in four was out of work, many families were too poor even to buy food, and 5000 banks had failed. Roosevelt promised a 'New Deal', and launched a programme which enabled banks to reopen and created jobs for the unemployed. He also began radio broadcasts to the nation, known as his 'Fireside Chats'. The success of these and later measures ensured his election as president again in 1936.

> *The only thing we have to fear is fear itself.*
> FRANKLIN D. ROOSEVELT
> First speech as president, 1933

In 1940, with World War II raging in Europe, Roosevelt was elected for a third term, the first and last president to be so. In December 1941, after the Japanese had bombed Pearl Harbor, America entered the war. Roosevelt guided the country through its darkest days, working closely with the leaders of Britain and the Soviet Union, Winston Churchill and Joseph Stalin. He won a fourth election in 1944, but only six months later, and with war victory in sight, he suddenly died. ◆

👁 **see also**
Churchill   Roosevelt, Eleanor
Roosevelt, Theodore   Stalin

Theodore Roosevelt

President of the United States of America from 1901 to 1908
Born 1858   Died 1919 aged 60

Theodore Roosevelt was born into a wealthy family. He was a weak child who suffered from asthma and he had to build up his health and strength. He was always known as 'Teddy', and cartoonists likened him to a bear. Toy makers began making stuffed animals that they called 'teddy bears'.

Roosevelt entered politics at the age of 23, but the death of his wife and his mother on the same day in 1884 shattered him, and he became a cattle-rancher in Dakota instead.

In 1898 Roosevelt led a cavalry regiment, the Rough Riders, in Cuba during the Spanish American War. Then he became vice-president of America in 1901. Six months later, when President McKinley was assassinated, Roosevelt became president.

As president, Roosevelt broke up trusts (big business monopolies), settled a damaging coal strike, and bought a strip of land to build the Panama Canal. Through his efforts, Panama became independent from Colombia.

After he was elected president in his own right in 1904, he helped to bring peace in a war between Russia and Japan and was awarded the Nobel Peace Prize in 1906.

When he retired, Roosevelt

hunted big game in Africa and led an expedition to explore the River of Doubt in Brazil, now called the Roosevelt or Teodoro River. ◆

👁 **see also**
Roosevelt, Eleanor
Roosevelt, Franklin D.

Diana **Ross**

American singer
Born 1944

Detroit singer Diana Ross had 18 hits with the 1960s all-girl group the Supremes on the Tamla Motown record label before she went solo in 1970, notching up over 40 more hits. Her voice is thin but radiates star quality. In a cleverly planned career, guided by Motown boss Berry Gordy Jr, she conveniently changed style from soul to pop, jazz, or disco to suit the times. She also appeared in several musical films, including *Lady Sings the Blues* (1972) and *The Wiz* (1978). Eventually she became a part-owner of Motown. ◆

Dante Gabriel **Rossetti**

British painter and poet
Born 1828   Died 1882 aged 53

Dante Gabriel Rossetti's father was an Italian political refugee who fled to England. He named his son after the great Italian poet Dante, but he was known by his other name, Gabriel. His sister Christina became a well-known poet, and although Gabriel was also a talented writer, he was more interested in painting. In 1848 he and some friends founded the Pre-Raphaelite Brotherhood, aiming to revive the sincerity and freshness of early Italian paintings (before the time of Raphael, whom they disliked).

In 1862 Rossetti's wife died and he was so devastated he buried the only manuscript of his poems with her; seven years later friends persuaded him to have the poems dug up and published. After his wife's death Rossetti became obsessed with another strikingly beautiful woman, Jane Morris, who was married to his business partner, the great designer William Morris.

▼ *Rossetti's* The Blessed Damozel. *He also wrote a poem with the same title.*

He painted her many times and his love for her broke up his friendship with her husband. At the end of his life Rossetti became an eccentric recluse (he kept a wide variety of unusual animals, including a wombat) and had become dependent on drugs and alcohol. ◆

👁 **see also**
Dante   Morris   Raphael

Gioachino **Rossini**

Italian composer
Born 1792   Died 1868 aged 76

Both of Gioachino Rossini's parents were professional musicians and they gave him his first lessons. From 1806 he studied at the Liceo Musicale in Bologna. His career in operatic composition began in 1810, and he found great success with his 1816 opera, *The Barber of Seville*. By 1829, when his greatest serious opera *William Tell* was produced in Paris, he had written no fewer than 39 operas – sometimes three or four a year. And then, quite suddenly, he stopped. For the rest of his life he wrote only songs, piano pieces, and a little church music, including the *Stabat Mater* and the *Petite Messe solennelle*. The reason for his early retirement seems to have been a mixture of ill-health, depression, and sheer exhaustion, plus a belief that his style of music had become rather out of date. Thus he produced no more of the brilliant comic operas, and powerful serious operas, that had delighted audiences throughout Europe. ◆

Mayer Amschel **Rothschild**

German founder of the Rothschild banking empire
Born *1744*   **Died** *1812 aged 68*

Mayer Amschel Rothschild had to give up being a student when his parents died, and he went to work in a bank instead. Gradually he built up his own banking business in Frankfurt and, with the help of his five sons, he started branches all over Europe.

The family fortune was made during the wars against Napoleon I, when they lent money to the warring countries. Later during the Industrial Revolution they made money buying and selling the stocks and shares of the new companies in Europe. ◆

👁 **see also**
Disraeli

Henri **Rousseau**

French painter
Born *1844*   **Died** *1910 aged 66*

Henri Rousseau worked for the Paris Customs Office and was given the nickname 'Le Douanier' (the customs officer). When he was 49 he devoted himself full-time to his hobby of art.

Rousseau was the most famous of all 'naive' painters, artists with no professional training who painted in a style that was in some ways childlike. His work is full of charm and freshness. Rousseau died a pauper, but was soon hailed as an artistic genius. ◆

👁 **see also**
Picasso

▶ *Henri Rousseau's jungle paintings depict brightly coloured worlds filled with apes and other wild animals lurking amongst the striking assortment of flowers and trees.*

J. K. **Rowling**

English children's writer
Born *1965*

Joanna Kathleen Rowling wrote her first story when she was six. At school she liked English best, but she also enjoyed foreign languages, and studied French at university.

Joanna wanted to write, but she had to work to earn a living. In 1990 she was working in Manchester, and on a train to London she had the idea for Harry Potter – a seemingly ordinary boy who one day receives an invite to go to Hogwart's School of Witchcraft and Wizardry.

The first Harry Potter book was finished in 1994, but it was two more years before it was published. The book was a hit with both children and adults, and won many prizes. Joanna was able to give up work and write full-time. By 2000, four Harry Potter books had been published, selling 30 million copies worldwide. In 2001 a film of the first book was a huge success, and Joanna received an OBE (Order of the British Empire) from the Queen. ◆

Jean-Jacques **Rousseau**

Swiss philosopher
Born *1712*   **Died** *1778 aged 66*

Jean-Jacques Rousseau's early life was a series of scandals and adventures, all later narrated with gusto in his *Confessions*, which were published after his death. After 1741 he settled in Paris and began making his reputation as a writer. His essay *Discourse on the Arts and Sciences* (1750), in which he praised the natural state of humankind, as opposed to the highly artificial society of 18th-century France, brought him fame and financial security.

In 1762 Rousseau published *Emile*, a novel about a young man's education, and *On the Social Contract*. The latter, with its revolutionary views on civil society, which Rousseau believed should be governed by 'the general will', attracted the hostility of the authorities. Rousseau fled to Switzerland and England for some years. He is remembered as a republican whose political ideas helped to fuel the French Revolution. ◆

Peter **Rubens**

Flemish painter and ambassador
Born 1577   Died 1640 aged 62

When he was 14 Peter Rubens became an apprentice painter in Antwerp; seven years later he became a master painter. When he was 23 he travelled to Italy to learn about art and to develop his own extraordinary talents.

He had a charming personality, and made friends easily. He became adviser as well as court painter to the Spanish rulers of Flanders, and they sent him to Spain and England. He spoke several languages well and combined the two careers of painter and diplomat.

When the demand for his paintings became too great, he set up a studio with several first-class assistants. They kept up a huge output of paintings which Rubens planned and finished off himself.

▲ *Ruben's painting* The Kidnapping of Ganymede *is full of movement and colour.*

His paintings (usually on biblical or mythological subjects) are crowded with figures, but seem spacious and light. His work is bold, energetic, full of colour, splendour, and optimism.

At the age of 53, four years after the death of his first wife, he married his second wife, a 16-year-old girl, Hélène Fourment. His interest in his new young family can be seen in the more domestic painting of his last ten years. ◆

Arthur **Rubinstein**

Polish-born American pianist
Born 1887   Died 1982 aged 95

Arthur Rubinstein was already a capable pianist when he was just three years old, and after a period of study in Berlin from the ages of 10 to 13, he began his international career. He made his first American tour in 1906. By this time he had given up studying, and this sometimes showed in some of his performances. Then in 1932 he withdrew from the concert platform for a period of intensive study and reassessment. Rigorous discipline was now added to a brilliant technique, and the success of his 1937 American tour swept away any doubts the critics may have had. He became an American citizen in 1941 and made concert appearances well into his 90s, specializing in the music of Mozart, Chopin, and Debussy. ◆

Bertrand **Russell**

British philosopher, pacifist, and campaigner
Born 1872   Died 1970 aged 97

Bertrand Russell came from an aristocratic family and had a privileged childhood – even though both his parents died before he was two years old.

He studied mathematics and philosophy at Cambridge University and this led to his most important philosophical work. He tried to show that all mathematics was derived from a few simple laws of logic. Later he extended these ideas to show that knowledge was based, via logic, on simple observations. Neither project was completely successful, but his ideas greatly influenced mathematics and philosophy. He was an excellent writer, and won the Nobel Prize for Literature in 1950. To the public, though, he was best known for his political and social views, and for his many broadcasts. He was a lifelong pacifist, and in 1958 helped to start the Campaign for Nuclear Disarmament (CND). ◆

Babe **Ruth**

American baseball player
Born 1895   Died 1948 aged 53

George Herman Ruth went to a school for poor children in Baltimore, which is where he began his baseball career as a pitcher with the Baltimore Orioles. Then, known to all the fans as 'Babe Ruth', he became a member of the Boston Red Sox and hit 29 home runs in 1919. The next year, playing for the New York Yankees, he hit 54 home runs and became so popular that by 1925 he was earning more money than the president of America. In 1927 he raised his record to 60 home runs in a season, and by the time he retired in 1935 he had scored a career total of 714. He is considered by some to be the greatest baseball player of all time. ♦

👁 **see also**
DiMaggio

Ernest **Rutherford**

New Zealand scientist who revealed the structure of atoms
Born 1871   Died 1937 aged 66

Ernest Rutherford came from a family of eleven children and grew up on his family's small farm in New Zealand. He was very clever and studied at university in New Zealand before going to Cambridge University.

At Cambridge he began work on the exciting new subject of radioactivity. He discovered that radioactive substances produce three different types of radiation. At this time, scientists were only just beginning to study the inside of atoms. For more than 2000 years atoms had been thought of as like

▲ *Ernest Rutherford was awarded the Nobel Prize for Physics in 1908 for his work on radioactivity.*

tiny marbles, but Rutherford's experiments showed that in the centre of an atom there is a tiny, heavy blob, the nucleus, and that most of the atom consists of empty space.

Rutherford gathered other brilliant scientists in his laboratory in Cambridge. These included James Chadwick (who discovered the neutron) and John Cockcroft (who built an atom-smashing proton accelerator). The work of these and others, like Marie and Pierre Curie, Enrico Fermi and Niels Bohr, began a new age of physics: the 'nuclear age'. It has produced radiation for treating cancer, nuclear power-stations which generate electricity, and also nuclear weapons. ♦

👁 **see also**
Bohr   Curie   Fermi

Mohammed Anwar el **Sadat**

President of Egypt from 1970 to 1981
Born 1918   Died 1981 aged 63

As a young officer in the Egyptian army, Mohammed Anwar el Sadat joined the revolt which overthrew King Farouk in 1952. In 1964 he became vice-president of Egypt to President Abdel Nasser, and when Nasser died in 1970, Sadat became president.

During the 1973 war between Israel and its Arab neighbours, the Egyptian army broke through Israel's defences. This proved that the Israelis were not unbeatable. After the fighting Sadat felt that Egypt was strong enough to make a separate peace deal with Israel, even though many other Arab nations did not agree with this. But Sadat knew that Egypt, a poor country, was just

▼ *President Sadat was much admired for his peace-making efforts.*

made poorer by constant fighting. In 1977 he flew to Jerusalem to talk with the Israeli prime minister, Menachem Begin. They were awarded the Nobel Peace Prize the following year for their efforts to bring peace in the troubled Middle East. A peace treaty was finally signed in 1979 in Washington following the so-called Camp David negotiations.

In 1981 Sadat was assassinated by an extreme Muslim group. ◆

see also
Begin   Nasser

Camille **Saint-Saëns**

French composer, pianist, and organist
Born *1835* **Died** *1921 aged 86*

Camille Saint-Saëns composed his first piece of music when he was three, and made his concert début at the age of 10, playing concertos by Beethoven and Mozart. He studied at the Paris Conservatoire, impressing everyone with his dazzling gifts as pianist, organist, and composer. There seemed to be nothing he could not do. And so it continued throughout his long, enormously prolific life. His compositions include 13 operas, of which *Samson et Dalila* (1877) is the most famous, 10 concertos (five of which are for piano), three symphonies, sacred and secular choral works, and a great many songs and piano pieces. He was also a great supporter of other composers' works, including those of Liszt and Schumann, and did much to revive an interest in Bach, Gluck, Mozart, and Rameau. ◆

see also
Bach   Liszt   Mozart   Schumann

▲ *Saladin's name literally means 'the Welfare of the Faith'.*

Saladin

Muslim soldier who fought against the Christian crusaders
Born *1137* **Died** *1193 aged 55*

Throughout his childhood, Saladin was taught how to fight and how to honour his God.

When he was 14, he became a soldier and fought against other Muslims in Egypt. Before Saladin could attack the Christian crusaders, he had to unite the different Muslim kingdoms. This took him 15 years to achieve. In 1187 he lead the Muslims against the Christians in the Holy Land. Saladin destroyed the Christian army at Hattin, recaptured Jerusalem, and resisted the new Christian attack led by Richard I of England.

Saladin could also be kind and gentle. He built schools, mosques, and canals, and encouraged scholars and theologians. ◆

see also
Muhammad   Richard I

Abdus **Salam**

Pakistani physicist
Born *1926* **Died** *1996 aged 70*

Abdus Salam studied in England. As professor of theoretical physics at Imperial College, London, he investigated the forces between the extremely small particles that make up the parts of an atom.

Salam was the first Pakistani to win a Nobel Prize when he shared the 1979 Physics Prize with Steven Weinberg and Sheldon Glashow. He was the first Director of the International Centre for Theoretical Studies in 1964, set up to help physicists from developing countries. ◆

Pete **Sampras**

American tennis champion
Born *1971*

As a child, Pete Sampras found an old tennis racquet and started hitting a ball against the garage door. His talent was encouraged by his parents and Pete turned professional when he was 16. Two years later he was one of the world's top ten players. That year he won the US Open, the first of his Grand Slam titles. He was the youngest ever winner in the men's singles.

In 1993 Pete became number 1 in the world and won Wimbledon for the first time. He went on to win the men's singles at Wimbledon a record 7 times. His total of 14 Grand Slam titles is also a record. ◆

José de **San Martin**

Argentinian soldier and statesman
Born *1778*   **Died** *1850 aged 72*

Although he was born in Argentina, José de San Martin lived in Spain from the age of six and was an officer in the Spanish army for 20 years. Then, in 1812, he was persuaded to switch sides and join the South American rebels who were fighting for independence from Spain. He raised an army in northern Argentina and then led them over the Andes to defeat the Spanish at Santiago, thus assuring the independence of Chile. He then landed his troops on the Peruvian coast and took control of the capital, Lima. He was given the title of Protector of Peru in 1821. In the following year he met with Simon Bolívar and, after some initial disagreement, he left the liberation of the rest of Peru to Bolívar. San Martin sailed to Europe where he lived for the rest of his life. ◆

see also
Bolívar

◀ *Agentinian soldiers salute a monument to José de San Martin, the general who played a vital part in the liberation of their country.*

Jean-Paul **Sartre**

French philosopher, playwright, and novelist
Born *1905*   **Died** *1980 aged 75*

Jean-Paul Sartre, who worked first as a teacher, gained attention as a philosopher with his book *Being and Nothingness* (1943). This is the most important French statement of existentialist philosophy, the philosophy which believes there is no such thing as inherited character and that to go from 'nothingness' into 'being', people must choose who they want to be and what they want to do. In short, human beings have to 'make' themselves by making conscious decisions.

Sartre joined the French Resistance against the invading German forces during World War II. His long novel *The Roads to Freedom* (1945–1949) draws on his experience of the French defeat at the beginning of the war. His existentialism continued to find expression in concerns over human relationships in plays such as *In Camera* (1944). In his later literary and political projects, Sartre usually worked with his long-time lover Simone de Beauvoir. ◆

Friedrich **Schiller**

German writer
Born *1759*   **Died** *1805 aged 45*

Apart from his friend Johann Goethe, Friedrich Schiller was the greatest German writer of his period. He is best known as a dramatist and poet, but he also wrote historical and philosophical works and translated plays by Racine and Shakespeare.

Schiller's first important work was the play *The Robbers* (1781); it is an attack on political tyranny and shows a passionate concern for freedom, the central theme of Schiller's work. In 1782 Schiller moved from Stuttgart to Mannheim, where he became resident playwright for the city's famous theatre. In 1794 he met Goethe in Weimar, and on his personal recommendation Schiller became professor of history at the nearby University of Jena.

Many of his plays were used as the basis for operas; his most popular play, *William Tell* (1804), was made into an opera by Rossini. His most famous poem is 'Ode to Joy' (1785), part of which Beethoven set to music in his *Ninth Symphony*. ◆

see also
Goethe   Rossini

Heinrich **Schliemann**

German-born American archaeologist
Born *1822*   **Died** *1890 aged 68*

By the age of 26 Heinrich Schliemann had already been a cabin-boy, a grocer, and a bookkeeper. His tremendous energy and determination enabled him to learn more than eight languages in ten years. He went on to make a fortune as a merchant in Russia. Then, in 1863, he retired from work, became an American citizen, and put all his energy and money into archaeology. It had long been an ambition of his to find an historical basis for the stories of the siege of Troy, as described in Homer's tale, the *Iliad*.

▲ *This stunning gold crown was one of the treasures Heinrich Schliemann discovered in his excavation of the ancient site of Mycenae in Greece.*

During an archaeological dig in Hissarlik, Turkey, which had begun in 1871, Schliemann discovered the fortifications of a city and some golden jewellery. He had found what many believed to be the city of Troy, as described by Homer. He carried out three more excavations at Hissarlik and later discovered the remains of a prehistoric civilization in Turkey. He also discovered the remains of the Mycenaean civilization in Greece between 1874 and 1876. ◆

see also

Homer

Arnold
Schoenberg

Austrian composer
Born 1874 Died 1951 aged 76

Arnold Schoenberg was a mainly self-taught composer. His highly romantic orchestral work, *Transfigured Night* (1900), brought him a lot of attention. However, before long he found that his music

no longer followed the rules that had served composers for nearly 300 years. He looked for an explanation and found it in the development of his own new scale system, where no note was considered more important than any other. He also believed that the notes should always appear in a strict sequence. His ideas appalled ordinary music lovers, but began to influence other composers.

▼ *Arnold Schoenberg would often give talks before perfomances of his challenging musical works to explain what they meant.*

Because his music met with opposition, Schoenberg was obliged to teach in order to earn a living. When he was forced to leave his teaching post in Berlin in 1933 by the Nazis (because he was Jewish), he settled in Paris and then in America, where he taught at the University of California. He is now regarded by many as one of the most revolutionary and influential composers of the 20th century. ◆

Erwin
Schrödinger

Austrian physicist
Born 1887 Died 1961 aged 73

After studying science in Vienna and serving in World War I, Erwin Schrödinger moved to Zurich, Switzerland. When he was 39 he developed a theory which described sub-atomic particles as waves. He applied his 'wave mechanics' to the hydrogen atom and got an equation which predicted results that other scientists had found but had not explained. He shared the 1933 Nobel Prize for Physics with Paul Dirac for this work.

Schrödinger tried hard to attach physical meaning to the symbols used in his equations but was never completely successful. Other scientists were happy to interpret wave equations as descriptions of the probable behaviour of particles, but Schrödinger himself never accepted this view.

In 1933 he fled in disgust from Hitler's Nazis: he was one of the few non-Jewish scientists to do so. He eventually found refuge in Ireland where he became senior professor at the Dublin Institute for Advanced Studies in 1940. ◆

see also

Bohr

▲ *This 19th-century painting shows Schubert playing his music to an admiring audience.*

Franz **Schubert**

Austrian composer
Born *1797* **Died** *1828 aged 31*

As a child, Franz Schubert showed a remarkable talent for music. His father taught him to play the violin, and his elder brother taught him the piano. When he was nine he began to study harmony and counterpoint (the art of adding melody as an accompaniment).

In 1808 he became a chorister of the imperial court chapel. He founded a students' orchestra in which he played and also sometimes conducted. By this time he was also writing music, including quartets for his family to play. When he left college, he became a schoolmaster like his father, although he soon gave it up to concentrate on composing.

In his short life Schubert wrote an amazing amount of music, including nine symphonies, several operas, much fine chamber music, and over 600 songs. He seldom had any money but he lived happily and had many friends who admired his music and encouraged him. ♦

Robert **Schumann**

German composer
Born *1810* **Died** *1856 aged 46*

Robert Schumann was an outstanding pianist and wrote many of his finest works for that instrument. He started studying law, but soon turned to music full-time. In 1832 he injured his right hand in an attempt to improve his playing technique and had to abandon all hopes of a concert career. After this set-back he concentrated on his work as a composer, but he also became known as an enthusiastic champion of German music.

His marriage to Clara Wieck (1840) proved to be very happy and resulted in a great outpouring of songs and piano music. She was a brilliant pianist herself and often performed his works, including the popular A minor Piano Concerto. Sadly, in 1854 Schumann's mental health gave way and he spent the rest of his life in an asylum. ♦

👁 **see also**

Brahms

Albert **Schweitzer**

German mission doctor, theologian, and musician
Born *1875* **Died** *1965 aged 90*

As a young man, Albert Schweitzer was brilliantly successful. He became a doctor three times over, first of philosophy, then of theology, and finally of medicine. He also studied music and gained an international reputation as an organist.

Schweitzer was a man of strong convictions and was passionate in his belief that all life was precious. Because of this, he left the concert halls and universities of Europe behind him and went to Lambarene in West Africa to work as a mission doctor. He started work in 1913 and

▼ *Albert Schweitzer passionately believed in what he called 'reverence for life'. His work as a missionary inspired many to follow his example.*

stayed there for the rest of his life. In 1963 the hospital at Lambarene treated 500 patients, although its methods were getting out of date.

Schweitzer received the Nobel Peace Prize in 1952 for 'efforts on behalf of the Brotherhood of Nations'. ◆

Robert **Scott**

English Antarctic explorer
Born *1868* ***Died*** *1912 aged 43*

Robert Falcon Scott, a British naval officer, was placed in command of a British Antarctic Expedition, and in 1901 sailed south in the ship *Discovery*. His party returned two years later, having reached further south than anyone else at that time.

In 1910 Scott, by then a captain, again travelled to the Antarctic, this time in an attempt to be first to the South Pole. The expedition was dogged by bad planning and bad luck. Within 200 miles of the Pole, Captain Scott set out on the final stretch with four colleagues: Oates, Wilson, Bowers, and Evans. They reached the South Pole on 18 January only to find that the Norwegian explorer Amundsen had beaten them by a month. Bitterly disappointed, they turned back, but were overtaken by blizzards, and died from starvation and exposure.

> *Great God! this is an awful place.*
>
> ROBERT SCOTT
> Comment on the South Pole in his diary.

The bodies of Scott and his colleagues were recovered eight months later. Their notebooks, letters, and diaries described the brave but grim events. The gallant manner of Scott's failure was much admired by the British people, and he became a national hero. ◆

see also
Amundsen

▲ *These are some of the items of clothing worn by Robert Scott on his first Antarctic expedition.*

Walter **Scott**

Scottish writer and poet
Born *1771* ***Died*** *1832 aged 61*

Walter Scott became one of the most famous writers in Europe. He was so popular that a railway station (Waverley) and a football team (Heart of Midlothian) were named after his novels. Although Scott was lame, he became a great walker and grew to love the Scottish Border countryside with its many legends.

After training in Edinburgh as a lawyer, he married and returned to the Borders. He enjoyed collecting the old Border ballads, and wrote poems of his own, such as 'Marmion' and 'The Lady of the Lake'. Their mixture of romance, history, and action was very popular.

His first novel, *Waverley*, mixed real people such as Bonnie Prince Charlie with characters that Scott had invented. It brought history to life in a way that no other writer had ever managed. *Waverley* was an instant success, and so were his other novels such as *Old Mortality, The Heart of Midlothian, Ivanhoe,* and *Rob Roy*.

Streams of people visited his home and tourists began visiting Scotland after reading his books. But in 1826 his publishing company collapsed, leaving huge debts. Scott managed to clear the debts by writing but died after six years of hard work. ◆

Mary **Seacole**

Jamaican nurse who helped in the Crimean War
Born *1805* ***Died*** *1881 aged 76*

Mary Seacole's mother was black and her father was a Scottish officer with the British army in Jamaica. Her mother taught her African cures for tropical illnesses, and Mary became known as a 'doctress' in Jamaica.

In 1854 the British army was sent to fight Russia in the Crimean War. Seacole went to England to join the nurses whom Florence Nightingale had taken to the Crimea. She was turned down because she was black, so she went out to the Crimea at her own expense and opened a store and eating-place near the front lines.

Seacole showed great bravery, going among the men with medicine and supplies of food. When the fighting was fierce she bandaged the wounded and comforted the dying. Her work was remembered by many soldiers who, when the war had finished, gave money to save her from poverty. ◆

Sequoya

Native American Indian who created the Cherokee alphabet
Born 1760   Died 1843 aged 83

Sequoya was probably the son of a British trader but he was brought up by his Cherokee mother. He was an artist and a warrior who fought for the US Army in the Creek War of 1813–1814.

Having served in the army, he felt it was important that the Cherokee people had their own writing system to keep them independent of white Americans. Adapting letters from English, Greek, and Hebrew, he came up with an alphabet of 86 symbols in 1821. He taught it to young people and it was soon in use in schools, books, and newspapers. His work helped thousands of Native Americans to read and write. Sequoya went on to negotiate on their behalf with the US government over resettlement of their lands.

In tribute to his contribution to American culture, his name was given to the giant redwood tree and to the Sequoia National Park in California. ◆

Georges **Seurat**

French painter
Born 1859   Died 1891 aged 31

Georges Seurat came from a wealthy family. Unlike many famous artists, he never had to worry about earning a living and could work how and when he pleased. He loved the colourful paintings of the Impressionists, such as Monet and Renoir, but he thought that he could take their ideas further. Working slowly and patiently, he devised a method of completely covering the canvas with tiny dots of pure, bright paint. From close up they looked like abstract patterns, but when viewed from the right distance the patterns blended together perfectly to create a scene that sparkled with light and colour. This technique was called 'Pointillism', from the French word 'point', meaning 'dot'. Seurat was being hailed as the brightest new star in French painting when he died very suddenly; the official cause was meningitis, but a friend said that he had killed himself with overwork. He loved painting so much that he usually had time for little else. ◆

👁 **see also**
Monet   Renoir

7th Earl of **Shaftesbury**

English aristocrat who helped the poor
Born 1801   Died 1885 aged 84

Anthony Ashley Cooper was an unhappy child. His father

▼ *Seurat's greatest work,* Sunday Afternoon on the Isle of the Grande Jatte *(1884–1886), is considered by many to be one of the landmarks of modern art.*

▲ *Shah Jahan's magnificent Taj Mahal. Many people from all over the world travel to see and marvel at it.*

was cold and distant, and his mother was selfish. Only his nurse, Maria Millis, loved him; she taught him his Christian faith and this inspired everything he did.

He entered parliament in 1826 and was determined to devote his life to helping the poor. He campaigned to bring in laws which helped many people in Britain's industrial cities. These laws ensured that children were no longer employed in textile mills; women and children did not work in coal-mines; and boys did not climb dangerous sooty chimneys to sweep them. He also helped to reduce the working day for adults in factories to ten hours.

He helped to start 'ragged schools' for very poor children, and the 'Arethusa Training Ship' to train boys for the merchant navy. He ran soup kitchens for the hungry, and improved conditions for the mentally handicapped. Though his family was rich (he became the 7th Earl of Shaftesbury when his father died in 1851), he was often quite short of money because he gave so much away. ◆

Shah Jahan

Indian Mogul leader
Born *1592*   **Died** *1666 aged 74*

In the 16th century, India was largely made up of independent states, each with its own ruler. One of the most important was the Mogul empire. Shah Jahan became ruler of this empire in 1627. During his reign, Mogul power extended and the capital at Delhi was rebuilt. In fact, Shah Jahan was always interested in architecture and many great buildings were erected during his time as emperor, the most famous being the Taj Mahal. This was built at Agra as a tomb when his favourite wife, Mumtaz Mahal, died after 17 years together.

Twenty thousand men worked on the Taj Mahal, producing a beautiful, white marble domed building, which gleamed in the sunlight and was reflected in the waters of a pool.

Shah Jahan became ill in 1657, and this caused a war between his four sons. Eventually Aurangzeb, the third son, killed his rivals, imprisoned his father, and seized the throne. When Shah Jahan died he was buried at the Taj Mahal with his wife. ◆

Shaka the Zulu

First great chief of the Zulu nation in southern Africa
Born *c.1787*   **Died** *1828 aged about 41*

Shaka was born the son of Senzangakona, a chieftain of the Zulu nation in southern Africa. His mother, Nandi, was an orphaned princess of the Langeni tribe. When he was a child, Shaka and his mother were banished from the Zulu villages by Senzangakona and had to go back to the Langeni. There they were treated very badly and were eventually banished by the Langeni too.

They found shelter with the Mtetwa tribe, and there Shaka became a warrior. After Senzangakona's death, Shaka returned to the Zulu as chieftain. He reorganized the Zulu army into regiments known as the *impi*, giving them more deadly *assegais* (stabbing spears), changing their battle tactics, and training them to march up to 80 km a day. This training made the Zulu the strongest nation in southern Africa.

When Shaka became chief, there were fewer than 1500 Zulu; by 1824 he ruled over 50,000 people because he incorporated defeated clans into the Zulu nation. He could, however, be a very cruel leader: when his mother died in 1827, he had 7000 Zulu put to death as a sign of his grief. Shaka was murdered in 1828 by his own half-brothers. ◆

 see also

Buthelezi   Cetshwayo

William **Shakespeare**

English playwright and poet
Born *1564*   **Died** *1616 aged 52*

William Shakespeare was the eldest child of the bailiff (mayor) of Stratford-upon-Avon. In 1582 Shakespeare married Anne Hathaway. Their first child, Susannah, was born the following year and twins, Hamnet and Judith, followed in 1585. Hamnet died when he was 11.

▲ *This miniature portrait of William Shakespeare was painted in 1588. Shakespeare died on 23 April (traditionally thought to be his birthday) in 1616, and was buried in Holy Trinity Church in his home town of Stratford.*

Nobody knows what Shakespeare was doing for a living in his early twenties, but by 1592 he was earning money as an actor and playwright in London while his wife and family remained in Stratford. He soon became a leading member of a theatrical company called the Lord Chamberlain's Men. In 1603, when James I succeeded Queen Elizabeth I on the throne, the company changed its name to the King's Men.

> *What are these,*
> *So withered, and so wild in their attire,*
> *That look not like th'*
> *inhabitants o' the earth*
> *And yet are on 't?*
>
> WILLIAM SHAKESPEARE
> *Macbeth*
> (description of the three witches)

Between 1599 and 1613 their main base was the Globe Theatre on the south bank of the River Thames, and in 1609 they acquired the Blackfriars Theatre in the City of London.

Shakespeare seems to have taken little or no interest in the printing or publication of his work, and one or two of his plays may have been lost. A complete collection was not published until seven years after his death. This so-called *First Folio* included all his plays except for *Pericles*. The number of plays which are wholly or mostly written by Shakespeare is generally agreed to be 37. He also wrote 154 sonnets.

Shakespeare's most famous plays are probably the four great tragedies, *Hamlet*, *Macbeth*, *Othello*, and *King Lear*. He also wrote popular comedies, such as *A Midsummer Night's Dream* and *Twelfth Night*, and many history plays. The best-known of these are *Julius Caesar* and *Antony and Cleopatra*, which deal with Roman history, and a long cycle of eight plays dealing with English history from the reign of *Richard II* to the reign of *Richard III*. Other favourites in the theatre are *The Merchant of Venice*, *Romeo and Juliet*, and *The Tempest*.

By 1597 Shakespeare was so successful that he was able to buy one of the finest houses in Stratford, New Place, and it was here that he retired with his family for the last few years of his life. ◆

Uday **Shankar**

Indian dancer and choreographer
Born *1900*   **Died** *1977 aged 77*

Uday Shankar undertook formal art training in Bombay and at the Royal College of Art in London in the 1920s. In London he met the famous ballerina Anna Pavlova and created two dances for her dance company.

He returned to India in 1929 and formed his own dance company which appeared regularly in Europe and the United States. With his brother, the sitarist Ravi Shankar, he explored ways of using folk dance as dance drama. Shankar used Western theatrical techniques to spread the popularity of traditional Hindu dance to Europe and America. Some fans of traditional dance disapproved of his experimental work, but many important and influential Indians supported what he was trying to do. ◆

 see also

Pavlova

George Bernard **Shaw**

Irish playwright
Born *1856*   **Died** *1950 aged 94*

George Bernard Shaw moved from Ireland to London at the age of 20 and had a go at writing novels. These were not very successful, but people did begin to take an interest in his magazine articles. Many of these were about politics, as the young Shaw was a keen supporter of the Fabian Society, a group of Socialists.

Shaw's first successful play was *Widowers' Houses*, performed in 1892. The play, which attacked

▲ *A poster for* My Fair Lady, *the 1964 musical film adaptation of George Bernard Shaw's play* Pygmalion.

slum landlords, upset those people who did not like to see themselves criticized on stage. Shaw went on to write many famous plays. *Saint Joan* is about Joan of Arc, who led the French army against the English in the Middle Ages. Many people know the story of his play *Pygmalion* because of the musical version, *My Fair Lady*.

However, Shaw's plays are more than just stories. They contain powerful arguments against things and ideas that Shaw considered unfair, dangerous, or silly. Shaw explained these ideas in prefaces or introductions to his published plays. He was awarded the Nobel Prize for Literature in 1925. ◆

Mary **Shelley**

English writer
Born *1797*   **Died** *1851 aged 54*

Mary Shelley was the daughter of Mary Wollstonecraft, a writer and feminist, and William Godwin, a novelist and writer on politics. At 16, Mary ran away with the poet Percy Bysshe Shelley. She married Shelley after his first wife's suicide in 1816.

Her novel, *Frankenstein,* a pioneering science-fiction story, was published when Mary was only 19. It tells how Frankenstein, a student, creates a living creature out of parts taken from dead bodies.

Mary also wrote short stories, biographies, and travel literature, including an entertaining account of the continental tour she and Percy undertook when they eloped, entitled *History of a Six Weeks' Tour* (1817). Mary continued to write after Percy was drowned in 1822. ◆

◉ **see also**
Shelley, Percy

Percy **Shelley**

English poet
Born *1792*   **Died** *1822 aged 29*

A lot of Percy Bysshe Shelley's work reflected his radical beliefs. He was expelled from Oxford University in 1811 for distributing a pamphlet, attacking religious belief, which he had written with a student friend. And no one would publish his long poem, *Queen Mab*, for fear of prosecution over its celebration of free love, republicanism, and vegetarianism, so he published it himself in 1813.

Shelley married 16-year-old Harriet Westbrook in 1811, but left her when he fell in love with another 16-year-old. This was Mary, daughter of William Godwin, the man whose writing had shaped Shelley's own ideas. They married after Harriet's suicide and spent the summer of 1816 on Lake Geneva with Lord Byron. In 1818 they left England to travel in Europe. They eventually settled in Italy, and it was here that Shelley wrote some of his greatest works, including *Prometheus Unbound* (1820), 'To a Skylark' (1820), and 'Adonais' (1821), written on the death of Keats. Shelley was drowned just a year later when his sailing boat, *Ariel*, overturned in a storm off the Italian coast. ◆

◉ **see also**
Byron   Keats   Shelley, Mary

▼ *This artistic impression of Percy Bysshe Shelley's funeral was painted in 1889, many years after Shelley's tragic early death.*

Shi Huangdi

First emperor of all China
Born *259 BC*   **Died** *210 BC aged 49*

Shi Huangdi's aim was to found an empire that would last 10,000 generations. In fact it collapsed four years after his death.

At 13 Shi Huangdi became ruler of Quin (Chin), the most powerful of the half-dozen states into which China was then divided. He conquered all the others and had created a single Chinese empire by 221 BC. He then united it by building roads and canals and making everyone obey the same laws and use the same weights and measures. All important officials were appointed directly by the emperor. Monuments and temples were built in his honour and frontier defences were improved to make a single Great Wall. When he died he was buried in a huge, elaborate tomb guarded by 10,000 warriors made of terracotta. ◆

▼ *Shi Huangdi's Great Wall is the only man-made structure that is visible from the Moon.*

Bill Shoemaker

American champion jockey
Born *1931*   **Died** *2003 aged 72*

Bill (Willie) Shoemaker was one of the world's most successful jockeys. When he retired in 1991, he had achieved 8833 wins from 40,350 mounts.

He was born prematurely weighing just 1.35 kg. However, his grandmother saved his life by putting him in a shoebox inside an open oven door for his first 24 hours. He grew to be only 1.5 m (4 ft 11 in) tall.

He began working with horses as a teenager and became a jockey in 1949. He was America's champion jockey ten times and also leading money winner ten times. He won top races such as the Kentucky Derby and Belmont Stakes several times.

In 1991 Shoemaker was injured in a car crash and confined to a wheelchair, although he still managed to train horses. ◆

👁 **see also**

Piggott

▲ *An early Sholes typewriter.*

Christopher Sholes

American inventor who developed the typewriter
Born *1819*   **Died** *1890 aged 71*

Christopher Sholes worked as a printer and as a newspaper editor but his main interest was inventing. He was so attracted by the idea of producing a letter-printing machine that he spent the rest of his life developing and improving the typewriter.

Sholes was granted a patent for a

typewriter in 1868 but he could not raise enough money to develop the idea. Eventually he sold his design to the Remington Arms Company. The first Remington typewriters went on sale in 1874. They only wrote in capital letters but they had many of the features we recognize today: levers struck an inked ribbon to print the letters and the paper moved along to space out the characters. Sholes also arranged the keys in almost exactly the same 'QWERTY' pattern found on modern typewriters and computer keyboards. ◆

Dmitry Shostakovich

Russian composer
Born 1906   *Died* 1975 aged 68

Dmitry Shostakovich's mother was a professional pianist and gave him his first lessons. From 1919 he studied at the Petrograd Conservatoire, but as his family was poor he helped out by playing the piano in a cinema. Success came early. Although his First Symphony was written in 1926 as a graduation exercise, it was hailed as a masterpiece. His career continued to prosper until 1936, when the newspaper *Pravda* suddenly attacked his opera *The Lady Macbeth of the Mtsensk District* for being a disgrace to the Soviet way of life and for a while he found himself out of favour. He was greatly admired during the war years – his Seventh Symphony was composed in Leningrad (now St Petersburg) while the city was under siege by the Nazis in 1941. Besides operas, ballets, choral, and instrumental works of every kind, Shostakovich wrote 15 symphonies and 15 string quartets

which are now considered to be among the most important of the 20th century. ◆

Jean Sibelius

Finnish composer
Born 1865   *Died* 1957 aged 91

Jean Sibelius wrote his first piece of music when he was ten, and began to study the violin in earnest four years later. In 1885 he enrolled at the University of Helsinki as a law student, but turned to music in the following year. His first ambition was to become a concert violinist, but he then turned to composing. Success came in 1892 with the symphonic poems *En Saga* and *Kullervo*. Both were based on Finnish legends. This delighted the Finns, who were struggling against Russian domination and were anxious to keep their culture alive. Sibelius completed the first of his seven symphonies in 1899. These, together with his violin concerto and symphonic poems, brought him international fame. But gradually he became disillusioned with the latest developments in music, and after completing the symphonic poem *Tapiola* in 1926 he gave up composing altogether. ◆

Siemens family

German family of engineers and industrialists
Werner von Siemens
Born 1816   *Died* 1892 aged 75
(Charles) William Siemens
Born 1823   *Died* 1883 aged 60
Frederick Siemens
Born 1826   *Died* 1904 aged 77

When Werner von Siemens was 24 his father died leaving him with nine brothers and sisters to look after. He took this

responsibility seriously and helped to build Europe's most important family of engineers.

Werner served in the army but his main interest was science and, in particular, electricity. In 1848 he set up the business that built Germany's first telegraph line.

Werner's younger brother (Charles) William also trained as a scientist and then went to England. Another brother, Frederick, joined William and the two of them worked on improving the furnaces used in industry. In 1856 they developed a 'regenerative' furnace that used hot, waste gases to heat the air being pumped into the furnace. This made glass-making much more efficient and replaced old-fashioned ways of making steel.

Frederick went back to Germany in 1867 to take over a large glassworks which another brother, Hans, had set up. William stayed in England and in 1883 was knighted by Queen Victoria in recognition of his contributions to science and industry. ◆

👁 **see also**

Bessemer

▼ *A cartoon of (Charles) William Siemens from* Punch *magazine, 1883.*

PUNCH'S FANCY PORTRAITS.—No. 146.

SIR C. W. SIEMENS, D.C.L., F.R.S., &c.

THE ELECTRIC KNIGHT-LIGHT.

▲ *Igor Sikorsky seen at the controls of the first flight of his invention, the Sikorsky VS-300, on 14 September 1939.*

Igor **Sikorsky**

Russian-born American aeronautical engineer
Born *1889*   **Died** *1972 aged 83*

As a boy in Russia, Igor Sikorsky built a model helicopter which flew, powered by a rubber band. Forty years later, in 1939, he built what was to be the world's first commercially successful helicopter. This was built in large numbers, mainly for military purposes, and was the forerunner of all modern helicopters.

In the years between, Sikorsky had trained as an engineer in Russia and in 1908, after meeting the aeroplane pioneer Wilbur Wright in Paris, he returned home to give serious attention to fixed-wing aircraft. In 1913 he built the first four-engined passenger aeroplane. In 1919 he emigrated to America. There he produced successful 'flying boats', which, in the 1930s, were used for passenger services across the Atlantic and the Pacific oceans. However, he still pursued his dream of a vertical take-off aircraft and this was realized with his VS-300 model in 1939. By 1957, when he retired, Sikorsky had seen the helicopter develop in power, size, and versatility. ◆

👁 **see also**
Wright brothers

Paul **Simon**

American singer and songwriter
Born *1942*

New York's folk-rock duo, Simon and Garfunkel, had many hit records during the 1960s and 1970s. The best known was probably 'Bridge over Troubled Waters' (1970). They split up after this record and Art Garfunkel turned mainly to film acting while Paul Simon pursued a solo career as a singer and songwriter. Although he was often dismissed in the early stages of his career as an imitator of Bob Dylan, Simon's work on albums like *There Goes Rhymin' Simon* (1973) and *Still Crazy After All These Years* (1975) showed him to be a sensitive and intelligent songwriter.

Simon and Garfunkel have played several concerts together since they originally split up. The most memorable was probably their concert in Central Park, New York, in 1981.

In 1986 Simon recorded the album *Graceland* with many top African musicians. Many people consider this celebration of African and American music to be his finest album to date. ◆

Frank **Sinatra**

American singer and film star
Born *1915*   **Died** *1998 aged 82*

Francis Sinatra was born in a tough neighbourhood in New Jersey, where he may have made the first underworld (organized crime) contacts for which he has often been criticized. He started as a singer when he was about 20

▼ *Frank Sinatra was particularly linked with the song 'My Way', which spent a record 122 weeks in the British pop charts from 1969 to 1971.*

and in 1939 was 'discovered' by bandleader Harry James. His style of singing romantic ballads with emotive and characteristic phrasing delighted his teenage fans, but he could also sing witty and moody numbers.

He began acting in films in the 1940s but was not taken seriously as an actor until the non-singing role of an American soldier in *From Here to Eternity* (1953), which won him an Oscar. He went on to star in many more films, both musicals and dramas. He continued to sing in live concerts even when he was in his seventies. ◆

Sitting Bull

Sioux Indian chief
Born *c.1834* **Died** *1890 aged about 56*

Sitting Bull was a Sioux Indian chief whose Indian name was Tatanka Iyotake. He is most famous for his part in the defeat of General Custer and his cavalrymen at the battle of Little Bighorn in 1876. This battle came about because the Americans broke the Sioux resettlement treaty, which Sitting Bull had agreed to in 1868.

After this battle, Sitting Bull and his followers were relentlessly pursued by the American army and were forced to escape to Canada. They returned to America in 1881 and Sitting Bull became famous once again, this time for his appearances in Buffalo Bill's Wild West shows. He finally settled on a reservation in South Dakota where he continued to lead the Sioux in their refusal to sell their lands to white settlers. He was killed shortly after while 'resisting arrest' during an uprising there. ◆

👁 **see also**
Buffalo Bill Custer

▲ *Sioux Indian Chief Sitting Bull was also a 'medicine man', and was believed to possess magical powers.*

Adam **Smith**

Scottish philosopher and economist
Born *1723* **Died** *1790 aged 67*

Adam Smith was educated at Glasgow and then Oxford University. In 1751 he returned to Glasgow as a professor of logic and moral philosophy and published his first major work, *The Theory of Moral Sentiments,* in 1759. He left Glasgow in 1764 to travel for two years as tutor to the Duke of Buccleuch. Upon his return he settled down to write his most famous book, *The Wealth of Nations.* This has become one of the most important books on economics. In it Smith explained the development of capitalism and how it made people better off. He also introduced his most famous idea, 'the invisible hand' of competition, which ensures that economic activity can produce prosperity for all even though individuals act only in their own self-interest. These ideas remain powerful today and have influenced

many governments. After completing this major work, Smith became commissioner of customs in Scotland and moved to Edinburgh, where he died two years later. ◆

> *There is no art which one government sooner learns of another than that of draining money from the pockets of the people.*
>
> ADAM SMITH, 1776

Charles Kingsford **Smith**

Australian pilot
Born *1897* **Died** *1935 aged 62*

Charles Kingsford Smith was educated in Australia and trained as an engineer. When World War I broke out he joined the Royal Flying Corps. After being wounded, he was made a flying instructor.

In 1924 he returned to Australia and became chief pilot for Western Australian Airways. Two years later he started his own airline. From then until his death, he made many record-breaking flights. He and co-pilot Charles Ulm flew round Australia in less than 11 days in 1927, and in 1928 they flew across the Pacific Ocean from California to Australia, the first people to do so. In 1930 they flew to England from Australia in just under 13 days, and in 1934 Smith and another co-pilot, Gordon Taylor, made the first west-to-east crossing of the Pacific.

In those days, long flights were frightening adventures and were full of risks. Smith's luck eventually ran out. One day in 1935, while flying from India to Singapore with co-pilot Thomas Pethybridge, his plane disappeared over the Indian Ocean. ◆

Jan **Smuts**

*Prime minister of South Africa from 1919
to 1924 and from 1939 to 1948*
Born *1870*   ***Died*** *1950 aged 80*

After going to school in southern Africa, Jan Christiaan Smuts went to Cambridge University where he was a brilliant student. In 1895 he went to Cape Town and began work as a lawyer.

In 1899 a war started between the British, who ruled the colonies of southern Africa, and the Boers (Afrikaners), who were white settlers of Dutch descent. Smuts fought against the British, and at the end of the war in 1902 he began to work for the colonies to become self-governing instead of being ruled by Britain.

The Transvaal area got its own government in 1907, and all the colonies were united into one country, the Union of South Africa, in 1910. The new Union remained part of the British empire.

During World War I, Smuts became a member of the War Cabinet in London. After the war, he became prime minister of South Africa from 1919 until 1924.

He became prime minister again in 1939, when South Africa allied itself to Britain in World War II. This time Smuts stayed in power until 1948, when he was defeated in the elections by Daniel Malan, who put forward 'apartheid' policies to keep the different races apart in South Africa. ◆

Garry **Sobers**

West Indian cricketer
Born *1936*

As a boy in Barbados, Garfield Sobers was good at all sports, but eventually he decided to devote himself to cricket. He was an excellent batsman, scoring a Test match record at the time of 365 not

◀ *This photograph was taken in 1914 when Jan Smuts was about to become an ally of Britain in World War I.*

out for the West Indies against Pakistan in 1958. He held this record until 1994 when Brian Lara scored 375 runs for the West Indies against England. Sobers could also bowl left-handed in two different styles: fast-medium and slow spin.

When he retired in 1974, his Test match record was 8032 runs, 235 wickets, and 109 catches, making him one of the best all-round cricketers in the world. He was also the first player to score six sixes in one over. ◆

Socrates

Ancient Greek philosopher
Born *c.469 BC*
Died *399 BC aged about 70*

At first Socrates followed his father's profession as a sculptor. Like most men at that time in Athens he also served in the army.

Turning later to philosophy, Socrates did not open a school or give public lectures as some philosophers did. He simply felt he had a mission to correct people's ignorance. His method was to engage people in 'question and answer' sessions. He was the first to use a set of rules, or logic, to discuss important matters. He questioned the way people thought and acted. We know about his ideas and teaching methods from his follower, Plato. Plato wrote down Socrates' ideas and published them.

Socrates upset some people in government and important positions in Athens. In 399 BC he was accused of corrupting young men by making them ask awkward questions about the society in which they lived. He was found guilty and the judges condemned him to death by drinking some poisonous hemlock. ◆

👁 **see also**

Plato

King **Solomon**

King of Israel during the 10th century BC
Born c.980 BC
Died c.922 BC *aged about 58*

Solomon succeeded his father, David, to the throne of Israel when he was about 20 years old. He strengthened the fortifications of Jerusalem and other cities and enlarged his army by adding horsemen and chariots. He made alliances with the rulers of Egypt and other nations, and planned a large programme of trade, industry, and construction. The first Jewish temple in Jerusalem was built during his reign and many foreign rulers came to visit his court.

Solomon had a reputation for being wise, but this wisdom was not shown in the way he ruled his land. He was extravagant and used heavy taxation and forced labour for his building programme. This caused hardship and unrest among the people. There was rebellion during his lifetime, and after he died Israel was divided again. The northern kingdom kept the name Israel while the southern part was called Judah. ◆

👁 **see also**
David

▼ *Solomon shown dictating the Bible's Book of Proverbs. It was once believed that he wrote three proverbs.*

Solon

Ancient Greek statesman
Born c.630 BC
Died c.560 BC *aged about 70*

Solon was born into a noble family in Athens but had little money. As a young man he worked as a merchant. He also took part enthusiastically in the political life of Athens, especially in its arguments and wars with other Greek states. In 594 BC he was appointed chief archon of Athens (nine archons, who were like magistrates, governed the city each year). Solon was told to create reforms to help the city out of its economic depression. His particular job was to calm the arguments which broke out among the rich nobles and the poorer people. The nobles not only controlled the running of the state but owned nearly all the land. The poor had to borrow from the rich, becoming slaves when they could not repay the debt. Solon made great changes immediately. He cancelled the debts and made laws to forbid slavery because of debt. He also made some important changes to the constitution so that all citizens could have some share in the government of their city-state. With these reforms, Solon helped to establish the first democracy. ◆

▲ *Solzhenitsyn's book* The Gulag Archipelago *(1973) is about the Soviet labour-camp network.*

Alexander **Solzhenitsyn**

Russian writer
Born 1918

In 1945 Alexander Solzhenitsyn was arrested for criticizing Stalin, the ruthless Russian leader. He spent eight years in labour camps and three more in exile before being released in 1956. In 1962 he caused a sensation with his book *One Day in the Life of Ivan Denisovich*, which described the effort it took to survive just one day in the appalling conditions of the labour camps. Some of his later writings, critical of the authorities, were banned in the Soviet Union. They were published in other countries, however, and in 1970 Solzhenitsyn was awared the Nobel Prize for Literature.

He was deported from the Soviet Union in 1974 and went to Germany before settling in America. He made an emotional return to Russia in 1994. ◆

Sophocles

Ancient Greek playwright
Born c. 496 BC
Died 406 BC aged about 90

In the 5th century BC, the Greek city of Athens was a very rich and lively place. Its inhabitants were especially keen on the arts and they encouraged artists and writers of all kinds. Every spring, Athens held a competition for new plays. In 468 BC, the winning plays were written by Sophocles.

Born near Athens, Sophocles studied music, poetry, and drama, and then started to write his own plays. During his long life he wrote 123 plays, and won the Athens drama competition 24 times. Seven of his plays have survived. They tell the sad stories of important people in Greek legends. They are so powerful and gripping that they are still performed today. ◆

Spartacus

Leader of a slave revolt against the Romans 74–71 BC
Date of birth unknown
Died 71 BC age unknown

Spartacus was a bandit who was captured in the province of Thracia (now north-eastern Greece and Turkey) and forced to be a slave. He was sold to be trained as a gladiator in Capua, Italy. In the gladiatorial school there he led an uprising of fellow gladiators against the cruelty of the owner. They escaped and were soon joined by other runaway slaves.

Spartacus' men easily defeated the first army of 3000 Roman soldiers sent against them. The army of slaves grew to about 90,000 men and for two years they defeated the Roman forces. Eventually, however, the rebellious slaves were defeated in a battle in which Spartacus was killed. Six thousand of his slave companions were captured and crucified. ◆

Steven **Spielberg**

American film director, writer and producer
Born 1947

As a boy, Steven Spielberg began using his father's cine-camera to film toy trains. At school he made several amateur science fiction films.

His big impact on the cinema came in 1975 with the tense thriller *Jaws*, which quickly made more money than any other film. After making *Close Encounters of the Third Kind* in 1977, he broke box-office records again with the success of *Raiders of the Lost Ark* (1981) and *E.T.* (1982), which made more than 700 million US dollars. His film *Jurassic Park* (1993), with its amazing dinosaur special effects, again broke all box-office records. In 1994 Spielberg was awarded his first Oscar for Best Director for his film *Schindler's List*. This black and white film about the Holocaust also won six other Oscars, including one for Best Film. ◆

Mark **Spitz**

American swimming champion
Born 1950

Mark Spitz began swimming at the age of two, and his father began to coach him seriously when he was eight. In 1968, when he was at Indiana University, Spitz predicted that he would win six gold medals at the Mexico Olympics. In fact, he won only two, both in the relay races. Embarrassed by this failure, he trained hard for the 1972 Munich Olympics. There he broke all records by winning seven gold medals in seven events, and in each of these events he set a new world record. ◆

Joseph **Stalin**

Dictator of the Soviet Union from the 1920s to 1953
Born 1879   Died 1953 aged 73

Joseph Vissarionovich Dzhugashvili's parents wanted him to be a priest, but he was expelled from his Christian

▼ *Steven Spielberg comes face to face with the star from one of his most famous films, E.T.*

college for his 'disloyal ideas'. Later he joined the Russian Social-Democratic Workers' Party and became a full-time revolutionary. He proved himself to be tough, brave, and dedicated, and was invited by Lenin to join the Bolshevik Party leadership in 1912. It was then that he took the name 'Stalin' (man of steel).

In 1917, Stalin was a loyal supporter of Lenin's seizure of power during the Revolution, and in 1922 he became secretary of the Communist Party (as the Bolsheviks were now known). However, as Lenin lay dying, he asked his comrades to remove Stalin from this important post because 'he is too rude and uncomradely'. But Lenin died in 1924 before any action could be taken.

In the years that followed, Stalin helped to build a strong nation through a series of Five-Year Plans intended to industrialize and modernize the Soviet Union. His greatest achievement was to lead his country, as 'Generalissimo', to victory over the Nazis in World War II. After this, Communist influence spread through much of Europe.

But all this was done at great human cost. Stalin arranged for all his rivals to be killed until he became dictator. Soviet people lived

in fear of arrest, torture, and execution by the notorious secret police (later called the KGB). Millions of people were sent to labour camps for opposing Stalin's wishes, and in the countryside millions more died of starvation during the 1920s and 1930s.

It was only after his death in 1953 that people felt free to criticize Stalin. The leaders of the Communist Party denounced him in 1956, and in 1961 his body was removed from its place of honour in the Lenin Mausoleum in Red Square. ◆

👁 **see also**

Lenin Trotsky

◀ It was the plight of poor families like this, forced to live in their car, that inspired Steinbeck's novels.

John **Steinbeck**

American writer
Born *1902* **Died** *1968 aged 66*

Most of John Steinbeck's writing explores America's agricultural society and the relationship between people and the land. This is hardly surprising considering that Steinbeck grew up in a farming region in California.

By 1935 Steinbeck had written several books and stories, but it was his novel *Tortilla Flat* that gave him his first popular success. This was followed by *Of Mice and Men*, a touching story of two very different farm workers. In 1939, Steinbeck's greatest work was published. *The Grapes of Wrath* is the story of a poor fruit-picking family migrating from America's dust bowl to California. His detailed and sympathetic portrayal helped bring the problems suffered by homeless farmers to the public's attention.

Steinbeck's later writing included novels, short stories, screenplays and also non-fiction. He was awarded the Nobel Prize for Literature in 1962. ◆

▼ A cartoon depicting Stalin as the captain of his country.

КАПИТАН СТРАНЫ СОВЕТОВ
ВЕДЕТ НАС ОТ ПОБЕДЫ
К ПОБЕДЕ!

Gloria **Steinem**

American women's rights campaigner
Born 1934

Gloria Steinem was born in Toledo, Ohio. During the 1960s she was involved in campaigns against racism and American involvement in the Vietnam war. In 1971 she helped to establish the National Women's Political Caucus, which encourages women to become politicians.

Steinem has been a leading campaigner for women's rights, determined to gain women more freedom in situations such as work, politics, and everyday life. She helped to found the Women's Actions Alliance to fight inequality, and in 1972 she launched *Ms.* magazine, which reports on issues affecting women. ◆

Ingemar **Stenmark**

Swedish world champion skier
Born 1956

Ingemar Stenmark learnt to ski at the age of five in his home village just outside the Arctic Circle. He won his first national championship at the age of eight and at 13 he was selected to train for the Swedish junior team. He went on to become the best skier in the world. He won three successive overall World Cup titles (1976–1978), and in 1980 won two gold medals at the Winter Olympics even though he had a metal plate in his ankle after breaking it the previous year. He retired in 1989, having won 15 World Cup championships for the slalom and giant slalom skiing competitions. His 86 wins made him the most successful skier of all time. ◆

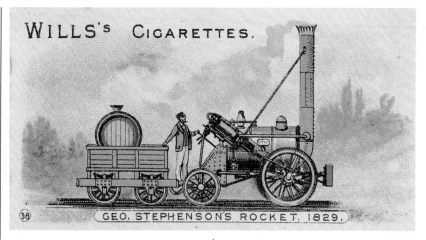

WILL'S CIGARETTES.

GEO. STEPHENSON'S ROCKET. 1829.

George **Stephenson**

English engineer and builder of the world's first public railway
Born 1781   Died 1848 aged 67

As a teenager George Stephenson had various jobs working with mining engines. He had never been to school, but he taught himself to read by attending night-classes. He became a colliery engineer, and in 1812 was appointed to be an engine-builder at Killingworth colliery, near Newcastle.

Stephenson spent the rest of his working life designing and building railways and railway locomotives. Between 1814 and 1826 he built railway engines for pulling coal. In 1823 he was put in charge of building a railway from Stockton to Darlington that would carry people. When it opened in 1825, Stephenson himself drove the engine which pulled the world's first steam-hauled passenger train. Stephenson's successes led to the building of railways throughout Britain. He also won a competition with his design for an efficient locomotive, called 'The Rocket', which was built by his son Robert. He used the money he had made from his inventions to set up

▲ *Stephenson's locomotive 'The Rocket' earned him £500 when it won a competition in 1829.*

schools for miners' children and night-schools for the miners so they could get an education. ◆

Robert Louis **Stevenson**

Scottish writer
Born 1850   Died 1894 aged 44

Robert Louis Stevenson was brought up in Edinburgh.

▼ *A fictional map of* Treasure Island, *from Robert Louis Stevenson's book of the same name.*

TREASURE ISLAND

When he left university he travelled abroad to escape the cold and wet Scottish climate. Stevenson's first books described his tours in Belgium and France, and his journey to California to marry an American, Fanny Osbourne.

Stevenson's exciting adventure story *Treasure Island* was published in 1883. This thrilling book about pirates and treasure was an instant success. Three years later his fame soared when the novel *The Strange Case of Dr Jekyll and Mr Hyde*, a fascinating horror story, was published.

In 1889 Stevenson and his family settled on the Polynesian island of Samoa. He continued to write, and the islanders called him 'Tusitala', meaning 'Storyteller'. ◆

Marie **Stopes**

Scottish founder of the first birth control clinic in London
Born 1880   Died 1958 aged 77

Marie Stopes was born in Edinburgh. She studied science in England and Germany and later also studied philosophy. She married when she was 31, but her marriage was unhappy and she and her husband soon separated.

At the time many people thought it was wrong to talk about sex and birth control. As a result they were ignorant when they got married, and this often caused problems. Because of her own unhappy marriage, Marie Stopes decided to do something about this. She wrote two books: *Married Love* and *Wise Parenthood*. The books explained sex, birth control, and family planning clearly. Some people were shocked by the books, but others were pleased and many wrote to Marie Stopes thanking her and asking for more information. In

1918 she married again. With her second husband she opened the first family planning clinic in 1921 in London. ◆

Harriet Beecher **Stowe**

American anti-slavery author
Born 1811   Died 1896 aged 85

Harriet Stowe was born in Connecticut, America, the seventh of nine children. In 1832 the family moved to Cincinnati, where she and her older sister Catherine set up one of the first colleges for women.

Stowe married a professor, and for the next 18 years she lived through one of the most dramatic periods in North American history. In the Southern states slave-owning was legal, but many of the Northern states had abolished slavery. Slaves from the South would often try to escape to the North and into Canada where they could be free. Only the Ohio River separated Stowe from a slave-holding community, and runaway slaves were sometimes sheltered on their way north by Stowe and her friends.

Her book *Uncle Tom's Cabin* describes in vivid, moving language the hardships and tragedy of a slave's life. It was read by more people than any other novel of its time, and influenced the decision to abolish slavery for good. ◆

◉ **see also**
Tubman

Antonio **Stradivari**

Italian maker of violins
Born 1644
Died 1737 aged 93

Antonio Stradivari began work as a pupil of Niccolo Amati, a violin maker, but he was soon putting his own label on the violins he made. Over the years he developed new shapes for his violins and a new kind of varnish, whose secret was never discovered. Soon a Stradivarius violin became a prized possession for musicians all over the world because of its powerful and penetrating tone. In his life, Stradivari made more than 1100 instruments, including lutes, guitars, and mandolins as well as violins. ◆

◀ *Because the sound of a Stradivarius violin is said to be the finest in the world, they are now among the most expensive violins to buy.*

311

Johann **Strauss I and II**

Two important members of a musical Austrian family
Johann I
Born *1804* **Died** *1849 aged 45*
Johann II
Born *1825* **Died** *1899 aged 73*

Johann Strauss I began his musical career as a violinist. Shortly after the birth of his son (Johann II) he formed his own orchestra and played in the inns and dance-halls of Vienna. Soon everyone was dancing to the waltzes and lively dance tunes he composed. His fame rapidly spread throughout Europe and he undertook many successful tours.

Johann II began writing music when he was six years old. However, his father did not want him to take up a musical career and he had to study in secret. It soon became clear that he was very talented. When it came to waltzes, no one could rival Johann II. He was the 'Waltz King' of Vienna. *The Blue Danube* and *Tales from the Vienna Woods* delighted everyone, as did his polkas, quadrilles, and marches. His operettas, such as *Die Fledermaus* (The Bat) (1874), were equally successful.

Johann I had other musical sons, Josef (1827–1870) and Eduard (1835–1916), who also wrote splendid dance tunes, but neither of them could rival their famous elder brother. ◆

Richard **Strauss**

German composer and conductor
Born *1864* **Died** *1949 aged 85*

Richard Strauss was a classical composer who became well-known for dramatic music which

▲ *Richard Strauss's opera* Salome *(1905) was based on an Oscar Wilde play.*

interpreted stories from literature or history. He was still composing when he was well into his eighties.

Born in Munich, Strauss was the talented son of a horn player. He started his musical training early and his first symphony was performed when he was 20. He then developed his own distinctive and bold personal style. He went on to compose many pieces which he called tone poems. His first great success in this style was *Don Juan* (1889). Later, he turned to opera and wrote the startling *Salome* (1905) and *Elektra* (1909). His most popular opera was probably *Der Rosenkavalier* (1911) which was in a more traditional style with tuneful waltzes. Strauss also wrote many songs and was a distinguished conductor. ◆

Igor **Stravinsky**

Russian composer and conductor
Born *1882* **Died** *1971 aged 88*

Although Igor Stravinsky showed an early talent for music, it was some time before he found his feet as a composer. His first great

success came with the ballets he wrote between 1910 and 1913 – *The Firebird, Petrushka*, and *The Rite of Spring* made him the most talked-about composer in Europe. However, many people were outraged by *The Rite of Spring* and thought it was simply a horrible noise.

Because of World War I and the Russian Revolution, Stravinsky decided to leave Russia. He lived first in Switzerland and then in America. His music also took a new turn. It still used interesting harmonies and exciting rhythms, but it was no longer as savage as it had been. As a conductor, he conducted *The Firebird*, which he turned into a concert suite, about a thousand times.

Even at the end of his life Stravinsky was still experimenting with new ways of writing music. When he died, the world lost one of the most adventurous musical explorers of all time. ◆

Achmad **Sukarno**

Indonesian president from 1945 to 1967
Born *1901* **Died** *1970 aged 69*

Achmad Sukarno originally trained as an engineer. He was also brilliant at making speeches and could talk in half-a-dozen different languages. He was a founder-member of the movement for Indonesian independence from Holland. While the Dutch ruled, he spent 13 years in prison or in exile abroad. During the Japanese occupation of Indonesia during World War II, he confirmed his position as the country's leading nationalist. After the Japanese surrender, Sukarno claimed the title of President of Indonesia in 1945. He then led the fight against a Dutch re-conquest. Firmly in power from 1950, he began to act like a world-leader overseas and a dictator at home, while Indonesia suffered increasing economic difficulties. He eventually lost power to the army in 1966 and General Suharto became president in 1967. ◆

Suleiman I

Muslim ruler of the Ottoman empire from 1520 to 1566
Born c.1494   Died 1566 aged about 71

Suleiman was the only son of Sultan Selim I. While his father was sultan (king), he became governor of Manisa in Asia Minor. There he learnt the skills that he needed when he became sultan of the Ottoman empire in 1520.

▼ *This map shows Suleiman's empire at its greatest extent. The Ottomans were a mighty sea power at this time and were feared throughout the area of the Mediterranean Sea.*

Under Suleiman's rule, the Ottoman empire prospered and expanded to its greatest extent. His first military success came when he conquered Belgrade in 1521. The following year he conquered the Mediterranean island of Rhodes, and then in 1526 he defeated the Hungarian armies in a battle at Mohács. In all, he made conquests in the Balkans, the Mediterranean, Persia (now Iran), and North Africa.

Suleiman gathered around himself many statesmen, lawyers, architects, and poets. Because he tried to modernize their laws, the Ottomans gave Suleiman the name *Kanuni*, which means 'Lawgiver'. In Europe, though, his opponents called him 'Suleiman the Magnificent'.

In his later life, Suleiman's reign was troubled by arguments between his three sons. Suleiman himself was still actively involved in military matters when he died during a siege in Hungary in 1566. ◆

Sultan of Brunei

Head of the state of Brunei from 1967
Born 1946

His Majesty Sultan Sir Muda Hassanal Bolkiah Mu'izuddin Waddaulah succeeded his father as Sultan of Brunei in 1967, when he was only 21. Up until that time he had been preparing for his future role of ruler of his country.

At the time of his succession to the throne, Brunei had been under British control for nearly 80 years. It became independent in 1984, and the Sultan became prime minister as well as ruler of the state. Brunei is an Islamic country, and the Sultan is regarded as the leader of the large Muslim community.

Brunei is a country which has become wealthy because of its petroleum industry. It has a high level of employment and well-developed systems of health care and education. ◆

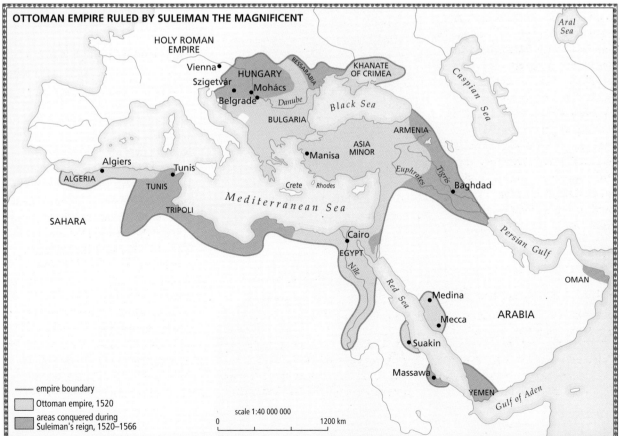

OTTOMAN EMPIRE RULED BY SULEIMAN THE MAGNIFICENT

empire boundary
Ottoman empire, 1520
areas conquered during Suleiman's reign, 1520–1566

scale 1:40 000 000
0   1200 km

Sun Yat-sen

Founder of the Nationalist Party which ruled China before the Communists
Born 1866   Died 1925 aged 58

While studying as a doctor in Hong Kong, Sun Yat-sen joined a group of revolutionaries who were intent on overthrowing the corrupt Manchu dynasty which ruled China. He made several journeys to China with a secret army but all attempts at revolution failed. From 1896, Sun Yat-sen lived in exile. Then, in 1911, there was a successful revolution against the rulers, and Sun Yat-sen returned to China and was proclaimed president.

The new republic of China was broken into districts which were ruled by warlords' armies. Because of the power of the warlords, Sun Yat-sen was president in a part of south China only. He founded the People's National Party to carry out his 'Three Principles of the People'. His first principle was a united China. The second was democracy or people's rights. The third was to create a nation where industry was modernized and peasants had enough land to feed their families. He began to build an army to march against the warlords, but died before it set out. ◆

◀ *Sun Yat-sen pictured with his wife.*

Joan Sutherland

Australian soprano
Born 1926

Joan Sutherland was taught to sing first by her mother, and then professionally in Sydney and at London's Royal College of Music. She made her début in London's Covent Garden in 1952 in Mozart's *The Magic Flute*. In 1959 her performance in the Covent Garden production of Donizetti's *Lucia di Lammermoor* established her as an outstanding soprano. Sutherland and her husband, who is a pianist and conductor, have toured the world's opera houses, specializing in 19th-century French and Italian opera, and have made many outstanding recordings. She retired in 1990. ◆

Shin'ichi Suzuki

Japanese violinist and founder of the Suzuki Method
Born 1898   Died 1997 aged 99

After studying the violin in Japan, and later in Berlin, Shin'ichi Suzuki and three of his brothers formed a string quartet. Later he founded the Tokyo String Orchestra.

Suzuki felt that everyone should learn to play an instrument. It occurred to him that if children could learn to speak by repeating simple words and phrases and gradually moving on to more complicated sentences, they might also be able to learn to play an instrument in the same way. So, he devised a method whereby young children could learn to play in easy stages, starting with simple tunes and repeating them day after day until playing became second nature.

The Suzuki Method spread all over the world. It is used to teach many kinds of instruments. ◆

▲ An illustrated scene from Gulliver's Travels. Although Swift mocked humankind in this and many of his other books, he showed great affection for many individual people.

Jonathan **Swift**

Irish-English author
Born *1667*   **Died** *1745 aged 77*

Jonathan Swift was born in Ireland of English parents. For 30 years he was Dean of St Patrick's Cathedral in Dublin, but was more famous as a writer of satire – fiction that is sometimes comic, sometimes serious, but always critical of people and their society.

His best-known satire is *Gulliver's Travels*, which describes the journeys of a ship's doctor, Lemuel Gulliver. He visits Lilliput, where everyone is tiny, then Brobdingnag, a land of giants. After more journeying, Gulliver arrives at a country ruled by gentle talking horses. These behave so much better towards each other than humans do that Gulliver longs to stay with them, dreading the return to his own world of back-biting, poverty and war. ◆

Irena **Szewinska**

Polish athletic champion
Born *1946*

Irena Kirszenstein began her athletics career as an 18-year-old at the 1964 Tokyo Olympics, where she won silver medals in the long jump and 200 m, and gold in the 4 × 100 m relay. The following year she broke the world record for the 200 m, the event for which she won another gold at the 1968 Mexico Olympics. By now she had married her coach, Janusz Szewinski.

As Irena Szewinska she carried on breaking the 200 m world record regularly into the 1970s, before winning a third Olympic gold medal in the 400 m at Montreal in 1976. By the time she retired she had become one of the best athletes ever, with ten European championship medals, seven Olympic medals, and four World Cup medals to her name. ◆

Sir Rabindranath **Tagore**

Indian poet, philosopher, and musician
Born *1861*   **Died** *1941 aged 80*

Rabindranath Tagore was born into a rich Bengali family and was sent to England to study law. He started writing poems at a very young age, and published his first poems when he was 17 years old. He also wrote a number of plays and novels. In his writing he tried to blend together the best traditions of Indian and European literature.

Tagore won the Nobel Prize for Literature in 1913, and was given a knighthood by the British government in 1915. He renounced this title in 1919 in protest against the Jallianwala Bagh incident in India, when a British general ordered troops to fire on an unarmed crowd, killing about 400 people. A song written and composed by Tagore was adopted as the national anthem of India in 1950. ◆

Tamerlane

Central Asian conqueror
Born *c.1336*   **Died** *1405 aged about 69*

Timur, later known as 'Tamerlane' or 'Tamburlaine' in the West, was the great-grandson of a minister of Genghis Khan. His ambition was to rebuild the empire of that great conqueror.

When he was about 20, Timur began to claim power over the other tribes in the area around Samarkand (now in Uzbekistan). By 1369, he had brutally defeated all his rivals. He now moved further afield. For the next 35 years he raided and conquered the regions from the Black Sea to the Indus. In 1404 he staged an immense celebration of his victories, displaying his captured treasures. His next great expedition was to be against China. He set out in 1405, but died on the way of a fever. He was buried in Samarkand.

Timur was lame in his right leg, and so the Persians called him 'Timur lenk', meaning 'Timur the lame', which became 'Tamerlane'. ◆

👁 **see also**

Genghis Khan

▶ *Tamerlane's burial place.*

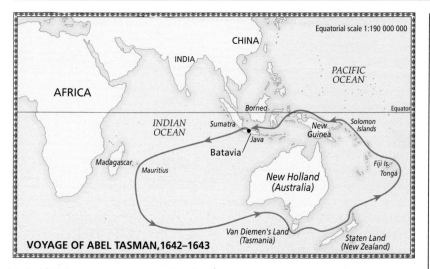

VOYAGE OF ABEL TASMAN, 1642–1643

▲ In 1642 Tasman set out to explore the South Pacific from Batavia in Java. He became the first European to reach the island now called Tasmania and to see New Zealand, Tonga, and Fiji.

Abel **Tasman**

Dutch explorer
Born c.1603
Died c.1659 aged about 56

Abel Tasman was a sailor who worked for a trading company called the Dutch East India Company. He was based in Java, then a Dutch colony and now part of Indonesia. In 1642 Anthony Van Diemen, the governor of the Dutch East Indies, sent Tasman to explore the seas further south in the hope of finding a route across the Pacific Ocean to Chile.

Tasman sailed west across the Indian Ocean, then turned south-east. Eventually he came to a forested coast, and named the territory 'Van Diemen's Land' (now called Tasmania). He then carried on east and found more land, which he named 'Staten Land' (now known as New Zealand). Heading back to Java, Tasman lost his way. He sighted Tonga and then Fiji before reaching home. He had also sailed right round Australia without knowing it! ◆

Elizabeth **Taylor**

British-born American film actress
Born 1932

Elizabeth Taylor was born in London, but grew up in Hollywood as a child actress. She appeared in films from the age of 10 and enjoyed great success in *National Velvet* in 1944.

She became one of the most glamorous stars of the 1950s and 1960s, and also attracted much attention because of her several short-lived marriages. She was married twice to the great Welsh actor Richard Burton, with whom she acted in *Cleopatra* (1963). She played the title role in this film and had to make 65 costume changes.

Her most memorable performances are of strong-minded women. She won Oscars for playing such women in *Butterfield 8* (1960) and *Who's Afraid of Virginia Woolf?* (1966). ◆

▼ Elizabeth Taylor in a Hollywood publicity shot. She started her career as a child actress in films such as Lassie Come Home.

Pyotr Ilyich **Tchaikovsky**

Russian composer
Born 1840   **Died** 1893 aged 53

If you like ballet or like listening to music, you will probably know and love Tchaikovsky. Songs and symphonies, operas and ballets, concertos and serenades all poured from his pen.

Pyotr (Peter) Tchaikovsky was born into a wealthy Russian family and grew up in the town of Votkinsk, near the Ural Mountains. He was sent to boarding school in St Petersburg when he was eight, and eventually became a law student. It was not until he was 23 that he decided to devote his life to music. He enrolled in Russia's first Conservatory of Music in St Petersburg, run by the brilliant pianist Anton Rubinstein.

When he was 26 he wrote his first symphony, and followed it with some piano pieces, the 'Children's Album', written for his nieces and nephews. He also wrote difficult piano works, like the piano concertos, which even Rubinstein and other top pianists could hardly play at the time. But it is his fairytale ballets that many people know: *Swan Lake*, *Sleeping Beauty*, and *The Nutcracker*.

Despite his great success and fame, Tchaikovsky was often unhappy, and he suffered seriously from depression. Nine days after conducting his moving Sixth Symphony, the *Pathétique*, he died. Some mystery surrounds the cause of his death; one theory is that he committed suicide after revelations of a scandalous affair. ◆

🔊 **see also**
Rubinstein

Kiri **Te Kanawa**

New Zealand soprano
Born *1944*

Five weeks after Kiri was born into a poor Maori family, she was adopted by Tom and Nell Te Kanawa, who named her Kiri, the Maori word for bell.

After winning many singing prizes in New Zealand and Australia, Te Kanawa studied at the London Opera Centre and then joined the Royal Opera Company. She made her Covent Garden début in 1970, her first major role being that of the Countess in Mozart's *The Marriage of Figaro*. She has specialized in the music of Mozart and Richard Strauss and made many outstanding recordings of opera and also of American musicals, such as Bernstein's *West Side Story*. ◆

🔊 **see also**
Bernstein   Mozart   Strauss

Thomas **Telford**

Scottish civil engineer
Born *1757*   **Died** *1834 aged 77*

Thomas Telford started his working life as an apprentice stonemason. But because of his

▲ *Telford engineered the Menai suspension bridge which connects the Welsh mainland to Anglesey.*

skills, hard work, and constant thirst for knowledge, Telford became one of Europe's leading civil engineers. His canals, bridges, harbours, and roads can be found all over Britain, still in use today.

In 1793 Telford was given his first big project: to build the Ellesmere Canal, linking the rivers Severn and Mersey. This canal made his reputation, and soon he was in great demand. He was an outstanding road builder too, and his road from London to the Welsh port of Holyhead was one of the most important routes in the country. His famous Menai suspension bridge still carries this road to the island of Anglesey.

In 1820 the Institution of Civil Engineers invited Telford to be its first president. He held this post until his death, and his influence greatly helped civil engineering become a respected profession. In 1963 the town of Telford in Shropshire was named after him. ◆

🔊 **see also**
Brunel

Shirley **Temple**

American child film actress
Born *1928*

Shirley Temple started acting in short films at the age of four, and was given a special Oscar when she was only five for her success in the film *Stand up and Cheer* (1934). Over the next few years she was America's favourite child star, usually playing the part of a little orphan who got her way with adults by smiling sweetly and dancing or singing.

Unfortunately, she did not succeed in becoming an adult actress and made her last film, *Fort Apache* (1948), at the age of 20. Under her married name, Shirley Temple Black, she has taken on various diplomatic roles. She became US representative to the United Nations in 1969 and then ambassador to Ghana in 1974, and to Czechoslovakia in 1989. ◆

Alfred, Lord Tennyson

English poet
Born 1809   *Died* 1892 aged 83

A lfred, Lord Tennyson, was born in Somersby, Lincolnshire, and educated at Trinity College, Cambridge.

By 1833 he had published two sets of poems which received bad reviews. This was followed by the death of his close friend, Arthur Hallam, and caused Tennyson to suffer a great depression. In the following nine years, Tennyson wrote and rewrote many poems but published hardly any.

This changed in 1842 with the successful publication of *Poems*. His elegy for Hallam, *In Memoriam*, was published in 1850 and he succeeded William Wordsworth as Poet Laureate in the same year.

Tennyson continued to enjoy great popularity with works such as *The Charge of the Light Brigade* and *Idylls of the King*, a retelling of the Arthurian legends. He was made a Baron in 1884. ◆

👁 **see also**
Wordsworth

Tenzing Norgay

One of the first two men to reach the summit of Mount Everest
Born 1914   *Died* 1986 aged 71

T enzing Norgay was a Sherpa, one of the Himalayan people who have the reputation of being hardy mountaineers. Tenzing made his first trip as a porter (load carrier) on the British expedition to Mount Everest in 1935. Over the next 15 years he made 17 more expeditions to the Himalayas and became an experienced

mountaineer and sirdar, a Sherpa leader.

In 1953 he was invited to lead the Sherpas on another British expedition to Everest. This was his nineteenth Himalayan climb. By now Tenzing was a major climber in his own right and he was selected to be in one of the assault parties to attempt the final climb to the summit. On 29 May, Tenzing and Edmund Hillary of New Zealand stood on the top of Everest, the first people to do so. ◆

👁 **see also**
Hillary

▶ *Tenzing Norgay and Edmund Hillary on their way to conquering Mount Everest in 1953.*

Mother Teresa

Christian missionary in India
Born 1910   *Died* 1997 aged 87

A gnes Gonxha Bojaxhiu grew up in a loving home in Albania. Like her brother and sister, she went to the local school, but by the time she was 12 she became a nun, taking the name Teresa.

In 1928 she was sent to India to teach at St Mary's High School convent in Calcutta. One day she felt that God needed her to be among the poorest, forgotten people of the city. So, in 1948 she left the convent, setting aside her nun's habit and putting on an Indian sari.

She moved into the slums of Calcutta, where she gathered together destitute children and sheltered them. In 1950 the Roman Catholic Church allowed her to start a new sisterhood, the Congregation of the Missionaries of Charity. She opened a Home for the Dying in Calcutta in 1952, as well as a leper colony called Shanti Nagar ('Town of Peace'). After that, Mother Teresa opened over 60 more schools, orphanages, and homes

▲ *Mother Teresa, also known as the 'saint of the gutter'.*

for the dying worldwide. In 1979 she received the Nobel Peace Prize, which she accepted on behalf of the poor and destitute everywhere. In 1990, after an illness, she retired from her most active work. ◆

Saint **Teresa of Avila**

Spanish nun
Born *1515*   **Died** *1582 aged 67*

Teresa came from a devoutly Christian family. As a child she read about the lives of the saints and wanted to follow their example. When she was a teenager, she became ill with fever. Believing she might die, she remembered her childhood dreams of heaven, and decided to become a nun. When she was better, she ran away from home and joined a Carmelite convent just outside the town.

The Carmelite order of nuns had been founded 400 years before. But standards of obedience to the rules had slipped, and Teresa was greatly disappointed by the nuns' behaviour. In 1562 Teresa began her mission to reform the Carmelite order. She insisted, for example, that the nuns slept on straw, wore rope sandals, and ate no meat. Teresa spent the last 16 years of her life travelling around Spain, restoring Carmelite houses to their original purity. ◆

see also
Augustine of Hippo

Valentina **Tereshkova**

Russian cosmonaut; the first woman to go into space
Born *1937*

Valentina Tereshkova spent her childhood on a farm. When she was older she worked in a tyre factory and then in a textile mill. But she had an adventurous spirit, and in her spare time she made as many as 163 parachute jumps.

Because of her lack of fear and her dedication, she was picked for space training in 1962. It was only a year later that she piloted a spacecraft, *Vostok 6*, in a group flight that lasted three days. Her spaceship made 48 orbits of the Earth.

Although she was a colonel in the Soviet air force, Tereshkova devoted herself to helping others in many spheres – as a figure in politics, as a diplomat on trips round the world, and as a campaigner for peace and women's rights. ◆

William Makepeace **Thackeray**

English writer
Born *1811*   **Died** *1863 aged 52*

The two most important novelists of Victorian times were probably Charles Dickens and William Makepeace Thackeray.

Thackeray was born in Calcutta, India, educated at public school and Cambridge University in England, and had an inheritance that enabled him to travel widely on the continent. In 1836 this money finally ran out and Thackeray began writing for newspapers and periodicals using false names such as Michael Angelo Titmarsh and George Savage Fitzboodle!

Thackeray wrote humorously about the English upper-middle classes, pointing out their faults and bad behaviour. His greatest work, *Vanity Fair*, was published in monthly instalments between 1847–1848. Other works of his include *The Book of Snobs*, *The Luck of Barry Lyndon*, *The Newcomes*, and *Henry Esmond*.

In contrast to his comic writing, Thackeray suffered tragedy in his private life. His second child died early and his wife suffered a permanent mental breakdown. Thackeray himself died suddenly one Christmas Eve. ◆

see also
Dickens

▼ *A portrait of Thackeray from 1867.*

Margaret **Thatcher**

British prime minister from 1979 to 1990
Born 1925

Margaret Thatcher was born Margaret Roberts. She studied chemistry at Oxford University and later became a barrister. Having been elected to Parliament in 1959, she gained her first cabinet post as Minister of Education in 1970. She replaced Edward Heath as Conservative Party leader in 1975.

In 1979 the Conservatives won the General Election, and Margaret Thatcher became the first woman prime minister of Britain. She at once set about lowering taxes and reducing government control of businesses. Later, many state-owned businesses like British Telecom were sold to private owners.

In 1982 Thatcher reacted quickly when Argentina invaded the British colony of the Falkland Islands. A British task force recaptured the

◀ *Thatcher was renowned for her tough style; she tolerated little disagreement, either from the opposition or from within her own party.*

islands, but many British and Argentinian soldiers died.

In 1983 she led the Conservatives to another election victory, and in 1987 she became the first prime minister in the 20th century to be elected to a third consecutive term of office.

Margaret Thatcher's toughness in foreign affairs led to her being called 'the Iron Lady' and she earned respect from many people throughout the world. By the end of 1990, though, her popularity had declined. She came under attack from colleagues in the cabinet who thought that her style of government was too domineering. Margaret Thatcher resigned after a contest for the leadership of the Conservative Party. She was made a life peer (Baroness Thatcher of Kesteven) in 1992. ◆

Themistocles

Ancient Greek statesman and soldier
Born c.528 BC
Died c.462 BC aged about 66

As leader of Athens and creator of its navy, Themistocles, an ambitious and daring man, saved Greece from being conquered by the Persians.

Not much is known about his early life. In 490 BC, he became an Athenian politician after the Greeks had defeated the Persians at the battle of Marathon. He favoured building a navy because he believed that the Persians would attack again, and that the war would be decided at sea. Aristides, the then leader of Athens, opposed this plan. He was banished in 482 BC and Themistocles took his place.

In 480 BC, a small force from Sparta fought the Persians to the death at Thermopylae. Then the new Athenian navy under Themistocles destroyed the Persian fleet at the battle of Salamis. In the following year, Athens and Sparta combined to overwhelm their common enemy.

In 470 BC, Themistocles was accused of conspiracy against Athens. He was exiled and fled to live in Persia. ◆

Dylan **Thomas**

Welsh poet
Born 1914   Died 1953 aged 39

Dylan Thomas was born in Swansea, Wales, and his strong feeling for the Welsh countryside and people runs through his best writing.

Thomas published his first book of poems and moved to London around the age of 20. While in London he met most of the famous writers of the time, and also

▼ *This portrait of a young Dylan Thomas is by the English painter Augustus John.*

developed a habit of long drinking sessions with his friends.

In 1949 he returned to Wales and wrote the radio play *Under Milk Wood*. The play celebrates, with affection and gentle humour, the characters of a small Welsh seaside town. Thomas, now famous for his poetry readings, was invited to America for a reading tour. However, the effects of alcoholism caught up with him and he collapsed and died while in New York. ◆

Daley **Thompson**

English decathlon champion
Born 1958

The decathlon involves ten different running, jumping, and throwing events in two days, so it takes a very good all-round athlete to win this competition. Daley Thompson is undoubtedly Britain's greatest ever decathlete.

After showing promise as a junior decathlete, Thompson became Commonwealth champion in 1978. He went on to win two Olympic gold medals (1980 and 1984), two European championships (1982 and 1986), and one world championship (1983). During this time he set four world record scores. He was the

▲ *Daley Thompson taking part in the 1988 Olympic Games in Seoul, Korea.*

first athlete ever to hold the World, Olympic, European, and Commonwealth titles all at the same time. ◆

Joseph **Thomson**

English physicist who discovered the electron
Born 1856   Died 1940 aged 83

In 1876, Joseph Thomson went to Trinity College, Cambridge. He stayed for the rest of his life becoming one of the university's most famous professors.

Thomson investigated the cathode rays given out when hot metals are placed in strong electric fields. (These are the rays used in television tubes.) He was trying to prove that these rays were streams of particles and not waves, as German physicists believed.

To solve the problem, Thomson built a 'vacuum' tube in which he could bend a beam of rays using magnetic and electric fields. He then calculated the mass and charge of the particles in the beam. In 1897 he announced his remarkable results. At that time scientists believed that the hydrogen atom was the smallest piece of matter:

Thomson's 'corpuscles' were about 1000 times lighter! He had found the first sub-atomic particle – the electron. He was awarded the Nobel Prize for Physics in 1906. ◆

👁 **see also**
Bohr   Rutherford

Jim **Thorpe**

American all-round athlete
Born 1887   Died 1953 aged 66

Jim Thorpe was an outstanding athlete at college. Later, at the 1912 Olympic Games in Stockholm, he became the first man to win gold medals in both the pentathlon and decathlon. Afterwards, Olympic officials took away his medals because he had previously played professional baseball for money. At that time, only amateurs (who did not get paid) could compete in the Games.

Thorpe then turned fully professional. He played major-league baseball from 1913 to 1919 and was also an outstanding American football player from 1917 to 1929.

It was not until after his death that Thorpe's victories at the Stockholm Games were officially recognized and his gold medal status was restored. ◆

Jacopo **Tintoretto**

Italian painter
Born 1518   Died 1594 aged 75

Jacopo Tintoretto's real name was Jacopo Robusti; his nickname comes from his father, who was a cloth dyer ('tintore' in Italian). He lived almost all his life in Venice, where he was the most successful painter of his time. Part of his success came from his crafty business methods. Once, when several artists were asked to submit sketches in competition for a ceiling painting, Tintoretto instead did a full-size painting and had it secretly raised in position the day before the competition was to be judged. This initiative won him the commission, but not surprisingly it made him unpopular with his fellow artists.

Tintoretto was a man of great energy who painted a huge amount of work for churches and public buildings in Venice. He worked there for more than 20 years on marvellously dramatic scenes from the life of Christ and the Virgin Mary. His style was very dynamic and energetic, but also full of tender human feelings. ◆

Titian

Italian painter
Born c.1488   Died 1576 aged about 88

Tiziano Vecellio (Titian's Italian name) was born in a village north of Venice. His family was not rich but was well respected because his father was a local official.

Titian trained to be a painter in the workshop of Giovanni Bellini, the most famous Venetian painter of his time. When Bellini died in 1516, Titian took over his post as the city's official painter. He worked on paintings for the great churches and families of Venice, and he became so successful and famous that kings and nobles from other parts of Europe also commissioned work from him.

Titian's wonderful skill in composing a painting enabled him to break all the traditional rules of how pictures should be arranged. He deeply impressed other artists in Venice by his modern, bold style. No other painter had placed the Madonna and Child in the corner of a picture and not in the centre, as Titian did. He used oil paint with sumptuous, glowing colours which suited the splendour and richness of the Venice of his time. In many of his later works, Titian often used his fingers instead of a brush to make finishing touches or highlights. ◆

👁 **see also**

Bellini

Josip **Tito**

President of Yugoslavia from 1953 to 1980
Born 1892   Died 1980 aged 87

Josip Broz was the son of a blacksmith in Croatia, which was then part of the Austrian empire. He was called up to fight for Austria against Russia in World War I. After the war he stayed in Russia to help the Communists, who had just come to power.

When he came home in 1920,

▼ *Salome with the Head of John the Baptist (1515) by the great Venetian artist Titian.*

Croatia was part of a new kingdom which soon took the name 'Yugoslavia'. As well as the Croats it included people of five other national groups, and was virtually ruled as a dictatorship.

In 1921 Tito founded the Yugoslav Communist Party. The government declared it illegal, so in the 1920s and 1930s he was either in prison for his beliefs or working for Communist causes in other countries, which is where he first used the undercover name 'Tito'.

In 1941, during World War II, the Germans invaded and occupied Yugoslavia. Tito built up a resistance force, the Partisans, and after many struggles they finally chased the Germans out and set up a new Communist state with Tito as leader. The homelands of all six national groups became equal republics in the state. At first Tito ran the government as the Soviet Union ordered, but in 1948 he broke away. His Partisan comrades stood by him and he kept Yugoslavia free from Soviet control. Although the government was still Communist, it gave the people more freedom and let workers and farmers manage their own factories and farms. Tito was eventually made president for life in 1974. ◆

Tokugawa Ieyasu

Japanese ruler
Born 1542 *Died* 1616 aged 74

Tokugawa Ieyasu was born at a time of endless civil wars in Japan. Growing up surrounded by spies, he learned to be tough and cunning. As a young warrior he supported the shogun (warlord) Oda Nobunaga in bringing large areas of Japan under his control. After Nobunaga's assassination Ieyasu married the sister of

▲ *The original jacket design for the first edition of Tolkein's* The Hobbit *(1937).*

Hideyoshi, who was very powerful and controlled a lot of land. Ieyasu promised that if Hideyoshi died he would help his baby son, Hideyori, inherit Hideyoshi's lands. However, Ieyasu broke his word and smashed Hideyori's supporters at the great battle of Sekijahara in 1600. He then took over his opponents' lands and was appointed shogun in 1603. He abdicated two years later but still controlled affairs. Ieyasu founded Edo (now Tokyo), which became Japan's biggest city. His family ruled for over 250 years, bringing economic strength and improved educational standards. After his death a fabulous shrine was built to honour him at Nikko. ◆

> *Think of being uncomfortable as normal and you will never be bothered by it.*
> TOKUGAWA IEYASU

J. R. R. **Tolkien**

South African-born English novelist
Born 1892 *Died* 1973 aged 81

When John Ronald Reuel Tolkien was three years old he and his younger brother returned from South Africa with their mother to live in the countryside around Birmingham, England. His father died before he could join them, and when Tolkien was 12 his mother died too. She left the boys in the care of a priest, Father Francis Morgan, who saw to it that they had a good education.

Tolkien became very interested in old languages and they remained a fascination for him for the rest of his life. He read Classics at Oxford University, and, after serving in the army during World War I, he returned to become a professor there from 1925 to 1959. However, he became most famous for the stories he made up to amuse his children. He invented creatures, like elves and hobbits, with their own languages, and gave them adventures. His first fantasy novel, *The Hobbit*, appeared in 1937, but it took him another 12 years to complete the three volumes of *The Lord of the Rings*. Since then, his books have sold millions of copies and have been read by people all over the world. ◆

Leo **Tolstoy**

Russian novelist
Born *1828* **Died** *1910 aged 82*

Leo Tolstoy was born into one of Russia's most famous noble families. His mother died when he was two and his father when he was eight, so he was brought up by his aunt. He did not go to school but was educated at home by a governess. He later studied at Kazan University, but left before finishing his course.

At the age of 23 he became an artillery officer in the Caucasus and took part in the Crimean War. He wrote his first stories during the war, drawing on his own early life. *Childhood* was published in 1852, followed by *Boyhood and Youth*. After taking part in the defence of Sevastopol, he wrote his famous *Sevastopol Sketches*.

During the 1860s and 1870s he spent much of his time and energy on studying education. He also published a magazine and wrote stories for children. It was during this period, 1863 to 1869, that he wrote *War and Peace*, considered by many to be the greatest novel in the world. It gives a picture of Russia just before and during the war against Napoleon in 1812. Next he worked on *Anna Karenina*, about a married woman's tragic love affair with a soldier. By the time the book was finished, Tolstoy was facing a crisis in his life. He was an aristocrat, but he was beginning to reject his life of luxury for the simple life of a peasant. In spite of his marriage and his writing, he felt he was living selfishly. He developed a new religious philosophy based on peace, love, and a humble life.

Finally, one night he felt that he must get away. He left his home secretly, but died of pneumonia at a railway station just ten days later. ◆

Tomás de **Torquemada**

Head of the Spanish Inquisition from 1483 to 1498
Born *1420* **Died** *1498 aged 78*

Tomás de Torquemada was born in Valladolid in northern Spain, where he later went to university. He then became a Dominican friar. When aged about 32 he was appointed head of the Dominican friars in Segovia. In Segovia he later met Princess Isabella and came to know her well.

▲ *During the Spanish Inquisition, Torquemada became famous for his severity and the harshness of his judgements.*

In 1474 Princess Isabella became Queen of Castile, the largest kingdom in Spain. Isabella was a Catholic Christian, but her subjects included Jews, Muslims, and Christians who had converted from the other religions. Isabella feared these groups. In 1478 an 'Inquisition' was established – a system of law courts which would examine Christians suspected of not being true Christians. At first the inquisition worked badly, so in 1483 Isabella placed Torquemada in charge.

Torquemada reorganized the inquisition, giving it new rules by which to operate. Its trials were often conducted in secret, under torture. Before Torquemada's death the inquisition tried about 100,000 cases and executed over 2000 people. Torquemada also persuaded Isabella to order Jews to become Christians or leave the country: about 50,000 eventually departed. ◆

👁 **see also**
Ferdinand and Isabella

Henri de **Toulouse-Lautrec**

French painter
Born *1864* **Died** *1901 aged 36*

Henri de Toulouse-Lautrec was the son of an aristocrat and as a boy loved sports and horse-riding. However, he had two childhood accidents that damaged the bones in his legs and this left him stunted. (He is sometimes described as a midget, but in fact he grew to be about 1.5 m (5 feet) tall). His large head made him look a grotesque figure, but he accepted his misfortune without bitterness, and never mentioned it except to make a joke about it. His father and uncle were amateur artists, and when he was 21 he was given money to set up his own studio in Paris. He became famous for his pictures of life in dance-halls, theatres, cafés, circuses, and brothels. He was also a brilliant poster designer for many of the stage stars of his time.

▲ *Toulouse-Lautrec made many paintings and drawings of life in the famous Parisian nightclub 'The Moulin Rouge', including this one of the singer Yvette Guilbert.*

Alcohol and venereal disease ruined his health, however. He suffered a breakdown in 1899 and died just two years later. ◆

Toussaint l'Ouverture

Caribbean anti-slavery leader
Born c.1743   **Died** 1803 aged about 60

Pierre Dominique Toussaint's father is said to have been an African chief who was taken as a slave to a sugar plantation in the French colony of St Domingue in the Caribbean. Toussaint was born there. He was clever, and his father helped him to learn to read French and Latin and study mathematics. He was freed from slavery in 1777.

In 1791 the other slaves on the island rebelled against their masters and Toussaint eventually became their commander, turning the rebels into a strong fighting force. By 1798 both the French colonists and the British invaders had been beaten. Toussaint's followers gave him the name 'l'Ouverture', meaning the opener of the way to freedom.

In 1802 the French emperor, Napoleon, sent in his army to recapture Toussaint's country. Toussaint agreed to make peace with the French commander, who promised to do him no harm. The promise was false and Toussaint was sent to prison in France, where he died. His soldiers rose up and defeated the French and renamed their free country Haiti. ◆

Trajan

Roman emperor
Born AD 53   **Died** 117 aged 64

Trajan was born in Spain and served with his father in the army before holding various posts in the running of the provinces of the empire. The Emperor Nerva adopted Trajan as his heir; he became emperor in AD 97 when Nerva died.

The Emperor Trajan then spent most of his reign at war, against the Dacians, Armenians, and Parthians. To mark his victory over the Dacians, Trajan built a huge public square (called a forum) in Rome and the column which is 38 metres high. From top to bottom it is carved with scenes from his military campaigns. Trajan's Column gives us a unique picture of military life, and death, in the Roman Empire, as its carvings show soldiers making camp, marching, and fighting.

Many public works were undertaken during Trajan's reign. He was a popular and respected emperor who commanded the loyalty of his subjects. ◆

👁 **see also**

Hadrian

▼ *This carved detail from Trajan's Column shows Trajan making a sacrifice before the departure of his troops to fight the Dacians in the war of 101–106.*

Anthony **Trollope**

English writer
Born 1815   *Died* 1882 aged 67

Anthony Trollope was a very busy Victorian writer. He wrote 47 novels, and many plays, short stories, and biographies and still had the time to pursue a career as a civil servant in the Post Office! In fact, it was Trollope who helped to introduce pillar boxes for letters in Great Britain. Trollope managed to combine his two jobs by writing a set amount of words every day before going to work.

As a writer, Trollope is best remembered for the *Barsetshire Chronicles*, a series of five novels about church life set in the fictional county of Barset; and *The Pallisers*, a series which explored political life. Trollope's interest in politics was lifelong and he stood unsuccessfully for Parliament in 1867. ◆

▼ *Anthony Trollope worked on his many books in his spare time.*

▲ *Leon Trotsky was one of the most important figures of the Russian Revolution.*

Leon **Trotsky**

One of the leaders of the Russian Revolution
Born 1879   *Died* 1940 aged 60

Lev Davidovich Bronstein was born of Jewish parents on a farm in the Ukraine, part of the Russian empire. He was expelled from university for political activities and was then banished to Siberia when he opposed the tsar's rule. He escaped from there and fled the country under his new name, Trotsky, which he took from one of his prison guards.

Trotsky returned to Russia in 1917 when the tsar had been overthrown. He joined Lenin's Bolshevik Party (later to become known as the Communist Party). He was one of the main organizers of the October Revolution when the Bolsheviks seized power. He then took charge of foreign affairs and defence, and built a new army, the Red Army, which won the bitter Russian civil war of 1918–1921.

Trotsky was a brilliant linguist, writer and speaker, but his impatience and bitter tongue made him many enemies in the Communist Party. After Lenin's death, he was deprived of power by Stalin. In 1927 he was expelled from the party, and two years later was driven out of the USSR. He was murdered with an ice-pick in Mexico on Stalin's orders. ◆

👁 **see also**
Lenin   Stalin

Pierre **Trudeau**

Prime minister of Canada from 1968 to 1984
Born 1919   *Died* 2000 aged 80

Pierre Trudeau became involved in politics when he supported the workers during a miners' strike at Asbestos, Québec, in 1950. In 1965 he was elected to parliament and he became prime minister in 1968. He insisted on the use of both French and English as the two official languages of Canada.

In 1982 he negotiated a new law which meant that Britain no longer had to give formal approval for amendments to the Canadian constitution. The same law also gave Canadians a Charter of Rights and Freedoms, which made sure that all people, including those from minority groups, would be treated fairly. He retired as prime minister in 1984. ◆

Harry S. **Truman**

President of the United States of America from 1945 to 1953
Born 1884   *Died* 1972 aged 88

Harry S. Truman became vice-president of the United

States of America in 1945. However, President Roosevelt died only 83 days later, and Truman suddenly found himself leader of the world's most powerful nation. At this time America was involved in World War II, and Truman took the decision to drop atomic bombs on Hiroshima and Nagasaki in Japan. This killed almost a million people but ended the war with Japan. After that he turned to Europe and provided Marshall Aid to help rebuild countries ravaged by war.

His main aim was to contain the power of the Communists in Europe and Asia. During his two terms of office, Truman helped to create the North Atlantic Treaty Organization (NATO) and led America into the Korean War in 1950. In 1951 he survived an assassination attempt by Puerto Rican nationalists. ◆

👁 **see also**
Roosevelt

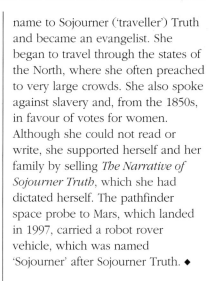

▶ Sojourner Truth's message to her audiences was that as Christians they should oppose slavery.

Sojourner **Truth**

American anti-slavery campaigner
Born c.1797
Died 1883 aged about 86

Sojourner Truth was born into slavery and was originally called Isabella. She was abused as a young woman and between 1810 and 1827 she had at least five children. Then in 1827 she was freed under a New York law that banned slavery. One of her first acts as a free woman was to fight for the release of her youngest son, who had been illegally sold into slavery.

She came to believe that God wanted her to preach His message of love, so in 1843 she changed her name to Sojourner ('traveller') Truth and became an evangelist. She began to travel through the states of the North, where she often preached to very large crowds. She also spoke against slavery and, from the 1850s, in favour of votes for women. Although she could not read or write, she supported herself and her family by selling *The Narrative of Sojourner Truth*, which she had dictated herself. The pathfinder space probe to Mars, which landed in 1997, carried a robot rover vehicle, which was named 'Sojourner' after Sojourner Truth. ◆

👁 **see also**
Douglass   Stowe   Tubman

Ts'ai Lun

Chinese inventor of paper
Born c.50   **Died** 118 aged about 68

Ts'ai Lun is remembered as the man who discovered how to make one of the simplest and most revolutionary of all inventions – paper. He was an important court officer who must have spent much of his working day dealing with the laws, letters, and tax returns which running the government of a country involves. According to the official history of his times, Ts'ai Lun made his discovery in the year 105. The raw materials he used to make the first paper included tree-bark, hemp, rags, and old fishing-nets. Paper made an excellent, smooth surface for elegant Chinese brush-writing and was much cheaper than the other materials that were usually used, such as vellum (soft, scraped leather), silk, or bamboo. The Chinese soon realized that this new invention had many possible uses – such as for writing on, for wrapping things, and for making lanterns and screens. ◆

Harriet **Tubman**

American anti-slavery worker
Born *c.1820*   **Died** *1913 aged about 93*

Harriet Tubman was born into slavery and as a child and young woman she worked under terrible conditions on the slave plantations in the southern states of America. Finally, however, she managed to escape. She made her way north on the 'Underground Railroad' – not a real railway but a famous escape system for runaway slaves. These slaves were taken to Canada or the northern states of America, where slavery was illegal. Escaping slaves were called passengers. The homes they hid in were called stations, and the escape organizers were called conductors.

Harriet Tubman became the most famous 'conductor' of all. Over a period of ten years she helped more than 300 slaves to escape, including her aged parents. She became known as the 'Moses of her people' because, like Moses, she led so many slaves into freedom. She opened schools for ex-slaves, and eventually settled in New York where she opened the Harriet Tubman Home for Aged Negroes. ◆

 see also

Douglass   Stowe   Truth

Jethro **Tull**

English agricultural engineer
Born *1674*   **Died** *1741 aged 66*

Jethro Tull studied at Oxford University and in 1699 qualified as a lawyer. However, the work did not really suit him and he turned to farming instead. To gain experience he travelled widely throughout Europe before settling down to farm on an estate in England.

At that time it was the custom for farmers to sow seed by hand, scattering handfuls as they walked up and down the fields. The crop then had to be weeded by hand. Tull invented a horse-drawn seed drill which sowed the seed in parallel rows. When the weeds appeared they could be removed by a horse-drawn hoe. He described his method in a famous book called *Horse-Hoeing Husbandry* (1731). However, mechanized agriculture was slow to be adopted in England, where labour was then plentiful and cheap, although it quickly became popular in North America where labour was scarce and expensive. ◆

J. M. W. **Turner**

English landscape painter
Born *1775*   **Died** *1851 aged 76*

Joseph Mallord William Turner, the son of a London barber, was an exceptionally talented child. At the age of 14 he became a student at the Royal Academy schools, and at 16 his work was first exhibited to the public.

After a sketching tour in Italy Turner became particularly interested in colour and light. His subject, nearly always landscape, seems to be a fantastic magical world of lighting effects, threatening weather conditions, and mysterious shadows. A friend described his way of working: 'He began by pouring wet paint onto the paper until it was saturated. He poured, he scratched, he scrabbled at it in a kind of frenzy, and the whole thing was chaos – but gradually as if by magic the lovely ship, with all its exquisite detail came into being. By lunch-time it was finished.'

Turner's energy was astonishing. He produced about 500 oil paintings and over 20,000 watercolours and drawings. In his will, he left the

▼ The Fighting Temeraire, *one of Turner's many dramatic works set at sea.*

majority of his paintings and his drawings to the British people; most are in the Tate Gallery, London. ◆

Marie **Tussaud**

French wax modeller
Born *1760*   **Died** *1850 aged 89*

Marie Grosholtz was just six years old when she was taught how to work in wax. Her portraits became so famous that by the time she was 20 she was living in the Palace of Versailles and working as the art teacher to Louis XIV's sister. In 1789 the French Revolution broke out, and during those terrible days Marie was called upon to make models of the severed heads of aristocrats, many of them her friends, after they had been killed by the revolutionaries.

Marie married a French engineer, François Tussaud, and in 1802 she received permission from Napoleon to take her waxwork collection to England. She began making models of important English men and women, as well as of notorious criminals who had been executed. In 1835 she set up a permanent exhibition in London, which still exists today. ◆

Tutankhamun

Ancient Egyptian boy-king
Born *c.1370 BC*
Died *1352 BC aged about 18*

The modern world discovered Tutankhamun, the Egyptian boy-king, in 1922, when the English archaeologist Howard Carter

▶ *The contents of Tutankhamun's tomb contained many works of art, like this solid-gold coffin, which are now displayed in a museum in Cairo, Egypt.*

uncovered his secret tomb. We call Tutankhamun the boy-king because he died young, after reigning for only nine years. He became the pharaoh (god-king) when he was only about ten years old through his marriage to the princess Ankhesenpaaten, who was the daughter of the pharaoh, Akhenaten, and his queen, Nefertiti. We are not sure who his parents were. ◆

Desmond **Tutu**

Archbishop of Cape Town from 1986
Born *1931*

Desmond Mpilo (meaning 'life') Tutu was the son of a primary school headmaster and a domestic servant. He soon discovered what it was like to be black and poor in South Africa. He trained to be a teacher, but in the 1950s the South African government decided that black children should only be given a basic education. Tutu could not accept this decision, so he left teaching to become a priest in the Anglican Church.

In the 1960s and 1970s he and his family spent some time in Britain. They were amazed at the civilized way they were treated compared to their experiences in South Africa. This made him speak out against *apartheid* (the policy of racial separateness and discrimination)

▲ *Desmond Tutu, one of the leading figures in the struggle against apartheid in South Africa.*

when he returned to his own country. In 1975 he became Dean of Johannesburg and could have lived in an area reserved for whites. Instead he chose to live in Soweto, a crowded township of a million black people. In 1984 he was awarded the Nobel Peace Prize for his 'non-violent struggle against apartheid'. ◆

👁 **see also**

de Klerk   Mandela

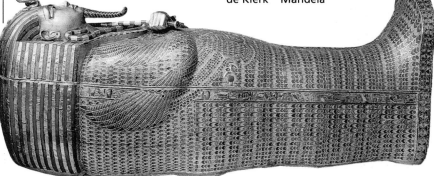

Mark **Twain**

American writer
Born *1835*   **Died** *1910 aged 74*

Mark Twain's real name was Samuel Langhorne Clemens. When he was four, his family moved to the small town of Hannibal on the Mississippi River, where his father opened a grocery store. He spent his childhood watching the giant lumber rafts and the steamboats on the river. When he was 11 his father died, and Sam left school to do odd jobs to earn money for his family.

At 13 he was apprenticed to a printer, and later began writing for local newspapers. Then, for almost four years, he worked as a pilot on the local steamboats; later he remembered those years as the most carefree of his life. After trying his luck next as a gold-miner he became a full-time writer, using the pen-name 'Mark Twain', a phrase from his steamboat days meaning 'two fathoms deep'.

He was a great storyteller and wrote in a brilliantly funny way about the Southern way of life. In *Tom Sawyer* (1876) and *The Adventures of Huckleberry Finn* (1884) he painted a wonderful

▼ *A publisher's advert for Mark Twain's story* Huckleberry Finn *(1884), with an illustration of the novel's leading character.*

MARK TWAIN'S NEW WORK,
"ADVENTURES OF
HUCKLEBERRY FINN"
(Tom Sawyer's Comrade.)
APPEARS FEBRUARY 18th
Prospectuses now ready.
Fine Heliotype of the author in each book.
Agents wanted.   Splendid Terms!
CHARLES L. WEBSTER & CO.
Publishers,
658 BROADWAY, NEW YORK CITY.

picture of life on and around the Mississippi, describing it exactly as the boys in the story would see it. He wrote many other novels and also a book about his travels. ◆

Pope **Urban II**

French pope who launched the First Crusade
Born *c.1042*   **Died** *1099 aged about 57*

Born in north-east France, Urban's original name was Odo de Lagery. He became a monk of the famous monastery at Cluny in France. In 1079 the Abbot of Cluny sent Odo to Rome. The pope, Gregory VII, was impressed by Odo, and made him a cardinal. In 1088 he was elected pope, and took the name Urban II.

A few years before, Muslim Turks from Asia had invaded the Holy Land, and had stopped European pilgrims from visiting the Holy Places known to Jesus. Many Europeans were angry about this, and wanted to do something. In 1095, at Clermont in France, Urban proclaimed a crusade (a word derived from the Spanish 'cruzada', meaning 'marked by the cross'). He appealed for fighting men from Europe to go and reconquer the occupied lands. Several armies set off. Jerusalem was captured from the Muslims on 15 July 1099. Urban died just a few days later. ◆

Rudolph **Valentino**

Italian-born American film actor
Born *1895*   **Died** *1926 aged 31*

Rudolph Valentino was born in Castellaneta, Italy. At 18 he travelled to America, where he

▲ *Rudolph Valentino in a publicity shot for* Son of the Sheik *(1926). His many female fans were devastated by his early death, which was caused by a perforated ulcer.*

worked as a dancer and a film 'extra'. He became a star during the 1920s, acting in films such as *The Sheik* (1921), *Blood and Sand* (1922), and *Son of the Sheik* (1926). He was adored by film fans for his handsome appearance in such romantic roles. His early death attracted thousands of fans to his funeral to mourn the most glamorous leading man of the silent film era. ◆

Cornelius **Vanderbilt**

American businessman
Born *1794*   **Died** *1877 aged 83*

Cornelius Vanderbilt was the son of a poor farmer and boatman in Port Richmond, New York. He left school at 11 and when he was 16 he borrowed money to buy a ferry boat. It was the first of a long series of business operations which would make him one of the richest men in the world.

Eventually Vanderbilt ran a very profitable steamship company. By 1846 he was a millionaire. Then, at the age of 70, he started to buy railroad companies, and made even more money. When he died he had amassed a fortune of 100 million dollars.

Vanderbilt is remembered as an example of the American dream. Americans have always proudly believed that people in their country can start from nothing and, by working hard, become rich and prosperous. Cornelius Vanderbilt was one of the first people to demonstrate this. ◆

Anthony **van Dyck**

Flemish painter
Born *1599*   **Died** *1641 aged 42*

Anthony van Dyck was a boy genius. He painted brilliant portraits while he was still in his mid-teens and by the time he was 20 he was the best painter in Flanders, apart from the great Rubens. He worked as Rubens' assistant for two years, and then branched out, travelling to England and then Italy, where he lived from 1621 to 1628.

After a four-year stay in Antwerp, his home town, he settled in England in 1632 as court painter to King Charles I, who knighted him. Charles was a great art lover and van Dyck painted many portraits of him and his family and also of his courtiers. These paintings were so elegant, poised, and dashing that they set a standard for 'society' portraiture for generations; Gainsborough was deeply influenced by them more than a century later. Van Dyck also painted religious scenes and

landscapes, but it is as a portraitist that he ranks among the greatest painters of all time. ◆

👁 **see also**
Gainsborough   Rubens

Jan **van Eyck**

Flemish painter
Born c. *1390*
Died *1441 aged about 50*

Jan van Eyck was one of the greatest European painters of his time. He spent most of his career in Bruges in Belgium, where he worked for Philip the Good,

Duke of Burgundy. Philip employed him on secret diplomatic missions as well as for his artistic skills. For centuries van Eyck was regarded as the inventor of oil painting. We know that it was in fact used before his time, but he was certainly one of the first to master the technique. His craftsmanship was superb and he created effects of glowing colour and exquisite detail that are still amazing to see. Because he showed the potential of oil paint so brilliantly, van Eyck is considered to be one of the most important figures in European art. ◆

▼ *Jan van Eyck's* The Arnolfini Marriage *(1434), a fine example of his skill in handling oil paint.*

Vincent **Van Gogh**

Dutch painter
Born 1853   Died 1890 aged 37

The son of a pastor (minister of a Protestant church), Vincent Van Gogh was taught that a meaningful life meant devoting oneself to others. He became deeply religious, and trained to be a missionary. However, his moody personality prevented him from being successful in the Church or in other jobs that he tried.

Van Gogh then taught himself to draw and paint. His dark and sombre early paintings show the miserable lives of the working poor. Later he went to France, where he experimented with clear, bright colours. His technique of excited, bold brushstrokes shows deep emotion and a sort of frenzy even when the subject itself is peaceful. His pictures are of the ordinary things in life: his bedroom, a chair, a bunch of sunflowers. He rarely painted any grand subjects.

Van Gogh spent the last two years of his life in southern France. He was very busy but often depressed and suffered periods of insanity; he cut off one of his own ears during one such crisis. After only ten years of painting, he committed suicide. He died poverty-stricken, having sold only one painting during his lifetime. ◆

▼ *Van Gogh's painting of* The Church at Auvers-sur-Oise *(1890).*

Ralph **Vaughan Williams**

English composer
Born 1872   Died 1958 aged 85

Ralph Vaughan Williams's family was wealthy and able to support him through an unusually long period of study at the Royal College of Music, Cambridge University, Berlin, and Paris. Although he started to compose when he was six, he developed very slowly. It was only in 1903, when he began to collect and study British folk-song, that his music began to find its own special voice. His music includes opera, choral works, concertos, chamber music, songs, and a series of nine important symphonies. He also wrote music for films, one of which, *Scott of the Antarctic*, became the basis for his Seventh Symphony (*Sinfonia Antarctica*). ◆

Diego **Velázquez**

Spanish painter
Born 1599   Died 1660 aged 61

Diego Velázquez, born in Seville, Spain, had one of the most continuously successful careers in the history of art. He produced masterpieces when he was still in his teens. When he was 24 he painted a portrait of King Philip IV of Spain. Philip was so impressed that he declared that from then on no other artist would be allowed to paint him.

Philip honoured Velázquez with various court posts in Madrid. These jobs only left Velázquez time to paint about three pictures a year. However, these include some of the finest portraits in the world. He depicted his subjects with great sympathy, whether he was portraying king or commoner. Even the wretched court fools kept to amuse the king were given a sense of dignity in Velázquez's portraits. ◆

Giuseppe **Verdi**

Italian composer
Born *1813*   **Died** *1901 aged 87*

The wonderful thing about Giuseppe Verdi is that the older he grew, the greater his music became. He wrote his last operas, *Otello* and *Falstaff*, considered to be his masterpieces, between the ages of 74 and 80, when most people have long been retired.

Verdi's parents were poor and his musical education was paid for by a neighbour, a wealthy merchant. Even so, he failed to gain entry to the Milan Conservatory of Music and had to study privately. His first opera, *Oberto*, was quite successful and he was asked to write more. But tragedy struck: his wife and two young children died within two months of each other. Verdi was heartbroken and vowed never to write another note.

▼ *A caricature of the famous Italian composer Giuseppe Verdi.*

Fortunately, he was tempted to write a new opera, *Nabucco*, and its success launched his career as Italy's most famous composer. His most popular operas include *Rigoletto* (1851), *La Traviata* (1853), and *Aida* (1871). They are loved for their bold tunes and the wonderful way he can make his characters come alive. Verdi also wrote a String Quartet (1873) and a famous Requiem (1874). ◆

Jan **Vermeer**

Dutch painter
Born *1632*   **Died** *1675 aged 43*

Not very much is known about Jan Vermeer's life. His father kept an inn, and Jan Vermeer may have worked there. He married at 21 and had 11 children. He became head of the Painters' Guild twice, and was well respected. But he ran up debts, particularly to his baker, to whom he gave two paintings in return for credit. After his death, his wife tried to buy back the paintings, but she also became bankrupt.

Vermeer did not become famous until 200 years after his death, when his paintings were recognized as masterpieces. He worked extremely slowly and produced only about 40 paintings. He painted Dutch people doing ordinary domestic jobs, but he handled light and colour so cleverly that his figures are solid and strong, yet serene and gentle. ◆

Jules **Verne**

French novelist
Born *1828*   **Died** *1905 aged 77*

Jules Verne used his knowledge of geography and science to give his exciting and imaginative

▲ *Jules Verne worked for a time writing the words for operas before turning to science fiction novels such as* Twenty Thousand Leagues Under the Sea, *from which this illustration is taken.*

stories a backdrop of realistic detail. What makes his novels even more intriguing is that in them he actually anticipated future scientific developments; he forecast the invention of aeroplanes, submarines, television, guided missiles, and even space satellites!

His first book, *Five Weeks in a Balloon* (1863), started life as a non-fiction essay about an exploration of Africa in a balloon but he rewrote it as an imaginative story at the suggestion of his publisher. Its instant success inspired Verne to write more 'science fiction' and adventure novels. Among the most famous are *Journey to the Centre of the Earth* (1864), *Twenty Thousand Leagues Under the Sea* (1869), and *Around the World in Eighty Days* (1873), which recounts the travels of Phileas Fogg. ◆

Paolo **Veronese**

Italian painter
Born *1528*   **Died** *1588 aged 60*

Paolo Veronese's real surname was Caliari. He was born in Verona (from which he gets his nickname), but he spent almost all his working life in Venice. There he ranked with Tintoretto as the leading painter at the end of the 16th century. This was a golden period in Venice's history, when the city grew rich as one of the world's most important trading centres.

Veronese's paintings are wonderfully colourful and decorative, reflecting Venice's success and material splendour. He tended to treat every subject like a glorious pageant and this got him into trouble with the religious authorities. They objected to what they considered irrelevant 'vulgar' figures in a painting he had done of *The Last Supper*. Veronese

▼ *In spite of his problems with Church authorities, Veronese, who painted this religious scene, was a devout Catholic.*

cleverly got round the problem by simply changing the title to *The Feast in the House of Levi* – the title of a less solemn dining scene from the Bible. ◆

👁 **see also**

Tintoretto

Hendrik **Verwoerd**

Prime minister of South Africa from 1958 to 1966
Born *1901*   **Died** *1966 aged 65*

Hendrik Verwoerd was the man who developed the apartheid (separation by race) system which enslaved South Africa's black population. Under apartheid black people were forced to live separately from whites and could only get low-paid jobs. Marriage between blacks and whites was forbidden.

Verwoerd was a university teacher and taught in Germany for a while. During World War II he edited a newspaper and was on the side of the Nazis. In 1950 he became South Africa's minister of native affairs, and it was then that he organized the apartheid policy. He became prime minister in 1958. When the other Commonwealth countries objected to apartheid he took South Africa out of the Commonwealth in 1961. He also introduced harsh measures to silence black opposition, including the banning of the African National Congress. In 1966 he was assassinated in parliament. ◆

👁 **see also**

De Klerk   Luthuli   Mandela

Andreas **Vesalius**

Belgian doctor, surgeon, and author
Born *1514*   **Died** *1564 aged 49*

Andreas Vesalius was a professor at Padua University, Italy, where he lectured in surgery. He had to teach anatomy and this was done using textbooks written by Galen, a Greek doctor who had lived over 1000 years earlier. Vesalius dissected many dead human bodies and realized that Galen's books were inaccurate. He thought they were probably based on animals rather than humans. Vesalius abandoned Galen's books and taught anatomy from his own knowledge of dissection.

In 1543 he published *On the Structure of the Human Body*, a remarkable set of anatomy textbooks, with drawings by a pupil of the painter Titian. Vesalius became famous, and was appointed court doctor to the Holy Roman Emperor, Charles V, and his son, Philip II of Spain. However, he was

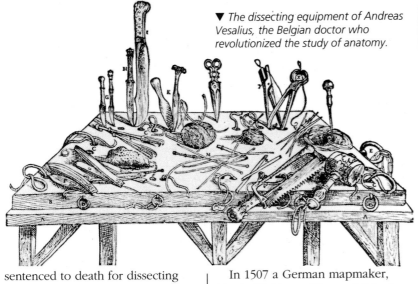

▼ *The dissecting equipment of Andreas Vesalius, the Belgian doctor who revolutionized the study of anatomy.*

sentenced to death for dissecting human bodies (which was then illegal). The sentence was lifted, provided he made a pilgrimage to Jerusalem. He made the journey but unfortunately died while on the way home. ◆

see also

Galen

Amerigo **Vespucci**

Italian explorer
Born 1451   Died 1512 aged 61

Amerigo Vespucci was an Italian merchant who settled in Spain as an agent for the Medici Bank. He was the contractor who organized the supplies for Christopher Columbus for his voyages to the west. In due course, Vespucci became chief navigator for the Medici Bank, making maps of the lands discovered by Columbus and other explorers.

As a navigator, Vespucci sailed across the Atlantic Ocean from Europe, and in 1501–1502 he explored the South American coast as far south as the Río de la Plata. It was then that he realized he was looking at another continent, not at parts of Asia as Columbus had believed.

In 1507 a German mapmaker, Martin Waldseemüller, published a map in which the newly discovered lands to the west were given a name. That name, he said, should be America, because he believed Amerigo had discovered it. In fact, Vespucci did not discover America, but he was one of the first people to realize it might be a separate continent and not part of Asia. ◆

see also

Columbus

Victor Emmanuel II

The first king of Italy from 1861 to 1878
Born 1820   Died 1878 aged 58

Victor Emmanuel II succeeded his father as king of the state of Sardinia-Piedmont in 1849. At that time Italy was divided into several small separate states. Through the middle years of the 19th century, politicians worked to create a united Italy from these states.

Victor Emmanuel had the imagination to see that the future for Italy lay with more democratic forms of government than there were at the time. He appointed Camillo Cavour as prime minister of Piedmont in 1852. They were both central figures in the period of political unrest that followed. Their vision of a united and liberated Italy, free from foreign rule and intervention, resulted in many battles. They enlisted the help of Giuseppe Garibaldi to help defeat the Austrians in northern Italy (with Napoleon III's France as their ally). Several years later, Garibaldi's forces also captured Sicily and Naples, and handed over the whole of southern Italy to Victor Emmanuel. A vote was taken to accept him as king and in 1861 Victor Emmanuel became the first king of a united Italy. Only the Vatican, a small state ruled by the pope, stayed independent, and remains so to this day. In 1870 Victor Emmanuel II made Rome his capital. ◆

see also

Cavour   Garibaldi

▼ *A cartoon caricature of Victor Emmanuel II from the English magazine* Vanity Fair *in 1870.*

Victoria

Queen of the United Kingdom from 1837 to 1901
Born *1819*   **Died** *1901 aged 81*

As a child, Victoria was lively and strong-willed. She could be moody, and had firm likes and dislikes, but she was sensible too. She was very interested in new inventions: she enjoyed travelling on some of the early railways, and photography fascinated her. She was musical and could draw well.

In spite of the fact that she was only 18 when she became queen, Victoria clearly had a clever understanding of the British political system. Although the real ruling was done by parliament, she succeeded in exerting some influence. At 21 she married her German cousin, Prince Albert. The queen was devoted to her 'dearest Albert', and they had nine children together. When Albert died suddenly of typhoid in 1861, Victoria was desperately unhappy. She refused to appear in public for some years, and wore black for the rest of her life. It was the prime minister, Benjamin Disraeli, whose tactful, flattering ways she liked, who finally managed to coax her into public life again.

During Victoria's 63-year reign, the longest in British history, the British Empire grew to a vast size, making Britain the richest country in the world. Her popularity now at its height, her Golden and Diamond Jubilees (marking 50 and 60 years on the throne respectively) were causes for huge celebrations. ◆

👁 **see also**

Disraeli   Gladstone

◀ During the Victorian age, as the 19th century is often known, Britain was one of the most powerful nations in the world. Its queen, Victoria, was a strong figurehead for the country's success. She was also Empress of India.

Pancho **Villa**

Mexican bandit and freedom fighter
Born *1877*   **Died** *1923 aged 46*

Imagine a gang of Mexican bandits galloping across a dusty plain – guns slung across their backs, bullets in cross-belts on their chests, sombreros hanging behind by their straps. That was Pancho Villa and his band.

Even Villa's early life is like a film script. It is said that as a young man he killed his boss's son because he assaulted his sister, and had to escape into the mountains.

Revolutions and governments came and went in Mexico at the turn of the century. Villa sometimes sided with the revolutionaries and sometimes fell out with them. Miraculously he stayed alive, even when he killed a number of Americans and President Wilson sent an army after him.

Eventually he made peace with the Mexican Government, and he was allowed to settle down as a farmer. Unfortunately, after a few years his luck ran out and he was assassinated by one of his old enemies. ◆

Virgil

Ancient Roman poet
Born *70 BC*   **Died** *19 BC aged 50*

Virgil was born near Mantua in Italy. Although his parents were not rich, he had a good education in Cremona, Milan, and Rome. He then returned to his family farm to write. Among his important poems are the series of poems called the *Eclogues* which are about the countryside and its people, and the series called the *Georgics* which are about farming.

Virgil's most important work is the epic poem (poem-story) called the *Aeneid* written at the request of the Emperor Augustus. It tells of the mythical hero Aeneas and his escape from the burning city of Troy, his adventures on his journey across the sea to Carthage and then to Italy, and his foundation of the city of Lavinium, south of Rome.

Although Virgil devoted the last 11 years of his life to writing the *Aeneid*, he did not finish it and ordered that the manuscript should be burnt after his death. However, the Emperor Augustus ordered it to be published. ◆

see also

Augustus

Vitruvius

Roman architect and writer on architecture
Lived during the 1st century BC

Marcus Vitruvius Pollio, an official architect (at one time in the service of Julius Caesar), was not well-known in his own lifetime. He became famous because of the ten books on architecture that he wrote in his old age and dedicated to Caesar Augustus. These books contain the only accounts of the rules that had guided Greek and Roman architects and builders. They describe the kind of skills that an architect in public service was then expected to have, including construction, water-engineering, and the control of public health.

His descriptions, particularly of measurement and ornament, were important to Italian architects of the 15th and 16th centuries (like Palladio), who wished to revive the architecture of Ancient Rome. ◆

see also

Palladio

Antonio **Vivaldi**

Italian composer
Born 1678   Died 1741 aged 63

Little is known of Antonio Vivaldi's early life, except that he was born in Venice and taught to play the violin by his father. He then trained as a priest and was ordained in 1703. In the same year he began to teach music at the Conservatorio della Pietà in Venice. The Conservatorio was an orphanage for girls which had a famous choir and orchestra. Vivaldi helped train the girls and wrote music for them to play. As his fame spread throughout Italy, he spent more and more time away from the Conservatorio and finally left there in 1738.

Vivaldi composed all kinds of music, including over 40 operas, but he is most famous for his concertos; he wrote over 500, nearly half for solo violin. He also wrote concertos for flute, oboe, bassoon, recorder, and mandolin. Some have descriptive titles, such as *The Four Seasons* and *The Hunt*, and their music cleverly conjures up the appropriate atmosphere. ◆

▼ This painting from 1723, by Francois Morellon La Cave, is the only known portrait of the composer Antonio Vivaldi.

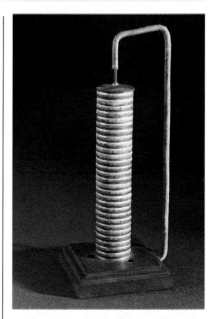

▲ The voltaic pile (the first electric cell) invented by Italian physicist Alessandro Volta. The volt (unit of electromotive force) is named after him.

Alessandro **Volta**

Italian inventor of the first battery
Born 1745   Died 1827 aged 82

A friend of Alessandro Volta's, a scientist called Luigi Galvani, wrote telling him about a puzzling experiment that he had done: he had hung a piece of frog muscle on a brass hook, and when the muscle came in contact with some iron wire it twitched. Some people thought that the muscle must be producing its own 'animal electricity', but Volta proved that it was the contact of the brass and the iron that produced the electricity and made the muscle twitch. Volta did many experiments with different metals. He made a pile of coins of two different metals, separated the coins with card soaked in salt solution and produced an electric current. This was the first battery. ◆

see also

Galvani

Voltaire

French writer and philosopher
Born *1694* **Died** *1778 aged 83*

The son of a wealthy lawyer, Voltaire was born Francois-Marie Arouet. In 1718 he adopted the pen-name Voltaire, and started to write plays and witty, hard-hitting articles. He was imprisoned for a year for criticizing the power of the French monarchy and the Church. In 1726 he was exiled to England, and after returning, he unfavourably compared British freedom with the censorship of France and he was finally chased out of Paris in 1734. In 1754 he went to Switzerland, where he spent the rest of his life. He wrote his famous novel *Candide* there in 1758. This describes the adventures of an innocent young man who believes that life is always for the best. With everything around him getting steadily worse, he finally decides that it is, after all, quite a dangerous world. ♦

◀ *Voltaire was persecuted for his belief that people had a right to think what they liked.*

Richard **Wagner**

German composer
Born *1813* **Died** *1883 aged 69*

Richard Wagner was brought up in a theatrical family and until the age of 15 he seemed more likely to become a playwright than a composer. In the end he did both, by writing the words and music for his own operas.

Wagner studied music at Leipzig University, but he really began to learn his trade when he worked in various German opera-houses. His own first attempts at opera failed. Then *Rienzi* and *The Flying Dutchman* were successful and his luck changed.

Wagner was not content with ordinary opera. He wanted something better, something that would combine all the arts into a music drama. In 1853 he began to write *The Ring of the Nibelungs*, a cycle (series) of four music dramas based on German legends.

He completed it in 1874. This magnificent production confirmed Wagner as one of the greatest musical geniuses the world has ever known. Wagner was as passionately interested in theatre as he was in music. In 1876 he opened his own opera house in Bayreuth, Germany, and it was here that the first performance of *The Ring of the Nibelings* took place. ♦

◀ *Derek Walcott collecting his Nobel Prize in December 1992.*

Derek **Walcott**

West Indian poet
Born *1930*

Derek Walcott was born in St Lucia and later went to the University of the West Indies. He then lived in Trinidad, founding a theatre workshop and writing plays which often combined singing with storytelling and dancing. He also wrote poetry which experimented with different types of English, including local dialect. Walcott was always fascinated by the ancient Greek writer Homer, finding many similarities between his descriptions of the Greek islands and the different islands of the Caribbean today. This influence found its way into Walcott's poem 'Omeros' (1989) and his own version of Homer's *The Odyssey*, both of which won him much fame. In 1992 Walcott was awarded the Nobel Prize for Literature – the greatest honour any writer can receive. ◆

👁 **see also**
Homer

Lech **Walesa**

Polish trade union leader, and president of Poland from 1991 to 1995
Born 1943

Lech Walesa started work as an electrician in the shipyards in Gdansk, Poland, in 1966. He soon became involved in protests against the Communist government's treatment of workers, and in 1976 he was sacked for his activities. In 1980 workers went on strike for higher wages and Walesa joined those who were occupying the yards. In the same year they created a new, independent trade union called Solidarity and 10 million workers throughout Poland registered to join.

The Communist government was alarmed at what was happening. Solidarity was banned and Walesa detained for nearly a year. He continued to fight for workers' rights and in 1983 was awarded the Nobel Peace Prize. Eventually the government gave way and Solidarity became legal again in 1989. The trade union became a political party and Walesa, as its leader, won a landslide victory against the Communists in the free presidential elections of 1990. ◆

Robert **Walpole**

First prime minister of Britain
Born 1676   Died 1745 aged 68

Robert Walpole became a member of parliament in 1701. Although he was briefly imprisoned in the Tower of London in 1712 for taking bribes, his hard work and attention to detail, and the support he received from King George I, enabled him to rise to a position of great influence. In 1721 he became first lord of the treasury and chancellor of the exchequer and so was the king's chief minister.

His policy of avoiding foreign wars and so keeping taxes down helped him keep power; so did his tactic of giving well-paid jobs as rewards to his own supporters. But his enemies attacked him for this type of corruption, and he became less popular. Finally in 1742 he was forced to resign.

The job of prime minister did not exist before Walpole. He helped create it by taking on the major responsibility for getting things done in the House of Commons. From Walpole's time onwards, the practice of having one chief (prime) minister continued, just as it does today. ◆

Andy **Warhol**

American artist
Born 1928   Died 1987 aged 59

Andy Warhol was the son of Czech immigrants to America; his original name was Andrew Warhola. In the 1950s he was a highly successful commercial artist, winning prizes for his shoe advertisements and earning huge sums. Then, in 1962, he became an overnight sensation when he exhibited pictures of Campbell's Soup cans and was hailed as a leader of Pop Art, which took its subjects from the worlds of advertising, packaging, and television. He produced his pictures by the commercial process of silk-screen printing, which meant they could be duplicated as many times as he wanted, with variations of colour if required. His fame grew rapidly with brightly coloured portraits of Marilyn Monroe and other celebrities. He also made films, often with a strong documentary feel like *Chelsea Girls* (1966) and wrote books, including *Popism* (1980). When he died he left a colossal fortune, but opinions on him are divided. To some he was a genius, to others merely a brilliant con-man. ◆

▼ *Andy Warhol first made his name with paintings of commercial products such as Campbell's Soup cans.*

Booker T. **Washington**

Founder of Tuskegee Institute, a famous college for black Americans
Born 1856   Died 1915 aged 59

When Booker Taliaferro Washington was nine years old, slavery in America was abolished. He had been a house servant, but he could read and wanted to teach. When he was 16 he travelled 500 miles with almost no money to a school for black teachers. To pay for their studies, all the students worked. Washington cleaned the school. Later, he started a college for black students at Tuskegee, Alabama. The students themselves built most of it and Washington persuaded some rich White Americans to give donations.

In a speech in 1895, Washington said that blacks and whites could be separate like fingers, but that they could work together like a hand. Some black leaders disagreed, but at that time Washington thought black people needed education and jobs more than civil rights. ◆

George **Washington**

The first president of the United States of America
Born 1732   Died 1799 aged 67

George Washington did not have much schooling, but he was always very practical. At 14 he helped to survey some frontier land. A year later he had his own surveying business, and in 1752 he inherited his brother's land.

Britain and France were then rivals, both owning colonies and both trying to control North America. As a soldier in the British army, Washington fought against the French for five years, and his exploits made him well known in Virginia, the British colony where he was born.

After the war, Washington settled down to be a farmer on his Mount Vernon plantation. However, he gradually came to believe that the American colonists had to fight for freedom from Britain. In 1775 he was made commander-in-chief of the colonists' army, and they began to fight what became known as the American Revolution (War of Independence).

Washington's perseverance and grit kept the rebels going. Often his troops were famished and sometimes they went barefoot in the snow. In 1783, after the war had been won, Washington went back to Mount Vernon. Although he was a national hero, he did not want public office.

Nevertheless, in 1789 he was unanimously elected the first president of the United States. He accepted the job, and his re-election in 1792, but he refused a third term. America's capital city was named in his honour. ◆

▼ *This painting shows George Washington (standing, left) and his troops crossing the River Delaware as they flee from the British after the battle of Whiteplains in 1776 during the American Revolution.*

Robert **Watson-Watt**

Scottish inventor of radar
Born 1892   Died 1973 aged 81

During World War I Robert Watson-Watt worked as a weather forecaster. He noticed that when there were thunderstorms about you could hear crackles on the radio. He wondered whether it might be possible to use these crackles to find out where the thunderstorms were.

In the years just before World War II, the British government asked Watson-Watt to find out whether it would be possible to use a beam of radio waves to heat up an enemy aeroplane so much that its bombs would explode in the air (rather as we now use microwaves to heat things in microwave ovens). He quickly proved that it would be impossible, but while doing the necessary sums he realized that a narrow beam of radio waves would bounce off an aeroplane. Thinking back to the crackles on the radio he devised a way of using the reflected waves from an aeroplane to find out how far away and in which direction that aeroplane was. Thus began the development of radar (radio detection and ranging). ◆

James **Watt**

Scottish designer of a new steam-engine
Born 1736   Died 1819 aged 83

Having trained as a mathematical instrument-maker, James Watt was given a model of Thomas Newcomen's steam-engine to repair. He studied the model carefully. It was clearly a clever idea to use steam pressure to drive an engine, but Newcomen's design did not work well; it was very inefficient and wasted a lot of fuel. Watt began to make improvements, which, over the next ten years, made the steam-engine much more effective. Then in 1775 he went into partnership with Matthew Boulton, a businessman, and began manufacturing steam-engines.

▲ Jean-Antoine Watteau's The Shepherd, *which is typical of the paintings that made him famous.*

▲ *A model of James Watt's design for a steam-engine.*

Watt's steam-engines began to transform British industry. Iron manufacturers used them to drive the great hammers which crushed the iron. The textile industry used the engine to power the new machinery invented by Richard Arkwright. In coal-mining, men and women no longer had to carry the coal to the surface in sacks as it could be lifted up by winding-gear powered by the Watt engine.

So although Watt did not invent the steam-engine it was because of his improvements that it became so effective. ◆

👁 **see also**
Arkwright   Newcomen   Stephenson

Jean-Antoine **Watteau**

French painter
Born 1684   Died 1721 aged 36

Jean-Antoine Watteau was the most important French painter of the early 18th century. He specialized in scenes called *fêtes galantes* (which can be translated as 'scenes of gallantry' or 'courtship parties'). They showed beautifully dressed young people idling away their time in dreamy, romantic settings. His style was exquisitely graceful and charming; it set the tone for the light-hearted approach followed by many 18th-century French artists. However, Watteau was not simply a frivolous painter. His pictures have an underlying feeling of sadness, for the people in them seem to realize that all earthly pleasure is short-lived. Watteau himself was cruelly aware that life is short, for he died young of tuberculosis. ◆

John **Wayne**

American film actor
Born 1907   Died 1979 aged 72

Marion Morrison worked behind the scenes in film studios before taking small acting parts, first under the name of 'Duke' Morrison and then from 1930 as John Wayne. His first leading role came in the western film *Stagecoach* (1939), and he went on to become the most famous star of westerns.

He also starred in war films like *Sands of Iwo Jima* (1950), and directed two films in the 1960s. His tough patriotic roles made him a national hero for many American film fans. In total, he made more than 175 films. He finally achieved Oscar success for his leading role in *True Grit* (1969). ◆

Josiah **Wedgwood**

English founder of the Wedgwood pottery factory
Born *1730*   **Died** *1795 aged 64*

The Wedgwood pottery firm founded by Josiah Wedgwood in 1759 still makes plates, bowls, cups, and saucers today. It is especially famous for its blue pottery ornaments, with delicate white patterns and scenes laid on the top.

▲ *Josiah Wedgwood developed the style of pottery using white figures in relief on a blue background, known as 'Jaspar ware', which is now world-famous.*

Josiah Wedgwood was born into a family who owned a pottery factory, and at the age of nine he began his career as a potter. He became an expert at the job and invented better materials and methods for producing top-class pottery. In 1759 he set up his own factory and became famous for a cream-coloured table service, called Queen's ware, that he made for King George III's wife, Queen Charlotte.

Josiah Wedgwood's grandson was the famous scientist Charles Darwin. ◆

👁 **see also**

Darwin

Chaim **Weizmann**

Russian-born first president of Israel
Born *1874*   **Died** *1952 aged 77*

At school in Russia, Chaim Weizmann became interested in science. He was extremely able but laws against Jews made entry into university difficult so he left Russia to finish his education. Manchester University offered him a job and he settled in England. During World War I he worked in a laboratory producing vital chemicals for explosives.

Weizmann believed passionately in Zion, an independent homeland for Jews in Palestine. Britain announced backing for the idea (the Balfour Declaration, 1917) and Weizmann travelled the world seeking the support of other nations. He became leader of a political group known as the Zionists.

After World War II the British governed Palestine and some Jews began a campaign of terror against them. Weizmann condemned this, and the Zionists dismissed him as their leader. But in the end Weizmann was needed to persuade the Americans to support a Jewish nation. In 1948 the nation was born and called Israel. Weizmann was elected its first president. ◆

Orson **Welles**

American film actor and director
Born *1915*   **Died** *1985 aged 70*

As a young actor Orson Welles became famous in 1938 for presenting a radio play about invaders from Mars as if it were a real newsflash. People listening to *The War of the Worlds* were terrified and thousands of them fled in panic. Welles had to apologize.

A few years later, Welles went to Hollywood to make his masterpiece of film direction, *Citizen Kane* (1941), in which he also starred as a selfish millionaire newspaper-owner. The new techniques he used for combining sound and pictures in this and other films, including *The Magnificent Ambersons* (1942), *Macbeth* (1948), and *Touch of Evil* (1958), inspired many other film directors. ◆

▼ Citizen Kane, *directed by and starring Orson Welles, is regarded by many as his greatest film.*

Duke of **Wellington**

One of England's greatest generals, and prime minister from 1828 to 1830
Born 1769   Died 1852 aged 83

Arthur Wellesley was born in Dublin, Ireland. He joined the army at the age of 18 and served in India for eight years, where he won a number of battles and became a major-general.

But it was in Spain and Portugal that he won his great reputation (for which he was made Duke of Wellington), during the Peninsular War against Napoleon's French armies. In 1812 and in 1813 the English attacked, with support from the Portuguese and Spanish troops, driving the French out of Spain and back into France.

When Napoleon escaped from Elba, Wellington lead the allied armies against him. At the battle of Waterloo in 1815, Wellington's troops defeated the French again.

After Waterloo Wellington continued to serve his country, holding many positions in government, including that of prime minister from 1828 to 1830. For a time he was unpopular because he did not want to give the vote to more people, fearing that it might lead to revolution as in France. But by the end of his long life most people had come to admire him. ◆

see also
Napoleon I

H. G. **Wells**

English novelist
Born 1866   Died 1946 aged 79

Herbert George Wells left school at 14 in order to train as a shopkeeper before deciding to go to university and become a teacher.

▲ *John Wesley holding a service during a storm while travelling to America.*

Then, after much hard work and continuing poverty, he became well-known as a novelist of science fiction. In his books he described air and submarine travel long before anyone believed such journeys were remotely possible. Always restlessly energetic, Wells also wrote his massive *An Outline of History* (1920) as well as popular works about science and politics. One of the best-known people of his time, Wells interviewed famous political leaders and was always ready with an opinion on world events. But it is as a novelist he is best remembered. *The Time Machine* (1895) and *The Invisible Man* (1897) have remained very popular and have also proved to be particular favourites with many film-makers. ◆

see also
Verne

John **Wesley**

English Christian evangelist who founded the Methodist Church
Born 1703   Died 1791 aged 88

John Wesley was the son and grandson of clergymen. Not surprisingly, he too chose to enter the Church and was ordained as a priest in 1728. With his brother, Charles, he formed a group of men who tried to lead methodical lives, praying and reading the Bible together, and going to church regularly. They were nicknamed 'methodists'.

In 1738 Wesley had an experience that changed his life. At a gospel meeting he felt his heart 'strangely warmed' and he knew that he was 'saved' by Jesus. From then on he committed himself to changing the lives of ordinary people through God's love. For 50 years he travelled all over England, holding services and preaching. Sometimes his meetings were held in churches, but often in fields and market-places. He organized 'methodist' societies and used ordinary people as preachers.

Although Wesley originally wanted to remain loyal to the Church of England, a split came in 1784 when Wesley broke Church rules by ordaining a group of Methodist preachers. Reluctantly Wesley watched his movement grow into a separate Church. ◆

Walt **Whitman**

American poet
Born 1819   Died 1892 aged 72

Walt Whitman was born on
Long Island, New York. He
was the third of eight children and
was five years old when his family
moved to Brooklyn.

Between 1838 and 1850, Whitman
took up a series of jobs including
teaching journalism and newspaper
editing. In 1855 he published *Leaves
of Grass*, a book of 12 poems.
During the next five years Whitman
revised this and wrote further
poems. By the third edition of
Leaves of Grass, there were over
130 poems in the book. This is
now regarded as one of the most
important books in American
literary history and Whitman is
known as the greatest American
poet of the 19th century.

During the American Civil War,
Whitman worked as a volunteer
nurse in Washington. His wartime
experiences formed the basis of his
poems printed in *Drum Taps* and
Sequel to Drum Taps.

In 1873 Whitman suffered a stroke
that paralysed him. He moved to
Camden, New Jersey, where he
lived by printing, writing, and
through donations from admirers. ◆

Frank **Whittle**

English inventor of the jet engine
Born 1907   Died 1996 aged 89

In 1927, as a 20-year-old flight
cadet studying at the Royal Air
Force College, Frank Whittle wrote
a paper on 'Future Developments in
Aircraft Design'. He suggested that
aeroplanes would soon be flying
at more than 800 km/h (the fastest
then was 300 km/h), at great
heights, and with jet engines rather
than propellers.

▲ *Frank Whittle's jet engine (above)
proved to be a great success when it
was tested in the aeroplane Gloster
E28/39 (top) in 1941.*

In 1929, Whittle tried to persuade
the Air Ministry that jet propulsion
was possible. His engine would
burn cheap fuel oil; the gases
produced would turn turbine
blades as they rushed out, and the
force of the gases would drive the
plane forward. However, the Air
Ministry was not interested, so
Whittle went back to flying.

Later, Whittle started a company
called Power Jets Ltd. The RAF let
him work full-time on his engine,
and it was tried, on the ground, on
12 April 1937. A special aeroplane,
the Gloster E28/39, was designed
to take the engine, and on 15
May 1941 it flew for the first time,
perfectly.

As Whittle had predicted, the jet
engine was more efficient at high
speeds and great altitudes, and by
1944 Power Jets Ltd. was producing
the first jet fighter. Whittle's jet
engine went on to power most
modern aeroplanes. ◆

William **Wilberforce**

*English leader of the campaign to end
slavery in the British empire*
Born 1759   Died 1833 aged 73

William Wilberforce was M.P.
for Hull from the age of 21.
His life's work began when he met
John Newton, the captain of a slave
ship, who had realized how wrong
it was to buy and sell human
beings. From 1785, Wilberforce
campaigned to stop the slave trade.
In 1807 parliament passed a law to
abolish it. But employers in the
West Indies still wanted slaves, and
the trade continued secretly. So
Wilberforce and his supporters
decided there must be a law
stopping people from owning
slaves at all. A law to abolish
slavery in the British empire
eventually went through Parliament
in 1833. ◆

▼ *These brutal-looking chains
are remnants from the cruel slave
trade which politician William
Wilberforce spent years
struggling to abolish.*

Oscar **Wilde**

Irish dramatist
Born 1854   Died 1900 aged 46

The son of a wealthy surgeon and of a poet, Oscar Wilde came from Dublin to Britain at the age of 20. Soon known as the wittiest man in London, he was also renowned for his flamboyant clothes. In the 1890s he wrote a number of brilliant comedies which were both funny and sharply critical of the times in which they were written. The best of these was *The Importance of being Earnest* (1895). Sadly Wilde was convicted in the same year of homosexual activities, at that time still illegal. The two hard years he spent in Reading Jail broke his spirit, and he died three years after his release. ◆

William I

King of England from 1066 to 1087
Born c.1027   Died 1087 aged about 60

William was born in Falaise, France. When he was about eight years old, his father died, and he became the Duke of Normandy.

William grew up to be tough, efficient, determined, and a brave fighter. Meanwhile the King of England, Edward the Confessor, had promised the English crown to William, his cousin. But Harold of Wessex, the strongest of the Anglo-Saxon nobles, also wanted to be king.

When King Edward died in 1066, Harold proclaimed himself king. William immediately built a great invasion fleet and crossed the English Channel. The Saxon and Norman armies met at the Battle of Hastings, where Harold was killed. William ruthlessly went on to conquer the rest of England, and became known as William the Conqueror. In 1086 he organized the greatest land survey that had ever been made; this culminated in the Domesday Book. ◆

▼ *The Bayeux Tapestry in France tells the story of the Norman Conquest of England and the events that led up to it.*

Andrew **Wiles**

English mathematician who solved Fermat's Last Theorem
Born 1953

Andrew Wiles was a quiet boy who liked puzzles and numbers. When he was ten, he read about a maths problem called Fermat's Last Theorem.

Fermat was a mathematician in the 17th century. He was supposed to have proved that there are no solutions to a simple set of equations ($x^n + y^n = z^n$.). But his proof had been lost, and no-one since had been able to work it out. Andrew resolved that he would prove Fermat's theorem.

Andrew studied maths at university, then got a job as a researcher. In 1986 he learned that a connection had been found between Fermat and a more recent maths problem. Andrew set to work to solve this new problem. In 1993 he thought he had found the proof, but there turned out to be a mistake. It was another year before he could say that he had solved Fermat's Last Theorem. ◆

ET VENIT AD PEVENESÆ

William III

King of Britain, Scotland, and Ireland from 1689 to 1702
Born 1650   Died 1702 aged 51

William of Orange was born in The Netherlands and was the Protestant ruler of the Dutch people. He was married to Mary, the eldest daughter of the Catholic king of England, James II.

William had one great aim: to stop the powerful Louis XIV of France from swallowing up more land in Europe. When, in 1688, William was invited by some leading English politicians to save England from the Catholic James II, he agreed, thinking that if he became the king of England he would be helped in his fight against the French. The plan met with virtually no resistance and in 1689 Parliament jointly offered him and Mary the crown of England, Scotland, and Ireland.

William was never a popular king, and the Catholic Irish people still supported James. William finally defeated James in Ireland at the battle of the Boyne in 1690. Many Irish Protestants today still call themselves 'Orangemen' because of William's victory. ◆

William of Sens

French mason and architect
Lived in the 12th century

William of Sens worked as a stonemason and architect in the days when the Christian Church was extremely powerful in Europe. Talented workmen travelled from country to country in the service of the Church. William came to Canterbury from Sens, a French city where a cathedral in the new Gothic style had just been finished. He had won a competition to

▲ *A view of the Choir at Canterbury Cathedral, much of which was built by William of Sens after the original had been destroyed by fire in 1180.*

design Canterbury's new cathedral in the most up-to-date French style. Three years later he had a tragic accident when he fell from the scaffolding. Although he was disabled, he was still able to continue the cathedral choir with the help of another architect, William the Englishman. After six years in England, William of Sens returned home where he died. ◆

William the Silent

Founder of the Republic of Holland
Born 1533   Died 1584 aged 51

William owned an immense amount of land and held the title of Prince of Orange. The Spanish king, Philip II, who ruled

The Netherlands at the time, appointed William the governor of Holland, Zeeland, and Utrecht in 1555. But from about 1561 William, with other great lords, began to openly oppose Spanish rule. Although the opposition was first about foreign control, it soon became a question of religion. The Spanish were Catholics but in The Netherlands the Protestant Christian religion was more dominant. By 1566 there was open rebellion against Spanish rule. Eventually William became the national leader against the Spaniards, and tried to unite the country. Although this did not last, William continued his fight against the Spaniards, who offered a reward for his assassination. In 1584 William was shot by a fanatical Catholic thought to be a Spanish agent.

William was known as 'the Silent' because he could be relied upon to keep secrets. ◆

⬤ **see also**

Philip II

▼ *A portrait of William the Silent painted when he was 46.*

Robbie **Williams**

British pop star
Born 1976

At school, Robbie Williams was always a joker. He was not very good at academic subjects, but he enjoyed sport and acting. Robbie left school at 16 to work as a salesman. One day he saw an advert in a paper for a fifth member of a pop group. He went for an audition, and got the job. The band was called Take That.

Take That were not immediately a success, but in 1991 they became hugely popular. From 1991 to 1996 they had a string of hit records in the UK. Robbie enjoyed being famous, but he didn't quite fit with the band's clean-cut image. In 1996 he fell out with the other members and left the group.

For a year after leaving Take That Robbie ran wild, and most people thought it was the end of his career. But Robbie had other ideas. In 1997 he released a solo album, *Life Thru a Lens*. The single 'Angels' was soon number one in the UK charts, and the album became a best-seller.

A string of number one UK singles and three more best-selling albums followed. Between 2000 and 2002, Robbie won six Brit awards and two MTV awards. He had success in the UK and the USA with the song *Somethin' Stupid*, a duet with the actress Nicole Kidman. ◆

Tennessee **Williams**

American writer
Born 1911   Died 1983 aged 71

Tennessee Williams, the adopted name of Thomas Lanier Williams, was born in Columbus, Mississippi, an area that provided the inspiration for many of his plays. After going to university, Williams supported his writing by taking various jobs before winning a grant from the Rockefeller Foundation for his play *The Battle of Angels* in 1940. This was followed by the award-winning play, *The Glass Menagerie* (1945).

Williams continued to confirm his status as an important playwright with *A Streetcar Named Desire* (1947) and *Cat on a Hot Tin Roof* (1955) which both won Pulitzer Prizes. They are notable for their brilliant dialogue and for scenes of high emotional tension.

Williams's early works are regarded as his best; in his later years he was often in ill health as he struggled with an addiction to alcohol and sleeping pills. ◆

Woodrow **Wilson**

President of the United States from 1913 to 1921
Born 1856   Died 1924 aged 67

Woodrow Wilson began his career as a lawyer, but soon turned to teaching. By 1890 he was a professor at Princeton University, and in 1902 he was elected its president. Then, in 1910, he was elected as the Democratic Governor of New Jersey.

Only two years later Wilson was elected president of America. When World War I broke out in Europe in 1914, Wilson kept America out of it, and was very popular at home for this. But in 1917 German submarines began sinking American merchant ships, so America declared war on Germany.

Just before the end of the war, Wilson outlined 'Fourteen Points' for a peace settlement. He persuaded other countries to agree to most of these points, including the setting up of the 'League of Nations' (an earlier form of the United Nations). However, the American Congress refused to let America join the League. Despite this, Wilson, now a sick man, was awarded the 1920 Nobel Peace Prize for helping to found the League. ◆

Thomas **Wolsey**

English cardinal and chief minister to Henry VIII
Born c.1474   Died 1530 aged about 56

Thomas Wolsey started his career as a priest. In Tudor England an ambitious boy from an ordinary family could still get to the top by being a priest, and Wolsey finally got a job at court. The young Henry VIII realized that Wolsey would serve him loyally and well. In 1515 the king made him chancellor. Wolsey also became Archbishop of York, and later a cardinal (a very senior priest in the Roman Catholic Church). He soon became richer than the nobles at Henry's court, and built wonderful palaces, including the huge Hampton Court.

In 1529 the king wanted the pope to give him a divorce from Catherine of Aragon. Wolsey tried his best to get it, but the pope refused. Henry seldom forgave failure. Wolsey was sent away to York, but would not stop meddling in politics. Henry summoned the elderly cardinal to London to accuse him of treason but Wolsey was sick and he died at Leicester Abbey on the way. ◆

👁 **see also**

Henry VIII

Stevie **Wonder**

American pop musician and singer
Born 1950

Steveland Morris of Saginaw, Michigan, was renamed Little Stevie Wonder at the age of ten by Berry Gordy Jr, the owner of Tamla Motown Records. Stevie is blind, but plays harmonica, piano, organ, and drums superbly. He had his first No. 1 hit, 'Fingertips' when he was only 13 years old. Twenty hits later, in the 1970s, he struck out in a new direction, adding funky electronic keyboards to his sound and singing about the problems faced by black Americans. ◆

Eldrick 'Tiger' **Woods**

American golfing star
Born 1975

Tiger Woods has been swinging a golf club almost since he could walk. By the age of three he was playing on a nine-hole course, with a cut-down golf club that his father made for him.

As an amateur golfer, Tiger won six US Amateur titles, then in1996 he turned professional. He won 6 of the 25 events he entered in his first season.

Next year, aged only 21, Tiger won the US Masters, one of the four top golfing events (Grand Slams). He was the youngest person ever to win a Grand Slam.

In 2000 Tiger won three of the four Grand Slam events. He also became golf's all-time highest money earner. In 2001Tiger won the US Masters, and became the first golfer in history to hold all four golfing Grand Slams at once. ◆

Virginia **Woolf**

British novelist
Born 1882   Died 1941 aged 59

Virginia Woolf had a restless, brilliant intelligence which was revealed in her essays and stories. An early believer in Women's Liberation, she was also fascinated by the act of writing itself.

In her novels, she breaks away from normal story-telling techniques in favour of a style closer to how we all actually think from moment to moment. In their thoughts, her characters often pass from the present to the past as one memory piles on another. Her characters also react to experience in a very personal way, describing events or sights immediately as they seem at that particular moment. This does not always make Woolf's writing easy to read, but she is always interesting and original.

Although she was a successful author and was part of a group of leading writers of the day, Woolf was not always happy. She finally committed suicide when she felt she was slipping once again into the deep depression which had tormented her for much of her life. ◆

◀ *Among Woolf's novels are* Mrs Dalloway *(1925),* To the Lighthouse *(1927), and* Orlando *(1928).*

Frank **Woolworth**

American founder of the Woolworth chain of stores
Born 1852   Died 1919 aged 67

▲ *The Woolworth Building in New York, built in 1913. At 241.4 m tall, it was the world's tallest building at the time.*

Early in his working life, Frank Woolworth had the idea for a new kind of shop. With help from his boss, W. H. Moore, he set up a 'five and ten cent' store in 1879 with a wide range of goods for sale at low prices. Customers flocked to his shop. His idea was also taken up by his brother, his cousin, and a few close friends, including W. H. Moore, who all opened similar businesses. In 1912 all these stores merged to form the F. W. Woolworth chain. The following year the company built the Woolworth Building in New York, which was for many years the world's largest skyscraper. By the time Woolworth died, there were more than 10,000 stores in the chain, including many in Canada, Britain, and Germany. ◆

William **Wordsworth**

English nature poet
Born *1770*   **Died** *1850 aged 80*

After studying at Cambridge University, William Wordsworth spent some time in France, where he fell in love with Annette Vallon, the daughter of a surgeon. But although they had a child, Wordsworth left her before they could marry. His money ran out and he had to return to England.

In 1798 he published his first collection of poems, *Lyrical Ballads*, in partnership with his great friend, the poet Samuel Taylor Coleridge. Wordsworth's poems caused a sensation because he wrote about ordinary events in plain language. One of his most famous poems, 'To Daffodils' starts:

I wandered lonely as a cloud
That floats on high o'er vales and
    hills,
When all at once I saw a crowd,
A host, of golden daffodils.

This new simplicity was a great contrast to the more showy types of poetry that were popular at the time.

Because both of his parents had died when he was a child, he was always close to his sister, Dorothy. In 1799 he moved to the Lake District and lived with Dorothy and also with his wife Mary, whom he married in 1802. The Lake District was an area he loved and its scenery inspired much of his writing. ◆

👁 **see also**
Tennyson

Christopher **Wren**

English mathematician, astronomer, and architect of St Paul's Cathedral
Born *1632*   **Died** *1723 aged 90*

It did not take people long to realize that Christopher Wren was very clever. After studying at Oxford University, he soon became a teacher there. He was particularly good at mathematics and physics. While still a young man, he was made a professor of astronomy at Oxford in 1661.

In London, in 1662, he helped to found a club of men keen to explore the world through science. King Charles II was very interested in it, and it was called 'The Royal Society'. Many outstanding men were members, including Robert Boyle and Isaac Newton. This society still exists today.

▶ *St Paul's Cathedral, which dominates the skyline in the City of London, is considered by many to be the finest building Wren designed.*

Wren began to design buildings, and proved to be brilliant at that as well. The chapel at Pembroke College in Cambridge and the Sheldonian Theatre in Oxford were among his earliest buildings. Then, in 1666, the Great Fire destroyed most of London. Wren drew up a plan for rebuilding the entire city. Sadly his plan was never used. However, St Paul's Cathedral needed to be rebuilt, and Wren was chosen to design it. The construction of his magnificent plan was completed in 1710.

Wren worked very hard: he rebuilt 52 London churches destroyed by the fire, and the list of other buildings he designed seems endless. He was knighted in 1672, and became President of the Royal Society in 1680. ◆

👁 **see also**
Boyle   Newton

Wright Brothers

American flying pioneers who built and flew the first aeroplane

Wilbur Wright
Born *1867* **Died** *1912 aged 45*
Orville Wright
Born *1871* **Died** *1948 aged 76*

Orville Wright was a champion cyclist, and so the two brothers set up a shop where they made and sold bicycles. Neither of the brothers had a proper education, but they had tremendous mechanical skills. They both enjoyed the new sport of gliding, and decided to try and build a bicycle with wings and a petrol engine to drive a propeller round.

By 1903 the Wright brothers had built *The Flyer*. It was a biplane (with two sets of wings) and the pilot lay flat across the lower wing. A series of bicycle chains and gears connected the engine to two propellers which rotated at about 450 times a minute. On 17 December 1903, at Kitty Hawk in North Carolina, Orville Wright made a 12-second flight over a distance of 36 m. This was the first aeroplane flight in history. Later that morning Wilbur flew for nearly a minute. They carried on building better aeroplanes and in 1905 Wilbur flew 38 km in a half-hour flight.

The brothers were the sons of a minister, Bishop Milton Wright. They never smoked or drank

▲ *In 1903 the Wright brothers made the first-ever powered flight in their hand-built aeroplane,* The Flyer.

alcohol, and neither of them married. Wilbur died of typhoid fever in 1912, and his brother Orville gave up building planes a couple of years later. ◆

Frank Lloyd Wright

American architect
Born *1867* **Died** *1959 aged 91*

Frank Lloyd Wright was the most prolific and versatile of the great architects of the 20th century. His career lasted almost 70 years (he worked almost to the day of his death) and he designed about 1000 buildings, of which about 400 were erected. He worked in a variety of styles and was highly inventive in his use of materials and architectural forms. Wright also wrote many books and articles (including an autobiography), through which he promoted his ideas. His ideal was 'organic architecture', in which buildings harmonize with their environment and their users.

Wright had achieved a considerable reputation by the time he was in his thirties. However, until he was about 60, most of his commissions were fairly small. From the late 1930s, though, he designed many large public buildings in America, including the Guggenheim Museum in New York. He was a forceful personality – one of the central figures of modern American cultural life. ◆

▶ *Wright said his inspiration for the Guggenheim Museum in New York was a child's spinning top.*

John **Wycliffe**

Medieval scholar who challenged the power of the Roman Catholic Church
Born c.1330   **Died** 1384 aged about 54

Nothing is known about Wycliffe until the 1360s. By then he was about 30 years old, studying and teaching theology at Oxford University.

In 1374 Edward III sent him to Flanders to negotiate with ambassadors from the Pope about the taxes that the King had to pay to Rome. Wycliffe questioned the Pope's right to collect money, and went on to challenge the wealth and power of the Catholic Church in general.

Over the next ten years his views became more and more extreme. Wycliffe attacked the authority of the Church, and encouraged people to pray directly to God. He issued the first translation of the Bible from Latin into English so that people could read the Bible for themselves. This was considered very shocking. He was condemned as a dangerous heretic (for not accepting Catholic teaching), and his writings were publicly burnt.

Wycliffe's ideas helped to inspire the 'Lollards', people who protested against the power of the Catholic Church. They in turn inspired the Protestants in the 16th century. ◆

👁 **see also**

Edward III

Xerxes

King of Persia from 485 BC to 465 BC
Born c.519 BC
Died 465 BC aged about 54

Xerxes came to the throne of the huge Persian empire on the death of his father Darius I. Darius had invaded the Greek mainland,

but his army had been thoroughly defeated by the Greeks at the battle of Marathon.

It was now important for Xerxes to show Persia's strength. He made preparations for the largest invasion the Greeks had ever seen. The army crossed into Greece by building a bridge of boats across the narrow straits, called the Hellespont (now the Dardanelles), which divided Greece from Asia Minor (now Turkey).

The two armies first clashed in 480 BC, at a narrow mountain pass called Thermopylae. Here a small Greek force held the pass against the Persians. However, the Persians managed to find a mountain track which led them round to the rear. They killed all but two of the 300 defenders. The way to Athens was now open to the Persians, and Xerxes' army captured the city.

The only hope for the Greeks was to defeat the Persians at sea. They did this at the famous sea battle of Salamis in 480 BC, and the Persian navy was destroyed. King Xerxes returned home, but his army stayed and was defeated in Plataea the next year. Persia was no longer a threat to Greece. ◆

👁 **see also**

Darius I

▲ *Persepolis was the capital of the Persian empire until it was burnt down after its capture in 331BC by Alexander the Great. Parts of it still remain intact (above).*

W. B. **Yeats**

Irish poet and dramatist
Born 1865   **Died** 1939 aged 73

William Butler Yeats went to school in London, but for his holidays he was sent to his grandparents in Sligo on the west coast of Ireland. He loved to listen to the Sligo people talk of fairies and ghosts, and of the time when great kings, queens, and warriors inhabited Ireland.

When he was older he collected the folklore and myths of Ireland, and helped to found a national theatre in Dublin. He met and fell in love with a woman called Maude Gonne, who inspired much of his greatest poetry but refused to marry him. In his later years, his poetry increased in power, drawing on the ancient myths and his personal emotions. Many of his best-known poems appeared in *The Tower* (1928), and *The Winding Stair* (1929). He won the Nobel Prize for Literature in 1923. ◆

◀ *The Russian president Boris Yeltsin pictured at the Helsinki Summit in 1992. Faced with severe economic problems and unrest among his people, he consistently called for international aid.*

Boris **Yeltsin**

Russian president who led his country to democracy
Born 1931

Boris Nikolayevich Yeltsin was born in Sverdlovsk in the Urals. He began work as a builder and joined the Communist Party in 1961. By 1968 he was a full-time party worker, and in 1976 was appointed First Secretary of the Sverdlovsk District Central Committee. Life in the Soviet Union changed in the 1980s when Mikhail Gorbachev became General Secretary of the Soviet Communist Party. The many changes he introduced were welcomed by Yeltsin, who became First Secretary of the Moscow City Party Committee in 1985. However, in 1990 Yeltsin ran for President against Gorbachev, and won easily. This gave him the authority to become a world figure. When there was an attempt to overthrow Gorbachev in 1991, Yeltsin bravely led the opposition to the coup. With the break-up of the Soviet Union into individual country states, Yeltsin continued to lead Russia to democracy. But economic problems caused a lot of discontent and Yeltsin made the decision to dissolve the Russian parliament in 1993 in order to push through his economic reforms. His Communist opponents led an armed uprising against him but Yeltsin was able to put this down with the help of his loyal troops. From 1996 he suffered from serious heart problems, and at the end of 1999 he retired from office. ◆

👁 **see also**
Gorbachev

Yoshida Shigeru

Japanese prime minister
Born 1878   Died 1967 aged 89

Born the son of a politician, Yoshida Shigeru studied politics at Tokyo University, and then made his career as a statesman and politician. He served as Japan's ambassador to Scandinavia, Italy, and Britain. However, the military in Japan did not trust his international outlook and he did not serve in office during World War II. He was imprisoned in June 1945 for recommending that Japan should surrender in the closing stages of the war, and then released three months later with the arrival of American Occupation troops. He then served as foreign minister from 1945 to 1946 and prime minister from 1946 to 1947 and 1948 to 1954. Yoshida opposed Communism strongly and favoured close links between Japan and America. Under his firm rule his defeated country rapidly regained its independence and started on its astonishing road to economic recovery. ◆

Brigham **Young**

American leader of the Mormon community
Born 1801   Died 1877 aged 76

Brigham Young was the ninth of 11 children. He had very little education and started work as a house painter.

In 1832 he became dissatisfied with the Methodist church that he had been brought up in, and became a Mormon. The Mormons are one of the many groups which have split off from other Christian Churches because of disagreements about their different beliefs.

▼ *The leaders of the Mormon settlers who journeyed to Utah in 1847 were very well organized, treating the migration almost like a military operation.*

In many parts of America, Mormons were disliked and were driven from their land. In 1847 Young became leader of the Mormons, and decided to find a new, peaceful home for them. He led 148 Mormon settlers to the Great Salt Lake of Utah and started what became Salt Lake City. By the time he died, 147,000 Mormons were living in Utah.

Brigham Young believed, like many Mormons, in polygamy, and had 27 wives and 56 children. ◆

Thomas **Young**

English physicist
Born *1773*   **Died** *1829 aged 55*

Thomas Young was very bright and could read when he was two. He studied medicine, but he was interested in physics, too.

Although Isaac Newton and other great scientists thought that light was a stream of particles, Young thought they were wrong. He proved that light is really a kind of wave. He also found out that our eyes can only detect three colours, and all the other colours can be made up of mixtures of these. In 1801 he was made a professor at the Royal Institution in London.

Young was also very good at languages. The famous Rosetta stone, which was over 2000 years old, was found in Egypt in 1799. It was carved in three languages: high-class Egyptian (hieroglyphics), everyday Egyptian (demotic), and Greek. Young was the first to publish an account of this important find, although it was a Frenchman, François Champollion, who first deciphered the hieroglyphics on the stone. ◆

👁 **see also**

Huygens   Newton

Emiliano **Zapata**

Mexican revolutionary
Born *1879*   **Died** *1919 aged 40*

▼ *For eight years Zapata led his peasant armies against the haciendas and successive heads of state in his quest to give land back to the people.*

For over 30 years (1877–1911) Mexico was ruled by the dictator Porfirio Diaz. The owners of haciendas (big estates) did not treat the poor peasants well. Emiliano Zapata, son of a peasant horse-dealer, was arrested at 18 for leading a protest against an estate-owner. When the revolution broke out against Diaz in 1910, Zapata was a strong supporter. His slogan was 'Land and Liberty'. By 1911 he controlled the southern state of Morelos. While the rest of Mexico slid into chaos, Zapata used his part-time farmers' army to re-establish order, chase landowners off their estates, and divide up their lands fairly among the peasants. In 1919 he was tricked into an ambush and assassinated by corrupt political rivals. But the revolution did eventually lead to land reform and the unselfish Zapata is revered in Mexico as a national hero. ◆

> *Men of the South! It is better to die on your feet than live on your knees!*
>
> EMILIANO ZAPATA

Emil **Zatopek**

Czechoslovakian athlete

Born *1922*   **Died** *2000 aged 78*

Emil Zatopek was the best long-distance runner of his day and possibly of all time. At the 1948 Olympics he won the gold medal for the 10,000 m and silver for the 5000 m. Then, at the 1952 Helsinki Olympics, he won the 5000 m and 10,000 m gold medals, and entered the marathon for the first time in his life. He won by 800 m (half a mile) to complete a unique treble.

His wife, Dana Zatopkova, also added to the family celebrations by winning the gold medal in the women's javelin competition. ◆

Ferdinand von **Zeppelin**

German airship builder
Born *1838*   **Died** *1917 aged 78*

In 1870 Paris was surrounded by the Prussian army. Ferdinand von Zeppelin, a Prussian officer, saw how the French used balloons to carry supplies into the besieged city. This got him thinking about designing an airship which, unlike balloons, could be controlled.

He designed his first hydrogen-filled airship and launched it in 1900. It did not fly well but Zeppelin improved the design and, before long, his airships were making flights lasting many hours. The German government ordered a whole fleet of them, and in

▼ *This World War I German propaganda poster shows one of Zeppelin's airships flying over New York. The slogan beneath reads 'Two days to North America', implying that it would be very easy for German zeppelins to reach and bomb American cities.*

IN 2 TAGEN NACH NORD-AMERIKA!
DEUTSCHE ZEPPELIN-REEDEREI

World War I used over a hundred 'zeppelins' to bomb enemy cities, including London.

Zeppelin started the first airship passenger airline in 1909. Although he died before intercontinental airship travel became a reality, by the 1930s huge zeppelins were flying across the Atlantic. The most famous were the *Graf Zeppelin*, which flew over 1,600,000 km, and the *Hindenburg*. Then, in 1937, the *Hindenburg* burst into flames killing 36 people. This and other disasters signalled the end of the airship era. ◆

Zhou Enlai

Prime minister of Communist China from 1949 to 1976
Born *1898*   **Died** *1976 aged 77*

Zhou Enlai believed that the answer to China's economic problems was to follow socialist ideas of sharing wealth. He went to study European political ideas in France, where he formed a branch of the new Chinese Communist Party. He returned to China and worked with other Communists to build up Chiang Kai-shek's Nationalist Party, until Chiang turned against the Communists in 1927. Zhou escaped and joined up with Mao Zedong and Deng Xiaoping. He took part in the Long March of 1934–1935, and became one of Mao's chief advisers.

After the creation of the People's Republic of China in 1949, Zhou became its first prime minister, holding the post until he died. During Mao's Cultural Revolution he actively restrained extremists and helped restore order. He also played a major role in building good relations with America, which previously had been the bitter enemy of Communist China. Zhou was a charming man and was admired and trusted by both Chinese and foreigners. ◆

👁 **see also**

Chiang Kai-shek   Deng Xiaoping
Mao Zedong

Emile **Zola**

French writer
Born *1840*   **Died** *1902 aged 62*

Emile Zola was one of the greatest figures in the 19th-century French literary world. He was famous not only for his novels, but also for the outspoken way in which he campaigned for social reform and other causes he believed in. His novels, of which he wrote more than 20, paint a carefully detailed panorama of French life at the time. Among the most famous are *Nana* (1880), about a prostitute, and *Germinal* (1885), about the working conditions of miners. In 1898 Zola wrote his famous letter, *J'accuse* (I accuse), to a newspaper denouncing the French justice system for wrongly convicting an army officer, Captain Dreyfus, of treason. Zola had to take refuge in England to escape imprisonment for libel; Dreyfus was later pardoned. ◆

👁 **see also**

Dreyfus

Zoroaster

Persian prophet
Born *c.628 BC*
Died *c.551 BC aged about 77*

According to tradition, Zoroaster was a priest who began to have visions when he was 30. He

▲ *A Zoroastrian coin from the 2nd century showing the symbol of the Zoroastrian faith, the fire altar.*

converted a local king to his beliefs when he was 40 and it is believed that he was murdered while praying at the altar when he was 77. The religion he founded, Zoroastrianism, became the official faith of three successive Persian (Iranian) empires, from the 6th century BC to the 6th century AD. Its scriptures included the 'Gathas', 17 hymns said to have been written by Zoroaster. Its worship focused on fire as a symbol of purity.

Zoroaster taught that there is only one God, that people are free to choose between good and evil forces, and that their lives will be judged at death and lead them to either Heaven or Hell. These ideas are all fundamental to Judaism, Christianity, and Islam, though it is not clear how these religions were affected by Zoroaster. A number of people in India, known as the Parsees, still follow Zoroastrianism. ◆

Ulrich **Zwingli**

Swiss religious reformer
Born 1484   Died 1531 aged 47

Ulrich Zwingli went to university in Vienna and Basle before being ordained a Roman Catholic priest in 1506. He served in the Swiss town of Glarus (1506–1516) and then in Einsiedeln (1516–1518). Around this time, many people wanted to reform the organization and teachings of the Catholic Church. Zwingli concluded that the Church needed to be more like that of Jesus's time. This new Church was to become known as the Protestant Church.

In 1518 Zwingli moved to Zurich, where he became minister of the city's cathedral. This position gave him some influence over the city's government, and in the next ten years, he and the town council converted the city to the Protestant faith. Their aim was to simplify church rituals; they removed paintings and statues from churches, and closed down monasteries. In 1525 they declared that the Zurich Church would no longer obey the pope.

Other Swiss cities also converted to Protestantism. Rural areas, however, wanted to stay within the Catholic Church. They sent an army against Zurich and in the ensuing battle at Kappel (1531), Zwingli was killed. ◆

👁 **see also**
Calvin   Luther

▼ *Swiss Protestant leader Ulrich Zwingli.*

Vladimir **Zworykin**

Russian-born American scientist
Born 1889   Died 1982 aged 93

Vladimir Zworykin graduated as an electrical engineer in Russia, and during World War I was a radio operator in the army. After the war he emigrated to America where his interest in radio led him to a career in the flourishing electrical industry.

In 1923 he invented the iconoscope, an image-scanning device. In the 1930s it was developed into the cathode-ray tube, which is at the heart of every modern television set. This all-electric system quickly replaced the relatively crude optical-mechanical system demonstrated by John Logie Baird in 1926.

Zworykin also helped to develop a device for enhancing night vision, and the electron microscope, a research instrument which gives much greater magnification than is possible with the more common optical microscopes. He earned many honours and, in 1977, he was named in the US National Inventors Hall of Fame. ◆

👁 **see also**
Baird   Marconi

Special Reference Section

Thematic Directory

Famous people by subject
pages 358-370

Can you name the most famous explorers of all time? Or the most influential composers? Can you think of any artists other than Michelangelo? Or any inventors apart from Thomas Edison? In this section the 1000 people in the book have been grouped together by their area of achievement, thus making it easy to answer such questions at a glance.

Chronological Directory

Famous people through the ages
pages 371-383

Did you know that Christopher Columbus was exploring the Americas at the same time that Leonardo da Vinci was painting his masterpieces? Or that Karl Marx was developing his Communist ideas at the same time that Emily Brontë was writing *Wuthering Heights*? Get a different perspective on history by looking under the various headings in this section to find out which famous men and women in this book were born and lived at the same time.

Thematic Directory

In this comprehensive directory, the 1000 famous men and women in this book have been divided into thematic categories, thereby linking them together by their area of achievement. For example, all the painters are grouped together, as are all the scientists, all the explorers, etc. In some cases, categories are further divided into time periods that reflect the dates of activity for the figures listed. However, some people cannot easily be placed in just one thematic group because of the variety of skills they possessed. For this reason you might find the same person under two, or even three headings.

Artists, Composers, and Writers

Painters and illustrators

Up to 1800

Bellini, Giovanni
Blake, William
Bosch, Hieronymus
Botticelli, Sandro
Bruegel, Pieter
Canaletto, Giovanni
Caravaggio, Michelangelo Merisi da
David, Jacques-Louis
Dürer, Albrecht
El Greco
Gainsborough, Thomas
Giotto di Bondone
Hals, Frans
Hogarth, William
Holbein, Hans
Leonardo da Vinci
Michelangelo Buonarroti
Piero della Francesca
Poussin, Nicolas
Raphael
Rembrandt van Rijn
Rubens, Peter
Tintoretto, Jacopo
Titian
Van Dyck, Anthony
Van Eyck, Jan
Velázquez, Diego
Vermeer, Jan
Veronese, Paolo
Watteau, Jean-Antoine

▶ Vincent van Gogh

1800 to 1900

Cézanne, Paul
Constable, John
Degas, Edgar
Delacroix, Eugène
Gauguin, Paul
Goya, Francisco de
Manet, Edouard
Monet, Claude
Munch, Edvard
Pissarro, Camille
Renoir, Pierre Auguste
Rossetti, Dante Gabriel
Rousseau, Henri
Seurat, Georges
Toulouse-Lautrec, Henri de
Turner, J. M. W.
Van Gogh, Vincent

1900 to present

Braque, Georges
Chagall, Marc
Dalí, Salvador
Escher, M. C.
Kandinsky, Wassily
Klee, Paul
Magritte, René
Matisse, Henri
Miró, Joan
Mondrian, Piet
Nolan, Sidney
O'Keeffe, Georgia
Picasso, Pablo
Pollock, Jackson
Rivera, Diego
Warhol, Andy

▶ Salvador Dali

Photographers

Cartier-Bresson, Henri
Daguerre, Louis
Fox Talbot, William
Muybridge, Eadweard
Niepce, Joseph

Architects

Bernini, Gianlorenzo
Brunelleschi, Filippo
Gaudí, Antoni
Griffin, Walter Burley
Gropius, Walter
Le Corbusier
Mackintosh, Charles Rennie
Michelangelo Buonarroti
Palladio

Pei, I. M.
Vitruvius
William of Sens
Wren, Christopher
Wright, Frank Lloyd

Sculptors, designers, and craftspeople

Bernini, Gianlorenzo
Brancusi, Constantin
Cellini, Benvenuto
Chippendale, Thomas
Degas, Edgar
Donatello, Donato
Epstein, Jacob
Fabergé, Peter
Giacometti, Alberto
Hepworth, Barbara

Michelangelo Buonarroti
Moore, Henry
Morris, William
Phidias
Rodin, Auguste
Stradivari, Antonio
Wedgwood, Josiah

▲ Christopher Wren

Composers

Up to 1900

Bach, J. S.
Beethoven, Ludwig van
Berlioz, Hector
Bizet, Georges
Brahms, Johannes
Bruckner, Anton
Chopin, Frédéric
Debussy, Claude
Dvořák, Antonín
Gilbert and Sullivan
Grieg, Edvard
Handel, George Frideric
Haydn, Franz Joseph
Liszt, Franz
Mahler, Gustav
Mendelssohn, Felix
Monteverdi, Claudio
Mozart, Wolfgang Amadeus
Mussorgksy, Modest
Paganini, Niccolò
Puccini, Giacomo
Purcell, Henry
Rimsky-Korsakov, Nikolay

Rossini, Gioachino
Saint-Saëns, Camille
Schubert, Franz
Schumann, Robert
Sibelius, Jean
Strauss I, Johann
Strauss II, Johann
Strauss, Richard
Tchaikovsky, Pyotr Ilyich
Verdi, Giuseppe
Vivaldi, Antonio
Wagner, Richard

▼ Ludwig van Beethoven

1900 to present

Bartók, Béla
Berlin, Irving
Bernstein, Leonard
Britten, Benjamin
Copland, Aaron
Debussy, Claude
Elgar, Edward
Gershwin, George
Holst, Gustav
Mahler, Gustav
Porter, Cole
Prokofiev, Sergei
Puccini, Giacomo
Rakhmaninov, Sergey
Ravel, Maurice
Rimsky-Korsakov, Nikolai
Rodgers, Richard
Schoenberg, Arnold
Sibelius, Jean
Strauss, Richard
Stravinsky, Igor
Vaughan Williams, Ralph

Writers

Novelists

Achebe, Chinua
Alcott, Louisa May
Angelou, Maya
Austen, Jane
Balzac, Honoré de
Brontë sisters
Bunyan, John
Camus, Albert
Carroll, Lewis
Cervantes, Miguel de
Chaucer, Geoffrey
Cocteau, Jean
Conrad, Joseph
Defoe, Daniel
Dickens, Charles
Dostoevsky, Fyodor
Doyle, Arthur Conan
Dumas, Alexandre
Eliot, George
Fitzgerald, F. Scott
Flaubert, Gustave
García Márquez, Gabriel
Gide, André
Goethe, Johann von
Golding, William
Gordimer, Nadine
Greene, Graham
Hardy, Thomas
Hawthorne, Nathaniel
Hemingway, Ernest
Hughes, Langston

Hugo, Victor
James, Henry
Joyce, James
Kafka, Franz
Kawabata, Yasunari
Kipling, Rudyard
Lawrence, D. H.
Maupassant, Guy de
Melville, Herman
Montgomery, L. M.
Nabokov, Vladimir
Orwell, George
Proust, Marcel
Rabelais, François
Sartre, Jean-Paul
Scott, Walter
Shelley, Mary
Solzhenitsyn, Alexander
Stevenson, Robert Louis
Stowe, Harriet Beecher
Swift, Jonathan
Thackeray, William
Tolkien, J. R. R.
Tolstoy, Leo
Trollope, Anthony
Twain, Mark
Verne, Jules
Voltaire
Wells, H. G.
Woolf, Virginia
Zola, Emile

◀ Mark Twain

Dramatists

Aristophanes
Barrie, J. M.
Brecht, Bertolt
Chekhov, Anton
Cocteau, Jean
Fugard, Athol
Goethe, Johann von
Havel, Vaclav
Hugo, Victor
Ibsen, Henrik
Kalidasa
Miller, Arthur
Molière
Racine, Jean
Sartre, Jean-Paul
Shakespeare, William
Shaw, George Bernard
Sophocles
Thomas, Dylan
Walcott, Derek
Wilde, Oscar
Williams, Tennessee

▶ Virginia Woolf

◀ Oscar Wilde

▼ William Shakespeare

▲ Beatrix Potter

Other writers

Borges, Jorge Luis
Cicero, Marcus
Diderot, Denis
Erasmus
Frank, Anne
Herodotus
Johnson, Samuel
Machiavelli, Niccolò
Nostradamus, Michael
Pepys, Samuel
Plutarch
Voltaire

▲ Lord Byron

Poets

Auden, W. H.
Basho
Baudelaire, Charles
Blake, William
Borges, Jorge Luis
Browning, Robert
Burns, Robert
Byron, Lord
Camoens, Luíz vaz de
Carroll, Lewis
Chaucer, Geoffrey
Coleridge, Samuel
Dante Alighieri
Dickinson, Emily
Donne, John
Eliot, T. S.
Emerson, Ralph Waldo
Frost, Robert
Goethe, Johann von
Hardy, Thomas
Homer
Hughes, Langston
Hugo, Victor
Iqbal, Muhammed
Kalidasa

Keats, John
Lawrence, D. H.
Lear, Edward
Longfellow, Henry Wadsworth
Milton, John
Omar Khayyam
Owen, Wilfred
Petrarch, Francesco
Plath, Sylvia
Poe, Edgar Allan
Pope, Alexander
Pushkin, Alexander
Schiller, Friedrich
Scott, Walter
Shakespeare, William
Shelley, Percy
Tagore, Rabindraneth
Tennyson, Alfred, Lord
Thomas, Dylan
Virgil
Walcott, Derek
Whitman, Walt
Wordsworth, William
Yeats, W. B.

Storytellers

Aesop
Andersen, Hans Christian
Barrie, J. M.
Blyton, Enid
Dahl, Roald
Grahame, Kenneth
Grimm brothers
Kipling, Rudyard
Lewis, C. S.
Malory, Thomas
Maupassant, Guy de
Milne, A. A.
Poe, Edgar Allan
Potter, Beatrix
Rowling, J. K.

Entertainers

Classical musicians

Bernstein, Leonard
Callas, Maria
Casals, Pablo
Liszt, Franz
Melba, Nellie
Menuhin, Yehudi
Pavarotti, Luciano
Paganini, Niccolò
Rachmaninov, Sergey
Rubinstein, Arthur
Sutherland, Joan
Suzuki, Shin'ichi
Te Kanawa, Kiri

Popular musicians (jazz, rock, and pop)

Armstrong, Louis
Berry, Chuck
Bowie, David
Brown, James
Charles, Ray
Clapton, Eric
Dylan, Bob
Ellington, 'Duke'
Fitzgerald, Ella
Franklin, Aretha
Hendrix, Jimi
Holiday, Billie
Holly, Buddy
Jackson, Michael
Jagger, Mick
John, Elton
King, B. B.
Lennon and McCartney
Madonna
Marley, Bob
Miller, Glenn
Mitchell, Joni
Presley, Elvis
Robeson, Paul
Ross, Diana
Simon, Paul
Sinatra, Frank
Williams, Robbie
Wonder, Stevie

Actors

Astaire, Fred
Bernhardt, Sarah
Bogart, Humphrey
Brando, Marlon
Chaplin, Charlie
Cruise, Tom
Davis, Bette
Dean, James
De Niro, Robert
Dietrich, Marlene
Eastwood, Clint
Gable, Clark
Garbo, Greta
Grant, Cary
Hanks, Tom
Hepburn, Katherine
Irving, Henry
Kean, Edmund
Keaton, Buster
Kidman, Nicole
Laurel and Hardy
Marx brothers
Monroe, Marilyn
Olivier, Lawrence
Pickford, Mary
Roberts, Julia
Sinatra, Frank
Taylor, Elizabeth
Temple, Shirley
Valentino, Rudolph
Wayne, John
Welles, Orson

Film makers and directors

Chaplin, Charles
Cocteau, Jean
De Mille, Cecil B.
Disney, Walt
Eastwood, Clint
Eisenstein, Sergei
Fellini, Federico
Ford, John
Goldwyn, Samuel
Griffith, D. W.
Hitchcock, Alfred
Kurosawa, Akira
Ray, Satyajit
Spielberg, Steven
Welles, Orson

▲ Marlene Dietrich

Dancers, choreographers, and other entertainers

◀ Harry Houdini

Astaire, Fred
Blondin, Charles
De Valois, Ninette
Fonteyn, Margot
Graham, Martha
Houdini, Harry
Nijinsky, Vaslav
Nureyev, Rudolf
Pavlova, Anna
Shankar, Uday

World Leaders and Rulers

Ancient leaders and rulers – before 1 AD

Alexander the Great
Antony, Mark
Asoka
Augustus, Emperor
Caesar, Julius
Chandragupta Maurya
Cicero
Cleopatra
Cyrus the Great
Darius I
David, King

Hammurabi
Hannibal
Herod
Khufu
Nebuchadnezzar II
Pericles
Pompey
Rameses II
Shi Huangdi
Solomon
Solon

Spartacus
Themistocles
Tutankhamun
Xerxes

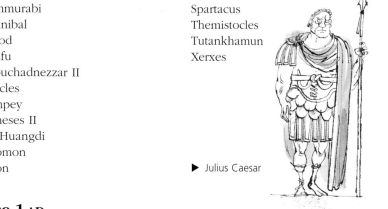

▶ Julius Caesar

Past and present rulers – since 1 AD

Europe

Alaric
Alfred
Boudicca
Canute
Catherine the Great
Charlemagne
Charles I (of England)
Charles II (of England)
Charles V (of France)
Christina (of Sweden)
Constantine the Great
Cromwell, Oliver
Edward I
Edward III
Edward the Confessor
Eleanor of Aquitaine
Elizabeth I
Elizabeth II
Eric the Red
Ferdinand and Isabella
Frederick I (Barbarossa)
Frederick II (the Great)
George I
George III
Gustavus Adolphus
Hadrian
Henry IV (of France)
Henry V (of England)
Henry VIII (of England)

Ivan the Terrible
James I
John
Justinian and Theodora
Llywelyn the Great
Louis XIV
Louis XVI
Macbeth
Maria Theresa
Marie Antoinette
Mary I
Mary, Queen of Scots
Napoleon I
Napoleon III
Nero
Nicholas II (of Russia)
Peter the Great
Philip II (of Spain)
Richard I
Richard III
Robert I
Suleiman I
Trajan
Victor Emanuel II
Victoria
William I
William III (and Mary II)
William the Silent

Rest of the world

Akbar
Atahualpa
Attila
Cetshwayo
Genghis Khan
Haile Selassie
Harun al-Rashid
Emperor Hirohito
Kublai Khan
Mehemet Ali
Minamoto Yoritomo
Mongkut
Montezuma II
Saladin
Shah Jahan
Sultan of Brunei
Tamerlane
Tokugawa Ieyasu

▶ Cleopatra and Mark Antony

Political leaders

Europe

Atatürk, Kemal
Attlee, Clement
Bismarck, Otto von
Blair, Tony
Borgia family
Brandt, Willy
Churchill, Winston
Clemenceau, Georges
De Gaulle, Charles
De Valera, Eamon
Disraeli, Benjamin
Franco, Francisco
Gladstone, William
Gorbachev, Mikhail
Havel, Vaclav
Hitler, Adolf
Khrushchev, Nikita
Kohl, Helmut
Lenin, Vladimir
Lloyd George, David
MacDonald, Ramsay
Mitterand, François
Mussolini, Benito
Peel, Robert
Pitt, William (the younger)
Rabin, Yitzhak
Stalin, Joseph
Thatcher, Margaret
Tito, Josip
Walesa, Lech
Walpole, Robert
Wolsey, Thomas
Yeltsin, Boris

Middle East

Arafat, Yasser
Begin, Menachem
Ben-Gourion, David
Hussein, Saddam
Khomeini, Ayatollah Ruhollah
Meir, Golda
Weizmann, Chaim

Americas and Canada

Adams, John
Bolívar, Simón
Bush, George W.
Castro, Fidel
Clinton, Bill
Davis, Jefferson

◀ Joseph Stalin

Eisenhower, Dwight
Grant, Ulysses S.
Jackson, Andrew
Jefferson, Thomas
Johnson, Lyndon B.
Kennedy, John Fitzgerald
King, William Lyon Mackenzie
Lincoln, Abraham
Macdonald, John A.
Madison, James
Monroe, James
Nixon, Richard
Pearson, Lester Bowles
Perón, Eva and Juan
Reagan, Ronald
Roosevelt, Franklin D.
Roosevelt, Theodore
Trudeau, Pierre
Truman, Harry S.
Washington, George
Wilson, Woodrow

▶ Eva Perón

Africa, Asia, and Australasia

Bhutto, Benazir
Bhutto, Zulfikar Ali
Chiang Kai-shek
De Klerk, F. W.
Deng Xiaoping
Gandhi, Indira
Gandhi, Mahatma
Haile Selassie
Hawke, Robert
Ho Chi Minh
Ito Hirobumi
Jinnah, Mohammed Ali
Kaunda, Kenneth
Kenyatta, Jomo
Lee Kuan Yew
Mandela, Nelson
Mao Zedong
Menzies, Robert
Mugabe, Robert
Nasser, Gamal Abdel
Nehru, Pandit Jawaharlal
Nkrumah, Kwame
Nyerere, Julius
Pol Pot
Qaddafi, Mu'ammar al-
Sadat, Mohammed Anwar al
Smuts, Jan
Sukarno
Verwoerd, Hendrik
Yoshida Shigeru
Zhou Enlai

◀ Mahatma Gandhi

Other leaders and politicians

Buthelezi, Gatsha
Cavour, Camillo
Collins, Michael
Franklin, Benjamin
Goebbels, Joseph
Goering, Herman
Hardie, James Keir
Kruger, Paul
Luthuli, Albert

Masaryk, Thomas
McCarthy, Joseph
Medici family
Metternich, Klemens
O'Connell, Daniel
Parnell, Charles
Rhodes, Cecil
Richelieu, Armand Jean
Torquemada, Tomás de

▶ Joseph Goebbels

Revolutionaries and military leaders

Alexander, Earl of Tunis
Charles Edward Stuart
Clive, Robert
Crazy Horse
Cromwell, Oliver
Custer, General George A.
Danton, Georges
Eisenhower, Dwight
Garibaldi, Giuseppe
Geronimo
Glyndwr, Owain
Grant, Ulysses S.
Guevara, Che

Hereward the Wake
Joan of Arc
Lafayette, Marquis de
Lawrence, T. E.
Lee, Robert E.
MacArthur, Douglas
Marlborough, Duke of
Minamoto Yoritomo
Montgomery, Bernard Law
Nelson, Horatio
Pétain, Henri Philippe
Revere, Paul
Rizal, José
Robespierre, Maximilien

Rommel, Erwin
Saladin
San Martin, José de
Shaka the Zulu
Sitting Bull
Sun Yat-sen
Tokugawa Ieyasu
Toussaint l'Ouverture
Trotsky, Leon
Wellington, Duke of
Zapata, Emiliano

◀ Che Guevara

◀ Giuseppe Garibaldi

▶ Joan of Arc

Civil rights leaders

Biko, Steve
Douglass, Frederick
Garvey, Marcus
King, Martin Luther, Jr
Malcolm X
Mandela, Nelson

Religious Leaders, Thinkers, and Reformers

Religious founders and followers

Abraham
Abu Bakr
Ali
Andrew, Saint
Aquinas, Saint Thomas
Augustine, Saint (of Canterbury)
Augustine, Saint (of Hippo)
Becket, Saint Thomas
Bernadette, Saint
Buddha
Calvin, John
Cranmer, Thomas
Dalai Lama
David, Saint
Eddy, Mary Baker
Fox, George
Francis of Assisi, Saint
George, Saint
Gobind Singh
Gregory I
Isaiah
Jesus
John XXIII, Pope
John the Baptist
John Paul II, Pope

Joseph
Knox, John
Loyola, Saint Ignatius
Luther, Martin
Mahavira
Mary
Moses
Muhammad
Nanak, Guru
Patrick, Saint
Paul, Saint
Penn, William
Ramakrishna
Teresa of Avila, Saint
Torquemada, Tomàs de
Tutu, Desmond
Urban II, Pope
Wesley, John
Wolsey, Thomas
Wycliffe, John
Young, Brigham
Zoroaster
Zwingli, Ulrich

Social reformers

Anderson, Elizabeth Garrett
Anthony, Susan Brownell
Baden-Powell, Robert
Barnardo, Thomas
Besant, Annie
Booth, William and Catherine
Brown, John
Butler, Josephine
Fry, Elizabeth
Fukuzawa, Yukichi
Montessori, Maria
Nightingale, Florence
Paine, Thomas
Pankhurst, Emmeline and Christabel
Roosevelt, Eleanor
Schweitzer, Albert
Seacole, Mary
Sequoya
Shaftesbury, 7th Earl of
Steinem, Gloria
Stopes, Marie
Teresa, Mother
Truth, Sojourner
Tubman, Harriet
Washington, Booker T.
Wilberforce, William

▶ Karl Marx

Thinkers and philosophers

Abelard, Peter
Aristotle
Aurobindo
Averroës
Avicenna
Bacon, Francis
Cicero, Marcus
Confucius
Descartes, René
Diderot, Denis
Diogenes
Empedocles
Erasmus, Desiderius
Hegel, Georg
Hobbes, Thomas
Hume, David
Ibn Khaldun

Keynes, John Maynard
Lao Tzu
Leibniz, Gottfried
Locke, John
Machiavelli, Niccolò
Malthus, Thomas
Marx, Karl
Mencius
More, Thomas
Nietzsche, Friedrich
Pascal, Blaise
Plato
Rousseau, Jean-Jacques
Russell, Bertrand
Sartre, Jean-Paul
Smith, Adam
Socrates

Scientists, Inventors, and Engineers

Physicists

Ampère, André-Marie
Becquerel, Henri
Bernoulli family
Bohr, Niels
Boyle, Robert
Bragg, William and Lawrence
Cavendish, Henry
Curie, Marie and Pierre
Einstein, Albert
Faraday, Michael
Fermi, Enrico
Foucault, Jean
Galvani, Luigi
Gay-Lussac, Joseph
Hahn, Otto
Hawking, Stephen
Heisenberg, Werner Karl
Hertz, Heinrich
Hooke, Robert
Huygens, Christiaan
Joule, James
Kelvin, William
Maxwell, James Clerk
Meitner, Lise
Newton, Isaac
Oersted, Hans Christian
Ohm, Georg
Oppenheimer, J. Robert
Planck, Max
Röntgen, Wilhelm
Rutherford, Ernest
Salam, Abdus
Schrödinger, Erwin
Thomson, Joseph
Volta, Alessandro
Watt, James
Young, Thomas

Chemists

Dalton, John
Davy, Humphry
Haber, Fritz
Hodgkin, Dorothy
Lavoisier, Antoine
Mendelèev, Dimitri
Pauling, Linus
Priestley, Joseph

Mathematicians

Aryabhata
Boole, George
Descartes, René
Euclid
Euler, Leonhard
Gauss, Karl
Hero of Alexandria
Leibniz, Gottfried
Mandelbrot, Benoit
Pascal, Blaise
Pythagoras
Russell, Bertrand
Wiles, Andrew

Astronomers

Bell, Jocelyn
Brahe, Tycho
Copernicus, Nicolaus
Eddington, Arthur Stanley
Galilei, Galileo
Halley, Edmund
Herschel, Caroline and William
Hipparchus
Hubble, Edwin
Kepler, Johannes
Laplace, Pierre
Lemaitre, Georges
Ptolemy

◀ Galileo Galilei

▼ Louis Pasteur

Biologists, physicians, and psychiatrists

Banting, Frederick
Barnard, Christiaan
Best, Charles
Crick, Francis
Darwin, Charles
Fleming, Alexander
Freud, Sigmund
Galen
Harvey, William
Hippocrates of Cos
Jenner, Edward
Jung, Carl

Koch, Robert
Leakey family
Leeuwenhoek, Anton van
Linnaeus, Carolus
Lister, Joseph
Mendel, Gregor
Mullis, Kary B.
Pasteur, Louis
Pavlov, Ivan
Vesalius, Andreas
Watson, James

Inventors, designers, and engineers

Up to 1800

Archimedes
Arkwright, Richard
Caxton, William
Crompton, Samuel
Fulton, Robert
Gutenberg, Johann
Hargreaves, James
Hero of Alexandria
Jacquard, Joseph-Marie
Leonardo da Vinci
McAdam, John
Mercator, Gerardus
Montgolfier brothers
Newcomen, Thomas
Niepce, Joseph
Telford, Thomas
Tull, Jethro
Volta, Alessandro
Watt, James

1800 to 1900

Babbage, Charles
Bell, Alexander Graham
Benz, Karl
Bessemer, Henry
Braille, Louis
Brunel, Isambard Kingdom
Colt, Samuel
Daguerre, Louis
Daimler, Gottlieb
Davy, Humphry
Diesel, Rudolf
Dunlop, John
Eastman, George
Edison, Thomas
Eiffel, Gustave
Fox Talbot, William
Hill, Rowland
Jacquard, Joseph-Marie
Krupp, Alfred
Lesseps, Ferdinand de
Lumière brothers
Marconi, Guglielmo
McAdam, John
Morse, Samuel
Niepce, Joseph
Nobel, Alfred
Otto, Nikolaus
Sholes, Christopher
Siemens family
Stephenson, George
Telford, Thomas
Zeppelin, Ferdinand von

▼ Isambard Kingdom Brunel

▼ Leonardo da Vinci

1900 to present

Baird, John Logie
Bardeen, John
Birdseye, Clarence
Biro, Laszlo
Braun, Wernher von
Carlson, Chester
Cockerell, Christopher
Cousteau, Jacques
Diesel, Rudolf
Eastman, George
Edison, Thomas
Ford, Henry
Hoover, William
Porsche, Ferdinand
Sikorsky, Igor
Watson-Watt, Robert
Whittle, Frank
Wright brothers
Zeppelin, Ferdinand von
Zworykin, Vladimir

Explorers and Adventurers

Pioneers and adventurers

Alcock and Brown
Amundsen, Roald
Armstrong, Neil
Batten, Jean
Blériot, Louis
Byrd, Richard
Cousteau, Jacques
Earhart, Amelia
Gagarin, Yuri
Glenn, John

Heyerdahl, Thor
Hillary, Edmund
Johnson, Amy
Lindbergh, Charles
Piccard, Auguste
Scott, Robert
Smith, Charles Kingsford
Tenzing Norgay
Tereshkova, Valentina

▶ Amy Johnson

Explorers and discoverers

Balboa, Vasco Núñez de
Banks, Joseph
Bering, Vitus
Bird, Isabella
Boone, Daniel
Cabot, John
Cartier, Jacques
Champlain, Samuel de
Columbus, Christopher
Cook, James
Cortés, Hernán
Dias, Bartolomeu
Drake, Francis
Eric the Red
Ericsson, Leif
Fa Hsien
Franklin, John

Gama, Vasco da
Hudson, Henry
Humboldt, Baron von
Ibn Batuta
Kingsley, Mary
La Salle, Rene
Lewis and Clark
Livingstone, David
Magellan, Ferdinand
Nansen, Fridtjof
Park, Mungo
Peary, Robert
Pizarro, Francisco
Polo, Marco
Raleigh, Walter
Tasman, Abel
Vespucci, Amerigo

◀ James Cook

◀ Marco Polo

Sports Stars

Ali, Muhammad
Beckenbauer, Franz
Bradman, Donald
Bubka, Sergey
Chiyonofuji
Comaneci, Nadia
Court, Margaret
DiMaggio, Joe
Fangio, Juan
Fraser, Dawn
Grace, W. G.
Graf, Steffi
Gretzky, Wayne
Henie, Sonja
Johnson, Michael
Jordan, Michael
Kasparov, Gary
Khan, Imran
Khan, Jahangir
Laver, Rod
Lenglen, Suzanne
Lewis, Carl
Louis, Joe

Maradona, Diego
Matthews, Stanley
Merckx, Eddy
Montana, Joe
Navratilova, Martina
Nicklaus, Jack
Owens, Jesse
Palmer, Arnold
Pelé
Piggott, Lester
Prost, Alain
Redgrave, Steve
Ruth, Babe
Sampras, Pete
Shoemaker, Bill
Sobers, Garry
Spitz, Mark
Stenmark, Ingemar
Szewinska, Irena
Thompson, Daley
Thorpe, Jim
Woods, Tiger
Zatopek, Emil

◀ Joe DiMaggio

Famous Characters

Arthur, King
Billy the Kid
Branson, Richard
Buffalo Bill
Calamity Jane
Capone, Al
Carnegie, Andrew
Casanova, Giovanni
Cavell, Edith
Crockett, Davy
Diana, Princess of Wales
Dreyfus, Alfred
El Cid
Fawkes, Guy
Gates, Bill
Getty, Jean Paul
Hearst, William Randolph
Heinz, Henry
Honda, Soichiro

Hughes, Howard
James, Jesse
Keller, Helen
Kellogg, William
Kelly, Ned
Lawrence, T. E.
Murdoch, Rupert
Oakley, Annie
Phidippides
Pocahontas
Rasputin
Rockefeller, John D.
Rothschild, Mayer Amschel
Schliemann, Heinrich
Tussaud, Marie
Vanderbilt, Cornelius
Villa, Pancho
Woolworth, Frank

◀ Calamity Jane

Chronological Directory

The 1000 famous men and women in this book have been divided into groups according to their date of birth. Thus, all the people who were born over 3000 years ago are linked together, as are those people who were born in the 1950s and 1960s. The timeline at the bottom of the pages can be used for quick and easy reference. A cross-reference (*see ...*) after some names guides you to the main article in the book where these people can be found.

2700 BC – 1001 BC

Khufu 26th century BC
Abraham 20th century BC
Hammurabi 18th century BC
Joseph 18th century BC
Tutankhamun c.1370 BC–1352 BC
Rameses II 13th century BC
Moses c.13th century BC
King David 10th century BC

1000 BC – 500 BC

King Solomon c.980 BC–c.922 BC
Homer 8th century BC
Isaiah 8th century BC
Nebuchadnezzar II c.630 BC–c.562 BC
Solon c.630 BC–c.560 BC
Zoroaster c.628 BC–c.551 BC
Mahavira c.599 BC–c.527 BC
Pythagoras c.582 BC–c.497 BC
Buddha c.563 BC–c.483 BC
Darius I c.558 BC–486 BC
Confucius c.551 BC–479 BC
Themistocles c.528 BC–c.462 BC
Xerxes c.519 BC–465 BC
Aesop 6th century BC
Cyrus the Great 6th century BC
Lao Tzu 6th century BC

499 BC – 200 BC

Sophocles c.496 BC–406 BC
Pericles c.495 BC–c.429 BC
Empedocles c.494 BC–c.434 BC
Phidias c.490 BC–c.430 BC
Herodotus c.484 BC–c.424 BC
Socrates c.469 BC–399 BC
Hippocrates of Cos c.460 BC–c.370 BC
Aristophanes c.450 BC–c.385 BC
Plato 429 BC–347 BC
Diogenes c.400 BC–c.325 BC
Phidippides 5th century BC
Aristotle 384 BC–322 BC
Mencius c.371 BC–c.289 BC
Alexander the Great 356 BC–323 BC
Euclid c.330 BC–c.260 BC
Chandragupta Maurya 4th century BC
Archimedes c.287 BC–212 BC
Shi Huangdi 259 BC–210 BC
Hannibal 247 BC–183 BC
Asoka 3rd century BC

199 BC – 1 BC

Marcus Cicero 106 BC–43 BC
Pompey 106 BC–48 BC
Julius Caesar c.100 BC–44 BC
Hipparchus 2nd century BC
Mark Antony 83 BC–30 BC
Herod c.74 BC–4 BC
Virgil 70 BC–19 BC
Cleopatra c.69 BC–30 BC
Augustus 63 BC–AD 14
Jesus c.4 BC–c.AD 29
John the Baptist c.4 BC–c.AD 28
Mary, mother of Jesus c.1st century BC
Spartacus 1st century BC
Vitruvius 1st century BC

0 AD – 499

Saint Andrew 1st century
Hero of Alexandria 1st century
Boudicca 1st century
Saint Peter 1st century
Saint Paul c.3–c.65
Nero 37–68
Plutarch c.46–c.120
Ts'ai Lun c.50–118
Trajan 53–117
Hadrian c.76–138
Ptolemy 2nd century
Galen c.130–c.200
Saint George 3rd century
Constantine the Great c.274–337
Saint Augustine of Hippo 354–430
Alaric 370–410
Saint Patrick c.390–c.460
Kalidasa 5th century
Fa Hsien 5th century
Attila 406–453
Aryabhata 476–c.550
Justinian 483–565

500 – 999

Saint Augustine of Canterbury 6th century
King Arthur 6th century
Saint David 6th century
Gregory I c.540–604
Muhammad c.570–632
Abu Bakr c.573–634
Ali c.600–661
Charlemagne 742–814
Harun al-Rashid c.764–809
Alfred 849–899
Eric the Red 10th century
Avicenna 979–1037
Canute c.994–1035

1000 – 1299

Leif Ericsson 11th century
Hereward the Wake 11th century
Edward the Confessor c.1003–1066
Macbeth c.1005–c.1057
William I c.1027–1087
Pope Urban II c.1042–1099
El Cid c.1043–1099
Omar Khayyam 1048–1123
Peter Abelard 1079–1142
William of Sens 12th century
Saint Thomas Becket 1118–1170
Eleanor of Aquitaine c.1122–1204
Frederick I c.1123–1190
Averroës 1126–1198
Saladin 1137–1193
Minamoto Yoritomo 1147–1199
Richard I 1157–1199
Genghis Khan 1162–1227
King John 1167–1216
Llywelyn the Great c.1172–1240
Saint Francis of Assisi 1182–1226
Kublai Khan 1215–1294
Saint Thomas Aquinas c.1225–1274
Edward I 1239–1307
Marco Polo c.1254–1324
Dante Alighieri 1265–1321
Giotto di Bondone c.1267–1337
Robert I 1274–1329

1300 – 1449

Ibn Batuta 1304–1368
Francesco Petrarch 1304–1374
Edward III 1312–1377
John Wycliffe c.1330–1384
Ibn Khaldun 1332–1406
Tamerlane c.1336–1405
Geoffrey Chaucer c.1340–1400
Owain Glyndwr c.1354–c.1416
Filippo Brunelleschi 1377–1446
Alfonso Borgia 1378–1458
Donato Donatello 1386–1466
Henry V 1387–1422
Cosimo Medici 1389–1464

Jan van Eyck c.1390–1441
Henry the Navigator 1394–1460
Thomas Malory 15th century
Johann Gutenberg c.1400–c.1468
Joan of Arc 1412–1431
Piero Medici 1414–1469
Piero della Francesca c.1415–1492
Tomás de Torquemada 1420–1498
William Caxton c.1422–1491
Giovanni Bellini 1430–1516
Roderigo Borgia 1431–1503
Sandro Botticelli c.1445–1510
Lorenzo Medici 1449–1492

1450 – 1499

Hieronymus Bosch c.1450–1516
John Cabot c.1450–c.1498
Bartolomeu Dias c.1450–1500
Christopher Columbus 1451–1506
Isabella of Spain 1451–1504 *see Ferdinand and Isabella*
Amerigo Vespucci 1451–1512
Ferdinand of Spain 1452–1516 *see Ferdinand and Isabella*
Leonardo da Vinci 1452–1519
Richard III 1452–1485
Desiderius Erasmus c.1466–1536
Vasco da Gama c.1469–1524
Niccolò Machiavelli 1469–1527
Guru Nanak 1469–1539
Albrecht Dürer 1471–1528
Nicolaus Copernicus 1473–1543
Francisco Pizarro c.1474–1541
Thomas Wolsey c.1474–1530
Vasco Núñez de Balboa c.1475–1519
Michelangelo Buonarroti 1475–1564
Cesare Borgia 1475–1507
Thomas More c.1477–1535
Lucrezia Borgia 1480–1519
Ferdinand Magellan c.1480–1521
Montezuma II c.1480–1520
Martin Luther 1483–1546
Raphael 1483–1520
Ulrich Zwingli 1484–1531
Hernán Cortés 1485–1547
Thomas Cromwell c.1485–1540
Titian c.1488–1576

Thomas Cranmer 1489–1556
Jacques Cartier 1491–1557
Henry VIII 1491–1547
Saint Ignatius Loyola 1491–1556
François Rabelais c.1494–1553
Suleiman I c.1494–1566
Hans Holbein 1497–1543

1500 – 1549

Benvenuto Cellini 1500–1571
Charles V 1500–1558
Atahualpa c.1502–1533
Michael Nostradamus 1503–1566
John Knox 1505–1572
Andrea Palladio 1508–1580
John Calvin 1509–1564
Gerardus Mercator 1512–1594
Andreas Vesalius 1514–1564
Saint Teresa of Avila 1515–1582
Mary I 1516–1558
Jacopo Tintoretto 1518–1594
Luíz vaz de Camoens 1524–1580
Pieter Bruegel c.1525–1569
Philip II 1527–1598
Paolo Veronese 1528–1588
Ivan IV 1530–1584
Elizabeth I 1533–1603
William the Silent 1533–1584
Francis Drake c.1540–1596
El Greco 1541–1614
Akbar 1542–1605
Mary, Queen of Scots 1542–1587
Tokugawa Ieyasu 1542–1616
Tycho Brahe 1546–1601
Miguel de Cervantes 1547–1616

1550 – 1599

Walter Raleigh c.1552–1618
Henry IV 1553–1610
Francis Bacon 1561–1626
Galileo Galilei 1564–1642
William Shakespeare 1564–1616
Henry Hudson c.1565–1611

James I 1566–1625
Samuel de Champlain 1567–1635
Claudio Monteverdi 1567–1643
Guy Fawkes 1570–1606
Michelangelo Merisi da Caravaggio 1571–1610
Johannes Kepler 1571–1630
John Donne 1572–1631
Peter Rubens 1577–1640
William Harvey 1578–1657
Frans Hals c.1581–1666
Armand Jean Richelieu 1585–1642
Thomas Hobbes 1588–1679
Shah Jahan 1592–1666
Gustavus Adolphus 1594–1632
Nicolas Poussin 1594–1665
Pocahontas 1595–1617
René Descartes 1596–1650
Gianlorenzo Bernini 1598–1680
Oliver Cromwell 1599–1658
Anthony van Dyck 1599–1641
Diego Velázquez 1599–1660

1600 – 1649

Charles I 1600–1649
Abel Tasman c.1603–c.1659
Rembrandt van Rijn 1606–1669
John Milton 1608–1674
Molière 1622–1673
Blaise Pascal 1623–1662
George Fox 1624–1691
Queen Christina 1626–1689
Robert Boyle 1627–1691
John Bunyan 1628–1688
Christiaan Huygens 1629–1695
Charles II 1630–1685
Anton van Leeuwenhoek 1632–1723
John Locke 1632–1704
Jan Vermeer 1632–1675
Christopher Wren 1632–1723
Samuel Pepys 1633–1703
Robert Hooke 1635–1703
Louis XIV 1638–1715
Jean Racine 1639–1699
Isaac Newton 1642–1727
Rene LaSalle 1643–1687

Basho 1644–1694
William Penn 1644–1718
Antonio Stradivari 1644–1737
Gottfried Leibniz 1646–1716

1650 – 1699

Duke of Marlborough 1650–1722
William III 1650–1702
Jakob Bernoulli 1654–1705
Edmund Halley 1656–1742
Henry Purcell 1659–1695
Daniel Defoe 1660–1731
George I 1660–1727
Mary II 1662–1694
Thomas Newcomen 1663–1729
Gobind Singh 1666–1708
Johann Bernoulli 1667–1748
Jonathan Swift 1667–1745
Peter the Great 1672–1725
Jethro Tull 1674–1741
Robert Walpole 1676–1745
Antonio Vivaldi 1678–1741
Vitus Bering 1681–1741
Jean-Antoine Watteau 1684–1721
J. S. Bach 1685–1750
George Frideric Handel 1685–1759
Alexander Pope 1688–1744
Voltaire 1694–1778
Giovanni Canaletto 1697–1768
William Hogarth 1697–1764

1700 – 1739

Daniel Bernoulli 1700–1782
John Wesley 1703–1791
Benjamin Franklin 1706–1790
Leonard Euler 1707–1783
Carolus Linnaeus 1707–1778
Samuel Johnson 1709–1784
David Hume 1711–1776
Frederick II 1712–1786
Jean-Jacques Rousseau 1712–1778
Denis Diderot 1713–1784

Maria Theresa 1717–1780
Thomas Chippendale c.1718–1779
Charles Edward Stuart 1720–1788
James Hargreaves c.1720–1778
Adam Smith 1723–1790
Immanuel Kant 1724–1804
Giovanni Casanova 1725–1798
Robert Clive 1725–1774
Thomas Gainsborough 1727–1788
James Cook 1728–1779
Catherine the Great 1729–1796
Josiah Wedgwood 1730–1795
Henry Cavendish 1731–1810
Richard Arkwright 1732–1792
Joseph Haydn 1732–1809
George Washington 1732–1799
Joseph Priestley 1733–1804
Daniel Boone 1734–1820
John Adams 1735–1826
Paul Revere 1735–1818
James Watt 1736–1819
Luigi Galvani 1737–1798
Thomas Paine 1737–1809
George III 1738–1820
William Herschel 1738–1822

1740 – 1759

Joseph Montgolfier 1740–1810
Thomas Jefferson 1743–1826
Antoine Lavoisier 1743–1794
Toussaint l'Ouverture c.1743–1803
Joseph Banks 1744–1820
Mayer Amschel Rothschild 1744–1812
Jacques Montgolfier 1745–1799
Alessandro Volta 1745–1827
Francisco de Goya 1746–1828
Jacques-Louis David 1748–1825
Johann von Goethe 1749–1832
Edward Jenner 1749–1823
Pierre Laplace 1749–1827
Caroline Herschel 1750–1848
James Madison 1751–1836
Joseph-Marie Jacquard 1752–1834
Samuel Crompton 1753–1827
Louis XVI 1754–1793

Marie Antoinette 1755–1793
John McAdam 1756–1836
Wolfgang Amadeus Mozart 1756–1791
William Blake 1757–1827
Marquis de Lafayette 1757–1834
Thomas Telford 1757–1834
James Monroe 1758–1831
Horatio Nelson 1758–1805
Maximilien Robespierre 1758–1794
Robert Burns 1759–1796
Georges Danton 1759–1794
William Pitt 1759–1806
Friedrich Schiller 1759–1805
William Wilberforce 1759–1833

1760 – 1779

Katsushika Hokusai 1760–1849
Sequoya 1760–1843
Marie Tussaud 1760–1850
Robert Fulton 1765–1815
Joseph Niepce 1765–1833
John Dalton 1766–1844
Thomas Malthus 1766–1834
Andrew Jackson 1767–1845
Baron von Humboldt 1769–1859
Mehemet Ali 1769–1849
Napoleon I 1769–1821
Duke of Wellington 1769–1852
Ludwig van Beethoven 1770–1827
William Clark 1770–1838 *see Lewis and Clark*
Georg Hegel 1770–1831
William Wordsworth 1770–1850
Mungo Park 1771–1806
Walter Scott 1771–1832
Samuel Coleridge 1772–1834
Klemens Metternich 1773–1859
Thomas Young 1773–1829
Meriwether Lewis 1774–1809 *see Lewis and Clark*
André-Marie Ampère 1775–1836
Jane Austen 1775–1817
Daniel O'Connel 1775–1847
J. M. W. Turner 1775–1851
John Constable 1776–1837
Karl Gauss 1777–1855
Hans Christian Oersted 1777–1851

Humphry Davy 1778–1829
Joseph Gay-Lussac 1778–1850
José de San Martin 1778–1850

1780 – 1799

Elizabeth Fry 1780–1845
George Stephenson 1781–1848
Niccolò Paganini 1782–1840
Simón Bolívar 1783–1830
Jacob Grimm 1785–1863
Davy Crockett 1786–1836
John Franklin 1786–1847
Wilhelm Grimm 1786–1859
George Ohm 1787–1854
Shaka the Zulu c.1787–1828
Lord Byron 1788–1824
Robert Peel 1788–1850
Louis Daguerre 1789–1851
Edmund Kean 1789–1833
Michael Faraday 1791–1867
Samuel Morse 1791–1872
Charles Babbage 1792–1871
Gioachino Rossini 1792–1868
Percy Shelley 1792–1822
Cornelius Vanderbilt 1794–1877
Rowland Hill 1795–1879
John Keats 1795–1821
Franz Schubert 1797–1828
Mary Shelley 1797–1851
Sojourner Truth c.1797–1883
Eugène Delacroix 1798–1863
Honoré de Balzac 1799–1850
Alexander Pushkin 1799–1837

1800 – 1809

John Brown 1800–1859
William Fox Talbot 1800–1877
7th Earl of Shaftesbury 1801–1885
Brigham Young 1801–1877
Alexandre Dumas 1802–1870
Victor Hugo 1802–1885
Hector Berlioz 1803–1869
Ralph Waldo Emerson 1803–1882

Benjamin Disraeli 1804–1881
Nathaniel Hawthorne 1804–1864
Mongkut 1804–1868
Johann Strauss I 1804–1849
Hans Christian Andersen 1805–1875
Ferdinand de Lesseps 1805–1894
Mary Seacole 1805–1881
Isambard Kingdom Brunel 1806–1859
Giuseppe Garibaldi 1807–1882
Robert E. Lee 1807–1870
Henry Wadsworth Longfellow 1807–1882
Jefferson Davis 1808–1889
Napoleon III 1808–1873
Louis Braille 1809–1852
Charles Darwin 1809–1882
William Gladstone 1809–1898
Abraham Lincoln 1809–1865
Felix Mendelssohn 1809–1847
Edgar Allan Poe 1809–1849
Alfred, Lord Tennyson 1809–1892

1810 – 1819

Camillo Cavour 1810–1861
Frédéric Chopin 1810–1849
Robert Schumann 1810–1856
Franz Liszt 1811–1886
Harriet Beecher Stowe 1811–1896
William Thackeray 1811–1863
Robert Browning 1812–1889
Charles Dickens 1812–1870
Alfred Krupp 1812–1887
Edward Lear 1812–1888
Henry Bessemer 1813–1898
David Livingstone 1813–1873
Giuseppe Verdi 1813–1901
Richard Wagner 1813–1883
Samuel Colt 1814–1862
Otto von Bismarck 1815–1898
George Boole 1815–1864
John A. Macdonald 1815–1891
Anthony Trollope 1815–1882
Charlotte Brontë 1816–1855
Ernest Werner Siemens 1816–1892
Frederick Douglass 1817–1895

Emily Brontë 1818–1848
James Joule 1818–1889
Karl Marx 1818–1883
George Eliot 1819–1880
Jean Foucault 1819–1868
Herman Melville 1819–1891
Christopher Sholes 1819–1890
Queen Victoria 1819–1901
Walt Whitman 1819–1892

1820 – 1829

Susan Anthony Brownell 1820–1906
Anne Brontë 1820–1849
Florence Nightingale 1820–1910
Harriet Tubman c.1820–1913
Victor Emmanuel II 1820–1878
Charles Baudelaire 1821–1867
Fyodor Dostoevsky 1821–1881
Mary Baker Eddy 1821–1910
Gustave Flaubert 1821–1880
Ulysses S. Grant 1822–1885
Gregor Mendel 1822–1884
Louis Pasteur 1822–1895
Heinrich Schliemann 1822–1890
Charles William Siemens 1823–1883
Charles Blondin 1824–1897
Anton Bruckner 1824–1896
William Kelvin 1824–1907
Paul Kruger 1825–1904
Johann Strauss II 1825–1899
Cetshwayo c.1826–1884
Frederick Siemens 1826–1904
Joseph Lister 1827–1912
Josephine Butler 1828–1906
Henrick Ibsen 1828–1906
Dante Gabriel Rossetti 1828–1882
Leo Tolstoy 1828–1910
Jules Verne 1828–1905
Catherine Booth 1829–1890
William Booth 1829–1912
Geronimo 1829–1909

1830 – 1839

Emily Dickinson 1830–1886
Eadweard Muybridge 1830–1904
Camille Pissarro 1830–1903
James Clerk Maxwell 1831–1879
Louisa May Alcott 1832–1888
Isabella Bird 1832–1904
Lewis Carroll 1832–1898
Gustave Eiffel 1832–1923
Edouard Manet 1832–1883
Nikolaus Otto 1832–1891
Johannes Brahms 1833–1897
Alfred Nobel 1833–1896
Gottlieb Daimler 1834–1900
Edgar Degas 1834–1917
Dimitri Mendeléev 1834–1907
William Morris 1834–1896
Sitting Bull c.1834–1890
Andrew Carnegie 1835–1919
Yukichi Fukuzawa 1835–1901
Camille Saint-Saëns 1835–1921
Mark Twain 1835–1910
Elizabeth Garrett Anderson 1836–1917
William Gilbert 1836–1911 *see Gilbert and Sullivan*
Ramakrishna 1836–1886
Georges Bizet 1838–1875
Henry Irving 1838–1905
Ferdinand von Zeppelin 1838–1917
Paul Cézanne 1839–1906
General George A. Custer 1839–1876
Modest Mussorgsky 1839–1881
John D. Rockefeller 1839–1937

1840 – 1849

John Dunlop 1840–1921
Thomas Hardy 1840–1928
Claude Monet 1840–1926
Auguste Rodin 1840–1917
Pyotr Ilyich Tchaikovsky 1840–1893
Emile Zola 1840–1902
Georges Clemenceau 1841–1929
Anton Dvořák 1841–1904
Ito Hirobumi 1841–1909
Pierre Auguste Renoir 1841–1919

Arthur Sullivan 1842–1900 *see Gilbert and Sullivan*
Edvard Grieg 1843–1907
Henry James 1843–1916
Robert Koch 1843–1910
Karl Benz 1844–1929
Saint Bernadette 1844–1879
Sarah Bernhardt 1844–1923
Henry Heinz 1844–1919
Friedrich Nietzsche 1844–1900
Nikolay Rimsky-Korsakov 1844–1908
Henri Rousseau 1844–1910
Thomas Barnardo 1845–1905
Wilhelm Röntgen 1845–1923
Buffalo Bill 1846–1917
Peter Fabergé 1846–1920
Charles Parnell 1846–1891
Alexander Graham Bell 1847–1922
Annie Besant 1847–1933
Thomas Edison 1847–1931
Jesse James 1847–1882
Paul Gauguin 1848–1903
W. G. Grace 1848–1915
Crazy Horse c.1849–1877
William Hoover 1849–1932
Ivan Pavlov 1849–1936

1850 – 1859

Horatio Kitchener 1850–1916
Tomas Masaryk 1850–1937
Guy de Maupassant 1850–1893
Robert Louis Stevenson 1850–1894
Henri Becquerel 1852–1908
Calamity Jane c.1852–1903
Antonio Gaudí 1852–1926
Frank Woolworth 1852–1919
Cecil Rhodes 1853–1902
Vincent Van Gogh 1853–1890
George Eastman 1854–1932
Oscar Wilde 1854–1900
Ned Kelly 1855–1880
Sigmund Freud 1856–1939
James Keir Hardie 1856–1915
Robert Peary 1856–1920
Henri Philippe Pétain 1856–1951
George Bernard Shaw 1856–1950

Joseph Thomson 1856–1940
Booker T. Washington 1856–1915
Woodrow Wilson 1856–1924
Robert Baden-Powell 1857–1941
Joseph Conrad 1857–1924
Edward Elgar 1857–1934
Heinrich Hertz 1857–1894
Rudolf Diesel 1858–1913
Emmeline Pankhurst 1858–1928
Max Planck 1858–1947
Giacomo Puccini 1858–1924
Theodore Roosevelt 1858–1919
Billy the Kid 1859–1881
Arthur Conan Doyle 1859–1930
Alfred Dreyfus 1859–1935
Kenneth Grahame 1859–1932
Georges Seurat 1859–1891

1860 – 1869

J. M. Barrie 1860–1937
Anton Chekhov 1860–1904
William Kellogg 1860–1951
Gustav Mahler 1860–1911
Annie Oakley 1860–1926
Nellie Melba 1861–1931
Fridtjof Nansen 1861–1930
José Rizal 1861–1896
Rabindranath Tagore 1861–1941
William Bragg 1862–1942
Claude Debussy 1862–1918
Mary Kingsley 1862–1900
Auguste Lumière 1862–1954
Henry Ford 1863–1947
William Randolph Hearst 1863–1951
David Lloyd George 1863–1945
Edvard Munch 1863–1944
Louis Lumière 1864–1948
Richard Strauss 1864–1949
Henri de Toulouse–Lautrec 1864–1901
Edith Cavell 1865–1915
Rudyard Kipling 1865–1936
Jean Sibelius 1865–1957
W. B. Yeats 1865–1939
Wassily Kandinsky 1866–1944
Ramsay MacDonald 1866–1937

Beatrix Potter 1866–1943
Sun Yat–sen 1866–1925
H. G. Wells 1866–1946
Marie Curie 1867–1934
Frank Lloyd Wright 1867–1959
Wilbur Wright 1867–1912
Fritz Haber 1868–1934
Charles Rennie Mackintosh 1868–1928
Nicholas II 1868–1918
Robert Scott 1868–1912
Mahatma Gandhi 1869–1948
André Gide 1869–1951
Henri Matisse 1869–1954

1870 – 1879

Vladimir Lenin 1870–1924
Maria Montessori 1870–1952
Jan Smuts 1870–1950
Marcel Proust 1871–1922
Rasputin 1871–1916
Ernest Rutherford 1871–1937
Orville Wright 1871–1948
Roald Amundsen 1872–1928
Aurobindo 1872–1950
Louis Blériot 1872–1936
Piet Mondrian 1872–1944
Bertrand Russell 1872–1970
Ralph Vaughan Williams 1872–1958
Sergey Rakhmaninov 1873–1943
Winston Churchill 1874–1965
Robert Frost 1874–1963
Gustav Holst 1874–1934
Harry Houdini 1874–1926
William Lyon Mackenzie King 1874–1950
Guglielmo Marconi 1874–1937
L. M. Montgomery 1874–1942
Arnold Schoenberg 1874–1951
Chaim Weizmann 1874–1952
D. W. Griffith 1875–1948
Carl Jung 1875–1961
Ferdinand Porsche 1875–1951
Maurice Ravel 1875–1937
Albert Schweitzer 1875–1965
Constantin Brancusi 1876–1957
Pablo Casals 1876–1973

Walter Burley Griffin 1876–1937
Muhammad Ali Jinnah 1876–1948
Muhammad Iqbal 1877–1938
Pancho Villa 1877–1923
Lise Meitner 1878–1968
Yoshida Shigeru 1878–1967
Albert Einstein 1879–1955
Otto Hahn 1879–1968
Paul Klee 1879–1940
Joseph Stalin 1879–1953
Leon Trotsky 1879–1940
Emiliano Zapata 1879–1919

1880 – 1884

Jacob Epstein 1880–1959
Helen Keller 1880–1968
Douglas MacArthur 1880–1964
Christabel Pankhurst 1880–1958
Marie Stopes 1880–1958
Mustafa Kemal Atatürk 1881–1938
Béla Bartók 1881–1945
Cecil B. De Mille 1881–1959
Alexander Fleming 1881–1955
Pope John XXIII 1881–1963
Anna Pavlova 1881–1931
Pablo Picasso 1881–1973
Georges Braque 1882–1963
Eamon De Valera 1882–1975
Arthur Stanley Eddington 1882–1944
Samuel Goldwyn 1882–1974
James Joyce 1882–1941
A. A. Milne 1882–1956
Franklin D. Roosevelt 1882–1945
Igor Stravinsky 1882–1971
Virginia Woolf 1882–1941
Clement Attlee 1883–1967
Walter Gropius 1883–1969
Franz Kafka 1883–1924
John Maynard Keynes 1883–1946
Benito Mussolini 1883–1945
Auguste Piccard 1884–1962
Eleanor Roosevelt 1884–1962
Harry S. Truman 1884–1972

1885 – 1889

Niels Bohr 1885–1962
D. H. Lawrence 1885–1930
David Ben-Gurion 1886–1973
Clarence Birdseye 1886–1956
Arthur Brown 1886–1948 *see Alcock and Brown*
Diego Rivera 1886–1957
Marc Chagall 1887–1985
Chiang Kai–shek 1887–1975
Marcus Garvey 1887–1940
Le Corbusier 1887–1965
Bernard Law Montgomery 1887–1976
Georgia O'Keeffe 1887–1986
Arthur Rubinstein 1887–1982
Erwin Schrödinger 1887–1961
Jim Thorpe 1887–1953
John Logie Baird 1888–1946
Irving Berlin 1888–1989
Richard Byrd 1888–1957
T. S. Eliot 1888–1965
T. E. Lawrence 1888–1935
Charlie Chaplin 1889–1977
Jean Cocteau 1889–1963
Adolf Hitler 1889–1945
Edwin Hubble 1889–1953
Pandit Jawaharlal Nehru 1889–1964
Igor Sikorsky 1889–1972
Vladimir Zworykin 1889–1982

1890 – 1894

Lawrence Bragg 1890–1971
Agatha Christie 1890–1976
Michael Collins 1890–1922
Charles De Gaulle 1890–1970
Dwight Eisenhower 1890–1969
Ho Chi Minh 1890–1969
Stan Laurel 1890–1965 *see Laurel and Hardy*
Groucho Marx 1890–1977
Vaslav Nijinsky 1890–1950
Alexander, Earl of Tunis 1891–1969
Frederick Banting 1891–1941 *see Banting and Best*
Chico Marx 1891–1961
Cole Porter 1891–1964
Sergei Prokofiev 1891–1953

Erwin Rommel 1891–1944
John Alcock 1892–1919 *see Alcock and Brown*
Francisco Franco 1892–1975
Jean Paul Getty 1892–1976
Haile Selassie 1892–1975
Oliver Hardy 1892–1957 *see Laurel and Hardy*
Josip Tito 1892–1980
J. R. R. Tolkien 1892–1973
Robert Watson-Watt 1892–1973
Herman Goering 1893–1946
Mao Zedong 1893–1976
Harpo Marx 1893–1964
Joan Miró 1893–1983
Wilfred Owen 1893–1918
Mary Pickford 1893–1979
Martha Graham 1894–1991
Jomo Kenyatta c.1894–1978
Nikita Khrushchev 1894–1971
Georges Lemaitre 1894–1966
Robert Menzies 1894–1978

1895 – 1899

John Ford 1895–1973
Buster Keaton 1895–1966
Babe Ruth 1895–1948
Rudolph Valentino 1895–1926
F. Scott Fitzgerald 1896–1940
Enid Blyton 1897–1968
Joseph Goebbels 1897–1945
Lester Bowles Pearson 1897–1972
Charles Kingsford Smith 1897–1935
Bertolt Brecht 1898–1956
Ninette de Valois 1898–2001
Amelia Earhart 1898–1937
Sergei Eisenstein 1898–1948
M. C. Escher 1898–1972
George Gershwin 1898–1937
C. S. Lewis 1898–1963
Albert Luthuli 1898–1967
René Magritte 1898–1967
Golda Meir 1898–1978
Henry Moore 1898–1986
Paul Robeson 1898–1976
Shinichi Suzuki 1898–1997
Zhou Enlai 1898–1976

Fred Astaire 1899–1987
Charles Best 1899–1978 *see Banting and Best*
Humphrey Bogart 1899–1957
Jorge Louis Borges 1899–1986
Al Capone c.1899–1947
Duke Ellington 1899–1974
Ernest Hemingway 1899–1961
Alfred Hitchcock 1899–1980
Yasunari Kawabata 1899–1972
Suzanne Lenglen 1899–1938
Vladimir Nabokov 1899–1977

1900 – 1904

Laszlo Biro 1900–1985
Aaron Copland 1900–1990
Ayatollah Ruhollah Khomeini 1900–1989
Uday Shankar 1900–1977
Louis Armstrong 1901–1971
Walt Disney 1901–1966
Enrico Fermi 1901–1954
Clark Gable 1901–1960
Alberto Giacometti 1901–1966
Werner Karl Heisenberg 1901–1976
Emperor Hirohito 1901–1989
Zeppo Marx 1901–1979
Linus Pauling 1901–1994
Achmed Sukarno 1901–1970
Hendrik Verwoerd 1901–1966
Langston Hughes 1902–1967
Charles Lindbergh 1902–1974
Richard Rodgers 1902–1979
John Steinbeck 1902–1968
Barbara Hepworth 1903–1975
Amy Johnson 1903–1941
Louis Leakey 1903–1972
George Orwell 1903–1950
Salvador Dalí 1904–1989
Deng Xiaoping 1904–1997
Marlene Dietrich 1904–1992
Cary Grant 1904–1986
Graham Greene 1904–1991
Glenn Miller 1904–1944
J. Robert Oppenheimer 1904–1967

1905 – 1909

Greta Garbo 1905–1990
Howard Hughes 1905–1976
Jean-Paul Sartre 1905–1980
Chester Carlson 1906–1968
Soichiro Honda 1906–1991
Dmitri Shostakovich 1906–1975
Katharine Hepburn 1907–2003
W. H. Auden 1907–1973
Laurence Olivier 1907–1989
John Wayne 1907–1979
Frank Whittle 1907–1996
John Bardeen 1908–1991
Donald Bradman 1908–2001
Henri Cartier-Bresson 1908
Bette Davis 1908–1989
Lyndon B. Johnson 1908–1973
Joseph McCarthy 1908–1957
Jean Batten 1909–1982
Kwame Nkrumah 1909–1972

1910 – 1914

Christopher Cockerell 1910–1999
Jacques Cousteau 1910–1997
Dorothy Hodgkin 1910–1994
Akira Kurosawa 1910–1998
Mother Teresa 1910–1997
Juan Fangio 1911–1995
William Golding 1911–1993
Ronald Reagan 1911–2004
Tennessee Williams 1911–1983
Wernher von Braun 1912–1977
Sonja Henie 1912–1969
Jackson Pollock 1912–1956
Menachem Begin 1913–1992
Willy Brandt 1913–1992
Benjamin Britten 1913–1976
Albert Camus 1913–1960
Mary Leakey 1913–1996
Richard Nixon 1913–1994
Jesse Owens 1913–1980
Joe DiMaggio 1914–1999
Thor Heyerdahl 1914–2002
Joe Louis 1914–1981

Tenzing Norgay 1914–1986
Dylan Thomas 1914–1953

1915 – 1919

Billie Holiday 1915–1959
Stanley Matthews 1915–2000
Arthur Miller 1915
Frank Sinatra 1915–1998
Orson Welles 1915–1985
Francis Crick 1916 *see Crick and Watson*
Roald Dahl 1916–1990
Yehudi Menuhin 1916–1999
François Mitterand 1916–1996
Indira Gandhi 1917–1984
John Fitzgerald Kennedy 1917–1963
Sidney Nolan 1917–1992
I. M. Pei 1917
Leonard Bernstein 1918–1990
Ella Fitzgerald 1918–1996
Nelson Mandela 1918
Gamal Abdel Nasser 1918–1970
Mohammed Anwar el Sadat 1918–1981
Alexander Solzhenitsyn 1918
Margot Fonteyn 1919–1991
Edmund Hillary 1919
Eva Perón 1919–1952
Pierre Trudeau 1919–2000

1920 – 1929

Federico Fellini 1920–1993
Pope John Paul II 1920
John Glenn 1921
Satayjit Ray 1921–1992
Christiaan Barnard 1922–2001
Julius Nyerere 1922–1999
Yitzhak Rabin 1922–1996
Emil Zatopek 1922–2000
Maria Callas 1923–1977
Nadine Gordimer 1923
Lee Kuan Yew 1923
Marlon Brando 1924–2004
Kenneth Kaunda 1924
Benoit Mandelbrot 1924
Robert Mugabe 1924

B. B. King 1925
Malcolm X 1925–1965
Margaret Thatcher 1925
Chuck Berry 1926
Elizabeth II 1926
Marilyn Monroe 1926–1962
Abdus Salam 1926–1996
Joan Sutherland 1926
Fidel Castro 1927
Maya Angelou 1928
Zulfikar Ali Bhutto 1928–1979
James Brown 1928
Gatsha Buthelezi 1928
Gabriel García Márquez 1928
Che Geuvara 1928–1967
Pol Pot 1928–1998
Shirley Temple 1928
Andy Warhol 1928–1987
James Watson 1928 *see Crick and Watson*
Yasser Arafat 1929
Anne Frank 1929–1945
Robert Hawke 1929
Martin Luther King, Jr 1929–1968
Arnold Palmer 1929

1930 – 1939

Chinua Achebe 1930
Neil Armstrong 1930
Ray Charles 1930–2004
Clint Eastwood 1930
Helmut Kohl 1930
Derek Walcott 1930
James Dean 1931–1955
Mikhail Gorbachev 1931
Rupert Murdoch 1931
Bill Shoemaker 1931–2003
Desmond Tutu 1931
Boris Yeltsin 1931
Athol Fugard 1932
Sylvia Plath 1932–1963
Elizabeth Taylor 1932
Yuri Gagarin 1934–1968
Gloria Steinem 1934
Dalai Lama 1935
Luciano Pavarotti 1935
Lester Piggott 1935

Elvis Presley 1935–1977
F. W. de Klerk 1936
Vaclav Havel 1936
Buddy Holly 1936–1959
Margaret Mahy 1936
Garry Sobers 1936
Dawn Fraser 1937
Saddam Hussein 1937
Valentina Tereshkova 1937
Rod Laver 1938
Rudolf Nureyev 1938–1993

1940 – 1949

John Lennon 1940–1980 *see Lennon and McCartney*
Jack Nicklaus 1940
Pelé 1940
Bob Dylan 1941
Muhammad Ali 1942
Aretha Franklin 1942
Stephen Hawking 1942
Jimi Hendrix 1942–1970
Paul McCartney 1942 *see Lennon and McCartney*
Mu'ammar al-Qaddafi 1942
Paul Simon 1942
Jocelyn Bell 1943
Robert De Niro 1943
Mick Jagger 1943
Joni Mitchell 1943
Lech Walesa 1943
Richard Leakey 1944
Diana Ross 1944
Kiri Te Kanawa 1944
Kary B. Mullis 1944
Franz Beckenbauer 1945
Eric Clapton 1945
Bob Marley 1945–1981
Eddy Merckx 1945
Steve Biko 1946–1977
George W. Bush 1946
Bill Clinton 1946
Sultan of Brunei 1946
Irena Szewinska 1946
David Bowie 1947
Elton John 1947
Steven Spielberg 1947

1950 – 1959

Richard Branson 1950
Mark Spitz 1950
Stevie Wonder 1950
Imran Khan 1952
Benazir Bhutto 1953
Tony Blair 1953
Andrew Wiles 1953
Chiyonofuji 1955
Bill Gates 1955
Alain Prost 1955
Tom Hanks 1956
Joe Montana 1956
Martina Navratilova 1956
Ingemar Stenmark 1956
Michael Jackson 1958
Madonna 1958
Daley Thompson 1958

1960 – 1969

Diego Maradona 1960
Nadia Comaneci 1961
Diana, Princess of Wales 1961–1997
Wayne Gretzky 1961
Carl Lewis 1961
Tom Cruise 1962
Steve Redgrave 1962
Sergey Bubka 1963
Michael Jordan 1963
Gary Kasparov 1963
Jahangir Khan 1963
J. K. Rowling 1965
Michael Johnson 1967
Nicole Kidman 1967
Julia Roberts 1967
Steffi Graf 1969

1970 onwards

Pete Sampras 1971
Tiger Woods 1975
Robbie Williams 1976

Picture Credits